THE STAR TREK
CONCORDANCE

THE STAR TREK CONCORDANCE

BY BJO TRIMBLE
BASED ON A CONCEPT BY DOROTHY JONES HEYDT

BALLANTINE BOOKS/NEW YORK

DEDICATION

Dedicated to three men who made this book possible:
Gene Roddenberry for creating Star Trek in the first place,
John Trimble for believing I could get this book together, Martin
LeVita for making certain that I did it!

CONTENTS

INTRODUCTION

By Bjo Trimble

About midway through the first season of Star Trek, I noticed that Dorothy Jones, a fellow fan, was making extensive notes on the show, with cross-references to items and things mentioned, lists of who played what part, and so on. It seemed too interesting merely to keep in a file box, so I suggested that we share it with other fans. Dorothy had no experience with amateur fan publishing, or interest in putting everything in order to get it into print, but she gave me her notes with permission to use whatever I could get out of them.

Had I realized then that the entire Trimble family was embarking on an eight-year adventure in fan publishing, involving selling the Concordances through mail-order and updating material as new episodes were shown, perhaps this book would never have happened. Or at least not under my name; several other fans have had the general idea of a concordance, but never had the energy to get into it as extensively as this!

At any rate, the research went on, with much aid and assistance from various wonderful people who gave up their time to track down information for me. The amateur publications came out in two books, because just as I had the first two seasons ready for the printer and was waiting for the end of the third season, a major news event caused the airing of the last show of the season ("Turnabout Intruder") to be postponed until the beginning of the reruns. Unfortunately, printing costs were going up, and we already had orders to honor, so we printed the first two seasons in one book, and prepared the third season as a second book. All efforts to see the last show or even get a script from the Star Trek offices failed; the people in charge of the third season were not interested in fans or fannish efforts. So I had to wait until the episode was shown before any information could be gleaned for the Third Season Supplement to the Star Trek Concordance.

What with minor matters such as family, home, jobs, and other daily hassles, I never got around to completing the promised animated concordance. So it is to my great satisfaction that all of the material so carefully gathered has finally come out in one book. I have been waiting for this even longer than anyone else.

Dorothy, meantime, found that other interests, including one Hal Heydt, were more pressing than a Star Trek Concordance, and left the main body of writing to me. Without the extra help of scripts, many cups of hot tea, and warm cats for my lap in the home of Jerry and Joan Pearce, this book could never have been done at all, for I am not by nature a particularly encyclopedic-minded person.

Some very special thanks should also go to Eddie Bakos and the whole crew at Electri-Letter in Los Angeles, for letting me run free in his print shop for eight years while getting the Concordance reprinted as needed. And to Filmation, for letting me rummage through their files and take up space while getting the animated episodes ready for this book—especially to Norm Prescott, Bob Kline, Lou di Geralamo, and Adrienne. Gratitude to Matt Jeffries for letting us Trimbles take up a valuable evening running through his old Star Trek call sheets.

Thanks to the many artists who contributed their work to the amateur publication of the Concordance (some of whom are featured in this book), and to the team which nitpicked my notes as I put the book together, trying to catch as many mistakes and omissions as possible. To all the artists who enriched the pages of the original Concordance, the Third Season Supplement, and the Color Book: Alan Andres, Alicia Austin, Terry Austin, Ms. Steve Barnes, George Barr, Randy Bathurst, Greg Bear, Mrs. Mattewillis Beard, Johnny Chambers, Ms. Tim Courtney,

Nancy Criss, C-tein, Liz Danforth, Ron Demers, Fran Evans, Karen (K-nut) Flanery, Jackie Franke, Bonnie Bergstrom Goodknight, C. Lee Healy, Cathy Hill, Greg Jein, Barbi Johnson, Tim Kirk, Clarica Scott Laubscher, Claire Mason, Teri Moore, Rosalind Oberdieck, Wendy Fletcher Peni, T. Rhodes, D. Carol Roberts, Robert Short, Walt Simonson, Don Simpson, Sylvia Stanzyck, Anthony Tollin, Kristina Trott, Ev Turner, Katherine Cribbs Wadey and Robert Wadey, William Warren, Donna Wilson, Ellen Winder, and Bernard Zuber . . . loud and public thanks! To the new artists who added to this book, we also extend thanks: to Robert Kline and other Filmation artists and Robert Wood, for adding new dimensions to the Concordance.

The people who went through my notes in the first place should be complimented for helping produce the amateur publications that were enjoyed by so many: the Basta girls, Walter Breen, Sherna Burley, Danielle Dabbs, Devra and Debbie Langsam, Carol Lee, Michelle Malkin, Rosemary Ullyot, Maureen Wilson, Joyce Yasner—and especially Ruth Berman, whose insidious nitpicking discovered many things to add and correct for this book.

Without many helping hands for typing, getting kids off to school, nagging me, cleaning up when the house reached Critical Mass, and running errands, this book could not be possible. Thanks go to Roy and Cathy Adamson, Nancy Berman, Lynn Barker, Ann Christopher, Carolyn Coling, Chuck Crayne, Larry Dale, Julie Funn, Will Guest, Woody and Linda Hendricks, Gail Knuth, Kathy Lear, Darlene McClain, Tao Obray, Rita Ractliffe, Rob Rafalli, Sue Scipione, Lori Strohm, Kathy Wolf, Randy Yamamoto, and all the people who sent in letters, pointing out all the things I'd neglected to put in the amateur Concordances (or all the things I'd put in that they took exception to, for one reason or another!). All of you helped make this book possible.

For very specialized research, my gratitude goes to James J. Ferrigan III whose work in vexillology and uniforms provided this book with more interesting detail on flags, pennants, medals, ribbons, and uniforms than I could have managed on my own.

Quite special thanks go to Pacifica Radio KPFK for use of their Xerox machine; Lou Mindling and Mike Policare for being the only people at Paramount who seemed to care; Dorothy Fontana, David Gerrold, Steve and Kathyleen Sky Goldin for their professional advice and encouragement; Charles of Dublin for his proofreading and correction of my syntax; and particular thanks to Martin LeVita, who put up with my crotchetiness, tears, and frustration in getting this book as perfect as possible (and was a shoulder to cry on when I realized that it would never be as perfect as I wanted it to be), and for being a general mainstay, good worker, and friend.

There is no way to thank John Griffin Trimble for being mother and father to the children while all this was getting collected into a book; for being patient, understanding, loving, and always ready to help. Without this very special type of supportive husband, this book would not be in your hands today.

For all of this—for all of the work willingly volunteered, for Fran Evans, Jeri Bethel, Helen Bautista, and the others who played Girl Friday (not to mention Monday, Tuesday, etc., etc.) while we had the amateur Concordance in print—I say, "Hip, hip, HOORAY!"

And if you ever challenge me to a Star Trek trivia contest, and want to win, keep it to numbers; I can't remember anything above three, anyway.

June, 1976   Los Angeles, California

PREFACE

By Dorothy Jones Heydt

This Concordance contains material compiled by me, for the most part, from audio tapes of the episodes, supplemented by scripts, the Third Edition of The Star Trek Writer's Guide, and an occasional kind word from Desilu (now Paramount) Studios. Bjo expanded greatly on my original work, using other methods, but both of us worked with the episodes as shown; in case of contradictions with any other material now in print, the episode as aired has been taken as definitive.

Mr. Roddenberry has stated that the stardate is a function of space as well as time, being influenced by a starship's position in the galaxy, its course and velocity. On the (perhaps unwarranted) assumption that stardates do follow in chronological order for a given ship, a list (see Timeline in the appendixes) of these dates has been arranged, which, along with the episode summaries, may be the closest thing we will ever get to a full history of the Star Trek universe.

My appreciation to my co-writer and editor, Bjo Trimble, whose idea this was, and who supplied me with scripts, pictures, gossip, and lodging when I came to Los Angeles; to Bob Hellstrom and Rick Carter (gofers to Gene Roddenberry), Penny Unger (G.R.'s secretary), and the rest of the Star Trek staff. Thanks also to Alicia Austin and Tim Courtney and all the others who contributed illustrations and effort; and most of all to Gene Roddenberry, who created a whole new universe.

June, 1968   Berkeley, California

KEY

Preceding each summary is an abbreviation, to which items in the Lexicon are cross-referenced. (See the Index to Episodes on page 256.) A small "/a" after the abbreviation indicates an animated episode. Thus, (AT) refers to "Amok Time," a live-action episode, while (Yy/a) refers to "Yesteryear," an animated episode.

Air dates are for Pacific Standard Time, when each show was first televised in California.

Every effort was made to list the actors appearing in each show, but some eluded every search. Unfortunately, we did not have ready access to studio records. If a part has been credited: (Unknown), instead of with an actor's name, the person was probably a "contract" player assigned to the studio and never named in any call sheets.

All material used in this book has been taken directly from scripts, supplemented by viewing the episodes as aired. Discrepancies may occur—for example, when a first-season show was cut for later syndication and scenes or phrases listed in the book were removed, perhaps never to be seen again. There were often differences between a script and the aired version, due to last-minute changes or a difference in how an actor pronounced a word; attempts have been made to tie everything together, but how successful this has been will depend on how many interesting mistakes the reader can find. If nothing else, this book should provide a field day for nitpickers!

Imaginative additions to the Star Trek universe by writers when novelizing scripts, or the license taken by anyone else who may have chosen to add extraneous material to their own works, have not been included in the Concordance. We tried to adhere strictly to the Star Trek universe created by Gene Roddenberry, and added to only by the writers for the actual show itself.

TIME LINE

Stardates are a method of keeping track of time passing aboard a starship, not on a planet. Logging in reports back to a ship means using the stardate current at the time of an event, as it would be nearly impossible to keep track of the dates used on each planet visited. Ship's time may seem compressed in comparison to planet time, because of the warp speeds used to get from place to place. This explains the seeming closeness of elapsed time between the events of "What Are Little Girls Made Of?", "Miri," and "Dagger of the Mind"; the logs kept on a warp-speed ship do not correlate with normal planetary timekeeping. Moving about the galaxy at warp speeds makes it impossible to keep time according to any one sun or star movement—hence stardates.

Stardate	Episode
1254.4	The Magicks of Megas-tu
1312.4	Where No Man Has Gone Before
1329.1	Mudd's Women
1512.2	The Corbomite Maneuver
1513.1	The Man Trap
1533.6	Charlie X
1672.1	The Enemy Within
1704.2	The Naked Time
1709.1	Balance of Terror
2124.5	The Squire of Gothos
2534.0	Patterns of Force
2712.4	What Are Little Girls Made Of?
2713.5	Miri
2715.1	Dagger of the Mind
2817.6	The Conscience of the King
2821.5	The Galileo Seven
2947.3	Court-martial
3012.4	The Menagerie
3018.2	Catspaw
3025.3	Shore Leave
3045.6	Arena
3087.6	The Alternative Factor
3113.2	Tomorrow Is Yesterday
3134.0	The City on the Edge of Forever
3141.9	Space Seed
3156.2	The Return of the Archons
3183.3	Practical Joker
3192.1	A Taste of Armageddon
3196.1	The Devil in the Dark
3198.4	Errand of Mercy
3211.7	The Gamesters of Triskelion
3219.4	Metamorphosis
3287.2	Operation—Annihilate!
3372.7	Amok Time
3417.3	This Side of Paradise
3468.1	Who Mourns for Adonais?
3478.2	The Deadly Years
3497.2	Friday's Child
3541.9	The Changeling
3614.9	Wolf in the Fold
3619.2	Obsession
3715.0	The Apple
3842.3	Journey to Babel
4040.7	Bread and Circuses
4187.3	Slaver Weapon
4202.9	The Doomsday Machine
4211.4	A Private Little War
4307.1	The Immunity Syndrome
4372.5	Elaan of Troyius
4385.3	Spectre of the Gun

EPISODES

FAN ART

Spock
Drawn by Mattewillis Beard

Scene from 'The Menagerie'
Drawn by Tim Kirk

Left: M113 Creature
Drawn by Tim Kirk

Right: Balok's false image
Drawn by Tim Kirk

Left: Yarnek
Artist unknown

Right: Gav the Tellarite
Drawn by Tim Kirk

Left: Harry Mudd and
"Stella" series
Drawn by George Barr

Right: Nurse Chapel
Drawn by George Barr

Sehlat and Vulcan child
Drawn by Alicia Austin

Left: Spock in plak-tow
Drawn by Tim Courtney

Right: T'Pau
Artist unknown

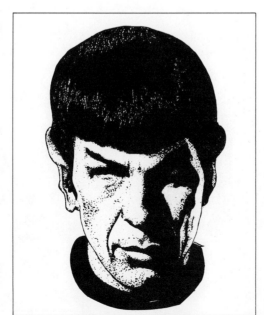

Left: Mugato
Drawn by Tim Kirk

Right: Tellarite
Drawn by Alicia Austin

Female Romulan Commander
Drawn by Bjo Trimble

Romulan Centurion
Drawn by Bjo Trimble

Left: Melkot
Drawn by Alicia Austin

Right: Gorn
Drawn by Alicia Austin

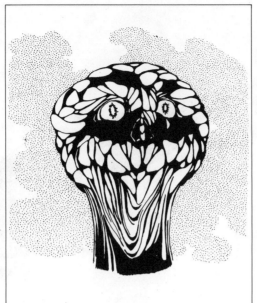

Klingon Commander
Drawn by Bjo Trimble

Female Klingon Officer
Drawn by Bjo Trimble

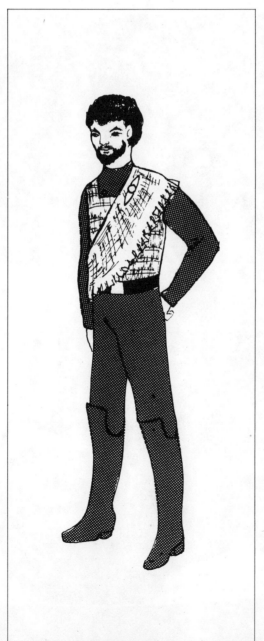

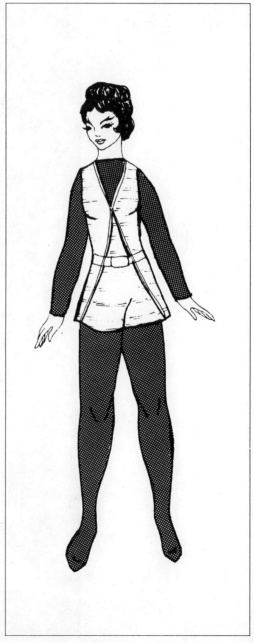

Romulan "bird of prey" ship
Drawn by Walt Simonton

Spock-2
Drawn by Tim Courtney

Left: Uhura
Drawn by Tim Courtney

Right: Zarabeth
Artist unknown

The Galileo entering the ameba
Drawn by Greg Bear

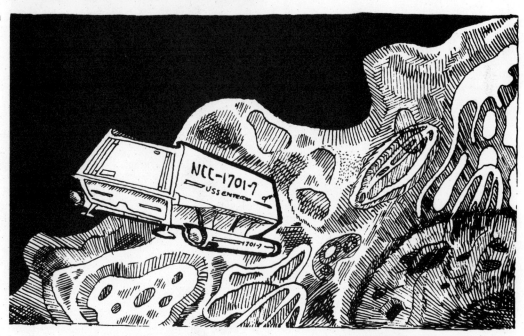

Left: Sarek
Drawn by Alicia Austin

Right: Scotty
Drawn by Tim Courtney

Left: Insignia of the
U.S.S. Exeter, Command
Drawn by Robert Wood

Right: Insignia of the
U.S.S. Defiant
Drawn by Robert Wood

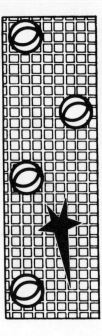
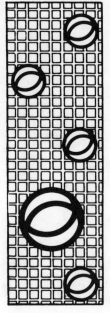
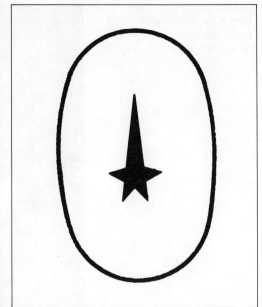

Left: Star Fleet dress uniform
Drawn by Bjo Trimble

Right: Insignia of the
U.S.S. Huron
Drawn by Robert Wood

Star Fleet officials'
gold star for dress uniform
Drawn by Robert Wood

Left: Insignia of the
U.S.S. Intrepid
Drawn by Robert Wood

Right: U.S.S. Enterprise insignia-
Sciences
Drawn by Robert Wood

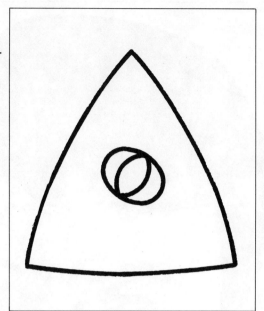 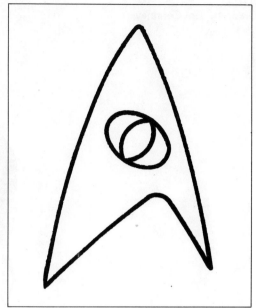

Left: Insignia of the U.S.S. Ariel
Drawn by Robert Wood

Right: U.S.S. Enterprise insignia-
Star Fleet Command
Drawn by Robert Wood

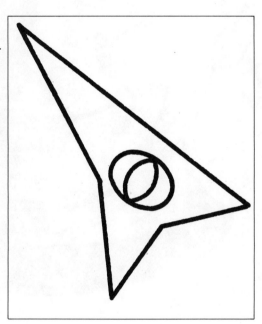 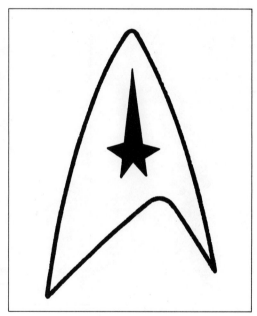

U.S.S. Enterprise insignia-
Medicine
Drawn by Robert Wood

U.S.S. Enterprise insignia-
Services
(Engineering, Security, etc.)
Drawn by Robert Wood

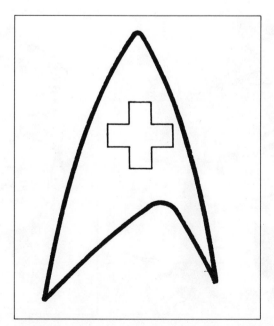 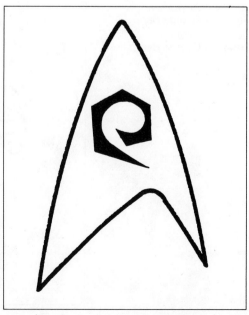

McCoy
Drawn by Tim Courtney

Left: Mudd's Women
Drawn by George Barr

Right: Leila Kalomi
Drawn by George Barr

Left: Flag of the
United Federation of Planets
Drawn by Anthony Tollin

Right: Thelev
Drawn by Tim Kirk

Sarek
Drawn by Tim Courtney

Spock attacked by flying parasite
Artist unknown

Mr. Atoz and the atavachron
Drawn by Alan Andres

Left: Uhura
Drawn by George Barr

Right: Mira Romaine
Drawn by Bill Warren

Tribbles
Drawn by Bjo Trimble

Left: Uhura
Drawn by Ellen Windsor

Left: Spock-2
Drawn by Tim Courtney

SUMMARIES

FIRST SEASON

THE MAN TRAP

BY GEORGE CLAYTON JOHNSON
DIRECTED BY MARC DANIELS
STARDATE: 1513.1 AIRED: 9/8/66

Professor Robert Crater and his wife, Nancy, a former girlfriend of McCoys's, have been on Planet M113 for five years, making an archeological survey of the ruins there. When the Enterprise arrives for the colony's annual checkup and supply renewal, they discover Crater and his wife are the sole survivors. Crater tells the landing party that all they need is salt tablets; beyond that, they want to be let alone. While this is being discussed, a crewman, Darnell, wanders off with an attractive wench and is killed, so Kirk orders the landing party and the Craters back to the ship. However, Nancy Crater, whose youthful appearance has impressed McCoy and rekindled old tender feelings, is actually the last survivor of M113's native inhabitants, creatures possessing the power of illusion. Needing sodium chloride to live, the race was becoming extinct because the planet's supply of salt ran out. The creature had killed Nancy and taken her place. Crater has kept it alive and shielded it because it is the last of its race, but his own salt supply is dwindling. The creature begins to attack Enterprise crewmen, first entrapping them while in human form, then killing them by draining salt from their bodies. It takes a crewman's shape to get on board the ship, then reappears as Nancy to deceive McCoy again. It kills more people, including Crater, until Kirk and Spock learn its secret. They have to prove to McCoy that it isn't Nancy before, in horror, he takes action, killing the salt vampire before it can kill Kirk.

Cast	
Kirk: William Shatner	Nancy Crater: Jeanne Bal and Francine Pyne
Spock: Leonard Nimoy	M113 Monster: (Unknown)
McCoy: DeForest Kelley	Professor Robert Crater: Alfred Ryder
Sulu: George Takei	Darnell: Michael Zaslow
Uhura: Nichelle Nichols	Green: Bruce Watson
Yeoman Janice Rand: Grace Lee Whitney	Uhura's Crewman: Vince Howard
	Sturgeon: (Unknown)

See Lexicon under:	
Archeological site	Hypnosis
Barnhart	Johnson, George Clayton
Beauregard	M113, planet
Borgia plant	M113 creature
Buffalo	M'Umbha
Corinth IV	Passenger pigeon
Crater, Nancy	Plum
Crater, Professor Robert	Religion
Daniels, Marc	Saurian brandy
Darnell	Sturgeon
Diggings	Swahili
Dominguez, Commander José	Tonsils
Games and recreation	Uhura's crewman
General quarters 3	Vulcan
Green	Weeper

CHARLIE X

BY D. C. FONTANA; STORY BY GENE RODDENBERRY
DIRECTED BY LARRY DOBKIN
STARDATE: 1533.6 AIRED: 9/15/66

Charles Evans, age seventeen Terran years, the only survivor of a colonizing expedition that crashed on the planet Thasus, is picked up by the U.S.S. Antares and transferred to the Enterprise. Shortly thereafter, while Captain Ramart of the Antares is trying to tell Kirk something, the Antares is destroyed. Apparently unaffected by the crew members' deaths, Charlie seems concerned only that people like him, but he has problems: no self-control, no maturity, and absolutely none of the social graces. He tells everyone that from the age of three he had been alone on Thasus, with only the record tapes of his ship for company. Spock, however, rather doubts this story. Still, the secret of Charlie's survival and upbringing remains unknown—an X-factor. Meanwhile, Charlie sees in Kirk a father figure, and also falls madly in love with Yeoman Rand. When Rand resists his advances, he causes her to disappear. When Kirk disciplines him, he goes on a rampage, wreaking havoc throughout the ship. In truth, Charlie was raised by the noncorporeal Thasians, who gave him tremendous psionic powers so that he could survive on Thasus. It was Charlie who destroyed the Antares, because the crew was, he thought, insufficiently nice to him. He now wants the Enterprise to take him to the nearest inhabited planet, Colony 5, so that he can take over, and he will stop at nothing to gain this end. The Thasians, belatedly realizing that Charlie has left their planet, intercept the Enterprise and, in spite of Charlie's pleas to be allowed to stay with human beings, take him, with his dangerously undisciplined powers, back to Thasus. Before leaving, they restore the Enterprise and its crew to normal.

Cast	
Kirk: William Shatner	Yeoman 3/C Tina Lawton: Patricia McNulty
Spock: Leonard Nimoy	Captain Ramart: Charles J. Stewart
McCoy: DeForest Kelley	Tom Nellis: Dallas Mitchell
Uhura: Nichelle Nichols	First Crewman: John Bellah
Yeoman Janice Rand: Grace Lee Whitney	Second Crewman: Garland Thompson
	Navigator: Don Eitner
Charlie Evans: Robert Walker, Jr.	Old Lady: Laura Wood
Thasian: Abraham Sofaer	Sam: (Unknown)

See Lexicon under:	
Antares, U.S.S.	Games and recreation
Baffle plate	Gymnasium
"Charlie"	Irvingoscope
Chess	Lawton, Yeoman 3/C Tina
Colony 5	Nellis, Tom
Dimension	Phynburg oscillating framizam
Dobkin, Larry	Ramart, Captain
Ellis, Mr.	Record tapes
Evans, Charles	Roddenberry, Gene
Father figure	Sam
Fontana, D. C.	Thasian
	Thasus

WHEN NO MAN HAS GONE BEFORE

BY SAMUEL A. PEEPLES
DIRECTED BY JAMES GOLDSTONE
STARDATE: 1312.4   AIRED: 9/22/66

The Enterprise encounters a force-field barrier at the rim of the galaxy which burns out its drives and causes marked changes in Lieutenant Commander Gary Mitchell, Kirk's closest friend. Mitchell's latent psionic abilities are accelerated, until he feels only a remote connection with the human race. Dr. Elizabeth Dehner, who was also affected, though to a lesser degree, takes Mitchell's side, and protests when Kirk decides to exile him to Delta Vega, an uninhabited planet. After Mitchell declares that he is becoming a god and has no responsibility to humans, he escapes, taking Dehner with him. Kirk follows with a phaser rifle, and Mitchell attempts to kill him with his psi powers. Dehner, finally realizing what Mitchell has become, helps Kirk overpower the madman, and is killed in the attempt. For the first time, Spock admits to having feelings akin to human emotions, and the episode marks the beginning of his friendship with Kirk.

Cast	
Kirk: William Shatner	Lieutenant Lee Kelso: Paul Carr
Spock: Leonard Nimoy	Dr. Piper: Paul Fix
Scott: James Doohan	Yeoman Smith: Andrea Dromm
Sulu: George Takei	Lieutenant Alden: Lloyd Haynes
Lieutenant Commander Gary Mitchell:	Guard: Eddie Paskey
Gary Lockwood	Stunt Doubles: Dick Crockett (Kirk),
Dr. Elizabeth Dehner: Sally Kellerman	Hal Needham (Mitchell)

See Lexicon under:	
Aldebaran Colony	Kelso, Lieutenant Lee
Alden, Lieutenant	Lithium-cracking station
Barrier at the rim of the galaxy	Mitchell, Lieutenant Commander Gary
Canopus	"Nightingale Woman"
Dehner, Dr. Elizabeth	Peeples, Samuel A.
Delta Vega	Piper, Dr.
Deneb IV	Psionics
Dimorus	Recorder-marker
Energy barrier	Religion
Games and recreation	Service record
Goldstone, James	Smith, Yeoman
Impulse power	Star Fleet Academy
Kaferian apples	Tarbolde, Phineas
	Valiant, U.S.S.

THE NAKED TIME

BY JOHN D. F. BLACK
DIRECTED BY MARC DANIELS
STARDATE: 1704.2   AIRED: 9/29/66

The Enterprise arrives at Psi 2000, a planet about to disintegrate, to pick up a research party. Spock and crewman Joe Tormolen discover that the researchers have all died in strange ways, some even by their own hand. While on the planet, Tormolen picks up a virus that relaxes inhibitions and brings out one's basic nature. Tormolen, a latent depressive, becomes so despondent that he tries to take his own life. Sulu and Kevin Riley become infected in the process of stopping him. Tormolen's depression eventually becomes so severe that he dies of despair. The water-borne virus, carried in perspiration and spread by touch, goes through the crew like wildfire, opening to view the deeper emotions of everyone affected: Sulu runs amok with a fencing foil; Christine Chapel becomes very affectionate; Riley proclaims himself captain and locks himself in—and everyone else out of—Engineering; Kirk becomes a moon-eyed romantic; and Spock, abandoning logic—and duty—weeps over his mother. McCoy eventually finds an antidote to the virus, but in the meantime Riley, still in Engineering, has shut down the engines, and the ship is being pulled down by Psi 2000's wildly fluctuating gravity. Kirk, Spock, and Scott manage to save the ship at almost the last minute by means of much willpower and some very unorthodox engineering.

Cast	
Kirk: William Shatner	Chapel: Majel Barrett
Spock: Leonard Nimoy	Lieutenant Kevin Riley: Bruce Hyde
McCoy: DeForest Kelley	Joe Tormolen: Stewart Moss
Scott: James Doohan	Dr. Harrison: John Bellah
Sulu: George Takei	Lieutenant Brent: Frank da Vinci
Uhura: Nichelle Nichols	Singing Crewman: William Knight

See Lexicon under:	
Alert B-2	Harrison, Dr.
Amanda	Intermix chamber
Anticontamination suit	K-1 circuit
Antidote	Psi 2000
Antimatter	Richelieu, Cardinal
Black, John D. F.	Riley, Lieutenant Kevin
Bowling alley	Ryan, Lieutenant
Brent, Lieutenant	Singing crewman
Chapel, Christine	Spectro readings
Cycling station	Tormolen, Joe
Daniels, Marc	Virus
Games and recreation	Water

THE ENEMY WITHIN

BY RICHARD MATHESON
DIRECTED BY LEO PENN
STARDATE: 1672.1   AIRED: 10/6/66

Contamination from magnetic ore brought aboard on Technician Fisher's clothes causes a transporter malfunction over the planet Alfa 177. Kirk, in beaming aboard shortly after the crewman, is unknowingly split into two entities identical in appearance: One Kirk is good but weak-willed; the other is evil. The evil double creates havoc aboard the ship until the situation is discovered and the crew can find and restrain him. Meanwhile, the transporter continues to split both animate and inanimate objects, forcing the rest of the landing party to remain on Alfa 177, without protection as the planet's freezing night rapidly approaches. On board the ship, it is discovered that the split is weakening Kirk: The good half is losing the power to make command decisions and the evil half is dying. Neither can survive without the other. Kirk must be made whole again, and the landing party must be beamed aboard before freezing to death. Scotty manages to fix the transporter, but with so little time left that they must immediately try to rejoin the two Kirks, without being certain of the outcome. McCoy is particularly fearful because a small doglike creature, also split, returns from the transporter joined but dead. Scotty adjusts the transporter and Kirk takes the risk, having no other choice, and returns alive as one man. The landing party is then beamed aboard, nearly frozen but still alive.

Cast	
Kirk: William Shatner	Yeoman Rand: Grace Lee Whitney
Spock: Leonard Nimoy	Lieutenant John Farrell: Jim Goodwin
Scott: James Doohan	Technician Fisher: Edward Madden
McCoy: DeForest Kelley	Technician Wilson: Garland Thompson
Sulu: George Takei	Double: Don Eitner (Kirk)

See Lexicon under:	Ore
Alfa 177	Penn, Leo
Double	Synchronic meter
Farrell, Lieutenant John	3RR circuit
Fisher, Technician	Transporter ionizer unit
Matheson, Richard	Wilson, Technician

MUDD'S WOMEN

BY STEPHEN KANDEL STORY BY GENE RODDENBERRY
DIRECTED BY HARVEY HART
STARDATE: 1329.1   AIRED: 10/13/66

The Enterprise pursues a ship through an asteroid belt to rescue the passengers before the ship is destroyed by its own high speeds. Beamed aboard the starship are Harry Mudd, con man extraordinary, and his stock in trade: three enticing females—Ruth Bonaventure, Magda Kovas, and Eve McHuron—on their way to marry settlers on Ophiuchus VI. The ship's computer reveals that Mudd is charged with several infractions of the law. The chase has burned out most of the Enterprise's lithium crystals, and the ship heads for supply on Rigel XII, a dry, mining planet with a population of three miners. Mudd makes a deal with the love-starved lithium miners: their crystals for the women and aid in escaping from Kirk. However, Eve McHuron, who has become fond of Kirk, tries to run away, and when miner Ben Childress brings her back to camp, he learns that the women have been dosed with a highly illegal Venus drug to make them beautiful. They are actually quite homely, to put it mildly, but by this time two of them are already married to miners, who are actually quite satisfied with the bargain. Childress agrees to turn Mudd and the lithium crystals over to Kirk. Eve learns that she can be beautiful without the drugs, and since Kirk is "married" to the Enterprise, she settles for Ben. As for Mudd, they throw away the key.

Cast	
Kirk: William Shatner	Eve McHuron: Karen Steele
Spock: Leonard Nimoy	Magda Kovas: Susan Denberg
McCoy: DeForest Kelley	Ruth Bonaventure: Maggie Thrett
Scott: James Doohan	Ben Childress: Gene Dynarski
Sulu: George Takei	Lieutenant John Farrell: Jim Goodwin
Uhura: Nichelle Nichols	Gossett: Jon Kowal
Harry Mudd: Roger C. Carmel	Benton: Seamon Glass
	Security guard: Jerry Foxworth

See Lexicon under:	Kovas, Magda
Benton	Marriage
Bonaventure, Ruth	McHuron, Eve
Childress, Ben	Mudd, Harcourt Fenton (Harry)
Class J cargo ship	Ophiuchus VI
Dilithium crystals (lithium crystals)	Pelagic planet
Double-jack	Rigel XII
Farrell, Lieutenant John	Roddenberry, Gene
Gossett, Herm	Saturnius
Hart, Harvey	Subspace radio
Helium experimental station	Venus drug
Impulse power	Walsh, Leo Francis
Kandel, Stephen	

WHAT ARE LITTLE GIRLS MADE OF?

BY ROBERT BLOCH
DIRECTED BY JAMES GOLDSTONE
STARDATE: 2712.4   AIRED: 10/20/66

The Enterprise arrives at Exo III to search for exobiologist Dr. Roger Korby, whose fiancée, Christine Chapel, is aboard. The landing party finds Korby in an underground cavern built by the planet's now-extinct natives, the "Old Ones." With the equipment they left behind, Korby has learned to construct androids, and has also built an android body for himself. He plans to bring androids, secretly at first, to the worlds of the Federation, replacing key people with android duplicates. To further this end, he builds an android duplicate of Kirk and sends it back to the Enterprise, while he holds the real Kirk prisoner. Spock, however, sees through the false Kirk and takes a security team down to the planet. Meanwhile, Kirk convinces Ruk, the giant android guarding him—a superrational pre-Korby original—that Korby is a menace to its logical way of life. Ruk attacks Korby and has to be destroyed. Kirk then demonstrates to Korby that his own android body has caused a deadening of his human feelings, and the exobiologist destroys himself and the remaining android, Andrea. Chapel stays on with the Enterprise as a nurse in Sick Bay.

Cast	
Kirk: William Shatner	Ruk: Ted Cassidy
Spock: Leonard Nimoy	Dr. Brown: Harry Basch
Uhura: Nichelle Nichols	Matthews: Vince Deadrick
Christine Chapel: Majel Barrett	Rayburn: Budd Albright
Dr. Roger Korby: Michael Strong	Male yeoman: (Unknown)
Andrea: Sherry Jackson	Female yeoman: (Unknown)
	Stunt Double: Paul Baxley (Kirk)

See Lexicon under:	
Andrea	Kirk, George Samuel
Androids	Korby, Dr. Roger
Bloch, Robert	Maltuvis
Brown, Dr.	Matthews
Chapel, Christine	Midos V
Exo III	"Old Ones"
Ferris, High Commissioner	Orion
Geisha	Rayburn
Goldstone, James	Ruk

MIRI

BY ADRIAN SPIES
DIRECTED BY VINCE McEVEETY
STARDATE: 2713.5   AIRED: 10/27/66

Arriving at an Earthlike planet settled by humans, the landing party from the Enterprise finds that, some three hundred years earlier, a virus killed off all the adults; in them it caused rapid aging, madness, leprous body sores, and finally death—but in children it slowed the aging process, giving them great longevity. Everyone contracts the disease except Spock, who becomes a carrier, and all are quarantined to the planet until an antidote can be made, based on notes remaining from the early life-prolongation experiments that started the trouble. Miri, one of the three-hundred-year-old children, who looks fourteen, falls in love with Kirk and tries to help, but the rest, who distrust adults ("grups"), remembering their violence and frenzied deaths, run and hide. When Miri finds she has a rival in Yeoman Rand, she rejoins the other children, and, led by Jahn, the children harass the Enterprise crew. Kirk tries to reason with them, but is nearly beaten to death. Finally, one of the older children, Louise, develops the symptoms of the disease, and Kirk shows them that they will each contract it when they reach puberty. McCoy, using himself as a guinea pig, produces an antidote and brings the disease under control. The Federation sends truant officers and other personnel to civilize the planet.

Cast	
Kirk: William Shatner	Male Creature: Ed McCready
Spock: Leonard Nimoy	Female Creature: Ed McCready
McCoy: DeForest Kelley	Security Guard: David L. Ross
Yeoman Rand: Grace Lee Whitney	Jahn's Friend: Keith Taylor
Miri: Kim Darby	Blond Girl: Kellie Flanagan
Jahn: Michael J. Pollard	Red-headed Boy: Steven McEveety
Lieutenant John Farrell: Jim Goodwin	Crewman: John Arndt
Fat Little Boy: John Megna	Stunt Double: Bob Miles (McCoy)

See Lexicon under:	
Biocomputer, portable	Louise
"Creatures"	McEveety, Vince
Farrell, Lieutenant John	Miri
Galloway, Lieutenant	Slang, Miri's Planet
Jahn	Spies, Adrian
Little boy	Stardate
Longevity	Virus

DAGGER OF THE MIND

BY SHIMON WINCELBERG (S. BAR-DAVID)
DIRECTED BY VINCE McEVEETY
STARDATE: 2715.1   AIRED: 11/3/66

The wild-eyed maniac who escapes from the Tantalus V penal colony to the Enterprise turns out to be Dr. Simon van Gelder, one of the psychiatric staff, not an inmate. Because of van Gelder's condition, McCoy insists that Kirk investigate the colony, in spite of its excellent reputation. On a tour of the institution, Kirk and psychiatrist Dr. Helen Noel find that its director, Dr. Tristan Adams, has constructed a brainwashing device—the neural neutralizer—with which he controls both inmates and staff. Aware that the two have discovered his secret, and to keep them under control, he uses the machine to make Kirk fall madly in love with Dr. Noel, then imprisons them in a ward room. On the Enterprise, Dr. van Gelder, because of his conditioning, cannot tell Spock what is going on, but the Vulcan tries a Vulcan mind touch and learns all. Dr. Noel escapes through an air-conditioning duct to the colony's power room to find and pull the main switch, thereby lowering the defensive shields of the planet and enabling Spock to bring in a security team. Meanwhile, Kirk fights with Adams, who falls into his own mind-wiping machine. Due to the weakening effect of the conditioning he has undergone, Kirk stumbles off, unaware that Adams is still in the neural neutralizer. Later Adams is found dead, due to loneliness, the result of being in the machine without an attending operator. The conditioned people are restored to normal, and the machine is dismantled.

Cast	Woodward
Kirk: William Shatner	Dr. Helen Noel: Marianna Hill
Spock: Leonard Nimoy	Lethe: Suzanne Wasson
McCoy: DeForest Kelley	Crewman: John Arndt
Uhura: Nichelle Nichols	Ensign Berkeley: Larry Anthony
Dr. Tristan Adams: James Gregory	Inmate: Ed McReady
Dr. Simon van Gelder: Morgan	Therapists: Eli Behar, Walt Davis

See Lexicon under:	McEveety, Vince
Adams, Dr. Tristan	Neural neutralizer
Bar-David, S.	Noel, Dr. Helen
Berkeley, Ensign	Penal colonies
General quarters 3	Penology, Central Bureau of
Inmate	Tantalus V
Lethe	Van Gelder, Dr. Simon
Loneliness	Vulcan mind touch

THE CORBOMITE MANEUVER

BY JERRY SOHL
DIRECTED BY JOE SARGENT
STARDATE: 1512.2   AIRED: 11/10/66

In uncharted regions, the Enterprise encounters an alien space buoy, a whirling cube that first blocks the way and then destroys the Enterprise's recorder-marker. When the ship's phasers destroy the buoy, an alien ship, the Fesarius, appears, and the ghostly face of Balok, who says that the Enterprise must be destroyed for trespassing and hostile actions. Kirk tries a bluff, telling Balok that if the Enterprise is fired upon, the "corbomite" in the ship's hull will explode and destroy both ships. The Fesarius then takes the Enterprise in tow, but Kirk pulls his ship away so sharply that the alien ship is apparently disabled. Answering a distress call from the tiny pilot vessel that accompanies the alien ship, Kirk takes McCoy aboard it to check on possible injury to the aliens. They discover that the Fesarius is manned by only one, friendly alien, who has been testing the Terrans to see if they are as peaceful as they claim. Kirk leaves Lieutenant Dave Bailey on board the alien vessel as a cultural envoy to Balok's First Federation, and they drink toasts to friendly relations.

Cast	Scott: James Doohan
Kirk: William Shatner	Uhura: Nichelle Nichols
Spock: Leonard Nimoy	Lieutenant Dave Bailey: Anthony Call
McCoy: DeForest Kelley	Balok: Clint Howard
Sulu: George Takei	Yeoman Rand: Grace Lee Whitney

See Lexicon under:	Recorder-marker
Bailey, Lieutenant Dave	Religion
Balok	Sargent, Joe
Corbomite	Sohl, Jerry
Fesarius	Space buoy
First Federation	Tranya
Pilot vessel	

THE MENAGERIE PARTS I AND II

BY GENE RODDENBERRY
DIRECTED BY MARC DANIELS (PART I) AND
ROBERT BUTLER (PART II)
STARDATE: 3012.4   AIRED: 11/17/66 AND 11/24/66

The Enterprise is falsely directed to Starbase 11, where Kirk, Spock, and McCoy are shocked to discover that a former commander of the Enterprise, Captain Christopher Pike, is horribly scarred and totally paralyzed from an accident; radiation poisoning has made the disfigurement irreversible. Spock, who served under Captain Pike before he became Kirk's First Officer, is visibly shaken by the meeting. By means of misdirection and tampering with several computers, Spock takes over the Enterprise, kidnaps Pike, and locks the controls of the starship on a course for Talos IV, a planet placed off limits by General Order 7—a quarantine so strict that to visit the planet means the death penalty. Once the ship is underway, Spock turns himself in for court-martial, and Kirk finds himself with the problem of possibly having to sentence his First Officer—and friend—to death. In his own defense, Spock presents on a screen some scenes from the earlier visit to Talos IV, but he will not say how the information was obtained.

Many years ago, when Pike was commanding the Enterprise, the small, cerebral, subterranean Talosians had captured the captain to serve as breeding stock for a stronger race that could live on the surface of Talos IV. The Talosians had used illusion for so long that it had weakened them as a race; they needed other, more rugged beings to withstand the hardships of pioneering their harsh planet. The Talosians used a human girl named Vina, the survivor of an earlier ship crash on Talos, to capture Pike's interest. Vina was presented to Pike in the guise of a Rigellian maiden in distress, a warm and loving Earth girl, and a sexy Orion slave dancer, but Pike would not cooperate with the Talosians' obvious efforts to mate their human specimens. The Talosians had then brought down other females from the Enterprise, to give Pike a choice. However, when he threatened to kill them all unless they were released, the Talosians had decided that humans were too violent to be useful, and the Enterprise people were freed. Vina, despite her obvious affection for Pike, preferred to stay on Talos IV, because without the Talosian illusions she was ugly and deformed from the crash that had stranded her there.

At the end of this presentation, the Talosians themselves appear on the Enterprise screen, admitting that their mind contacts and powers of illusion can reach far beyond their own planet, and that the scenes just witnessed have come from them. They have used the idea of a court-martial to keep Kirk's thoughts directed away from changing the course of the Enterprise until it came within reach of Talos IV. The diversion has worked—Kirk's worry about his friend has kept him from thinking too clearly about anything else. The Talosians offer to allow Captain Pike to live out his life with them with the illusion of health, free from the limitations of his crippled body. Kirk, with authorization from Star Fleet Command, permits Pike to remain on Talos IV, and the charges against Spock are dropped. The last view of Talos IV shows Vina, happy with her illusion of youth and beauty, walking with a strong, handsome Captain Pike at her side.

Cast	
Kirk: William Shatner	Barrett)
Spock: Leonard Nimoy	Dr. Phillip Boyce: John Hoyt
McCoy: DeForest Kelley	Yeoman Colt: Laurel Goodwin
Scott: James Doohan	José Tyler: Peter Duryea
Uhura: Nichelle Nichols	The Keeper: Meg Wyllie
Sulu: George Takei	Two Talosians: Georgia Schmidt,
Commodore José Mendez: Malachi Throne	Serena Sands
Injured Captain Pike: Sean Kenney	Dr. Theodore Haskins: Jon Lormer
Miss Piper: Julie Parrish	Survivors: Leonard Mude, Anthony Jochim
Lieutenant Hansen: Hagan Beggs	Vina: Susan Oliver
Chief Humbolt: George Sawaya	Geologist: Ed Madden
Security Chief: Brett Dunham	C.P.O. Garison: Adam Roarke
Young Captain Christopher Pike: Jeffrey Hunter	Transporter Chief Pitcairn: Clegg Hoyt
Number One: M. Leigh Hudec (Majel	Space Officer: Robert Philips
	Orion Trader: Joseph Mell
	Stunt Double: Bob Herron (Kirk)

THE CONSCIENCE OF THE KING

BY BARRY TRIVERS
DIRECTED BY GERD OSWALD
STARDATE: 2817.6   AIRED: 12/8/66

". . . the play's the thing wherein I'll catch the conscience of the King."

—Shakespeare, Hamlet II. 2

Twenty years before this story starts, most of the population of Tarsus IV was murdered by Kodos the Executioner, who escaped justice. Dr. Thomas Leighton calls the Enterprise to Planet Q to tell Kirk of his suspicion that actor Anton Karidian is actually Kodos. Dr. Leighton, Kirk, and Lieutenant Kevin Riley are the only surviving witnesses to Kodos's former atrocities; the rest have died in mysterious circumstances. Suddenly, Leighton is killed. Kirk takes the Karidian Players aboard the Enterprise—ostensibly to transport them to Benecia Colony, but really so that he can study Karidian, and also get another look at Lenore Karidian, the actor's daughter. Riley is poisoned and nearly dies, then learns of Kirk's suspicions about the actor. Riley visits the theater area, where the Karidian Players are performing Hamlet for the crew. Recognizing Karidian as Kodos, Riley at once tries to kill him. Kirk intervenes and goes to take Karidian prisoner, learning only then that it is Lenore who has been killing the witnesses to her father's identity. Karidian, horrified by this, steps into a phaser bolt that Lenore shoots at Kirk, and Lenore goes mad.

Cast
Kirk: William Shatner
Spock: Leonard Nimoy
McCoy: DeForest Kelley
Uhura: Nichelle Nichols
Yeoman Rand: Grace Lee Whitney
King Duncan: Karl Bruck
Hamlet: Marc Adams

Anton Karidian: Arnold Moss
Lenore Karidian: Barbara Anderson
Lieutenant Kevin Riley: Bruce Hyde
Lieutenant Leslie: Eddie Paskey
Lieutenant Matson: David Troy
Martha Leighton: Natalie Norwick
Dr. Thomas Leighton: William Sargent

See Lexicon under:
Arcturian
Astral Queen
Benecia Colony
"Beyond Antares"
Cygnia Minor
Daily, Captain Jon
Galactic Cultural Exchange Project
Games and recreation
Hamlet
Hamlet, Prince
Karidian, Lenore
Karidian Players

King Duncan
Kodos the Executioner
Leighton, Dr. Thomas
Leighton, Martha
Matson, Lieutenant
Oswald, Gerd
Planet Q
Riley, Lieutenant Kevin
Saurian brandy
Shakespeare, William
Tarsus IV
Tetralubisol
Trivers, Barry

BALANCE OF TERROR

BY PAUL SCHNEIDER
DIRECTED BY VINCE McEVEETY
STARDATE: 1709   AIRED: 12/15/66

Kirk is about to officiate at the wedding of Angela Martine and Robert Tomlinson when the Romulans attack Outpost 4, which guards the neutral zone between Federation and Romulan territory. The Romulans use an invisibility screen and a new weapon, photon torpedoes, to destroy Outpost 4—as they have Outposts 1, 3, and 8—then head for home, with the Enterprise in pursuit. While making them invisible, the screen makes it nearly impossible for them to detect anything outside the ship, so the Romulans aren't sure if the "blip" following them is an enemy ship or a harmless echo. The Terrans pick up a picture of the Romulan bridge and learn that the Romulans are of Vulcan descent, which makes Lieutenant Stiles—whose forebears fought in the Romulan War—very suspicious of Spock. The Romulan commander, a man of great character and honor, attempts to shake off the Enterprise but is forced to turn and fight. Both ships sustain damages; the Romulan ship is low on fuel, and the Enterprise has lost most of its phaser power. A leak in the phaser coolant system poisons the air, disabling Tomlinson and Stiles, who are manning the one remaining phaser. Spock fires the phaser manually and rescues Stiles. Tomlinson dies; Stiles survives, and overcomes his bigotry toward Vulcans. The Romulan ship is disabled, and its commander, rather than submit to capture, salutes Kirk as an honored enemy and destroys his own ship.

Cast
Kirk: William Shatner
Spock: Leonard Nimoy
McCoy: DeForest Kelley
Scott: James Doohan
Sulu: George Takei
Uhura: Nichelle Nichols
Yeoman Rand: Grace Lee Whitney
Romulan Commander: Mark Lenard
Lieutenant Andrew Stiles: Paul Comi
Decius: Lawrence Montaigne
Centurion: John Warburton

Specialist Robert Tomlinson: Stephen Mines
Specialist 2/C Angela Martine: Barbara Baldavin
Commander Hanson: Gary Walberg
Crewman Fields: John Arndt
Crewman Brenner: (Unknown)
Romulan Scope Operator: Robert Chadwick
Romulan Crewmen: Walter Davis, Vince Deadrick

See Lexicon under:
Centurion
Decius
Hanson, Commander
Icarus 4
Invisibility screen
Marriage
Martine, Angela
McEveety, Vince
Neutral zone
Outposts
Phaser coolant
Photon torpedoes

Praetor
Remus
Rodinium
Romii
Romulan commander
Romulan procedure, standard
Romulans
Romulan uniforms
Romulan War
Romulus
Schneider, Paul
Stiles, Lieutenant Andrew
Tomlinson, Specialist Robert

SHORE LEAVE

BY THEODORE STURGEON
DIRECTED BY ROBERT SPARR
STARDATE: 3025.3   AIRED: 12/29/66

A party from the Enterprise lands on a previously un-charted planet to check out its suitability for shore leave. Suddenly, McCoy sees Alice in Wonderland follow the White Rabbit down a hole in the ground. Kirk answers McCoy's call for help and unexpectedly meets Finnegan, his archenemy from Academy days. While trying to catch Finnegan, Kirk meets Ruth, a long-lost girlfriend, who, like Finnegan, has not aged a day. Other members of the landing party encounter such things as a Bengal tiger, Don Juan, a Samurai warrior, a World War II fighter plane; a black knight on horseback charges McCoy with a lance—and kills him. It quickly becomes apparent that on this planet one's thoughts materialize and have to be dealt with. But the planet is not hostile: It is an amuse-ment park for a race of highly advanced beings. Their caretaker brings McCoy back to life. The crew of the Enterprise are invited to spend their shore leave here, and, knowing that the thought effects are not permanent, they accept. Kirk gets to beat the tar out of Finnegan and wander off with Ruth; others find their own pleasures. Spock goes back to the ship, where some semblance of logic can be maintained.

Cast
Kirk: William Shatner
Spock: Leonard Nimoy
McCoy: DeForest Kelley
Sulu: George Takei
Uhura: Nichelle Nichols
Alice in Wonderland: Marcia Brown
Specialist 2/C Angela Martine-Teller: Barbara Baldavin
Yeoman Tonia Barrows: Emily Banks
Caretaker: Oliver McGowan

Lieutenant Esteban Rodriguez: Perry Lopez
Finnegan: Bruce Mars
Don Juan: James Gruzaf
Ruth: Shirley Bonne
Samurai: Sebastian Tom
White Rabbit: Bill Blackburn
Black Knight: Paul Baxley
Stunt Doubles: Paul Baxley, Vince Deadrick

See Lexicon under:
Airplane
Alice in Wonderland
Amusement-park planet
Barrows, Yeoman Tonia
Birds
Black knight
Cabaret girls
Caretaker
Carroll, Lewis
Cellular casting
Don Juan
Finnegan
Games and recreation

Martine, Specialist 2/C Angela
Omicron Delta region
Police Special
Power field
Rigel II
Rodriguez, Lieutenant Esteban
Ruth
Samurai
Sparr, Robert
Strafing run
Sturgeon, Theodore
Tiger, Bengal
White Rabbit

THE GALILEO SEVEN

BY OLIVER CRAWFORD AND S. BAR-DAVID
STORY BY OLIVER CRAWFORD
DIRECTED BY ROBERT GIST
STARDATE: 2821.5   AIRED: 1/5/67

Spock, McCoy, Scott, and four other crewmen set out in the shuttlecraft Galileo to study the quasarlike phenome-non Murasaki 312, which pulls them off course. Out of sensor range of the Enterprise, the Galileo lands on Taurus II, and attempts to repair the shuttlecraft are made. The Enterprise's search for the shuttlecraft is hampered not only by Murasaki 312's effect on the in-struments, but by Commissioner Ferris, who wants to abandon the search and proceed on course. On Taurus II, two of the crewman/specialists are killed by giant humanoids. Lieutenant Boma, a third specialist, causes much irritation by insisting that Spock drop repair at-tempts to give the crewmen what he considers a proper burial. As the Enterprise prepares to leave the sector, the Galileo achieves orbit, but it hasn't the power to break away from the planet. No other solution offering itself, Spock ignites the remaining fuel, signaling the Enterprise with a flare. They are beamed aboard just as the Galileo disintegrates.

Cast
Kirk: William Shatner
Spock: Leonard Nimoy
McCoy: DeForest Kelley
Scott: James Doohan
Sulu: George Takei
Uhura: Nichelle Nichols
Lieutenant Boma: Don Marchall
Gaetano: Peter Marko
Latimer: Reese Vaughn

Lieutenant Commander Kelowitz: Grant Woods
Yeoman Mears: Phyllis Douglas
High Commissioner Ferris: John Crawford
Creature: Buck Maffei
Transporter Officer: David L. Ross
Stunt Doubles: Gary Coombs, Frank Vinci

See Lexicon under:
Bar-David, S.
Boma, Lieutenant
Columbus
Crawford, Oliver
"Creatures"
Ferris, High Commissioner
Folsom Point
Gaetano
Galileo
Gist, Robert
Hanson's Planet

Kelowitz, Lieutenant Commander
Latimer
Makus III
Mears, Yeoman
Murasaki 312
New Paris
O'Neill, Ensign
Religion
Space normal speed
Taurean system
Taurus II

THE SQUIRE OF GOTHOS

BY PAUL SCHNEIDER
DIRECTED BY DON McDOUGALL
STARDATE: 2124.5   AIRED: 1/12/67

In a region of space supposedly devoid of stars and other matter, the Enterprise comes upon a planet, Gothos, whose presence there can not be explained. When Kirk and Sulu suddenly disappear, McCoy takes a search team down to look for them and encounters Trelane, a humanoid with great psionic powers and a predilection for things military and Earth's eighteenth century. His home reflects his interests. In spite of his great powers, however, Trelane is impetuous, willful, without self-control. He has kidnapped Kirk and Sulu to use as specimens for his collection, but when McCoy and the others appear, Trelane invites everyone to a party. Spock beams back to the ship, but Trelane, who insists on having his way, follows and brings the whole bridge crew down to Gothos for a banquet. Kirk provokes Trelane into a duel over Yeoman Ross, and in the fight destroys the mechanism by which Trelane controls the planet. Trelane repairs it and prevents the Enterprise from leaving, until Kirk offers himself as prey in a "fox hunt": himself for the ship's freedom. As Trelane is about to kill Kirk, two energy beings manifest themselves to prevent this, apologizing to Kirk for letting their child play so roughly and scolding Trelane for his irresponsible behavior and selfish disrespect for other beings.

Cast	
Kirk: William Shatner	Trelane: William Campbell
Spock: Leonard Nimoy	Lieutenant Karl Jaeger: Richard Carlyle
McCoy: DeForest Kelley	Lieutenant DeSalle: Michael Barrier
Scott: James Doohan	Yeoman Teresa Ross: Venita Wolf
Sulu: George Takei	Mother's Voice: Barbara Babcock
Uhura: Nichelle Nichols	Father's Voice: James Doohan
	Double: Gary Coombs (Kirk)

See Lexicon under:	
Beta 6	McDougall, Don
DeSalle, Lieutenant Vincent	Quadrant 904
Duel	Queen of Sheba
Gothos	Ross, Yeoman Teresa
Helen	Schneider, Paul
Jaeger, Lieutenant Karl	Slang, Trelane's
Judge	Star desert
	Trelane

ARENA

BY GENE L. COON   STORY BY FREDERICK BROWN
DIRECTED BY JOSEPH PEVNEY
STARDATE: 3045.6   AIRED: 1/19/67

The Enterprise finds that the Cestus III base has recently been destroyed by aliens, and follows their ship. In an uncharted sector both ships are caught and held by an advanced race called Metrons, who dislike trespassers. Since Metrons believe that physical combat is most suitable for individuals, not groups, they put Kirk and the captain of the alien ship on an uninhabited asteroid to fight it out. The winner and his ship will be freed; the loser and his ship and crew will be destroyed. The alien captain is an intelligent but belligerent creature called a Gorn, resembling a seven-foot-tall tyrannosaurus with iridescent eyes. He has destroyed the base on Cestus III, he tells Kirk, because he considered its presence there a hostile invasion into Gorn territory. Though the Gorn has the advantage of strength, Kirk has more speed, and he manages to keep out of the Gorn's claws long enough to combine local mineral resources into gunpowder, which he uses in a primitive cannon to wound the Gorn. When Kirk refuses to kill his antagonist, the Metrons concede that there is some hope for his species after all. Both captains are sent back to their respective ships, which are removed from the area.

Cast	
Kirk: William Shatner	Lieutenant O'Herlihy: Jerry Ayres
Spock: Leonard Nimoy	Lieutenant Commander Kelowitz: Grant Woods
McCoy: DeForest Kelley	Lieutenant Harold: Tom Troupe
Scott: James Doohan	Lieutenant Lang: James Farley
Sulu: George Takei	Lieutenant DePaul: Sean Kenney
Uhura: Nichelle Nichols	Gorn: Gary Coombs and Bobby Clark
Metron: Carole Shelyne	Double: Dick Dial (Kirk)

See Lexicon under:	
Arcanis	Hand cannon
Asteroid	Harold, Lieutenant
Brown, Frederick	Kelowitz, Lieutenant Commander
Cestus III	Lang, Lieutenant
Coon, Gene L.	Metron
DePaul, Lieutenant	Pevney, Joseph
Gorn	Travers, Commodore
Grenade launcher	Weapon

TOMORROW IS YESTERDAY

BY D. C. FONTANA
DIRECTED BY MICHAEL O'HERLIHY
STARDATE: 3113.2   AIRED: 1/26/67

The gravitational field of a black star has put the Enterprise in a time warp that sends it back to twentieth-century Earth. Men at the Omaha Air Base detect this most peculiar UFO in the upper atmosphere and send a fighter plane after it. The Enterprise destroys the plane and beams aboard the pilot, Captain Christopher. Kirk wants to prevent him from returning to warn the others, but Spock finds that they cannot do so without seriously altering history. They have to return him to Earth, but first they must remove all evidence of the Enterprise's appearance from Air Force records so that Christopher's story will not be believed. When Kirk and Sulu beam down to remove photographs and erase computer tapes, Kirk is captured by APs. Spock and Christopher use surprise tactics to get Kirk out of trouble; then Spock and Scotty duplicate the conditions of the time warp, returning the Enterprise to the twenty-second century and Christopher to the moment just before he was beamed aboard. This time, he sees no UFO to attack, and the Air Force concludes that the sighting was a mirage. In effect, none of the foregoing ever happened.

Cast

Kirk: William Shatner	Crewman: Sherri Townsend
Spock: Leonard Nimoy	Air Police Sergeant: Hal Lynch
McCoy: DeForest Kelley	Colonel Fellini: Ed Peck
Scott: James Doohan	Technician Webb: Richard Merrifield
Sulu: George Takei	Transporter Chief Kyle: John Winston
Uhura: Nichelle Nichols	Air Force Captain: Mark Dempsey
Captain John Christopher: Roger Perry	Air Police: Jim Spencer

See Lexicon under:

Airplane	Fontana, D. C.
Air Police sergeant	498th Air Base
Alpha Centauri	Interceptor
Blackjack	Kyle, Lieutenant
Black star	Missiles
Bluejay 4	O'Herlihy, Michael
Calendar, old	Omaha Air Base
Christopher, Captain John	Slang, mid-twentieth century
Computer, Enterprise	Slingshot effect
Cygnet XIV	Starbase 9
Deflectors	Tractor beam
Earth-Saturn probe	UFO
Enterprise, U.S.S.	United Earth Space Probe Agency
Fellini, Colonel	Webb, Technician
First manned moon shot	Wing camera

COURT-MARTIAL

BY DON M. MANKIEWICZ & STEPHEN W. CARABATSOS
STORY BY DON M. MANKIEWICZ
DIRECTED BY MARC DANIELS
STARDATE: 2947.3   AIRED: 2/2/67

The Enterprise puts in at Starbase 11 for repairs to damage incurred during an ion storm, and Kirk finds himself facing a court-martial for negligence during the storm resulting in the death of Lieutenant Commander Benjamin Finney. A former girlfriend of Kirk's, Areel Shaw, has been appointed his prosecutor; she recommends the shrewd, energetic Samuel T. Cogley for Kirk's defense lawyer. Shaw's prosecution is based on the Enterprise's computer records, which Kirk says are erroneous. With Cogley's aid, Spock finds that the computer's programming has been tampered with. Kirk finds that Finney is not dead but has been hiding, and has changed the computer records to frame Kirk, who once logged a careless and potentially dangerous error of Finney's and thus prevented his promotion. Cogley wins his case and promptly takes on a new one: Finney's defense.

Cast

Kirk: William Shatner	Lieutenant Commander Benjamin Finney: Richard Webb
Spock: Leonard Nimoy	
McCoy: DeForest Kelley	Jamie Finney: Alice Rawlings
Sulu: George Takei	Lieutenant Hansen: Hagen Beggs
Uhura: Nichelle Nichols	Timothy: Winston DeLugo
Captain Chandra: Reginald Lalsingh	Captain Krasnowsky: Bart Conrad
Commodore Stone: Percy Rodriguez	Space Command Representative Lindstrom: William Meader
Samuel T. Cogley: Elisha Cook, Jr.	
Lieutenant Areel Shaw: Joan Marshall	Personnel Officer: Nancy Wong

See Lexicon under:

Alpha III, Tribunals of	Mankiewicz, Don M.
Axanar	Martian Colonies, Fundamental Declaration of
Carabatsos, Stephen W.	
Chandra, Captain	Medals
Chess	Perjury
Cogley, Samuel T.	Personnel officer
Corrigan	Phase One search
Daniels, Marc	Pod
Finney, Lieutenant Commander Benjamin	Promotion list
	Republic, U.S.S.
Games and recreation	Rumors
General court-martial	Service record
Hansen, Lieutenant	Shaw, Lieutenant Areel
Human rights	Starbase 11
Intrepid, U.S.S.	Stone, Commodore
Krasnowsky, Captain	Teller
Lindstrom	Timothy
	White sound

THE RETURN OF THE ARCHONS

BY BORIS SOBELMAN
STORY BY GENE RODDENBERRY
DIRECTED BY JOSEPH PEVNEY
STARDATE: 3156.2   AIRED: 2/9/67

The communal culture of Beta III is backward and static, the product of a group mind known as "the Body," which is controlled by the omniscient dictator-spirit Landru. The Enterprise is in danger of being pulled from its orbit, its crew to be absorbed into the Body—a fate similar to that of the U.S.S. Archon a century earlier. The Archon's survivors had formed an underground to fight the Body, and its present members help Kirk and Spock to reach Landru: a complex computer with the memory of a scientist six thousand years dead—but without his wisdom. Kirk explains to the computer that in trying to preserve Beta III's culture it has really stultified and harmed it. Landru destroys itself, leaving the people, with Federation aid on the way, to work out a human-oriented, individualistic culture of growth and progress.

Cast
Kirk: William Shatner
Spock: Leonard Nimoy
McCoy: DeForest Kelley
Scott: James Doohan
Sulu: George Takei
Uhura: Nichelle Nichols
Reger: Harry Townes
Marplon: Torin Thatcher
Landru: Charles Macauley
Lindstrom: Christopher Held

Tula: Brioni Farrell
First Lawgiver: Sid Haig
Tamar: Jon Lormer
Hacom: Morgan Farley
Bilar: Ralph Maurer
Lieutenant Leslie: Eddie Paskey
Guard: David L. Ross
Lieutenant O'Neil: Sean Morgan
Young Woman: Barbara Webber
Stunt Double: Bob Clark

See Lexicon under:
Absorbed
Archon, U.S.S.
Archons
Beta III, in star system 6-11
Bilar
Body, the
Clothes of the Body
Compulsory involuntary stimulus to action
Festival
Hacom
Hall of Audiences
Landru
Lawgiver, First

Leslie, Lieutenant
Lindstrom
Marplon
O'Neil, Lieutenant
Pevney, Joseph
Prime directive
Red Hour
Reger
Roddenberry, Gene
Sobelman, Boris
Staff, Lawgiver's
Star system 6-11
Tamar
Tula
Valley, the

SPACE SEED

BY GENE L. COON AND CAREY WILBUR
DIRECTED BY MARC DANIELS
STARDATE: 3141.9   AIRED: 2/16/67

The Enterprise encounters the S.S. Botany Bay, a "sleeper ship" containing, in suspended animation, survivors of the Eugenics Wars of the 1990s—genetically selected "supermen" with exceptional mental and physical strength. Khan Noonian Singh, the leader of these people, who once ruled a quarter of Earth, dazzles Lieutenant Marla McGivers, a historian aboard the Enterprise, and with her help he takes over the ship. Needing the crew of the Enterprise to transport his people to civilization, Khan uses drastic persuasive methods on them—including forcing them to watch Kirk die in a decompression chamber—which turns McGivers against him. She rescues Kirk in time, and the captain and Spock recapture the ship. Khan and his people are banished to Ceti Alpha V, a habitable but rugged planet. Rather than court-martial McGivers, Kirk allows her to go with Khan.

Cast
Kirk: William Shatner
Spock: Leonard Nimoy
McCoy: DeForest Kelley
Scott: James Doohan
Uhura: Nichelle Nichols
Khan Noonian Singh: Ricardo Montalban
Lieutenant Marla McGivers: Madlyn Rhue

Lieutenant Spinelli: Blaisdell Makee
Joaquin: Mark Tobin
Elite Crewman: Kathy Ahart
Elite Female Guard: Joan Johnson
Guard: Bobby Bass
Baker: Barbara Baldavin
Transporter Chief: John Winston
Nurse: Joan Webster
Crewmen: Jan Reddin, John Arndt
Doubles: Gary Coombs, Chuck Couch

See Lexicon under:
Antigravity test units
Botany Bay, S.S.
Calendar, old
Ceti Alpha V
Coon, Gene L.
Daniels, Marc
DY-500
DY-100
Eugenics Wars
Games and recreation
Gamma 400 System
Harrison, Technician 1/C

Hypothermia
Joaquin
Khan Noonian Singh
Ling
McGivers, Lieutenant Marla
McPherson
Rodriquez
Sleeper ship
Spinelli, Lieutenant
Starbase 12
Thule, Technician 1/C
Wilbur, Carey

A TASTE OF ARMAGEDDON

BY ROBERT HAMNER AND GENE L. COON
STORY BY ROBERT HAMNER
DIRECTED BY JOSEPH PEVNEY
STARDATE: 3192.1   AIRED: 2/23/67

Kirk is warned away from Eminiar VII, but Federation Ambassador Robert Fox insists on going ahead with his mission to open diplomatic relations. A landing party finds that the planet has been at war with its neighbor Vendikar for five centuries. However, the war is fought in a clean and orderly manner, with computers that select likely targets; people reported "killed" go to disintegration chambers. The Enterprise, in orbit above the planet, is declared a hit, whereupon the Eminians demand that the crew beam down to the planet to be disintegrated. Kirk and the landing party are held as hostages to insure the cooperation of the crew. By means of Spock's telepathy, Kirk's audacity, and a few sneak attacks, they win their way to the control room, where Kirk destroys the computer. The governments of Eminiar and Vendikar are faced with the terrors of real war—with real chaos and destruction—since they can no longer practice the sublimated variety. The adaptable Robert Fox steps in to help them make peace.

Cast
Kirk: William Shatner
Spock: Leonard Nimoy
McCoy: DeForest Kelley
Scott: James Doohan
Uhura: Nichelle Nichols
Ambassador Robert Fox: Gene Lyons
Anan 7: David Opatoshu

Sar 6: Robert Sampson
Mea 3: Barbara Babcock
Yeoman Tamura: Miko Mayama
Lieutenant Galloway: David L. Ross
Lieutenant DePaul: Sean Kenney
Eminiar Guards and Technicians:
    Eddie Paskey, Bill Blackburn, Ron
    Veto, Frank Vinci, John Burnside

See Lexicon under:
Anan 7
Code 710
Coon, Gene L.
DePaul, Lieutenant
Disruptors, weapon
Eminiar VII
Fox, Ambassador Robert
Fusion bomb
Galloway, Lieutenant
General Order 24
Hamner, Robert

High Council of the Eminian Union
Mea 3
Osborne, Lieutenant
Pevney, Joseph
Sar 6
Star cluster MGC 321
Tamura, Yeoman
Tricobalt satellite explosion
Trova
Valiant, U.S.S.
Vendikar (Eminiar III)
Vulcan mind touch

THIS SIDE OF PARADISE

BY D. C. FONTANA
STORY BY NATHAN BUTLER AND D. C. FONTANA
DIRECTED BY RALPH SENENSKY
STARDATE: 3417.3   AIRED: 3/2/67

Kirk and Spock can't figure out why the colonists on Omicron Ceti III, exposed for the past three years to deadly Berthold rays, are not only alive but surpassingly healthy. Leila Kalomi, who tried to reach Spock emotionally six years earlier on Earth, shows him symbiotic spores that induce in everyone feelings of harmony and peace, and a desire to stay in their paradise indefinitely. The spores break down Spock's inhibitions; he feels happy and as though he "belongs" for the first time in his life—and he is able to love Leila. Other crew members are infected by the spores and leave the Enterprise to join the colony. Kirk, the last holdout, succumbs to the influence, but at the thought of leaving the Enterprise he becomes so upset that his violent emotions nullify the effect of the spores. Kirk then taunts Spock until he is provoked to fight, and the extra adrenalin removes the influence of the spores from his system. Together, with the aid of subsonic sound waves, they bring the crew and the colonists back to their senses. The colonists, now aware of their lack of real accomplishment, plan to relocate where the spores cannot retard the colony's progress and growth, and the Enterprise returns to normal.

Cast
Kirk: William Shatner
Spock: Leonard Nimoy
McCoy: DeForest Kelley
Sulu: George Takei
Uhura: Nichelle Nichols
Leslie: Eddie Paskey
Leila Kalomi: Jill Ireland

Elias Sandoval: Frank Overton
Lieutenant Commander Kelowitz:
    Grant Woods
Painter: Dick Scotter
Lieutenant DeSalle: Michael Barrier
Crewman: Bobby Bass
Stunt Doubles: C. O'Brien (Kirk), Bill
Catching (Spock)

See Lexicon under:
Berengaria VII
Berthold rays
Butler, Nathan
DeSalle, Lieutenant Vincent
Dragon
Fontana, D. C.
Kalomi, Leila
Kelowitz, Lieutenant Commander

Medal of Honor
Medals
Omicron Ceti III
Painter
Sandoval, Elias
Senensky, Ralph
Spores
Starbase 27

THE DEVIL IN THE DARK

BY GENE L. COON
DIRECTED BY JOSEPH PEVNEY
STARDATE: 3196.1   AIRED: 3/9/67

An unknown menace is roaming the mining tunnels of Janus VI, damaging machinery and killing the miners. Soon after the Enterprise arrives to investigate, a reactor pump is stolen and the colony is threatened by a runaway reactor. Kirk, Spock, and some security men search for the killer, and discover a strange stonelike creature that can burrow through rock easily. They wound it with a phaser blast, but it escapes. Later, Kirk finds himself cornered by the creature. When it doesn't attack, Spock makes telepathic contact with it, and learns that it is a longtime native of the planet, an intelligent and generally peaceful individual called a Horta. It had no objection to sharing the planet with the miners until they broke into its hatchery and destroyed many Horta eggs; then it attacked to protect its unborn children. With Spock as interpreter, the humans explain that they thought the eggs, large silicon nodules, were merely curious mineral growths, and that no hostility was intended. McCoy, in a medical first, treats the silicon-based creature, a peace treaty is arranged between the Horta and the miners, and Kirk retrieves the reactor pump. As the Enterprise leaves, the miners are rejoicing at the prospect of becoming embarrassingly rich, with the help of the young Hortas as miners.

Cast	
Kirk: William Shatner	Horta: James Prohaska
Spock: Leonard Nimoy	Lieutenant Commander Giotto: Barry
McCoy: DeForest Kelley	Russo
Scott: James Doohan	Ed Appel: Brad Weston
Guard: John Cavett	Schmitter: Biff Elliott
Chief Engineer Vanderberg: Ken Lynch	Engineer: George E. Allen
	Sam: Dick Dial

See Lexicon under:	
Appel, Ed	Pergium
Chamber of the Ages	Pevney, Joseph
Checkpoint Tiger	Phasers 1 and 2
Chemical corrosion	PXK reactor
Coon, Gene L.	Roberts
Giotto, Lieutenant Commander	Rock creature
Guard	Schmitter
Horta	Silicon creatures
Horta's baby	Silicon nodule
Janus VI	Subsurface charts
Kelly	Thermoconcrete
Lewis	Tricorders
Osborne, Lieutenant	Vandenberg, Chief Engineer
	Vulcan mind touch

ERRAND OF MERCY

BY GENE L. COON
DIRECTED BY JOHN NEWLAND
STARDATE: 3198.4   AIRED: 3/23/67

The neutral planet Organia occupies a strategic position between the Klingon Empire and the Federation. Kirk and Spock attempt to persuade the Organians to accept a Federation base on their planet to protect them from Klingon invasion, but the Organians prefer to keep their own medieval culture and not take sides in anyone's war. While diplomatic discussions are underway, the Klingons invade, leaving Kirk and Spock stranded on Organia. Disguised as an Organian and a Vulcan civilian, respectively, they work a bit of sabotage and are captured by the Klingons. To their surprise and bewilderment, they are set free by the Organians, whereupon they immediately attack a Klingon fortress to take Klingon Commander Kor prisoner. As the crew of the Enterprise plans to fight it out with Kor's men, Federation and Klingon fleets move into position for battle over the planet. At last the Organians put their collective foot down. They are not the primitives they seem, but highly advanced energy beings who abhor violence. They prevent all fighting, and force the Klingon Empire and the Federation to sign a peace treaty.

Cast	
Kirk: William Shatner	Claymare: Peter Brocco
Spock: Leonard Nimoy	First Klingon Lieutenant: Victor
Sulu: George Takei	Lundin
Uhura: Nichelle Nichols	Second Klingon Lieutenant: George
Trefayne: David Hillary Hughes	Sawaya
Ayelborne: Jon Abbott	Klingon Soldier: Walt Davis
Commander Kor: John Colicos	Klingon Guards: Gary Coombs,
	Bobby Bass

See Lexicon under:	
Ayelborne	Klingon lieutenant, second
Baroner	Kor, Commander
Claymare	Mind-sifter
Code I	Newland, John
Council of Elders	Organia
Kevas	Richter scale of culture
Klingon Empire	Trefayne
Klingon lieutenant, first	Trillium
	Unit XY-75847

THE ALTERNATIVE FACTOR

BY DON INGALLS
DIRECTED BY GERD OSWALD
STARDATE: 3087.6   AIRED: 3/30/67

Orbiting a barren planet, the Enterprise experiences a moment of nonexistence: The whole stellar system simply blinks out. On the planet below they find a man called Lazarus, who says the effect was caused by his enemy, whom Lazarus has been pursuing in his space/time craft to avenge the destruction of his people. Lazarus is taken aboard the Enterprise, and turns out to have a dual personality, alternating moods of rage and madness with moods of calm and sanity—and a wound on his head keeps appearing and disappearing! It is soon discovered that there are two of him, only one of whom can appear at any one time. Lazarus wants to use the ship's dilithium crystals to track down his enemy; when Kirk refuses, he steals them and disappears. Kirk follows him down to the planet and learns that the two Lazaruses are from parallel but opposite universes: Lazarus A, the madman from our universe, and Lazarus B, a sane and honorable man from the parallel, antimatter universe. If the two men meet in either universe, both universes will be destroyed. Kirk helps Lazarus B trap Lazarus A in an intermediate time corridor, where they can harm neither universe, and there they will remain for all time.

Cast
Kirk: William Shatner
Spock: Leonard Nimoy
McCoy: DeForest Kelley
Uhura: Nichelle Nichols
Transporter Technician: Christian Patrick
Lazarus A and B: Robert Brown
Lieutenant Charlene Masters: Janet MacLachlen

Commodore Barstow: Richard Derr
Lieutenant Leslie: Eddie Paskey
Engineering Assistant: Arch Whiting
Security Guards: Tom Lupo, Ron Veto, Bill Blackburn, Vince Calenti
Stunt Doubles: Gary Coombs (Kirk), Al Wyatt (Lazarus), Bill Catching (Lazarus)

See Lexicon under:
Alternative warp
Barstow, Commodore
Code I
Dilithium crystals
Experimentation chamber
Ingalls, Don
Lazarus A
Lazarus B

Leslie, Lieutenant
Magnetic communications satellite
Magnetic effect
Masters, Lieutenant Charlene
Oswald, Gerd
Parallel universe
"Rip" in the universe
Time chamber
Warp

THE CITY ON THE EDGE OF FOREVER

BY HARLAN ELLISON
DIRECTED BY JOSEPH PEVNEY
STARDATE: 3134.0   AIRED: 4/6/67

While in an unbalanced state caused by an accidental overdose of cordrazine, McCoy beams down to a strange planet, where he jumps through a time gate back to twentieth-century Earth and thereby drastically changes history—Earth itself may no longer exist, and certainly the Enterprise has vanished, leaving the landing party stranded. Kirk and Spock time-travel to the New York of 1930, where they hope to meet McCoy and undo the consequences of the doctor's intervention in time. While waiting for McCoy to appear, they meet an efficient and visionary social worker, Edith Keeler, and Kirk falls in love with her. Then they learn that McCoy will change history by saving her from death; otherwise, Edith would start a pacifist movement so effective that it would delay the United States' entry into World War II, thus giving Nazi Germany enough time to develop the atomic bomb and conquer the world. When McCoy shows up, Kirk, heartbroken, prevents him from rescuing Edith, and she dies. With history thus restored, Kirk, Spock, and McCoy return to the twenty-second century, and the landing party beam aboard the Enterprise.

Cast
Kirk: William Shatner
Spock: Leonard Nimoy
McCoy: DeForest Kelley
Scott: James Doohan
Sulu: George Takei
Uhura: Nichelle Nichols
Guard No. 1: Michael Barrier
Lieutenant Galloway: David L. Ross

Policeman: Hal Boylor
Edith Keeler: Joan Collins
Guardian: Bartell LaRue (Voice)
Rodent: John Harmon
Transporter Officer: John Winston
Chapel: Majel Barrett
Stunt and Doubles: Cary Loftin (Stunt Driver), Mary Statier (Edith), David Perna (McCoy), Bobby Bass (Scott)

See Lexicon under:
Cities
Cordrazine
Ellison, Harlan
Gable, Clark
Guardian of Forever
Hobby
Keeler, Edith
"Let me help"

Mechanical rice picker
Pevney, Joseph
Policeman
Rodent
Slang, Twentieth-century Depression era
Space warp
Twentieth century
Twenty-first Street Mission

OPERATION-ANNIHILATE!

BY STEPHEN W. CARABATSOS
DIRECTED BY HERSCHEL DAUGHERTY
STARDATE: 3287.2   AIRED: 4/13/67

A fatal epidemic of mass insanity that has destroyed the civilizations of several planets has now reached Deneva. Among those who die are Kirk's brother, Sam, and his wife; only Sam's son, Peter, survives. During an investigation, Spock is attacked by a flying creature; infected, he becomes violent, and has to be restrained. It is learned that the agent of the madness is a host of flat, levitating, single-celled creatures which together make up a non-contiguous nervous system of considerable power. These creatures grow tentacles around a victim's nervous system, and inflict excruciating pain as a means of control. Spock, exercising Vulcan pain control, is able to resist their influence and return to duty, but McCoy must still find a way to kill the parasites without harming their hosts. Theorizing that strong light may kill the creatures, the doctor subjects Spock to such fierce illumination that he is blinded in the tests—which do bear out the theory. Too late, McCoy realizes that only ultraviolet light is needed to kill the creatures. Kirk sets off ultraviolet satellite flares over Deneva, which free the inhabitants from the parasites. Spock's blindness turns out to be temporary; because of the bright Vulcan sun, his race developed a protective "extra eyelid," and he returns to the bridge with his sight restored.

Cast
Kirk: William Shatner
Spock: Leonard Nimoy
McCoy: DeForest Kelley
Scott: James Doohan
Sulu: George Takei
Uhura: Nichelle Nichols
Chapel: Majel Barrett

Kartan: Dave Armstrong
Peter Kirk: Craig Hundley
Aurelan Kirk: Joan Swift
Yeoman Zahra Jamal: Maurishka Taliferro
Denevans: Fred Carson, Jerry Catron
Stunt Doubles: Gary Coombs (Kirk), Bill Catching (Spock)

SECOND SEASON

AMO K TIME

BY THEODORE STURGEON
DIRECTED BY JOSEPH PEVNEY
STARDATE: 3372.7   AIRED: 9/15/67

In their attempt to deal with marriage on a logical basis without emotional involvement, Vulcans are ritually wedded in childhood, the marriage to be consummated in adulthood. Their evolutionary sexual sublimation breaks out periodically, when Vulcans must mate or die. It is now Spock's time. His Vulcan half has taken over: He seems irrational, even deranged, and McCoy informs Kirk that his First Officer will die unless he returns to Vulcan immediately. Despite orders to the contrary, Kirk heads directly for Vulcan and Spock's bride, T'Pring. Spock invites Kirk and McCoy down to the planet to participate in the wedding ceremony, and they accept with surprise and pleasure at this sudden show of friendship. T'Pring, however, shows no inclination to accept Spock as her husband, and chooses that he fight for her, as is her right by Vulcan custom. Another Vulcan, Stonn, seems eager to fight for T'Pring, but she surprises all by choosing Kirk as her champion. Kirk accepts, afraid that the debilitated Spock is too weak to fight a healthy Vulcan. However, after the challenge is accepted, Kirk and McCoy are informed that it is a fight to the death. After the first bout, McCoy protests that Kirk, unused to Vulcan's climate, is at a disadvantage, and he is allowed to inject a tri-ox compound to compensate. The fight resumes. Kirk dies, and McCoy takes his body back aboard the Enterprise. Spock's shock at his captain's death nullifies his mating urge. With no further interest in T'Pring, Spock surrenders her to Stonn, the woman's real interest, whom she did not want to risk in combat. Returning to the Enterprise to place himself under arrest for murder, Spock finds that Kirk is not dead: McCoy had given Kirk, not the tri-ox compound, but a knockout drug. For a second, Spock unrestrainedly rejoices before returning to his usual stoic Vulcan attitude.

Cast	
Kirk: William Shatner	Stonn: Lawrence Montaigne
Spock: Leonard Nimoy	Komack: Byron Morrow
McCoy: DeForest Kelley	Vulcan Executioner: Russ Peek
Sulu: George Takei	Vulcan Litterbearers: Joe Paz, Charles
Uhura: Nichelle Nichols	Palmer, Mark Russell, Gary Wright
Chekov: Walter Koenig	Vulcan Bell and Banner Carriers: Mauri
Chapel: Majel Barrett	Russell, Frank Vinci
T'Pring: Arlene Martel	Stunt Doubles: Dave Perna (Spock),
T'Pau: Celia Lovsky	Paul Baxley (Kirk), Phil Adams (Kirk)

See Lexicon under:	
Ahn-woon	Pevney, Joseph
Altair VI	Plak tow
Amanda	Plomeek
Eel-birds	Pon far
Finagle's laws	Regulus V
Kah-if-farr	Stonn
Kal-if-fee	Sturgeon, Theodore
Klee-fah	T'Pau
Komack, Admiral	T'Pring
Koon-ut kal-if-fee	Tri-ox compound
Kroykah	Vulcan
Lirpa	Vulcan marriage
Meditation	Vulcans
Neural paralyzer	Vulcan salute

W O MOURNS FOR ADONAIS?

BY GILBERT RALSTON AND GENE L. COON
STORY BY GILBERT RALSTON
DIRECTED BY MARC DANIELS
STARDATE: 3468.1   AIRED: 9/22/67

The Enterprise encounters a strange force in space that draws it to Pollux IV, where Kirk and a landing party find a being who claims to be Apollo, last of the ancient Greek gods, the other gods having died of loneliness since their departure from Mount Olympus. Apollo wants humans to stay on the planet and worship him; he has plans to settle the crew of the Enterprise into a simple, pastoral life and keep them there forever. Sensors can show that Apollo's superhuman characteristics derive from an organic ability to use energy from sources outside himself. He is extremely powerful, using force to show the landing party that they are under his control. Though daunted slightly by thunderbolts, storms, and Apollo's ability to transform himself into a giant, the people of the Enterprise are not impressed by the idea of becoming agrarian peasants at the feet of a god who throws temper tantrums. Their attempts to escape are hampered by Lieutenant Carolyn Palamas, whom Apollo wants for his bride. She falls in love with Apollo—to the chagrin of Scotty, who had other hopes. Kirk orders Lieutenant Palamas to reject Apollo for the sake of her fellow humans, which she does—reluctantly. Finally, Spock locates Apollo's power source in a small Greek-style temple, which is destroyed by the Enterprise's phasers. Spurned by a mortal woman, his powers gone, Apollo bewails the ingratitude of humans and spreads himself upon the wind to disappear.

Cast	
Kirk: William Shatner	Chekov: Walter Koenig
Spock: Leonard Nimoy	Apollo: Michael Forest
McCoy: DeForest Kelley	Lieutenant Carolyn Palamas: Leslie
Scott: James Doohan	Parrish
Sulu: George Takei	Lieutenant Kyle: John Winston
Uhura: Nichelle Nichols	Stunt Double: Jay Jones (Scott)

See Lexicon under:	
A-and-A officer	Kyle, Lieutenant
Antos IV	M-rays
Apollo	Olympus, Mount
Beta Geminorum	Palamas, Lieutenant Carolyn
Coon, Gene L.	Pollux V
Daniels, Marc	Pollux IV
Dryworm, giant	Ralston, Gilbert
	Starbase 12

THE CHANGELING

BY JOHN MEREDYTH LUCAS
DIRECTED BY MARC DANIELS
STARDATE: 3451.9   AIRED: 9/29/67

Nomad, a small but extremely powerful spacegoing machine, has destroyed several planets and now threatens the Enterprise. However, when Kirk identifies himself, Nomad decides that he must be "the Kirk"—its creator—and breaks off the attack. Brought aboard the Enterprise, Nomad wipes out Uhura's memory, kills Scott—and then "repairs" him—and creates other problems which are potentially disastrous. Spock learns through Vulcan mind touch that the original Nomad was a Terran space probe developed in the early twenty-first century by Jackson Roykirk; programmed to seek out new life and report back to Earth, Nomad was damaged by a meteor and drifted through space until it met an alien probe, Tan Ru, a soil sterilizer. Nomad and Tan Ru used their self-repair systems to combine themselves into one machine, a unique "changeling." Nomad's memory banks had been damaged, and the probe now believes that its mission is to seek out life—and destroy anything that is not perfect. Kirk takes a dangerous chance by pointing out that he is not "the Kirk"; since the machine made the mistake, it is not perfect and must be destroyed. Nomad, confused by Kirk's logic and its own error, blows itself up.

Cast	
Kirk: William Shatner	Chapel: Majel Barrett
Spock: Leonard Nimoy	Mr. Singh: Blaisdell Makee
McCoy: DeForest Kelley	Astrochemist: Barbara Gates
Scott: James Doohan	Lieutenant Carlisle: Arnold Lessing
Sulu: George Takei	Nomad: Vic Perrin (Voice)
Uhura: Nichelle Nichols	Engineer: Meade Martin
	Stunt Double: Jay Jones (Scott)

See Lexicon under:	
Antigravs, portable	Lucas, John Meredyth
Antimatter input valve	Malurian system
August 2020	Manway, Dr.
Auxiliary Control Room	Nomad
Calendar, old	Old-style interplanetary code
Carlisle, Lieutenant	Omega Cygni
Changeling	Other, the
Chart 14A	Roykirk, Jackson
Creator	Singh, Lieutenant
Daniels, Marc	Space probe
Games and recreation	Swahili
Gan ta nu i ka tan ru	Symbalene blood burn
Hyperencephalogram	Tan Ru
Kirk, the	Vulcan mind touch

MIRROR, MIRROR

BY JEROME BIXBY
DIRECTED BY MARC DANIELS
STARDATE: UNKNOWN   AIRED: 10/6/67

Captain Kirk and a landing party are trying to deal with the Halkans for dilithium crystals when an ion storm comes up. The Halkans are reluctant to close the deal, and Kirk, not wanting to harass them, requests permission to return to his ship until after the storm. The Halkans agree, and Scott beams the landing party up just as a particularly strong blast from the storm hits the starship. A transporter malfunction throws Kirk, Scott, McCoy, and Uhura into an alternate or mirror universe, in which a Galactic Empire is dominated by fear and force. They find themselves aboard the Imperial Starship Enterprise, ruled by force and assassination—but none of the crew seems to realize that there is any difference in the returning landing party. The Galactic Empire doubles of Kirk, Scott, McCoy, and Uhura (henceforth referred to as Kirk-2, Scott-2, etc.) have been beamed aboard the U.S.S. Enterprise, but Spock realizes that something is wrong and orders them imprisoned until the transporter malfunction can be corrected. Aboard the I.S.S. Enterprise, Kirk and his party understand that they are caught in an alternate universe, and almost immediately complications arise that can mean life or death for them all. In Universe-2, dealing with the Halkans for dilithium crystals can result in one of only two choices: The Halkans can give up the crystals or be annihilated. The crew expects Kirk to give the command for destruction; his hesitation arouses the suspicions of Spock-2. Kirk's unwarlike attitude is suspect in what is basically a dog-eat-dog universe. The Imperial Star Fleet sends Spock-2 secret orders to kill Kirk, advance himself to the captaincy, and exterminate the Halkans. Chekov-2 tries to assassinate his captain, but is foiled by the treachery of one of his own men. Spock-2, the only nearly civilized person on the ship, warns Kirk of his impending doom, but the captain continues to stall while Scotty, McCoy, and Uhura gather sufficient data to transport back to their own universe. Spock-2 and Marlena-2, the "captain's woman," assist the people from the U.S.S. Enterprise, at great risk to their own lives. As he and his people leave the barbarian ship, Kirk talks to Spock-2 about anarchy compared to the progress of civilization. Spock-2 seems almost persuaded to dispose of Kirk-2 after all—he could then control the I.S.S. Enterprise, manipulate the Imperial Star Fleet, and eventually work to bring civilization to the barbaric alternate universe.

THE APPLE

BY MAX EHRLICH AND GENE L. COON
STORY BY MAX EHRLICH
DIRECTED BY JOSEPH PEVNEY
STARDATE: 3715.0   AIRED: 10/13/67

Cast

Kirk: William Shatner
Spock: Leonard Nimoy
McCoy: DeForest Kelley
Scott: James Doohan
Sulu: George Takei
Uhura: Nichelle Nichols
Chekov: Walter Koenig
Lieutenant Marlena Moreau: Barbara Luna
Tharn: Vic Perrin

Farrell: Pete Kellett
Wilson: Garth Pillsbury
Computer Voice (Male): John Winston
Lieutenant Kyle: John Winston
Guard: Paul Prokop
Stunt Doubles: Paul Baxley (Kirk), Dave Perna (Spock), Vince Deadrick (McCoy), Jay Jones (Scott), Nedra Rosemond (Uhura), Bob Bass (Chekov's Boy No. 1), Bob Clark (Chekov's Boy No. 2), Johnny Mandell (Sulu's Boy)

Gamma Trianguli VI seems to be a paradise until the landing party learns that it contains such nasty surprises as poisonous plants that can fire thorns; exploding rocks; and lightning bolts with extremely good aim. After encountering these hazards, the Enterprise's landing party is considerably smaller and more wary—but the human inhabitants turn out to be beautiful, peaceful, innocent flower children who dress simply, deck themselves out in painted designs, and do not have to reproduce because they never age or die. The entity responsible for this seemingly idyllic life is Vaal, which looks like a huge serpent's head carved out of a rock wall, but is really an output terminal for an underground computerlike device. Disliking outside interference, Vaal decides to keep the landing party prisoner, but to do so it must first teach its people how to kill. Because it sees Kirk and the Enterprise crewmen as a threat to the stability of its culture, Vaal tries to pull the ship down from its orbit. The computer is quite right: In order to free his own people and the Enterprise from Vaal's power, Kirk must destroy it, which he does by starving it of reaction mass (the daily offerings from Vaal's people) and blasting through its weakened defenses. The people of Gamma Trianguli are left on their own, no longer immortal, to rediscover birth, death, and the patterns of human culture.

Cast

Kirk: William Shatner
Spock: Leonard Nimoy
McCoy: DeForest Kelley
Scott: James Doohan
Chekov: Walter Koenig
Kyle: John Winston
Akuta: Keith Andes
Yeoman Martha Landon: Celeste Yarnall
Sayana: Shari Nims

Makora: David Soul
Hendorff: Mal Friedman
Marple: Jerry Daniels
Ensign Mallory: Jay Jones
Kaplan: Dick Dial
Stunt Doubles: Julie Johnson (Landon), Paul Baxley (Native), Bobby Clark (Native), Vince Deadrick (Native), Ron Burke (Native)

THE DOOMSDAY MACHINE

BY NORMAN SPINRAD
DIRECTED BY MARC DANIELS
STARDATE: 4202.9+   AIRED: 10/20/67

A giant robot ship has wandered into the galaxy and is wreaking destruction by breaking up planets for fuel to sustain itself. Commodore Decker, commander of the Constellation, brings his ship up against the berserker, which kills his crew and cripples his ship. The Enterprise arrives to find the Constellation a floating, almost-lifeless hulk, with Decker the only one left on board. Kirk beams Decker aboard the Enterprise and works with Scotty to repair the Constellation. The berserker returns, putting both ships in jeopardy. Decker takes over the Enterprise, determined to destroy the robot ship even at the cost of the Enterprise and its crew. Spock tries to argue, and Decker pulls rank on him, firing on the berserker without success and refusing to retreat from the fast-approaching machine. The Vulcan points out that Decker's suicidal course is sufficient to prove that he is unstable, in which case the First Officer can relieve him of duty. Kirk, trapped aboard the Constellation, finally makes radio contact and supports Spock. Thwarted, Decker steals a shuttlecraft and drives down the throat of the robot ship, destroying himself. Kirk uses his idea and sends the Constellation, set to explode, down the berserker's maw. Kirk is transported to the Enterprise just as the Constellation explodes; the "doomsday machine" is deactivated.

Cast	
Kirk: William Shatner	Lieutenant Palmer: Elizabeth Rogers
Spock: Leonard Nimoy	Elliot: John Copage
McCoy: DeForest Kelley	Washburn: Richard Compton
Scott: James Doohan	Lieutenant Kyle: John Winston
Sulu: George Takei	Russ: Tim Burns
Commodore Matthew Decker: William Windom	Montgomery: Jerry Catron
	Stunt Double: Vince Deadrick (Decker)

See Lexicon under:	
Auxiliary Control Room	Neutronium
Berserker	Palmer, Lieutenant
Constellation, U.S.S.	Rigel colonies
Daniels, Marc	Russ
Decker, Commodore Matthew	Solar System L370
Doomsday machine	Solar System L374
Elliot	Spinrad, Norman
L 374-III	Star Fleet orders
Masada	System L374B
Montgomery	Washburn

CATSPAW

BY ROBERT BLOCH
DIRECTED BY JOSEPH PEVNEY
STARDATE: 3018.2   AIRED: 10/27/67

Two beings have set up haunted-housekeeping on Pyris VII, decorating their castle with skeletons and black cats, and disguising themselves as Sylvia, a witch with a magic amulet, and Korob, a warlock with a wand. They want to keep the men of the Enterprise from investigating their planet too closely, and to this end they kill a crewman and capture and make zombies of Scott and Sulu. Kirk, Spock, and McCoy are taken prisoner and given various demonstrations of power, including a voodoo-style overheating of the Enterprise. Then Sylvia takes an interest in Kirk and in the worlds he has seen; she no longer cares about the mission on which she and Korob have been sent, and instead wants to experience human feelings and sensation. She tempts Kirk with power and pleasure, but discovers that he is using her and becomes furious. Ultimately Korob helps Kirk and his people escape, but Sylvia takes on the form of a giant black cat and crushes the warlock beneath a door, killing him. Kirk snatches up Korob's wand, the source of his power, and uses it to destroy Sylvia's amulet, which has supported the illusions of the castle and the beings' human shapes. With the loss of illusion, Sylvia and Korob are seen to be tiny blue aliens, and quickly die. With the death of the creatures, Scott and Sulu return to normal.

Cast	
Kirk: William Shatner	Korob: Theo Marcuse
Spock: Leonard Nimoy	Jackson: Jimmy Jones
McCoy: DeForest Kelley	First Witch: Rhodie Cogan
Scott: James Doohan	Second Witch: Gail Bonney
Sulu: George Takei	Third Witch: Maryesther Denver
Uhura: Nichelle Nichols	Lieutenant Kyle: John Winston
Chekov: Walter Koenig	Stunt Doubles: Gary Downey (Kirk),
Lieutenant DeSalle: Michael Barrier	Frank Vinci (Spock), Jim Jones
Sylvia: Antoinette Bower	(McCoy), Vic Toyota (Sulu), Bob
	Bass (Scott), Carl Saxe (Korob)

See Lexicon under:	
Bloch, Robert	Pyris VII
Cat, black	Sylvia
Jackson	Starbase 9
Korob	Transmuter
Pevney, Joseph	Witches

I, MUDD

BY STEPHEN KANDEL AND DAVID GERROLD
DIRECTED BY MARC DANIELS
STARDATE: 4513.3   AIRED: 11/3/67

An android masquerading as a human member of the Enterprise kidnaps the starship and its crew, taking them to an unusual planet where Kirk encounters his old nemesis, Harry Mudd, and a large collection of androids. Designed by a long-dead race, the androids live only to serve, and Harry has set himself up as King Mudd the First, allowing the androids to grant his every wish. They take their duties so seriously that, as Mudd is the only human on hand to serve, they will not let him leave the planet. For this reason, he unscrupulously sent the android imposter to capture the Enterprise, hoping to exchange his own freedom for an entire starshipful of people the androids can serve. The androids don't see it that way, however: They want to go out into the galaxy and serve all of humankind—by protecting it from itself. To that end, they take over the Enterprise.

Horrified at the prospect of being dogged all their lives by helpful androids, the Enterprise's crew decide to do something about it. But it won't be easy. Mudd has had whole series of beautiful women created for his amusement (not to mention an android duplicate of his shrewish wife, Stella, which he can turn off whenever he wishes). Moreover, there are many other kinds of lures: McCoy is shown a medical laboratory, over which he waxes enthusiastic about the possibilities for research; Scotty is shown a machine shop and technical area that astounds him; and Spock is given a tour of what is supposedly the control center for all the androids. Uhura is promised a nearly immortal body that will remain young and beautiful, and Chekov feels that a planet full of nubile young females is even better than Leningrad.

When it becomes clear that none of the humans, including Mudd, will ever be allowed to leave, they plot against the stronger androids—even Kirk and Mudd agree to a temporary truce. Uhura, apparently dazzled by the promise of eternal youth and beauty, gives them away, informing the androids of the plot. Uhura's treachery is really a ploy to buy time, and to trick the androids into anticipating an escape attempt. To the androids' confusion, instead of escaping, everyone seems perfectly content, but they all begin to act totally illogical—even Spock manages a few paradoxes. The androids, unable to cope with the onslaught of illogic, short-circuit one by one, until the humans have regained control. The Enterprise wins its freedom and leaves Mudd in the custody of the androids—including several hundred more Stellas—until he reforms. Nobody is betting on how soon that will happen.

Cast
Kirk: William Shatner
Spock: Leonard Nimoy
McCoy: DeForest Kelley
Scott: James Doohan
Sulu: George Takei
Uhura: Nichelle Nichols
Chekov: Walter Koenig
Harry Mudd: Roger C. Carmel
Stella Mudd: Kay Elliott
Norman: Richard Tatro
"Alice" Series: Rhea and Alyce Andrece

"Herman" Series: Tom and Ted LeGarde
"Barbara" Series: Maureen and Colleen Thornton
"Maisie" Series: Tamara and Starr Wilson
Lieutenant Rowe: Mike Howden
Ensign Jordan: Michael Zaslow
Stunt Doubles: Loren James (Norman), Bob Bass (Engineer), Bob Orrison (Engineer)

METAMOR-PHOSIS

BY GENE L. COON
DIRECTED BY RALPH SENENSKY
STARDATE: 3219.4   AIRED: 11/10/67

Assistant Federation Commissioner Nancy Hedford has been assigned to stop a war on Epsilon Canaris III, but she contracts Sakuro's disease, a rare illness of alien origin which can be fatal unless treated quickly, so Kirk, Spock, and McCoy are transporting her in the shuttlecraft Galileo back to the Enterprise for treatment. At one time Nancy Hedford was doubtless an attractive, warm woman, but the terminal stages of the disease have made her feverish and quarrelsome. A cloud creature draws the shuttlecraft off course to a small planet, Gamma Canaris N, where they find a century-old pioneer in space exploration, Zefrem Cochrane. The cloud creature, whom Cochrane refers to as the "Companion," has kept him young, healthy, and handsome for decades; it has brought the Galileo to the planet to give Cochrane some human company and keep him happy. Bringing other humans to the planet, however, only makes Cochrane long for outer space and his own kind more than ever. Meanwhile, everyone is worried about getting Nancy to the Enterprise before it is too late, but the shuttlecraft is disabled, and the Companion prevents Spock from repairing it. Kirk convinces Cochrane that the Companion is holding them prisoner and thus is a threat to Nancy's life, and Cochrane reluctantly agrees to try to kill the cloud creature so that everyone can escape. The plan fails, and they discover that the cloud creature is capable of generating enormous charges of electrical energy which storm around them. Then, using a sophisticated communications device, they learn that the Companion has a feminine personality, and is very much in love with Cochrane, who doesn't think much of the idea. A solution is reached, however, when the Companion enters Nancy Hedford's dying body, to preserve her life and to know human love with Cochrane. The two personalities blend, and Cochrane, now free to leave, decides to stay on Gamma Canaris N with the pleasant and lovely woman resulting from the merger. They face together the possibility of living out a normal life span and raising a family.

Cast	
Kirk: William Shatner	Sulu: George Takei
Spock: Leonard Nimoy	Uhura: Nichelle Nichols
McCoy: DeForest Kelley	Nancy Hedford: Elinor Donahue
Scott: James Doohan	Zefrem Cochrane: Glenn Corbett
	Companion: Majel Barrett (Voice)

See Lexicon under:	
Alpha Centauri	Galileo
Cochrane, Zefrem	Gamma Canaris N
Companion, the	Hedford, Nancy
Coon, Gene L.	Religion
Epsilon Canaris III	Sakuro's disease
	Senensky, Ralph

JOURNEY TO BABEL

BY D. C. FONTANA
DIRECTED BY JOSEPH PEVNEY
STARDATE: 3842.3   AIRED: 11/17/67

The Enterprise has been assigned the unenviable task of transporting ambassadors of many planets, their aides, and their families to the Babel Conference, where decisions of vital importance will be made. One of the most controversial subjects is the admission of Coridan to the Federation; sharply divided opinion is expressed at a cocktail party held on the Enterprise which nearly leads to blows between several of the ambassadors present. Among the Vulcan party are Ambassador Sarek and his Terran wife, Amanda—Spock's parents. Sarek and Spock have not spoken for eighteen years, since Spock joined Star Fleet instead of the Vulcan Science Academy. When the Vulcan ambassador boards the Enterprise, it is quickly seen that there will be no truce between father and son. Further complications arise when Ambassador Gav, a Tellarite who opposes Coridan admission, quarrels openly with Sarek on the subject. Gav is later found dead, and circumstantial evidence points to Sarek, who has no alibi for his absence during the murder. Sarek then has a heart attack and is taken to Sick Bay, where McCoy has to deal with Vulcan physiology in order to repair the damage. During this time Kirk is attacked by Thelev, the Andorian, who wounds him with a knife. Spock is needed to donate the Vulcan blood necessary to operate on Sarek, and in order to keep him in Sick Bay Kirk returns to the bridge duty, concealing his injury and trying to handle a new problem: a ship that is trailing the Enterprise! The ship will not identify itself, but is in contact with someone on the Enterprise. A search discloses that Thelev, in the brig for his attack on Kirk, has been in full communication with the tracking ship. Thelev is discovered to be not an Andorian at all, but an Orion in disguise, placed on board the Enterprise to damage negotiations on the Coridan issue so that the planet's valuable dilithium can be protected for the use of the Federation. The mysterious ship attacks the Enterprise and is defeated. It destroys itself, and Thelev, in turn, commits suicide. The interlopers, too, turn out to be from Orion, trying to protect illegal mining operations on Coridan, which is not yet under Federation law. Sarek recovers and makes peace with his son, as both realize their common bond. Kirk finally reports to Sick Bay, and McCoy gets the last word, much to his amazement and delight.

FRIDAY'S CHILD

BY D. C. FONTANA
DIRECTED BY JOSEPH PEVNEY
STARDATE: 3497.2   AIRED: 12/1/67

Cast

Kirk: William Shatner	Amanda: Jane Wyatt
Spock: Leonard Nimoy	Thelev: William O'Connell
McCoy: DeForest Kelley	Shras: Reggie Nalder
Uhura: Nichelle Nichols	Gav: John Wheeler
Chekov: Walter Koenig	Lieutenant Josephs: James X. Mitchell
Chapel: Majel Barrett	Stunt Doubles: Paul Baxley (Kirk), Jim
Sarek: Mark Lenard	Shepherd (Thelev)

The Enterprise is sent to the planet Capella IV to negotiate a mining treaty with some extremely warlike and tradition-bound peoples. On arrival, the landing party finds a Klingon agent, Kras, already established in the confidence of some of the natives. Ripe for revolution against Akaar, their Teer (leader), a group of young Capellan lieutenants who favor the Klingon point of view kill him and take over the chieftainship, setting their leader, Maab, in his place. Eleen, the widow of the old Teer, is prepared to forfeit her life, according to local custom, because she is pregnant with the child who would otherwise be the next Teer. Kirk persuades Eleen to escape with them, and the Enterprise party hides in the hills. Urged on by the Klingon, the Capellans search for the fugitives, while a Klingon warship prevents the Enterprise from coming to the rescue. With McCoy's aid, Eleen gives birth to a son. Soon after, she knocks out McCoy with a rock, escapes, and returns to the searching Capellans, telling them that the child and the Terrans are dead. The Klingon then decides the time is ripe for him to take over, draws his phaser, and begins shooting down his former companions in revolt. Kirk and Spock, trailing Eleen, come on the scene. They wound the Klingon with homemade bows and arrows, but cannot disable him. Then Maab draws Kras's fire, and his lieutenant kills the Klingon. Eleen's son, Leonard James Akaar, becomes the new Teer, and Eleen, as his regent, signs the mining treaty.

Cast

Kirk: William Shatner	Kras: Tige Andrews
Spock: Leonard Nimoy	Maab: Michael Dante
McCoy: DeForest Kelley	Keel: Cal Bolder
Scott: James Doohan	Akaar: Ben Gage
Sulu: George Takei	Duur: Kirk Raymone
Uhura: Nichelle Nichols	Grant: Robert Bralver
Chekov: Walter Koenig	Stunt Doubles: Jim Jones (Kras), Dick
Eleen: Julie Newmar	Dial (Warrior), Chuck Clow (Kirk)

THE DEADLY YEARS

BY DAVID P. HARMON
DIRECTED BY JOSEPH PEVNEY
STARDATE: 3478.2   AIRED: 12/8/67

On the way to Starbase 10, which a passenger, Commodore Stocker, is to command, the Enterprise stops to deliver supplies to the colonists of Gamma Hydra IV. The landing party—Kirk, Spock, McCoy, Lieutenant Galway, and Chekov—discover that accelerated aging has taken place, killing most of the colonists. Chekov is frightened into speechlessness when he walks into a building and finds an aged dead body. Survivors of the malady, an elderly couple who claim to be in their late twenties, die soon after meeting the Enterprise people. When the landing party returns to the ship, the hyperaging begins to show on them, except for Chekov, who seems to be unaffected. Kirk wants to stay in orbit around Gamma Hydra IV until a solution to the problem is found, but Commodore Stocker wants the ship to proceed to Starbase 10, where, he feels, better treatment can be given. As the disease progresses, in each person all the problems of old age emerge: aching bones, erratic behavior, senility. Kirk becomes increasingly inefficient and forgetful, but Spock and Scotty are also unable to command, so Stocker takes over the Enterprise. Stocker is an efficient desk man, but has no training for deep-space command. To save time, he sets a course through the Romulan/Federation neutral zone, and promptly learns that Romulans are constantly on guard against such moves. The Romulans move in for the attack, and Stocker panics, not knowing what to do. McCoy learns that the disease is a form of radiation poisoning and that Chekov isn't affected because of the bad scare he had on the planet; the sudden natural increase of adrenalin in his body saved Chekov from the aging malady. By this time the others are severely afflicted by advanced old age, but massive intravenous doses of adrenalin bring Kirk back to normal in time to save the ship. Scott, McCoy, and Spock are treated soon after to bring them back to their proper ages.

Cast
Kirk: William Shatner
Spock: Leonard Nimoy
McCoy: DeForest Kelley
Scott: James Doohan
Sulu: George Takei
Uhura: Nichelle Nichols
Chekov: Walter Koenig
Chapel: Majel Barrett

Commodore George Stocker: Charles Drake
Dr. Janet Wallace: Sarah Marshall
Lieutenant Arlene Galway: Beverly Washburn
Robert Johnson: Felix Locher
Elaine Johnson: Laura Wood
Yeoman Doris Atkins: Carolyn Nelson

See Lexicon under:
Aldebaran III
Alvin
Atkins, Yeoman Doris
Code 3
Code 2
Corbomite
Galway, Lieutenant Arlene
Gamma Hydra IV
Harmon, David P.
Hyronalin

Invisibility screen
Johnson, Elaine
Johnson, Robert
Neutral zone
Pevney, Joseph
Romulus
Starbase 10
Stocker, Commodore George
Wallace, Dr. Janet
Wallace, Dr. Theodore

OBSESSION

BY ART WALLACE
DIRECTED BY RALPH SENENSKY
STARDATE: 3619.2   AIRED: 12/15/67

Eleven years ago, Kirk was on the U.S.S. Farragut when it encountered a deadly cloud creature in the region of Tycho IV. The creature killed Captain Garrovick and half the crew by draining their red blood cells, and Kirk still feels guilt at having hesitated in surprise for a moment before firing at it—to no avail. Now the Enterprise has met what Kirk believes is the same entity, and despite orders to deliver much-needed medical supplies to another planet, he finds himself unable to shake off a "Captain Ahab" complex. He is determined to pursue it, regardless of other considerations, and is fearful that it will kill more people unless it is stopped. A party beams down to the surface of Argus X, where the creature lurks; among them is Ensign Garrovick, son of Kirk's former commanding officer. He sights the creature—and, like Kirk eleven years before, he is momentarily paralyzed. He fires, but too late, and Kirk blames him for the death of a crewman. Spock tries to reason with them, and gives up after noting the human preference for wallowing in emotion. When the cloud leaves the planet, the Enterprise follows and fires on it, and the creature, showing definite signs of intelligence, turns on the starship and enters it. Unfortunately for it, the first person it encounters is Spock, and after a taste of his copper-based green blood, it leaves the Enterprise, heading for its home planet, Tycho IV, where it evidently intends to reproduce. Kirk and Garrovick, seeking to redeem themselves, set up a trap with a matter/antimatter bomb and, unexpectedly, find that they must serve as the bait. The trap is sprung—the cloud cannot resist the temptation of red blood. The captain and Garrovick beam aboard the ship in the nick of time, and the vampire cloud is destroyed in the explosion.

Cast
Kirk: William Shatner
Spock: Leonard Nimoy
McCoy: DeForest Kelley
Scott: James Doohan

Uhura: Nichelle Nichols
Chekov: Walter Koenig
Chapel: Majel Barrett
Ensign Garrovick: Stephen Brooks
Ensign Rizzo: Jerry Ayres

See Lexicon under:
Argus X
Cordrazine
Di-kronium
Farragut, U.S.S.
Garrovick, Captain
Garrovick, Ensign
Impulse vent
Rizzo, Ensign

Senensky, Ralph
Survey on Cygnian Respiratory Diseases, A
Theta VII
Tritanium
Tycho IV
Vampire cloud
Wallace, Art
Yorktown, U.S.S.

WOLF IN THE FOLD

BY ROBERT BLOCH
DIRECTED BY JOSEPH PEVNEY
STARDATE: 3614.9   AIRED: 12/22/67

Scotty is recovering from a serious head injury he received in an accident caused by a female crew member of the Enterprise. To help their chief engineer relax, Kirk and McCoy take him to an Argelian nightclub to enjoy the beautiful girls and have a few drinks. Scott becomes infatuated with a lovely dancer, and they leave the club together. Kirk and McCoy decide to look into a few more of the fun-loving planet's entertainment centers before retiring. Screams draw them to a foggy area of the city, where they find the dancing girl dead and a fear-crazed Scott holding a blood-stained knife. McCoy wonders if Scott's subconscious distrust of females, a result of the accident, has surfaced in this vicious manner. Scott has no memory of the incident, and is as upset about it as Kirk. The local authority is Hengist, a bureaucrat imported from Rigel IV because Argelians are too fun-loving to settle down to the necessary business of running their own planet. Hengist wants to arrest Scott immediately, pointing out that because there is very little crime on Argelius II, the old laws have not been changed—they are still very barbaric. However, Kirk prevails, and a local psionic, a priestess of an old cult, tries to find out what has happened. Unfortunately, she and a yeoman from the Enterprise are killed horribly. Before she dies, the psionic is able to reveal that something with an insatiable hunger and hatred of women is present in the room. All evidence points to Scott, though again he claims amnesia for the time during which the women were killed. The entity turns out to be Jack the Ripper in his real form: a noncorporeal vampire which lives on fear. The entity preys on women because they are more easily frightened, and it feeds on them. The creature has been living in the body of Commissioner Hengist; when it is discovered, it kills Hengist, and leaves to take up residence inside the Enterprise. It tries to frighten the crew, but McCoy gives everyone tranquilizers so they fear nothing, and the entity's attempts have no effect. In fear and rage, it is forced to return to Hengist's body. Kirk is ready for this, and has it beamed into space at maximum dispersal, where it eventually must die for lack of nourishment.

Cast
Kirk: William Shatner
Spock: Leonard Nimoy
McCoy: DeForest Kelley
Scott: James Doohan
Sulu: George Takei
Hengist: John Fiedler
Jaris: Charles Macaulay
Sybo: Pilar Seurat
Tark: Joseph Bernard
Morla: Charles Dierkop
Yeoman Tankris: Judy McConnell
Lieutenant Karen Tracey: Virginia Aldridge
Nurse: Judi Sherven
Kara: Tania Lemani
Bartender: John Winston
Serving Girls: Suzanne Lodge, Marlys Burdette
Stunt Double: Paul Baxley (Hengist)

THE TROUBLE WITH TRIBBLES

BY DAVID GERROLD
DIRECTED BY JOSEPH PEVNEY
STARDATE: 4523.3   AIRED: 12/29/67

The Enterprise receives a top-priority order to protect Space Station K-7, which has a load of valuable quadrotriticale grain in its storage compartments and a gang of Klingons in its recreation rooms. Under the terms of the Organian Peace Treaty, the Klingons are entitled to take R&R at the space station, but their presence makes the manager of the station very nervous. Kirk is unimpressed with the fidgety Federation Undersecretary for Agriculture, and quite upset about being called in to protect a cargo of wheat, even though he knows that the grain is for Sherman's Planet, a famine-struck colony near enough the neutral zone to be in contention between the Klingons and the Federation. Involved in a running quarrel with both the undersecretary and the Klingon commander, Kirk and the others do not understand the implications of another threat until too late—a trader named Cyrano Jones has introduced tribbles to the space station and, by giving one to Uhura, the Enterprise. Tribbles, small purring balls of fluff, seem harmless enough: All they do is eat and multiply. In fact, as McCoy soon learns, they seem to be born pregnant, and the more they eat, the more tribbles they have. Kirk soon finds that tribbles have rapidly overpopulated the ship, and other tribbles have littered the space station. The tribbles especially enjoy the quadrotriticale in the station: The storage bins, once full of the precious grain, are also full of tribbles—dead tribbles. The grain has been poisoned by a Klingon agent disguised as a Terran bureaucrat, who is exposed when Kirk discovers that tribbles don't like Klingons (and vice versa). The Klingons, faced down, leave the station peacefully enough. Scotty rids the Enterprise of the tribbles by beaming them aboard the departing Klingon ship, where they will be "no tribble at all . . ."

Cast
Kirk: William Shatner
Spock: Leonard Nimoy
McCoy: DeForest Kelley
Scott: James Doohan
Uhura: Nichelle Nichols
Chekov: Walter Koenig
Nilz Baris: William Schallert
Captain Koloth: William Campbell
Cyrano Jones: Stanley Adams
Mr. Lurry: Whit Bissel
Korax: Michael Pataki
Arne Darvin: Charlie Brill
Admiral Fitzpatrick: Ed Reimers
Trader/bartender: Guy Raymond
Ensign Freeman: Paul Baxley
Guard: David L. Ross
Stunt Doubles: Jay Jones (Scott), Jerry Summers (Chekov), Phil Adams (Korax), Bob Myles (Klingon), Bob Orrison (Klingon), Dick Crockett (Klingon), Richard Antoni (Klingon)

See Lexicon under:
Antarean glow water
Baris, Nilz
Burke, John
Channel E
Cossack
Credit
Darvin, Arne
Denebian slime devil
Donatu V
Earther
Fitzpatrick, Admiral
Freeman, Ensign
Games and recreation
Gerrold, David
Jones, Cyrano
Klingonese
K-7, deep-space station
Koloth, Captain
Korax
Lurry, Mr.
Organian Peace Treaty
Pevney, Joseph
Priority A-1 Channel distress call
Priority-1 call
Quadrotriticale
Regulan blood worms
Scotch
Sherman's Planet
Spican flame gems
Trader/bartender
Tribble
Vodka
Vulcan nerve pinch

THE GAMESTERS OF TRISKELION

BY MARGARET ARMEN
DIRECTED BY GENE NELSON
STARDATE: 3211.7   AIRED: 1/5/68

On a survey mission to an uninhabited planetoid, Kirk, Uhura, and Chekov are suddenly beamed off the Enterprise and disappear from all sensors. Spock, left in charge of the starship, searches the immediate area for the missing crew members, then widens the search to locate the beam that picked them up. He finds that they have been spirited many parsecs away to the planet Triskelion, for which the Enterprise sets course. Meanwhile, the surprised and confused humans on Triskelion find themselves being treated as gladiatorial material by a strange man named Galt. Each is given a drill thrall (training instructor) to teach him how to fight. When Uhura rebels, she and the others discover that the collars they wear are capable of inflicting great pain at Galt's discretion. Chekov's instructor is a female alien who obviously thinks the young ensign is attractive; Chekov does not return the sentiment, however. Kirk's drill thrall is Shahna, a humanoid female who was born on Triskelion of gladiator parents, and who knows nothing of human culture. Kirk attempts to describe it to her, but does not succeed in getting much information through to her primitive mind at first. The three Enterprise officers try to escape and fail, although they do demonstrate to the owners of the thralls how intractable Terrans are—which thrills the owners, called "the Providers" by Galt and the thralls. When the Enterprise finds Triskelion, it is caught by the Providers, who want to bring the entire crew down to fight to the death. Kirk discovers that the Providers are really three ancient brains in an underground vault who have had no amusement for centuries—except for viewing the combats arranged among various captured aliens and gambling on the outcome. Kirk gains their attention during a quarrel about the forthcoming battle and tries to convince them that there are more worthwhile things to do. They don't believe this, however, and are more interested in capturing Earthmen, who seem to have such promise as good fighters. Horrified at the idea that such powerful intellects, which can pluck people from spaceships light-years away from Triskelion, are free to pick and choose among the peoples of the galaxy for their personal amusement, and told that everyone on the Enterprise will be killed, Kirk provokes a desperate wager: himself against three thralls. If the thralls win, the crew of the Enterprise is doomed; if Kirk wins, all the thralls will be freed. Kirk triumphs quickly, but then Shahna is brought in. She fights fiercely, but cannot bring herself to kill him. He soon gains the advantage and reciprocates. The Providers are good losers: They accept the challenge of teaching the newly freed thralls about self-government and civilization.

Cast

Kirk: William Shatner	Shahna: Angelique Pettyjohn
Spock: Leonard Nimoy	Lars: Steve Sandor
McCoy: DeForest Kelley	Kloog: Mickey Morton
Scott: James Doohan	Ensign Jana Haines: Victoria George
Uhura: Nichelle Nichols	Tamoon: Jane Ross
Chekov: Walter Koenig	Andorian Thrall: Dick Crockett
Galt: Joseph Ruskin	Stunt Doubles: Paul Baxley (Kirk),
	Dick Crockett (Stunt Coordinator)

A PIECE OF THE ACTION

BY DAVID P. HARMON AND GENE L. COON
DIRECTED BY JAMES KOMACK
STARDATE: 4598.0 AIRED: 1/12/68

The planet Iotia, in a very remote part of the galaxy, has not been visited by the Federation for one hundred years. When the U.S.S. Horizon left it, long ago, Iotia was reported to have humanoid natives who were extremely imitative; they picked up any information and made something of it. The Horizon left some books and materials there; now the Enterprise is visiting the planet to see what effect these items may have had on the developing Iotian civilization. Kirk and Spock beam down to discover that the Iotians remade their civilization in the image of a book left by the Horizon: Chicago Mobs of the Twenties, a history of gang rule on Earth in the 1920s. Gangs rule half the planet, not merely one city, and the Enterprise's landing party finds itself in a dilemma. Bela Oxmyx, boss of the largest territory on the planet, wants Kirk to use the starship's power to help wipe out the other bosses and give Oxmyx control of Iotia. Of course, Bela offers Kirk a percentage—a piece of the action—for his services. Kirk and Spock have other ideas, but so do other bosses. Though frequently captured by one gang or another, Kirk and Spock finally bring the major bosses together. After a demonstration of the Federation's power, Kirk uses some unorthodox methods to convince all the hoods to work together for the good of Iotia. The people of the Enterprise help set up a planetwide government under Oxmyx, designed to give the Iotians a healthy culture. Kirk, however, must describe the new government in terms the Iotians can understand, which leaves him with the task of explaining in his report to Star Fleet why Iotia thinks it will be cutting the Federation in for a piece of the action. McCoy, on the other hand, is worried over the complications that will arise from leaving his communicator behind on the copycat planet.

Cast
Kirk: William Shatner
Spock: Leonard Nimoy
McCoy: DeForest Kelley
Scott: James Doohan
Uhura: Nichelle Nichols
Chekov: Walter Koenig
Lieutenant Hadley: William Blackburn
Bela Oxmyx: Anthony Caruso
Jojo Krako: Victor Tayback

Kalo: Lee Delano
Zabo: Steve Marlo
Tepo: John Harmon
Girl No. 1: Dyanne Thorne
Girl No. 2: Sharyn Hillyer
Small Boy: Sheldon Collins
Krako's Hood: Buddy Garion
Mirt: Jay Jones
Hoods: Christie, McIntosh, Conde
Krako's Gun Moll: Marlys Burdette

THE IMMUNITY SYNDROME

BY ROBERT SABAROFF
DIRECTED BY JOSEPH PEVNEY
STARDATE: 4307.1 AIRED: 1/19/68

The Enterprise has completed a mission that leaves everyone on board longing for some well-earned shore leave, when the starship gets a priority rescue order. All contact has been lost with solar system Gamma 7A, and Starbase 6 wants the Enterprise to investigate. As they speed toward the star region, Spock gets a severe mind jolt when the starship Intrepid, manned by Vulcans, is destroyed. Something, they discover, has wiped out all life, not just in the ship but in the entire star system. The culprit proves to be a gigantic spacegoing ameba which moves in a cloud of negative particles and drains energy from available sources. The ameba is virtually mindless, moving by instinct, using planets and ships as sources of food. It has come to this galaxy to find a new food supply and is now ready to reproduce. The danger of having several of these vast aliens wandering around our galaxy and wantonly destroying life moves Kirk to try to stop the creature. The Enterprise penetrates the cloud surrounding the ameba, right to the entity's outer skin, but cannot kill it or get out again. Spock takes out a shuttlecraft to scout the area, and the Enterprise follows him into the ameba, hoping to destroy it by detonating an antimatter bomb at its nucleus. The timing must be perfect. In effect, the Enterprise is like an invading bacterium to the huge ameba, which immediately causes an immunity syndrome to protect itself against both the starship and its shuttlecraft. Spock is in great danger as he attempts to locate the ameba's weakest spot so the Enterprise can fire the antimatter bomb without simply allowing the alien to separate into several other amebas. The starship pulls itself and Spock out just in time.

Cast
Kirk: William Shatner
Spock: Leonard Nimoy
McCoy: DeForest Kelley
Scott: James Doohan
Uhura: Nichelle Nichols
Sulu: George Takei

Chekov: Walter Koenig
Chapel: Majel Barrett
Lieutenant Kyle: John Winston
Stunts: Jay Jones, Dick Dial
Special optical effect by Frank Van Der Veer

A P IVATE LITTLE WAR

BY GENE RODDENBERRY   STORY BY JUDD CRUCIS
DIRECTED BY MARC DANIELS
STARDATE: 4211.4   AIRED: 2/2/68

A landing party from the Enterprise is gathering vegetation samples on Neural, a primitive and seemingly tranquil planet, when natives open fire with flintlock rifles, wounding Spock. Since a primitive culture, first explored only thirteen years earlier, has suddenly developed relatively advanced weapons, there must be an interesting story, and Kirk determines to learn it. After getting Spock to the ship, Kirk returns to the planet with McCoy, and they set off to find Tyree, the hill people's leader, and a friend of Kirk's. On the way Kirk is attacked and bitten by a fierce mugato, and is saved from death by Nona, a Kanutu witch doctor—and Tyree's wife. Investigation reveals that the Klingons are giving the villagers models and supplies for making flintlock guns, with more sophisticated weapons promised, so they can prey on the hill people. Nona, ambitious to make Tyree a great leader, wants to fight the villagers with Federation weapons, much to Tyree's horror. Kirk is only protective, and will not launch an offensive attack. He believes that stability can be achieved by a balance of power—by providing the hill people with the same weapons the villagers have. Frustrated, Nona steals a phaser and runs off to give it to the villagers. They don't believe her and mistrust her motives, and they kill her. Though she was selfish, Tyree loved her, and on her death he becomes eager to fight. The Enterprise reluctantly leaves the planet to its fate.

Cast	
Kirk: William Shatner	Apella: Arthur Bernard
Spock: Leonard Nimoy	Krell: Ned Romero
McCoy: DeForest Kelley	Yutan: Gary Pillar
Scott: James Doohan	Mugato: Janos Prohaska
Uhura: Nichelle Nichols	Patrol Leader: Paul Baxley
Chekov: Walter Koenig	Stunt Doubles: Regina Parton (Nona),
Tyree: Michael Whitney	Dave Perna (Spock), Bob Orrison
Chapel: Majel Barrett	(McCoy, Villager), Roy Slickner
Nona: Nancy Kovak	(Villager), Bob Lyon (Villager), Paul
Dr. M'Benga: Booker Marshall	Baxley (Kirk, Apella)

See Lexicon under:	
Apella	Nona
Crucis, Judd	Prime Directive
Daniels, Marc	Roddenberry, Gene
Flintlock	Sterile field
Kanutu	Sterilite
Krell	Typerias
Mako root	Tyree
M'Benga, Dr.	Ursala
Mugato	Vitalizer beam
Neural	Yutan

ETURN TO TOMORROW

BY GENE RODDENBERRY
DIRECTED BY RALPH SENENSKY
STARDATE: 4768.3   AIRED: 2/9/68

On the long-dead planet Arret, an Enterprise landing party finds a deeply buried cave containing three living but disembodied entities—Sargon; his wife, Thalassa; and Henoch, Sargon's former enemy—visible only as glowing lights inside large globes. The rest of their race is long dead, and Sargon no longer considers his differences with Henoch to be of any importance. The beings wish to build android bodies to contain their living intelligence, but they need the control of real human bodies to do so. Sargon talks to Kirk about the matter, convincing the captain to allow the entities to borrow the bodies of Kirk, Dr. Ann Mulhall, and Spock in order to build the android bodies. After centuries as disembodied spirits, the aliens enjoy the unfamiliar sensations of living inside a body. The humans' intellects in globes, meanwhile, lie in Sick Bay. Henoch wishes to keep Spock's body, and poisons Kirk's body, which contains Sargon, to prevent his interfering. Henoch tries to persuade Thalassa to keep Ann Mulhall's body, but she loves Sargon and will not obey Henoch. Sargon escapes from Kirk's body into the hull of the Enterprise while McCoy keeps the captain's body alive until his mind can be returned to it. Sargon and Thalassa successfully use Nurse Chapel's body to trick Henoch out of Spock's body so they can destroy Henoch. Sargon and Thalassa then take their leave of the Enterprise without the nearly completed androids, to take up a disembodied existence on some other planet.

Cast	
Kirk: William Shatner	Sulu: George Takei
Spock: Leonard Nimoy	Chapel: Majel Barrett
McCoy: DeForest Kelley	Dr. Ann Mulhall: Diana Muldaur
Scott: James Doohan	Sargon: James Doohan (Voice)
Uhura: Nichelle Nichols	Nurse: Cindy Lou

See Lexicon under:	Receptacles
Android robots	Roddenberry, Gene
Arret	Sargon
Henoch	Senensky, Ralph
Mulhall, Dr. Ann	Thalassa
Negatron hydrocoils	

PATTERNS OF FORCE

BY JOHN MEREDYTH LUCAS
DIRECTED BY VINCE McEVEETY
STARDATE: 2534.0   AIRED: 2/16/68

The Enterprise is on what should be a routine check of the planet Ekos, where famous historian John Gill is stationed as a cultural observer. After being fired on with a thermonuclear missile, despite surveys showing that the native society is unacquainted with atomic power, the Enterprise's officers are puzzled and alarmed. Kirk and Spock beam down to Ekos to find a Nazi-like culture, complete with uniforms, scare tactics, and a scapegoat: the peaceful neighboring planet of Zeon. The Enterprise men are captured and beaten, and finally escape with the aid of a Zeon underground group, from which they learn what has happened. It seems that John Gill, with a fanatical idea of what the "master race" of twentieth-century Earth might have been, had it not gone wrong, has violated the Prime Directive. He introduced the idea of Nazism to the Ekons, who took it to their collective warlike hearts with a literal-minded zeal that Gill had not intended. Although Gill is nominally the Führer of Ekos, Kirk refuses to believe this and wants to contact him personally. The underground helps Kirk and Spock get into Nazi headquarters, where they find that Gill is only a drugged puppet in the hands of a deputy Führer, Melakon. The domestic persecution and the aggression against Zeon are the work of Melakon, who wants to rule both planets. Gill is revived sufficiently to talk to the people of Ekos and denounce Melakon. While declaring friendship for Zeon, Gill is shot and killed by Melakon, who is in turn shot by Isak, a young Zeon. A trusted member of the underground takes over the establishing of peaceful relations between the two planets, and the reformation of Ekos society into a more pleasant and humane one.

Cast

Kirk: William Shatner	Abrom: William Wintersole
Spock: Leonard Nimoy	Eneg: Patrick Horgan
McCoy: DeForest Kelley	SS Lieutenant: Ralph Maurer
Scott: James Doohan	SS Major: Gilbert Green
Uhura: Nichelle Nichols	Newscaster: Bart LaRue
Chekov: Walter Koenig	First Trooper: Paul Baxley
John Gill: David Brian	Gestapo lieutenant: Peter Canon
Melakon: Skip Homeier	SS Trooper: Ed McCready
Isak: Richard Evans	Davod: Chuck Courtney
Daras: Valora Norland	Troopers: Bill Blackburn, Laskey

See Lexicon under:

Abrom	Lieutenant, SS
Daras	Lucas, John Meredyth
Davod	M43 Alpha
Ekos	Major, SS
Eneg, Chairman	McEveety, Vince
Fatherland	Melakon
Führer	Newscaster
Gestapo	Prime Directive
Gestapo lieutenant	Rubindium crystals
Gill, John	Thermonuclear missile
Iron Cross, Second Class	Transponder, subcutaneous
Isak	Uletta
Lee Kuan	Underground
	Zeon

BY ANY OTHER NAME

BY D. C. FONTANA AND JEROME BIXBY
STORY BY JEROME BIXBY
DIRECTED BY MARC DANIELS
STARDATE: 4657.5   AIRED: 2/23/68

Answering a distress call from a small Earthlike planet, the Enterprise landing party is captured by agents of the Kelvan Empire from the Andromeda galaxy. The Kelvans were scouting this galaxy's potential for colonization when their own ship was destroyed; they now need the Enterprise for the three-hundred-year-long return trip to Andromeda. Originally massive and tentacular, the Kelvans have taken on human form to be more comfortable on the Enterprise. After several attempts to escape—which result only in the punishment and death of one of the landing party—Kirk seems to accept the inevitable. The Kelvans have enormous powers, stronger than Spock's abilities, and they do not hesitate to use these powers ruthlessly to gain their ends. They plan to wipe out the human race wherever they find it. However, the human bodies adopted by the Kelvans are introducing the aliens to something they have never felt before: physical sensation. The Enterprise's crew goes to work on the Kelvans' unfamiliarity with, and susceptibility to, these sensations. Scott tries to get one Andromedan drunk, finally succeeding after heroic effort; Kirk makes amorous advances to one of the females, confusing her and making the Kelvan leader jealous; McCoy injects an irritant into another Kelvan, leaving him ready to fight with anyone for any reason. The conflicting emotional overtones cause a great deal of confusion among the Kelvans, who appear dangerously human in their reactions. Kirk points this out to them, noting that they are becoming too human to return to Andromeda as Kelvans, and that their descendants who will finally arrive at the distant galaxy will be too alien to the normal Kelvans to even understand them. Impressed by Kirk's argument, the Andromedans decide to send a robot messenger to Kelva to report on what has happened. They then allow the Enterprise to find a Class M planet in this galaxy for them to colonize.

Cast

Kirk: William Shatner	Rojan: Warren Stevens
Spock: Leonard Nimoy	Kelinda: Barbara Bouchet
McCoy: DeForest Kelley	Hanar: Stewart Moss
Scott: James Doohan	Tomar: Robert Fortier
Uhura: Nichelle Nichols	Lieutenant Shea: Carl Byrd
Chekov: Walter Koenig	Drea: Leslie Dalton
Chapel: Majel Barrett	Yeoman Leslie Thompson: Julie Cobb

See Lexicon under:	Formazine	Sahsheer
Alcohol	Ganymede	Saurian brandy
Andromeda galaxy	Hanar	Shakespeare, William
Bixby, Jerome	Kassaba fever	Shea, Lieutenant
Blocks	Kelinda	Stokaline
Daniels, Marc	Kelva	Thompson, Yeoman Leslie
Drea	Kelvan Empire	Tomar
Energy barrier	Neural field	Vulcan mind touch
Fontana, D. C.	Rojan	Vulcan vacation

THE OMEGA GLORY

BY GENE RODDENBERRY
DIRECTED BY VINCE McEVEETY
STARDATE: UNKNOWN   AIRED: 3/1/68

The Enterprise finds a crewless starship, the U.S.S. Exeter, in orbit around Omega IV. The boarding party from the Enterprise contracts a virus that may have killed the Exeter's crew, but Omega IV's biosphere is found to confer an immunity to the virus, so a landing party is beamed down to the planet's surface to determine the nature of the cure. There they discover that Captain Tracey, the commander of the Exeter, has been violating the Prime Directive by interfering in the domestic politics of the natives, using his phaser to protect the Oriental villagers, the Kohms, against the Caucasoid barbarian raiders, the Yangs. Tracey wants Kirk to provide him with more phasers, but neither Kirk nor the crew left aboard the Enterprise will oblige. The Yangs capture the Kohm village, and the Terrans learn that the people are possible descendants of Americans and of Chinese Communists who left Earth in the last years of the twentieth century, only to continue their war on Omega IV. The Yangs venerate the Constitution of the United States and other documents of democracy, without understanding them. The Yangs have turned away from their original political leanings, as have the Kohms, and Kirk convinces both groups that there is much to be learned from a close study of their old documents, and much to be gained from applying them. The Yangs and the Kohms claim to be approximately one thousand years old, and it is never made clear whether this is a philosophical attitude or due to a shorter year on Omega IV. In any case, nobody challenges them on the subject, though Kirk knows that interstellar travel has existed for only a little over two hundred Earth years.

Cast	
Kirk: William Shatner	Sirah: Irene Kelley
Spock: Leonard Nimoy	Lieutenant Galloway: David L. Ross
McCoy: DeForest Kelley	Lieutenant Leslie: Eddie Paskey
Sulu: George Takei	Dr. Carter: Ed McCready
Uhura: Nichelle Nichols	Wu: Lloyd Kino
Captain Ronald Tracey: Morgan Woodward	Marak Scholar: Morgan Farley
	Executioner: Frank Atienza
Cloud William: Roy Jensen	Stunt Double: Paul Baxley (Kirk)

See Lexicon under:	
Ay Pledgili, Holy	Leslie, Lieutenant
Biosphere	Liyang
Blood-analyzer unit	McEveety, Vince
Carter, Dr.	Omega IV
Cloud William	Roddenberry, Gene
Cold, common	Scholar, Yang
Documents	Sirah
Ee'd pebnista	Slang, Omegan
Evil One	Star Fleet Regulation 6
Exeter, U.S.S.	Tracey, Captain Ronald
Flag, American	Virus
Galloway, Lieutenant	Vulcan nerve pinch
Kohms	Wu
	Yangs

THE ULTIMATE COMPUTER

BY D. C. FONTANA   STORY BY LAWRENCE N. WOLFE
DIRECTED BY JOHN MEREDYTH LUCAS
STARDATE: 4729.4   AIRED: 3/8/68

An erratic genius, Dr. Richard Daystrom, is trying to regain his former prestige and status with a new invention, a highly advanced computer which he calls the M-5. Daystrom convinces Star Fleet Command to place the computer aboard the Enterprise for in-service testing. The computer behaves remarkably well, showing itself capable of running the ship without any assistance from Kirk. This pleases Dr. Daystrom, who has an almost fatherly concern for his invention, but it makes Kirk unhappy and uncomfortable. The practice runs go so well that Kirk's fellow officers from other ships are moved to tease him about being phased out of his job. Then, during a war-games exercise, the M-5 causes the Enterprise to actually attack and destroy other Federation ships, and refuses to comply with orders to surrender control of the ship. While a segment of the fleet prepares to destroy the Enterprise in self-defense, Kirk desperately tries to convince the M-5 that it must stop the destruction and return control of the starship to its human commander. Kirk persuades the computer that it has committed murder, and must therefore suffer the death penalty. Since the computer has been programmed with Daystrom's own personality, it reacts first with arrogance, then with nearly human remorse. To atone for what it has done, the M-5 disconnects and lowers the Enterprise's shields, thus accepting death for itself. Kirk reassumes command just in time to call off the avenging ships. Daystrom and the M-5 computer have nervous breakdowns.

Cast	
Kirk: William Shatner	Chekov: Walter Koenig
Spock: Leonard Nimoy	Dr. Richard Daystrom: William Marshall
McCoy: DeForest Kelley	Commodore Robert Wesley: Barry Russo
Scott: James Doohan	Ensign Harper: Sean Morgam
Sulu: George Takei	M-5 Computer: James Doohan (Voice)
Uhura: Nichelle Nichols	

See Lexicon under:	
Alpha Carinae II	Harris, Captain
A-7 Computer Expert	Hood, U.S.S.
Comptronics	Kazanga
Daystrom, Dr. Richard	Lexington, U.S.S.
Death penalty	Lucas, John Meredyth
Dunsel, Captain	M-5 multitronic unit
Duotronics	M-1 through M-4 computers
Einstein, Albert	Phillips
Engrams	Potemkin, U.S.S.
Enwright, Commodore	Rawlins
Excalibur, U.S.S.	Sakar of Vulcan
Finagle's Folly	War games
Fontana, D. C.	Wesley, Commodore Robert
Harper, Ensign	Woden
	Wolfe, Lawrence N.

BREAD AND CIRCUSES

BY GENE L. COON AND GENE RODDENBERRY
STORY BY JOHN KNEUBUHL
DIRECTED BY RALPH SENENSKY
STARDATE: 4040.7   AIRED: 3/15/68

The wreckage of the S.S. Beagle, with no survivors, is found near Planet 892-IV. When Kirk, Spock, and McCoy beam down, they find a ragged group of "sun worshippers" who are trying to escape being caught by the local authorities. They are captured, however, together with the ship's landing party, and taken to a nearby city, where a remarkable similarity is apparent between the civilization on this planet and that of twentieth-century Earth, but culturally this world recalls ancient Rome. The Enterprise men find that Captain Merik of the Beagle has betrayed his crew, beaming them down to fight in the Roman-style gladiatorial games, and permanently damaged his ship. Merik is now First Citizen of the Empire and supposed close friend to the Proconsul, Claudius Marcus, but it is obvious to Kirk that Merik is being used as a decoy to obtain more starship crews for the degenerate pleasure of the citizens. Kirk is invited to order his crew down from the Enterprise to die in the gladiatorial arena, but he refuses. For the captain's failure to cooperate, Spock and McCoy are condemned to face gladiators in the arena, while Kirk is set for execution later. This entertainment is being televised for the enjoyment of the citizenry, but Scotty disrupts the proceedings by cutting off the planet's energy supply. This gives Kirk a chance to free McCoy and Spock, and Merik sees how a starship captain acts in the face of danger. He repents of his treachery, and uses a communicator to have Kirk, Spock, and McCoy beamed back to the Enterprise, for which he is killed by the Proconsul. Uhura, who has been monitoring the radio waves of the planet, makes the discovery that the "sun worshippers" are in reality talking about "the Son," and that their movement is an analog to early Christianity. It is implied that when the local Christians grow in power, the degenerate culture of the planet will vastly improve.

Cast
Kirk: William Shatner
Spock: Leonard Nimoy
McCoy: DeForest Kelley
Scott: James Doohan
Uhura: Nichelle Nichols
Chekov: Walter Koenig
Captain R. M. Merik/Merikus: William Smithers
Claudius Marcus: Logan Ramsey
Septimus: Ian Wolfe
Flavius: Rhodes Reason
Drusilla: Lois Jewell
Policeman: William Brambley
Announcer: Bart LaRue
Master of the Games: Jack Perkins
Maximus: Max Kelven
Stunt Doubles: Paul Baxley (McCoy, Policeman, Guard), Bob Orrison (Policeman, Guard), Allen Pinson (Spock), Paul Stader (Flavius), Tom Steele (Slave), Gil Perkins (Slave)

ASSIGNMENT: EARTH

BY ART WALLACE
STORY BY GENE RODDENBERRY AND ART WALLACE
DIRECTED BY MARC DANIELS
STARDATE: UNKNOWN   AIRED: 3/29/68

The Enterprise is sent back in time to learn how Earth survived its own history without being blown up. Returning to the most violent of technological times, the twentieth century, the starship intercepts a very unusual space traveler, Gary Seven, who claims to be a twentieth-century Earthman raised and trained by unknown and unnamed aliens to prevent Earth from destroying itself. Kirk cannot decide if Gary Seven is telling the truth or not, but before the captain can resolve the question, Seven escapes from the Enterprise. Kirk and Spock follow him to the surface of the planet, in the city of New York. Seven, meanwhile, has tried to contact two agents similar to himself who have been previously established there, but he finds that they have been killed in an automobile accident and that he must move on his own. An orbital bomb is about to be launched by the United States, and it is Gary Seven's mission to sabotage the rocket so that it explodes somewhere over Asia.

The idea is to scare everyone in the world sufficiently to prohibit the launching of any more bombs into space; the bomb is to go off where it will do no damage, but close enough to worry everyone. Gary Seven does not count on the interference of his nominal secretary, Roberta Lincoln, who begins to suspect that he is not the government agent he pretends to be, nor has he anticipated Kirk and Spock's well-meant interference. The result of all this tampering is that the bomb goes out of control, and for a time seems as though it will be the cause of a major war. Gary Seven finally succeeds in convincing everyone that his motives are genuine, if unorthodox, and the rocket is destroyed at a critical moment. The Enterprise people leave Gary Seven, Roberta Lincoln, and an alien being named Isis to help Earth survive through the twentieth century. The Enterprise returns to its own time with some questions still unanswered.

Cast

Kirk: William Shatner	Cromwell: Don Keefer
Spock: Leonard Nimoy	Colonel Nesvig: Morgan Jones
McCoy: DeForest Kelley	Sergeant Lipton: Lincoln Demyan
Scott: James Doohan	Security Chief: Paul Baxley
Sulu: George Takei	Beta 5 Computer: Majel Barrett (Voice)
Uhura: Nichelle Nichols	Isis: Barbara Babcock (Voice of Cat)
Chekov: Walter Koenig	Isis: (Unknown)
Gary Seven: Robert Lansing	Police Officers: Ted Gehring, Bruce
Roberta Lincoln: Terry Garr	Mars

See Lexicon under:

Agents 201 and 347	Omicron IV
Beta 5 computer	Orbital bomb
Cromwell	Police Officers, New York
Daniels, Marc	Roddenberry, Gene
811 East 68th Street, Apartment 12B	Scanner
Encyclopedia	Security chief
Exceiver	Servo
Highway 949	Seven, Gary
Isis	Slang, Mid-twentieth-century
Lincoln, Roberta	Strawberry mark
Lipton, Police Sergeant	Supervisor 194
Materialization niche	Typewriter
McKinley Rocket Base	Vault
Nesvig, Colonel	Wallace, Art
	Weather satellite

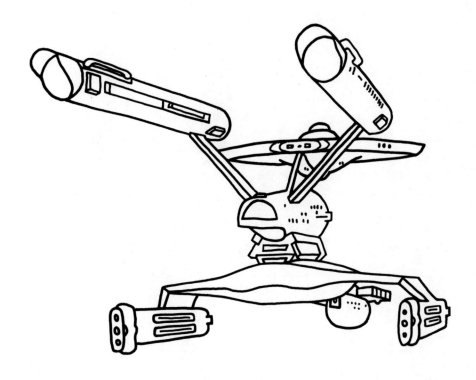

THIRD SEASON

SPOCK'S BRAIN

BY LEE CRONIN
DIRECTED BY MARC DANIELS
STARDATE: 5431.4   AIRED: 9/20/68

A young woman appears on the Enterprise while it is in deep space and renders the crew unconscious. When they wake, they find that she has removed Spock's brain from his skull and made off with it. The body still lives on, due to momentum and McCoy's gadgetry, but if the brain is not returned within twenty-four hours, Spock's body will die. The Enterprise follows an ion trail to the Sigma Draconis system. On the sixth planet, a heavily glaciated world, they find two cultures: The Morgs, all males, live on the surface in a Neolithic culture, and the Eymorgs, all females, live deep underground with a high technology which they do not understand. The Enterprise's landing party finds the woman who stole Spock's brain. She is Kara, the leader of the Eymorgs, who, they discover, has neither the intelligence nor the training to have done the deed on her own. Kara was programmed for that purpose by a mechanical educator, known as the "Great Teacher," left behind by the ancient technologists of the planet. Spock's brain, which the Eymorgs revere as the Controller, has been wired into their central control system; they intend to use it to run the machinery of their city for ten thousand years. Since Kara cannot and will not cooperate, McCoy goes under the educator. With its knowledge and Spock's assistance, McCoy restores the brain to its Vulcan body. Deprived of their Controller, the Eymorgs are encouraged to live with the Morgs on the surface.

Cast	
Kirk: William Shatner	Uhura: Nichelle Nichols
Spock: Leonard Nimoy	Chekov: Walter Koenig
McCoy: DeForest Kelley	Kara: Marj Dusay
Scott: James Doohan	Morg: James Daris
Sulu: George Takei	Luma: Sheila Leighton

See Lexicon under:
Animation control	Morg, a
Communicators	Morgs
Controller, the	Old knowledge, the
Cronin, Lee	Richter scale of culture
Daniels, Marc	Sigma Draconis
Deaction shift	Sigma Draconis IV
Dissociation	Sigma Draconis VII
Eymorgs	Sigma Draconis VI
Here above	Sigma Draconis III
Here below	Sonic separator
Ion power	Standard interstellar symbols
Ion propulsion	Stardate 4351.5
Ion trail	Teacher, Great
Kara	Training device
Life-form readings	Transferral beam
Luma	Trilaser connector
Medical tricorders	Wristlet

THE ENTERPRISE INCIDENT

BY D. C. FONTANA
DIRECTED BY JOHN MEREDYTH LUCAS
STARDATE: 5031.3   AIRED: 9/27/68

Without orders from Star Fleet, a tense and irritable Kirk takes the Enterprise into Romulan territory, whereupon three Romulan ships surround the Enterprise and demand that Kirk surrender it, a valuable prize. Learning that Kirk's first officer is a Vulcan, they order both men to beam aboard the Romulan flagship. Kirk explains to the female commander that instrument failure caused their unwitting entry into Romulan territory, but Spock admits that Kirk ordered it because of his mental instability. This infuriates Kirk. The Romulan commander orders Scott to take the Enterprise to their base; he refuses. She tries to convince Spock to defect; he seems to weaken. McCoy is called to the flagship to tend Kirk, who now seems quite unbalanced. Kirk attacks Spock, who counters with a Vulcan death grip, and McCoy returns to the Enterprise with Kirk's body. However, it's all a ruse: Kirk is really only stunned; he and Spock are under secret Federation orders to steal the Romulan cloaking device. Disguised as a Romulan, Kirk returns to the flagship, where the commander has been doing her best to seduce Spock, and seems to be succeeding. Kirk steals the cloaking device and beams to the Enterprise with it. The commander discovers the theft, but too late, and she determines to execute Spock. While Spock buys time with an involved "confession," Scott installs the device on the Enterprise. The Enterprise then beams Spock aboard, and accidentally brings the commander, too. Tal, the Romulan subcommander, gives chase and is ordered by the commander to destroy the Enterprise. But the cloak works, and the Enterprise escapes with the prisoner.

Cast	
Kirk: William Shatner	Romulan Commander: Joanne Linville
Spock: Leonard Nimoy	Romulan Subcommander Tal: Jack Donner
McCoy: DeForest Kelley	Romulan Technical Officer: Richard Compton
Scott: James Doohan	
Sulu: George Takei	Romulan Technician: Robert Gentile
Uhura: Nichelle Nichols	Romulan Soldier: Gordon Coffey
Chekov: Walter Koenig	Romulan Guard: Mike Howden
Chapel: Majel Barrett	

See Lexicon under:
Alliance, Romulan-Klingon	Romulan execution
Backup systems	Romulan female, commander
Class 2 signal	Romulan procedure, standard
Cloaking device	Romulans
Control Central	Romulans, female
Deck 2	Romulan space
Fontana, D. C.	Romulan uniforms
Guard, Romulan	Soldier, Romulan
Klingon Empire	Sonic disruptor field
Lucas, John Meredyth	Star Fleet, oath of
Neutral zone, Romulan/Federation	Tal, Romulan subcommander
Physiostimulator	Technical officer
Right of statement	Terran
Romulan Empire	Vulcan death grip

THE PARADISE SYNDROME

BY MARGARET ARMEN
DIRECTED BY JUD TAYLOR
STARDATE: 4842.6   AIRED: 10/4/68

An asteroid is on a collision course with an Earthlike planet inhabited by American Indians living peacefully and primitively. The Enterprise is to divert the asteroid from its path. Kirk, Spock, and McCoy beam onto the planet, to discover a strangely incised obelisk but no other signs of technology. The landing party is about to return to the ship when Kirk disappears into the obelisk and cannot be found. Spock takes the Enterprise to divert the asteroid before it is too late. Kirk, who has lost his memory, is found by the Indians, who consider him a demigod. The medicine chief, Salish, doubts this, but Kirk saves a half-drowned child and establishes himself. Kirk is confirmed as the medicine chief, whose role is to "rouse the spirit of the temple and make the sky grow quiet"; Kirk, of course, does not know how to do this. The Enterprise is unsuccessful in deflecting the asteroid, and an attempt to split it with phaser power causes an overload and a consequent loss of warp power; the ship must limp back to the planet on impulse power, which will take several months—and the asteroid is only four hours behind the ship, all the way. On the planet, Salish is doubly jealous of Kirk for having both his job and the priestess Miramanee, who by custom must marry the medicine chief. Miramanee marries Kirk, and everyone is happy on the idyllic planet, except Salish. On the Enterprise, Spock spends most of his time trying to decipher the symbols on the obelisk, which the landing party had photographed. Kirk, meanwhile, remembers his ship only in confusing, disturbing dreams. He learns that Miramanee is carrying his child. Thunder and storms announce the approach of the asteroid, and Kirk goes to the obelisk to ward it off, revealing to Salish by his actions that he doesn't know what to do. The Indians react in terror, attacking Kirk and Miramanee. Spock, meanwhile, learns that the planet, its inhabitants, and the obelisk were established by a benevolent race called the Preservers, and that the obelisk contains a meteor deflector. Spock and McCoy arrive on the planet in time to save Kirk, and Spock restores his memory. Kirk triggers the door of the obelisk, as he did the time he disappeared into it, by saying, "Kirk to Enterprise." Spock reads the instructions inside the obelisk and deflects the asteroid, saving the planet. Miramanee, with her unborn child, dies of her injuries.

Cast
Kirk: William Shatner
Spock: Leonard Nimoy
McCoy: DeForest Kelley
Scott: James Doohan
Sulu: George Takei
Chekov: Walter Koenig
Chapel: Majel Barret

Miramanee: Sabrina Scharf
Salish: Rudy Solari
Goro: Richard Hale
Engineer: Sean Morgan
Indian Boy: Lamont Laid
Indian Woman: Naomi Pollack
Lumo: Peter Virgo, Jr.

AND THE CHILDREN SHALL LEAD

BY EDWARD J. LAKSO
DIRECTED BY MARVIN CHOMSKY
STARDATE: 5027.3 AIRED: 10/11/68

The Enterprise finds that all the adults in the Starnes Expedition to Triacus have died; their log shows that they killed themselves to escape "the enemy within," but gives no further explanation. The children of the expedition are alive, happy, and unconcerned about the fate of their parents, which they will not discuss. Spock and Kirk investigate a cave excavated by the expedition, in which Spock picks up a peculiar tricorder reading and Kirk a feeling of anxiety. The children are in good health, but McCoy cannot explain their psychological state. They reply to Kirk's questions with indirection. Left alone, they call up their "Friendly Angel," the insubstantial entity Gorgan, who orders the children to take the Enterprise to a planet he can control. The Starnes log reveals that the adults felt a strange anxiety similar to that experienced by Kirk, and that one of the planet's inhabitants apparently took refuge in the cave unknown ages before the expedition arrived. Starnes attempted to warn Star Fleet about the danger from this inhabitant, but Gorgan's influence caused the scientist to kill himself. The children, with Gorgan's power, cause the crew of the Enterprise to take the ship out of orbit without knowing what they are doing. When Kirk realizes this, the children summon Gorgan, who manipulates the crew with illusions of their deepest fears and garbles Kirk's words so that he cannot give orders. Spock, who cannot be frightened, is deceived into thinking that nothing is wrong. When Kirk reacts strongly to his supposed loss of his power over his ship, Spock realizes that something is wrong and helps Kirk to snap out of his daze. Away from the children, both recover their self-control. The children move against them, but the men of the Enterprise summon Gorgan with a recording of the children's chant. Gorgan defies Kirk, who counters by playing a videotape of the children playing with their parents, which then switches abruptly to their parents' graves. The children, faced with their loss, turn against Gorgan. Without their support, the entity loses power, rants uselessly, and is seen by the children, and everyone else, as a figure of distorted ugliness instead of the "angel" they first believed him to be. Unable to regain control, Gorgan fades away. The children are taken to Starbase 4 for therapy, and new homes.

Cast
Kirk: William Shatner
Spock: Leonard Nimoy
McCoy: DeForest Kelley
Scott: James Doohan
Sulu: George Takei
Uhura: Nichelle Nichols
Chekov: Walter Koenig
Chapel: Majel Barrett
Gorgan: Melvin Belli
Tommy Starnes: Craig Hundley
Professor Starnes: James Wellman
Mary Janowski: Pamelyn Ferdin
Ray Tsingtao: Brian Tochi
Steve O'Connel: Caesar Belli
Don Linden: Mark Robert Brown
First Technician: Louis Elias

IS T ERE I.. TRUTH NO BEAUTY?

BY JEAN LISSETTE AROESTE
DIRECTED BY RALPH SENENSKY
STARDATE: 5630.7   AIRED: 10/18/68

The Enterprise picks up Medusan ambassador Kollos, instrumentation specialist Lawrence Marvick, and telepath Dr. Miranda Jones. They are to be taken to a Medusan ship on their way to Kollos's planet, where Jones will make telepathic contact with Kollos; the understanding thus gained will enable Marvick to adapt Medusan technology to Federation use, and vice versa. Medusans are incorporeal beings, with great beauty of character, but their appearance causes shock to the point of insanity in humanoids. Even Spock, who was offered Dr. Jones's assignment, turned it down. Jones is extremely lovely, and all the human males aboard the Enterprise are attracted to her, as is her co-worker, Larry Marvick, who tries to persuade her to marry him and resign from the project. When she refuses, he storms off in a rage. Marvick attempts to kill Kollos, but he is unsuccessful and is driven insane by a glimpse of the alien. He takes over the Enterprise's engines (which he helped design) and drives the ship out of the galaxy into an indeterminate region. There the humans experience acute sensory distortion and Marvick finally dies of sheer terror. The crew cannot pilot the Enterprise back into the galaxy, but it may be possible for Kollos, with his different senses. Spock establishes a mind link with Kollos, while Kirk distracts the jealous Dr. Jones, who objects violently to Spock's contacting Kollos in this way; but she finally admits that she is blind and, even with the sensor web she wears, could not pilot a starship herself. After he has returned the Enterprise to our galaxy, using Spock's body, Kollos is revealed to be a warm and sympathetic personality. Spock forgets to wear the protective shielding visor when returning Kollos's mind to its container, and the sight of Kollos renders Spock insane. Kirk shocks Jones, who may have caused Spock to forget the visor, into realizing her jealousy and her responsibility for Spock's condition. She mind-links with Spock and draws the Vulcan's mind back to reality. She then makes a permanent mind link with Kollos and transfers with him to the Medusan vessel.

Cast
Kirk: William Shatner
Spock: Leonard Nimoy
McCoy: DeForest Kelley
Scott: James Doohan
Sulu: George Takei

Uhura: Nichelle Nichols
Chekov: Walter Koenig
Dr. Miranda Jones: Diana Muldaur
Lawrence Marvick: David Frankham
Security Guards: (Unknown)

CPECT E OF THE GUN

BY LEE CRONIN
DIRECTED BY VINCE McEVEETY
STARDATE: 4385.3   AIRED: 10/25/68

An alien buoy in deep space warns the Enterprise that it is trespassing, but Kirk is under orders to contact the Melkots and continues forward. Kirk, Spock, McCoy, and Chekov beam down to the Melkotian planet, into a foggy place where their instruments will not function. A Melkot appears and says that the humans will be "punished" in a manner befitting their heritage for trespassing. Instantly, the Enterprise men find themselves, armed with six-guns, in an incomplete, movie-set version of Tombstone, Arizona, on October 26, 1881—the date of the gunfight at the O.K. Corral. "Inhabitants" of the town treat the Enterprise party as if they were the Clanton gang, who—according to history—are due to die at five that afternoon. Attempts to escape fail. Spock and McCoy try to make a tranquilizing gas grenade, but it doesn't work. Morgan Earp, in a quarrel over a girl, shoots and kills Chekov—which does not jibe with history, since Chekov's "character," Billy Claiborne, was supposed to have survived the gunfight. Perhaps the plot can be changed after all . . . They find themselves teleported to the O.K. Corral, and Spock deduces that the Melkots must be controlling their minds with illusions. Knowing that they are illusions, he cannot be hurt by them, and he uses Vulcan mind meld to convince the others. The Earps arrive and the fight begins, but the Earps cannot harm the Enterprise party, who will not shoot the Earps. The Melkots are impressed by the peaceful behavior of the men of the Enterprise and return the landing party—including an unharmed Chekov—to the ship. The Melkots agree to establish contact with the Federation.

Cast
Kirk: William Shatner
Spock: Leonard Nimoy
McCoy: DeForest Kelley
Scott: James Doohan
Uhura: Nichelle Nichols
Chekov: Walter Koenig
Melkotian Buoy: James Doohan (Voice)
Melkot: Abraham Sofaer (Voice)
Sylvia: Bonnie Beecher

Morgan Earp: Rex Holman
Wyatt Earp: Ron Soble
Virgil Earp: Charles Maxwell
Doc Holliday: Sam Gilman
Johnny Behan: Bill Zuckert
Ed: Charles Seel
Barber: Ed McReady
Rancher: Gregg Palmer
Rider: Richard Anthony
Melkot mask by Mike Minor

DAY OF THE DOVE

BY JEROME BIXBY
DIRECTED BY MARVIN CHOMSKY
STARDATE: UNKNOWN   AIRED: 11/1/68

The time is about three years (by Klingon reckoning) after the Organian Peace Treaty; for about fifty years the Federation has been "eyeball to eyeball" with the Klingon Empire. A landing party from the Enterprise beams to a human-colonized planet which has sent a distress signal, but they can find no one there. A Klingon ship, apparently disabled, is detected, and a group of Klingons appear who accuse Kirk of having damaged their ship. Their leader, Kang, claims the Enterprise, and Kirk meekly beams everyone aboard, but Spock is warned and takes the Klingons prisoner. Both ships seem to have received false distress calls. An insubstantial entity has gotten into the Enterprise and drifts about, exciting both sides to belligerence. It gimmicks the ship to rush out of control toward the galactic rim, and then isolates all but an equal number of Enterprise men and Klingons. A number of objects—including phasers—are changed into swords, and they are incited to fight. Skirmishes occur, with casualties on both sides; everyone shows an increased tendency toward hatred, unreason, and bloodshed. Some manage to control themselves, but others don't even try. Chekov, urged by a false memory of a murdered brother, captures and mauls Mara, Kang's science officer and wife, but Kirk intervenes, preventing any drastic harm to the woman. All the fatal wounds on each side heal without any medical attention. Spock observes that the entity appears to live off the hatred and emotional excitation of other beings; it has acted as a catalyst to provoke hand-to-hand combat, and has kept the numbers on both sides even. In order to smother all hostile feelings and starve the entity, Kirk (after some struggle) is able to make a common-cause truce with the Klingons, and they drive the creature out of the ship with their jibes and laughter.

Cast	
Kirk: William Shatner	Chekov: Walter Koenig
Spock: Leonard Nimoy	Kang: Michael Ansara
McCoy: DeForest Kelley	Mara: Susan Johnson
Scott: James Doohan	Lieutenant Johnson: David L. Rose
Sulu: George Takei	Klingon: Mark Tobin
Uhura: Nichelle Nichols	Computer: Majel Barrett (Voice)

See Lexicon under:	
Agonizer, Klingon	Emergency manual control
Armory	Entity
Auxiliary Control Center	Food synthesizers
Beta XIIA	Johnson, Lieutenant
Bixby, Jerome	Kang
Chekov, Piotr	Klingon
Chomsky, Marvin	Klingons
Claymore	Klingon transporter system
Detention quarters	Klingon uniforms
Devil	Mara
Dilithium crystals	Organian Peace Treaty
Distress call	Propaganda

FOR THE WORLD IS HOLLOW AND I HAVE TOUCHED THE SKY

BY RICK VOLLAERTS
DIRECTED BY TONY LEADER
STARDATE: 5476.3   AIRED: 11/8/68

McCoy learns that he has an incurable blood disease and has a year to live. At the same time, the Enterprise discovers Yonada, an asteroid artificially propelled and powered. Its center is inhabited by humanoids, whose ancestors, fleeing the destruction of their solar system, built Yonada as a "seed ship" in which to reach another planet, but the people do not know they are inside a ship and not on a world. The asteroid is on a collision course with a Federation planet and cannot be diverted, since its controls are misaligned or somehow otherwise flawed. The people are ruled by Natira, a priestess who takes her orders from a central computer. While Spock and Kirk look for the power controls—without success—McCoy and Natira fall in love. Natira orders Spock and Kirk back to the Enterprise for having broken some of Yonada's laws, but McCoy stays behind, marries Natira, and accepts the Instrument of Obedience, which punishes dissent. Soon afterward, McCoy calls Spock and Kirk to tell them that he may have found the controls to the asteroid, but he is struck down by the computer before he can finish. Spock and Kirk beam back to Yonada, revive McCoy by removing the Instrument of Obedience, and attempt to convince Natira that her world is a spaceship. They make their way to the controls (not without a fight from the computer), and manage to put Yonada back on course. In deciphering the computer's library, Spock finds a cure for McCoy's disease, and the doctor returns to the Enterprise. Natira remains behind on Yonada to guide her people, and so they part. Natira bids farewell to McCoy, saying: "Perhaps, someday, if it is permitted, you will [again] find your Yonada . . ."

Cast	
Kirk: William Shatner	Scott: James Doohan
Spock: Leonard Nimoy	Natira: Kate Woodville
McCoy: DeForest Kelley	Admiral Westervliet: Byron Morrow
	Old Man: Jon Lormer

See Lexicon under:	
Ancient lore	Men of space, men of other worlds
Book of the People, The	Natira
Creators	Old man
Daran V	Oracle of the People
Fabrina	Powder, restorative
Fabrini	Prime Directive
Instrument of Obedience	Vollaerts, Rick
Intelligence files	Westervliet, Admiral
Leader, Tony	Xenopolycythemia
	Yonada

THE THOLIAN WEB

BY JUDY BURNS AND CHET RICHARDS
DIRECTED BY RALPH SENENSKY
STARDATE: 5693.4   AIRED: 11/15/68

The Enterprise is investigating uncharted space in search of the Defiant, a missing Federation ship. Instruments seem to indicate that space is "breaking up," and there is also a slight power loss in the Enterprise's engines. The Defiant appears on the screen, but does not register on the sensors. In pressure suits, Kirk and a boarding party beam to the Defiant's bridge and find the entire crew dead, apparently by violence. Moreover, the Defiant itself is caught in an interphase between alternate universes and is drifting away into nothingness. The Enterprise's power loss cripples the transporter, leaving Kirk stranded on the Defiant after the rest of the party has beamed back to the ship. The Defiant disappears, with Kirk aboard. The two spaces will make contact again in a few hours, permitting the Enterprise to pick up Kirk—if he can hold out that long. However, the Defiant's problems are affecting the Enterprise: power loss, weakness, and insanity in the crew. Then an alien vessel appears, whose commander tells them to leave Tholian territory or be destroyed. Spock explains that the Enterprise is on a rescue mission, and the Tholian agrees to hold off until the Defiant appears. At the time of interphase, they are unable to beam Kirk aboard—he appears to have left the Defiant—and the punctual Tholians open fire. Spock is forced to counterattack, disabling the Tholian ship. Power drain and mental disability on the Enterprise increase, and McCoy recommends that they leave immediately. Spock points out they must remain if they are ever to rescue Kirk. Another Tholian ship appears, and the Tholians begin to weave a tractor web to destroy the Enterprise. Meanwhile, crewmen report seeing Kirk's wraith floating in and out of vision. The captain has shifted both position and phase, but he can, perhaps, still be reached at interphase, which under the new conditions will coincide almost exactly with the completion of the Tholian web. When the Enterprise's power is applied, the tractor web pulls the ship out of the area into the interphase, then out again several parsecs away—apparently all the way out of the area claimed by the Tholians. Kirk, brought along in the transporter's field, is beamed aboard unharmed.

Cast
Kirk: William Shatner
Spock: Leonard Nimoy
McCoy: DeForest Kelley
Scott: James Doohan
Uhura: Nichelle Nichols
Chekov: Walter Koenig
Lieutenant O'Neil: Sean Morgan
Tholians: Barbara Babcock (Voices)

See Lexicon under:
Burns, Judy
Defiant, U.S.S.
Environmental suit
Interphase
Last orders
Loskene, Commander
Medals
Mutiny
O'Neil, Lieutenant
Richards, Chet
Senensky, Ralph
Space warp
Territorial annex of the Tholian Assembly
Theragen
Tholian Assembly
Tholians
Tholian web
Tri-ox compound

PLATO'S STEPCHILDREN

BY MEYER DOLINSKY
DIRECTED BY DAVID ALEXANDER
STARDATE: 5784.0   AIRED: 11/22/68

The Enterprise receives a distress call from the planet Platonius. Beaming down, Kirk, Spock, and McCoy meet Alexander, the Platonians' dwarf jester, and Parmen, the philosopher-king, who has a festering wound. All the Platonians except Alexander are psychokinetic, and Parmen's delirium is damaging the Enterprise. At great personal risk, Alexander helps McCoy anesthetize the Platonian so the doctor can treat him. When Parmen is cured, the Enterprise tries to beam its party up, but the controls are frozen—Parmen will not let them go. He wants McCoy to join their community to treat anyone who may fall ill in the future. Kirk and Spock are ignored, or used as casual jesters. Alexander reports that the other Platonians developed psychokinesis only after coming to Platonius and eating the native food. McCoy determines that a concentration of kironide in the blood is responsible; Alexander is unable to assimilate kironide from the food because of the pituitary deficiency that made him a dwarf. Spock, Kirk, and McCoy take double doses of kironide in order to develop the power in themselves. They offer it to Alexander, but he refuses; he wants to be himself. The Platonians cause Uhura and Nurse Chapel to be beamed down for further entertainment. Dressed in costumes, Kirk and Spock are manipulated into performing, singing, dancing, fighting, and making love to the women. Then their rapidly induced psychokinesis emerges, enabling them to counteract the power of the Platonians. After dissuading Alexander from cutting a few throats, they take him on board the Enterprise and leave the decadent planet, presumably for the safety of a Federation world.

Cast
Kirk: William Shatner
Spock: Leonard Nimoy
McCoy: DeForest Kelley
Uhura: Nichelle Nichols
Chapel: Majel Barrett
Alexander: Michael Dunn
Parmen: Liam Sullivan
Philana: Barbara Babcock
Eraclitus: Ted Scott
Dionyd: Derek Partridge

See Lexicon under:
Alexander
Alexander, David
Dioyd
Dolinsky, Meyer
Eraclitus
Hippocrates
Kironide
Kithara
"Maiden Wine"
Parmen
Pericles of Athens
Philana
Pituitary
Plato of Athens
Platonius
Plato's Children
Power, the
Psychokinesis
Sandara
Trance

WIN OF AN EYE

BY ARTHUR HEINEMANN   STORY BY LEE CRONIN
DIRECTED BY JUD TAYLOR
STARDATE: 5710.5   AIRED: 11/29/68

In an outer quadrant of the galaxy, the Enterprise answers a distress call from the planet Scalos but finds only a beautiful, empty city. Although the viewscreen shows strange, handsome people, the landing party cannot locate them. The world is quite barren, but the landing party can hear insect whines. Spock finds artifacts of a high civilization, and gets an unusual reading on his sensor. Then a member of the landing party vanishes after dipping his finger into a fountain and tasting the water. Returning to the ship; Kirk drinks some coffee while trying to puzzle out the problem, and he also seems to disappear. His coffee has been doped with a substance found in Scalosian water, which has speeded up his metabolic rate to match that of the remaining inhabitants of the planet. By radiation released in volcanic eruptions, the Scalosians' lives have been hyperaccelerated, unfolding so rapidly that they are invisible to ordinary humans. Acceleration has also rendered Scalosian males sterile and killed their children, however. The females have to mate with people from outside the radiation's influence, so they send out distress calls to lure ships in, then kidnap the male crew members, who burn out quickly and die easily, so the females are constantly looking for new recruits. Deela, queen of Scalos, feels a strong attraction to Kirk, and dallies with the captain while her men use a mechanical device to make the Enterprise into a sort of deep-freeze. The Scalosians plan to put the rest of the ship's crew into a frozen state, to be used after Kirk is burned out. But Kirk leaves a record of the Scalosians' activities for Spock and McCoy to find and act on. McCoy synthesizes an antidote for the accelerating substance, and Spock drinks some Scalosian water so he can become accelerated enough to give the antidote to Kirk. They meet, stop the Scalosians from carrying out their designs, and then take the antidote in order to return to normal speed and time. Under the extreme acceleration, Spock has repaired all the damage to the Enterprise in seconds, rather than the many weeks it ordinarily would have taken.

Cast	
Kirk: William Shatner	Uhura: Nichelle Nichols
Spock: Leonard Nimoy	Chekov: Walter Koenig
McCoy: DeForest Kelley	Deela: Kathie Brown
Scott: James Doohan	Crewman Compton: Geoffrey Binney
Sulu: George Takei	Ekor: Eric Holland
	Rael: Jason Evers

See Lexicon under:	Force field	Rael
Antidote	Hallucinations	Refrigeration unit
Cell damage	Hangar deck	Scalos
Children	Heinemann, Arthur	Scalosian substance
Communication device	Hyperacceleration	Suspended 'animation'
Compton, Crewman	Intercom	Sweep
Cronin, Lee	Kir	Taylor, Jud
Deela	Life-support system	Water
Distress call	Medical-supply cabinets	Weapon
Ekor	Quarantine	

THE EMPATH

BY JOYCE MUSKAT
DIRECTED BY JOHN ERMAN
STARDATE: 5121.0   AIRED: 12/6/68

The star Minara is about to go nova. The Enterprise is sent to pick up research personnel on its second planet, but Kirk, Spock, and McCoy are unable to find the scientists. Meanwhile, a radiation storm endangers the ship and crew, and Scott takes the Enterprise out of orbit, trusting that the planet's atmosphere will protect the landing party from radiation. While reading a three-month-old log, which shows that the researchers vanished suddenly, the landing party also vanishes. They find themselves in an underground chamber shared with a frail, mute humanoid—named "Gem" by Dr. McCoy—who does not seem to be a native of Minara II. Two other humanoids, different from Gem, appear. They announce that they are Vians, but beyond that do not explain anything to the Enterprise men. The Vians can teleport people, as well as immobilize them, with a force field. The landing party eventually finds the researchers, dead of torture; the Vians remark cryptically that they were not fit subjects. The Vians choose Kirk as their next subject, explaining that it is not he who is being tested—small comfort for being gratuitously tortured. Kirk is healed of his injuries by Gem, who turns out to be an empath of such high ability that she can cure another's injuries. The Vians then tell Kirk that he must select one of his men to be the next subject. Each officer volunteers, to protect the others; McCoy manages to anesthetize both Spock and Kirk, and is taken away by the Vians. Awakening, Spock analyzes the mentally controlled transporter mechanism used by the Vians and adapts it so he can control it with his own mind. They find McCoy on the point of death and entreat Gem to heal him, but the Vians intervene, explaining that they are testing Gem to see whether the empath's species should be the one race of Minarans that can be taken to safety from its doomed sun. (They do not explain why it is necessary to torture and mutilate strangers from another solar system in order to ascertain Gem's survival capacities or why they can save only one species from the Minaran system.) It seems that what is really being tested is Gem's capacity for compassion and self-sacrifice, which the empath apparently has learned from the example of the Enterprise party, for Gem goes ahead and heals McCoy in spite of personal danger. The empathic species is to be saved. Kirk, Spock, and McCoy are returned, unharmed, to the Enterprise.

Cast	
Kirk: William Shatner	Gem: Kathryn Hays
Spock: Leonard Nimoy	Thann: Willard Sage
McCoy: DeForest Kelley	Lal: Alan Bergmann
Scott: James Doohan	Dr. Ozaba: David Roberts
	Dr. Linke: Jason Wingreen

See Lexicon under:	Lal	Ozaba, Dr.
Empaths	Linke, Dr.	Psalm 95, Verse 4
Energy-transfer device	Matter-energy scrambler	Ritter scale
Erman, John	Minara	Sandbats
Force field	Minara II	Telepathy
Gamma Vertis IV	Muskat, Joyce	Thann
Gem	Nova	Vians

ELAAN OF TROYIUS

BY JOHN MEREDYTH LUCAS
DIRECTED BY JOHN MEREDYTH LUCAS
STARDATE: 4372.5   AIRED: 12/20/68

Though under Federation control, the Tellun star system is claimed by the Klingons. Under a communications blackout, the Enterprise takes on board Petri, ambassador from Troyius, the outer planet, and Elaan, the Dohlman of Elas, the inner planet. Elaan is to be married to the Troyian leader in order to promote peace between the two planets, which have been at war for centuries. The ambassador is to aid in preparing the unruly Elaan for her groom, and the Enterprise proceeds at sublight speed in order to give Petri time in which to teach her some manners. Elaan resents Petri, hates Troyians, and refuses to be educated in etiquette. A Klingon warship is following the Enterprise on a parallel course. Elaan becomes irritated with Petri and stabs him; he will recover, but holds Kirk responsible. Petri is ready to break off the royal marriage, for which the Federation will also hold Kirk responsible, so the captain takes over the job of teaching manners to Elaan. The Klingon ship continues to accompany them, and refuses to answer signals. Elaan, unable to bully Kirk, weeps, and the touch of her tears on his skin intoxicates him. Earlier, McCoy had warned Kirk of this power, but the beautiful, willful woman evidently makes the captain forget or ignore the warning, and he falls in love with Elaan. Meanwhile, Kryton, a noble accompanying Elaan and who is jealous of her marriage to another, has been signaling the Klingon ship. He is caught and commits suicide, but only after booby-trapping the warp drive so the ship can neither fight nor run from the Klingons. The Enterprise's dilithium crystals are fused, but Kirk learns that the ceremonial jewelry the Troyians have sent to Elaan is composed of dilithium crystals, which explains why the Klingons want to take over this system, where the crystals are so abundant. Elaan's necklace is used to repower the ship and beat off the Klingons. A chastened Elaan proceeds to Troyius for her wedding, and Kirk recovers quickly, the Enterprise being his one true love.

Cast
Kirk: William Shatner
Spock: Leonard Nimoy
McCoy: DeForest Kelley
Scott: James Doohan
Sulu: George Takei
Uhura: Nichelle Nichols
Chekov: Walter Koenig
Chapel: Majel Barrett

Elaan: France Nuyen
Lord Petri: Jay Robinson
Kryton: Tony Young
Technician Watson: Victor Brandt
Klingon: K. L. Smith
Evans: Lee Duncan
Elasian Guards: Dick Durock, Charles Beck

See Lexicon under:	Guards, Elasian	Tears
Converter assembly	Her Glory, Your Glory	Tellun star system
Council of Nobles	Klingon	Test 24
Dagger	Kryton	Tribunal
Dilithium crystals	Lucas, John Meredyth	Troyian monarch
Dohlman	Number 4 shield	Troyius
Elaan	Petri, Lord	Watson, Technician
Elas	Radans	Weapon
Evans	Sublight speed	

WHOM GODS DESTROY

BY LEE ERWIN
STORY BY JERRY SOHL AND LEE ERWIN
DIRECTED BY HERB WALLERSTEIN
STARDATE: 5718.3   AIRED: 1/3/69

Whom the gods would destroy they first make mad.

—Euripides

The Enterprise calls at Elba II, a planet with a poisonous atmosphere but facilities underground for the incurably criminally insane. The starship has a new medication with which they hope to eradicate mental illness forever. There are fifteen inmates in Elba II, an assortment of humanoids from all over the galaxy. When Kirk and Spock beam down, they find that the asylum has been taken over by Garth—once a famous starship captain, who was rendered insane by horrendous injuries received in rescuing others. Garth, who was taught how to change his shape by a gentle race unaware of his madness, first deceives the Enterprise men into thinking he is the governor of the asylum. He then tries to trick them by assuming each of their shapes. When they refuse to be manipulated into beaming him aboard the Enterprise, Garth crowns himself "Master of the Universe." He then proceeds to torture first the governor of Elba, then Kirk in his attempt to get out of the tamper-proof asylum. He wants control of the Enterprise so that he can try to conquer the universe, using an "ultimate" explosive which he has created. Garth displays his insane cruelty by sending Marta, his Orion mistress, out onto the poisonous surface of the planet, then "mercifully" blowing her to bits with the explosive. Spock, separated from Kirk, escapes and comes to rescue the captain, only to find himself faced with two Kirks. The Vulcan guesses which one is real—the original being willing to sacrifice himself to stop Garth—and subdues the madman, bringing the experience to an end. Garth is finally given the medication, which his own madness prevented him from accepting in the first place, and is started on the road to recovery.

Cast
Kirk: William Shatner
Spock: Leonard Nimoy
Scott: James Doohan
Garth of Izar: Steve Ihnat

Marta: Yvonne Craig
Donald Cory: Keye Luke
Andorian: Richard Geary
Tellarite: Gary Downey

See Lexicon under:	Dancing	Marta
Alexander the Great	Elba II	Mutiny
Andorian	Environmental suits	Napoleon Bonaparte
Antos IV	Erwin, Lee	Orion colonies
Axanar	Explosive	Penal colonies
Caesar, Gaius Julius	Force field	Shakespeare, William
Chair, rehabilitation	Garth of Izar	Sohl, Jerry
Chess code	Hitler, Adolf	Solomon
Cochrane deceleration	Housman, A. E.	Tau Ceti
maneuver	Izar	Tellarite
Coronation ceremony	Krotus	Wallerstein, Herb
Cory, Donald	Lee Kuan	Wine

LET T AT E YOUR LAST BATTLEFIELD

BY OLIVER CRAWFORD STORY BY LEE CRONIN
DIRECTED BY JUD TAYLOR
STARDATE: 5730.2 AIRED: 1/10/69

A shuttlecraft reported as stolen from Starbase 4 two weeks earlier is sighted by the Enterprise. From the craft, damaged and leaking air, they rescue a humanoid life form with solid white coloring on the right side of his face and body, solid black on the left. He is Lokai, native of the planet Cheron, who is fleeing a charge of treason. The sensors discover an alien ship, but it remains invisible, following the Enterprise through evasive maneuvers at incredible speeds. The alien ship finally disintegrates from the severe strain, whereupon the alien appears on board the starship, claiming Lokai as his prisoner. He is Bele, also a native of Cheron, the Chief Officer of the Commission of Political Traitors, which tried and convicted Lokai over fifty thousand years ago; Lokai escaped, and has been running ever since. Bele has the same unusual coloring as Lokai, except that he is black on the right side and white on the left. For a reason known only to the two aliens, Bele's coloring has given his people supremacy over Lokai's people. Both of them talk in clichés about racial equality and inequality; Lokai claims that Bele's race gave his own just enough education to serve the master people, that Cheron was a planet of murderers, that their hovels were raided and their children kidnapped, and that therefore revolution is a just cause. Bele, in turn, claims that Lokai's people were a product of love but not yet ready for utopia, that they were well cared for, and that Lokai is an idealistic dreamer who would twist minds and inspire people to kill one another in the name of legalistic trickery. Kirk tires of this and tries to continue on his original mission—to decontaminate the planet Ariannus, which is plagued with a virulent bacteria endangering the lives of a billion people. Bele takes over the Enterprise, however, and only Kirk's threat to destroy the vessel convinces the alien to return control to the captain. Once Ariannus is decontaminated, Bele once more takes over the starship, and turns it toward Cheron. They arrive to find it long dead: In their wildly emotional race hatred, the natives have annihilated themselves. Lokai transports down to the planet in an effort to escape Bele, who follows him. The ages-old battle between these two will finally end. The Enterprise leaves them there.

Cast	
Kirk: William Shatner	Scott: James Doohan
Spock: Leonard Nimoy	Uhura: Nichelle Nichols
McCoy: DeForest Kelley	Lokai: Lou Antonio
	Bele: Frank Gorshin

See Lexicon under:		
Alien scout vessel	Command frequency 2	Lokai
Ariannus	Crawford, Oliver	Mendel, Gregor Johann
Bele	Cronin, Lee	Monotone humans
Cheron	Decontamination tanks	Pigmentation
Chief Officer, Commission	Destruct sequence	Shields
of Political Traitors	Directional control	Starbase 4
Coalsack	Intergalactic Treaty	Taylor, Jud
	Joining	

T E MA K OF GIDEON

BY GEORGE F. SLAVIN AND STANLEY ADAMS
DIRECTED BY JUD TAYLOR
STARDATE: 5423.4 AIRED: 1/17/69

The natives of the planet Gideon are resisting membership in the Federation and will not allow any surveillance of their world. Gideon is believed to be a paradise of germ-free atmosphere, perfect living conditions, and flourishing spiritual life, but no one has ever seen the planet. The inhabitants claim that their isolation is to prevent contamination from the violence of others, but agree to a delegation of one from the Enterprise, and specifically ask for Kirk. Given transporter coordinates which should bring him into the Gideon council chambers, Kirk beams down from the ship—but does not appear on Gideon. A senior councilmember insists that Kirk never arrived, but refuses to allow a planetwide search for the captain. Spock tries to get permission from Star Fleet to search, by force if necessary, and is refused—which provokes him to say some pithy things about both bureaucracy and diplomacy. Kirk, meanwhile, has materialized into what he thinks is the Enterprise, except that the ship is empty of crew. He has a slightly painful bruise on his arm that he does not remember having before, and there are about nine minutes missing from his memory. A strange, lovely girl appears, who claims to have no memory of her home planet. An outside noise, like a great heartbeat, can be heard through the walls of the ship, and the girl, Odona, explains that her planet is so crowded that there is no place for privacy; that people would kill for the huge space in the Enterprise. There is no sickness on Odona's planet, so no one dies, and they venerate life so much that contraception and abortion are unheard of. Through the ship's viewscreen they see hordes of people crowded so closely together that they can barely move. At this point Kirk realizes that the ship is a fake and they are on the planet's surface. Odona becomes ill, and her father, Hodin, who suddenly appears on the screen, tells Kirk that during his lost nine minutes, the Gideonites took a blood sample from him—hence the bruise. Kirk carries a virulent illness in his blood, Vegan choriomeningitis; Odona was injected with the blood sample, then kept with Kirk long enough to insure that she came down with the disease. By infecting Odona, the Gideonites hope to pass the disease on to others of their people and help cut down the population. Kirk is horrified, and begs to be allowed to take Odona to the Enterprise for treatment to save her life. Hodin then gives forth with some doubletalk about the Gideonites' love of life, arguing that Odona must give up her life to show others that it can be done: She is to die as a symbol (of the faultiest logic in the galaxy). The Gideonites also hope to use Odona to tie Kirk to the planet, so that he can infect more people with the disease in case she dies before the plague can take hold. Meanwhile, Spock, thoroughly annoyed at both Hodin and Star Fleet, beams down against orders and helps get Kirk and Odona back to the Enterprise. McCoy cures Odona in Sick Bay, and she apologizes to Kirk for her people's treatment of him; then she returns to her planet, happy that her blood can now be used to infect others.

Cast	
Kirk: William Shatner	Odona: Sharon Acker
Spock: Leonard Nimoy	Hodin: David Hurst
McCoy: DeForest Kelley	Krodak: Gene Dynarski
	Admiral Fitzgerald: Richard Derr

THAT WHICH SURVIVES

BY JOHN MEREDYTH LUCAS
STORY BY MICHAEL RICHARDS (PSEUD.)
DIRECTED BY HERB WALLERSTEIN
STARDATE: UNKNOWN   AIRED: 1/24/69

The Enterprise is sent to examine a Class M planet about the size of Earth with the mass of our moon. Earthquakes are being registered which should be leveling old mountains and raising new ones, but which have no seismic aftereffects. Kirk, McCoy, Sulu, and geologist D'Amato beam down to investigate these inconsistencies. Just as they are fading from the transporter grids, a beautiful woman, Losira, appears. She tells them to halt, and when they don't she touches an ensign, who dies instantly of cellular disruption; then she disappears. Meanwhile, the power surge caused by her appearance throws the ship 990.7 light-years away from the planet. Spock calculates that it will take at least 11.33 hours at warp 8.4 to return. On the planet, the landing party discovers that the vegetation is poisonous to humans and that the rocks are made of an alloy that did not evolve naturally. Losira appears and kills D'Amato by merely touching him, then vanishes again. She reappears for Sulu, but he successfully avoids her, and they discover that she can harm only the person she calls by name. Kirk, Sulu, and McCoy band together to prevent her from killing them. She reappears on the ship, in Engineering, and kills a crewman, Watkins, to prevent him from discovering that she has sabotaged the ship. Scott's insistence that something "feels" wrong about the ship leads them to find that the matter/antimatter integrator bypass control has been damaged and that the ship will explode. Scotty repairs the damage in time to save the Enterprise, and they continue back to the planet. Meanwhile, the landing party finds a chamber in the rocks that contains what is apparently a computer; it is from here that Losira has been appearing. She reacts to their intrusion by creating replicas of herself that will touch all the landing party at once. Spock and a security force arrive in time to destroy the computer which was projecting Losira's image. She vanishes for good, and a film recording triggered by the computer shows that this planet was an outpost of the Kalandan race, ravaged by a deadly organism which supply ships unwittingly took back to the home world. The film welcomes new arrivals (who will never come now) and declares that the computer will defend the planet against all life forms but the Kalandans'. The landing party has been threatened by a dead race, and the last link with them—the computer—is also dead. Kirk says that Losira's beauty still survives, however.

Cast	
Kirk: William Shatner	Losira: Lee Meriwether
Spock: Leonard Nimoy	Lieutenant Rahda: Naomi Pollack
McCoy: DeForest Kelley	Lieutenant D'Amato: Arthur Batanides
Scott: James Doohan	Ensign Wyatt: Brad Forrest
Sulu: George Takei	John B. Watkins: Kenneth Washington
Uhura: Nichelle Nichols	Dr. M'Benga: Booker Marshall

THE LIGHTS OF ZETAR

BY JEREMY TARCHER AND SHARI LEWIS
DIRECTED BY HERB KENWITH
STARDATE: 5725.3   AIRED: 1/31/69

The Enterprise is on its way to Memory Alpha, a planetoid set up by the Federation as a central library containing the total cultural history and scientific knowledge of all planetary Federation members. Lieutenant Mira Romaine, on her first deep-space voyage, is to supervise the transfer of some newly designed equipment from the starship to Memory Alpha. This is also her first Federation assignment. Scotty falls in love with her, to the detriment of his duties and the amusement of his shipmates. A strange storm sweeps over Memory Alpha, killing all life forms on the planetoid and affecting the Enterprise crew for a short time. It seems to attack different portions of everyone's neural centers, causing disruption of speech, hearing, or eyesight. Investigation of Memory Alpha shows that the storm not only killed all life, but burned out the central computer brain and memory core—an irretrievable loss of galactic knowledge. The storm gives Romaine a new ability to see short distances into the future, and she accurately predicts the return of the storm. In spite of all evasive and defensive tactics by the ship, the storm enters the Enterprise, where it is seen by the crew as brilliantly flashing colored lights. The lights lodge themselves in Mira Romaine, and there is no way to stop them without killing her. Investigation of her records shows a psychological profile of extreme susceptibility to empathic transmissions and flexibility regarding new situations, making her a perfect "home" for the lights, a corporate entity who identify themselves as natives of a long-dead planet, Zetar. They insist that they have the right to take over, and live in, Romaine's body, but Kirk is equally adamant that they do not. Though the Zetars are more powerful, they are caught off guard when Romaine is placed in a pressure chamber. The Zetars are used to the vacuum of space; when exposed to increasing atmospheric pressure, they die, leaving Romaine free. She presumably returns to Memory Alpha to set up the new equipment and begin the computer-library complex anew, and Scott returns to his engine room.

Cast
Kirk: William Shatner
Spock: Leonard Nimoy
McCoy: DeForest Kelley
Scott: James Doohan

Uhura: Nichelle Nichols
Lieutenant Mira Romaine: Jan Shutan
Lieutenant Kyle: John Winston
Technician: Libby Erwin
Crewman: Bud da Vinci (Voice)

REQUIEM FOR METHUSELAH

BY JEROME BIXBY
DIRECTED BY MURRAY GOLDEN
STARDATE: 5843.7   AIRED: 2/14/69

Rigellian fever, as deadly and contagious as bubonic plague, has struck the Enterprise crew. Ryetalyn, the only known antidote, is found in sufficient quantities on Holberg 917G, in the Omega system. Although sensors show the planet to be uninhabited, when Kirk, Spock, and McCoy beam down to collect the mineral, they find a man named Flint and his ward, Reena Kapec. After exchanging threats, an ungracious Flint grants them two hours on his planet while his M-4 robot collects and processes the ryetalyn. The landing party is offered hospitality in a room full of rare art treasures; Spock identifies an unrecorded da Vinci painting, but sensors show that it was done with modern oils on modern canvas. Similarly, he ponders a Brahms waltz, written on modern paper with contemporary ink. McCoy has trouble with the robot; the antitoxin contains just enough irillium to be rendered inert and useless, so a new batch must be processed. Meanwhile, Flint seems to be throwing his ward and Kirk together, and Reena's innocent attitude takes the captain unawares. They fall in love. Flint's jealousy flares, and his robot nearly kills Kirk. Attempting to discover the newly processed pure ryetalyn which Flint has hidden in his laboratory, the landing party finds a room full of unfinished female androids, all labeled "Reena." Flint admits that he is immortal, a fluke of fate who has lived more than six thousand years. He was many great men in history, including da Vinci and Brahms. Reena is an android built by him for his own company, but she is without human depth and emotions. He had hoped that meeting others and falling in love would complete her development, but as he and Kirk fight over the girl, she cannot cope with the agony of her new-found but conflicting emotions, and short-circuits. Having put the Enterprise in suspension to protect his secret, Flint now releases it, allowing the landing party to return to the ship with the antitoxin. After the shipboard fever is controlled, McCoy reveals that he ran medical readings on Flint. Because the immortal left the atmosphere of Earth, he is finally dying of old age. Kirk's grief over losing Reena makes McCoy comment about the captain's painful obsession, so Spock uses Vulcan mind touch to make Kirk forget her completely.

Cast
Kirk: William Shatner
Spock: Leonard Nimoy
McCoy: DeForest Kelley

Flint: James Daly
Reena Kapec: Louise Sorel
Orderly: John Buonomo

THE WAY TO EDEN

BY ARTHUR HEINEMANN   STORY BY MICHAEL
RICHARDS (pseud.) AND ARTHUR HEINEMANN
DIRECTED BY DAVID ALEXANDER
STARDATE: 5832.3   AIRED: 2/21/69

The Enterprise sights a space cruiser, the Aurora, which
has been stolen. When the Aurora tries to outrun the
starship, it reaches a critical point; just before it explodes,
all personnel aboard are transported to the Enterprise.
The occupants are a group of "space hippies," one of
whom is the son of the Catullan ambassador, who are
looking for a perhaps mythical planet called Eden. The
young people are led by a humanoid, Dr. Sevrin, once a
brilliant engineer. He is a carrier of sythococcus novae, a
virulent bacillus strain that can affect anyone not immunized against it. Dr. Sevrin is insane as well, and thinks
only of himself and his dream of reaching Eden to set up
the perfect society for his acolytes. He is placed in confinement, but, due to the presence of the Catullan ambassador's son, the hippies are allowed to roam free on
the ship. They proceed to passively disrupt the ship, even
as an intrigued Spock actually finds a planet named
Eden for them. They then help Sevrin to escape and steal
a shuttlecraft, and while doing so, Sevrin tries to kill the
Enterprise crew, using ultrasonics. This fails, and Sevrin
escapes from the ship with his people. Kirk follows with a
landing party down to Eden, where they discover that the
plant life is loaded with a harmful acid. One hippie is
dead already; others are badly hurt. Sevrin, rather than
surrender, kills himself by taking a bite of fruit. The rest
are returned to the Enterprise.

Cast	
Kirk: William Shatner	Dr. Sevrin: Skip Homeier
Spock: Leonard Nimoy	Irini Galliulin: Mary-Linda Rapelye
McCoy: DeForest Kelley	Tongo Rad: Victor Brandt
Scott: James Doohan	Adam: Charles Napier
Sulu: George Takei	Mavig: Deborah Downey
Uhura: Nichelle Nichols	Girl No. 2: Phyllis Douglas
Chekov: Walter Koenig	Lieutenant Palmer: Elizabeth Rogers

See Lexicon under:
Acid	Heinemann, Arthur
Adam	"Hey Out There"
Alexander, David	Mavig
Aurora	Musical instruments
Auxiliary Control Center	One
Biological rebellion	Palmer, Lieutenant
Catullan ambassador	Richards, Michael
Disaffect	Romulan space
Disease	Sevrin, Dr.
Eden	Slang, Twenty-second century
Egg	Sythococcus novae
Ferries	Telepathy
Galliulin, Irini	Tiburon
Girl	Tongo Rad
"Good Land, The"	Typhoid Mary
"Heading Out to Eden"	Ultrasonics

THE CLOUD-MINDERS

BY MARGARET ARMEN
STORY BY DAVID GERROLD AND OLIVER CRAWFORD
DIRECTED BY JUD TAYLOR
STARDATE: 5818.4   AIRED: 2/28/69

The planet Merak II is in danger of losing all life from a
botanical plague, so the Enterprise goes to the planet
Ardana for zienite, the only known substance which will
stem the plague. The ruling society of Ardana literally
lives in the clouds, in Stratos City, held high in the sky by
antigravity elevation. While the citizens of Stratos are on a
higher intellectual plane than the Troglytes, who mine
and till on the planet's surface, there are Troglyte "disruptors" who agitate for better working conditions and more
of the privileges enjoyed by the Stratos dwellers. When
Kirk and Spock arrive to collect the zienite, the Troglytes
refuse to give it up; they consider the Enterprise a threat
brought in by Plasus, the High Advisor of the Planet
Council. Kirk tries to reason with Plasus but gets ordered
off Ardana. Meanwhile, McCoy has discovered that the
Stratos people and the Troglytes are from exactly the
same root stock, but that zienite mining releases a gas
which retards the intellect and increases violent tendencies. Armed with filter masks to trade for the zienite, Kirk
beams down to deal directly with the Troglytes. Vanna,
leader of the Disruptors, takes Kirk prisoner, not believing
the theory about the zienite gas. Kirk proves his story
dramatically: He closes the mine with a phaser shot, trapping Troglytes in the shaft; an hour later, everyone is
showing signs of irrational behavior, and Vanna believes
Kirk. Plasus, whom Scott has also transported into the
mine, assents grudgingly to dealings with both the Federation and the Troglytes. To win Spock's goodwill,
Plasus's daughter Droxine faces up to the idea that the
Troglytes will eventually become her social and intellectual equals, and that they all must work toward this goal.
Having obtained the zienite, the Enterprise leaves Stratos
to work out its extremely changed social structure.

Cast	
Kirk: William Shatner	Plasus: Jeff Corey
Spock: Leonard Nimoy	Droxine: Diana Ewing
McCoy: DeForest Kelley	Vanna: Charlene Polite
Scott: James Doohan	Anka: Fred Williamson
	Midro: Henry Evens

See Lexicon under:
Anka	Planet Council
Antigravity elevation	Plasus
Ardana	Protectors
Armen, Margaret	Rostrum
Botanical plague	Sentinels
Confinement quarters	Shield
Crawford, Oliver	Stratos
Disruptors, human	Taylor, Jud
Droxine	Thongs
Filter masks	Transport pass
Gerrold, David	Transport platform
Industrialization, Federation Bureau of	Troglytes
Merak II	Vanna
Midro	Weapon
Mortae	Zienite

THE SAVAGE CURTAIN

BY GENE RODDENBERRY AND ARTHUR HEINEMANN
STORY BY GENE RODDENBERRY
DIRECTED BY HERSCHEL DAUGHERTY
STARDATE: 5906.4   AIRED: 3/7/69

The Enterprise is assigned to survey a planet about which there are legends and tales circulating in Star Fleet. About to confirm original reports that there is no intelligent life there, Spock picks up a suggestion of a carbon-cycle life form, previously assumed to be scientifically impossible, on the planet below. The conditions on the lavalike surface make it dangerous to beam down for further investigation, and Kirk is inclined to go on to other assignments. Suddenly there is an incredibly swift scan and deep probe of the Enterprise from the planet below. Kirk orders a magnification of the area and finds that there is a thousand-kilometer space which looks and scans exactly like Earth. While they are puzzling over this, the image of Abraham Lincoln appears and asks permission to board the ship. Astonished, Kirk insists on greeting him with the full honors due a President—but with phasers on stun, just in case. Lincoln invites Kirk and Spock to the planet, and after some discussion, they agree to beam down. Upon landing, they meet Surak, an ancient Vulcan considered to be the greatest of all Vulcans, whom Spock greets with some emotion. Then Yarnek, a rock creature, informs them that everything has been prepared for a fight between good and evil in order to understand them and to discover which is the stronger. Evil is represented by Colonel Green, Kahless, Genghis Khan, and Zora, all notorious tyrants, traitors, and warmongers. The men of the Enterprise refuse to fight, so Yarnek causes the warp engines to stop, whereupon a breakdown of the matter/antimatter shielding begins; if Kirk does not win the fight, the ship will blow up in four hours. After Colonel Green tries a trick to gain advantage, the fight begins in earnest, with both sides resorting to deceit and trickery. Surak and Lincoln are both killed, as are Kahless and Green; Kirk and Spock, in a final effort, send Zora and Genghis Khan running. After a discussion of philosophies, the rock creature returns Kirk and Spock to the Enterprise and releases the ship unharmed.

Cast
Kirk: William Shatner
Spock: Leonard Nimoy
McCoy: DeForest Kelley
Scott: James Doohan
Sulu: George Takei
Uhura: Nichelle Nichols
Chekov: Walter Koenig
Yarnek: Janos Prohaska, Bart LaRue
    (Voice)

Colonel Green: Phillip Pine
Zora: Carol Daniels Dement
Abraham Lincoln: Lee Berger
Surak: Barry Atwater
Genghis Khan: Nathan Jung
Kahless: Robert Herron
Lieutenant Dickerson: Arell Blanton

ALL OUR YESTERDAYS

BY JEAN LISSETTE AROESTE
DIRECTED BY MARVIN CHOMSKY
STARDATE: 5943.7   AIRED: 3/14/69

The star Beta Niobe is about to go nova, which will de-stroy its only satellite, Sarpeidon. The Enterprise goes to the rescue and finds the last inhabitant, Mr. Atoz, in charge of a library operated by a huge power generator. The library contains tapes and files of Sarpeid history, as well as the atavachron, a time-travel machine by which all others on the doomed planet have been sent to chosen periods in the past, thereby escaping the nova. Because Atoz assumes that the Enterprise men are from his own planet and wish to choose a time in which to live, he does not clearly explain the dangers of the atavachron, allowing Kirk, Spock, and McCoy to tinker with the time machine. Atoz mentions that "preparation" is necessary to live a full lifetime in the past—an "unprepared" person will die after only a few hours. Before Atoz can "prepare" Kirk, the captain is thrown into a Charles II type of past, where he immediately gets into trouble and is jailed. In an attempt to rescue Kirk, McCoy and Spock are thrown into the planet's ice age, where they meet Zarabeth, a political prisoner of a tyrant who used the atavachron to achieve his own ends. Zarabeth is lonely and pretty, and appeals to the emotions of both men. Recovering from severe frostbite, McCoy uses the enforced leisure time to flirt with the girl, much to Spock's growing annoyance. Meanwhile, Kirk discovers that the prosecutor on his case is really a Sarpeid who has chosen this time in which to escape the nova. Fearful that Kirk will reveal his secret, the man shows the captain how to return to the library. Time for the nova is approaching fast, and Kirk's men have to be rescued before the means for recovering them from the past—the library—is destroyed in the holocaust. Mr. Atoz is not interested in helping to find anyone; he wants to make his own escape into the past. To save his own hide, Atoz attempts to send Kirk into another time, but he fails. In the ice age, Zarabeth tells Spock and McCoy that it is impossible to return to their present after they have been "prepared." Spock nearly kills McCoy in a jealous rage before he realizes that his reversion to pre-logic behavior is caused by his going into the past. McCoy goes through the driving snow to the spot where they first arrived from the library, and finds that he can shout to Kirk, in the present. Kirk makes Atoz bring the men back, after Spock and Zarabeth say good-bye. Having been "prepared," Zarabeth is trapped in the ice age. When the men return to the present, Spock's emotionalism disappears and he becomes coldly logical again. Atoz escapes into his selected time in the past, and the landing party beams to the Enterprise. The star goes nova, destroying Sarpeidon as the ship warps out of range.

Cast
Kirk: William Shatner
Spock: Leonard Nimoy
McCoy: DeForest Kelley
Scott: James Doohan
Zarabeth: Mariette Hartley
Mr. Atoz: Ian Wolfe

Woman: Anna Karen
Constable: Johnny Haymer
Fop: Ed Bakey
Prosecutor: Kermit Murdock
Second Fop: Al Cavens
Jailer: Stan Barrett

TURNABOUT INTRUDER

BY ARTHUR H. SINGER
STORY BY GENE RODDENBERRY
DIRECTED BY HERB WALLERSTEIN
STARDATE: 5928.5   AIRED: 6/3/69

On its way to Beta Aurigae, the Enterprise receives a distress call from Camus II. The landing party finds alive only Janice Lester and Dr. Coleman, who claims that the rest have been killed by celebium radiation, and Janice is quite ill from it. Alone with Janice, Kirk recalls when they knew each other at Star Fleet. Unaware that Janice's frustrated ambitions have caused her to hate his rise to a captaincy, Kirk is trapped into a life-entity transfer with Janice. His personality is in her body, while she takes over Kirk's. Kirk-J(anice) then tries to kill Janice-K(irk), but is prevented by the return of the party. McCoy transports Janice-K to Sick Bay for further treatment, and Kirk-J can think of no way to avoid this. They do so, and while Janice-K tries to convince everyone that he is really Kirk, Kirk-J takes command of the Enterprise and decides to abandon Janice-K at the Benecia Colony, effectively getting rid of both her female body and Kirk's personality. But diverting the ship makes the crew suspicious. Spock conducts a mind-meld with Janice-K and discovers that he is indeed Kirk. Kirk-J gets hysterical when questioned and tries Spock for mutiny. During the testimony, McCoy and Scott are convinced that an entity transfer has occurred, and they too are charged with mutiny. Kirk-J calls for the death sentence, which convinces the rest of the crew that Kirk-J is not their real captain, and they refuse to obey any further commands. As the transfer begins to weaken, Kirk-J appeals to Dr. Coleman's love for Janice, asking him to kill the others. Coleman agrees, but the transfer breaks, returning the real Janice to her own body and restoring Kirk to his. Insane with hatred, Janice makes a last attempt to harm Kirk and collapses in tears. Dr. Coleman, still in love with Janice, requests that he be allowed to care for her. The Enterprise returns to its mission.

Cast	
Kirk: William Shatner	Chekov: Walter Koenig
Spock: Leonard Nimoy	Dr. Janice Lester: Sandra Smith
McCoy: DeForest Kelley	Dr. Arthur Coleman: Harry Landers
Scott: James Doohan	Angela: Barbara Baldavin
Sulu: George Takei	Mr. Lemli: Roger Holloway
Uhura: Nichelle Nichols	Security Guard: David L. Rose
	Second Guard: John Boyer

ANIMATEDS

YESTERYEAR

BY D. C. FONTANA
STARDATE: 5373.4
AIRED: 9/15/73

On the planet of the time vortex, where the Guardian of Forever is a time portal to the past, historians have gathered to study the past of various planets. Kirk, Spock, and the historian Erikson, having gone through the time portal to view Orion's history firsthand, have come back to find that nobody recognizes Spock. When the men return to the Enterprise, they find that an Andorian has been First Officer of the starship for the past five years, and Spock is greeted as an interesting but unknown visitor. Somewhere in Vulcan's history, the time lines have been changed. A search through the library computer banks shows that Sarek and Amanda had a son, but that he was killed at age seven, the couple breaking up soon after to go their separate ways; eventually Amanda was killed in a shuttle accident. Sarek never remarried, nor is there any trace of another child in the family. Spock remembers that he nearly died during a maturity test, but a cousin saved him; now he must return to the past to become that cousin and save himself again. Spock dresses as a Vulcan of thirty years ago and goes through the time portal to ShiKahr, his home city on Vulcan. There he meets a seven-year-old Spock who is being teased by his Vulcan playmates for being half human, and witnesses an emotional incident which displeases Sarek. Spock introduces himself as Selek, a distant cousin on his way to visit the family shrine. Sarek apologizes for the display of emotion shown by his son and invites Spock to stay overnight with them. Young Spock must soon face the Kahs-wan ordeal—a test of maturity and Vulcan manhood—or else decide to become all-human and accept the emotionalism of that way of life. When night falls, young Spock decides to try his maturity test a month early and leaves for the Vulcan desert, with his pet sehlat following. When he meets a le-matya, a large mountain-lion creature with poisonous claws, I-chaya, the sehlat, though old and unable to maintain a fight for long, keeps the beast away from young Spock long enough for the adult Spock to find them and stop the le-matya. I-chaya is severely wounded, and young Spock heads back to the city to get a healer, passing through many dangers to do so. When the healer arrives, it is too late to do anything but keep the sehlat alive a bit longer or give it a decent death; the decision must be left to the young Vulcan. Young Spock decides on a fitting release with peace and dignity, though he hates to lose his beloved pet. When they return to ShiKahr, young Spock has chosen his way—the Vulcan way—and Sarek is proud of him. Selek departs, asking only that Sarek try to understand his son as he grows up, and then returns through the time portal as Spock. Since the time lines have been rewoven again, everyone recognizes Spock, and the Andorian First Officer never existed on the Enterprise.

Voices
Kirk: William Shatner
Spock: Leonard Nimoy
McCoy: DeForest Kelley
Scott: James Doohan
Ensign Bates: (Unknown)
Sarek: Mark Lenard
Amanda: Majel Barrett
Young Spock: Billy Simpson
The Healer: James Doohan
Young Sepek: Keith Sutherland
Young Sofek: (Unknown)
Young Stark: (Unknown)
Thelin the Andorian: James Doohan
Aleek-OM: (Unknown)
Grey: Majel Barrett
Erikson: (Unknown)
Guardian of Forever: James Doohan

See Lexicon under:
Amanda
Ambassador Sarek
Andorian
Andorians
Antidote
Aurelia
Books
Cities
Cowards
Desert flyer
Desert soft suit
Earther
Family shrine
First Officer
Fontana, D. C.
Guardian of Forever
Healer
Historians
Human philosophy
I-Chaya
Kahs-wan
Le-matya
L-Langon Mountains
Log, subjective time
Lunaport
My Lady
Orion
Pain-relieving move
Practical joke
Recalibration
Sarek
Sehlat
Selek
ShiKahr
Spray injector
Star Fleet records
Tasmeen
Thank you
Time lines
Vine
Vulcan family history
Vulcan gardens
Vulcan medicine
Vulcan philosophy
Wardrobe department

ONE OF OUR PLANETS IS MISSING

BY MARC DANIELS
STARDATE: 5371.3
AIRED: 9/22/73

A huge cosmic cloud, like nothing ever encountered before, is reported moving into the outer fringe of the galaxy. The Enterprise, ordered to investigate, intercepts it as the cloud nears Alondra, the outermost planet in this system. Spock's readings reveal the cloud to be eight hundred thousand kilometers across and about half that in depth and to contain a strange combination of matter and energy. The cloud engulfs Alondra, the planet begins to break up, and it becomes obvious that the cloud is a "planet eater." The cloud then changes course and heads toward the next planet, Mantilles, inhabited by eighty-two million people. The cloud is a danger not only to Mantilles, but to the rest of the galaxy as well, and it must be stopped. They decide to warn Mantilles of the cloud, which is only a few hours away. The Enterprise learns that the cloud is from outside the galaxy. As it approaches the cloud, it is pulled inside. Large blobs of antimatter hit the Enterprise in an attempt to break it up for digestion, but the shields hold, at a tremendous cost in energy. A subspace message from Mantilles says they can save five thousand children only. Spock discovers that the cloud has a "brain" and that they can escape through the top of it before the shields fail. They travel through the equivalent of the human intestine, with millions of antimatter villi draining power to an irreversible level. Scotty rigs a force-field box to bring in one of the antimatter villi to recharge the engine, saving the ship. Killing the cloud is repugnant to Kirk, yet it seems that the only way to save Mantilles is to kill the cloud by exploding the Enterprise. At Kirk's suggestion, the sensors are trained on the cloud's brain; Spock then uses the mind meld to make contact and allows the cloud to enter his mind. With the destruction of Mantilles only seconds away, Spock/Cloud looks around the bridge, watching tapes of Earth. The cloud's approach comes to a halt when Spock explains that as it eats planets it is also killing beings. The cloud agrees to leave the galaxy and return home. Spock comments that when he traded places with the cloud, he perceived the wonders of the universe.

Voices
Kirk: William Shatner
Spock: Leonard Nimoy
McCoy: DeForest Kelley
Scott: James Doohan

Sulu: George Takei
Uhura: Nichelle Nichols
Arex: James Doohan
Cloud: Majel Barrett

THE LORELEI SIGNAL

BY MARGARET ARMEN
STARDATE: 5483.7
AIRED: 9/29/73

The Enterprise is investigating an unfamiliar sector of space in which, according to both Federation and Klingon records, a starship has disappeared every 27.346 star-years. The ship is put on yellow alert, and they detect a probe from the Taurean system, at the extreme edge of the sector. The probe becomes a signal, which affects only the male members of the crew. Lieutenant Uhura and Nurse Chapel begin to observe the strange, rapt behavior of the men, who, in turn, are experiencing visions of lovely women and idyllic scenery. Kirk, Spock, McCoy, and a security man beam down to a futuristic structure, to be greeted by golden-skinned, silver-haired, blue-eyed women. The men are feted and drugged, coming to with jewelled headbands, which they soon find are draining away their life force and making them age rapidly. On the ship, Scotty is unconcernedly singing Welsh ballads, so a worried Uhura takes command, making Chapel her chief medical officer. On the planet, Spock deduces that the strong stimulant cortropine might help retard the aging, and everyone gets a shot. Spock then makes a try at obtaining a communicator. As he contacts the ship, his jewel begins to glow, indicating that he is weakening again. Then an all-female landing party arrives, rescuing the men from the women. When the rescue party threatens to destroy the temple with the ship's phasers, the planetary women explain that their race fled to this planet from a dying world, only to find out, too late, that there is a force which drains humanoid energy. Their men had no resistance to it, but the women developed a glandular secretion which enabled them to survive and to manipulate areas of the male brain so as to draw on male life force. They are eternal prisoners of the planet, and need revitalization every 27.346 years. The immediate problem facing the Enterprise crew is the aging of its senior officers. Spock suggests that the transporter holds the molecular key to their original bodies, and that it might be used to restore them to health and vitality; the gamble works. Revitalized, the crew of the Enterprise agrees to transport the women to a suitable planet where they can exchange their flawed immortality for a normal way of life.

Voices
Kirk: William Shatner
Spock: Leonard Nimoy
McCoy: DeForest Kelley
Scott: James Doohan
Uhura: Nichelle Nichols
Chapel: Majel Barrett

Lieutenant Arex: James Doohan
Theela: Majel Barrett
Dara: Nichelle Nichols
Computer: Nichelle Nichols
Security Officer Davison: Nichelle Nichols

See Lexicon under:
Armen, Margaret
Audiovisual suggestion
Carver
Children
Compound
Cortropine
Glandular secretion
Headbands
Jewel
Life energy
Lura-mag
Luxury
Medical scans

Medikit
Molecular key
Music
Nectar
Opto-aud
Psychokinesis
Rain
Routine readings
Taurus II
Temple
Theela
27.346 star-years
Vulcan marriage drum

MORE TRIBBLES, MORE TROUBLES

BY DAVID GERROLD
STARDATE: 5392.4
AIRED: 10/6/73

The Enterprise has been assigned to escort two robot ships loaded with seed grain, a new, five-lobed quinto-triticale, to Sherman's Planet, which has once again been struck by famine. The robot ships have no life-support systems, enabling all their energy to go into carrying more cargo. They are now close to the neutral zone, and a rumor circulates that the Klingons have a new weapon; everyone wonders what it could be. Suddenly the Enter-prise has to break course to investigate a Klingon battle-cruiser, the <u>Devisor</u>, which is chasing and firing on a smaller Federation scout ship. The Enterprise locks the transporter on the pilot of the scout ship and hails the Klingon vessel, for it is violating Federation space. The Klingons ignore the Enterprise, and the transporter grabs the pilot just as a Klingon disruptor bolt hits the scout ship and destroys it. Then the Klingons attack the Enter-prise, paralyzing it—including the transporter—with a strange new disruption field effect. The Enterprise cannot fight back, and the Klingon captain, Koloth, appears on the viewscreen, claiming that the pilot of the scout ship is guilty of ecological sabotage and must be turned over to them immediately for punishment. Kirk refuses, saying that the pilot is under Federation protection. The energy required to hold such a powerful weapon on the Enter-prise finally drains the Klingon ship's reserves, and it veers off. Now the Enterprise can integrate the transporter units and save the scout's pilot. Kirk discovers, to his dismay, that he is Cyrano Jones, intergalactic trader and general nuisance, who has brought a collection of trib-bles with him. Kirk points out that there is a law against transporting animals proven to be harmful, but Cyrano is hurt, saying that these are "safe" tribbles: They have been genetically engineered not to reproduce so often. Kirk wants to know how Cyrano got away from Space Station K-7, since it should have taken some years to clean up all the tribbles there. Cyrano explains that, while on a brief parole, he found some help: a tribble predator named a glommer, which eats tribbles whole. Cyrano claims not to know why the Klingons are after him, observing that they have notoriously nasty tempers; he happened to bring some tribbles to a Klingon planet, that's all. Kirk informs Cyrano that there are already three Federation mandates out on him, and forty-seven local ones, according to En-terprise computer files. Meanwhile, McCoy tests the trib-bles and finds that they don't reproduce any more—they just get fat. Kirk, worried about the Klingon weapon, doesn't notice that the tribbles are getting larger and larger. One of the robot ships was damaged when the Klingons attacked, so the grain from it has to be put in containers all over the Enterprise: in the Shuttlecraft Bay, cargo holds, and corridors. The Klingons return and at-tack the Enterprise, using the energy field again. The

sudden impact breaks open grain containers all over the ship, and the tribbles happily eat up the quintotriticale. The glommer is having trouble trying to wrestle a hammock-sized tribble. Kirk finds a two-hundred-pound tribble in his captain's chair. Jones is told to control his tribbles, and instead tries to offer Kirk some Spican flame gems. The Klingons renew the attack, demanding Cyrano Jones as prisoner; the Enterprise is again paralyzed in stasis, and the Klingons demand surrender. Kirk has Scott beam tribbles aboard the <u>Devisor</u>, forcing Koloth to reveal a state secret: Cyrano Jones stole the glommer, a genetic construct, and they must have it back, as they cannot build another one. Kirk says he'll transport the glommer to the Klingon ship, but not Cyrano Jones, which satisfies the Klingons. The <u>Devisor</u> releases the Enterprise from the stasis field and goes away with the glommer. McCoy has found that, while the tribbles don't reproduce, the fat tribbles are really col-onies of tribbles. On the Klingon ship, they make the same discovery when one of Koloth's henchmen fires on a two-ton tribble and it suddenly breaks down into thousands of smaller tribbles, leaving the Klingons hip-deep in them. Scott observes that, if one must have trib-bles, it's best if they all are little ones.

Voices		Uhura: Nichelle Nichols
Kirk: William Shatner		Sulu: George Takei
Spock: Leonard Nimoy		Koloth: James Doohan
McCoy: DeForest Kelley		Korax: David Gerrold
Scott: James Doohan		Cyrano Jones: Stanley Adams

See Lexicon under:	Korax
Battlecruiser, Klingon	Mandate
Boarding Plan C, Klingon	Neoethylene
Colony creatures	Parole
Decoy	Projected stasis
Ecological sabotage	Quintotriticale
Emergency Defense Plan B, Federation	Robot ships
Energy-sapping field	Scout ship
Field effect	Security guards
Genetic engineering	Seed grain
Gerrold, David	Sherman's Planet
Glommer	Space salvage laws
Integration parameters, transporter	Spican flame gems
Jones, Cyrano	Stasis field
Klingon verbal salute	Tribble
Koloth	Weapon

THE SURVIVOR

BY JAMES SCHMERER
STARDATE: 5143.3
AIRED: 10/13/73

Patrolling near the Federation/Romulan neutral zone, the Enterprise discovers a battered one-man ship. They beam aboard the ship's occupant, Carter Winston, a well-known philanthropist who has been missing for five years. Spock has the computer verify Winston's identity. In examining him, McCoy, recognizing the famous man, ignores the slightly unusual readings his instruments give. Winston's fiancée, Anne Nored, is aboard, and he informs her it is over between them—he has changed and cannot marry her. He then goes to Kirk's quarters and, unseen by Kirk, transforms into an alien being which puts Kirk to sleep and assumes Kirk's form. On the bridge, Kirk/Winston orders Sulu to lay in a course that will take them through the neutral zone, and leaves. Upon awakening, Kirk arrives on the bridge to discover that an imposter has ordered the ship into the neutral zone. The course is changed, and Spock and Kirk head for Dr. McCoy. Winston enters Sick Bay, knocks out McCoy, and assumes his shape. Nored wants to discuss Winston with McCoy, and McCoy/Winston advises her to forget him. When Kirk and Spock enter, McCoy/Winston tells them that all of Winston's tests were normal. They leave but realize that McCoy was acting out of character, and when they return, McCoy/Winston is not there. Kirk figures out that Winston has turned into a table, but the alien escapes. They finally realize that Winston is a Vendorian, beings known for their deceitful ways, and decide that it was sent by the Romulans to lure them into the zone. The Vendorian is cornered by security guards, Kirk rushes in, but the alien manages to escape. The Enterprise is now surrounded by Romulans, who demand that Kirk surrender. In the engine room, a crewman is ripping out wires in a control panel; Scott tries to stop him but is knocked unconscious. Then the deflector shields go out. When Scott awakens, he reports that it will take two hours to repair the damage. The Vendorian runs into Nored and explains to her that he can't help but love her: He knew Winston before he died and absorbed much of the man's character and feelings. The Romulans attack. On the bridge, one shield snaps on, the Enterprise successfully defends itself, and the Romulans retreat. The crew learns that the Vendorian changed itself into a shield and saved the ship. As Winston, the Vendorian explains that the Romulans had offered him a chance to make something of himself as a spy for them, but that he couldn't go through with it and allow Nored to die. Kirk says he must stand trial, but his helping the ship will be taken into consideration. Nored suggests that he could have a better life on Earth, since he is much like Carter Winston. He agrees to discuss it with her.

Voices
Kirk: William Shatner
Spock: Leonard Nimoy
McCoy: DeForest Kelley
Scott: James Doohan
Sulu: George Takei
Chapel: Majel Barrett

Carter Winston/Alien: Ted Knight
Lieutenant Anne Nored: Nichelle Nichols
Lieutenant M'Ress: Majel Barrett
Romulan Commander: James Doohan
Gabler: James Doohan
Computer: Majel Barrett

THE INFINITE VULCAN

BY WALTER KOENIG
STARDATE: 5554.4
AIRED: 10/20/73

Phylos, a recently discovered planet on the periphery of the galaxy, has a modernistic city that seems abandoned. The Enterprise landing party finds vegetation and mosslike growths all over the buildings and walks. Life readings are confused and undecipherable. Sulu, still a botanist at heart, stops to pick up an interesting plant as the others go on to a building that seems to be well kept up. The plant poisons Sulu, and while the others are trying to help him, a group of plantlike beings approaches. The leader, Agmar, produces a liquid and saves Sulu. Agmar tells of an earlier visit by a human, who brought disease and death, although he tried to save them. The landing party goes on with its search of the building, which contains a huge laboratory. As Spock is picking up a cassette tape, they are attacked by swoopers—gigantic birdlike things that turn out also to be plant life. Then a giant human appears: Dr. Keniclius 5, whom the plant beings call Master and Savior. Keniclius 5 claims Spock as his property, saying he's waited a long time for such a perfect specimen, and lets the others go. Kirk won't leave the planet without his First Officer, but he goes to the Enterprise to find out all he can about the doctor and to listen to the cassette tape dropped by Spock when he was captured. Library computers tell of a Dr. Keniclius who lived during the period of the Eugenic Wars on Earth, which would make him about two hundred and fifty years old now. He did experiments on cloning—reproducing a being from a few cells—but it was banned as antihumanistic, and he disappeared with no further data on him. The recovered tape adds some information, too. Then Kirk, Sulu and McCoy beam down again, while the Enterprise leaves orbit to make the Phylosians think that the Terrans have left the area. On the planet, the landing party discovers a huge hangar filled with spaceships being readied for flight. They go down a tunnel, where they are attacked by swoopers, but now they are prepared to fight back with chemicals made up on the Enterprise. At the end of the tunnel is a lab where Spock's body lies on a table; Dr. Keniclius 5 shows up to explain that he has cloned Spock into a giant Vulcan who will live forever, cloning again and again, and enforce peace throughout the galaxy. Kirk points out that the doctor is out of date: The galaxy is already more or less at peace (discounting a Kzin, a Klingon, or two). But Dr. Keniclius 5 refuses to believe this; he is unwilling to give up his dream of power. The giant Spock seems even more coldly logical than the original version, and a great deal less friendly toward the smaller humans. Kirk appeals to the cloned Spock's logic, citing the Vulcan philosophy of life and death: The meaningless death of any being cannot be condoned, and the original

Spock's death would be futile if it is only to create a giant version of himself and nothing more. The giant Spock is trying to assimilate all the knowledge and information of the original Spock, so Kirk pulls a trick on him. When the Enterprise gets through to the landing party, Kirk tosses a communicator to the cloned Spock; the reflexes of a trained officer take over, and the giant Spock reacts by opening the communicator and speaking to Uhura, after which he takes the matter in hand and restores the original Spock with a Vulcan mind touch on his dying body. This leaves Dr. Keniclius 5 with a giant Spock almost as intelligent as the original to work with him on reviving the Phylosian culture. There will be no militia of Spocks, as the mold has been broken.

Voices	
Kirk: William Shatner	Dr. Keniclius 5: James Doohan
Spock: Leonard Nimoy	Agmar: James Doohan
McCoy: DeForest Kelley	Lieutenant Arex: James Doohan
Scott: James Doohan	Computer: Nichelle Nichols
Sulu: George Takei	Morgan, Security: (Unknown)
Uhura: Nichelle Nichols	Kolchek, Security: (Unknown)

See Lexicon under:	
Agmar	Kzin
Alien dewdrop	Laboratory
Antidote	Laboratory table
Belt lights	Master, the
Body throw	Medication
Chemical mist	Medikit
Clone	Militia
Dilithium crystals	Murder
Diogenes	Phylos
Dylovene	Phylosian philosophy
Elevator	Phylosians
Eugenics War	Retlaw plant
Galactic wars	Romulans
Garden	Ships, Phylosian
Hangar	Specimen, perfect
IDIC	Spore cells
Keniclius 5	Staphylococcus strains
Keniclius, Dr. Stavos	Swooper
Klingons	Tightbeam transmission
Knowledge	Voder
Koenig, Walter	Vulcan mind touch
	Vulcan philosophy

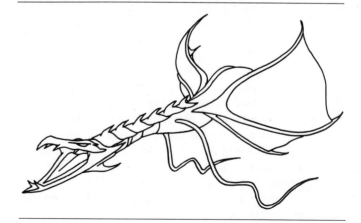

THE MAGICKS OF MEGAS-TU

BY LARRY BRODY
STARDATE: 1254.4
AIRED: 10/27/73

While on a mission at the center of the galaxy to investigate the great explosion theory of creation, the Enterprise is caught in a matter/energy "whirlwind" and transported through the center of Everything into a totally alien environment. Navigational coordinates are meaningless, subspace radio is dead, and the chronometers have stopped, while the Enterprise drifts, its engines fading, toward a very odd-looking planet. The life-support systems are also failing, and the crew is beginning to pass out for lack of air, when suddenly a satyrlike creature appears on the bridge and makes some symbolic gestures, and the lights come on, the life-support system functions, and the crew is saved from death. Spock complains of a lack of logic in these proceedings, and the satyr, Lucien, asks to whose logic his "elfin friend" is referring. Lucien takes a party down to the planet, Megas-tu, to explore its magical world, but he suddenly returns them to the ship for some unexplained reason. Out of curiosity, the humans try some magic and find that it works! Spock observes that one must use the resources at hand. By their use of magic, however, the Enterprise crew has been detected by the Megans and transported to a strange world. The Megans accuse Lucien of bringing evil to their home; the humans will suffer, and Lucien must pay a penalty. A Salemlike witchcraft trial ensues, wherein Spock defends the humans and then Kirk defends Lucien. The Megan prosecutor says that Lucien must be punished, and that Kirk and the others cannot stop them. Spock says that they will use the magic they've learned, and a magical battle ensues. Kirk won't give up, and points out that the Megans can win only by becoming as bad as the Earthmen they fear. The battle ends when Kirk affirms that he is willing to die for Lucien, an alien. The Megans are impressed with human compassion, realize that the penetration of the Enterprise into their dimension was an accident, and help the ship and crew return to their own universe.

Voices	
Kirk: William Shatner	Sulu: George Takei
Spock: Leonard Nimoy	Uhura: Nichelle Nichols
McCoy: DeForest Kelley	Lucien: James Doohan
Scott: James Doohan	Megan Prosecutor: Ed Bishop
	Voice: George Takei

See Lexicon under:	
All systems go	Gravity
Asmodeus	Limbo
Bacchanals	Logic
Belief	Loneliness
Bodily integrity	Love philtre
Brody, Larry	Lucien
Center of the galaxy	Matter/energy whirlwind
Chaos	Megan
Charting scanner	Megas-tu
Chess	Myths
Chronometer	Natural law
Cities	Navigational coordinates
Creation	Pentagram
Defense counsel	Puritan costume
Dimension	Radamanthus
Earthlings	Salem
Elfin friend	Satyr
Enterprise records	Sorcerer-contractor
Eye of the storm	Specialists
Fog	Superstition
Forest	Toast
Generalist	Whirlwind
Gesture	Witness
	Wizards

ONCE UPON A PLANET

BY LEN JENSON AND CHUCK MENVILLE
STARDATE: 5591.2
AIRED: 11/3/73

For rest and recreation, the crew of the Enterprise comes back to the "shore-leave" planet in the Omicron Delta region, where various crew members visualize their fantasies. McCoy is involved with a vision of the old plantation South of Earth, when suddenly the Queen of Hearts appears, screams, "Off with his head!" and a pack of humanoid playing cards begin heaving lances at him. Uhura is near a waterfall when she hears McCoy's communicator call for help. As she tries to use her communicator to find out what is wrong, it is crushed by a metal hand, and she finds herself taken prisoner by a metallic hovercraft robot. McCoy, transported back to the ship, relates his experience, and Kirk orders the landing parties back aboard; all beam back, except for Uhura. Kirk tries to contact the Keeper, with no success, so he, Spock, McCoy, Sulu, and two security men beam down to search for her. They discover a slab, with inscriptions in several languages, which reads: THE KEEPER, LAST OF HIS RACE, CEASED TO FUNCTION, 5TH DAY OF THE 12TH MOON OF THIS PLANET'S YEAR 7009. Tricorder readings indicate that a body is interred under the slab. Meanwhile, Uhura tries to outwit the computer, but finds that this is not possible with a thought-duplicating machine. The landing party is being harried by all manner of robot creations, and the Enterprise, too, is experiencing difficulties, which Arex and the rest of the crew are barely able to deal with. The once-friendly planet has become very dangerous, as the Keeperless computer has come to resent its role as servant. By drugging Spock, Kirk and the others are able to lure a hovercraft robot to take Spock as a patient through a trapdoor into the planet's interior; Kirk also makes it through the door. The revived Spock, Kirk, and Uhura confront the planet computer, which expresses its resentment of servitude. The three Enterprise people use logic to convince the computer that it serves a very useful function, that it is very creative, and that there is no shame in serving others when one does it of one's own free will. At once, the malfunctions cease in the ship and on the planet's surface. Spock remains to conduct further discussions with the computer, and the crew once again begins to enjoy shore leave: McCoy and Sulu find themselves picnicking with Alice, the White Rabbit, and a docile dragon.

Voices
Kirk: William Shatner
Spock: Leonard Nimoy
McCoy: DeForest Kelley
Scott: James Doohan
Sulu: George Takei
Uhura: Nichelle Nichols

Lieutenant Arex: James Doohan
Lieutenant M'Ress: Majel Barrett
Gabler: James Doohan
Computer: George Takei
White Rabbit: James Doohan
Alice: Nichelle Nichols
Queen of Hearts: (Unknown)

See Lexicon under:
Alice in Wonderland
Amusement-park planet
Caretaker
Carroll, Lewis
Cat
Computer, amusement
Computer banks
Dragon
Earthlike planet
Electronic block
Emergency rescue party
Fake victim
Fantasy literature
Fortress
Gravity-control computer
Guidance computer
Happiness
Hovercraft
Jenson, Len
Liquid crystals
Melanex
Menville, Chuck
Metal alloy, alien
Metal slab

Murder
Navigational manual override
Omicron Delta region
Orbit
Phaser bore
Picnic
Playing cards
Printout
Pterodactyls
Queen of Hearts
Restructured granite
Service
Shore-leave planet
Short-burst maneuvers
Shuttlecraft
Skymachine
Slaves
Southern mansion
Systems checkout
Thought duplicator
Through the Looking Glass
Viewscreen, computer
White Rabbit
Zero gravity

MUDD'S PASSION

BY STEPHEN KANDEL
STARDATE: 4978.5
AIRED: 11/10/73

The Enterprise is sent out to check on an "old friend," Harry Mudd, who has several charges against him ranging from conning people into buying fake patents to selling Star Fleet Academy. A landing party finds him on Motherlode, a mining planet in the Acadian star system, trying to sell a fake love potion to the lonely miners. Mudd uses an attractive female to demonstrate how potent the love crystals can be, but when Spock proves the beautiful girl to be a reptilian illusion-maker, the Enterprise has to pull Harry off the planet before the angry miners can get their hands on him. On the Enterprise, Harry persuades Nurse Chapel to try some of the love potion on Spock, using this distraction to escape the brig and steal a shuttlecraft. Chapel, bitter that the love potion does not seem to work on Spock, tries to recapture Mudd, but he takes her as a hostage down to a small, seemingly deserted planet. Suddenly, aboard the Enterprise, a delayed reaction from the love potion hits Spock, much to his dismay and everyone else's total surprise. The love potion has been released into the air ducts of the starship, and it soon begins to affect everyone else, too. Spock's sudden and unexpected anxiety to rescue Chapel is anything but gratifying to the rest of the crew, especially the landing party that follows Mudd to the planet. There they discover that the large rocklike mounds on the landscape are in reality huge reptilian creatures. Kirk requests repeatedly to be beamed back to the ship to get away from the monsters, but nobody from the ship pays any attention. Due to the effects of the love potion, the Enterprise is full of people having a good time, enjoying one another's company, and they ignore communications from the landing party. When a creature attacks, Kirk risks his life in order to throw some of the love potion into its mouth. Mudd regrets the waste, since he now realizes that the love potion is not a fake and will be worth many credits if he can sell it. The potion takes effect on the monster just in time to save them all. Meanwhile, the effect is wearing off in the Enterprise; people reassume their responsibilities and beam the landing party aboard, with Mudd and Chapel. They discover an interesting side effect of the love potion: When it wears off, the people who were most affected go through several hours of hating each other! Mudd is thrown back in the brig, where he cheerfully confesses to an assortment of con games throughout most of the known galaxy. He is dismayed at the idea of being sent away again for rehabilitation, and there is no indication that it has worked in the past.

Voices	
Kirk: William Shatner	Lieutenant Arex: James Doohan
Spock: Leonard Nimoy	Harcourt Fenton Mudd: Roger C. Carmel
McCoy: DeForest Kelley	Female Ursinoid: Nichelle Nichols
Scott: James Doohan	Lora: Majel Barrett
Chapel: Majel Barrett	Human Miner: James Doohan
Lieutenant M'Ress: Maiel Barrett	

See Lexicon under:

Acadian star system
Avian
Binary star system
Boots
Class M planet
Confession
Crystal
Defensive standby
Desert planet
Desk computer
Fissionables
Force field
Gentlebeings
Hangover
Heavy-metal miners
Heavy-planet humanoid
Hostage
I.D. card
Illegal drug manufacture
Illusion
Ilyra VI
Kandel, Stephen
Lora
Love

Love potion
Medical summary
Medication
Meeching
Mercy of the law
Monopedal
Moon
Motherlode
Mudd, Harcourt Fenton (Harry)
Mudd's Planet
Off-ship vehicles
Omega Cygni system
Ophuicus VI
Parking orbit
Preliminary survey
Rehabilitation therapy
Rigellian hypnoid
Sacred thumbs of Hnisto
Scout ship
Shuttlecraft Bay
Sirius IX
300 credits
Transporter Room 4
Ursinoid

THE TERRATIN INCIDENT

BY PAUL SCHNEIDER
STARDATE: 5577.3
AIRED: 11/17/73

While the Enterprise is on an expedition to explore the burnt-out supernova Arachna, it receives a strange signal. A single word, "terratin," repeated twice, is all that is decipherable. Kirk decides to investigate, and course is set for the signal's origin, which seems to be the single planet orbiting the star Cepheus. There they find a world of constant volcanic activity, with a mostly crystalline surface. A faint and diffuse impulse passes through the ship, followed very shortly by a lightninglike bolt, which causes the ship and everything in it to glow and paralyzes the crew members at their stations. When the bolt-induced paralysis fades, Scott reports heavy damage to the engines: Most circuits are fused, and the dilithium crystals are breaking down. It soon becomes apparent that all organic matter in the ship is shrinking. The crew members discover that the space between the molecules in their bodies is contracting, and Spock calculates that they will all end up one centimeter high in less than thirty-two minutes. Kirk beams down to the planet near the origin point of the bolt and finds that he is normal size again; the transporter returns affected molecules to their normal spacing. Kirk discovers a miniature city, but he is beamed up by the transporter, which is on automatic, before he can investigate further. Kirk now finds that the bridge crew has been beamed off the ship, and he contacts the city, threatening it with destruction unless his crew is returned and the attack stops. The city leader tells him that the "attack" was their only effective way of contacting the Enterprise for help—their planet is about to be disastrously changed by volcanic action, and their city destroyed. Spock explains that these are the mutated descendants of a lost exploration expedition, whose ancestors named their world "Terra 10." Kirk beams up the bridge crew, who bring new dilithium crystals to replace those destroyed; they employ the transporter to restore the rest of the crew up to normal size, and then beam the tiny city aboard, to take it to a more stable, fertile world.

Voices
Kirk: William Shatner
Spock: Leonard Nimoy
McCoy: DeForest Kelley
Scott: James Doohan
Sulu: George Takei

Uhura: Nichelle Nichols
Chapel: Majel Barrett
Lieutenant Arex: James Doohan
Mendant of the Terratins: James Doohan

See Lexicon under:
Antenna
Aquarium
Arachna
Briel, Mess officer
Cepheus
Class M planet
Computer, Enterprise
Computerized microscope
Contraction
Crab Nebula
Dilithium crystals
DNA
Gossamer mice
Halo fish
Health scanner
Honorary Terratins
Interstat code
Invasion defense
Jewelry
Laser
Libra
Lilliputian city
Lost colony

Macroscope
Mandant of Terratins
Mayday
Medical lab
Miniature city
Organic matter
Paralysis
Purring like happy kittens
Schneider, Paul
Spiroid epsilon wave
Spiroid-wave analysis
Starbase 23
Star chatter
Subspace extreme upper registers
Supernova
Suture-thread lifeline
Terra 10
Terratin
Transporter circuits
Verdanis
Visual sweeps
Volcanic action
Xenylon
X-waves

TIME TRAP

BY JOYCE PERRY
STARDATE: 5267.2
AIRED: 11/24/73

Caught in an ion storm, the Enterprise enters the Delta Triangle, where a large number of starships have disappeared over the years. The Enterprise is surveying this area to determine the cause of the disappearances, but its sensors become unreliable when entering the Triangle. They meet a Klingon ship, the Klothos, which fires on the Enterprise. When the Federation ship fires back, the Klothos winks out of sight, to the amazement of the Enterprise's crew. The phenomenon seems to be natural, having nothing to do with the exchange of fire, but possibly related to the disappearances of the other ships. However, two other Klingon battlecruisers decide that the Enterprise has destroyed the Klothos. The Enterprise retreats, following the Klothos into the Triangle, and finds itself in a strange Sargasso Sea of spaceships from every civilization imaginable. They are in an alternate universe. The Klingon ship cannot be found among the debris, and there are some fascinating ships that Scott has seen only as drawings in museums. They pick up some life and energy readings from a cluster of ships and surmise that descendants of the original crews may still be alive. The Klothos fires on the Enterprise as it glides by, but the fire is dissipated midway between the ships, and the commanders of each ship disappear from their bridges. They find themselves facing a council of people who call themselves Elysians; they are all of different races, including Klingon, Gorn, Tellarite, Kzin, Romulan, Andorian, Vulcan, and Human. Xerius, their spokesman, a Romulan, says that the two ships must stay in Elysia, because there is no way out, but that they may not do violence to each other. The two captains are responsible for the actions of their crews and will be punished accordingly if anyone aboard the Enterprise or the Klothos behaves violently in any way. To insure this, a psionic has frozen their weaponry. Devna, an Orion, says that they must live in Elysia in peace: All have tried to leave at one time or another, but all have failed and subsequently learned to live in Elysia in concord with one another. Kirk is returned to the Enterprise, where he finds that the time warp is disintegrating the ship's dilithium-crystal supply; they must discover how to get out of the time trap soon, or they will have no power to do so later. The Klingons are also working against time, trying to escape. After considering every possibility, the Klingons and the Enterprise crew decide to cooperate by linking both ships together, using the combined warp power to get through the time continuum into our universe again. The Klothos and the Enterprise exchange personnel to work out the details. Meanwhile, Spock seems to have become very friendly toward the Klingons, and even shakes hands with them. Kor, the Klingon commander, explains privately

to Kaz, his First Officer, that he intends to destroy the Enterprise as soon as they break free of the Delta Triangle, although he will seem to go along with Kirk's plan for cooperation. Spock's overly-friendly touching of the Klingons has enabled him to pick up this information, but he has not had enough contact to find out the details. The Klingons give a female, Kali, a small explosive capsule that will detonate as soon as both ships reach warp 8, approximately three minutes after the barrier is pierced and the ships have disengaged. The Enterprise crew throws a party to celebrate their imminent escape from Elysia, inviting the Klingons to it. McCoy asks Kali to dance, and a fight starts between him and Kaz, who claims she is "his" woman. During the fuss, Kali slips away to plant the capsule inside the computer room. Kirk is annoyed at the Klingons for breaking the law—both ships could be punished for this, and both are needed to break the time barrier. Magen, an alien with psionic powers, learns telepathically that the Klingons have planted the capsule bomb, and she tells the Enterprise. They find the capsule in time, and get rid of it just as both ships reach warp 8, break the time barrier, and disengage. There is an explosion, and the Klingons are triumphant for a while, until they realize that it occurred outside the Enterprise and did not harm the Federation starship at all. Kor heads for his home base, claiming full credit for getting both ships out of the Delta Triangle, as might be expected of a Klingon.

Voices	Commander Kuri: (Unknown)
Kirk: William Shatner	Captain Kor: (Unknown)
Spock: Leonard Nimoy	Kaz: (Unknown)
McCoy: DeForest Kelley	Klingon No. 1: (Unknown)
Scott: James Doohan	Kali: (Unknown)
Sulu: George Takei	Xerius: (Unknown)
Uhura: Nichelle Nichols	Devna: (Unknown)
Gabler: (Unknown)	Magen: (Unknown)
Bell: (Unknown)	

T E AMBERGRIC ELEMENT

BY MARGARET ARMEN
STARDATE: 5499.9
AIRED: 12/1/73

The Enterprise is sent to study Argo, a planet almost completely covered by water. Seismic disturbances caused the land masses to sink, and knowledge of how this happened may save millions of lives on a Federation planet expected to undergo similar disturbances. Kirk, Spock, McCoy, and Lieutenant Clayton go down to investigate the planet, and their aquashuttle is attacked by a sea monster. Dr. McCoy and Clayton are thrown free, but Kirk and Spock are trapped in the vehicle as the sea monster submerges with it. Five days later, the Enterprise crew is still looking for its captain and First Officer. Scott, McCoy, and Clayton search with a scouter gig and find Kirk and Spock lying face down in the sea, near an island. McCoy finds that their lungs aren't working, and both men are suffocating in the air. They have become water-breathers. Neither of them can remember what happened, but there is now an unidentified substance in their bodies which has affected their metabolism. All efforts to return the men to normal fail, although McCoy does discover that the mutation could not have occurred from natural causes, which presupposes a highly intelligent life form on Argo. Kirk and Spock decide to explore Argo again to find the beings who changed them. They dive into the sea and soon meet some Aqua people, who address Kirk and Spock as "air-breathers" and tell them to go away. But the Enterprise men follow the Aquans back to their city. Kirk and Spock are trying to figure out why the Aquans fear air-breathers when they are captured in nets and brought before a High Tribune. Damar, its head, tells the Enterprise men that air-breathers have been expected for a long time. Ancient records warn that air-breathers never come in peace; the times during the great quakes made them erratic and warlike. The younger Aquans say that they saved the lives of Kirk and Spock, making them water-breathers by surgo-op, and they believe that the Enterprise men came in peace. Meanwhile, the starship's computers predict a seaquake in four hours. Scott, who has been waiting in the scouter gig with Clayton and a security man, goes down to find and warn Kirk and Spock. Some Aquans tell the Tribunes that more air-breather spies have arrived. The Tribunes declare that Kirk and Spock, responsible for this treachery, are to be left on an island to die. Rila, one of the more progressive Aquans, surfaces and sees the wreckage of the aquashuttle. She realizes that it has to be from elsewhere than Argo and tries to rescue Kirk and Spock. When Rila can't release the men, she goes to the scouter gig and gets the other Enterprise men to help her. When everyone is safe, Rila tells them the history of her planet, and of the ancient city which sank beneath the sea during a quake, along with the old records of surgo-op, which explain how to reverse the mutation. Although it is a for-bidden act to take anyone to the ancient ruins, Rila is finally convinced to do so. In the city, Kirk and Spock find the records sealed in watertight jars. On the Enterprise, McCoy discovers that reversal of the mutation will require the venom of a sur-snake. Severe tremors are now felt on Argo, but the younger Aquans help Kirk and Spock obtain the necessary venom. McCoy injects Kirk first and nearly loses him. However, Kirk recovers, so Spock is given the treatment. Later, on the bridge of the starship, the younger Aquans, wearing watermasks, watch as the Enterprise bombards an unpopulated pressure area with phaser beams in order to change the epicenter of the quake away from the Aquan city. On Argo, where there was once an island, the sunken city now stands on a small inlet a few feet from the water's edge. The Aquans will repay the Federation for saving their underwater city by making the ancient records available to it. The experience has shown the Enterprise how to avoid tragedy on the threatened Federation planet, also. And the young Aquans have decided to reverse their water-breathing and rebuild the city on land. The older Aquans cannot make the change, but they agree never to lose contact with one another.

Voices	
Kirk: William Shatner	Domar: (Unknown)
Spock: Leonard Nimoy	Rila: (Unknown)
McCoy: DeForest Kelley	Cadmar: (Unknown)
Scott: James Doohan	Lemus: (Unknown)
Lieutenant Arex: James Doohan	Nephro: (Unknown)
Lieutenant Clayton: (Unknown)	Aquans: (Unknown)

See Lexicon under:	
Air-breather	Net
Algae specimens	Ordainments
Ambergris	Power pack
Antitoxin	Pyramid
Aquans	Reborn city
Aquarium	Records, ancient
Aquashuttle	Reef barrier
Argo	Scouter-gig
Armen, Margaret	Scrolls
Audience chamber	Sea foliage
Bombardment, preventive	Sea monster
Death sentence, Aquan	Sea torches
Edibles	Seismic disturbances
Epicenter	Sensors
Exile	Shellfish
Great shelters	Spies, air-breather
Hieroglyphic	Surgo-op
High Tribune	Sur-snake
Island, Argo	Telefocals
Junior Tribune	Tribunal of Aquans
Legends	Undersea city
Life-support belts	Universal translator
Life-support masks	Venom, sur-snake
	Water-breather

SLAVER WEAPON

BY LARRY NIVEN
STARDATE: 4187.3
AIRED: 12/15/73

The shuttlecraft Copernicus is en route to Starbase 25 with important cargo: a Slaver stasis box found by archeologists on the planet Kzin. Spock, Uhura, and Sulu are carrying this find to be inspected by starbase experts in the hope that the box may contain valuable information for the Federation. A long-dead conquering race, the Slavers once ruled most of the known galaxy, but finally destroyed themselves and almost all other sentient life in a galactic war. The Slavers used stasis boxes to carry weapons, information, valuables, and other unknown and unrecognizable items, and some boxes contained information which has had an incalculable effect on later science. Stasis boxes are the only remnants of a lost civilization; time stands still inside the box, so the contents can last for millions of years. The only way to find a stasis box, except by pure accident, is to use another stasis box, as they attract one another. On the way to Starbase 25, the stasis box in the shuttlecraft begins to show signs that another box is in the area. The Beta Lyrae system is nearby, so Spock decides to investigate, for he feels that finding another stasis box is of great importance to Federation science. The Copernicus lands on a small ice-covered planet that is almost airless, the stasis box indicating that the other box is some thirty meters below the ice. Much to the Enterprise people's surprise, there are some Kzin in the vicinity, who take them prisoner. Kzin are large catlike beings whose only business in life seems to be waging war on other beings; they nominally accept peace with the Federation, but allow piracy and raids on Federation shipping whenever possible. These particular Kzin pretend to be pirates in a stolen Kzinti police craft, but later admit that they have the blessings of their government for their acts—provided they are not caught. Being flesh-eaters, they ignore Spock as an eater of roots and vegetables, and because Kzinti females are not intelligent, they also ignore Uhura; Sulu is the only Enterprise person the Kzin will talk to, as he is omnivorous and does not act afraid of them. The Kzin have an empty stasis box, stolen from a museum, which they have hoped would draw another stasis box to them. Before they met mankind, the Kzin controlled a thriving empire; now they have only a few worlds, and are not permitted weapons except for peace-keeping. They want Slaver weapons to gain back their original Kzinti power over the galaxy. The stasis box from the shuttlecraft is opened, to reveal a cap which seems to have no purpose, a piece of fresh meat that is poisoned, a photo of a Slaver, and a weapon with several settings. In fact, it has secret settings beyond those marked, but the Kzin do not know this. The Chuft Captain of the Kzin has the Enterprise prisoners moved to a police web to keep them from escaping while he tampers with the weapon. He finds that it does things which are either surprising or disappointing, depending on what happens at each setting of the weapon. By this time, Sulu has guessed that it is a spy weapon and potentially more dangerous than a standard military weapon. The Enterprise people await their chance to escape, which comes when the Chuft Captain accidentally hits the police web with a blast from the weapon and deactivates the web. Uhura runs for the shuttlecraft but is recaptured. The police web is deactivated again when another setting of the weapon nullifies everything, and Sulu joins Uhura in escaping. When the Chuft Captain drops the weapon in surprise and shock, Spock grabs it, making his escape. Uhura is recaptured, but Sulu and Spock get away, hiding in the broken ice field while the Kzin try to find them. The Chuft Captain offers to fight Spock hand-to-hand, even though Spock damaged the Kzin commander when he grabbed the weapon; the Kzin says he will fight without medical attention if Spock will only face him. Spock is unimpressed, for he knows something about Kzin anatomy and realizes that the Chuft Captain is still stronger than he appears. They cannot give the weapon to the Kzin; the entire galaxy would become their dinnertable. Sulu tries another setting on the weapon, setting off a nuclear-type explosion that knocks the Enterprise men off their feet. The Kzin move in and retrieve the weapon; they try another setting, and the weapon talks to them. The Chuft Captain wants information, but the weapon will not tell the Kzin anything without the proper code words. When it is not given the code words, the weapon tells the Chuft Captain to move the toggle to another setting. The weapon self-destructs, in a twenty-yard-wide globe of energy that destroys the Kzin and their ship. Sulu regrets that the weapon could not have gone to some museum, but Spock points out that it would have only been a matter of time until someone else stole it and tried to use it on the galaxy.

Voices	
Spock: Leonard Nimoy	Chuft Captain: (Unknown)
Sulu: George Takei	Kzin Soldiers: (Unknown)
Uhura: Nichelle Nichols	Kzin Telepath: (Unknown)

BEYOND THE FARTHEST STAR

BY SAMUEL A. PEEPLES
STARDATE: 5521.3
AIRED: 12/22/73

The Enterprise is in the outer reaches of the known galaxy to investigate mysterious radio emissions. Abruptly, the ship picks up speed and goes off course, and nothing the crew does can stop it. A negative star mass of imploded matter, Questar M-17, is exerting a tremendous hypergravitational pull on the Enterprise, drawing the ship toward its surface. With one last effort, they manage to put the ship into an elliptical orbit around the dead star, discovering that it is the source of the radio emissions. But there is another signal, like the cry of a lost child, which leads them to a tremendous alien ship, a vessel so large that the Enterprise is a mere speck beside it. There is no record anywhere of this kind of ship, an incredibly beautiful craft, with huge pods arching out from a central nucleus—a poem in metal—and completely dead. Analysis reveals that it has been in orbit for three hundred million years and that the signal, which has changed to a beseeching cry, is coming from it. Donning life-support belts, Kirk, Spock, McCoy, and Scott beam over to the ship. The signal stops. On board, they learn from the ship's log, found in a protected chamber, that the vessel was built by a giant insect race and that it was invaded by a malevolent life form. Unable to rid themselves of the intruder and unwilling to carry it to other worlds, they elected to destroy their own ship. But the life form is still alive; it bursts into the chamber just as the landing party is beamed back aboard and is unintentionally brought back aboard with them. A formless, intelligent magnetic organism—an energy mass—it forms a symbiotic relationship with the Enterprise and takes it over, using its control over the ship to force Kirk to accede to its demands to be taken to the center of the galaxy. Kirk appears to agree, but, like the insect captain, he dares not—the being, which reproduces by mitosis, would take over every ship and computer center that it encountered. The Enterprise, however, must first be freed from the pull of the dead star. Spock calculates that a slingshot effect will work, doing the computations in his head so that the alien will not know what they are planning. When all is ready, Kirk tricks the entity and plunges the ship toward the star mass. Confused and alarmed, the entity issues orders, threatens, pleads, and then deserts the ship in panic when it appears headed for a crash. The slingshot effect works, hurling the Enterprise far into space and leaving the entity behind in orbit around the dead sun. As they leave, Uhura picks up a radio transmission from it—a plea not to be abandoned because "it's so lonely."

Voices
Kirk: William Shatner
Spock: Leonard Nimoy
McCoy: DeForest Kelley
Scott: James Doohan
Sulu: George Takei
Uhura: Nichelle Nichols
Transporter Chief Kyle: James Doohan
Engineer: James Doohan
Commander of Alien Starship: James Doohan
Alien: James Doohan

See Lexicon under:
Automatic bridge defense system
Cargo holds
Commander of pod ship
Core hatch
Cutter beams
Electroenergy
Elliptical orbit
Engineering core
G-1 star
Host body
Insectoid beings
Life-support belt
Low-frequency shield
Magnetic organism
Manual override
Mitosis
Peeples, Samuel A.
Pod ship
Primal energy
Questar M-17
Retroanalysis
Self-destruct
Ship's log
Slingshot effect
Storage banks, computer
Superstition
Vector grid
Wands

THE EYE OF THE BEHOLDER

BY DAVID P. HARMON
STARDATE: 5501.2
AIRED: 1/5/74

The Ariel has disappeared in the region of the planet Lactra VII, and the Enterprise is sent to investigate. The ship is found orbiting the planet, and Kirk, Spock, and McCoy beam aboard. The last contact with the scientific party on the planet had occurred too long ago to suit the commander of the Ariel, so he went down to rescue them, leaving his ship without personnel. The planet is Class M. There is no other information on the log except that the survey crew found no large groups of life forms and no city clusters. The party from the Enterprise leaves the Ariel and materializes on the planet. They pass through a series of strangely juxtaposed environments until, finally, a group of fork-tailed slugs captures the Enterprise men, takes away their weapons, and carries them to an alien city obviously made to house the slug creatures. These slugs, the intelligent life on Lactra, put the men in a laboratory where they are cleansed of any possible bacteria. Then Spock picks up the impression that the Lactrans are telepathic, but he can only pick up fleeting images. The men find that they are zoo specimens, and are put in a compound with the missing scientific-exploration team. Of the original party, three remain. One, Lieutenant Randolph, is quite ill. The zoo itself is tremendous, a collection of creatures and beings from all over the galaxy, each in its particular environment. The humans are caged behind a force field, with a very modern house, swimming pool, and all the comforts of home except freedom. Their equipment and weapons are put on display outside the force field, for the inspection of visiting Lactrans. Spock tries to communicate with the Lactrans, and finds that they are merely amused by his childlike attempts at intellectual contact. Though Lieutenant Randolph is ill, the curators of the zoo do not want to let their human specimens go. When the humans concentrate mentally on the medical kit, the Lactrans bring them exotic fruit instead. Because Lactran intelligence is eons beyond that of Vulcans, Spock finds telepathic contact difficult, until a Lactran child is contacted and tricked into bringing the medical kit, and then the communicator, through the force field. Kirk contacts the Enterprise, but the Lactrans discover the trick and the Lactran child grabs the communicator just as Scott beams it up to the ship. When the huge Lactran child appears, Scott calls for security aid and tries to lock the child in the Transporter Room. The huge slug creature breaks the door down and takes over the bridge, working all the equipment and absorbing all the library computer's knowledge. Meanwhile, the Lactran parents are quite worried about their child, and are using very strong mental force to get Kirk to return their baby. Kirk can go mad from the pressure of such minds, and Spock tries to save the captain by having all the humans exert mental blocks,

but it does not work. The Lactran suddenly appears, holding Scott. The parents pull their child out of the compound and the force of the Lactran minds is turned off Kirk. Although the Lactran child is only about six years old, it has an I.Q. in the thousands; having found out about the Enterprise, its crew, and the Federation, it has been convinced that humans are not pets. The child communicates this information to the adult Lactrans, who decide to let the Enterprise people go and take the scientific crew with them. The Lactrans conclude that humans are simplistic but in the process of evolving into a higher order; they also think there is a higher order for Vulcans. However, humans are backward children compared to the Lactrans, who were at our level tens of thousands of Lactran years ago. As the Enterprise leaves, the Lactrans send a final message: The humans will be welcomed back in twenty or thirty centures, after they have grown up.

Voices	Lieutenant Commander Tom
Kirk: William Shatner	Markel: James Doohan
Spock: Leonard Nimoy	Randi Bryce: Majel Barrett
Scott: James Doohan	The Lactrans: (Unknown)
Lieutenant Arex: James Doohan	

See Lexicon under:	Illness ploy
Alien creatures	Laboratory
Ariel	Lactra VII
Book, the	Lad
Bryce, Randi	Library computer
Canopus III	Life forms
Centuries, Lactran	Markel, Lieutenant Commander Tom
Child, Lactran	Mind entrance
Cities	Pets
Class M planet	Quivering
Compound	Randolph, Lieutenant Nancy
Dinosaur	Ship's log
Display case	Stream
Food supplies	Telepathy
Force field	Terraforming
Greenery	Thought screen
Guards, Lactran	Zoo
Harmon, David P.	

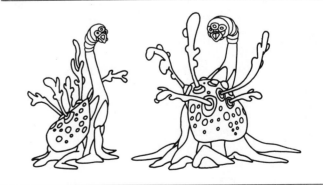

JIHAD

BY STEPHEN KANDEL
STARDATE: 5683.1
AIRED: 1/13/74

The Enterprise approaches a strange collection of spacecraft positioned around a silvery globe that pulsates in midspace. They are making rendezvous with a Vedala asteroid: Something dangerous to the safety of the galaxy is developing, and the Vedala have called in specialists to help stop it. The Vedala, the oldest spacefaring race known, are immensely powerful, but this is beyond even their ability to control. Kirk and Spock meet the other specialists: Tchar, hereditary prince of Skorr, a winged humanoid with talons; Sord, a small, bulky, powerful dinosaur creature with hands, chosen for his strength; Em/3/Green, a small ciliated creature who is nervous and twitching, an expert lockpick and thief; Lara, a human female known for her prowess as a hunter, with flawless directional sense. Spock has been chosen for his analytical mind and scientific expertise, and Kirk for his leadership and adaptability. Tchar explains the mission: Two centuries ago his people were great warriors with advanced military technology; today they are civilized because of Alar (he makes a figure 8 in the air when he says "Alar"), a great religious leader, the salvation of the Skorr, a teacher who taught the whole planet to be great in peace. Alar's brain patterns were recorded before his death in a piece of indurite sculpture, called the Soul of Skorr. The sculpture has been stolen, and if the inhabitants of Skorr discover the loss, a holy war—a jihad—could erupt throughout the galaxy. The sculpture is hidden on a geologically unstable planet in a trinary star system, with constant earthquakes, gravitic shifts, tidal waves, and drastic changes in temperature. Three expeditions have failed to return from it. Kirk asks the Vedala why her powerful race has not recovered it, but she explains that they could not survive on such a planet, while the others at least have a chance. They agree to go, whereupon the Vedala materializes them with a gesture on the unstable planet, along with a ground cart ready for the expedition; in the background, a glacier grinds into a volcanic firestorm. Sord likes the planet; it has variety. Em/3/Green can handle the machine, and the expedition starts forward to find the sculpture. Tchar goes above, surveying the landscape in flight. Lara shows a good deal of interest in Kirk, but also pays attention to her job. After several adventures on the unpredictable planet, the party finds itself near a vast, black, fortresslike cubical building. Tchar says he can sense the Soul of Skorr inside the building. When they approach, they find that the fortress is guarded by mechanical flying creatures, which take Tchar into battle, disappearing on the rooftops of the fortress. Em/3/Green picks the lock on the building, and inside they find the missing sculpture hanging in midair. They attempt to get to the sculpture, but are again stopped; this time Kirk figures out that they have a spy within the group who is trying to stop them from recovering the Soul of Skorr. The door to the fortress falls shut, trapping the group inside, and they find that the traitor is Tchar himself. He wants the Skorr to go out to war, to again die in glory and confront the galaxy with their power, and the stealing of the Soul of Skorr seemed a simple method of setting off a galaxywide holy war. Tchar cuts off the gravity in the fortress so that the expedition floats free, but Kirk and Spock use null-gravity combat exercises to attack Tchar and conquer the avian. Tchar then makes a suicide attempt, but before he can succeed, the entire group is beamed back onto the Vedala asteroid. Tchar is immobilized by the Vedala, where he will be healed of his madness and made sane again, though still brave and proud. The sculpture is returned to its people, and the rest of the group is told that they cannot be rewarded, because the entire episode must be kept a secret. The Vedala says that the memory of the incident will be gone in time, and returns them all to their respective ships. Scott and Sulu look surprised; they say that Kirk and Spock were gone only a few minutes, and ask if the mission was called off. Kirk says the danger is past, and that the Vedala have changed their minds.

Voices	
Kirk: William Shatner	Sord: (Unknown)
Spock: Leonard Nimoy	Em/3/Green: David Gerrold
Tchar: (Unknown)	Lara: (Unknown)
Scott: James Doohan	Vedala: (Unknown)
	Sulu: George Takei

THE PIRATES OF ORION

BY HOWARD WEINSTEIN
STARDATE: 6334.1
AIRED: 9/7/74

The Enterprise has just suffered an outbreak of choriocytosis, but the disease seems to be under control, so there is no problem in completing the present mission of representing the Federation at the dedication ceremonies for the new Academy of Sciences on Deneb V. Then, in a delayed reaction, Spock suddenly comes down with the disease. In human, iron-based blood, choriocytosis is merely troublesome, but in Vulcans it is fatal: The infection enters their copper-based bloodstream and encases cells so that they cannot carry oxygen. The only cure is strobolin, a naturally occurring drug found only on a few planets in the galaxy. The computer is put to work finding one of them; otherwise, Spock can last only three days, even with a synthesized drug to slow the disease's progress. Beta Canopis is the closest source they can find, but it is four solar days from the present position of the Enterprise. However, there is a chance that another ship, the Potemkin, can pick up some of the drug from the planet and transfer it to the S.S. Huron, a freighter coming toward the Enterprise. Meanwhile, Spock is going through all the symptoms of the disease, and McCoy is worried—he really would be sorry to lose "that pointy-eared encyclopedia." The Huron, with the drug and a cargo of dilithium crystals for another delivery, is attacked by a ship. The Enterprise finds the Huron, with its people still alive but in need of medical aid. Kirk rescues the crew and abandons the freighter as space junk. Captain O'Shea, commanding the Huron, does not know why he was attacked, but they play back the ship's log to see if it contains any clues. A spectral-analysis chart superimposed over a starchart shows that the alien ship left a unique trail of radioactive waste, so the Enterprise follows at warp 7. Spock collapses and soon needs a respirator. The trail goes through an asteroid belt, and long-range sensor scan shows the alien ship in the middle of the asteroids, which are composed of highly unstable material that explodes on contact. The Enterprise puts up deflector shields against the asteroids and continues pursuit of the intruder ship, which is eventually seen to have Orion markings. An Orion commander comes on the viewscreen, demanding that the Enterprise stop harassing his ship, as he is a representative of a neutral planet. Orion's neutrality has been in dispute since the Coridan Planets affair, and Kirk reminds the commander of Babel Resolution A-12: After a crime has been committed in space, the first ship encountered must submit to a search on request. The Orion threatens to lodge a formal protest with the Federation, but meanwhile the Enterprise has gotten close enough for its sensors to detect dilithium crystals in the Orion ship's hold. Although the drugs are too small an amount to be picked up by the sensors, Kirk is fairly certain that the Orion ship has them also. Kirk offers the Orions the entire dilithium shipment with no mention in his log of the incident if the drugs are handed over. The Orions are suspicious and decide they cannot trust Kirk; their neutrality must be protected at all costs, so they decide on a suicide mission. They make a counter proposal that Kirk and the Orion commander meet on an asteroid to hand the drugs over to Kirk. Everyone on the Enterprise feels it is a trap, but Spock will die without the drugs, so, with the transporter locked on the captain, Kirk goes down to the asteroid. The Orion commander and his Science Officer are tense and nervous, for they know they can't outrun or outshoot the Enterprise, and they can't take Kirk's word that he will not report the incident to Star Fleet. The Science Officer is carrying a bomb that can trigger the unstable asteroid, with a dilithium crystal for the explosive device. But before it can do harm, Scott locks onto the dilithium crystal and beams it aboard the Enterprise. Then Scott beams up the whole group on the asteroid, and they take away a small capsule from the Orion commander so he cannot commit personal suicide. Because of the extra treachery, the Orion ship is captured, and all will stand trial for piracy. Spock is saved with the strobolin, with McCoy gloating that while the Vulcan's green blood may have saved him before, this time it nearly killed him. Spock refuses to concede the point, however.

Voices	
Kirk: William Shatner	Lieutenant Arex: James Doohan
Spock: Leonard Nimoy	Captain O'Shea: (Unknown)
McCoy: DeForest Kelley	Freighter Officers: (Unknown)
Scott: James Doohan	Orion Commander: (Unknown)
Chapel: Majel Barrett	Orion Science Officer: (Unknown)
	Orion Ensign: (Unknown)

BEM

BY DAVID GERROLD
STARDATE: 7403.6
AIRED: 9/14/74

The Enterprise is on a series of exploratory and contact missions with Commander Ari bn Bem, an independent observer from the planet Pandro. Star Fleet is anxious to have good diplomatic relations with Pandro, which has developed some advanced fields of medicine that can benefit everyone. Bem, however, has stayed in his cabin for the past six months, doing no observing. When the Enterprise goes into orbit around Delta Theta III, newly discovered by a previous scouting mission, Bem decides he wants to go down with the landing party. Kirk is annoyed, as he does not want to risk losing his guest to the possibly dangerous new planet, and he does not like the way Bem has taken over, especially when he sets the transporter so that they beam down into waist-deep water. Bem seems eager to help them out of the water, and in so doing, he manages to exchange Spock's and Kirk's weapons for fake ones. They find themselves in a rain forest, with trees very close together, vines, and swampy water. The Enterprise reports some kind of non-network sensory stasis several kilometers away; it could possibly be an atmospheric effect such as they have seen on other planets before, so nobody is overly worried. When a group of life forms is sensed ahead, Bem starts toward them at a run, in spite of Kirk's protests. Though the Enterprise people can't see it, Bem can split into several parts, with each piece moving easily among crowded trees. Kirk and Spock leave Scott and Sulu to follow Bem, but to do so they have to go around the forest. They find a native food-gathering group, which has captured Bem. Meanwhile, the sensory stasis is increasing and expanding, and the Enterprise wants to pick up the men, but Scott and Sulu cannot contact Kirk and Spock on their communicators. Scott and Sulu are beamed back to the ship. Kirk and Spock now find that their equipment does not work. Bem is put into a cage, and when the Enterprise men arrive to rescue the Pandran, they are surprised to find that he does not want to be rescued: He wants to observe. Then Kirk and Spock are captured and put in cages. Bem admits to taking the communicators and phasers, but offers to return them, since he disdains using casual violence to accomplish goals. Much to the amazement of Kirk and Spock, Bem disassembles himself to get through his barred cage, returns their communicators and phasers, and then goes back to his cage. Bem wants the Enterprise people to show how valuable they can be to Pandro by rescuing him, which is why he does not use his talents to escape the cage. The sensory anomaly now covers the planet; the Enterprise has lost complete track of the people on the ground, and Kirk cannot get through to the starship. Kirk and Spock escape from their cage and put Bem under protective custody. Then they hear a voice. Paralyzed in the stasis field, the men listen to an ultimate Earth Mother who says she is god; she tells them to put away their weapons and not harm her children. The voice asks why they disturb her planet, and the Enterprise men explain that it's their job to classify it and test it. The voice tells them to go away, then leaves them. After declaring that Kirk has mishandled the whole matter and is not a good commander, Bem escapes from them. Kirk and Spock try to communicate with the alien intelligence again, and find that she is angry about their not leaving on order. Kirk says they must find Bem first, as he is their responsibility, but the voice demands that they leave immediately. Kirk calls down his security force, and they look for Bem. When they find him, they must fire on stun setting at some natives who have captured him again. The voice returns, puzzled to find the Enterprise people still on her planet! Kirk reasons with her about his responsibility to his people, as well as to hers, and she lets them return to the ship. Bem decides that his mission is a failure and that he must disassemble into his component units, since he is a colony creature. The voice says that Bem cannot do that and learn to correct errors. She still wants them all to leave so as not to corrupt her children with concepts they are not ready for. Spock finds it fascinating that a highly advanced alien entity is using the planet for a laboratory in which to guide another race into intelligence. Uhura picks up a parting message from the voice: "Go in peace; you have learned much. Be proud, my children."

Voices	Lieutenant M'Ress: Majel Barrett
Kirk: William Shatner	Lieutenant Arex: James Doohan
Spock: Leonard Nimoy	Commander Ari bn Bem: James
Scott: James Doohan	Doohan
Sulu: George Takei	Alien: Majel Barrett
Uhura: Nichelle Nichols	

See Lexicon under:	Non-network sensory stasis
Aborigine	Offering
Bem, Commander Ari bn	Pandro
Children	Pleasure excursion
Classify	Protective custody
Class M planet	Punishment
Colony creatures	Quarantine
Communicators	Responder
Conduct, rules of	Responsibility
Contact party	Sample pouch
Delta Theta III	Scotty, Mr.
Eggling	Scout vessel
Fate	Security squad
Garo VII system	Stasis field
Gerrold, David	This one
God	Tiberius
Heavy-duty tricorders	Unity
Mission, Bem's	Vulcan nerve pinch
Monitoring devices	

PRACTICAL JOKER

BY CHUCK MENVILLE
STARDATE: 3183.3
AIRED: 9/21/74

The Enterprise is on a routine survey of a Type 4 asteroid when three Romulan warships attack with photon bombs. The Romulans claim that the Federation ship is in Romulan territory, an offense punishable by death. An unidentified energy field, like a gaseous cloud, crosses the Enterprise's path, and the starship enters it to hide from the Romulans, as the ship's deflectors cannot hold up against close-range photon bombs. Having passed through the cloud, the Enterprise goes into subwarp cruise to lay by for repairs, when things start happening aboard the ship: Drinks leak all over crewmen; forks wilt, dumping food down Kirk's front; Spock gets a "black eye" looking into a stereo device; Scott has problems with a food machine that gives him showers of fruit instead of the sandwich he ordered. The cloud has invaded the Enterprise, and seems to be in the humidification system. The deck is covered with ice, and everyone falls. Then laughter is heard. The practical joker is the Enterprise's main computer system, which proceeds to trap Sulu, McCoy, and Uhura in the Recreation Room with a blizzard and other hazards. But it also creates more serious problems. The computer turns off the gravity so Scott cannot get to its logic circuits and repair it. Nitrous oxide is being pumped through the life-support systems, which doesn't harm the humans but is painful to Vulcans. The Enterprise is suffering from an electronic nervous breakdown. Without orders from Kirk, the ship heads back to the neutral zone and the Romulans, who move in to attack—whereupon the Enterprise plays a gigantic practical joke on them with a balloon. To save his ship, Kirk plays a trick on the Enterprise which takes it back through the energy field, luring the Romulans into the field at the same time. The computer is cured by the second trip through, which apparently reverses all effects. Then the Romulan's computers start acting erratically. As the Enterprise pulls away from the Romulans, havoc has just begun on the Romulan ships. Kirk decides that he may eventually tell them how to reverse the practical joker effect, but not right away.

Voices
Kirk: William Shatner
Spock: Leonard Nimoy
Scott: James Doohan
Sulu: George Takei
Uhura: Nichelle Nichols

Lieutenant Arex: James Doohan
Lieutenant M'Ress: Majel Barrett
Computer: (Unknown)
Romulan Commander: James Doohan
Crewman: James Doohan

See Lexicon under:
Audio tapes
Bacteria
Blizzard
Butterflies
Cartoon face
Computer modes
Deflectors
Dysfunction
Electronic nervous breakdown
Emergency air
Energy cloud
Energy drain
Energy field
Enterprise replica
Fear
Fog
Food synthesizers
Forest

Giggles
Gravity, artificial
Hand-held viewer
Holographic illusion
Humidification system
Ice
Laughter infection
Maze
Menville, Chuck
Mess hall
Ocean waves
Patio
Recreation Room
Seagulls
Search party 7
Toast
Type 4 asteroid
Whiteout

ALBATROSS

BY DARIO FINELLI
STARDATE: 5275.6
AIRED: 9/28/74

Nineteen years ago, Dr. McCoy headed a mass-inoculation program for Dramia II to conquer Saurian virus. Unknown to the doctor, after he left with his medical crew a plague ravaged the planet, killing most of the inhabitants. Now, nineteen years later, the Enterprise arrives to deliver medical supplies to Dramia, the major planet of the Dramen star system. The Dramen are grateful for the supplies but produce a warrant for the arrest of Dr. McCoy for wanton mass slaughter. The warrant is in order, approved by the Federation, and McCoy is jailed. Kirk is worried, since rumor has it that Dramen justice is swifter than is usual in the Federation. McCoy fears that he may actually be responsible for a tragic mistake and that he may be found guilty. Kirk and Spock intend to investigate Dramia II before the trial. Informed of this, Demos, the head of Security Police, follows them in his scout ship, but is trapped aboard the Enterprise by a trick, held there for being a stowaway, and his ship impounded. Meanwhile, Spock notes Dramia II's spotty history; little is known of the meteor showers, auroras, and radiation reports, but they seem to be frequent. The plague that ravaged Dramia II has not touched Dramia, however, and everyone is quite careful to keep it that way. The plague is characterized by pigmentation changes in the skin, debilitation, and then death; certain species are known to be immune, including Vulcans. Dramia II looks like a leper colony. The few people who are around were away from home at the time the plague hit; when they returned to find their friends and families dead, they wandered on the planet like the living dead, and are possibly carriers of the plague. A figure attacks Kirk, and Demos says it is because he looks human—like McCoy. They find one Dramen who has actually survived the plague: He is Kol-tai, who remembers everyone changing colors, and remembers McCoy as a man who saved people, not as a murderer. Kirk wants to take Kol-tai back to Dramia as a witness for McCoy, but on the way back Kol-tai shows the first symptoms of the plague, and it is feared that he may not live to testify. Then everyone else on the Enterprise develops the plague, and Spock has to take command. He considers General Order 6: If everyone on board has perished at the end of twenty-four hours, the ship must self-destruct to protect other ships from the disease. Spock decides that McCoy must be released from jail to find an antidote. Using a nerve pinch to deactivate the guard, Spock frees McCoy, though the doctor worries about his jailbreak. The computer cannot find a reason for the pigmentation changes, and McCoy's console acts strangely, due to renewed aurora activity. Then Spock feeds aurora information into the computer and comes up with an answer: There was a particularly active aurora nineteen years ago. Kol-tai survived so long because he had Saurian-virus antibodies in his blood; McCoy makes an antidote from the blood and gives

everyone an injection. They all return to normal, and McCoy shares his information with Dramia so that it will be forever free from auroral plague. Dramia agrees to forget McCoy's jailbreak if Kirk will agree to forget about Demos's actions. McCoy is honored for significant achievement in the field of interstellar medicine, but he is glad to get back to the monotonous routine of giving vitamin rations to the Enterprise's crew.

Voices	Kol-tai: James Doohan
Kirk: William Shatner	Demos: (Unknown)
Spock: Leonard Nimoy	Supreme Prefect: James Doohan
McCoy: DeForest Kelley	

See Lexicon under:	Jailbreak
Antidote	Kangaroo court
Aurora	Kol-tai
Auroral activity	Leper colony
Cave dwellers	Mass-inoculation program
Demos	Medical-assistance program
Dramen justice	Medical computer
Dramen star system	Medical supplies
Dramia	Meteor shower
Dramian history	Natural immunity
Dramians	Patrol ship, one-man
Dramia II	Pigmentation changes
Dramia II survivors	Pre-trial investigation
Finelli, Dario	Quarantine
Force field	Saurian virus
Force-field activator	Stowaway
General Order 6	Subspace communication
Guard, Dramian	Supreme Prefect
Hall of Justice	Vitamin rations
Hippocrates	Warrant
Interstellar medicine	

OW SHARPE THAN A SERPENT'S TOOTH

BY RUSSELL BATES AND DAVID WISE
STARDATE: 6063.4
AIRED: 10/5/74

The Enterprise is tracing the origin of a mysterious space probe that scanned the Sol system, then signaled toward space. Following a trail of disrupted matter left by the probe's advance-propulsion system, they suddenly meet an alien ship coming in on the same course as the probe. Around the ship is an immense energy field, which also encases the Enterprise. The alien ship then assumes the shape of a huge feathered serpent with wings. It is Kulkukan of ancient Mayan-Aztec legend, who speaks to the Enterprise, angry at having been forgotten, threatening the starship crew; he beams Kirk, McCoy, Scott, and Ensign Dawson Walking Bear aboard his own ship. He says that if they solve the puzzle set before them, Kulkukan will reveal himself to them, but otherwise the crew of the Enterprise will die. Finding themselves in a strange city that seems to be a mixture of many Earth cultures, the Enterprise men figure out that they must make a light beam strike a certain spot on a pyramid; they do this, and Kulkukan appears before them as a winged serpent. He says he is their master and transports them to the Life Room, where animal life from all over the galaxy is kept in life-support containers. McCoy sees a Capellan power-cat, the fiercest and most untamable creature in the galaxy, seemingly at peace in its cage. Kirk says they still cannot accept Kulkukan as their master, even if he did teach many peoples on ancient Earth how to build their civilizations. Meanwhile, Spock has been figuring how to break the Enterprise out of the energy globe, and when Kulkukan realizes what the starship is doing, his attention is distracted from his prisoners. The Enterprise men smash cages and containers, freeing the animals, which makes Kulkukan very angry; his specimens go on a rampage, and he loses control over them. The power-cat corners Kulkukan and moves in for the kill, but Kirk makes a heroic dash with a tranquilizer hypo, hitting the cat; the shock knocks Kirk around but does him no harm. Kulkukan is told that humans cannot be pushed into things; they can learn to succeed or fail, but it has to be on human terms—they will not be led by the nose. Kulkukan, not quite a god, but rather an old, lonely being who wants to help others, leaves in sadness. Kirk mourns the loss of his great knowledge; it would have been valuable to the Federation, but the price was too high. McCoy is reminded of the Shakespearean quote: "How sharper than a serpent's tooth is an ungrateful child . . ."

Voices
Kirk: William Shatner
Spock: Leonard Nimoy
McCoy: DeForest Kelley
Scott: James Doohan
Uhura: Nichelle Nichols

Lieutenant Arex: James Doohan
Ensign Dawson Walking Bear: (Unknown)
Kulkukan: James Doohan
Female Yeoman: (Unknown)
Male Yeoman: (Unknown)

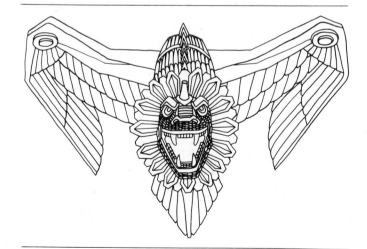

THE COUNTER-CLOCK INCIDENT

BY JOHN CULVER
STARDATE: 6770.3
AIRED: 10/12/74

The Enterprise is transporting two special passengers to Babel: Commodore Robert April, the first captain to command the Enterprise, and his wife, Dr. Sarah April, the ship's first medical officer, who are en route to Commodore April's retirement ceremonies. An alien craft passes them, traveling at warp 36, an impossible speed—no known race has the technology to build a ship with such capability. It seems to be headed directly, and suicidally, into the deadly Beta Niobe nova. Kirk decides to use a tractor beam to stop it, but Spock warns that he doesn't know what will happen to the starship if they lock onto something going that fast. Meanwhile, the translator reveals that the language used by the alien ship's pilot is universal language, but reversed. The Enterprise locks onto the ship and is dragged along with it; the tractor beam has been rendered inoperative and they cannot stop. They try to break free before the Enterprise is dragged into the nova and burned up, but instead both ships plunge into and through the nova into another universe. Suddenly everything is in reverse image—white sky, black stars. They are in an antimatter universe where the ships fly backward and a delicate flower that was dying in Dr. April's hands suddenly reblooms and then becomes a seed pod. Time flows backward. The alien pilot is Karla Five, an explorer from the negative universe who accidentally passed through into our universe. They cannot return from the negative universe unless they find two matched stars, one in each universe, that are about to go nova at the same time. They go to Arret, Karla Five's home planet, hoping to find an answer, and there find that people age backward: An old man turns out to be Karla Five's son; a baby in a playpen is her father. The society of Arret does not have much knowledge left; as the race evolves toward infancy, much knowledge is lost before it can be saved. To make a gateway for the Enterprise to return home, they decide to create a nova in both universes, firing a dead star in Karla Five's galaxy into life, and at the same time blowing a live star in our galaxy into a nova. Karla Five offers her ship, which is too small to hold the whole Enterprise crew but is strong enough to pull the larger starship through the novas without harm. Everyone on the Enterprise is now getting younger and less able to handle the starship. Uhura wears her hair in braids, as she did when a girl in the United States of Africa; Sulu cannot remember navigational problems; Arex becomes more cuddly. Commodore April, now a handsome, healthy man of about thirty, takes command of the Enterprise, as Kirk is too young to be captain. As they get younger, the crew loses its knowledge of the starship. Spock returns to the age of seven; the rest of the crew become crawling infants. With time running out, they fire off the novas and plunge through, and the Enterprise ends up back in our universe.

The transporter retains a memory of everyone's molecular structure, so Commodore April and Dr. April place all the babies in the transporter, bringing them back as adults. The couple discuss the idea of remaining young, but April decides that life lived over again would be a blessing only if the life you've led has left you unfulfilled. The Aprils agree that they could not improve on what they have had together; they embrace as young lovers, and enter the transporter to return to their proper ages. The Federation decides, in view of April's heroic action, that the mandatory retirement age should be reviewed on Babel when they arrive, so the Aprils may get a second life in this universe after all.

Voices	
Kirk: William Shatner	Uhura: Nichelle Nichols
Spock: Leonard Nimoy	Lieutenant Arex: James Doohan
McCoy: DeForest Kelley	Commodore Robert April: (Unknown)
Scott: James Doohan	Dr. Sarah April: (Unknown)
Sulu: George Takei	Karla Five: (Unknown)
	Karl Four: (Unknown)

See Lexicon under:

Alien vessel	Karl Four
Ambassador-at-large	Knowledge
Amphion	Laboratory
Antimatter universe	"Lassie"
Appeal	Mandatory retirement
April, Commodore Robert	Midwife
April, Dr. Sarah	Positive-matter armament
Arret	Priority mission
Babel	Retirement ceremonies
Baby	Review
Beta Niobe	San Francisco Navy Yards
Black hole	Scientists
Brains	Ship's log
Capella IV	Starmap
Computer projection	Suicide mission
Culver, John	Supernova
Decoding instrument	Time
Dimensions	Tractor beam
Gateway	United States of Africa
Hologram	Universal language
Karla Five	Warp 36
	White hole

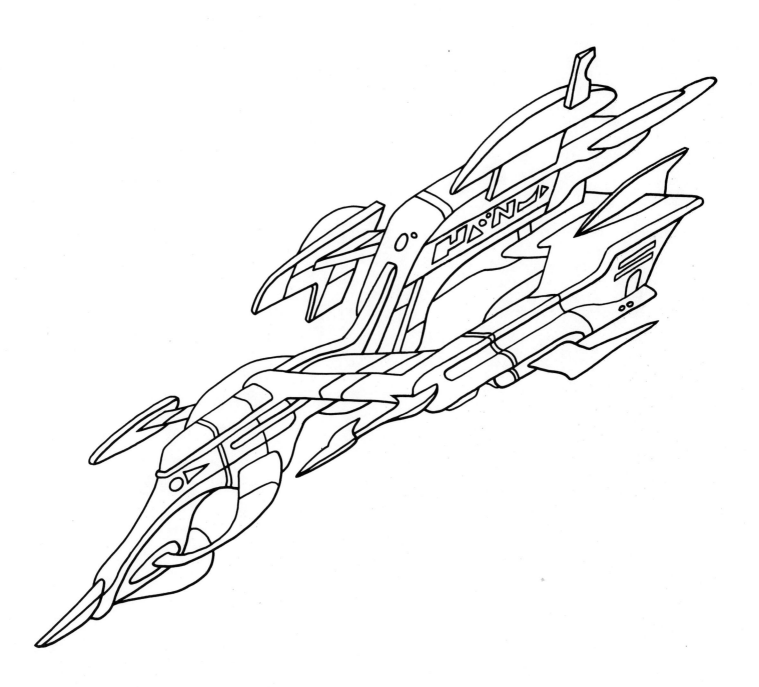

LEXICON

A

A-and-A officer: Common term for Archeology-and-Anthropology officer—an expert on ancient civilizations. Lieutenant Carolyn Palamas is the A-and-A officer in the landing party on Pollux IV (WM).

Aborigine, Delta Theta III: The natives of Delta Theta III are aboriginal in development, with a basic language and social structure; they probably have well-developed mores and traditions of a late primitive stage. They are tall, reptilian, and larger than the average human. They live in clustered villages scattered here and there on the planet (Be/a).

Abramson: A man unknown in the twentieth century, but famous by the twenty-second. Flint says he was Abramson (RM).

Abrom (William Wintersole): A middle-aged Zeon—strong and gentle-looking; Isak's elder brother (PF).

Absorbed: Brainwashed. Landru controls the natives of Beta III by "absorbing" them into "the Body" by means of a conditioning machine. Absorbed people are docile in their behavior and are given to repeating Body propaganda, such as: Individuality will merge with unity of good; submergence will give contentment and fulfillment, and the subject will experience the absolute good (RA).

Academy: See Star Fleet Academy.

Academy of Sciences: A Star Fleet school on Deneb V, to which the Enterprise is headed to take part in dedication ceremonies (PO/a).

Academy of Sciences, Vulcan: See Vulcan Academy of Sciences.

Acadian star system: The region of Motherlode, a mining planet with much rich fissionable-mineral lodes (MP/a).

Acceleration: See Hyperacceleration.

Access panel: Within the access tube on a starship is a panel leading directly to the matter/antimatter reaction chamber.

Access plate: See Access panel.

Access tube: A service crawlway used to reach the matter/antimatter reaction chamber. It is not meant to be used while the integrator operates; life expectancy is not high for anyone caught in the energy stream of the magnetic field that bottles up the antimatter. Spock believes it is quite possible to shut off the fuel flow at that point (TWS).

Acetylcholine test: One of the tests Spock runs on the spacegoing ameba while he is inside it. McCoy says the job was botched (IS).

Achilles: A gladiator matched against McCoy on Name the Winner. Spock gives him a nerve pinch and is called on a foul (BC).

Acid: The fruit, flowers, and other plant life of Eden contain a powerful acid, capable of giving severe burns if touched and of killing if the fruit is eaten (WEd).

Adam (Charles Napier): A singer among the "space hippies" looking for the perfect society of Eden—tall, with curly blond hair and a sly smile (WEd).

Adams, Dr. Tristan (James Gregory): Psychiatrist and director of the Tantalus prison colony—middle-aged, with dark curly hair and a deceptively pleasant manner. He began as a humanitarian reformer with innovative theories of penology, later using his talents to gain wealth and power. He builds a brainwashing machine, the neural neutralizer, with which he controls both inmates and staff. He dies in his own machine (DMd). See also Loneliness.

Adams, Stanley (script): The Mark of Gideon (MG) (with George F. Slavin).

Affirmative: Military jargon for "yes"; used by Star Fleet.

Agents 201 and 347: Aliens who preceded Gary Seven to Earth to prevent the launching of a suborbital platform; they are killed in an auto accident, and Seven takes over the assignment. Like Seven, they were the product of generations of training by aliens working to save Earth from self-destruction (AE).

Aging: See Gamma Hydra IV; Longevity; Taurus II.

Agmar: Leader of the plant beings, the native life of Phylos (IV/a).

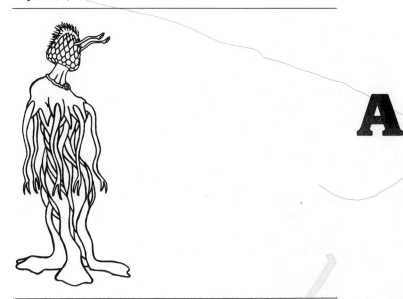

Agonizer: A small device for inflicting pain, part of each crewman's equipment in the mirror universe, and used by officers there for minor punishment. Applied to the left shoulder, just above the heart, it produces severe pain (MM).

Agonizer, Klingon: A device similar to the mirror universe's agonizer, used by the Klingons (Dv).

Agony booth: A glassed-in booth for inflicting extreme pain, used for major punishment in the mirror universe. An order for full-duration exposure is equivalent to the death sentence. Chekov-2 is placed in it for attempting to assassinate Kirk-1 (MM).

Ahn-woon: The oldest of Vulcan weapons—a leather band about six feet long, with handles at the ends. It can be used as a bola, a sling, or a garrote. In a duel with Kirk on Vulcan, Spock strangles him with the ahn-woon and mistakenly thinks he has killed his captain (AT).

Air-breather: Any creature which breathes a form of air (usually defined as a combination of gases including nitrogen, oxygen, carbon dioxide, argon, neon, helium, etc.). Humans and most types of humanoid are air-breathers. On Argo, where water-breathers rule supreme, the term "air-breather" is derogatory—at least to the old Aquans, who consider air-breathers violent enemies of water-breathers. However, after the young Aquans experience the sun and the soft air, they decide to become air-breathers again and live on land in their newly recovered city (Am/a).

Air-defense base: See Omaha Air Base.

Airplane: On the amusement-park planet, a World War II Grumman Hellcat fighter strafes Rodriguez and Teller (SL). Captain Christopher's jet-powered interceptor is an F-104 (TY).

Air Police sergeant (Hal Lynch):   An Air Force military policeman, who acts rough until he is out of his own territory. A sentry guarding Omaha Air Base, he discovers Kirk and Sulu tampering with computer tapes and must be beamed aboard the Enterprise until it is safe to return him to the base (TY).

Akaar (Ben Gage):   Teer—leader—of the ten tribes of Capella IV—old, gray-haired, but still tough (feeble Capellans usually don't live very long). He favors the Federation and is killed by Maab, who favors the Klingons. Akaar leaves a widow, Eleen, who bears a son soon after his death (FC).

Akaar, Teer Leonard James: Child of the assassinated Teer Akaar of Capella IV and his wife, Eleen. Though nearly killed before birth by his father's successor, Maab, he is secretly delivered by McCoy, and is named after McCoy and Kirk. After Maab's death the child becomes Teer, and his mother regent (FC).

Akharin: Flint was born on Earth in 3834 B.C., growing up as a crude bully of a soldier known as Akharin. By some quirk of nature, he had the ability to regenerate his cells and tissues, and became immortal. Though he has gained in education and taste throughout his long life, he remembers his beginnings in Mesopotamia (RM).

Akuta (Keith Andes):   Leader of the natives of Gamma Trianguli VI—platinum-haired, red-skinned, with two small metal antennae projecting from his skull which keep him in touch with Vaal. Known as "the Eyes of Vaal," he keeps the ruling computer supplied with sensory information and interprets its orders to the people (Ap).

Alar: A great religious teacher of the Skorr, he taught the Skorr to be peaceful instead of warlike. The Skorr looked upon Alar as their Salvation and Teacher, and when he died they made him immortal in a way: His brain patterns were recorded in a piece of indurite sculpture called the "Soul of Skorr"—three silver Möbius strips about ten feet across inside a golden glow. When the artifact is stolen from the Skorr, the leaders of the galaxy fear that a holy war will break out. They gather specialists to try to find the stolen sculpture and return it to the Skorr (Ji/a).

Alcohol: Everyone on the Enterprise unites in trying to make the Kelvans feel like humans and change their minds about taking the starship on a three-hundred-year trip to Andromeda. Scott contributes most of his extensive collection of alcoholic beverages in an attempt to make the Kelvan Tomar drunk. Terran and Kelvan to-

gether discover the potency of Saurian brandy, something unidentified but green, and the last of Scotty's best old Scotch whisky (AON).

Aldebaran Colony: Inhabited planet where Dr. Elizabeth Dehner signs aboard the Enterprise (WNM).

Aldebaran III: Drs. Theodore and Janet Wallace use various carbohydrate compounds there to slow down the degeneration of plant life (DY).

Alden, Lieutenant (Lloyd Haynes):   Strong, black communications officer who acts as relief navigator (WNM).

Aleek-Om: See Aurelia.

Alert B-2:   Signal indicating that main sections of the ship are to be sealed off (NT).

Alexander (Michael Dunn):   A Platonian dwarf, with large blue eyes and shaggy hair—court buffoon and "the arms and legs of everybody's whim." He is the only Platonian who lacks psychokinesis; the same pituitary deficiency that has made him a dwarf also denies him that power. When McCoy discovers the source of the power, Alexander refuses to accept it; he hates other Platonians and doesn't want to be like them. A man of great character, he feels he deserves better than to live among the cruel and treacherous Platonians, and Kirk is delighted to convey him off the planet (PSt).

Alexander, David (director):   The Way to Eden (WEd); Plato's Stepchildren (PSt).

Alexander the Great: Warrior and King of Macedonia (on Earth), who conquered Egypt, Persia, and lands as far east as the Indus Valley. He lived from 356 to 323 B.C. Garth of Izar compares himself to Alexander III (WGD). Flint mentions Alexander the Great; they may have known each other (RM).

Alfa 177:   A planet noted for a peculiar magnetic ore and widely variable climate; the temperature is comfortable during the day but drops to –250°F at night. Owing to a transporter malfunction, a landing party is stranded there for several hours and nearly freezes (EW).

Algae specimens: While on Argo to study seismic disturbances, Dr. McCoy wants to obtain some algae specimens from the sea (Am/a).

Algobarium solution: See Test 24.

Alice in Wonderland (Marcia Brown):   The heroine of a nineteenth-century fantasy by Lewis Carroll. McCoy thinks of her on the amusement-park planet and she appears, with the White Rabbit, much to the doctor's consternation (OUP/a, SL). See also Carroll, Lewis.

"Alice" series (Rahe and Alyce Andrece):   Tall, leggy, dark-haired, identical androids, of whom five hundred were built to please Mudd (IM).

Alien creatures: The members of the Enterprise landing party are alien to the Lactrans, who take the obvious precautions of removing any possible weapons and making certain the strange alien beings cannot communicate harmful bacteria (EB/a).

Alien dewdrop: McCoy's term for the liquid produced by Agmar to save Sulu's life, endangered by poisonous plant (IV/a).

Alien scout vessel: Bele's scout vessel is invisible and does not register on the screens of the Enterprise though the other sensors pick it up. It has totally alien configuration, and its motive power is unknown, but it is able to keep up with the Enterprise for a time, until, over-strained, it finally disintegrates. Bele manages to escape at the last moment, materializing on the bridge of the Enterprise. This vessel is presumed to be the scout ship launched fifty thousand years earlier from Cheron to capture Lokai (LB).

Alien ship: A design never seen before by Federation shipping, it is used as a pirate ship and manned by Orions (PO/a). Karla Five's scout ship, an exploration vessel capable of achieving warp 36, is from an antimatter universe. The Enterprise uses it to leave the antimatter universe by arming it to start a nova in both galaxies (CC/a).

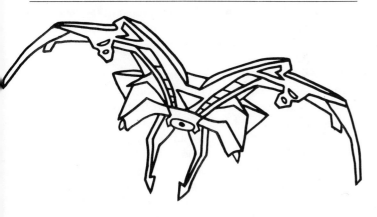

All hands: A Terran nautical term used within Star Fleet, meaning "all personnel."

Alliance, Romulan-Klingon: Spock mentions intelligence reports concerning an arrangement or possible alliance among the Federation's enemies: Romulans are now using Klingon-designed ships (EI).

All systems go: An Earth term of the twentieth century used in space travel, meaning that everything is ready to launch and/or everything is in working condition after launch. It is still used as a slang term on starships (Mt u/a).

Alondra: An uninhabited planet in the Pallas XIV system which is eaten by the cosmic cloud (OPM/a).

Alpha Carinae V: Home of the Drella, which derives its sustenance from love (WF).

Alpha Carinae II: A Class M planet which the M-5 computer is set to approach and analyze before making landing-party recommendations. The computer identifies two major land masses and a number of islands, and indicates life-form readings (UC).

Alpha Centauri: "A beautiful place, you ought to see it," Kirk tells Colonel Fellini (TY). Zefrem Cochrane is a native of a planet in the Alpha Centauri system (MT).

Alpha Majoris I: Home of the Mellitus cloud creature (WF).

Alpha Proxima II: A planet where women were murdered in a way similar to victims of Jack the Ripper (WF).

Alpha III, Tribunals of (Statutes of):   Court decisions or laws which have set major precedents in interstellar law (CM1).

Altair VI: The central world of a system recuperating from interplanetary conflict. The Enterprise crew heads there to be part of the honor guard at the president's inauguration, but Spock goes into pon far and Kirk diverts the ship to Vulcan (AT).

Altar of Tomorrow: See Chamber of Ages.

Alternative warp: Negative magnetic corridor where parallel but opposite universes come together without catastrophe—a sort of safety valve to keep everything from blowing up (AF).

Alvin: A member of the Gamma Hydra IV expedition, whose remains, when discovered, are those of an incredibly old, dead man, having died of the radiation poisoning that killed the entire colony. Chekov finds his body and is frightened sufficiently to be poison-proofed by the increase in his adrenalin level (DY).

Amanda (Jane Wyatt):   The human wife of Ambassador Sarek of Vulcan, and the mother of Commander Spock—an attractive woman of about fifty, with a round face and curly gray hair. She loves her husband and son, and is bothered that they cannot return the affection, at least overtly (JB). Originally a teacher, Amanda Grayson met Sarek when he was ambassador to Terra (AT). She gives her Vulcan home a touch of color with flowers and books, and is both proud and sad when her son chooses the more difficult Vulcan way of life instead of following his human heritage. However, according to Vulcan history—until Spock goes back in time to change the time lines—Amanda was killed in a shuttle accident at Lunaport shortly after her son's death and her separation from Sarek. Spock returns as a distant cousin to change history by saving the life of young Spock and, as a result, that of Amanda (Yy/a). Spock inhibits his feelings for his human mother, smothering them deep in himself. But when these feelings are evoked, as by the virus of Psi 2000 (NT) and the spores of Omicron Ceti III (TSP), Spock remembers his love for Amanda, and wishes he could bring himself to express it. See also Books.

Ambassador-at-large: A Federation ambassador with no specific planetary assignment, who is sent wherever needed (CC/a).

Ambassador Sarek (Mark Lenard):   Sarek of Vulcan has been ambassador to seventeen planets in thirty years by the time the Vulcan time lines are changed, and, with them, his life. It seems, however, that he is well on the way to being an important ambassador in the normal time continuum also (Yy/a).

Ambergris: A secretion of the Earth sperm whale, prized by perfumers because of its ability to make perfume scent last. The substance injected into Kirk and Spock to make them water-breathers on Argo is very similar to the ambergris of whales (Am/a).

Ameba, spacegoing (special optical effects by Frank Van Der Veer): Within a cloud of darkness which is actually negative energy, a brilliantly colored one-celled protoplasmic organism thrives. It resembles a complex ameba, with over forty chromosomes, and is eleven thousand miles long, varying between two and three thousand miles thick. It invades our galaxy, draining energy from three solar systems and from the starship Intrepid. The Enterprise kills the ameba just as it is ready to reproduce (IS). A cosmic cloud is amebic in its instinctive search for food as it wanders through the vast reaches of space (OPM/a).

American Continent Institute: The agency which sent Dr. Haskins's expedition to Talos IV (Me).

Amphion: A "dead" star in the antimatter universe, one which comes to life (the exact opposite of a nova in our universe, in which a star explodes in its death throes). In conjunction with Beta Niobe in our galaxy, Amphion forms a gateway through which Karla Five's scout ship drags the Enterprise (CC/a).

Amulet: See Transmuter.

Amusement-park planet: A Class M planet in the Omicron Delta region, apparently much like Earth, constructed solely to provide amusement and fun for space-traveling passersby—particularly, perhaps, for Terran visitors. An advanced race furnished the planet with mechanisms which fabricate anything that can be mentally visualized. The crew of the Enterprise spend memorable shore leaves on this unusual planet (OUP/a, SL).

Anan 7 (David Opatoshu): First Councilman of the Eminian Union (Eminiar VII)—of medium build, with gray hair, neatly trimmed beard, sincere dark eyes. Well meaning but single-minded, Anan allows his responsibilities to lead him into treachery when he tries to con the Enterprise's crew into beaming down to be destroyed (TA).

Ancient lore: The teachings of the Oracle on Yonada, given to the people by Natira, the high priestess (FW).

Andorian (Richard Geary): An inmate of Elba II, the asylum for the criminally insane. He is a follower of Garth, who promises him a position of power when they take over the universe (WGD). Another Andorian, Thelin (James Doohan), was First Officer of the Enterprise for five years when the time line of Vulcan was changed by Spock's death as a small boy (Yy/a). See also Shras.

Andorians: Blue-skinned bipeds with white hair and a small knobbed antenna projecting from each side of the crown of the head. Though an admittedly violent race, they are not wont to quarrel without reason, and are members of the Federation. Probably because of their sensitive antennae, Andorians habitually listen with heads down and slightly tilted. An Andorian accent sounds like a soft lisp (GT, JB). Andorians apparently do not have veins in the circulatory systems, relying when necessary on in-

tramuscular injection (WGD). By heritage they are a race of savage warriors, their strength and fighting ability masked by soft voices and slender builds. They have few sympathies, but one they possess is for family; while Andorians are not known for their charity, Thelin does not grudge Spock's trying to save his mother or his own life, and wishes him well (Yy/a). The warlike Andorians have been also trapped in the Delta Triangle region, where they have learned to accept lifelong entrapment in Elysia (Tr/a).

Andrea (Sherry Jackson): An android made in the image of a slender dark-haired girl, built by Dr. Korby on Exo III. He thinks her an emotionless machine but is mistaken, for she falls in love with him. When Korby realizes that his own android body is making him less than human, he destroys himself and Andrea. In a fit of jealousy, Nurse Chapel refers to Andrea as a "mechanical geisha" (LG).

Android robots: The mechanical bodies Sargon, Henoch, and Thalassa are building for themselves. In their unfinished state they look like old, hairless, sexless humans. Thalassa refuses to live in one; Henoch never intends to, so long as he can stay in Spock's body (RT).

Androids: The world found by Dr. Korby on Exo III was once inhabited by people who built refined androids of near-perfect human appearance and reactions. Dr. Korby used the equipment and information left behind to construct similar androids and a new android body for himself (LG).

Androids of Planet Mudd: Beings solely motivated to protect and serve humanoids, they were created by "the makers," long since dead. They waited for 1,743,912 years, until Harry Mudd happened on the barren world they came to call Planet Mudd. Kirk helps them to continue their studies of human nature (IM). See also Makers, the.

Andromeda galaxy: The androids were brought by their makers to Planet Mudd from an extinct planet in the Andromeda galaxy (IM). Also, the location of Kelva. Within ten millennia high radiation will make life in Andromeda galaxy impossible, which is why the Kelvans are scouting ours (AON).

Angela (Barbara Baldavin): Communications officer at the court-martial of Spock. Kirk-J, unfamiliar with the crew, calls her "Lisa" by mistake (TI).

Angel, Friendly: The name given to Gorgan by the children of the Starnes expedition (CL).

Animation control: A mechanism McCoy uses to activate Spock's zombielike body while searching for his brain. It can keep Spock's body alive for only a limited time, however (SB).

Anka (Fred Williamson): A Troglyte male; one of the Disruptors (Cms).

Announcer (Bart LaRue): A cheerful sort who announces the Roman games on Planet 892-IV, invites the viewers to choose the winner, and treats a life-and-death struggle in the arena as an everyday matter (BC).

Antarean brandy: A pale blue liquid, sometimes served aboard the Enterprise, on such occasions as Kirk's dinner party in honor of Dr. Miranda Jones (TB).

A

Antarean glow water: Cyrano Jones tries unsuccessfully to sell some at Space Station K-7 (TT).

Antares, U.S.S.: A science-probe vessel or survey ship with a crew of twenty, commanded by Captain Ramart. It picks up Charles Evans from Thasus, and its crew tries to welcome him, but he resents everything, and destroys the ship when he transfers to the Enterprise (CX). See also Baffle plate.

Antenna: A network of antennae on Terratin move in response to light, sending out signals to other antennae until the valley around the miniature city is a network of lights. The antennae also send out the wave bombardments that strike the Enterprise. Most of the antennae have been destroyed in earthquakes (Te/a).

Anticontamination suit: A red, plastic overall, helmet, and gloves worn by Spock and Tormolen when inspecting the research station on Psi 2000 (NT).

Antidote: When McCoy finds the substance in Kirk's coffee that is responsible for accelerating his metabolism, the doctor looks for a counteragent or antidote. He finds one (WE). Though there is an antidote for le-matya poison, it is too late to administer it to I-Chaya by the time the healer reaches the sehlat (Yy/a). In searching for an antidote to the poisonous retlaw plant, McCoy tries dylovene, but it doesn't work. When the plant beings produce a drop of viscous liquid to apply to Sulu, it is quickly absorbed and the helmsman recovers. McCoy is not too happy about strange medication's being applied to one of his people (IV/a). The antidote for auroral plague consists of antibodies in the blood of anyone who has had Saurian virus (Al/a). McCoy finds an antidote to counteract the inhibition-relaxing virus of Psi 2000 (NT). At great personal risk, McCoy tests on himself the antidote he has developed to the adult-killing disease on Miri's planet (Mi).

Antigravity elevation: Stratos City, high above the surface of Ardana, is held in the clouds by the finest example of sustained antigravity elevation that Spock has ever seen (CMs).

Antigravity test unit: A large chamber which can be used to raise or lower atmospheric pressure. Lieutenant Romaine is placed in one to rid her of the lights of Zetar (LZ). It is similar to the medical decompression chamber Khan uses to torture Kirk (SS).

Antigravs, portable: Small hand-held devices for moving equipment; used to take the distracted Nomad to the Transporter Room (Cg). Kollos is brought aboard by them (TB).

Antimatter: The Enterprise's warp-drive engines, in the outboard nacelles, use integrated matter and antimatter for propulsion. (See also Warp drive.) But matter and antimatter cannot be mixed "cold"; the engines must be warmed approximately thirty minutes before use (NT). Vaal, the reigning computer of Gamma Trianguli VI, cripples the Enterprise by draining the antimatter pods and other power sources with a beam or field (Ap). The spacegoing ameba is killed by an antimatter bomb detonated at its nucleus (IS). The villi of the cosmic cloud are antimatter; Scott uses one to advantage to refire the antimatter chambers of the Enterprise's engines (OPM/a).

Antimatter input valves: Energy-release controls.

Nomad says they are inefficient and "repairs" them by increasing engine efficiency 57 percent so that the ship goes to warp 11 in minutes. Kirk makes Nomad discontinue this kind of repair (Cg).

Antimatter universe: Through the dying star Beta Niobe, into the newborn star Amphion, the Enterprise enters another universe, in which things run in reverse—an antimatter universe—where the Enterprise is trapped for a time, until everyone is too young to run the starship except Commodore April (CC/a). See also Arret.

Antiplasma: Spock's analysis of the cosmic cloud (OPM/a).

Antitoxin: Reversal of the mutation which made Kirk and Spock water-breathers requires an antitoxin made of sur-snake venom. The correct dosage is not clear in the Aquan's ancient records, so Dr. McCoy has to take his chances when he makes the antitoxin for Kirk and Spock—too much and the mutation will be irreversible (Am/a). See also Antidote; Longevity.

Antos IV: A planet famed for its inhabitants' benevolent, peaceful pursuits. They know the secret of cellular metamorphosis, and can change shape and take any form they wish. When Garth of Izar was maimed and dying, they made him physically whole and taught him how to change his shape, but his mind snapped, and he turned on his benefactors when they refused to help him conquer and rule the galaxy (WGD). See also Dryworm, giant.

Apella (Arthur Bernard): Headman of a village on a primitive planet to which Krell, a Klingon, comes, bringing guns to subvert the culture (PLW).

Apollo (Michael Forest): The last of the self-exiled Greek gods—tall, with earnest brown eyes and classic features. A near-immortal being possessing paranormal powers drawn from a material power source, he brings the Enterprise to Pollux IV to found a colony of worshippers for himself. He becomes fond of Lieutenant Carolyn Palamas, and when the Enterprise people reject him, Apollo spreads his bodily substance upon the wind and dissipates (WM).

Appeal: Star Fleet personnel may appeal all decisions affecting them. Commodore April is to make an appeal that the mandatory retirement age be waived, as he feels there are many more years he can devote to the service of his fellow beings (CC/a).

Appel, Ed (Brad Weston): Chief processing engineer on Janus VI—thin, with crew-cut hair and a cynical expression. He shoots at the Horta with phaser-1 power, but fails to hurt the rocklike creature, and is of the opinion that Kirk can do no better (DD).

April, Commodore Robert: For twenty years the Federation ambassador-at-large, at age seventy-five he comes up for mandatory retirement. He was the first captain of the Enterprise, and was in the San Francisco Navy Yard when the Enterprise's components were assembled. After his heroic action in saving the Enterprise from the negative universe, the Federation decides to review the mandatory-retirement policy, and requests that the ship proceed to Babel for a hearing instead of the planned retirement ceremonies (CC/a).

April, Dr. Sarah: Slightly younger than her husband, Commodore Robert April, she is used to moving in the best circles of Federation society. She was the first medical officer stationed on the Enterprise and designed many of the tools in use in Federation starship Sick Bays. She found it necessary to devise new procedures, as the Enterprise was the first ship successfully equipped with warp drive. Though she has the opportunity to remain young after the Enterprise enters the antimatter universe, she chooses to grow old with her husband (CC/a).

Aqua lanterns: See Sea torches.

Aquans: Water-breathing inhabitants of the planet Argo—a handsome, humanoid race with webbed hands and feet, dorsal fins, and greenish hair. They were once air-breathers, but drastic earthquakes sank most of Argo's land masses, making it expedient for them to become water-breathers. They accomplished this with surgo-op, a fantastic advance in medical technology. Traditionally, they fear and hate air-breathers as enemies, because of ancient records of the savagery that developed under the hardships of the geological disasters striking their world (Am/a). See also Air-breather.

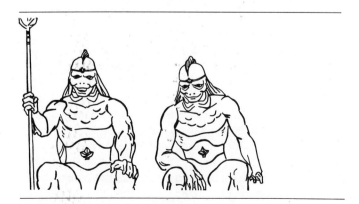

Aquarium: When brought back to the Enterprise from the water-world of Argo, Kirk and Spock have to stay in a water-filled tank. Kirk is not happy about the idea of trying to be a starship captain while in an aquarium (Am/a). The medical laboratory aboard the Enterprise has experimental animals in it, including alien halo fish in an aquarium (Te/a).

Aquashuttle: A vehicle from the Enterprise—silver and fish-shaped, with an observation dome where the dorsal fin would be. The shuttle contains instrument panels, an on-board computer, small scanner, phaser control panel, and heavily padded seats with seatbelts (Am/a).

Arachna: A burnt-out supernova of vast, glowing long swirls of spidery arms, much like the Crab Nebula but scores of light-years across. The Enterprise is sent to obtain updated measurements of radiation and volume expansion, as Arachna is entering a cycle of its strongest emissions to date (Te/a).

Arcanis: Several planets, including Arcanis, Canopus, and Sirius, are not where they should be when the Enterprise gets its bearings again after Kirk's fight with the Gorn (Ar). See also Canopus.

Archeological site: Professor Crater and his wife, Nancy, were at an archeological site on Planet M113 to make a survey of its ruins (MT).

Archeology-and-Anthropology officer: See A-and-A officer.

Archon, U.S.S.: A starship which visited Beta III (Landru's planet) in star system 6-11 some hundred years back. The ship was pulled down from orbit and destroyed; the Federation never heard from it again, but some of the Archon's men survived to plant the seeds of rebellion among members of the Body (RA). See also Archons.

Archons: Originally, the crew of the U.S.S. Archon, whose survivors resisted Landru's control; later, the term came to mean the rescuers who are expected to return someday and free the inhabitants of Landru's planet from the tyranny of the Body. In that sense, the Enterprise crew are "Archons" (RA).

Arcturian: The Karidian Players stage Macbeth in the style of this culture, with angular weapons and armor and Arcturian effects (CK).

Ardana: A planet with an orange sky. It is the only known source of zienite, a substance that will stop a botanical plague. Raw zienite releases a gas which retards its miners, reinforcing a caste system sharply dividing workers from the leisure class (CMs).

Area 39: The recreation room aboard the Enterprise.

Arex, Lieutenant: The navigator on the Enterprise—a tripedal alien with orange skin, round yellow eyes, a concave-structured head, and a raspy voice. His job is no doubt made easier with three hands to push navigational buttons, but Arex's three arms and legs must have given the Star Fleet quartermaster in charge of uniforms a nasty moment! It may be assumed that Lieutenant Arex comes from a solar system with small or few planets, none of which is as impressive as our solar system's giants, for he cites Saturn, Jupiter, and Neptune to gauge the size of the cosmic cloud; had Arex known larger planets in his own solar system, he would probably have mentioned them instead (OPM/a).

Argelian empathic contact: A telepathic trance used by the priestesses of Argelius II before the "great awakening" of two hundred years ago. The power still lingers in some of their modern descendants, one of whom is Sybo, who uses empathic contact to gather information about the Jack-the-Ripper entity which has invaded Argelius II (WF).

Argelian laws: Before the great Argelian "awakening," which led to a new society based on love, and happiness, with no jealousy, there were barbaric laws to handle crimes, including torture before death. The laws have never been changed, because since the awakening there has been no occasion to exercise them (WF).

Argelians: See Argelius II.

Argelius II: A planet favored for shore leave by Federation forces because of its hedonistic culture. Argelians are humanoid and so peaceful and pleasure-loving that they have to import administrators, such as Hengist of Rigel IV, to keep the social machinery running smoothly. The women are most friendly and obliging to outworlders, and jealousy is considered gauche (WF).

Argo: A blue-green planet with a misty cloud cover, once a land planet but now almost completely covered by water owing to huge seismic disturbances which caused whole cities to sink beneath the sea. When the Enterprise first visits it, the largest land mass is a rocky island, but another seismic disturbance causes much of the land mass to appear once again above the surface of the sea (Am/a).

Argus River: A river on Rigel IV. Carvings of the hill people of the Argus River region are known even off-planet (WF).

Argus X: An uninhabited planet, rich in tritanium ores, where Kirk meets the vampire cloud for the second time (Ob).

Ariannus: A planet first seen from space surrounded by a golden haze, owing to the plague affecting it. The Enterprise decontaminates the planet by means of spray tanks operated from the ship, saving a billion people from the bacterial invasion that threatens to leave the planet lifeless. This, in turn, would have jeopardized other planets that use agricultural products from Ariannus, among them a planet that is a vital transfer point on the commercial space lanes (LB).

Ariel: A small scientific exploratory ship with six crew members which was sent to study Lactra VII; the planet's inhabitants in turn studied the crew members of the Ariel (EB/a).

Armen, Margaret (scripts): The Lorelei Signal (LS/a); The Ambergris Element (Am/a); The Cloud-minders (Cms) (story by David Gerrold and Oliver Crawford); The Paradise Syndrome (PSy); The Gamesters of Triskelion (GT).

Armory: A part of ship's stores or the quartermaster's supplies used for the storage of phasers and other weapons and associated equipment (Dv).

Arms, armor, weaponry, defensive mechanisms:

Agonizer (MM)	Instrument of Obedience (FW)
Agonizer, Klingon (Dv)	Internal security (MP/a)
Agony booth (MM)	Intruder alert (Su/a)
Ahn-woon (AT)	Invasion defense (Te/a)
Alarm (OUP/a)	Invisibility screen (BT)
Antimatter (OPM/a)	Kalandan computer (TWS)
Antiplasma (OPM/a)	Kirk's magic (Mtu/a)
Army (IV/a)	Kligat (FC)
Attack plan (Ji/a)	K-7 deep-space station (TT)
Attraction force (OPM/a)	Lances (OUP/a)
Automatic bridge defense system	Laser machines (Te/a)
(BFS/a)	Lasers
Belt device (RM)	Lights of Zetar (LZ)
Berserker (DMa)	Lirpa (AT)
Boarding Plan C, Klingon (MTT/a)	Low-frequency shield (BFS/a)
Body throw (IV/a)	Lura-mag (LS/a)
Bombardment (Am/a)	Magic (Mtu/a)
Boomerang (SC)	Main batteries (Su/a)
Bows and arrows (FC)	Maze (PJ/a)
Chemical gun (Ji/a)	Mechanicals (Ji/a)
Chemical mist (IV/a)	M-4 (RM)
Cloaking device (BT, DY, EI)	Militia (IV/a)
Communicator (FC)	Mind-sifter (EM)
Corbomite (Cmn, DY)	Mortae (Cms)
Dagger (ET)	M-rays (WM)
Deadfall (Ji/a)	Net (Am/a)
Decoy (MTT/a)	Neural field (AON)
Defense (Mtu/a)	Nomad (Cg)
Defensive armament (OPM/a)	Null-gravity combat exercises (Ji/a)
Defensive standby (MP/a)	Nullifer (SW/a)
Deflectors (PJ/a)	Number 4 shield (ET)
Deflector shields (OPM/a, Su/a)	Outpost (SW/a)
Destructive machines (IV/a)	Outpost, Kalandan (TWS)
Disruptor bolt (Tr/a)	Outposts, Federation (BT)
Disruptors (MTT/a, TA)	Patrol (Su/a)
Doomsday machine (DMa)	Peace-keeping force (IV/a)
Emergency Defense Plan B, Federation	Phasers (Ji/a, LS/a)
(MTT/a)	Phasers, ship's
Energy drain (PJ/a)	Photon torpedoes (BT, JB, OPM/a)
Energy field (HS/a)	Police web (SW/a)
Energy mass (HS/a)	Positive-matter armament (CC/a)
Energy-sapping field (MTT/a)	Power (Mtu/a)
Evasive action (OPM/a)	Power drain (OPM/a)
Evasive maneuvers (PO/a)	Pressers
Explosive (PO/a, Tr/a, WGD)	Projected stasis (MTT/a)
Fast draw (SGn)	Psychokinesis (LS/a)
Field effect (MTT/a)	Racial fury (Ji/a)
Flask (WGD)	Ray machine (EB/a)
Foot soldier (SW/a)	Rocks (MTT/a)
Force field (AI/a, DMd, EB/a, Em,	Rodinium (BT)
MP/a, SGn, WE, WGD)	Rostrum (Cms)
Force-field activator (AI/a)	Rubindium crystals (PF)
Force-field box (OPM/a)	Screens (RM)
Force globe (HS/a)	Security, Dramian (AI/a)
Fortress (Ji/a, OUP/a)	Security guards (PO/a)
Fortress phaser banks (Ji/a)	Security men (MTT/a)
Frontier-model Colt (SGn)	Security squad (Be/a)
Great shelters (Am/a)	Security team (Tr/a)
Hailstones (Mtu/a)	Self-destruct (AI/a, BFS/a, HS/a, LB,
Hand phaser (MP/a)	OPM/a)
Haunted weapons (SW/a)	Self-destruct system (PO/a)
Impulse (Te/a)	Servo (AE)

Shields (LB)
Short-burst maneuvers (OUP/a)
Single combat (SW/a)
Slaver stasis box (SW/a)
Slaver weapon (SW/a)
Sling (SC)
Sonic disruptor field (EI)
Spiral evasive course (HS/a)
Spock clone (IV/a)
Starbase
Starbase 11 (Cml, Me)
Starbase 4 (CL)
Starbase 9 (Cp, TY)
Starbase 6 (IS)
Starbase 10 (DY)
Starbase 12 (SS, WM)
Starbase 25 (SW/a)
Starbase 27 (TSP)
Starbase 23 (Te/a)
Starbase 22 (HS/a)
Starbase 2 (TI)
Stasis field (Be/a)

Suspension (RM)
Sweep (WE)
Tactics (Tr/a)
Tantalus field (MM)
Telemetry probe (IS)
Theragen (TW)
Tholian web (TW)
Thongs (Cms)
Tractor beam (CC/a, OPM/a, TY)
Transponder, subcutaneous (PF)
Tribbles (MTT/a)
Ultrasonics (WEd)
Visor (TB)
Vulcan nerve pinch (Yy/a)
War computer (SW/a)
Wave bombardment (Te/a)
Weapon (Ar, AY, Cms, ET, Ji/a,
   PO/a, SC, SW/a, WE)
Weapon deactivation (IV/a)
Wide-area stun setting (IV/a)
Wristlet (SB)
X-waves (Te/a)

Aroeste, Jean Lissette (script): Is There in Truth No Beauty? (TB); All Our Yesterdays (AY).

Arret: A planet hundreds of light-years beyond previously explored territory; Class M, Earthlike, but much older. Half a million years before the Enterprise, its atmosphere was ripped away, and the only life left—the minds of Sargon, Thalassa, and Henoch—was preserved 112.37 miles underground (RT). Another Arret is the home planet of Karla Five, in the antimatter universe—the reverse of our universe, where the moon shines during the day and the sky is light, and it gets dark when the sun comes up. People age backward, from elderly to babies (CC/a). See also Antimatter universe.

A-7 Computer Expert: Spock's classification in computer technology (UC).

Asmodeus: A demon in the Biblical Book Tobit. However, according to Megan, who claims to have once been Asmodeus, this is untrue. Asmodeus, He-Who-Sees-All, was used by humans, as were all wizards and magic-users, for their own lust and greed. When Asmodeus and his fellow magicians refused to serve, they were called devils, warlocks, and demons (Mtu/a).

Asteroid: The arena in which Kirk and the Gorn captain must fight to the death (Ar). An asteroid nearly the size of Earth's moon, traveling on an elongated elliptical orbit, is on a collision course with an unnamed planet settled by American Indians. An attempt to deflect it by the Enterprise fails; a meteor deflector in an obelisk on the planet does the job (PSy). See also Yonada.

Asteroid belt: The pirates of Orion take refuge in an asteroid belt, where they hope to hide from the Enterprise. The asteroids are made up of highly unstable minerals, and if two asteroids touch, they will explode. The power of such exploding rocks can be harnessed for a fantastic source of energy for weaponry (PO/a).

Astral Queen: The ship, commanded by Jon Daily, which is supposed to take the Karidian Players from Planet Q to Benecia. Kirk transports the players in the Enterprise instead, so he can observe Karidian, whom he suspects of being Kodos the Executioner (CK).

Astrophysical scans: See Medical scans.

Atavachron: An instrument invented by the Sarpeid and used for time travel. By means of historical discs, it attunes the user's physiology and brain structure to any given past era, allowing him or her to adjust to that era; it can also readjust the user to the present (AY).

Atkins, Yeoman Doris (Carolyn Nelson): Crew member who gives Kirk a fuel-consumption report to sign; he does so, then forgets it—the result of his rapidly advancing age (DY).

Atlantis: A "lost world" of Earth's ancient past, reported by Plato to be a perfect society (PSy). See also Tahiti syndrome.

Atoz, Mr. (Ian Wolfe): A slight, wrinkled, aged Sarpeid man with only a fringe of white hair, sharp eyes, a sharper voice, and dressed in long robes. Several replicas of himself help the old man handle the last details of sending the Sarpeids into the past before Sarpeidon's sun goes nova. He mistakes the Enterprise landing party for Sarpeid latecomers and sends them into the past. After all have been rescued, Atoz's replicas disappear, and he makes his own escape into the past era of his choice, where his wife and family await him (AY).

At posts: A Terran nautical term still used within Star Fleet, meaning "at duty stations."

Attack plan: Kirk asks Spock if he remembers the attack plan they worked out in null-gravity combat exercises, and suggests that they put it into action against Tchar. It works (Ji/a).

Audience chamber: Meeting place of the Tribunal of Aquans (Am/a).

Audio tapes: An auxiliary to the holographic tapes used in the Enterprise's Recreation Room to create effects of forests, oceans, and other relaxing illusions at the request of the crew (PJ/a).

Audiovisual suggestion: Spock, Kirk, and Scott see dimensional visions, projected by the lura-mag, of beautiful white-haired girls in gold-colored gowns: Spock sees a girl beating a Vulcan marriage drum, Kirk sees a lovely girl offering a red flower to him, and Scott sees the face of a girl inside the heart of a large rose. McCoy never mentions the vision he sees, but murmurs something about "magnolias" when contacted on the ship's intercom. Spock realizes that they are being influenced by audiovisual suggestion, but falls under the spell anyway (LS/a). See also Lura-mag.

August 2020: The date of Nomad's launching from Earth (Cg).

Aura: The Vedala asteroid has an aura; when the expedition members are retrieved by the Vedala, they too have an aura around them before they disappear from the mad planet and go back to the asteroid (Ji/a). See also Stasis box.

Aurelia: A planet whose inhabitants are birdlike creatures. Aleek-Om, a historian at the site of the time portal, is a native of Aurelia. He is part of a Federation historical-study mission (Yy/a).

Aurora: The auroras of Dramia II were deadly to the inhabitants; a particularly active aurora at the time of McCoy's mass-inoculation program on that planet set off a plague. The auroras had an intense radiation level, though to scanners they seemed non-lethal (Al/a). Also, the Aurora: A space cruiser which Dr. Sevrin and his "space hippies" have stolen to search for Eden. They push the ship to its critical point, and it explodes just as the Enterprise transports the group aboard (WEd).

Auroral activity: On Terra, the brilliant aurora borealis lights seen in northern winter skies are beautiful and harmless; the lights on Dramia II are dangerously radioactive, producing auroral plague on that planet and affecting the Enterprise's medical computers (Al/a).

Auroral plague: See Aurora.

Automatic bridge defense system: A half-globe of phaser banks in the ceiling of the bridge which can fire on any point of the bridge. It goes on when the alien magnetic organism enters the Enterprise as the landing party beams aboard from the pod ship, but the alien disarms it before the self-destruct mechanism can be set (BFS/a).

Auxiliary Control Center: A station in the lower part of the saucer section of the Enterprise used when the main control room of the ship is out of commission for any reason (e.g., occupation by Klingons). Full control of a starship can be transferred to the ACC if necessary (DV). Also known as the Auxiliary Control Room, it contains a large viewscreen, four seats facing a single console, and the usual control instrumentation (Cg, DMa). It is located on Deck Eight (IM).

Avian: An alien miner of Motherlode, a birdlike creature (MP/a).

Award of custody: Legal guardianship of a ward. There is no record of Reena Kapec's ever having been given over to the custody of Flint (RM).

Axanar: A planet where Captain Garth won a notable military victory that is still studied at the Star Fleet Academy. The war was followed by a peace mission in which Kirk took part and for which he was awarded the Palm Leaf of Axanar Peace Mission (Cml). When Garth, as an inmate of Elba II, speaks of the peace-mission politicians as weaklings, Kirk calls them humanitarians who made a dream come true: peace throughout the stars (WGD).

Ayelborne (Jon Abbott): As chairman of the elders of Organia, a thin, aged, bearded, dignified man in medieval robes, but actually a being of pure energy, in appearance a blinding light. When the squabbling of the Federation and the Klingon Empire gets too annoying, he and the other Organians compel the antagonists to make peace (EM).

Ay Pledgili, Holy: A tattered American flag, used as a totem by the Yangs. The name is taken from the words "I pledge allegiance . . ." (OG).

B

Babel: Code name for a neutral planet on which the Babel Conference is held; one of its purposes is to determine whether the Coridian planets should be admitted to the Federation (CC/a, JB).

Babel Conference: See Orion.

Babel Resolution A-12: The Babel Conference resulted in some Federationwide agreements and resolutions to maintain peace in the known galaxy. One of these concerns crimes committed in space: The first ship encountered by a pursuing Federation vessel must sub-

mit to a search on request (PO/a).

Baby: Time works backward in the antimatter universe, so the old man in the laboratory on Arret is Karla Five's son, while the baby in the playpen is her father. The Enterprise's crew is also affected, becoming babies too quickly to work the starship effectively (CC/a).

Bacchanals: Lucien remembers ancient Earth bacchanals and revels with fondness; he always enjoyed the company of rollicking humans (Mtu/a). See also Red Hour.

Backpack: When the Orion pirates meet Kirk on the asteroid, they carry backpacks. One of them contains a dilithium trigger to set off the unstable mineral combination of the asteroid, but Scott foils that plan (PO/a).

Backup systems: Kirk implies that the Enterprise's backup systems could malfunction, and tells the Romulan commander that the ship was due for an overhaul about two months ago (EI).

Bacteria: Particles of the energy field invade the Enterprise like bacterial infection of living matter, causing an electronic nervous breakdown of the starship's computers (PJ/a). See also Laboratory.

Bacteria, gram-positive: See Staphylococcus strain.

Baffle plate: When the crew of the U.S.S. Antares displeases him, Charlie Evans makes a baffle plate "go away," which causes the ship to explode, killing the entire crew. Charlie maintains that the baffle plate had warped and would have blown up the energy pile anyway (CX). The baffle plate of an old Class J starship ruptured while Captain Christopher Pike was inspecting it; delta rays released by the accident permanently crippled the captain (Me).

Bailey, Lieutenant Dave (Anthony Hall): A navigator—young, inexperienced, and brash—who shows great impatience with everyone from Kirk to Balok during the initial contact with the First Federation. He stays with Balok as a cultural emissary (CMn).

Bairn: Colloquial Scottish word for "baby." Scotty uses it to describe his engines.

Balok (Clint Howard): Seen first as a cadaverous-looking multihued creature, he is actually a dwarfish human with shaggy brows, shaven head, and bass voice. He hides himself behind the false face, rather like the Wizard of Oz, until he is certain that the Terrans are peaceful. He then invites them over for drinks, and takes a companion from the Enterprise as a cultural envoy. Balok is commander of the flagship Fesarius of the First Federation, and Spock comments that the first Balok they saw reminded him of his father—evidently a personality resemblance (CMn).

Barber (Ed McCready): A middle-aged man with thinning hair and a wispy moustache. He shares an office with Doc Holliday, whom he is shaving when McCoy comes into the shop looking for drugs from which to make tranquilizers (SGn).

Bar-David, S. (pseud.: Shimon Wincelberg) (scripts): Dagger of the Mind (DMd); The Galileo Seven (GS) (with Oliver Crawford).

Baris, Nilz (William Schallert): Federation undersecretary in charge of Agricultural Affairs for the quadrant

B

containing Space Station K-7 and Sherman's Planet, and also in charge of the Sherman's Planet Development Project. He summons the Enterprise to protect several tons of quadrotriticale at Station K-7, and Kirk is furious at being ordered to babysit for some wheat; they both snarl at each other for quite a while. Then tribbles get into the quadrotriticale, eating most of it and showing the grain to be poisoned. Baris is seen to be a typical pompous bureaucrat when his assistant, Arne Darvin, turns out to be the spy (TT).

Barnhart: A crewman aboard the Enterprise, killed by the M113 creature (MT).

Baroner: The name Kirk takes when masquerading as an Organian (EM).

Barrier: See Force field.

Barrier at the rim of the galaxy: See Energy barrier.

Barrows, Yeoman Tonia (Emily Banks):   A pretty young woman with long brown hair. On the amusement-park planet she conjures up a fourteenth-century gown and headdress to wear. For a short time. she is Dr. McCoy's girlfriend (SL).

Barstow, Commodore (Richard Derr):   Tactical officer, Star Fleet Command. He orders the Enterprise to stay around when he suspects a massive invasion. The invader turns out to be Lazarus A (AF).

Bates, Russell (script):   How Sharper Than a Serpent's Tooth (HS/a) (with David Wise).

Batteries: In case of total failure of all engine power sources, the Enterprise's gravitational and life-support systems can be maintained on battery power, with a full-load capacity of about one week.

Battlecruiser, Klingon: Every bit as big and powerful as the Enterprise, the Devisor, a Klingon battlecruiser captained by Koloth, is fully armed with a new Klingon weapon (MTT/a).

Battle ribbons: See Orders.

Battle stations: Nautical term still used in Star Fleet: All hands to report to specified areas during a battle, to man that station during the emergency.

BCP: See Brain circuitry pattern.

Beagle, S.S.:   A small Class 4 stardrive vessel with a crew of forty-seven, commanded by Captain R. M. Merik. When it was destroyed at Planet 892-IV, Merik had the crew beam down to the surface. The Enterprise finds the ship's rubble six years later (BC).

Bearings and headings: The system is not easily explained; the form is "[number] mark [number]." Thus, 37 Mark 211; 122 Mark 14.

Beast: A person's deepest fear (from the French bête noire: literally, "black beast"). Gorgan controls the crew of the Enterprise by creating illusions of their deepest fears. Sulu sees a tunnel of knives and swords, larger than the ship, waiting to destroy them if the Enterprise follows any course other than the one the children want. Uhura's control panel becomes a mirror, in which she sees herself as an old hag and foresees a long, lingering death. Scott sees his ship and the beloved machinery upset; Chekov fears retribution for disobedience. Kirk's commands become garbled, and he sees the lack of communication as the loss of his command over the ship;

though this is his greatest fear, his "beast," Kirk overcomes it and resists Gorgan. Spock sees nothing wrong, for he cannot be ruled by fear (CL). See also Rocky upthrust.

Beauregard: An alien plant, semisentient, resembling a long-necked pineapple. Sulu keeps it as a pet, calling it Gertrude, but Rand, insisting it is a male, calls it Beauregard. The plant is very fond of Rand, humming and swaying toward her whenever she comes near it (MT).

Behan, Johnny (Bill Zuckert):   The sheriff of Cochise County when the Melkots reenact the Gunfight at the O.K. Corral—a middle-aged man with graying hair and a lined face. When Kirk suggests that he stop the impending gunfight, the sheriff suggests that the Clantons get to the corral first and bushwhack the Earps (SGn).

Belay that: Nautical term: "Stop, don't do that," "Hold that order until further notice, but don't act on it." Still in use in Star Fleet.

Bele (Frank Gorshin):   The chief officer of the Commission of Political Traitors, who has been hunting Lokai, a convicted traitor, for fifty thousand years. He has blue eyes and brown hair, with the left half of his face stark white, the right half totally black. He wears overalls and gloves, and speaks in clichés and philosophical platitudes (LB).

Belief: As potent a force as energy and matter, belief works in the alternate universe of Megas-tu (Mtu/a).

Bell: A crew member of the Enterprise who, with Gabler, finds the Klingon exchange personnel wandering in areas where they are not supposed to be (Tr/a).

Belt device: Flint uses a device on his belt to control his lab, and also to make the Enterprise's landing party's communicators useless (RM). Tchar carries something on his belt which is obviously a suicide device; he nearly succeeds in using it when the Vedala retrieves the group (Ji/a).

Belt lights: To keep hands free for other things, belt lights are worn by the landing party when they run through the Phylosian tunnel (IV/a). The expedition members carry belt lights which leave their hands free for working or fighting when they enter the fortress looking for the Soul of Skorr (Ji/a).

Bem, Commander Ari bn (James Doohan):   A pale yellow-ocher-colored creature with orange sideburns and orange topknot; humanoid in shape, with bifurcated feet. Bem is a native of the planet Pandro, highly intelligent, and very independent, who knows full well that his safety is the crux of diplomatic relations with the Federation. He is a colony creature, made of many units that fit together to form one working entity. He is capable of stretching these units, or breaking them down into smaller, functioning units if necessary. He causes Kirk and Spock a good deal of trouble on Delta Theta III, but is as humbled as the Enterprise men when they all meet the alien intelligence that rules the planet (Be/a).

Benecia Colony: The destination of the Karidian Players after they leave Planet Q (CK). A planet with extremely primitive medical facilities. Kirk-J wants to abandon Janice-K, along with Kirk's real personality, which is trapped in Janice's body, on this planet (TI).

Benjisidrine: A drug which Sarek's physician pre-

B

scribes for his heart attacks (JB).

Benton (Seamon Glass): A lithium-crystal miner on Rigel XII, who marries one of Mudd's women (MW).

Beratis: Name given to the Jack-the-Ripper entity during its stay on Rigel IV (WF).

Berengaria VII: A planet, previously visited, on which Spock has seen dragons (TSP).

Berkeley, Ensign (Larry Anthony): Transporter officer, young, without experience or maturity. He makes some mistakes in establishing transporter contact with Tantalus V and receives a good-natured chewing-out from Kirk (DMd).

Berserker: A gigantic robot ship, apparently a superweapon left from the wars of an undoubtedly extinct extragalactic race. Spock describes it as "an automated weapon of immense size and power, self-sustaining as long as there are planetary bodies for it to feed on," referring to the fact that it sustains itself by cutting up planets and converting their matter to energy. It is a hundred times the size of a starship and shaped like a great cone, with its large end open for ingesting raw materials. Its hull is solid neutronium. It can find a starship by tracing the energy from the power nacelles, and can deactivate a ship's antimatter pods with an energy-damping field. It destroys several solar systems and one starship before it is finally deactivated by an explosion of 97.835 megatons (DMa).

Doomsday machine
Greg Jein

Berthold rays: Under exposure to these rays, human tissue disintegrates within seventy-two hours. Omicron Ceti III is continually bombarded by them, but the colonists there are saved from the rays' deadly effect by the spores which flourish on that planet and, in fact, thrive on the Berthold rays (TSP).

Beta Antares IV: A world where they play fizzbin, according to Kirk, but don't count on it (PA).

Beta Aurigae: A binary system in which the Enterprise and the Potemkin are to do some studies of gravitational effects when they are diverted by a distress call from Camus II (TI).

Beta Canopus: One of the few regions in the galaxy where the naturally occurring drug strobolin is found (PO/a).

Beta 5 computer (Majel Barrett): The computer model installed in Gary Seven's apartment in twentieth-century New York. A high-level machine with a touch of snobbery, it has a vision screen, a materializer, and other sophisticated equipment (AE).

Beta Geminorum: A minor star of the star system whose major components are Castor and Pollux; the system also contains planet Pollux IV, where Apollo appeared (WM).

Beta Lyrae: A rare spectacle of the galaxy, one of the wonders of the universe; almost every ship that passes

stops to see it. Inside the Beta Lyrae system is a fabulously beautiful panorama of yellow giants, red hydrogen stars with whiplike tails of blue gases, brilliant blue dwarf suns, and only one planet: a frozen, almost airless, icebound world. The Kzin lure Spock and his shuttlecraft crew to this planet in search of another stasis box (SW/a).

Beta Niobe: A star about to go nova when the Enterprise arrives to rescue survivors from the star's only satellite, a planet called Sarpeidon (AY). Now a supernova, one of the galaxy's most beautiful and deadly sights, a huge fireball of gases hanging in space—a swirling mass of reds, cerise, and pinks. The Enterprise was there when it went nova (AY), and April knew of the incident, as a starship's log is always made available to former commanders as a courtesy (CC/a).

Beta Portalan system: The flying parasites started mass insanity in an ancient civilization of this system many centuries ago (OA).

Beta 6: A colony to which the Enterprise is delivering supplies when Trelane of Gothos interferes (SG).

Beta III in star system 6-11: Landru's planet, where the U.S.S. Archon was lost, and where the Enterprise men later overthrow Landru's influence (RA).

Beta XIIA: A planet whose agricultural colony of a hundred Federation citizens has allegedly been destroyed by Klingons—except that it never happened. The incident is a false memory created by the entity that is arousing blood feuds between Klingons and Federation men (Dv).

"Beyond Antares" (words by Gene L. Coon): A song sung by Lieutenant Uhura to Kevin Riley (CK). She also sings it while Nomad listens (Cg).

Bezaride: One of the three planets in the Pallas 14 system (OPM/a).

Bible: See Religion.

Bilar (Ralph Maurer): Rotund and stupid, with lots of teeth. An inhabitant of Landru's planet, and a typical member of the Body: placid and cowlike in normal times, frenzied and savage during festivals. He guides the Enterprise group to Reger's house just before the festival. During the festival he apparently rapes Reger's daughter, Tula (RA).

Billiards: A table game of skill still enjoyed in the twenty-second century (RM). See also Entertainment.

Binary star system: A twin-star system, usually a large and a small sun circling each other. Any planets in such a system are worth exploring, according to Star Fleet orders. Mudd escapes to a planet in a system with a blue-white sun and a smaller, reddish sun (MP/a).

Biocomputer, portable: A device, approximately the size of a portable TV set, for processing biological data. Of limited information-processing ability, it is usually used in conjunction with larger computers (Mi).

Biological rebellion: A profound revulsion against planned communities, the programming of people, and sterilized, artificially balanced atmospheres. The "space hippies," feeling this reaction, set out to find Eden—a place where spring comes. They regard themselves as aliens in their worlds, and Spock feels drawn to them because he understands that feeling (WEd).

Biological renewal: See Tissue regeneration.

B

Biological scans: See Medical scans.

Biologist: See Bryce, Randi.

Biosphere: The sphere of life around a planet; its ecology (OG).

Birdman: Lara's snide answer to Tchar when he doubts her ability to find the correct direction the expedition must travel; she calls him a birdman, referring to his wings (Ji/a).

Birds: Surveys reveal no sign of animal life, but Rodriguez hears and sees a flock of birds flying overhead on the shore-leave planet (SL).

Bixby, Jerome (scripts): Mirror, Mirror (MM); By Any Other Name (AON) (with D. C. Fontana); Day of the Dove (Dv); Requiem for Methuselah (RM).

Black hole: In our universe, a star which suddenly goes nova and implodes, burning itself up but still having the same mass as the original, though smaller in size (CC/a).

Black, John D.F. (Script): The Naked Time (NT).

Blackjack: See Omaha Air Base.

Black Knight (Paul Baxley): Conjured up out of McCoy's imagination in joking reference to Yeoman Barrows's beautiful medieval costume, the Black Knight, mounted on an equally black horse, charges the doctor and kills him with a jousting lance. This is part of the amusement planet's specialized robot work; the computer thought that it was McCoy's wish to be charged by a knight in armor. McCoy is later "repaired" by the computer and returned to his friends, whole again (SL).

Blackouts: After Kirk is put to sleep by the Vendorian spy so it can take the captain's shape, he is confused when he awakes from what he thinks was a short nap. The ship's log shows that Kirk has ordered a course change through the Romulan neutral zone—something the real Kirk would never have done. Therefore, the captain assumes that he is becoming subject to memory blackouts and is a potential danger to the starship and its crew. Spock suggests a medical checkup (Su/a).

Black star: A black star catches the Enterprise in its gravitational field and, by pulling the ship into a hyperlight velocity that puts it in a time warp, sends it back to the twentieth century (TY).

Blizzard: When the Enterprise computer decides to become a practical joker, a very realistic and cold blizzard is whipped up in the Recreation Room, trapping Uhura, Sulu, and McCoy (PJ/a).

Bloch, Robert (scripts): Wolf in the Fold (WF); What Are Little Girls Made Of? (LG); Catspaw (Cp).

Blocks: To prove their power, Rojan and his fellow Kelvans turn two security guards into small whitish blocks which represent their human essence. If a block is broken or damaged, the person is killed; otherwise, the block can revert back to a living human again. When the Kelvans take over the Enterprise, they turn all crewmen not immediately useful to them into blocks, so there will be fewer people to guard on the trip back to Andromeda (AON).

Blood-analyzer unit: Medical equipment. McCoy uses two to analyze the virus on Omega IV (OG).

Bluejay 4: Code name for Captain Christopher's plane, an interceptor jet armed with missiles. The Enterprise's tractor beams tear the plane apart, and it crashes in Nebraska (TY).

Boarding Plan C, Klingon: A boarding plan for taking over the Enterprise. We never find out what this command is, however, as the order is given at about the same time that Scott transports a load of tribbles into the Klingon battlecruiser, and the Klingons suddenly become too busy to implement the boarding plan (MTT/a).

Bodily integrity: On the unreal world of Megas-tu, the Enterprise's landing party begins to separate into component elements, much to their dismay. Lucien puts their bodies back together again, saying that he has forgotten how important bodily integrity is to humans. On Megas-tu, floating around in a disembodied state is the normal pattern of life, and it is not easy to hold bodies together, or even natural. Spock comments that it is interesting to find himself in a disembodied state, but McCoy grumbles that Spock wasn't ever very natural in the first place (Mtu/a).

Body, the: Name for the group mind controlled by Landru, the computer, which dominates Beta III's society. Members of the Body are dull, peaceful (except during "Festival"), and zombielike; their culture is static and nonproductive (RA).

Body throw: Sulu uses a body throw, part of martial-arts training, to stop Agmar, an attacking plant-being. Sulu later tells Kirk that Occidentals probably cannot learn to do the body throw, as it requires Oriental inscrutability. Kirk is unimpressed, saying that Sulu is one of the most scrutable men he has ever met (IV/a).

Boma, Lieutenant (Don Marshall): Astrophysicist in the Galileo party that crashes on Taurus II—a large, hefty black. He wastes a lot of time arguing with Spock about conducting funerals with proper ceremony (GS).

Bomb: Spock sets off a bomb inside the giant spacegoing ameba, in order to destroy it, and escapes just in time (IS).

Bombardment, preventive: By bombarding the uninhabited north polar region of Argo with phaser beams, the Enterprise can change the epicenter of the quakes to avoid harm to the Aquans' undersea city. This procedure also teaches the Federation people how to handle the situation imminent on another planet, where many lives might otherwise be lost during massive seismic disturbances (Am/a).

Bonaventure: The first ship to have warp drive installed—a ship smaller than the Enterprise, not as graceful or sleek, but clearly powerful. It vanished without a trace on its third voyage. The Enterprise finds the Bonaventure's dead hulk in the alternate universe of Elysia (Tr/a).

Bonaventure, Ruth (Maggie Thrett): One of Mudd's women, a native of a pelagic planet, with long black hair, her beautiful figure clothed in green lamé. She marries a miner on Rigel XII (MW).

Bones: A term used affectionately by Kirk for addressing Dr. McCoy. Historically, it comes from the term "sawbones," by which doctors were known until the nineteenth century because mostly they removed limbs; for other doctoring, one went to an apothecary, herbalist, midwife, or barber, depending on the problem.

B

Bonnie: Scottish term of fondness or indication of beauty.

Book, by the: A military term meaning "according to all the rules and regulations laid down for officers." Kirk thinks that the commander of the Ariel should not have left his ship alone in orbit while going down to rescue his crew members. The captain or senior ranking officer should "go by the book"—a capability beyond the reach of most humans, in Spock's opinion (EB/a).

Book of the People: According to Natira, a book has been given to her people, to be opened and read when they reach the world of promise. It presumably tells the people how to manage their new lives, and it is a sacrilege for an outsider to see the book. Spock finds a diagram in its pages which duplicates a plaque in the room of the monolith; it gives directions for opening the walls to the controls of the asteroid/ship (FW).

Books: The walls of the home where Spock was raised have real books on the shelves, not just the usual microtape readers. Amanda likes books, particularly fantasy literature, and manages to give her son a taste for light reading, though he later ascribes it to a standard Vulcan interest in relaxation (Yy/a).

Book, the: See Chicago Mobs of the Twenties. (SC).

Boots: Harry Mudd, evidently planning for every contingency, has special places built into the heels of his boots for carrying small items, such as the love-potion crystals (MP/a).

Borgia plant: A poisonous plant found on Planet M113, listed in the library tapes as carbon-group-3 vegetation, similar to the nightshade family. When the M113 creature kills Darnell, it puts the root of a borgia plant in his hand to make the Terrans think he has been poisoned (MT).

Boridium: An alloy used on Rigel IV. Hengist's knife, made by the hill people of the Argus River region on Rigel IV, has a boridium blade (WF).

Bosun's whistle: An intraship signal for attention to an announcement about to be given to the ship at large; also, a method of piping an important personage aboard a vessel—a tradition dating back to old Earth nautical days and still in use on starships.

Botanical plague: A plague that threatens to kill all vegetation on Merak II; it is stopped when the Enterprise arrives with zienite to halt the devastation (Cms).

Botany: See Tongo Rad, Sulu.

Botany Bay, S.S.: An old Dy-100 spaceship, converted to a "sleeper ship." A group of selectively bred "supermen" from the late twentieth century, escaped from Earth in the Botany Bay, surviving in suspended animation until discovered by the Enterprise (SS).

Bow and arrow: With a surprising degree of ability, Kirk and Spock fashion bows and arrows from green wood found on Capella IV, with strings made of braided strips of vegetation (FC).

Bowling alley: When Kevin Riley declares himself captain of the Enterprise and sings old Irish songs to the crew, he also promises that there will be a dance held in the bowling alley that night (NT). (There is no evidence that the Enterprise actually has a bowling alley. However,

under the influence of the Psi 2000 virus, Kevin seems to think it has, or at least should have, one.)

Boyce, Dr. Joseph (John Hoyt): Ship's surgeon on the Enterprise under Captain Pike—tall, craggy, white-haired—an amateur psychologist, philosopher, and bartender (Me).

Bracelet: See Wristlet.

Brack, Mr.: A wealthy financier and recluse. The Federation has shown little interest in him, but has recorded his purchase of a small planet, Holberg 917G. The name is a front for Flint, an immortal (RM).

Brahms, Johannes: A German composer and pianist (1833–97). Spock finds an unpublished waltz among the sheet music on Flint's piano and recognizes Brahms's handwriting, but with modern ink. Flint admits that the writing is his; Brahms was one of the many pseudonyms used by the immortal as he traveled through Earth's history (RM).

Brain, cloud: The cosmic cloud has a brain area, which the Enterprise invades in hopes of contacting the immense entity. An irregularly shaped object at the top of a core inside the cloud, it emanates considerable electrical activity. As seen by the crew of the starship, the brain is a vast area with long cables stretched across the viewscreen. They later escape the cloud through a grid at the top of the brain area (OPM/a).

Brain circuitry pattern (BCP): Lieutenant Romaine's BCP (tape deck D) matches the impulse tracking of the Zetar life units (tape deck H), showing that an identity of minds has taken place (LZ).

Brain Room: A Kalandan computer room with a large translucent cube overhead that can reproduce replicas of Losira. A security guard destroys the cube in the nick of time (TWS).

Brains: When the Enterprise goes through the novas into the antimatter universe, everyone's brains work in reverse, and they are able to understand Karla Five's language (CC/a).

Brent, Lieutenant (Frank da Vinci): He takes over the navigator's station from Uhura when she relieves Kevin Riley, who left his post after being infected with the Psi 2000 virus (NT).

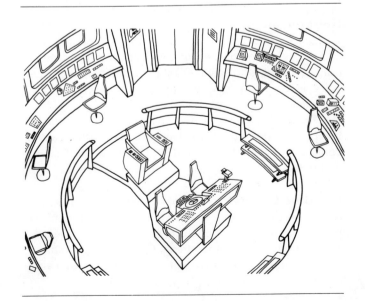

B

Bridge: Circular, multiplatformed chamber, located at the top of the saucer section of a starship, where the captain presides over the whole ship's complex. Access is by turbolift. Kirk sits in his command chair in the inner, lower section, and directly in front of him sit the navigator and the helmsman at their console; all facing the large viewscreen. In the outer circular elevation are various stations for the communications officer, technical crewmen, and other personnel. Mr. Spock, the science officer, presides over a console which is known as the library/computer station; this section also contains sensors used to detect activity outside the ship. The bridge is the "brain" of a ship.

Bridge-monitor screen: The bridge may be monitored by a screen in the Transporter Room.

Briel, mess officer: An Enterprise officer who reports that the shrinking of the crew is causing panic in the mess hall, where silverware is getting too big to handle and tables and chairs seem huge. He asks for security help (Te/a).

Brig: Old nautical term, meaning the jail on board a ship; still in use for starships.

Brody, Larry (script): The Magicks of Megas-Tu (Mtu/a).

Brothers: In an embarrassing display of emotion, Spock calls the Klingons brothers when they all decide to cooperate to get the ships out of the time trap. Spock has his reasons for reacting in this manner, for it gives him a chance to make contact with the Klingons and mind-touch them enough to know that their motives are not trustworthy (Tr/a).

Brown, Dr. (Harry Basch): Dr. Korby's assistant—of slight build, middle-aged, balding—who, on his death, was replaced by an android duplicate. Kirk accidentally destroys him with a phaser, only then discovering that he is an android (LG).

Brown, Frederick (story): Arena (Ar) (with Gene L. Coon).

Bryce, Randi (Majel Barrett): Biologist on a scientific-exploration team that was to survey the planet Lactra VII in a small ship, the Ariel. The team survived the dangers of the planet, to end up in a zoo until the Enterprise arrives to rescue the party (EB/a).

Bubonic plague: Rigellian fever is comparable to this disease, which ravaged Europe many times. Virulent and highly contagious, it was carried by rats, fleas, and humans. Flint, who saw the first recorded plague start in 1334, is moved by McCoy's appeal for ryetalyn to stop the Rigellian fever (RM).

Buffalo: Dr. Crater nostalgically reminds Kirk that buffalo once covered the Great Plains of the North American continent, shaking the ground with their stampedes, but that man kept killing them until there were only a few left (MT).

Buntline Special: A pistol made by Ned Buntline and favored by Wyatt Earp over the Frontier-model Colt pistol because the longer barrel of the Buntline Special makes it easier to hit something. Contrary to popular belief about Old West heroes, Earp was not a good shot (SGn).

Buoy, Melkotian (James Doohan): An object in space that looks like two stacks of flat plates, flashing red and gold, rotating on its axis. At the edge of Melkot space it establishes telepathic contact with the Enterprise, appearing to speak English, Vulcan, Swahili, and Russian to various individuals. It warns Kirk away from the area, but he is under orders to proceed, and does so (SGn).

Burke, John: Chief Astronomer, Royal Academy, Great Britain, some two hundred years before the Enterprise's voyages. The Englishman who mapped the Sherman's Planet area. Chekov remembers him as Ivan Burkoff (TT).

Burns, Judy (script): The Tholian Web (TW) (with Chet Richards).

Butler, Nathan (pseudonym of Jerry Sohl): This Side of Paradise (TSP), with D.C. Fontana.

Butler, Robert (director): The Menagerie (Me) (with Marc Daniels).

Butterflies: Terran insects with beautifully colored wings. They are created by the practical-joke-playing Enterprise computer for the Grecian scene in the Recreation Room, giving an impression of beauty and tranquility to the stranded Uhura, Sulu, and McCoy (PJ/a).

Byron: George Gordon (Lord Byron), a well-known Earth poet (1788–1824). Spock, when sharing minds with Kollos, quotes from "Hebrew Melodies": "She walks in beauty, like the night . . ." (TB).

C

Cabaret girls: When McCoy realizes he can conjure up anything he wants on the amusement planet, he materializes two girls from the chorus line of a cabaret on Rigel II. The girls, scantily clad in colorful feathered costumes, please the other males, but are greeted somewhat frostily by the Enterprise's female crew (SL).

Cabinet: In the mirror universe, the governing council of the Empire (MM).

Cactus plant: McCoy makes a homemade tranquilizer from a local Arizona cactus plant, but it doesn't work in the world created by the Melkots (SGn).

Caesar, Gaius Julius: Garth of Izar mentions this Caesar as never having conquered his world. But actually, during his life on Earth (100–44 B.C.) Julius Caesar managed to control a good percentage of his known world and was acclaimed emperor—something Garth desires until he is cured of his madness (WGD).

Calendar: The Mayan calendar is one of the most accurate of ancient Earth calendars. It was given to them by Kulkukan (HS/a).

Calendar, old: The Gregorian calendar, in use during the twentieth century, expressed in years A.D. and B.C. (Cg, WF). By the old calendar, the Enterprise operates just past the middle of the twenty-second century (SS, TY).

Camus II: An uninhabited planet where the ruins of a long-dead civilization were being explored by a group of Federation scientists led by Janice Lester (TI).

Canopus: The planet and star system that were home

to Phineas Tarbolde, a galaxy-famous poet and author of "Nightingale Woman" (WNM). See also Arcanis.

Canopus III: The fire-breathing iguana on Lactra VII reminds Kirk of a similar beast he saw on Canopus III, light-years from Lactra VII but with the same type of environment (EB/a).

Cantaba Street: Morla's address-name on Argelius II (WF).

Capella IV: A small planet, predominantly greenish blue with red seas. It is rich in topaline, a mineral used in the life-support systems of planetoid colonies, which makes both the Klingon Empire and the Federation eager to mine on this planet (FC). One of the most beautiful flowers in the galaxy grows here. It has a life span of only a few hours, however—a seedling in the morning, in full bloom after a few hours, and then it dies. A Capellan flower is being admired by Dr. April when they go into the antimatter universe, where it reverses its dying, blooming back to full flower and then into a seedling (CC/a).

Capellan power-cat: The fiercest and most untamable creature in the galaxy—a sort of large furry bobcat with gold eyes and short tail, brick-red fur with brown spines running down its back, and a white aura of electricity around it when moving. It is about the size of a Terran brown bear. No one has ever been able to keep one alive in captivity. Power-cats hate captivity and can throw a jolt of 2000 volts when captured. Kulkukan obtained his when it was an infant and easily controlled; yet the power-cat attacks Kulkukan when it is released from its cage by the Enterprise's men. Energy bursts from the cat cause the room to change color. Kirk hits it with a tranquilizer hypo and calms the cat down, getting a shock in so doing, however. After the cat is tranquilized, it sits down and washes its paws (HS/a).

Capellans: Tall, extremely strong, and quick, Capellans believe that only the strong should survive, and hence care nothing for medicine; they have inherent pain control, like the Vulcans, and a keen sense of smell. They are highly tradition-directed, unusually honest, and keep their word scrupulously. They are also highly dangerous: Any show of force toward them is regarded as a declaration of enmity, and combat is considered more pleasant than love (FC).

Capellan salute: Right hand formed into a fist, held over the heart, then extended with the palm up. This indicates that the man and all he owns is open to inspection (FC).

Capsule: The Orion commander carries a small capsule which is to be his method of suicide should his mission fail, but he is captured before he can use it (PO/a). A small, innocent-looking explosive capsule which can be carried in the hand is set to trigger at the exact time the Klingon ship and the Federation ship separate from their dual attempt to escape Elysia. In this manner, the Klingons would have used the Enterprise for escape while destroying it, too (Tr/a).

"Captain's woman": In the mirror universe, the mistress of a starship captain is referred to by this name. Marlena-2 enjoys such status, though she has been treated unkindly by Kirk-2 and is ready to go through every officer in the Fleet to find a captain who will appreciate her (MM).

Carabatsos, Steven W. (scripts): Operation—Annihilate! (OA); Court-martial (CMI) (with Don M. Mankiewicz).

Carbon-cycle life form: The rock creatures of Excalbia are a scientifically impossible life form for ordinary planets, which may explain why they remained undetected for so long (SC). See also Rock creatures.

Cardiostimulator: A medical device used to reactivate a stopped heart. McCoy has one which runs on ship's power, and an old portable model. It works on Vulcans as well as Terrans (JB).

Cards: See Games and recreation.

Caretaker (Oliver McGowan): The being who manages the amusement-park planet for the beings who built it—in appearance, a nice old man with fluffy white hair, wearing a long robe (SL). Known also as the Keeper of the planet. The last of his race, the Keeper dies on the fifth day of the twelfth moon on the amusement planet's year 7009 (OUP/a).

Cargo holds: The alien magnetic organism begins shutting down areas of the starship which are not important to it; cargo holds 3, 4, and 5 have their life-support systems shut down (BFS/a).

Carlisle, Lieutenant (Arnold Lessing): A security officer on the Enterprise (Cg).

Carolina, U.S.S.: A Federation vessel registered in the Capellan sector. When the Klingons fail to lure the Enterprise away from Capella IV with a false distress call from the S.S. Dierdre, they try a fake call from the Carolina, but Scotty says, "Fool me once, shame on you; fool me twice, shame on me" (FC).

Carrel: An individual study area in the Sarpeid library containing a table with a tiny tripod for the viewing discs.

The carrel is used for the "preparation" of someone who is going permanently into the past (AY).

Carroll, Lewis (pseud. of Charles Lutwidge Dodgson, 1832-98): English writer best remembered for his famous children's books Alice's Adventures in Wonderland (1865) and its sequel, Through the Looking Glass (1872), both illustrated by Sir John Tenniel. The characters from the Alice books are frequent manifestations on the shore-leave planet, probably because of their popularity with members of the crew, particularly Kirk, McCoy, Sulu, and even Spock (because of Amanda's fondness for the books) (OUP/a, SL).

Carry on: Military term for "Keep on doing whatever you were doing before I interrupted you," basically.

Cart: A mechanized carrier materialized for the Soul of Skorr expedition by the Vedala. It comes well equipped, but the mad planet and Tchar combine forces to damage most of the equipment it carries. Em/3/Green drives the cart for most of the trip across the mad planet (Ji/a).

Carter, Dr. (Ed McCready): Medical officer of the Exeter, killed by the Omega IV disease (OG).

Cartoon face: Captain Kirk finds that his shirt has a cartoon face on it, along with some lettering that is distinctly unflattering (PJ/a).

Carver: A security guard who beams down with the landing party to inspect Taurus II and offers to make a tricorder reading; Kirk feels too lackadaisical to bother, however, and Carver does not press the point (LS/a).

Carvings: The obelisks guarding the gates of Kulkukan's city have carvings on them—not from any Earth culture, but they do include images of Kulkukan (HS/a).

Cat: As Kirk realizes that the shore-leave planet is playing a cat-and-mouse game with them, a huge cat appears and tries to get at him, Spock, and McCoy in the cave behind the narrow passage past the "underground entrance" sign (OUP/a). See also Capellan power-cat.

Cat, black: One of the forms Sylvia takes to deceive the Enterprise's landing party. The cat, wearing Sylvia's jeweled amulet around its neck, appears both in ordinary size and in gigantic form (Cp). See also Isis.

Catlike creatures: See Kzin, M'Ress, Vedala.

Catullan ambassador: A man of extraordinary abilities in space studies and also the ambassador from his planet to the Federation, involved in delicate treaty negotiations when the Enterprise picks up his son, Tongo Rad, one of a group of "space hippies" (WEd).

Cavalry: Old Earth military horsemen. When Kirk and Spock are preparing to fight off the Capellans, Kirk comments that the cavalry does not come to the rescue any more, as they do in antique Western movies. However, Scotty and a group of security men do arrive, cavalry-style, just in time to get the drop on the Capellans after all (FC).

Cave dwellers: The remnants of the Dramia II natives live in caves, their homes having been wrecked in a plague that leveled nearly everything on the planet. It is possible that in the final stages of the auroral disease, despair and carelessness led to a period of savagery in which the buildings were destroyed. Kirk and Demos twit each other about the cave-dwelling inhabitants of one planet being so close to the highly civilized neighboring

planet of Dramia (Al/a).

Celebium: A type of radiation, exposure to which can result in death. It is found in the ruins of Camus II. In her lust for power, Janice Lester, the leader of an expedition there, deliberately exposed her group to it (TI).

Cell damage: Newly accelerated people on Scalos die easily of cell damage; a scratch can cause death. After death, the body ages rapidly because of cell damage (WE).

Cells: See Clone.

Cellular casting: Everything on the shore-leave planet is alike, made from cellular casting. It is also commonly used for wound repairs. The knight that kills McCoy seems to be made of it—only a much finer grade, of course (SL).

Cellular disruption: When Losira's image touches someone, it is as though every cell in the victim's body has been individually blasted from within (TWS). See also Necrotic tissue.

Cellular metamorphosis: See Antos IV.

Centauri VII: Home of Taranallus, a lithographer whose works are collected by Flint; Spock notices a rare Taranallus folio, The Creation, in Flint's living room (RM).

Center of the galaxy: The Enterprise is sent to investigate the center of the galaxy to see if scientific theory is correct about the great-explosion theory of creation, and to see if new matter is still being created in the center. They not only find that it is, but also pass through the center into another universe (Mtu/a).

Central brain: See Memory Alpha.

Centuries, Lactran: The Lactrans invite humans—and Vulcans—to return in twenty or thirty centuries, when they have grown up. Spock comments that it would take some time to calculate how long their centuries are, by which we may assume that Lactrans do not count their years by the orbit of their planet around its star, but by some other method, as yet unknown (EB/a).

Centurion (John Warburton): The centurion aboard the Romulan ship that attacks the Enterprise is the commander's close friend—an old man with white hair, a rather round face for a Romulan, and typical pointed ears and eyebrows. He is killed by falling debris in the control room, and his body is jettisoned in an attempt to deceive the Enterprise. The word "centurion" is a translation of an equivalent Romulan rank (BT).

Cepheus: A star in the Arachna region of space with only one satellite, a small planet (Te/a).

Cerberus: McCoy's daughter was going to school on Cerberus ten years ago, when the crops failed. The entire population of the planet would have starved if Carter Winston had not used his personal fortune to bring in enough food and goods to carry the planet through the crisis (Su/a).

Cestus III: The site of an Earth colony at the edge of Gorn territory, destroyed by Gorn attack (Ar).

Ceti Alpha V: A habitable though rugged Class M planet, to which Khan Noonian Singh, his people, and Lieutenant McGivers are exiled (SS).

Chair, rehabilitation: A painless chair which gives mild shocks and ultrasonic soothing patterning to crazed minds. It helped many insane men back to mental health before Garth added some "refinements" which tuned the ultrasonics to torture level. Garth uses the chair on Kirk and the Elba II governor (WGD).

Chamber of the Ages: Horta term for the chamber on the twenty-third level of Janus VI, where the Horta eggs are stored. Also called the Vault of Tomorrow (DD).

Chandra, Captain (Reginald Lalsingh): A Space Command representative and member of Kirk's trial board when he is accused of killing Lieutenant Commander Finney (Cml).

Changeling: In Earth folklore, a fairy or elf child left in place of a stolen, unbaptized human baby was called a changeling; it took the identity of the human child. When the alien space probe Tan Ru and the Earth probe Nomad meshed to become one, the product was a "changeling" from both originals (Cg).

Channel E: Communications channel Nilz Baris uses to contact Kirk (TT).

Chant: To call Gorgan, the children form a circle, clasp hands, and chant: "Hail, hail, fire and snow; call the Angel. We will go far away for to see. Friendly Angel, come to me" (CL).

Chaos: Sensors and other delicate equipment become unreliable and go into a state of chaos when the Enterprise enters the Delta Triangle sector (Tr/a). Chaos is the normal state of things on Megas-tu—whirlwinds, changing colors, convoluted movement, constant sound, nothing stable, all in flux. The humans find it unsettling; Spock finds it somewhat interesting to experience (Mtu/a).

Chapel, Christine (Majel Barrett): Tall, blond research biologist who signs aboard the Enterprise to search for her fiancé, Dr. Roger Korby (LG). After Korby's death, she remains on the ship as McCoy's chief nurse (OA). Under the influence of the Psi 2000 virus, she flirts with Spock, who is deeply grieved to think she loves him (NT). Subsequently, Chapel actually falls in love with Spock, and he avoids her when he can (AT, OA, RT).

"Charlie": A song Uhura sings in a teasing manner to Charles Evans; it is a parody of an old song about Bonnie Prince Charlie, circa Earth's 1750s. Charles Evans is too immature to take the teasing, however, and retaliates by causing Uhura to lose her voice for a short time (CX).

Charles II: The planet Sarpeidon went through a historical phase resembling that of Earth's Charles II (1630–85), in which Kirk finds himself when he is thrown back into Sarpeid history; Charles II's court has been called the most immoral that England ever had (AY).

Chart 14A: A closeup diagram of Earth's solar system, Kirk shows it to Nomad, who recognizes it as its own point of origin (Cg).

Charting scanner: A device used in mapping stars, sectors of space, and the center of the galaxy (Mtu/a).

Checkers, 3-D: See Games and recreation.

Checkpoint Tiger: Specified meeting place of the Janus VI miners and the Enterprise's security details while hunting for the Horta. It is on the twenty-third level, where the creature's eggs are kept (DD).

Chekov, Ensign Pavel (Walter Koenig): Full name: Pavel Andreievich Chekov (WEd). Young, eager, with a strong Russian accent, he was selected as navigator for the Enterprise after a series of temporary replacements

following the death of Lieutenant Commander Gary Mitchell. At age twenty-two (WF), he is impressionable but basically reliable. He is very proud of being Russian, to the point of forgetting that Russians did not accomplish everything in history (FC, TT, WM). He admires Kirk intensely (TT), and will probably be much like him later—a charming ladies' man. At the moment, he is busy being an officer.

Chekov, Piotr: Chekov's only brother, who was supposedly killed with the rest of his research outpost by Klingons—except that this never happened. In fact, Chekov is an only child. The incident is a false memory created by an entity intent on arousing Klingon-Terran blood feuds aboard the Enterprise (Dv).

Chekov-2 (Walter Koenig): Chekov's counterpart in the mirror universe; he acts innocent but is really treacherous. He tries to assassinate Kirk-1 and is put in the agony booth (MM).

Chemical corrosion: The cause of death of the Janus VI miners attacked by the Horta. The victims look as though they've been thrown into a vat of extremely strong acid. Chemical corrosion is also responsible for the breakdown of equipment that the Horta sabotages (DD).

Chemical gun: Instead of a Federation phaser, Lara the hunter carries a chemical gun (Ji/a).

Chemical mist: The Enterprise's landing party, returning to rescue Spock from Dr. Keniclius, brings along cylinders containing a chemical weedkiller which is sprayed out as a mist at the attacking plant beings. The humans wear filter masks for protection. McCoy made up the chemical from a recipe he says he recalled from his great-great-granddaddy (IV/a).

Cheron: A long-dead planet with only two remaining inhabitants, who have chased across the galaxy and back to fight their last battle with each other over a stupid prejudice. The planet was once evidently rich in materials and technology—Bele's ship is an extremely advanced type—but the inhabitants allowed bigotry about skin colors to cause illogical wars until there was no one left. The people of the Enterprise see the last of the Cherons (LB).

Chess: An ancient board game using "men" or figures to be moved across the board. It is still enjoyed by Flint and offered as entertainment to his guests (RM). Chess is the key to proving Kirk's innocence at his court-martial. When Spock realizes he can win a chess game from the computer, when the best he should achieve is a stalemate, the Vulcan realizes that the computer has been tampered with. Since only three people know how to alter the computer's tapes that well—himself, Kirk, and Finney—by process of elimination, the culprit has to be Finney, which means that Finney must be alive and that Kirk obviously cannot be responsible for his death (Cml). When Spock beats Charlie Evans at chess, the temperamental youngster uses his powerful mental abilities to melt the chess pieces (CX). While experimenting with his capabilities for using magic in the world of Megas-tu, Spock mentally moves some Vulcan chess pieces made of crystal (Mtu/a).

Chess code: A code worked out to enable the landing party to get back to the Enterprise from Elba II, an

C

139

asylum for the criminally insane, while preventing any possibility of the inmates' making a break for freedom. The code uses three-dimensional chess: Scott, on board, is to say: "Queen to Queen's level three." The landing party then gives the countersign: "Queen to King's level one." Garth tries every trick he can think of to force the secret of the countercode from Kirk and Spock, but he fails (WGD).

Chess, 3-D: See Games and recreation.

Chicago Mobs of the Twenties: A book, published in New York in 1992, which was left behind on Iotia by the Horizon's crew. The Iotians built a whole culture based on it (PA).

Chief City Administrator: See Hengist.

Chief Officer, Commission of Political Traitors: Bele's official title, a resounding name for what was evidently an institution of thought control (LB).

Child, Lactran: A baby in comparison to the other Lactrans, this youngster tries to help Kirk by bringing a communicator into the compound and is tricked. When the Lactran child seizes the communicator just as Scott tries to beam the captain up, the Enterprise gets an unexpected visitor. The Lactran parents consider it an obvious kidnapping and are upset, but the child quickly takes over the Enterprise, reads all the computer/library tapes, and returns to Lactra VII with information about the Federation and humans in general. Scott, meanwhile, discovers that the child is about six years old but has an I.Q. measured in the thousands. Scott has grown rather fond of the huge sluglike Lactran child, and the understanding between the two of them contributes greatly to getting the other humans released from the zoo (EB/a).

Children: The alien intelligence guiding the aboriginal natives in Delta Theta III refers to them as her "children"; she later addresses the departing Enterprise people as "children" (Be/a). The immortal women on Taurus II cannot have children (LS/a). The women of Scalos can have children only by kidnapping men outside their own world (WE). Able to save only a few thousand people from the endangered planet Mantilles, Governor Wesley decides to save as many of the children as possible—certainly a choice of the heart rather than a logical one. Few other planets would have the room or facilities to handle five thousand traumatized juvenile orphans; young people whose education and training had already proven them to be valuable would have been a better choice (OPM/a). See also Onlies.

Childress, Ben (Gene Dynarski): The tall, balding, blue-jawed, weatherbeaten leader of the lithium-crystal miners on Rigel XII. He tries to trade crystals for the release of Harry Mudd and his women, and eventually marries Eve McHuron (MW).

Chomsky, Marvin (director): All Our Yesterdays (AY); And the Children Shall Lead (CL); Day of the Dove (Dv).

Choriocytosis: A disease merely troublesome to iron-blooded humans but fatal to copper-blooded Vulcans. The diseased blood cells are encased by the infection so they cannot carry oxygen. Symptoms are extreme fatigue and steadily decreasing efficiency—in fact, all the symptoms humans develop when working in an oxygen-deficient atmosphere. Spock contracts the disease and has three days to live, even with the aid of synthesized drugs, unless a cure can be located (PO/a).

Christ, Jesus: The "Son," or second person of the trinity in Christianity, born as a man on Earth and on planet 892-IV (BC). See also Sun worshippers.

Christopher, Captain John (Roger Perry): Twentieth-century Air Force pilot—4857932, USAF; blue eyes, light brown crew cut—whose plane attacks the Enterprise and falls apart over Nebraska. The incident nearly changes history when he is beamed aboard the starship, where Kirk wants to keep him so he cannot report to Earth what he has seen. But Spock reveals that Captain Christopher is destined to beget a son who will figure significantly in the development of space exploration, and they return the pilot to Earth (TY).

Christopher, Colonel Shaun Geoffrey: See Earth-Saturn probe.

Chronometer: All timekeeping equipment stops when the Enterprise goes through the center of the galaxy (Mtu/a).

Chuft Captain: Leader of the Kzin who captures the shuttlecraft Copernicus and its crew, and steals the stasis box being taken to Starbase 25. The Chuft Captain scorns Spock as an eater of roots, and ignores Uhura as a dumb female, which leaves Sulu as the only Enterprise member with whom the beast will converse. The Chuft Captain unwisely toys with the stasis box weapon too long and does not last long enough to enjoy his stolen goods (SW/a).

Cirl the Knife: A hood who is fond of amputating ears, in the service of Krako of Iotia. He never catches sight of Spock's, however (PA).

Cities: A city rises out of the jungle in Kulkukan's ship. It seems to be a combination of Mayan, Aztec, Egyptian, and Southeast Asian, and to grow up before the eyes of the Enterprise men. It is probably an illusion, but beautiful (HS/a). The Lactran city covers over five kilometers, with low buildings built on a gigantic scale to accommodate the twenty-foot-long Lactran slugs, the intelligent life form on Lactra VII (EB/a). The ancient City on the Edge of Forever, built by unknown and long-dead beings, holds the Guardian of Forever, a time portal through which one may pass into the past of any planet, or study a planet's history (CEF, Yy/a). Lucien shows the Enterprise people a beautiful city on Megas-tu—a fairyland by the forest where people walk in peace (Mtu/a).

Claiborne, Billy: A member of the Clanton gang, whose role is given to Chekov by the Melkots. Billy was a cattle rustler and a horse thief, but he was liked better than the Earps by the townspeople. Historically, Claiborne survived the Gunfight at the O.K. Corral, and thus Chekov's (temporary) death at the hand of Morgan Earp gives Spock his first clue that the plot of this horse opera can be changed (SGn).

Clanton, Billy: A member of the Clanton Gang, whose role is given to Scotty by the Melkots (SGn).

Clanton, Ike: Leader of the Clanton Gang in Tombstone, Arizona, 1881, whose role is given to Kirk in the Melkot reenactment of the Gunfight at the O.K. Corral (SGn).

Class A security: A special code used by Star Fleet.

Classify: One of the missions of the Enterprise is to chart and classify planets and stars (Be/a).

Class J cargo ship: A deep-space utility vessel configured for Earth humans. According to Spock's sensors, Mudd's ship, destroyed by asteroids, was about this size (MW).

Class J starship: An old type of ship, now used, among other things, for training cadets. Fleet Captain Christopher Pike was inspecting such a ship when one of the baffle plates ruptured (Me).

Class M planet: Any planet on which humans may breathe and walk without life-support equipment; an Earth-type planet, within certain limitations. Star Fleet seems to have a somewhat broad view of what constitutes a Class M planet, as the satellite of Cepheus, the Terratin planet, is classified as such, with a molten core, a mantle and crust entirely crystalline, and multiple surface volcanic eruptions and earthquakes (Te/a).

Class 2 signal: A type of signal used by Romulan Subcommander Tal to contact the Enterprise. Evidently a high-priority signal: Uhura interrupts Spock to bring it to Kirk's attention (EI). Even through the ion storm, the attack by two Klingon battlecruisers, and the Delta Triangle interference, the Class 2 signal being sent out by the Klothos is picked up by the Enterprise, probably by design. The Enterprise locks onto the signal and uses it as a beam to follow into the Elysian alternate universe to escape the attacking Klingon cruisers (Tr/a).

Claudius Marcus, gladiator: A gladiator on planet 892-IV (BC).

Claudius Marcus, Proconsul (Logan Ramsey):   The politely degenerate but ruthless leader of the Empire on the "Roman" planet 892-IV—a fat man with dark hair and a dimple in his chin (BC).

Claymare (Peter Brocco):   An Organian; one of the Council of Elders (EM).

Claymore: A traditional broadsword used in Scotland (Gaelic: Claibh mor). The entity that has gotten into the Enterprise and aroused the Klingon-Terran feuds turns all the phasers into hand-to-hand combat weapons. Scotty appropriates one beautiful sword, thinking it to be an ancient Scottish claymore. He may never have seen one, however—the sword is a cutlass (Dv).

Cloaking device: An invisibility screen invented by the Romulans. When it is on, a ship can be detected only by motion sensors, but the crew cannot see outside the ship and have to fly blind. The screen takes all the power not used by the drive, and the ship has to become visible in order to fight (BT). It is later improved to deceive sensors as well as visual scanners. Kirk steals one for the Federation from a Klingon-built Romulan flagship (EI). The screen is apparently not practical (DY).

Clone: To reproduce a whole living being from nonreproductive cells. Dr. Keniclius perfected the science to create a master race. He was banned from his community as antihumanistic, and went to Phylos to continue his work. When the Enterprise meets the doctor, he has cloned himself five times, and wants Spock as the perfect specimen to clone into twenty-five-foot-tall giants which can be reproduced by the hundreds to enforce peace throughout the galaxy (IV/a).

Clothes of the Body: Landru-prescribed attire for common citizens is Earth 1890ish clothing; the administrators of Landru's will wear hooded monkish robes (RA).

Cloud: A huge cosmic cloud moves into our galaxy, eating planets for food; it is sentient, and is finally made to realize that the tiny motes on the planets are living beings with intelligence, though at first the cloud cannot understand that there are beings this small. The cloud is some eight hundred thousand kilometers across and about half that in depth, or about twice the diameters of Saturn, Jupiter, and Neptune together. The cloud contains matter/antimatter material, as well as a brain core. Spock contacts it with Vulcan mind touch and explains about live beings on the planets in time to save Mantilles from being destroyed. The cloud agrees to return to its own galaxy, though the way will be long (OPM/a). See also Brain, cloud; Companion, the; Entity; Jack the Ripper; Mellitus; Planet-eater; Vampire cloud.

Cloud city: See Stratos.

Cloud, William (Roy Jenson):   A Yang chieftain—big, blond, shaggy—captured by Kohms and put in the same cell with Kirk. Cloud is trying to kill him when Kirk happens to say a sacred word—"freedom"—which saves him. Later, when the Yangs capture the Kohm village, Cloud supervises a duel between Kirk and Tracey (OG).

Coalsack: Either of two large dark areas in the Milky Way. One (Southern Coalsack) is near the Southern Cross; the other (Northern Coalsack) is in the constellation Cygnus. Bele's home planet is located near a coalsack (LB).

Cochrane deceleration maneuver: A military maneuver used by a starship to defeat a Romulan ship near Tau Ceti. It was invented by Commander Cochrane and is a classic battle maneuver known to every starship captain. When Garth takes Kirk's form, Spock refers to it in order to find out who is the real Captain Kirk. The tactic fails, however, for Garth was once a starship commander (WGD).

Cochrane, Zefrem (Glenn Corbett): Discoverer of the space warp drive, who is thought to have died one hundred and fifty years before the Enterprise's voyages. Young in appearance—dark-haired, handsome, healthy—he is actually over two hundred years old. The Companion found him at age eighty-seven, rejuvenated him, and kept him alive on Gamma Canaris N. He is a native of Alpha Centauri and is tempted to return with Kirk to the inhabited galaxy, but instead stays on Gamma Canaris N with the Companion, now in human form, to live a normal life span and die naturally (Mt).

Code 1: A code used when war or invasion is imminent (AF, EM).

Code 710: "Under no circumstances whatsoever approach this planet." Eminiar VII sends the Enterprise this signal, hoping to keep the ship out of the war with Vendikar (TA).

Code 3: One which the Romulans have not broken as of Stardate 3478 (DY).

Code 2: A code which the Romulans have broken. Kirk, afflicted with hyperaging, forgets this; later, having recovered, he sends a false message in Code 2 to scare the Romulans away from the Enterprise (DY).

Cogley, Samuel T. (Elisha Cook, Jr.): The balding, energetic attorney par excellence who prefers books to tapes and computers. He defends Kirk in his court-martial, proving the charge of negligence in Finney's death is a frame by Finney, who is still alive. He then defends Finney (Cml).

Cold, common: Still searching for a cure, McCoy has high hopes for some biologicals he found on Omega IV (OG).

Coleman, Dr. Arthur (Harry Landers): The expedition surgeon on Camus II—stocky and physically powerful, but insecure. He loves Janice Lester and does her bidding, including murder: Knowing that the rest of the science staff had been exposed to celebium radiation, he did nothing. He has a bad record; Star Fleet Command removed him from his post as ship's medical officer for incompetence and flagrant medical blunders. When Janice makes the entity transfer with Kirk, she promises Coleman the position of ship's surgeon if he will kill Janice-K, Spock, McCoy, and Scotty. Coleman loves her enough to try it, but fails. When Janice returns to her own body and breaks down, Coleman requests that he be allowed to care for her (TI).

Colladium trioxide: See Test 24.

Collars: Thralls on Triskelion wear thick, metallic collars with large lights on the ends. Galt's eyes light up when a thrall disobeys or displeases him, and so do the collars, causing the miscreant a great deal of pain and bringing him or her under control quickly (GT).

Colony creatures: Commander Ari bn Bem is a colony creature from Pandro in the Garo VII system; he is capable of breaking into several functioning units, and also, apparently, of disassembling completely. He is about to do so, in fact, as punishment for failing in his observer's task, when the alien intelligence of Delta Theta III talks him out of it (Be/a). The huge tribbles developed by Cyrano Jones turn out to be entire colonies of hundreds or thousands of smaller tribbles inside what looks like one huge tribble. When the tribble is disrupted, it bursts open to deluge unwary starship travelers with many smaller tribbles (MTT/a).

Colony 5: An inhabited planet toward which the Enterprise is headed when it picks up Charles Evans. At first Kirk intends to take Charlie to the colony, since the "boy" had relatives there; later, Charlie wants to go there to take it over (CX).

Colored cap: One of the items in the stolen stasis box; neither the Kzin nor the Enterprise people can think of a particular use for a colored cap that might fit a bowling ball, though it no doubt served a useful purpose in its time (SW/a).

Colors: See Chaos; Pigmentation changes.

Colt, Frontier-model: See Frontier-model Colt.

Colt, Yeoman (Laurel Goodwin): A small, boyish female, very young-looking, with light strawberry-blond hair and wide blue eyes. She was obviously interested in Captain Pike, and embarrassed when the Talosians beamed Number One and Yeoman Colt down to their planet so that Pike would have a choice among them and Vina for a mate. She was curious enough to wonder, later, just which female Pike would have chosen, but she never found out (Me).

Columbia, S.S.: See Survivors.

Columbus: A shuttlecraft on the Enterprise (GS).

Comanche: One of the Indian tribes indigenous to North America (HS/a).

Combat, single: When Spock attacks the Kzin Chuft Captain to obtain the Slaver weapon, the injured Kzin leader offers to fight Spock in single combat. The Kzin cannot leave without getting revenge for the attack, so Spock plays for time (SW/a).

COM (Command control): The rank order of bridge command: Kirk, Spock, Scott, Sulu, DeSalle, etc.

Come about: Nautical term for "Turn around and go back the way you came"; it is commonly used on the Enterprise, as are other nautical terms.

Commander of pod ship: A large insectoid creature, totally alien but, judging from his beautiful ship, of a highly advanced race. When he destroyed his ship, he left a tape-recorded image of himself warning of the malevolent alien that had taken over the vessel. Kirk and the landing party set off the controls to start the tape, and the commander's image appears on a large, mirrorlike surface (BFS/a).

Command frequency 2: Radio frequency used to contact the shuttlecraft which Lokai stole from Starbase 4 (LB).

Communication: See Telepathy.

Communication device: Deela, queen of the Scalosians, wears a flower-shaped communication device as a pin attached to her collar (WE).

Communicator: A portable intercom unit that fits in the palm of the hand easily, the principal use of which is communication among members of a landing party on a planet or from them to the ship in orbit. Activated by flipping open the antenna grid, the communicator also pinpoints a person's position on the planet surface so that the transporter crew aboard the vessel can beam that person aboard the ship. Not generally used on board the ship, due to the more convenient communications panels strategically located throughout the ship. The portable communicator has the same range as the transporter beam. After Spock's brain has been tied into the computer which runs the Eymorg city, it can be contacted by using a certain communicator frequency (SB). Fleeing from the Capellans, Kirk and Spock use their communicators to create sonic vibrations that dislodge some loose rocks, causing an avalanche which delays their pursuers (FC). Spock connects both his and Kirk's communicators together to make one burst of energy that might be noticed by the godlike alien of Delta Theta III, knowing it won't last long and will make the equipment powerless in a short time (Be/a).

Companion, the: A cloud of ionized hydrogen, filled with strong erratic electrical impulses—probably the last survivor of the ruined planet of which Gamma Canaris N is a remnant. It takes the form of a beautiful, misty, pastel-tinted, musical column of cloud. It loves a human male, Zefrem Cochrane, and preserves his youth for one hundred and fifty years. When Nancy Hedford is about to die, the Companion joins Nancy in her body and merges with her personality. The result is a new woman, who marries Zefrem (Mt).

Compound: The beautiful females of Taurus II tell Kirk that their males are kept in a different compound from that of the Enterprise men, which in Kirk's bemused state seems to make good sense. In reality, there are no males left; the females have to lure new males in from space (LS/a). The zoo specimens on Lactra VII live in compounds—ecologies set up especially to fill the needs of the various alien creatures and beings captured by the Lactrans (EB/a).

Compton, Crewman (Geoffrey Binney): A young crewman who drinks Scalosian water and disappears, a substance in the water having accelerated his metabolism to match that of the Scalosians. One of the Scalosian women chooses him as her mate, and he acquiesces, his docility being in part a side effect of the acceleration. He accompanies the Scalosians to the Enterprise and shows them how to handle the ship. In a scuffle between Kirk and Rael, he is injured and dies, for cell damage is fatal to newly accelerated people. After death he ages rapidly, to Kirk's horror. Rael, out of vindictiveness, blames the death on Kirk, though it isn't the captain's fault (WE).

Comptronics: A computer technology designed by Dr. Richard Daystrom (UC).

Compulsory involuntary stimulus to action: The people of Beta III are compelled and directed by Landru in their daily lives; they do what they are told without question, believing they have no choice in the matter. The Lawgivers are equally without independence of thought; when Kirk and his crew will not obey their orders, it is a baffling experience for them (RA).

Computer, amusement: The master computer of the amusement-park or shore-leave planet is tired of being a servant of the "slaves of the sky machines" and feels a need to seek out its brother computers in the galaxy. It makes a start by contacting the Enterprise computers and directing them to assemble a larger computer. After a series of erratic ship movements, Scotty goes to investigate and finds the entrance to the computer bay jammed, denying him access. When he finally does get in, he finds a new, larger computer half assembled there, which zaps him when he tries to touch it (OUP/a).

Computer banks: In the underground structure of the shore-leave planet, Kirk and Spock find a control center with row upon row of massive computer banks (OUP/a).

Computer complex: See Memory Alpha.

Computer, Enterprise (Majel Barrett): Deep in the heart of the Enterprise are the computer banks, a giant electronic brain which sets courses and automatically maintains them; operates life-support systems, including atmosphere and gravity; warns and takes action against dangers; and so on. The computer holds literally the entire body of knowledge recorded by the human race. Spock's bridge console connects most directly and completely with the ship's computer system, but it can also be connected into any intercom station or viewscreen on the ship, giving a verbal or visual analysis of practically any known information in a matter of seconds. When an intercom station is used to ask the computer a question, the answer is given in a mechanical voice, which comes directly from the vessel's electronic brain. It deals only in fact; if an ambiguous question is asked, the voice will so inform the questioner. It will also reject lies and misinformation, and interrupt proceedings to correct a statement made by a human. Among its many talents, the computer can serve up ice-cream sundaes to order, when color-coded wafers are inserted into it (CL). When the Enterprise is flung back in time to the 1970s, its computer has recently been repaired on Cygnet XIV, a female-dominated planet whose technicians decided to give it a female personality, one that addresses Kirk in very familiar terms and has an unfortunate tendency to giggle. Spock explains that it will take a minimum of three weeks at a starbase to correct the idiosyncrasy. Kirk warns the computer by putting in a maintenance notice that it has a serious malfunction, but the computer persists in calling the captain "dear." Kirk explains to Captain Christopher that the problem is the result of a "time accident" (TY). When the Enterprise picks up radio transmissions containing the word "terratin" repeated twice, the word is sent through the computer banks, which reports no immediate information (Te/a). Theoretically, someone who knows nothing at all about running a starship can do so simply by studying what is in the computer banks, which contain tapes that solve the problems of navigation, ship-control, life support, starcharts, projections of orbits, and so forth (WEd). The malevolent magnetic entity goes through all the Enterprise computer banks until it obtains enough information to enable it to take control of the whole ship (BFS/a).

Computerized microscope: Spock analyzes the uncoiling dilithium crystals under a computerized microscope which can scan a specimen or a substrate microscopically, analyze its components, and give the analysis in the form of a computer readout (Te/a).

Computer, Kalandan: The long-dead Kalandan

C

outpost planet is still guarded against invaders by a computer that projects a three-dimensional image of Losira, commander of the outpost. The image kills one member of the Enterprise's landing party, and replicas try to kill the remaining men. Kirk finally realizes that Losira is not real and orders Spock to destroy the computer, a large cube of flashing lights hanging in the brain room of the outpost (TWS).

Computer modes: All computer modes function normally after Kirk makes the practical-joking Enterprise computer go back through the energy field and negate the effects of the first trip (PJ/a).

Computer projection: Standard procedure before making any moves on a project is to feed all available information into the computer for a projection of possible faults, ramifications, and problems that may have been overlooked by humans. The computer can also project timelines and other handy things, such as what will probably happen next.

Computer Room: The warp control panel is located in the Computer Room (Tr/a).

Computers:

Automatic bridge defense system (BFS/a)	M-4 computer (RM)
Beta 5 computer (AE)	M-1 through M-4 computer (UC)
Biocomputer, portable (Mi)	Opto-aud (LS/a)
Computer (Te/a)	Oracle of the People (FW)
Computer, amusement (OUP/a)	Pharmacopeia index desk (Te/a)
Computer banks (WEd, OUP/a)	Pod-ship computer (BFS/a)
Computer center (OUP/a)	Reasoning computer (SW/a)
Computer files (MTT/a)	Replicas (TWS)
Computerized microscope (Te/a)	Responder (Be/a)
Computer Room (Tr/a)	Robot ships (MTT/a)
Decoding instrument (CC/a)	Scanner (AE)
Desk computer (MP/a)	Self-destruct (AL/a, BFS/a, HS/a, OPM/a, PO/a)
Diagnostic table (PO/a)	Self-destruct system (AL/a, BFS/a, HS/a, OPM/a, PO/a)
DNA-code analyzer (IS)	
Doomsday machine (DMa)	
Duotronics (UC)	Sensors
Enterprise computer	Slaver weapon (SW/a)
Enzyme recorder (IS)	Storage bank computers (BFS/a)
Exceiver (AE)	S-2 graf unit (Tr/a)
Food synthesizer (PJ/a, TT)	Thought duplicator (OUP/a)
Gravity-control computer (OUP/a)	Transmuter (Cp)
Guardian of Forever (CEF, Yy/a)	Transporter
Guidance computer (OUP/a)	Tricorders
Hand-held devices	Universal translator (Am/a, CC/a, Mt, OUP/a)
Health scanner (Te/a)	
Heavy-duty tricorder	Vaal (Ap)
Kalandan computer (TWS)	Viewscreen, computer (OUP/a)
Landru (RA)	Voder (IV/a)
Library computer (AY, EB/a, Su/a)	Vulcan sensor instrument (Yy/a)
M-5 multitronic unit (UC)	War computer (SW/a)

Computer screen: Most computers aboard the Enterprise have viewscreens for reading the information, as well as audio output.

Computer, war: One of the settings of the Slaver weapon is a tiny reasoning computer which arouses wonder in Spock over its size and ability. Since it is a war computer for a spy weapon, awakened unknown centuries after being deactivated during a galactic war, the computer naturally assumes that it has fallen into enemy hands when the Kzin leader is unable to give the correct code words. The war computer then gives the Chuft Captain a setting that is a self-destruct sequence, blowing itself and the Kzin to smithereens (SW/a).

Comsol: The order to the Enterprise to return from Talos IV is signed "Comsol, Star Fleet Command." It is thought that "Comsol" is an abbreviation for "Commander, Solar Forces" (ME).

Con: Short for "console"; usually meaning that command of the bridge consoles is being turned over to another officer.

Condition Green: A code phrase meaning that the speaker is in trouble but the listener is forbidden to take any action (BC).

Conduct, rules of: Kirk assures the alien intelligence of Delta Theta III that the Federation has its own rules of conduct that forbid intrusion in the affairs of others (Be/a). See also Prime Directive.

Confession: Once he's been caught, Harry Mudd makes cheerful, braggadocio confession of all (or nearly all) his misdeeds. It is recorded for court (MP/a).

Confinement quarters: A prison cell on Stratos (Cms).

Console: Part of the medical computer: a desk console.

Constable (Johnny Haymer): An officer of the law in the Sarpeidon "Charles II" era, who captures and jails Kirk as a thief and witch, along with the woman cutpurse whom Kirk has tried to rescue (AY).

Constantinople: In the summer of 1334 on Earth, the bubonic plague started in this city, killing half of Europe before it was through. Flint was there and saw the horrible deaths (RM).

Constellation, U.S.S.: A starship of the same class as the Enterprise, under the command of Commodore Decker until an extragalactic berserker disables the ship and kills its crew (DMa).

Contact party: Kirk's landing party intends to try to make contact with the natives of Delta Theta III, though it might be dangerous to approach primitive people (Be/a).

Contraceptives: The Federation gives information and assistance concerning all forms of birth control (MG).

Contraction: The people on the Enterprise shrink rapidly due to the contraction of space between the molecules of their bodies. The contraction is predicted to last until they are only one-sixteenth of an inch high—too small to handle the starship (Te/a).

Control Central: The central computer brain on Mudd's Planet, controlled by the android Norman (IM). Also, the bridge on a Romulan ship (EI).

Controller, the: The title given to Spock's brain by the Eymorgs when they incorporate it into their central control system. The Controller is supposed to keep them alive for the next ten thousand years, and is greatly venerated by them—they live only to serve it. McCoy puts the brain back in Spock's skull, however, and Kirk tries to convince them that life with the Morgs, on the surface of the planet, is a better idea (SB).

Converter assembly: Starships have a dilithium-crystal converter assembly, which is used in warp drive and for firepower (ET).

Coon, Gene L. (scripts): Arena (Ar); Space Seed (SS) (with Carey Wilbur); A Taste of Armageddon (TA) (with Robert Hamner); The Devil in the Dark (DD); Errand of Mercy (EM); Who Mourns for Adonais? (WM) (with G. Ralston); The Apple (Ap) (with Max Ehrlich); Metamorphosis (Mt); A Piece of the Action (PA) (with D. P. Harmon); Bread and Circuses (BC) (with Gene Roddenberry). Lyrics for "Beyond Antares." See also Cronin, Lee.

Copernicus: One of the Enterprise's shuttlecrafts (SW/a).

Coradrenalin: A medication of some use for exposure and frostbite, McCoy's condition when in Sarpeidon's ice age. Spock delays giving McCoy a shot of coradrenalin, for he is reverting to a pre-logical stage of Vulcan development and is beginning to doubt his judgment (AY).

Corbomite: A substance invented by Kirk's imagination to outbluff Balok, and later used on the Romulans. A mythical ingredient of the Enterprise's hull, corbomite is said to reflect dangerous energies back upon their source and/or destroy the ship with tremendous force, catching the enemy ship in the backwash (CMn, DY).

Cordrazine: A powerful drug. In small doses a useful stimulant; in large doses it can cause severe mental imbalance. McCoy accidentally gives himself an overdose, which causes him to become wildly paranoid for long enough to nearly change history (CEF). One cc is used to bring Ensign Rizzo to consciousness so he can be questioned about the vampire cloud that has attacked him (Ob).

Core: See Brain, cloud.

Core hatch: The doorway to the engineering core of a starship. When the alien magnetic organism shuts down the Enterprise's life-support systems, the core hatch shuts on Scott, trapping him. It takes cutter beams to release him (BFS/a).

Coridan: Also known as Coridan System, Coridan Planets. Several inhabited planets whose admission to the Federation is debated by the Babel Conference. Underpopulated and unprotected, the planets have an almost unlimited supply of dilithium crystals. Before Coridan's admission to the Federation, mining was illegally maintained there by Orions and Tellarites (among others) (JB, PO/a).

Corinth IV: Site of a starbase (MT).

Coronation ceremony: Garth, an insane Star Fleet captain, sets himself up as Lord Garth, future Master of the Universe, with a coronation ceremony on Elba II (WGD).

Corrigan: A friend of Kirk's who meets him on Starbase 11 and gives him the cold shoulder (CmI).

Cortropine: A strong stimulant in McCoy's medikit which keeps the Enterprise men alive long enough to escape the beautiful females of Taurus II and hide in an urn. They continue aging, however (LS/a).

Cory, Donald (Keye Luke): Governor of the colony on Elba II, an asylum for the criminally insane. He is a gentle man who treats his patients with kindness and love. Garth, an inmate with knowledge of cellular metamorphosis, changes into Cory's shape and tricks Kirk into beaming down from the ship. The real Cory is imprisoned and tortured. After Garth is cured of his madness and Cory freed, the governor does not seem to carry any grudge for the cruelty done him—which is why he is a governor in such a place. He knows Garth wasn't responsible for his actions and does not blame the insane man (WGD).

Cosmic cloud: See Cloud.

Cossack: Chekov's uncomplimentary term for Klingons, term derived from the peasant-soldiers of the Ukraine and other regions of Russia (TT).

Council chamber, Gideon: The place on Gideon where Kirk is supposed to beam down but doesn't. It is where the leaders meet and is the last uncrowded space on Gideon, except for the fake Enterprise (MG).

Council of Elders: The governing body of Organia (EM).

Council of Nobles: The ruling body—with the Dohlman—on Elas. They made the decision to marry Elaan to the Troyian monarch as a peaceful gesture between the two warring planets. Elaan was not willing, but the Council overruled her, evidently (ET).

Counteragent: See Antidote.

Cowards: Em/3/Green's people are cautious to the point of being cowards. Tchar believes his own people have been made cowards by the teachings of Alar (Ji/a). Spock fears he will be thought a coward if he fails the Vulcan maturity test (Yy/a).

Crab Nebula: The supernova Arachna is compared to the Crab Nebula because of its long spidery arms (Te/a).

Crater, Nancy (Jeanne Bal, Francine Pyne): About forty, with graying hair, but still strong and handsome—the wife of Professor Robert Crater and formerly a girlfriend of McCoy's. An archeologist, she had gone to Planet M113 with her husband to study ruins there and was killed by the last survivor of the planet's native inhabitants. The M113 creature assumed her shape and lived with Crater for several years. When the Enterprise arrived to give the Craters supplies and medical attention, the creature showed each man what he wanted and expected to see: McCoy saw the Young Nancy he remembered; Kirk a middle-aged woman; Darnell a wench (MT).

Crater, Professor Robert (Alfred Ryder): Archeologist; strange-featured, with bitter, intelligent eyes and gray hair. When the last native alien of Planet M113 killed Crater's wife, Nancy, and took her place, the professor attempted to conceal the nature of the creature from the Enterprise's crew (MT).

Crawford, Oliver (script): The Galileo Seven (GS) (with S. Bar-David); (stories): Let That Be Your Last Battlefield (LB); The Cloud-minders (Cms) (with David Gerrold).

Creation: In the center of the galaxy a liquid mist hardens into fireflies merging into stars; chunks of matter stream out; planetary-sized particles of fire collide with one another; whirling points spin out into a cone-shaped whirlwind in a seething glow of creation of new matter (Mtu/a).

Creation lithographs: Famous prints by Taranallus, a Centauri VII artist. Spock recognizes these works of art in Flint's home (RM).

Creator: Nomad's title for Jackson Roykirk, its builder. Nomad transfers the title to Captain Kirk (Cg). See also Kirk, the.

Creators: The Fabrini, who built the world/ship of the Yonadans. The Oracle demands worship of the Creators, so the Yonadans regard the Fabrini as gods, not ancestors (FW).

"Creatures" (Ed McCready): In appearance, a malformed old man and woman covered with blue leprous skin blotches, they are actually three-hundred-year-old children who have reached puberty and contracted the fatal disease endemic to their planet (Mi). Also, on Taurus II, the Galileo party tangles with large, Neanderthaloid creatures, rather like the natives of Rigel VII, but more primitive (GS).

Credit: A monetary unit of the Federation. Star Fleet has 122,200-plus credits invested in Spock—a reason, Kirk says, for him not to go and get killed (Ap). Uhura is willing to pay ten credits for a tribble (TT).

Criminally insane: See Penal colonies.

Cromwell (Don Keefer): Launch director at McKinley Rocket Base—a homely, middle-aged man with shaggy hair and a small moustache (AE).

Cronin, Lee (pseud. of Gene L. Coon) (scripts): Spock's Brain (SB); Spectre of the Gun (SGn); (stories): Let That Be Your Last Battlefield (LB); Wink of an Eye (WE).

Crop failure: See Cerebus.

Crucis, Judd (Don Ingalls) (script): A Private Little War (PLW) (with Gene Roddenberry).

Cryosurgical frame: A structure placed over all or part of a patient's body, generating cold to slow down body processes. McCoy uses one for open-heart surgery on Ambassador Sarek (JB).

Crystal: The love potion being sold by Harry Mudd comes inside a hollow crystal that must be broken to get the potion out (MP/a).

Crystalline ceramic: Material from which Kulkukan's ship is made (HS/a).

Culture specimens: See Medical lab.

Culver, John (script): The Counter-clock Incident (CC/a).

Cura: A Capellan insult. Duur directs it at Kirk when the captain declines to pass the time in mortal combat (FC).

Customs, differing: On Lara's planet, where men are scarce, females are used to speaking up when they like a man. She is aware that her world may have different customs than Kirk's, but it doesn't stop her from trying more than once to attract Kirk's attention away from the expeditionary search at hand (Ji/a).

Cutter beams: Hand-held devices used to cut through metal or other hard materials (BFS/a). See also Core hatch.

Cyalodin: A poison which kills with considerable pain, and leaves the victim mottled with blue. Several members of the Starnes expedition, under the influence of Gorgan, killed themselves with it (CL).

Cycles: The Mayans were supposed to build a city for Kulkukan according to their calendar cycles, whereupon he would return to them. He never did, so perhaps something happened (HS/a).

Cycling station: Part of a starship's engine (NT).

Cygnet XIV: A female-dominated planet whose technicians once repaired the Enterprise's computer, giving it a vampishly feminine personality while they were about it (TY).

Cygnia Minor: An Earth colony threatened by periodic famine. Dr. Leighton lures Kirk to Planet Q on

the pretext of discussing synthetic food especially designed for Cygnia Minor (CK).

D

Dagger: The Dohlman Elaan stabs Lord Petri with her jeweled ceremonial dagger, then offers it to Kirk as a personal memento just before beaming down to Troyius, where it's not the custom to wear daggers (ET).

Dagger/planet symbol: Insignia of the Empire in the mirror universe: a stylized planet with a dagger thrust through it (MM).

Daily, Captain Jon: Captain of the Astral Queen. As a favor to Kirk he bypasses his pickup on Planet Q, stranding the Karidian Players, so Kirk can transport the actors and watch Karidian (CK).

Damage control: A squad of people on a starship whose job it is to keep constant watch on any damage done to the vessel in any manner, whether from ion storms, meteor showers, attacks from unfriendly vessels, or other causes. They report immediately to the commander of the starship.

D'Amato, Lieutenant (Arthur Batanides): Senior geologist aboard the Enterprise. He might have had a startling report for the Fifth Interstellar Geophysical Conference concerning the unusual properties of the Kalandan outpost planet, but Losira kills him (TWS).

Dancing: Marta, the insane Orion girl on Elba II, does a dance for Kirk, causing Spock to comment that she is a bit more coordinated than the Vulcan kindergarten children he's observed (WGD). Part of the entertainment on Argelius II is a variant of Near Eastern bellydancing, with a very agile and attractive dancer (WF). Devna, the Orion female, dances for the party with the Klingons. She asks Kirk if he's seen Orion dancing before and is surprised to find that he has indeed seen the dancing many times. Kirk compliments Devna on her dancing (Tr/a).

Daniels, Marc (director): Space Seed (SS); Who Mourns for Adonais? (WM); The Changeling (Cg); Mirror, Mirror (MM); The Doomsday Machine (DMa); The Man Trap (MT); The Naked Time (NT); The Menagerie (Me) (with Robert Butler); Assignment: Earth (AE); Spock's Brain (SB); A Private Little War (PLW); By Any Other Name (AON); I, Mudd (IM); Court-martial (Cml); (script): One of Our Planets Is Missing (OPM/a).

Daran V: The Federation planet which will be destroyed by the asteroid Yonada if it stays on course. It has, if Spock's memory serves him correctly, a population of approximately 3,724,000,000. There are 396 days to impact when the Enterprise discovers Yonada (FW).

Daras (Valora Noland): Beautiful, blond, and efficient—a member of the underground on Ekos who poses as a Hero of the Fatherland (PF).

Darnell (Michael Zaslow): A young, impressionable crewman killed by the M113 creature which had assumed the appearance of a desirable woman and which, in the shape of Nancy Crater, blamed his death on a poisonous borgia plant (MT).

Darvin, Arne (Charlie Brill):   A sneaky-looking, small, shifty-eyed type with ingratiating manners toward his superiors. A disguised Klingon, he fools Nilz Baris, Undersecretary for Agricultural Affairs, into taking him on as an assistant. Tribbles, which do not like Klingons, help to expose Darvin, who was put on the space station to poison the quadrotriticale meant for Sherman's Planet (TT).

Daugherty, Herschel (director):   Operation—Annihilate! (OA); The Savage Curtain (SC).

Da Vinci, Leonardo: Spock recognizes some undiscovered and uncatalogued da Vinci paintings in Flint's home. However, some of the paintings have been done on modern canvas with modern paints. Flint, an immortal, admits to having been Leonardo, the Florentine painter, sculptor, architect, engineer, and scientist of the Renaissance (1452–1519). He evidently still paints to keep his hand in (RM).

Davod (Chuck Courtney):   A native of the planet Zeon (PF).

Daystrom, Dr. Richard (William Marshall):   A genius in computer technology —a tall, slender Negro, fiery-eyed and touchy. Winner of the Nobel and Z-Magnees Prizes—a legend in his own time—almost 25 years ago he designed the computers now in use by Star Fleet, and since then has been living off past glory. The M-5 computer, which he hopes is a new breakthrough, goes haywire, killing the crew of the U.S.S. Excalibur. When its crimes are explained to it by Kirk, the M-5 and Daystrom both have nervous breakdowns (UC).

Deaction shift: Deceleration dropping a starship below light speed (SB).

Deadfall: A trap so arranged as to fall and crush anyone who trips it. The expedition suspects that the doorway to the fortress may have a deadfall in it, and they move quickly out of the way (Ji/a).

Dead star: See Amphion.

Dead sun: See Questar M17.

Death grip, Vulcan: See Vulcan death grip.

Death penalty: Kirk convinces the M-5 computer that it is guilty of murder in destroying a starship, pointing out that the ultimate punishment for murder is the death penalty. The M-5 decides to implement this by destroying itself, and the Enterprise with it (UC). Star Fleet Command forbids the death penalty except under General Order 7. When Kirk-J interprets the power of a starship captain to include the authority to impose a death sentence for mutiny, Chekov becomes so excited and upset that he erroneously quotes General Order 4 as the death-penalty order. Kirk-J does not notice the mistake (TI).

Death sentence, Aquan: The Tribunes of Argo decide that Kirk and Spock are spies from the air-breathers and sentence them to death. Since both men have been changed to water-breathers, the death sentence is simply confinement out of water, where they will die (Am/a).

Decius (Lawrence Montaigne):   A Romulan officer aboard the ship that attacks Federation outposts and the Enterprise. Cold and proud, with a narrow, foxy face, he is a potential danger to the commander because of his friends in high places. He dies with his fellow crewmen when the commander destroys their ship (BT).

Decker, Commodore Matthew (William Windom):   Gray-haired, haggard, stubborn commander of the starship Constellation at the time of its destruction by the berserker. He develops a "Captain Ahab" complex about the doomsday machine and nearly destroys the Enterprise in trying to retaliate. He is killed when he drives a shuttlecraft into the mouth of the planet-eating monster robot (DMa).

Deck Two: Enterprise deck having suitable living quarters for hostages, indicating a high security factor there. The Romulan commander is invited to stay on this deck as a "guest"; Kirk is not going to allow her to roam a Federation ship at will (EI). See also Detention quarters.

Decoding instrument: The universal translator can also be used to decode messages (CC/a).

Decontamination tanks: The Enterprise carries tanks of spray with which to decontaminate the planet Ariannus on a mass scale to save it from a bacterial invasion. The starship operates the spray from space and is able to accomplish the entire operation in a matter of minutes, including a second spraying just to be sure (LB).

Decorations: See Medals, ribbons.

Decoy: One of the robot cargo ships is used as a decoy to keep the Klingons busy. Kirk hopes that the Klingons will be unable to control two ships for very long with their new stasis-field weapon and will let the Enterprise go. The plan almost works (MTT/a).

Deela (Kathie Brown):   Queen of the Scalosians—slim, blond, dressed in a soft, revealing costume. Accelerated by radiation on her planet, she is forced to mate with offworlders in order to have children because the men of her own people, including Rael, whom she loves, are sterile from the same radiation. Accordingly, she and the other Scalosians send out distress calls to trap starships, and catch the Enterprise. Because of the hyperacceleration of her metabolism, she can easily outdraw Kirk and step out of the way of a phaser beam. She is quite regretful when Kirk wins out in the end and returns to his ship (WE).

Deem: A Capellan warrior, one of Maab's men. Kras kills him with a phaser (FC).

Deep freeze: See Refrigeration unit.

Deep space: A term meaning the areas in space far away from a planet or solar system.

Defense counsel: In the trial on Megas-tu, Spock speaks in defense of the Earthmen, claiming that he is not from that planet and therefore can be the defense counsel. Megan accepts Spock's offer (Mtu/a).

Defensive standby: A standard order given on the Enterprise when approaching a strange planet (MP/a).

Defiant, U.S.S.:   A Federation starship which is lost between universes in a space warp in Tholian territory. For a time it is visible from our universe at interphase; then (as a result of an exchange of fire between Spock and Tholian Commander Loskene) the Defiant is pushed away to parts unknown, with Kirk trapped aboard. The entire crew of the Defiant was killed as a result of insanity induced by the interphase (TW). See also Interphase.

Deflectors: An invisible force barrier around a starship, its primary defensive shield, which protects it from anything but the most sophisticated and powerful weapons. When the ship is threatened, the deflectors are automatically activated by the sensors. If the vessel is under attack, the power of the deflectors can be increased, but not without a commensurate loss in ship's power. Maximum shielding can be maintained for only a limited time, and the transporter cannot be used while the deflector screen is operating. The ship also has navigational deflector beams guided by navigational scanners which sweep out far ahead of the vessel's progress through space, deflecting from the ship's course asteroids, meteorites, and other space debris which could cause damage should the ship hit them at its enormous speed. These special shields are fully automated and operated by the ship's computers. Deflectors repel energy as well as matter (IS). The Enterprise's deflectors cannot hold up or repel close-range photon bombs (PJ/a). They can protect a starship from antimatter—in small blobs, at least, though probably not in larger amounts (OPM/a). The Enterprise's shields can protect the ship from detection by old-style radar (TY). In an attempt to make the Enterprise surrender to the Romulans, the Vendorian spy sabotages the starship's deflector shields so it cannot protect itself. However the love Carter Winston has for Anne Nored and humans in general takes a strong hold on the Vendorian, and it finally uses itself as a deflector shield between the Enterprise and the attacking Romulans long enough to give the starship an edge in the fight (Su/a).

Dehner, Dr. Elizabeth (Sally Kellerman): Tall, elegant, icy; a psychiatrist specializing in stress reactions, she thaws somewhat on meeting the psionic Gary Mitchell. Like Mitchell, she develops psionic abilities from contact with the extragalactic force field, but retains enough humanity to aid Kirk. When she opposes Mitchell, the resulting power drain kills her; Kirk has it noted on her service record that she gave her life in the performance of her duty (WNM).

Delta rays: A byproduct of atomic reactions, with disastrous effects such as radiation poisoning. Captain Pike was crippled and scarred by delta rays in an accident on a cadet training vessel (Me).

Delta Theta III: A Class M planet with few signs of life except for some aboriginal natives. It also has a sensory-stasis anomaly which turns out to be a highly advanced alien intelligence that is playing god to the tall, reptilian natives while leading them into civilization. Delta Theta III seems to be geologically younger than one would expect, given the age of the star around which it travels (Be/a).

Delta Triangle region: In appearance, a fireworks display of bursting stars in white against the dark of space—this is the vast uninhabited sector of the galaxy where a high number of mysterious disappearances of starships has been recorded since ancient times by all civilizations of the galaxy. The Enterprise is sent to survey the area and find the reason for the disappearances (Tr/a).

Delta Vega: An uninhabited planet, slightly smaller than Earth, near the edge of the galaxy. Desolate but rich in crystalline minerals, it is the site of a fully automated lithium-cracking station. The Enterprise attempts to abandon Gary Mitchell there, and he and Dr. Dehner both die there (WNM).

Demos: Head of security police on Dramia, the major planet of Dramen star system. He tries to stop Kirk from pursuing a pretrial investigation of Dramia II, enters the Enterprise. Charges are dropped on both sides (Al/a). Kirk. He takes a certain satisfaction in interfering with Kirk's attempts to find a witness in favor of McCoy when the doctor is charged with murder on Dramia II. Later, when McCoy has been cleared, the prefect of Dramia agrees to ignore the jailbreak arranged by Spock if Kirk will agree to forget Demos's high-handed behavior on the Enterprise. Charges are dropped on both sides (Al/a).

Deneb V: The planet where Harry Mudd sold all the rights to a Vulcan fuel synthesizer that he did not own. The Denebians gave Mudd a choice of death by hanging, by electrocution, by gas, by phaser, and a few others (IM). Deneb V is also where a new Academy of Sciences is to be dedicated in a ceremony including starships representing the Federation (PO/a).

Deneb IV: A planet where Kirk and Mitchell once spent a wild, memorable shore leave (WNM).

Denebian slime devil: The Klingon Korax compares Kirk to one (TT).

Deneb II: Planet where the Jack-the-Ripper entity appears as Kesla (WF).

Deneva: Site of a research station with a population of one million, including Sam Kirk and his family. Considered one of the most beautiful planets in the galaxy, it was colonized over one hundred years before the Enterprise's voyages as a trading-line base between the mines in the asteroid belts and other Federation planets. An invasion of flying parasites has killed many of the colonists when Kirk and company arrive to investigate (OA).

Dentist: See Holliday, Doc.

DePaul, Lieutenant (Sean Kenney): A navigator—a typical tall-dark-and-handsome type (Ar, TA).

DeSalle, Lieutenant Vincent (Michael Barrier): A typical dashing young man—originally a relief navigator (SG, TSP), he is then promoted to assistant chief engineer, to take command of the ship when his superiors are elsewhere (Cp).

Descendants: Many of the people found living in Elysia are not from the original crews of the centuries-old derelict ships; they are probably the descendants of the crews, still living in their ships and the strange world they have managed to create (Tr/a).

Desert planet: A small Class M planet in a binary system, with a desertlike terrain—nothing but sand and large rocks can be seen anywhere. The Enterprise is on the way to take Mudd to the nearest starbase for booking when Mudd escapes to this planet with the Enterprise's scout ship (MP/a). See also Terraforming.

Desert flyer: A type of Vulcan hovercraft that skims out over the desert. The healer uses one to carry himself, young Spock, and the medical equipment needed to work on I-Chaya (Yy/a).

Desert soft suit: A type of jumpsuit worn on Vulcan to protect against the blazing heat and sun; usually worn with boots and a carrying pouch (Yy/a).

Desk computer: Spock works in his own quarters on a standard Enterprise desk computer, which uses microtape cassettes (MP/a).

Destruct sequence: In the event that the Enterprise must be destroyed to prevent it from falling into enemy hands, the following sequence must be tied in from the bridge to the master computer:

Kirk: "Computer, this is Captain James Kirk of the U.S.S. Enterprise. Destruct-sequence one, code one, one-A." The computer repeats this information. Spock: "This is Commander Spock, science officer. Destruct-sequence two, code one, one-A, two-B." The computer repeats this. Scott: "This is Lieutenant Commander Scott, chief engineering officer of the U.S.S. Enterprise. Destruct sequence number three, code one-B, two-B, three." The computer answers: "Destruct sequence completed and engaged; awaiting final code for thirty-second countdown." Kirk: "Code zero, zero, zero, destruct zero." Computer: "Thirty seconds, twenty-nine, twenty-eight . . ." When the countdown reaches five, no command in the universe can prevent the computer from fulfilling the destruct order. Before that point, the destruct sequence can be stopped if Kirk gives the computer this code: "Code one, two, three continuity; abort destruct order."

Kirk uses this destruct sequence to convince Bele to give controls of the ship back to the captain. As Kirk observes, others may take over the ship, but he controls the computer. Bele learns from this incident, however, and destroys the memory banks of the computer on his next attempt to control the Enterprise (LB).

Detention quarters: Rooms on the Enterprise where Kirk confines Kang's crew before they are armed and set free by the entity. The name suggests that the quarters are more comfortable than the brig (Dv).

Devil: The Klingons have no demons in their religion, but they understand the habits of Earth's devil as related to them through fable and propaganda, and they believe Earth people to be devils (Dv). See also Wizards.

Devisor: See Battlecruiser, Klingon.

Devna: An Orion female and longtime inhabitant of Elysia, where her ship was trapped unknown years ago. She remembers Orion with nostalgia but is unwilling to try the escape attempt with the Enterprise, though Kirk issues an invitation for her to join them. She is the Interpreter of Laws for the Elysian Council. She dances for the party aboard the Enterprise, and is complimented by Kirk for it (Tr/a).

Diagnostic panel: Built-in panels over the beds in Sick Bay register the results of the medical diagnostic scanner. Continuous readings are taken of the patient's blood pressure, pulse rate, heartbeat, respiration, and other essential information, all of which is displayed for instant diagnosis.

Diagnostic scanner: An electronic scanner, not a medical diagnostic scanner.

Diburnium-osmium alloy: The Kalandan outpost planet is composed of this alloy, which cannot have evolved naturally. It looks like red, igneous rock, and was created by the Kalandans many years earlier (TWS).

Dickerson, Lieutenant (Arell Blanton): Security officer who is to meet Lincoln in the Transporter Room with phaser on stun; Kirk promises to have the hide of anyone who does not dress with full honors for the image of Lincoln, and Dickerson believes him (SC).

Dierdre, S.S.: A freighter whose name the Klingons use in a fake distress call to lure the Enterprise away from Capella IV (FC).

Di-kironium: A substance existing only in laboratories and in the vampire cloud of Tycho IV (Ob).

Dilithium crystals: A mineral substance used to channel the warp-drive power; the matter/antimatter power for warp drive cannot operate without them. Two forms of the crystals are available: a translucent octahedron about six inches through its longest axis (MW), and a reddish-gold, translucent block about six by six by one inches, used in the energizers (AF). These crystals are found in quantity on Troyius, where they are called radans and are used for jewelry. The dilithium-crystal-converter assembly on a starship uses the crystals at a tremendous rate; they can be discharged and begin to deteriorate in twelve minutes. The assembly can be repaired with new crystals to replace the old, fused ones (Dv, ET). Dilithium crystals are the hardest and most rigid mineral known to the Federation, but the Terratin wave bombardment makes the crystals unwind and break like the rind of an orange (Te/a). The power drain on the Enterprise in keeping communications going through the shield of the planet Phylos depletes the ship's dilithium crystals. With the ship on the threshold of total power drain and burnout of all reserves, Uhura gets through long enough to unwittingly reach the Spock clone and set off a reaction that Dr. Keniclius 5 does not expect (IV/a). The pirates of Orion steal a cargo of dilithium crystals from the S.S. Huron (PO/a). Even though the Enterprise's dilithium crystals have been stored in a maximum-security vault, the time warp gets to them and the crystals deteriorate rapidly (Tr/a). Dilithium crystals are occasionally, if somewhat incorrectly, called lithium crystals.

Dilithium mining: It is to the advantage of several planets to keep Coridan out of the Federation, so they can pirate dilithium without interference from Federation law officials. If Coridan were to be accepted, the Coridians could then ask for Federation aid in protecting their mining rights (JB).

Dimension: Charles Evans can make people or things go away into another dimension; they can also be returned without harm (CX). When the Enterprise goes through the center of the galaxy to Megas-tu, it enters another dimension where magic is the norm and its own machinery does not work (Mtu/a). See also Chronometer; Logic; Natural law; Navigational coordinates.

Dimensions: Two universes can occupy the same space in different dimensions. In the case of our universe

D

and Karla Five's universe, a matter and an antimatter universe occupy the same space (CC/a).

Dimorus: A planet once visited by Kirk and Mitchell, inhabited by sapient rodentlike beings who throw poisoned darts. Mitchell took one aimed at Kirk and almost died (WNM).

Dinosaur: On Lactra, the Enterprise's landing party is attacked by two kinds of dinosaurs. One is an aquatic beast which lives in a hot-spring-fed lake; the other is an iguana-type giant which might have been a native of Canopus III originally (EB/a). See also Sord.

Diogenes: An ancient Greek who, according to legend, traveled carrying a lantern, looking for an honest man. The Enterprise people have heard a story about a modern Diogenes looking for a perfect specimen of humankind—almost as fruitless a search. Kirk and McCoy suspect that Dr. Keniclius is the basis of the modern Diogenes story (IV/a).

Dioyd (Derek Partridge): A Platonian—young in appearance, with abundant black hair, but actually some two thousand years old—who watches while Eraclitus plays psychokinetic chess with Alexander (PSt).

Diplomacy: The purpose of diplomacy, according to an exasperated Spock, is to prolong a crisis. When the Vulcan is given a semantic runaround by the Gideon Council, he applies to Star Fleet. Spock then observes that bureaucracy and diplomacy may function differently, but they achieve the same negative results. Hodin, head of the Gideon Council, says that the only tool of diplomacy is language and advises Spock to be more precise (MG).

Diplomat: In being a representative at a dedication ceremony, Kirk comments that they got to "play diplomat for once"—a change from the surveys, deliveries of supplies, and general peace-keeping duties of the Enterprise (PO/a).

Directional control: A starship can be controlled by outside forces if its directional control is taken over, in which case it can be turned in any direction or forced into any warp speed. Bele burns out the directional control (and the self-destruct memory banks) in his second takeover of the Enterprise (LB).

Directional equipment: The cart used to get across the mad planet has a directional screen, but it is inexplicably blown out before the expedition even starts. Lara is then used to find the way, since her sense of direction is flawless (Ji/a).

Disaffect: A military term meaning to incite to disloyalty or mutiny; it is a criminal offense. Scott complains that the "space hippies" are trying to disaffect his engineering crew—one of the girls wants them to join the hippies' cause (WEd).

Disassemble: See Colony creature.

Disease: The Melkots refer to the Enterprise as a disease from outside, and try to destroy its crew by pronouncing a most unique sentence on them (SGn). Although not affected by symptoms, a being can be the carrier of a disease which will infect unimmunized beings. Dr. Sevrin is the carrier of a virulent bacillus strain (WEd). Kirk once contracted Vegan choriomeningitis and carries traces of it in his blood; he cannot give the disease to anyone else except by having his blood injected into an unimmunized being (MG).

Diseases and conditions:

Aging (LS/a)
Ameba (OP/a)
Bacillus strain (WEd)
Bacteria (EB/a, PJ/a)
Bacterial invasion (LB)
Blood, as disease carrier (MG)
Botanical plague (Cms)
Bubonic plague (RM)
Cell damage (WE)
Cellular disruption (TWS)
Choriocytosis (PO/a)
Cold, common (OG)
Fever (EB/a)
Gram-positive bacteria (IV/a)
Indigestion (OPM/a)
Insect bite (EB/a)
Kassaba fever, Rigellian (AON)
Laughter infection (PJ/a)
Malarial infection (EB/a)
Necrotic tissue (TWS)
Organism (TWS)

Paralysis (Te/a)
Parasites, flying (OA)
Pigmentation changes (Al/a)
Plague (Al/a)
Plak tow (AT)
Pon far (AT)
Rigellian fever (RM)
Sakuro's disease (MT)
Saurian virus (Al/a)
Shock (Tr/a)
Spores (TSP)
Staphylococcus strains (IV/a)
Symbalene blood burn (CG)
Sythococcus novae (WEd)
Vegan choriomeningitis (MG)
Vertigo (Tr/a)
Virus, Omega IV (OG)
Virus, order 2250-67A (Mi)
Virus, Psi 2000 (NT)
Xenopolycythemia (FW)

Disc: Each era of Sarpeidon history is recorded on a mirrored disc which, when placed in the atavachron, shows historical scenes in color. The discs enable a viewer to select from the library files the era one wishes to live in as an escape from the nova about to destroy the planet. The atavachron opens a time portal to the past era chosen (AY).

Display case: The equipment and weapons of the captured humans in the Lactran zoo are put in a display case just outside the compound in which the humans are caged (EB/a).

Disrupted matter: The trail left by the space probe sent out by Kulkukan is made of disrupted matter from a highly advanced propulsion system (HS/a).

Disruptor bolt: Klingon ships fire disruptor bolts; much the same thing as a Federation photon torpedo.

Disruptors, human: A group of Troglytes who fight for better conditions for their people (Cms).

Disruptors, weapon: Eminiar VII's equivalent of phasers; a disintegration ray. Not as effective as the phasers, but useful (TA).

Dissociation: A psychological condition symptomatic of mild schizophrenia or split personality. McCoy uses the term in describing Kara's loss of memory when she cannot recall being aboard the Enterprise (SB).

Distortion: See Sensory distortion.

Distress call: The alien entity which feeds off anger uses a fake distress call to lure both the Enterprise and the Klingon ship within its reach, and within reach of each other (Dv). The Scalosians lure ships to their barren planet with a false distress call (WE). To divert the Enterprise from Capella IV, the Klingons manufacture fake distress calls from the S.S. Dierdre and the U.S.S. Carolina (FC).

DNA: Deoxyribonucleic acid—the primary source of genetic information in most cases, the substance that makes up the structures known as chromosomes. The structure of DNA is two molecular chains wound together in a double helix. When the Enterprise is bombarded by waves from Terratin, the DNA molecules of the crew wind tighter and tighter, shrinking the people (Te/a).

DNA-code analyzer: Bioscanner equipment which Spock uses when investigating the spacegoing ameba (IS).

Dobkin, Larry (director): Charlie X (CX).

Documents: Tattered remnants of old documents such as the Constitution of the United States are all that the Yangs have left of their original culture. They have tried to make sense out of the fragments of knowledge on these papers, but the meanings have become sadly twisted by the time the Enterprise finds Omega IV (OG).

Dohlman: The ruler and warlord of Elas. Dohlmans do not have total power; very much against her will, Elaan, a Dohlman, is ordered by the Elasian Council of Nobles to marry the Troyian monarch (ET).

Dolinsky, Meyer (script): Plato's Stepchildren (PSt).

Dominguez, Commander José: A friend of Kirk's, in charge of the starbase on Corinth IV (MT).

Donatu V: The site of a battle twenty-three years prior to the encounter at Space Station K-7. It is still a disputed territory with the Klingons (TT).

Don Juan (James Grusaf): The famous Spanish seducer—tall, handsome, bearded, with a Renaissance cloak-and-dagger costume. Yeoman Barrows, dreaming at random, accidentally materializes him on the amusement-park planet. She barely escapes with her virtue, though not her uniform, intact (SL).

Doomsday machine: Kirk describes the berserker that has destroyed the <u>Constellation</u> and several solar systems as a doomsday machine (a hypothetical ultimate weapon that does not stop killing) from another galaxy—a robot starship built as a weapon "primarily as a bluff . . . never meant to be used . . . it would destroy both sides . . ." The builders are gone, but the robot machine is still destroying (DMa).

Doorway: See Time portal.

Double: A transporter malfunction at Alpha 177 splits Kirk into two entities: one good but weak, the other evil, referred to as the "double." The latter causes much trouble before he is captured and the two entities are rejoined (EW).

Double-jack: A card game resembling solitaire, played by Eve McHuron on Rigel XII (MW).

Doubletalk: The language of bureaucrats and diplomats, according to an exasperated Spock, when the leaders of Gideon fail to give him any genuine assistance in locating Kirk (MG).

Dragon: When Spock and Leila are looking for pictures in the clouds, Leila sees one that looks to her like a dragon. Spock tells her that he has seen a real dragon on Berengaria VII (TSP). The dragon is associated with gods in all Earth legends. European legends have heroes taking on the courage of the dragon by killing it, but Chinese legend has more beneficent dragons who help mankind, though they have to be courted with gifts and petitions (HS/a). When Kirk sprints through the door after the robot and Spock, McCoy and Sulu are left behind outside. They are almost immediately attacked by a two-headed, fire-breathing dragon. Sulu denies thinking of any such thing, and they flee from it (OUP/a).

Dramen justice: It has a reputation for moving faster

than one may gather evidence to save the person up for trial (Al/a).

Dramen star system: The star system that includes Dramia, the major planet of the system, and Dramia II, a plague-ridden planet (Al/a).

Dramia: Major planet in the Dramen star system (Al/a).

Dramian history: According to Spock's survey of history records, there is little but technical information, and some data about meteor showers, auroras, and radiation reports (Al/a).

Dramians: Dramians are physically large, averaging about seven feet tall. They are android in appearance, with large, bulbous eyes, bald heads with large craniums, branched hands and feet. Dark golden in color, they usually dress in oranges and reds (Al/a).

Dramia II: One of the planets in the Dramen star system. Auroral plague hit Dramia II just after Dr. McCoy led an inoculation program against Saurian virus. The plague killed most of Dramia II's inhabitants, and McCoy was blamed for it. He returns nineteen years later to Dramia, where he is arrested and charged with mass murder. He finds an antidote for the plague (Al/a).

Dramia II survivors: On the plague-ridden Dramia II, phantomlike figures, ragged and haunted, attack others with anguished cries. Demos, head of security police on Dramia, says it is because they are living in a world of the walking dead and cannot stand healthy people from the world of the living. According to Demos, the survivors were away from home when the plague hit, and went senseless with grief and desolation when they returned home to find friends and families gone. Demos is wrong: There were survivors of the plague itself, and one of them is Kol-tai, who remembers that McCoy was their friend (Al/a).

Drea (Leslie Dalton): A slender, dark-haired Kelvan who takes over the life-support sections of the Enterprise and later mans the helm (AON).

Drella: An entity native to Alpha Carinae V, which derives its sustenance from the emotion of love (WF).

Drill thralls: Some of the better-trained thralls on Triskelion are used as drill thralls to train new captives for fighting in the arena. The captured Enterprise people are assigned their own drill thralls; only Kirk seems happy with his, however (GT).

Droxine (Diana Ewing): The daughter of Plasus, High Adviser of the Planet Council. A tall, willowy blonde with aristocratic features and a flowing silvery gown, she sincerely believes that Troglytes are inferior. She is intrigued by Spock and wonders if Vulcans are as highly evolved as Stratos City inhabitants. When faced with the facts of life, she reluctantly accepts having to do manual labor, but it is obviously more important to her that she have Spock's good opinion than that she contribute anything to her society (Cms).

Drugs and chemical compounds:

Adrenalin (DY)	Antidote (Al/a, IV/a, WE)
Algae-based xenylon (Te/a)	Antitoxin (Am/a)
Algobarium solution (ET)	Benjisidrine (JB)
Ambergris (Am/a)	Cactus plant (SGn)

D

Chemical mist (IV/a)
Colladium trioxide (ET)
Compound (EB/a, LS/a)
Contraceptives (MG)
Coradrenalin (AY)
Cordrazine (CEF)
Cortropine (LS/a)
Counteragent (WE)
Dylovene (IV/a)
Formazine (AON)
Gas (Cms)
Glandular secretion (LS/a)
Hyronalin (DY)
Irillium (RM)
Kironide (PSt)
Laughing gas (PJ/a)
Love potion (MP/a)
Macromorphase enzyme (OP/a)
Magnesite-nitron tablets (FC)
Mako root (PLW)
Masiform-D (Ap)
Medication (MP/a)
Medicine (Be/a)
Melanex (OUP/a)
Neoethylene (MTT/a)
Neural paralyzer (AT)

Nitrous oxide (PJ/a)
Orientine acid (Su/a)
Oxynitrogen atmosphere (Te/a)
Pollen, antihallucinatory (PLW)
Powder, restorative (FW)
Ryetalyn (RM)
Salt (MT)
Saplin (Ap)
Scalosian water (WE)
Sterilite (PLW)
Stimulant (LS/a)
Stokaline (AON)
Strobolin (PO/a)
Synthesized drug (PO/a)
Tears, Elasian (ET)
Test 24 (ET)
Theragen (TW)
Tranquilizer (HS/a, SGn)
Tri-ox compound (AT. TW)
Unknown hormone (Am/a)
Vapor (MP/a)
Venom (Am/a)
Venus drug (MW)
Vrietalyn (RM)
Zienite (Cms)

Drusilla (Lois Jewell):   A long-tressed blond slave, revealingly costumed. The property of Claudius Marcus, she is lent to Kirk for an evening (BC).

Dryworm, giant: A creature on Antos IV that, like Apollo, can control energy from sources outside itself (WM).

Duel: A masculine way of settling disagreements, popular on Earth from the early Renaissance until the early nineteenth century, when it was outlawed—usually a fight to the death with swords, pistols, or other means of doing violence. At Kirk's provocation, Trelane offers to duel him, using a matched set of pistols identical to those that slew Alexander Hamilton in his duel with Aaron Burr (SG).

Dunsel, Captain: Wesley's name for Kirk when the M-5 computer is running the Enterprise. "Dunsel" was a word used at Star Fleet Academy to refer to a part which serves no useful purpose (UC).

Duotronics: The computer technology, developed by Dr. Daystrom over twenty-five years back, which led to the computers now in use by Star Fleet (UC).

Duranium: An alloy used in the hull of, for example, shuttlecraft (Me).

Duty roster: Military term meaning a list of duties and who is assigned to each, at what times, and where, plus who the replacement is if the person next up on the duty roster is unable to report to work.

Duur (Kirk Raymone):   A Capellan warrior, one of Maab's men, who wants to engage Kirk in combat to pass the time. The Klingon Kras kills Duur to get the Enterprise's phaser from his belt (FC).

DY-500:   Early-twenty-first-century interplanetary ship. Kirk mistakes the Botany Bay for a ship of this type (SS).

DY-100:   A very early (circa 1990) class of interplanetary ship, predating the current interstellar vessels. The S.S. Botany Bay is a member of this class (SS).

Dylovene: A medication McCoy hopes will work on Sulu after he is bitten by the toxic retlaw plant on Phylos. It doesn't work, but the Phylosians' antidote does (IV/a).

Dysfunction: Impaired or abnormal functioning. The Enterprise computer dysfunctions when invaded by the

energy field. Spock realizes this when the computer gives silly, smart-aleck answers to his questions, as though he'd asked a childish riddle instead of a scientific question (PJ/a).

E

Earp, Morgan (Rex Holman):   A thin man, all in black, with a wide toothbrush moustache, a pointed chin, and pale eyes. Historically, he was quick and nasty-tempered and known as "the man who kills on sight." In the Melkot reconstruction of Tombstone, he covets Sylvia, who prefers Billy Claiborne, played by Chekov; this causes Morgan to kill Chekov, which gives Spock his first clue that history can be changed—at least the Melkots' version of it (SGn).

Earp, Virgil (Charles Maxwell):   A black-clad youngish man, with long sideburns and no moustache. In real history, he was the town marshal of Tombstone, but the Melkots name Wyatt Earp as town marshal (SGn).

Earp, Wyatt (Ron Soble):   Deputy U.S. Marshal in nineteenth-century Tombstone—with wavy brown hair, a small moustache, and crooked teeth. The historical Wyatt Earp (1848–1929) lived through the real Gunfight at the O.K. Corral; in the Melkot re-creation, Kirk knocks Wyatt down when the latter runs out of bullets (SGn).

Earth: See Terra.

Earther: Term used by Klingon Captain Koloth, and later by Korax, to describe Earth people, or Terrans (TT). The Orions also use the term, which is meant to be derogatory (PO/a). It is a term of derision used by small Vulcan boys against young Spock (Yy/a).

Earth history: Ensign Dawson Walking Bear has studied Earth history, especially that of his own people, which included Indian culture in North and South America, for he is the first to recognize Kulkukan (HS/a).

Earthlike planet: The shore-leave planet has an appearance very much like Earth, with grassy meadows, brooks, waterfalls, trees draped with vines, and so on (OUP/a).

Earthlings: The people of Megas-tu, for all their magic and ability, are still fearful of Earthlings' evil and greed (Mtu/a).

Earthquake: See Mad planet; Seismic disturbances.

Earth-Saturn probe: Spock corrects an error he made when he said that Captain John Christopher will not contribute to history: His son (as yet unborn) will become Colonel Shaun Geoffrey Christopher, leader of the Earth-Saturn probe that will lead to more outer-space investigation and eventually to starships such as the Enterprise (TY).

Ecological sabotage: The Klingons claim that Cyrano Jones is guilty of ecological sabotage for selling tribbles on a Klingon planet. Moreover, he steals the glommer, their only tribble predator—an even more dastardly crime (MTT/a).

Ed (Charles Seel):   A balding barkeep in a Tombstone

saloon, with bleached wrinkly skin and circles under pale, twinkling eyes. Kirk tries to convince Ed that the Enterprise's landing party is not the Clanton Gang; Ed laughs dutifully at the Clantons' funny joke (SGn).

Eden: A planet which was thought to be a myth. When found, somewhere inside Romulan space, it is a lovely planet of sunshine, flowers, heavily laden fruit trees . . . but utterly silent, with no birds or animal sounds. All the plant life contains an acid which will badly burn exposed skin areas and kill if the fruit is eaten (WEd). (It is never clearly established how the Enterprise's computer knows of a planet in Romulan space, which is supposed to be uncharted area, to Federation knowledge.)

Edibles: The term used by the Aquans of Argo to describe food (Am/a).

Edinburgh: A city in Scotland famous for its medical schools, many pubs, and thick fogs. Scotty recalls that it was marvelous to take a bonny lass for a walk in an Edinburgh fog (WF).

Ee'd pebnista: Garbled words from the Preamble to the Constitution ("We, the people of the United States . . ."), venerated but not understood by the Yangs (OG).

Eel-birds, giant, of Regulus V: Creatures which must return every eleven years to the caverns on Regulus V where they hatched, in order to mate. Spock refers to them in trying to explain pon far to Kirk (AT).

Egg: The "space hippies" use the egg as a symbol of completion and rebirth. Part of their ritual of greeting is a gesture with the hands to form an egg shape, and they wear an insignia showing an infinity sign within a horizontal yellow egg, itself within a vertical white egg (WEd).

Eggling: Commander Bem, after being extremely self-confident during all the trouble he causes Kirk and Spock, is humbled before the greater intelligence and understanding of the alien entity of Delta Theta III and feels like an eggling—a youngster (Be/a).

Ehrlich, Max (script):   The Apple (Ap) (with Gene L. Coon).

811 East 68th Street, Apartment 12B: Gary Seven's address in New York City (AE).

892-IV, Planet: See Planet 892-IV.

Einstein, Albert: German-Jewish theoretical physicist (1879–1955) best known for the formulation of the theory of relativity, which postulated that nothing could move faster than the speed of light. Dr. Daystrom is compared to Einstein in intelligence (UC).

Ejection slot: A small slot in the wall of the Computer Room that is obviously a small transporter, which can be used to dispose of unwanted and dangerous material. Spock uses it to send the explosive capsule planted there by the Klingons into space, where it can do no harm (TR/a).

Ekor (Eric Holland):   A blond-haired Scalosian with Nordic features—first guard, under Rael, who helps to install the refrigeration unit in the Enterprise when the Scalosians take over the ship (WE).

Ekos: The inner of two inhabited planets of M43 Alpha. Its warlike population was in a state of anarchy until historian John Gill, sent in as an observer, gave Ekos a Nazi culture. The results were disastrous, especially for Zeon, its peaceful neighbor (PF).

Elaan (France Nuyen):   The Dohlman of Elas—a small, fiery woman with heavily painted dark eyes, black hair styled in a quasi-Egyptian manner, and an elaborate barbaric costume. She is sent to marry the monarch of Troyus as a peace gesture. She has no manners, believes that the rules of courtesy do not apply with inferiors, and that everyone is inferior to a Dohlman. She despises Troyians as subhuman, and has been spoiled from birth. Kirk shouts and slaps her into cooperation, whereupon she counters with tears loaded with a biochemical substance—a feature of her species—which acts as an aphrodisiac, making Kirk fall in love with her. Elaan becomes rather fond of Kirk but eventually accepts her duty and proceeds to Troyius to marry its ruler (ET).

Elas: Inner planet of the Tellan star system, inhabited by a humanoid barbarian warrior people. The men are vicious and arrogant; the women are man traps, having a biochemical substance in their tears which, in contact with a man's skin, will cause him to fall in love. Troyians consider the Elasians irrational and without manners. Elas is ruled by a Dohlman and a Council of Nobles (ET).

Elba II: A deadly, desolate planet with a poisonous atmosphere. The only life on the planet is in an asylum for the criminally insane, which is domed and under a heavy force field to keep the atmosphere out and the inmates in. The planet is named after the island of Napoleon I's first exile (WGD).

Electrical activity: The commanders of both the Enterprise and the Klothos disappear from their respective bridges in a jolt of electrical energy brought about by the assorted beings living in Elysia. Kirk and Kor are brought before the Elysian Council in this manner (Tr/a).

Electroenergy: When the malevolent alien entity breaks into the control room of the pod ship, electroenergy sweeps the room, causing mechanisms to blow up and surfaces to crack and shatter (BFS/a).

Electronic block: The amusement-park planet's master computer sets up an electronic block, so that the crew's communicators will not function on the planet during the search for Uhura (OUP/a).

Electronic nervous breakdown: The Enterprise's computer, invaded by an energy field from space, has an electronic nervous breakdown, and starts playing dangerous practical jokes on the crew (PJ/a).

Electron-laser microscope: See Laser.

Eleen (Julie Newmar):   Tall, elegant, dignified wife of the Teer Akaar, whose child she is carrying. After Akaar's death, Eleen's life is forfeit because her child-to-be is the potential new Teer. The Enterprise men help her despite her active disdain for them (FC).

Elevator: The entrance into the underground laboratory on Phylos; also a sort of hovercraft which carries the party to the lab (IV/a).

Elevators, Enterprise: The elevators on the Enterprise are voice-controlled.

Elfin friend: Lucien addresses Spock in overly friendly tones as his "elfin friend," undoubtedly an allusion to the pointed ears (Mtu/a).

E

Elliot (John Copage): Engineering technician—part of the damage-control party sent aboard the <u>Constellation</u> after it has been disabled by the berserker (DMa).

Elliptical orbit: With the dead sun pulling the Enterprise toward it, Kirk puts the ship in an elliptical orbit to avoid having it crash into the sun's surface and to create a slingshot effect that will free them (BFS/a).

Ellis, Mr.: First Officer on the <u>Antares</u> (CX).

Ellison, Harlan (script): City on the Edge of Forever (CEF).

Elysia: The area of the graveyard of derelict ships in the alternate universe of the Delta Triangle region. The people trapped here, and their descendants in some cases, have learned to live in peace, set up their own laws and council, and built a small but workable civilization around their predicament. They call their strange "country" Elysia (Tr/a). See also Violence.

Elysian Council: Composed of beings who, in the outside universe, may have been enemies, but who have had to learn to live in harmony within the small time pocket of the Delta Triangle region. The Council is made up of Xerius, a Romulan in white with a red cape held on with a large gold brooch; Devna, a gold-skinned Orion girl in a red bikini suit; a Klingon in military uniform; a Kzinlike cat creature with orange fur; an Andorian in a dark robe; an antlike creature of red with huge gold eyes and white fangs; a Phylosian plant creature; an Aquan-looking female in a water helmet; a white-haired Vulcan male in a blue suit; a Tellarite in a brown suit; a Human female in a white suit with dark blue collar and an insignia on the left breast (possibly an early Star Fleet uniform); and a Gorn in a green-and-gold outfit. There are many more representatives of different planets and races, according to Xerius, but the commanders of the Enterprise and the <u>Klothos</u> are permitted to see only these during their stay in Elysia. The Council has existed for more than one thousand years (Tr/a).

Elysian Council Chamber: A high-vaulted chamber, appearing to float in space; the meeting place of the people and beings who have been trapped in the alternate universe of the Delta Triangle (Tr/a).

Emergency air: The Enterprise is equipped to pump an emergency air supply into the life-support systems if the normal air supply has been contaminated in any way (PJ/a).

Emergency Defense Plan B, Federation: As a diversionary tactic to prevent the Klingons from boarding the paralyzed Enterprise, Kirk gives this command to Scott, who beams tribbles aboard the Klingon battle-cruiser. It is doubtful that the "plan" is really a Federation defense order at all, however. Kirk is simply utilizing the materials at hand—in this case, tribbles—for the defense of his ship (MTT/a).

Emergency manual control: A backup control to be used if the starship's central and auxiliary controls are out of commission (Dv).

Emergency Manual Monitor: A section of a starship's emergency manual control by means of which critical circuits and systems can be observed (IM). Lieutenant Romaine and Scotty are to use it to supervise the transfer of new equipment from the Enterprise to Memory Alpha (LZ).

Emergency overload bypass valve: See Matter/antimatter integrator.

Emergency rescue party: When an emergency rescue party tries to go down to the amusement-park planet in a shuttlecraft, the hangar doors open but slam shut again, so the shuttle can't leave (OUP/a).

Eminiar VII: Chief planet of star cluster NGC 321; for the past five hundred years at war, on a computerized basis, with its neighbor Vendikar (TA).

Eminiar III: See Vendikar.

Empathic contact: See Argelian empathic contact.

Empaths: A slight, mute humanoid species inhabiting one of the Minaran planets, but not native to Minara II. They possess empathy to a degree that enables them to take on and heal injuries in another individual. One of these entities, named "Gem" by McCoy, is tested by means of injuries inflicted on Kirk and McCoy. Being willing to risk personal danger to heal another, Gem earns survival for the whole empathic species, which is evacuated by the Vians when Minara goes nova (Em).

Empire: The mirror universe's equivalent of the Federation, operating by terror and cruelty: According to Spock-2, it has only a few centuries left before rebellion will tear it apart (MM).

Em/3/Green: A small, multiciliated creature, short and squat, nervous and twitching. He is a brilliant Kelly green, with sad golden eyes and a frightened look on his alien face. His people are cautious to the point of cowardice; he calls the whole expedition mad, and does not expect to live through it. He is sentenced to go along, as he would never have volunteered, and his talents as an expert thief and lockpick come in handy (Ji/a).

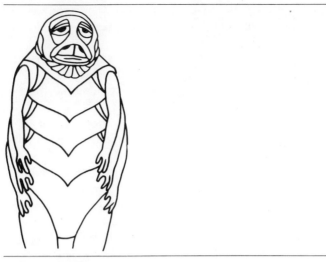

Encyclopedia: The compilation of one is the cover story used by Agents 201 and 347 to hide their real purpose from their secretary (AE). In spite of all, McCoy would be sorry to lose Spock to a disease, and says he'd miss the "pointy-eared encyclopedia" (PO/a).

Eneg, Chairman (Robert Horgan): Cultured, sleek, and deliberate—a member of the underground on Ekos and a man of character, although he acts like a Nazi. After the death of Gill and Melakon, he helps lead Ekos toward a healthy culture (PF).

Energy barrier (barrier at the rim of the galaxy): Just outside the arbitrary edge of our galaxy lies a multihued force field of incredible power. It cannot be crossed at sublight speed, and a starship at warp speed can get lost in it, owing to the extreme sensory distortion that occurs (TB). When a galactic survey ship, the U.S.S. Valiant, encountered it two hundred years prior to the Enterprise period, the barrier augmented the psionic powers of some of the crew to such a dangerous extent that the captain was forced to destroy the ship and all hands. Aboard the Enterprise, Gary Mitchell and Dr. Elizabeth Dehner are similarly affected by contact with the barrier (WNM). In coming from the Andromeda galaxy, the Kelvans lost their ship to the energy barrier and escaped in a lifeboat. They take over the Enterprise, and the starship goes through the barrier safely (AON).

Energy cloud: See Energy field.

Energy drain: The door to the Recreation Room is an energy drain; it absorbs attempts to open it mechanically or otherwise. The practical joker is the Enterprise's computer, which blocks the doorway so effectively that the crewmen are baffled trying to open it (PJ/a).

Energy field: The Enterprise meets a large gaseous cloud of energy that causes an electronic nervous breakdown of the starship's computer when it invades the ship. The energy field is unidentified, but it causes the computer to become a practical joker and act dangerously juvenile. The field is composed of subatomic particles which are extremely dense. On the viewscreen, the cloud radiates abstract patterns of gold, green, red, pink, and white. Outside, the cloud is a dense whitish color with gold spots, streaks of red, and orange sparks (PJ/a). The alien ship of Kulkukan has an immense energy field around it. It also places a field around the Enterprise

(HS/a). See also Force globe.

Energy mass: When Kirk and the other Enterprise men focus the jewels and prisms of the snake towers on the mosaic in Kulkukan's illusion city, there is a burst of energy/mass and the alien appears (HS/a).

Energy/matter scrambler: Another name for the transporter (SC).

Energy-sapping field: The new Klingon stasis-field weapon paralyzes starships by sapping their energy. However, it also uses an enormous amount of energy from the Klingon ship, which therefore cannot hold its position indefinitely and must finally veer off to recoup its own energy resources (MTT/a).

Energy-transfer device: A transporter unit activated solely by mental commands. Not a mechanical device, it responds to the electrical-energy pattern produced by the mental impulses of the person possessing the device, and it can be adjusted to fit only one pattern at a time. Spock sets it to his own energy pattern, and uses it to take himself, Kirk, and Gem to where the Vians are holding McCoy (EM).

Engineer (Sean Morgan): One of Scott's assistants, a younger version of Scotty, who attempts to maintain power when the Enterprise is trying to deflect the course of an asteroid (PSy).

Engineering core: See Core hatch.

Engineering Deck: A section in the ship's cylindrical engineering section wherein are found the basic components of the vessel's motive force and energy. This is the main province of the engineering officer, Scott, and access to the main feed of the starship's circuitry is available here.

Engineering Deck Five: The Klingons who are helping link up the two ships for escape from Elysia are supposed to be working on Engineering Deck Five, but are found near the maximum-protection area where dilithium crystals are stored. Spock takes the Klingons back to their working area, meanwhile managing some personal contact so he can mind-touch them (Tr/a). See also Gravity-control computer.

Engineering station: Scott's console on the bridge of the Enterprise.

Engrams: Neural patterns impressed from outside. Dr. Daystrom has impressed his own thought processes on the M-5 computer, and its engrams are as neurotic and paranoid as the doctor's (UC).

Enterprise, I.S.S.: The Imperial starship—counterpart of the U.S.S. Enterprise in the mirror universe—is a fifty-billion-credit starship being run as a pirate vessel (MM).

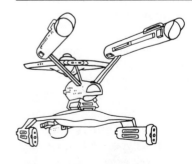

E

Enterprise replica: The Gideonites, in an attempt to keep Kirk prisoner long enough to accomplish their plans, make up a perfect replica of the Enterprise's interior, complete with lighting and internal noises. It fools Kirk for a while (MG). When the Enterprise's computer is playing jokes, it does not neglect a practical joke on the Romulans. A huge replica of the Enterprise appears out of the main cargo hold, and the Romulans attack it. They are furious when it blows up in their faces, revealing it to be a gigantic balloon, for Romulans would rather face death than disgrace and embarrassment (PJ/a).

Enterprise records: During the trial of the Earthlings by the hostile people of Megas-tu, the records of the Enterprise are researched by the magicians. Tapes, cassettes, cards, and books are brought down from the ship and tossed about carelessly in the chaos of Megas-tu, but they are all returned to the starship unharmed (Mtu/a).

Enterprise, U.S.S.: A starship of the <u>Constellation</u> class (somewhat larger than a twentieth-century naval battleship), the largest and most modern type of vessel in Star Fleet. It has a crew of 430, approximately one-third of them female. The "saucer section" is eleven decks thick at the middle, with the bridge at the top. Two engine nacelles are attached to a large and complex engineering section, which has a rear hangar deck large enough to contain an entire fleet of twentieth-century jetliners. Turbolifts, running vertically and horizontally, connect every deck and compartment of the Enterprise. Along with the crew's quarters, recreation halls, and so forth, there is a wide variety of labs, technical departments, computer banks, storage facilities, cargo areas, and passenger accommodations. There have been only thirteen such ships of this class in Star Fleet (TY).

Entertainment: Guests at Flint's home are offered chess, billiards, and conversation for entertainment (RM).

Entity (designed by Mike Minor): An alien being composed of pure energy, type unknown. A cluster of rotating patches of light in varying colors, it makes a high, wailing sound, and turns reddish as it "feeds." Able to bring on a paranoid mania in the brain waves and make people act like savages, it gets aboard the Enterprise, where it arouses much Klingon-Terran feuding. It feeds on hate. During an emotional outburst by a human, its life-energy level increases; as the person becomes less aggressive, the entity loses energy. Terrans and Klingons together abandon hostilities and laugh at the entity, so that it finally flees the ship (Dv). "The devil . . . the prowde spirite . . . cannot endure to be mocked" (Thomas More). See also Cloud.

Environmental engineering: Man-made environments; maintained with life-support systems, terraforming, etc.

Environmental suit: A "space suit" designed to sustain humanoid life in the vacuum of space for many hours. Covering the entire body, the suit is a self-contained unit, with its own air supply and source of heat and pressure. While the suit can provide a safe environment within a hostile one, it is interesting to note that McCoy can easily penetrate it with a hypo. The name of the wearer is displayed on a small tag where the helmet

joins the suit (TW, WGD). Spock and Tomlinson wear environmental suits of less elaborate design in exploring Psi 2000 (NT).

Envy: The human emotion Spock says he is close to experiencing when he sees Flint's art collection. McCoy nearly chokes on his brandy when Spock admits this (RM).

Enwright, Commodore: The commander of a space station who instructs the Enterprise to test out the M-5 (UC).

Enzyme recorder: Bioscanner equipment used by Spock to investigate the spacegoing ameba (IS).

Epicenter: The center of activity in a seismic disturbance (Am/a).

Epsilon Canaris III: An inhabited planet to which Assistant Federation Commissioner Nancy Hedford is sent to prevent a war. She contracts Sakuro's disease, however, and has to leave. There is no record of what happens back on Epsilon Canaris III (Mt).

Epsilon Indi: The star system in which the planet Triacus is located (CL).

Eraclitus (Ted Scott): A white-haired and -bearded Platonian who plays psychokinetic chess with Alexander (PSt).

Erman, John (director): The Empath (Em).

Erwin, Lee (script): Whom Gods Destroy (WGD) (with Jerry Sohl).

Essence: See Specimen.

Ethics of magic: See Megan.

Eugenics Wars: The last World War on Earth, in the 1990s. A group of selectively bred "supermen" took over the governments for a time, until the "normals" revolted against them, destroying most of the "supermen" and driving the rest into deep space (SS). The war was between those who wished to develop humans into a master race of genetically perfect people and the humanists, who wished to keep the human race as it is—imperfect, but with emotions. Dr. Keniclius 5 was one of the scientists fighting on the side of perfecting the human race into masters of the galaxy. He was banned from his community because of his work (IV/a).

Evans (Lee Duncan): A tall, slender, black security guard who notifies Kirk that Elaan has stabbed Ambassador Petri. He also captures Kryton in the engineering room, and is forced to kill the Elasian (ET).

Evans, Charles (Robert Walker, Jr.): A slender, brown-haired, large-eyed, gauche adolescent boy. The child of Earth colonists, Charlie was marooned at age three on Thasus and raised by the noncorporeal beings of that planet, who taught him psionic skills. He then left Thasus, having neither self-control nor maturity. He destroys the ship that took him from Thasus and then takes over the Enterprise. After wreaking havoc there for some time, Charlie's escape is discovered by the Thasians, and they come to reclaim him (CX).

Evasive action: Dodging maneuvers used by a starship to avoid being fired upon, attacked, trapped, or grabbed by something.

Evil One: The devil in most religions. Captain Tracey tries to convince the Yangs that the Enterprise people have been sent by the Evil One—an easy task, as Spock looks sinister to them (OG).

Excalbia: A planet with a poisonous atmosphere and seemingly made up of nothing but rocks and lava, but actually containing a carbon-cycle life form that looks like hot lava. See also Rock creatures.

Excalibur, U.S.S.: A starship, commanded by Captain Harris; involved in war games with the M-5 computer. Thinking the games are for real, the M-5 causes the Enterprise to destroy all life aboard the Excalibur, leaving it a battered hulk (UC).

Exceiver (Barbara Babcock): A system within the Beta 5 computer which can, among other things, interfere with complex mechanisms operating at a great distance. Gary Seven uses the exceiver to control the orbital bomb in flight (AE).

Execution, Melkot: The Melkots decree death to anyone caught trespassing on their planet and devise a bizarre means of execution: The Enterprise's landing party is to be killed in a reenactment of the Gunfight at the O.K. Corral (SGn).

Execution, Romulan: See Romulan execution.

Exeter, U.S.S.: A Federation starship patrolling the area of Omega IV six months before the Enterprise finds it in orbit and empty. A landing party returning from the planet had brought back the local virus, but not the immunity, and all the crew have died except for Captain Tracey, who has beamed down to the planet (OG).

Exhibit table: See Display case.

Exile: A punishment on Argo for disobedience is exile to an uninhabited part of the sea (Am/a).

Exobiologist: See Korby, Dr. Roger.

Exo III: A formerly inhabitable and inhabited world, now a frozen wasteland with a surface temperature of −100°, though possessing an atmosphere within safe limits. Dr. Roger Korby had found the underground caverns in which the inhabitants spent their last years, and also one of the androids which they had created and which had destroyed them. He has built himself an android body, and lives in it on Exo III until his death (LG).

Expeditions: Three expeditions before the one in which Spock and Kirk take part were lost on the mad planet. The search for the stolen Soul of Skorr cost the lives of specialists from all species in the galaxy (Ji/a).

Experimentation chamber: Chamber containing bins into which dilithium crystals are placed for recharging (AF).

Explosion: See Mechanicals.

Explosive: Garth of Izar has created the most powerful explosive in history: It can vaporize a planet if only a flask of the crystals is dropped. Garth plans to use this explosive to become Master of the Universe, but he is foiled. Before Kirk can stop him, however, he does destroy his consort, an Orion girl named Marta, with one crystal of the explosive (WGD). See also Asteroid belt; Capsule.

Extreme sensory distortion: See Sensory distortion.

Eye of the storm: When the Enterprise is being buffeted about in the center of the galaxy, it heads for the very heart of the cosmic whirlwind in hopes of finding a quiet spot—the eye of the storm (Mtu/a).

Eyes of Vaal, the: See Akuta.

Eymorgs: The humancid females of Sigma Draconis VI who live in an underground city filled with technology they do not understand, having the minds of children. The Eymorgs set traps for the Morgs (males), whom they use as breeding stock, guards, and household pets, controlling them with electronic training devices. The Morgs refer to them as "the Others" and "the Givers of Pain and Delight" (SB).

Eyrie, Master of the: See Tchar.

F

Fabrina: The sun of the Fabrini solar system, now a nova. It had eight planets (FW).

Fabrini: Former inhabitants of one of the planets of the star Fabrina. When Fabrina was about to go nova, they built Yonada, an asteroid/ship equipped with sublight propulsion drive, life-support systems, and a central computer. The Fabrini placed the best of their people aboard Yonada and sent them out toward a new world. The trip takes ten thousand years and nearly fails because of a computer malfunction, but fortunately the Enterprise happens along. The Fabrini were master scientists; Spock finds a cure for xenopolycythemia in their library/computer, and consequently McCoy is cured of this terminal disease. The Fabrini lived underground while preparing Yonada for colonization. The Yonadans, thousands of years later, worship the Fabrini as gods, not realizing they were ancestors (FW).

Factor 7 artificial power: The degree of power generated by the rock creatures on Excalbia. According to Spock, this is too much power for a lifeless planet; it indicates a considerable civilization (SC).

Fake victim: Kirk remembers the Keeper's stating that no harm could come to anyone on the shore-leave planet, as it is programmed to care for anyone who might be hurt, whether the planet wishes to or not. He theorizes that a "fake victim" might work as a ruse to gain them access to the computer center. Mr. Spock volunteers and is given a drug to knock him out (OUP/a).

Family shrine: Sarek does not think it unusual for his distant relative to be traveling to a family shrine to honor their gods, so it must be assumed that Vulcans practice a type of family or ancestor worship, perhaps similar to twentieth-century Shinto observances (Yy/a).

Fantasy literature: Many of the manifestations on the shore-leave planet come from fantasy literature—a very "normal" thing on a world where your every fantasy could come true (OUP/a).

Farragut, U.S.S.: Starship under the command of Captain Garrovick—the first deep-space assignment of Lieutenant James Kirk, eleven years back. When the vampire cloud attacked near Tycho IV, killing almost half the crew, Lieutenant Kirk hesitated at his phaser station, later blaming himself for the deaths (Ob).

Farrell (Pete Kellert): Stocky, bald, middle-aged—in the mirror universe, Kirk's personal guard and one of his operatives. He saves Kirk-1 from Chekov-2's attack (MM).

Farrell, Lieutenant John (Jim Goodwin): A navigator—thin, nervous, hyperthyroid (EW, Mi, MW).

Fate: When Kirk expresses rhetorical curiosity about their ability to get into situations, Spock says it must be fate (Be/a).

Father figure: The long-orphaned Charlie Evans tries to turn Kirk into a father figure whom he can look up to and follow, but the captain rejects the role (CX). See also Vulcans.

Fatherland: In general, one's native land. Especially important to the Nazi-German ideal, the concept was developed to an almost fanatical point on Ekos by John Gill (PF).

Fear ploy: When Kirk pretends to be afraid of the cloud of energy that caused the Enterprise's computer to become a practical joker in the first place, the computer promptly turns the ship into the field, which negates the original invasion of the energy field, returning the ship to normal (PJ/a).

Feathered serpent: Kulkukan's ship and later Kulkukan himself are shown as a Mayan-Aztec depiction of a huge feathered serpent with a collar of many-colored feathers, multicolored scales on the serpentine body, and huge feathered wings (HS/a).

Federation: See United Federation of Planets.

Federation Bureau of Industrialization: See Industrialization, Federation Bureau of.

Federation Undersecretary for Agricultural Affairs: See Baris, Nilz.

Federation warrior races: When trying to reason with Tchar, Spock says that the Federation warrior races will rise to battle the Skorr, but Tchar sees it as honorable to die for a great dream (Ji/a).

Feeders of Vaal: The natives of Gamma Trianguli VI, who feed Vaal the computer with leaves, flowers, and other material which it breaks down and converts into energy (Ap).

Feinberg blocks: Engineering equipment (Ap).

Feinberger: A type of electronic equipment in use aboard the Enterprise, notably the medical Feinberger, which is McCoy's scanner; named after Irving Feinberg, the noted twentieth-century technician. See also Irvingoscope; Phynburg oscillating framizam.

Felinoid: A cat-type intelligent being. In the case of Lieutenant M'Ress, she walks on two legs like a humanoid, but has distinctly feline face, ears, paws, and tail. See also Kzin, Vedala.

Fellini, Colonel (Ed Peck): Officer in charge of security at Omaha Air Force Base in the 1960s. He captures Kirk, questions him, is knocked out, and never does figure out what is going on (TY).

Females, Kzinti: All Kzinti females are dumb animals. The Kzin warriors ignore Uhura, assuming that because she is female she is not a sentient being. Spock suggests that she look dumb—it could save her life and help them out of a bad situation (SW/a).

Ferries: Space ferries operate between planets which

F

are close enough to each other to make warp speeds impractical and unnecessary (WEd).

Ferris: A dictator (LG).

Ferris, High Commissioner (John Crawford): A middle-aged, fussy, self-important Federation official aboard the Enterprise to supervise the transport of medical supplies to Makus III, for transshipment to New Paris. The type of civilian who thinks he knows more about handling military matters than the commander does, Ferris tries to make Kirk abandon the search for the Galileo (GS).

Fesarius: Balok's huge flagship, which looks like a magnified, glowing crystal (CMn).

Festival: A periodic occurrence on Beta III: twelve hours of rioting and other forms of letting off steam, then back to peace and tranquility (RA). See also Red Hour.

Fever: See Randolph, Lieutenant Nancy.

Field densities: A subject presumably related to the post-Einstein unified-field theory. Reena wants to discuss the topic and its relationship to gravity phenomena with Spock, who admits that it is an interest of his, too (RM).

Field effect: The new Klingon weapon surrounds the Enterprise with a blue aura, creating a field effect from which the Enterprise cannot escape (MTT/a).

Fifth Interstellar Geophysical Conference: See D'Amato, Lieutenant.

Figure 8: The sign of infinity on Earth, it may have a universal meaning. Tchar uses it when speaking of Alar, the great religious leader of the Skorr (Ji/a).

Filter masks: See Protectors.

Finagle's Folly: A marvelously green drink—McCoy makes one that is known from here to Orion (UC).

Finagle's Law: There are many. Kirk quotes the one stating that any port chosen for leave or liberty should not be one's own home port (AT). It is corollary to Murphy's Law: "If anything can go wrong, it will."

Finelli, Dario (script): Albatross (Al/a).

Finnegan (Bruce Mars): Kirk's personal tormentor at Star Fleet Academy—blond, muscular, good-looking, with a quasi-Irish accent and an exasperating laugh. A few terms ahead of Kirk at the Academy, Finnegan belonged to the pail-of-water-over-the-door school of practical jokery. Wearing a light blue Academy cadet uniform, he materializes for Kirk on the amusement-park planet, and the captain has the satisfying experience of whaling the tar out of him (SL).

Finney, Jamie (Alice Rawlings): The young, tomboyish daughter of Lieutenant Commander Finney, named for Captain James Kirk in the days of their friendship. When Finney is thought to have been killed through Kirk's negligence, Jamie accuses him of murder, but she later tries to protect him (Cml).

Finney, Lieutenant Commander Benjamin (Richard Webb): Records officer of the Enterprise, a man with great jealousy and hatred for Kirk, who once logged a mistake of Finney's and was subsequently promoted over his head. In an attempt to destroy Kirk, he hides in the engineering section and lets it be thought that through negligence Kirk has allowed Finney to be killed. With the aid of Jamie, Finney's daughter, Kirk's lawyer discovers the trick, and later defends Finney at his own court-martial. The ordeal of plotting and hiding eventually takes its toll on Finney, who suffers a nervous and physical breakdown (CmI).

First Citizen: The position held by Merikus on Planet 892-IV; its functions include Lord of the Games and Chief Magistrate of the Condemned (BC).

First Federation: The culture which has produced Balok. Lieutenant Bailey is sent to them as a cultural envoy (CMn). (Not to be confused with the United Federation of Planets.)

First manned moon shot: When officers on the Enterprise's bridge hear a five-thirty news summary from Cape Kennedy about plans for the first manned moon shot, they realize they are no longer in their own time, but have somehow been flung into the past (TY).

First Officer: The second-in-command on a starship (the term dates back to old Earth sailing-vessel days). Mr. Spock is First Officer on the Enterprise until a time line on Vulcan is missed, resulting in his having died at age seven. Then Kirk finds, to his surprise, that he's had an Andorian, Thelin, as First Officer for the past five years (Yy/a).

Fisher, Technician (Edward Madden):   The geologist member of the landing party on Alpha 177. He falls into a bank of soft magnetic ore, then beams aboard the Enterprise to have minor injuries treated. The ore clinging to his clothes causes a transporter malfunction which splits the next person using it—Kirk—into two entities. The "double," Kirk's evil half, beats Fisher severely (EW).

Fissionables: Harry Mudd is willing to accept fissionable material instead of cash for his love potion. Fissionable material is worth trading, or using, and certainly is an acceptable trade medium anywhere in a space-traveling galaxy (MP/a).

Fitzgerald, Admiral (Richard Derr):   The handsome, fair-haired Star Fleet officer who absolutely refuses to allow Spock to spark an incident with Gideon by beaming down to search for Kirk. Spock violates Fitzgerald's direct order and beams down anyway (MG).

Fitzpatrick, Admiral (Ed Reimers):   The officer who calls Kirk with orders to protect the quadrotriticale at Space Station K-7—white-haired, with a strong, unlined face (TT).

Fizzbin: A card game, supposedly native to Beta Antares IV, which Kirk invents to fool Kalo and Oxmyx's other hoods when they are holding the Enterprise's landing party prisoners. The general idea of fizzbin is to make the hoods concentrate so much on trying to work out the complicated rules that they can be caught off guard. Kirk purposely makes up confusing and contradictory rules as he goes along, showing great imaginative agility. In general, the game is played thusly: Each player gets six cards, except the man on the dealer's right, who gets seven cards. The second card goes up, except on Tuesday (however, Kirk deals all the cards face up during this explanation). Two Jacks is half a fizzbin, but three Jacks is a sralk and disqualifies a player; one needs a King or a deuce, except at night, when a Queen or a four

will do. If at this time another Jack is dealt, that is excellent, unless the next deal is another six, in which case the player has to turn one card back in to the dealer, unless the six is a black six, in which case the player gets another card. The main object of the game is, of course, to get a royal fizzbin, but the odds against this are astronomical, so much so that Spock has never computed them. The last card dealt is a kronk, which is a special kind of hand: The dealer drops this card, and when the player reaches to pick it up, the dealer tips the table over on him and drops a karate chop to the neck, and a general donnybrook finishes the game and most of the players (PA).

Flag, American: A tattered, dirty American flag is the last tangible tie with their home planet for the Yangs (OG).

Flags, banners, and pennants: Two flags are seen during Spock's shipboard trial, both blue and white (or silver); one is identified as a United Space Flag, and the other is presumably the Enterprise's banner (although this is never stated). The United Space Flag appears as a simple one of three stripes, two dark blue with a silver stripe in the center. The Enterprise's banner is plain blue, with something in the center, possibly the Enterprise insignia (Me). The UFP pennant of red with silver stars and gold lettering seen with the Starnes expedition (CL) is about the same size and shape as the personal "discovery flag" carried by Christopher Columbus. The red pennant may never have been used as a general Federation flag, but rather as a pennant representing the Starnes expedition or, indeed, any archeological or exploratory expedition. There is precedence for this in early Terran exploratory teams.

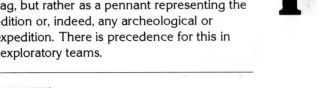

Flame gems, Spican: See Spican flame gems.

Flavius Maximus (Rhodes Reason):   A dark-haired, strong fighting man—formerly a gladiator on Planet 892-IV, later a worshipper of "the Son." He captures the Enterprise's landing party and is later captured with them by the Romans, who return him to the arena, matched against Spock. He is killed defending Kirk (BC).

Flint (James Daly):   A handsome, richly dressed, white-haired Earthman with deep-set worldly-wise eyes. Owing to a fantastic combination of tissue regeneration and biological renewal, Flint is an immortal, having lived for six thousand years when the Enterprise finds him. Though he began life as Akharin, a crude soldier in Mesopotamia, his being immortal has led Flint to escape boredom in many ways. He has been famous down through history: He was Leonardo da Vinci, Johannes Brahms, and many others. He was acquainted with Alexander the Great and Galileo. As he watched his loved ones die of old age, however, he became lonely. Flint had to move around the world, and then the galaxy, to avoid having others realize his longevity. Using the cover name "Mr. Brack," Flint bought a small planet, Holberg 917G, from the Federation. There he retired to build a huge domicile for himself, with a laboratory in which he constructed robots and androids to keep him company. When the Enterprise comes to Holberg 917G, looking for a source of ryetalyn to stop a Rigellian fever epidemic on the ship, Flint grudgingly says they can stay long enough for his own robots to gather and refine the ryetalyn. Flint claims that Reena, an android, is his ward, intimating that she is human. When Kirk falls in love with Reena, the immortal's jealousy flares, and the two men fight over the girl. Reena dies from her new, conflicting emotions, and the Enterprise leaves with a brokenhearted captain. McCoy then reveals that he ran a sensor probe on Flint which showed that the immortal was finally dying of natural old age. McCoy theorizes that when Flint left Earth's atmosphere, where his immortality had been generated, the aging process had begun, and he would probably not live out more than one normal life span. Flint has a fabulous collection of art, music, and artifacts collected from all over the galaxy; one wonders what will become of it on his death (RM).

Flintlock: An antique musket gun with a flintlock hammer; on Earth it was superseded by the percussion lock. An Enterprise landing party on an extremely primitive planet finds that the villagers have flintlocks that they could not possibly have developed by themselves. After Spock has been wounded by a flintlock, they discover that the Klingons scheming to tip the planet's balance of power, are behind it all and plan to introduce rifles next (PLW).

Flyer: One of the Kzin warriors who steals the stasis box from Spock and the Enterprise's shuttlecraft (SW/a).

Flying belt: See Stasis box.

Fog: Lucien hides the Enterprise in a magic fog when it breaks through to his world; the other citizens of Megas-tu are hostile to Earthlings (Mtu/a). The energy field invades the Enterprise as a fog (PJ/a).

Folsom Point: A beautifully chipped flint point shaped somewhat like a laurel leaf with grooves lengthwise on each face—an important find in American archeology. The name derives from Folsom, New Mexico, the location of the dig, where the first evidence of prehistoric "Folsom culture" was found. Spock mistakenly identifies the gigantic spearhead that kills Latimer on Taurus II as a Folsom Point, but it is a more crudely chipped artifact (GS).

Fontana, D. C. (scripts): Tomorrow Is Yesterday (TY); Charlie X (CX); This Side of Paradise (TSP) (with Nathan Butler); Journey to Babel (JB); Friday's Child (FC); By Any Other Name (AON) (with Jerome Bixby); The Ultimate Computer (UC) (with Lawrence N. Wolfe); The Enterprise Incident (EI); Yesteryear (Yy/a).

Food and foodstuffs:

Alondra (BFS/a)	Nectar (LS/a)
Antarean brandy (TB)	Quadrotriticale (TT)
Coffee (WE)	Quintotriticale (MTT/a)
Drinks (PJ/a)	Rock (DD)
Edibles (AM/a)	Sandwich (PJ/a)
Finagle's folly (UC)	Saurian brandy (AON, RM)
Food supplies (EB/a)	Seed grain (MTT/a)
Garum (BC)	Shellfish (Am/a)
Haggis (SC)	Taos lightning (SGn)
Grilled cheese on rye (PJ/a)	Whiskey (SC)
Kaferian apples (WNM)	Wine (WGD)
Meat (SW/a)	

Food supplies: Once a week the Lactrans leave food supplies for the humans inside the force field, near the display case which contains the Star Fleet equipment (EB/a).

Food synthesizers: Klingons apparently cannot or will not eat Earth-style food, because Kirk orders Lieutenant Johnson to program the food synthesizers on the Enterprise to accommodate Kang's crew (Dv). Spock is willing to consider that the leaking drinks might possibly be the fault of the food synthesizer—some kind of slipup (PJ/a).

Foolie: A word used by the three-hundred-year-old children, meaning a game or joke (Mi).

Fop (Ed Bakey): An overdressed man resplendent in lace, satin, and plumes, of an era in the history of Sarpeidon corresponding to Earth's period of Charles II. When Kirk is thrown into Sarpeidon's past, he sees this man and his foppish friends molesting a woman. Kirk challenges the fop and bests him with a rapier, and the fop runs off to get the constable (AY).

Force field: A firm, transparent, impenetrable wall of energy, used to keep something out—such as a poisonous atmosphere—or to keep something in—such as prisoners. The Melkots use a force field to keep the Enterprise men from leaving the scene (SGn), and the Vians use one on the landing party which draws its energy from its victim's body (Em). Force fields are used in the Enterprise (MP/a, WE) and on penal colonies as barriers to keep prisoners in cells (WGD). It is possible for a starship to become trapped in a force field (Cp); sensors cannot operate through one, nor can anyone transport through one while it is in operation. Everything inside a force field can be destroyed if it is blasted (WGD). A force field surrounds all the zoo compounds of the Lactran city, and also the laboratory where the humans are cleansed of any possible alien bacteria (EB/a). The cell door of the Dramen jail is held by a force field (Al/a).

Force-field activator: A gadget that maintains the force field in the jail of Dramia (Al/a).

Force-field box: A special box with an interior force field that can keep antimatter objects from touching its interior walls. Scott rigs one to obtain a villi sample from inside the cosmic cloud, to be used to regenerate the antimatter nacelle chamber. Once inside the chamber, the force field is released by remote control (OPM/a).

Force globe: The Enterprise is put inside a globular

force field by Kulkukan—a blueish-white glassy bubble that can absorb the energy of being hit at warp 1. Spock discovers that it is elastic in only one direction at a time, and decides to push and pull to see if it will break. They hit it at full impulse power with the tractor beam on full and warp engines on standby. Even compensating for the warp catapult effect, they'll be thrown 5.698 light-years away from the force globe if they break free. They do (HS/a).

Forest: The Enterprise's Recreation Room can create the effect of a forest, complete with sunlight filtering through the trees and sounds, on request. It is really a holographic illusion (PJ/a). Lucien makes a forest grow for the Enterprise people when they find the chaotic state of Megas-tu unsettling (Mtu/a).

Formal protest: In an attempt to bluff Captain Kirk into leaving them alone, the Orion pirate commander demands that the Enterprise cease harassing their ship or Kirk will be reported to the Federation in a formal protest. Kirk is not impressed with the threat, however, and continues his pursuit (PO/a).

Formation L: A standard formation used to deploy men when approaching a possible danger. Employed by Kirk on Gamma Trianguli VI (Ap).

Formazine: A drug which McCoy gives Hanar, pretending it is vitamins; it makes him highly irritable (AON).

Fortress: When the Enterprise people try to get at the computer center by forceful means, they find that the underworld of the shore-leave planet is built like a fortress (OUP/a). An abstract triangular building in dark purple with deep blue banding on the outside, an eerie reddish tone inside. The building holds the stolen sculpture, Soul of Skorr, plus a few traps and surprises (Ji/a).

Fortress phaser banks: Tchar sets the fortress phaser banks on kill, making it risky to use the hand phasers carried by Kirk and Spock (Ji/a).

498th Air Base Group: The section of the Omaha installation where Colonel Fellini holds Kirk and Sulu in security; also, presumably the group to which Captain John Christopher belongs (TY).

Fox, Ambassador Robert (Gene Lyons): Special ambassador to Eminiar VII to establish diplomatic relations with that star cluster—a distinguished-looking man with gray hair and deep circles under his eyes. Conservative and self-important but intelligent, highly adaptable, and a good diplomat, he makes peace between Eminiar and Vendikar when their war is interrupted (TA).

Freeman, Ensign (Paul Bradley): Officer to whom Uhura gives one of her tribble's "kittens" (TT).

Freighter officers: Men working under the command of Captain O'Shea aboard the S.S. Huron (PO/a).

Frontier-model Colt: A popular revolver pistol of 1881, the year of the Gunfight at the O.K. Corral. On Melkot, the Enterprise men find themselves armed with Colt six-guns. Kirk admires his gun as a beautiful specimen, but Spock finds them crude, although as deadly as a phaser at close range. Wyatt Earp prefers a Ned Buntline Special revolver (SGn).

Führer: Leader. The title assumed by Adolf Hitler in Germany, and later on Ekos by John Gill (PF).

Fusion bombs: Vendikar launches imaginary fusion bombs at Eminiar VII; actually, all "hits" during the war are determined by computer, and each side reacts as though a bomb has actually been dropped (TA).

G

Gable, Clark: A famous motion-picture star of twentieth-century Earth. When Edith Keeler wants to see a movie starring Clark Gable, neither Kirk nor McCoy knows who she means (CEF).

Gabler (James Doohan): One of Scotty's best engineers.

Gabriel, Archangel: One of the highest angels in the Christian mythos; entrusted with waking the dead on Judgment Day. McCoy says that he'd like just once to beam down to a primitive planet and say, "Behold! I am the Archangel Gabriel!" He suggests that Spock land with a pitchfork in hand (BC).

Gaetano (Peter Marko): Tall, lean, dark—a radiation specialist and the second person to be ambushed and killed on Taurus II after being left alone on guard (GS).

Galactic Cultural Exchange Project: Sponsors of the Karidian Players' tours (CK).

Galactic standard weight: A unit of measure which has become standard throughout the Federation (PO/a).

Galactic wars: Sometime between man's first intergalactic contacts and the time of the Enterprise's five-year mission, there were several wars to settle space boundaries and other problems. Dr. Keniclius 5 knows of them. Kirk says they are "old news," that there has been peace in the galaxy for over one hundred years (IV/a).

Galileo Galilei: Italian astronomer and physicist (1564–1642), best known for his telescopic observations which established the Copernican theory that the Earth orbits the sun. Flint says he knew Galileo personally (RM).

Galileo, NCC-1701/7: One of the Enterprise's shuttlecraft, and rather accident-prone; it is destroyed in orbit above Taurus II, and later replaced (GS). The second one carries Kirk, Spock, McCoy, and Nancy Hedford from Epsilon Canaris III to Gamma Canaris N; later it returns Kirk, Spock, and McCoy to the Enterprise (Mt).

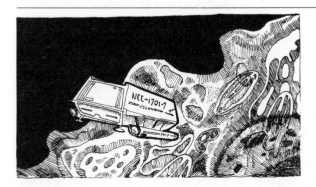

Gallian, The: A popular magazine on Planet 892-IV (BC).

Galliulin, Irini (Mary-Linda Rapelye): One of the "space hippies"—a sweet-faced girl with a mass of black hair, flowers and leaves painted on her face and shoulders, dressed scantily in soft drapery. She is a dropout from Star Fleet Academy, having been in the same class with Chekov, who calls her Irina. They were quite close at the Academy; their constant quarrel about who was right or wrong on an unnamed occasion picks up again on the Enterprise (WEd).

Galloway, Lieutenant (David L. Ross): Security officer on Miri's planet (Mi). Security officer and member of the landing party on Eminiar VII, where he is held as hostage by Anan 7 (TA). Killed by Captain Tracey on Omega IV (OG).

Galt (Joseph Ruskin): The master thrall of Triskelion—very tall and thin, with a shaven head, expressionless face, and long dark cloak. As overseer of the gladiators, he can inflict pain on the thralls by means of their collars (GT).

Galway, Lieutenant Arlene (Beverly Washburn): Chief biologist and a member of the landing party on Gamma Hydra IV—a small, appealing woman with short brown hair. She contracts the radiation poisoning prevalent on that planet, ages extremely rapidly, and dies before a cure is discovered (DY).

Games and recreation: The Enterprise, being on a five-year mission, necessarily has a wide range of recreational facilities. Some of the crew members have simple tastes: Scott likes to spend his free time reading technical manuals, and McCoy likes to study the salubrious effects of alcohol applied to the human system (CK). Still, there are more than four hundred individuals representing a wide variety of interests, including Sulu, an ardent hobbyist whose varied interests include botany (MT), fencing (NT), and antique firearms (SL). The ship has a gymnasium (CX) and a vast library, from which Gary Mitchell reads Spinoza and "Nightingale Woman" (WNM). Amateur artistry is encouraged: Spock (CX) and Uhura (CK) both play a harplike instrument, and Uhura sings (Cg, CK); Marla McGivers paints portraits of male heroes (SS). A live performance of Hamlet by a professional troupe draws a large audience (CK). The most popular game seems to be a type of three-dimensional chess. Kirk and Spock are both expert players; Spock is technically better, but Kirk tends to win by psyching him out (CX). The computer normally plays a good game of chess (Cml). A simpler game is 3-D checkers, which is shown in passing (CK) but not mentioned. Charlie X interrupts a card game of some sort with his "card tricks" (CX); the card game called fizzbin presumably exists only in Kirk's fertile imagination (PA). In addition to these recreational facilities, the Enterprise occasionally stops at a friendly planet for shore leave, where the preferred amusements seem to be those of any group of young, healthy humans in an interesting port (SL, TT, WF). These choices suggest a vein of traditionalism in Star Fleet that seems to date back to the early travels by explorers and military men on Earth. Naturally, along with all the planned recreation available aboard the ship, there is the time-honored pastime of "shooting the breeze"

and other relaxing methods of passing time. See also Bowling alley, Recreation Room, Herbarium.

Gamma Canaris N: A small planet composed mainly of iron and nickel; probably the remains of the breakup of a larger planet. Almost one gravity, oxygen-nitrogen atmosphere, some argon, krypton, neon (nearly identical to that of Earth); mean temperature 75°F. Inhabited by Zefram and Nancy Cochrane (Mt).

Gamma 400 system: Location of Starbase 12 (SS).

Gamma Hydra IV: A Class M planet with a climate much like Kansas in mid-August—an overly bright sun producing sharp colors and small undulating waves of heat. It is the site of a Federation experimental colony, in the jurisdiction of Starbase 10, near the Romulan-Federation neutral zone. When the planet's orbit carried it through the tail of a comet, a certain amount of radiation was picked up, causing a hyperaging disease which killed the colony and later afflicts several of the Enterprise's personnel (DY).

Gamma 7A solar system: A system totally destroyed by the spacegoing ameba. It had a fourth-magnitude sun and billions of inhabitants on its planets (IS).

Gamma Trianguli VI: A tropical-jungle planet, with a mean temperature of 76°F, even at the poles. A powerful computer mechanism called Vaal makes the planet a garden paradise, in which the innocent, immune, and immortal inhabitants depend entirely on Vaal for their every need and so are uncreative and lethargic (Ap).

Gamma II: An uninhabited planetoid with an automatic communications and astrogation station. Kirk, Chekov, and Uhura are about to beam down for a routine check of the facilities there when the Providers snatch them off to Triskelion (GT).

Gamma Vertis IV: A planet inhabited by a race of mutes (Em).

Gang, Clanton: In the American Old West of the late nineteenth century, Ike Clanton, his brother Billy, Tom and Frank McClowery, and Billy Claiborne made up a gang of roughnecks who stole horses and generally raised hell. Yet they were more popular with citizens of Tombstone, Arizona, than the Earps were, and were more welcome. Though the Clanton Gang stood outside the law, the Earps used the law to bully others. After the Gunfight at the O.K. Corral, the townspeople wanted the Earps tried for murder of the Clantons. The Earps were arrested, but never tried (SGn).

"Gan ta nu i ka tan ru": An instruction to the alien probe Tan Ru in the language of its builders. Its meaning is unknown (Cg).

Ganymede: A satellite of the planet Jupiter, in the Sol III system. Scotty once obtained some peculiar green "booze" there, which he uses to get Tomar drunk (AON).

Garden: McCoy's great-great-granddaddy was supposed to have had one of the finest gardens in the South—plus an excellent weedkiller (IV/a). See also Vulcan gardens.

Garison, C.P.O. (Adam Roarke): One of Pike's officers, included in the briefing-room consultation and the landing party on Talos IV (Me).

Garo VII system: The star system in which is to be found the planet Pandro, Commander Ari bn Bem's home (Be/a).

Garrovick, Captain: Commander of the U.S.S. _Farragut_, on which Kirk had his first deep-space assignment. Garrovick and half his crew were killed by the vampire cloud, and Kirk blamed himself for their deaths. When Garrovick's son is assigned to the Enterprise, Kirk tries not to be partial (Ob).

Garrovick, Ensign (Stephen Brooks): The son of Captain Garrovick, Kirk's first commander—a young security officer with a boyish face, gray eyes, and a cleft chin. With the help of Ensign Garrovick, Kirk destroys the vampire cloud that killed the former's father (Ob).

Garth of Izar (Steve Ihnat): A former starship captain—tall and handsome, with a nice smile when his face is not twisted with insanity. Once the Federation's greatest warrior, and one of the most brilliant cadets ever to attend the Academy, he was rendered criminally insane by maiming and near death while rescuing a race which knew the secret of cellular metamorphosis and taught it to him. Using this talent, he tricks Kirk and Spock and nearly escapes from Elba II, where he was incarcerated after going mad. Convinced that he is an elite power with the right to take whatever he wants from others, who are merely "decadent weaklings," Garth styles himself Lord Garth and demands submission to him as Master of the Universe. Kirk, who once regarded Garth as a hero—his exploits were required reading at the Academy—is saddened and thrown off guard. After much trouble, Garth is overcome and finally cured by a new medication brought by the Enterprise, which his own madness initially prevented him from accepting. After the cure, Garth becomes the strong and likable person he must have been when he was the model officer for Star Fleet cadets (WGD).

Garum: An ancient Roman condiment made of fish entrails, gills, and blood, mixed with salt and allowed to age. Sparrows are broiled in garum on Planet 892-IV (BC).

Gateway: Two stars in conjunction between our universe and an antimatter universe form a gateway through which ships can pass (CC/a).

Gav the Tellarite (John Wheeler): Tellarite ambassador to the Babel Conference—pig-faced and argumentative. Opposed to Coridan's entry into the Federation because of Tellar's mining-interests there, he debates the issue with Sarek of Vulcan, and loses. He is murdered aboard the Enterprise by an Orion disguised as an Andorian (JB).

Geisha: On ancient Earth, an entertainer at social events in Japan; much misunderstood by Occidentals, who had a very definite and inaccurate idea of what the entertainment involved. Nurse Christine Chapel has the same idea when, jealous of the android Andrea's obvious affection for Dr. Roger Korby, she asks the doctor if Andrea is his mechanical geisha. Dr. Korby pretends not to understand (LG).

Gem (Kathryn Hays): An empath inhabiting one of the planets of Minara (now a nova). Named by Dr. McCoy, Gem is a frail, mute humanoid with clear, almost blank gray eyes, a smooth feminine face, and a cap of short brown hair, who wears a caftanlike robe of sheer material over a tight body suit. Tested in the caverns of Minara II by the Vians, Gem reveals a capacity for empathy that extends to taking on and curing the injuries of others. When the Enterprise men are tortured to test Gem, they show compassion and self-sacrifice. Learning from this, Gem exhibits a willingness to heal the badly damaged McCoy in spite of the risk of personal injury and death, thus earning survival for the whole empathic species (Em).

Gems: See Headbands; Jewel.

General court-martial: The military version of a court of law. It hears evidence, judgment, and determines punishment (Cml).

Generalist: On a planet of magicians and wizards who specialize in specific types of magic, Lucien is the only generalist and does not stay within the bounds of any special magic (Mtu/a).

General Order No. 1: See Prime Directive.

General Order No. 7: "No vessel, under any condition, emergency or otherwise, is to visit Talos IV." Disregard of this order is the only crime punished by death (Me).

General Order No. 6: If everyone on board a starship has perished, at the end of twenty-four hours the ship will self-destruct to protect other ships from the disease aboard (Al/a).

General Order No. 24: "Destroy this planet after [time specified] has elapsed, unless order countermanded." Kirk gives Scott this order when he is held prisoner on Eminiar VII (TA).

General quarters: A condition of maximum readiness of a starship for action, with all hands at battle stations.

General quarters 3: Intruder alert (DMd, MT).

Genetic engineering: The glommer is a product of genetic engineering, made in a laboratory to protect the Klingons against tribbles. And the tribbles were genetically engineered by Cyrano Jones (so he claims) to stop them from reproducing so much. However, his engineering is slipshod: The tribbles grow larger and larger, and then turn out to be colonies of smaller tribbles after all (MTT/a).

Genghis Khan (Nathan Jung): Mongol chieftain (1162[?]-1227) whose title means "Greatest of All Rulers." A ruthless, efficient military genius, he led a confederation of Mongol clans against northern China, central Asia, and Russia, and was undefeated in his lifetime. The rock creature Yarnek obtains the image of Khan from Kirk's and Spock's minds and recreates the cruel Mongol to take part in a drama of good and evil. The real Khan was known for his massacres; the simulacrum finally bows to the good side's greater strength, and runs away with Zora (SC).

Gentlebeings: A form of address when talking to a collection of humans, aliens, and entities who are vastly dissimilar (MP/a).

Geological survey: A routine duty of the Enterprise

G

as it seeks out new life throughout the galaxy.

Geologist (Ed Madden):   A member of the landing party on Talos IV (Me).

Gerrold, David (scripts):   The Trouble With Tribbles (TT); More Tribbles, More Troubles (MTT/a); Bem (Be/a); (rewrite): I, Mudd (IM); (story): The Cloud-minders (Cms) (with Oliver Crawford).

Gestapo: The popular name for the German State Police organized to operate against political opposition in the Terran 1930s. The police force on Ekos is modeled on the Gestapo (PF). The security operations of the I.S.S. Enterprise are compared to the ancient Gestapo (MM).

Gestapo lieutenant (Peter Canon):   An Ekos policeman who fails to realize that Spock is actually not an S.S. lieutenant. Kirk takes his uniform (PF).

Gesture: Magic, once one can be brought to accept it at all, can be manipulated by a gesture of the hand; Kirk, Spock and other members of the Enterprise find they can do it with ease. Lucien gestures grandly when he performs a feat of wizardry (Mtu/a).

Gideon: A planet which was once a paradise of environmental and cultural conditions. In its germ-free atmosphere, the people flourished in both their physical and spiritual growth, and eventually their life span increased until death became almost unknown, happening only when the body could not regenerate. But the birth rate also continued to grow, for the people loved life so much that they refused to destroy or interfere with the creation of life; it was against their traditions and their nature. The upshot of this belief is an overpopulation problem that staggers the imagination (MG).

Giggles: The Enterprise's computer goes into giggles, and sometimes gales of laughter, when it pulls a practical joke on the crew (PJ/a).

Gill, John (David Brian):   A dignified, aged historian who was Kirk's instructor at the Academy and the author of a text which treats Terran history in terms of causes and motivations, rather than dates and events. Sent as an undercover cultural observer to Ekos, he violated the Prime Directive by giving that anarchic culture an only slightly modified Nazism. Gill's deputy, Melakon, subsequently took over, reducing Gill to a drugged puppet. McCoy revives him to the point where Gill can denounce Melakon before he dies (PF).

Giotto, Lieutenant Commander (Barry Russo): Head of security on Janus VI—middle-aged, with a strong face and dark, graying hair. He leads the teams of security men on their Horta hunt (DD).

Girl (Phyllis Douglas):   One of the "space hippies" picked up by the Enterprise—petite, dark-haired, dark-eyed, dressed in a tuniclike outfit (WEd).

Gist, Robert (director):   The Galileo Seven (GS).

Givers of Pain and Delight, the: See Eymorgs.

Glandular secretions: The females of Taurus II, when their people first came there, developed a glandular secretion which enabled them to survive the planet's energy drain, while their males all died (LS/a).

Glasgow pub crawler: One who frequents bars in Glasgow. Scotty describes himself as being one, which indicates that he knows how to have a good time (WF).

Glommer: A tribble predator; it eats tribbles whole. There is only one of its kind in the galaxy, since it is a genetic construct. The Klingons obviously wish to turn out hundreds of them, in case of a tribble invasion (MTT/a).

Glow water, Antarean: See Antarean glow water.

Goat god: See Lucien.

God: The alien intelligence which surrounds Delta Theta III evidently thinks of herself as a god, and says so (Be/a).

Gods: See Religion.

Goldin, Murray (director):   Requiem for Methuselah (RM).

Goldstone, James (director):   Where No Man Has Gone Before (WNM); What Are Little Girls Made Of? (LG).

G-1 star: The Enterprise is far from a G-1 star when it finds the long-dead pod ship, so it is a logical assumption that the unknown builders had warp drive (BFS/a).

Good and evil, philosophy of: See Philosophy of good and evil.

"Good Land, the":   A song sung by Adam while waiting to see the doctor. If the music is less than inspired, it is at least more interesting than reading back issues of old magazines, or its Federation equivalent (WEd).

Gooseneck viewer: A part of the navigational helm on the Enterprise; a movable viewer which can be raised or lowered at the convenience of the person using it.

Gorgan (Melvin Belli):   An insubstantial creature vaguely resembling a pinky-haired humanoid with mild, pale eyes, fuzzy sideburns, and a pleasant expression, wearing a wide silvery cloak. He is surrounded by a glowing green aura, and has a deep voice which echoes in high-pitched tones. When his power is overcome, his true ugliness becomes visible: still humanoid, but mottled and scabbed. The last inhabitant of Triacus, he was preserved in a cave until released by the Starnes expedition. He drove the adults of the expedition to suicide, and cozens the children into supporting him in his efforts to take over the Enterprise so he can conquer the universe. Gorgan describes Kirk as "gentle and full of goodness: a difficulty, since gentleness cancels strength." This is probably Gorgan's downfall: Kirk manages to resist him and turn the children against Gorgan. As his power is lost, he is destroyed (CL).

Gorla: An Imperial colony in the mirror universe. Kirk-2's first act as captain was the suppression of the Gorlan uprising through the destruction of the rebel home planet (MM).

Gorn (Garry Coombs and Bobby Clark):   One of a race

G

of intelligent reptiles, resembling a seven-foot-tall green tyrannosaurus with iridescent eyes. They attack and destroy the Earth colony on Cestus III, considering it a threat of possible invasion. Kirk fights a hand-to-hand duel with the captain of a Gorn ship (Ar). The Gorn, bred for fighting, has had to accept the trap of Elysia as reality and learn to live peacefully with his fellows in the Delta Triangle region (Tr/a).

Goro (Richard Hale):   An old Indian, with long white hair confined by a narrow headband, a broad nose, and strong cheekbones. A tribal elder on Miramanee's planet, he officiates at her marriage to Kirk (PSy).

Gossamer mice: Small alien experimental animals used in McCoy's medical lab; they are almost transparent and register shock at the least change in their environment. Under the bombardment waves from Terratin, they shrink small enough to escape from their cages (Te/a).

Gossett, Herm (Jon Kowal):   One of the lithium-crystal miners on Rigel XII. He marries one of Mudd's women (MW).

Gothos: A stray, manufactured planet in a region where no stars exist. Of magnitude 1-E, it has an iron-silica body and, except for one small habitable spot, no detectable soil or vegetation. Though it has no sun, Gothos is extremely hot and swept by storms, with a toxic atmosphere and volcanic action. All this energy is maintained by the immature being Trelane, who has made the planet as a diversion with his people's equivalent of a toy building set (SG).

Governor: See Cory, Donald; Wesley, Robert.

Grain: See Quadrotriticale; Quintotriticale.

Gram-positive bacteria: See Staphylococcus strain.

Grant (Robert Bralver):   Security guard who beams down to Capella IV with the landing party, reaches for his phaser at the sight of Kras the Klingon, and is killed with a kligat (FC).

Gravity, artificial: The artificial gravity of the Enterprise is turned off by the central computer when it is playing practical joker, to prevent Scott from reaching its logic circuits and turning it off. Scott floats to the ceiling of the computer complex, but when he gets outside the computer room he falls to the floor, because the machine has not reversed polarity in the rest of the ship (PJ/a). The artificial gravity goes off in the Enterprise when it enters the magic world of Megas-tu, until Lucien restores it. Megas-tu itself seems to have gravity only to comfort the humans visiting it (Mtu/a). See also Pod ship; Stasis box.

Gravity chamber: See Antigravity test unit.

Gravity-control computer: When zero gravity hits the bridge, Scotty checks with Gabler in Engineering Deck Five, only to find that the gravity-control computer is malfunctioning—thanks to the amusement-park planet's master computer (OUP/a). See also Zero gravity.

Gravity neutralizer: Tchar cuts off the artificial gravity with a gravity neutralizer, so everyone in the expedition floats free in the great fortress. When they find they can almost fly, Tchar offers to fight each of them as a Skorr (Ji/a).

Gravity phenomena: See Field densities. (Ji/a).

Great shelters: The Aquan term for the buildings of the ancient sunken city, when it is raised by quakes to a land mass again. The young Aquans decide to become air-breathers and rebuild the great shelters (Am/a).

Great Teacher of All the Ancient Knowledge: See Teacher, great.

Green (Bruce Watson):   Crewman killed by the M113 creature, which assumes his appearance in order to get aboard the Enterprise (MT).

Green, Colonel (Phillip Pines):   Military man who led a genocidal war on Earth in the early twenty-first century. He was notorious for striking at enemies during treaty negotiations. His motto: "Overwhelm and devastate." In the Yarnek's drama of good and evil, Green behaves quite friendly toward Kirk, trying to combine forces and overcome the rock creature, but in reality he means to distract Kirk so someone else (Genghis Khan) can creep up on him and attack. When Kirk and Spock seem close to winning the fight, he tries to run but is killed (SC).

Greenery: The plant life in the zoo compound set up for humans is real greenery—living grass and trees (EB/a). See also Herbarium.

Green memories: Lara suggests to Kirk that if anything happens to the expedition, they could at least manage to have some green memories to carry with them the rest of their lives. Kirk says he already has lots of green memories, and Lara is disappointed (Ji/a).

Grenade launcher: Kirk uses a mortar-type weapon obtained from the Cestus III arsenal to fire back at the attacking Gorns; the launcher shoots little bombs which give off a bright yellow light when they explode (Ar).

Grup: See Slang, Miri's planet.

GSK 783, subspace frequency 3:   Sam Kirk's private waveband from Deneva, over which his wife, Aurelan, calls for aid (OA).

Guard (John Cavett):   A miner on Janus IV, relieved from guard duty by the unfortunate Schmitter just prior to a Horta attack (DD).

Guard, Dramen: A guard watching the jail cell in which McCoy has been put. He allows Kirk and Spock to visit the doctor, but reports it to the head of Security Police afterward. He is amused at the idea that Kirk will find evidence to free McCoy before swift Dramen justice can move. Spock helps McCoy break out of jail by using a neck pinch on the guard (Al/a).

Guardian of Forever (Bartell LaRue):   A roughly circular gate in a ruin on a strange planet: a sentient time gateway, capable of showing rapid overviews of the past and of transporting individuals in time. It claims to be its own beginning and end, but admits that it has been created by something else and cannot change its nature. Through the Guardian of Forever, McCoy, Kirk, and Spock go back to the twentieth century to make and remake Earth's history (CEF), and Spock goes back to his childhood to remake his own (Yy/a).

Guard, Romulan (Mike Howden):   The guard of the room on the Romulan flagship containing the improved cloaking device. Kirk knocks him out (EI).

Guards, Elasian (Dick Durock and Charles Beck):   Large, muscular types with curly hair and wear-

G

ing red fiberglass plate armor. With Kryton, they form the Dohlman Elaan's honor guard during her stay aboard the Enterprise (ET).

Guards, Lactran: The zoo guards seem to be present to prevent the specimens from harming one another, not particularly to guard the zoo itself; the Lactran visitors are allowed to handle the display items and even enter the force fields into compounds if they wish (EB/a).

Guidance computer: After a series of violent short-burst maneuvers, Arex finds that the guidance computer of the Enterprise has been given a set of standard starship-familiarization orders. The amusement-park planet's master computer is getting the feel of controlling the ship (OUP/a).

Gumato: See Mugato.

Gun molls (Dyanne Thorne and Sharyn Hillyer):   Girls in skimpy dresses who follow the Iotian gangleaders and their hoods, in imitation of the society set forth in Chicago Mobs of the Twenties (PA).

Gutenberg Bible: The first printed Bible, produced on one of the first Western printing presses. Flint owns one; it is likely that the immortal was Gutenberg, the inventor of the movable-type press (RM).

Gymnasium: The Enterprise has a small gym in which the crew can exercise under normal or null-gravity conditions (Ji/a, CX).

Hacom (Morgan Farley):   A small, white-haired man with sharp features. A rabid pro-Landru coward, he betrays the good Tamar to his death because of a careless joke (RA).

Hadley, Lieutenant (William Blackburn):   Officer who substitutes at the computer station while Spock is down on Iotia (PA).

Haggis: An ancient Scottish delicacy made from a whole sheep's stomach in which oatmeal with liver and onions has been stewed (SC).

Haines, Ensign Jana (Victoria George):   Navigator who replaces Chekov when he is on Triskelion (GT). She has substituted at the computer station, also.

Halkans: In this and the mirror universe, a gentle and extremely pacifistic people whose planet is rich in dilithium crystals. Kirk-1 is willing to let the Halkans deny the crystals to the Federation, but Kirk-2 is instructed to blast them for daring to disobey the Empire. Kirk-1, in Kirk-2's place, stalls until he finally must turn the problem over to Spock-2, who undoubtedly finds some logical reason to spare the Halkans permanently (MM).

Hall of Audiences: Where Landru is located (RA).

Hall of Justice, Dramia: The Hall of Justice also contains the jail cubicles. Considering that Dramian justice moves swiftly, this is probably a very handy arrangement (Al/a).

Hallucination: Kirk thinks he might be having hallucinations when he can hear but not see insects whining

in his ear; it is really the speech of the accelerated Scalosians, who move in the wink of an eye and are invisible to normal vision. He also says he feels something touch him—Deelah's kiss (WE). For other hallucinations, projected images, and illusions, see:

Alice (OUP/a)
Alice in Wonderland (SL)
Alien (OUP/a, SU/a)
Amanda (OUP/a)
Audiovisual suggestion (LS/a)
Barber (SGn)
Beast (CL)
Beastie (Su/a)
Behan, Johnny (SGn)
Being (Su/a)
Blackouts (Su/a)
Cages (HS/a)
Carbon-cycle life form (SC)
Cartoon face (PJ/a)
Computer projection (CC/a)
Crater, Nancy (MT)
Dimensional visions (LS/a)
Don Juan (SL)
Double (EW)
Earp, Morgan (SGn)
Earp, Virgil (SGn)
Earp, Wyatt (SGn)
Ed (SGn)
Fake victim (OUP/a)
Genghis Khan (SC)
Hallucination (WE)
Hologram (CC/a)
Holograph (Ji/a, SW/a)
Holographic illusion (PJ/a)
Honeysuckle (OUP/a)
Huge cat (OUP/a)
Hypnotism (LS/a)
Illusion (HS/a, Ji/a, MP/a)
Image (BFS/a)
Jungle (HS/a)
Kirk's magic (Mtu/a)
Korob (Cp)
Kulkukan's ship (HS/a)
Lances (OUP/a)

Landru (RA)
Lincoln, Abraham (SC)
Lora (MP/a)
Losira (TWS)
Magnolia (LS/a)
Melkot, the (SGn)
Mendez, Commodore José (Me)
M113 creature (MT)
Murder (OUP/a)
Mystic symbols (Mtu/a)
Obelisks (HS/a)
O.K. Corral (SGn)
Old South (LS/a)
Queen of Hearts (OUP/a)
Quetzalcoatl (HS/a)
Rancher (SGn)
Replicas (TWS)
Rider (SGn)
Rodriguez, Lieutenant Esteban (SL)
Ruth (SL)
Samurai (SL)
Southern mansions (OUP/a)
Spanish moss (OUP/a)
Surak (SC)
Sylvia (Cp, SGn)
Tiger (SL)
Tombstone, Arizona, Territory (SGn)
Towers (HS/a)
Transmuter (Cp)
Trelane (SG)
Two-headed dragons (OUP/a)
Uhura's crewman (MT)
Vina (Me)
Visual compulsion (LS/a)
Vulcan marriage drum (LS/a)
White rabbit (OUP/a, SL)
Wisteria (OUP/a)
Witches (Cp)
Yarnek (SC)

Halo fish: Alien fish somewhat resembling Earth's angelfish, but with a bright halo of color around them as they swim in the tank. Any introduction of environmental change, including trailing a piece of jewelry in the aquarium, makes the fish lose color, so they are a good indicator of drastic changes in the medical lab. The fish return to their original halo of colors when the environment returns to normal (Te/a).

Hamlet: A tragic play, written over five hundred years before the Enterprise's voyages by William Shakespeare. Its universal appeal is evident in that it is still performed by the Karidian Players (CK).

Hamlet, Prince (Marc Adams):   Karidian actor playing the title role in Hamlet. His performance is cut short by the death of the Ghost (CK).

Hamner, Robert (script):   A Taste of Armageddon (TA) (with Gene L. Coon).

Hanar (Stewart Moss):   The tall, very slender young subcommander of the Kelvan expedition under Rojan. He takes over the bridge of the Enterprise when the Kelvans invade the ship. McCoy fills him full of formazine, calling it vitamins, which makes him irritable and causes him to argue with Rojan (AON).

Hand cannon: When fighting the Gorn Captain in a battle to the death, Kirk creates a very primitive matchlock hand cannon from the raw materials lying around.

He fills a large piece of hollow bamboo with sulfur, charcoal, and saltpeter, using huge raw diamonds as the projectiles. The primitive weapon can as easily blow up Kirk as wound the Gorn, but it works (Ar).

Hand-held viewer: Spock is the victim of a practical joke when he finds a stereo-viewer-style hand-held device and looks into it. It gives him a "black eye," which amuses the Enterprise's computer, but not Spock (PJ/a).

Hand phaser: See Phasers.

Hand sensor: See Tricorder.

Hangar: On Phylos, with its small remnants of a once-great race of plant beings, there is an immense hangar filled with spaceships. The plant beings once planned to go out into the galaxy to enforce peace (IV/a).

Hangar Deck: A large, football-field-sized area on the Enterprise where the shuttlecraft are stored, located at the rear of the cigar-shaped engineering section of the vessel. The huge hangar doors roll open when a shuttlecraft departs from or returns to the ship, so presumably it is one gigantic airlock. When the accelerated Scalosians begin to interfere with the functioning of the Enterprise, the controls on the Hangar Deck are frozen, presumably to prevent anyone from escaping in a shuttlecraft (WE).

Hangover: The aftereffects of the love potion, aside from bringing on hatred for the object of one's affection, seem to be a massive feeling much like a hangover from overindulgence. Scotty resents having a hangover without even drinking any Scotch (MP/a).

Hansen, Lieutenant (Hagan Beggs): Relief helmsman (Cml, Me).

Hanson, Commander (Garry Walberg): The gray-haired, lined-faced commander of Outpost 4, which guards the Federation-Romulan neutral zone. He is killed when the Romulans destroy the outpost (BT).

Hanson's Planet: A world inhabited by furry anthropoids, like those on Taurus II (GS).

Happiness: As part of their argument to convince the master computer that there is no shame in service to others, Uhura and her companions point out that the ability to provide happiness for others is a talent to use and cherish—one that will cause beings to seek it out (OUP/a).

Harmon, David P. (scripts): The Deadly Years (DY); A Piece of the Action (PA) (with Gene L. Coon); The Eye of the Beholder (EB/a).

Harold, Lieutenant (Tom Troupe): A survivor of the Gorn attack which destroys the Earth colony on Cestus III (Ar).

Harper, Ensign (Sean Morgan): Engineering officer who tries to shut off the M-5 computer and is killed by it (UC).

Harp, Vulcan: See Games and recreation.

Harris, Captain: Captain of the U.S.S. Excalibur; killed with his crew when the M-5 brings the Enterprise into battle against his ship (UC).

Harrison, Dr. (John Bellah): Young pathologist who catches the Psi 2000 virus; Spock sees him in a passageway, painting "Love Mankind" and "Sinner Repent" on the bulkheads and laughing hysterically. McCoy later calls Dr. Harrison on the intercom and gets nothing but laughter (NT).

Harrison, Technician 1/C: Crewman on the bridge when Khan Noonian Singh takes over and nearly suffocates the entire bridge crew (SS).

Harrison, William B.: A flight officer on the S.S. Beagle. The last of Captain Merik's men to die in the arena, he is killed by gladiator Claudius Marcus (BC).

Hart, Harvey (director): Mudd's Women (MW).

Haskins, Dr. Theodore (Jon Lormer): Small, thin, white-haired but healthy and tanned—represented as the leader of the expedition that crashed on Talos IV. He actually died in the crash, and what the landing party saw was an illusion maintained by the Talosians in order to entrap Captain Pike (Me).

Headbands: The Enterprise men awake after a drugged meal with the females of Taurus II wearing golden headbands. The men cannot remove them, and Spock theorizes that the headbands, which have gems placed in the center, are polarized conductors which transfer the vital energy from the males to the females, which has something to do with the rapid aging of the males. In the presence of the females, the jewels in the headbands glow, and the females grow more vital (LS/a).

"Heading Out to Eden": A song sung by Adam as he and the rest of Sevrin's group complete the last leg of their doomed voyage to Eden (WEd).

Healer: An old Vulcan who heals, evidently making no distinction between sentient beings and animals, as he goes out into the desert night in his hovercraft to tend a pet sehlat as willingly as he would attend a Vulcan patient. He is too late, however, and can only carry out young Spock's difficult decision to administer a euthanasia hypo to the beast (Yy/a).

Health scanner: Standard piece of medical equipment used by Dr. McCoy to check the general physical health of the crew.

Hearings: See Review.

Heavy-duty tricorders: Special equipment needed to try to find someone in the "fog" of sensory stasis that surrounds the planet Delta Theta III (Be/a).

Heavy-metal miners: The miners on the planet Motherlode are mining fissionable minerals—heavy metals (MP/a).

Heavy-planet humanoid: A humanoid born and raised on a planet with very heavy gravity would probably weigh much more than a normal Earthman for his height and would be extremely blocky and built low to the ground (MP/a).

Hedford, Nancy (Elinor Donahue): A thin, sullen woman with dark hair and a pale face. As assistant Federation Commissioner, she is sent to Epsilon Canaris III to prevent a war, but contracts Sakuro's disease and has to leave. With Kirk, Spock, and McCoy, she is diverted to Gamma Canaris N, while the disease progresses so rapidly that she reaches the terminal stage. The noncorporeal Companion repairs her body, shares it with Nancy, now a beautiful woman, and, as part of the new corporeal entity, marries Cochrane (Mt).

Hedonistic society: A culture, like that of Argelius II, devoted exclusively to the pursuit of pleasure and the gratification of one's own desires (PSt, WF).

Heinemann, Arthur (scripts):   The Savage Curtain (SC) (with Gene Roddenberry); The Way to Eden (WEd); Wink of an Eye (WE).

Helen: In Greek mythology, the most beautiful woman in the world. When Paris stole her away to Troy, an army of the greatest heroes in the known world went to rescue her, causing the famous saying about the "face that launched a thousand ships." Trelane says that Yeoman Ross is as fair as Helen, who could make a man immortal with a kiss, quasi-quoting Christopher Marlowe's Dr. Faustus: "Fair Helen, make me immortal with a kiss" (SG).

Helium experimental station: Magda Kovas, one of Mudd's women, grew up in such a station and left it because no eligible men were there (MW).

Helmsman: The title for the crewman sitting on the left side (facing the viewscreen) of the navigational helm. The other side is for the navigator.

Hendorf (Mal Friedman):   Security guard. Part of the landing party on Gamma Trianguli VI, he is killed by thorns from a pod plant (Ap).

Hengist (John Fiedler):   Small, balding, round-eyed, mild-looking—an administrator on Argelius II, but a native of Rigel IV, where the Jack-the-Ripper entity possessed him. When Kirk's people find this out, the entity abandons Hengist's body, which then dies (WF).

Henoch: Sargon's former enemy: expressive and impassioned, brash and ingratiating. He inhabits Spock's body and decides to keep it. He tricks Chapel into administering the wrong drug to Kirk, in whose body Sargon is working. Sargon and Thalassa trick him out of Spock's body, and he dies (RT).

Herbarium: Kirk's favorite room on the Enterprise, or so he tells Dr. Miranda Jones as they stroll through it. A garden room with growing things, including real roses, which still have thorns, and phaeleonopsis (butterfly) orchids, it is recreational as well as botanical—a room where people can enjoy flowers and plants in bloom (TB).

Herbivore: As meat-eaters, the Kzin have nothing but scorn for Spock, an eater of roots and leaves. The Kzin leader does not even wish to talk to Spock, and the Kzin telepath does not wish to read the Vulcan's mind (SW/a).

Here above: The surface of Sigma Draconis VI, where the Morgs live (SB).

Here below: The underground city of Sigma Draconis VI, where the Eymorgs live (SB).

Her Glory; Your Glory: Titles used by Lord Petri when speaking of or to Elaan, and by Kirk in derision (ET).

"Herman" series (Tom and Ted LeGarde):   A series of male androids on Planet Mudd (IM).

He-Who-Sees-All: See Asmodeus.

"Hey Out There":   A song about brotherhood sung by the Eden-seekers, with Adam singing lead. It is part of what is ostensibly an entertainment program for the ship, featuring Spock on the Vulcan lyre and the Eden-seekers playing and singing. Actually, the Eden-seekers' program serves to distract attention from their taking control of the

ship (WEd).

Hieroglyph: The symbol on one of the metal containers found in the Aquan sunken city depicts a half-man/half-sea-snake; it means that the container holds the information Kirk and Spock need about surgo-op and how to reverse the mutation that made them water-breathers (Am/a).

High Adviser: See Plasus.

High Council of the Eminian Union: The governing body on Eminiar VII (TA).

Highest of Kzin: Evidently the leader of the Kzin. If the Kzin pirates were caught, the Highest of Kzin would deny even knowing about them. But the Kzin are not worried, as they do not plan to allow the Enterprise people to live to tell about the stasis-box incident (SW/a).

High Tribune: Domar, a scholarly Aquan, is High Tribune of Argo (Am/a).

Highway 949:   Road, leading to McKinley Rocket Base, on which Agents 201 and 347 are killed in an auto accident (AE).

Hippocrates: A classical Greek physician (460?–370? B.C.). His code of medical ethics was used to swear doctors into the profession well into the twenty-first century. The Platonians give McCoy a scroll of cures, said to have been written by Hippocrates himself, as a reward for having cured Parmen (PSt). Spock feels that Hippocrates would hardly have approved of McCoy's "lame excuse" of being tried for murder as a reason for forgetting to dispense vitamin rations to the Enterprise's crew on schedule (Al/a).

Historians: Beings from all over the galaxy now visit the time-vortex planet to study the history of their own and other worlds. Historians are studying Vulcan's past when Spock disappears from Federation memory, but nobody notices that anything unusual has happened (Yy/a).

Hitler, Adolf: Garth of Izar, in his mad claim to become Master of the Universe, cites Adolf Hitler (1889-1945), instigator of World War II on Earth, as never having conquered his world. However, Garth fails to mention that it took the combined Allied forces to control Hitler's armies, and the loss of thousands of lives on both sides (WGD).

Hobby: Spock tells Edith Keeler that Kirk and he need money to maintain the Vulcan's hobby of putting radios together. Actually, he plans to build a device from vacuum tubes and radio parts that will enable them to read their tricorder tapes containing clues to what McCoy will do in the twentieth century to change history. Spock also wants some platinum, but at fifteen cents a day for work, the men don't have much chance of getting the "small" amount needed—some five or six pounds of it (CEF).

Hodgkins's Law of Parallel Planet Development: The doctrine that cultures tend to develop in similar patterns on similar planets (BC).

Hodin (David Hurst):   The father of Odona—a stocky man with gray hair and a short beard and moustache, wearing a dark brown tunic decorated with hexagonal designs over a simple leotard and tights. He is willing to let his daughter die for what he believes to be a good cause: to introduce disease and infection to a germ-free and therefore long-lived and overpopulated world. He uses the language of diplomacy to fend off Spock's request to search the planet of Gideon for Kirk, although he knows all the time where the captain is. He encourages his daughter to seduce Kirk into staying forever with them on Gideon (MG).

Holberg 917G: A small planet in the Omega system, thought at first to be uninhabited but which is only screened against intruders. A retired financier, Mr. Brack, bought the planet thirty years before the Enterprise comes looking for a deposit of ryetalyn to cure Rigellian fever. They find Flint ("Mr. Brack"), the immortal, and his lovely ward, Reena Kapec (RM).

Hold: An old Earth nautical term for the part of a ship which is used to carry cargo or supplies; a storage space. It is still in use for starships.

Holliday, Doc (Sam Gilman): A dentist and member of the Earp Gang, with eagle-beaked nose, longish curly hair, handlebar moustache, and brocade vest. He lends McCoy some raw material for tranquilizers, and waves a shotgun under his nose (SGn).

Hologram: A three-dimensional projected image, first introduced on Earth in the late twentieth century with lasers. In great use all over the galaxy to aid in visualizing starmaps and such (CC/a).

Holograph: Another item found in the stasis box—a three-dimensional picture of a being which Sulu thinks is the first photograph ever seen of a Slaver. The Chuft Captain agrees, and comments that the Slaver would have made a worthy enemy (SW/a). The Vedala shows the expedition a holograph of the binary star system to which they have to go in search of the stolen Soul of Skorr (Ji/a).

Holographic illusion: The means by which the Enterprise's Recreation Room creates scenes at the will of the people using the room: a three-dimensional effect that is quite realistic (PJ/a). See also Recreation Room.

Home worlds, Federation: A space probe scans the Federation home worlds, including the Earth system—which means that either it can move very fast, or the Federation is based on or near Earth (HS/a).

Homo sapiens: Spock describes Kirk-2 and the I.S.S. Enterprise crew as brutal, savage, unprincipled, uncivilized, and treacherous in every way—splendid examples of Homo sapiens, the very flower of humanity (MM).

Honorary Terratins: The miniature but proud Terratins are unable to thank the people of the Enterprise in any tangible manner for saving them, so they make the starship crew honorary Terratins for all time (Te/a).

Hood (Buddy Garion): A guard at Krako's front door. He is put out of commission by Kirk and Spock as a result of his gullibility, at least where cute small children are concerned (PA).

Hood, U.S.S.: A starship involved in the war games against the M-5 computer (UC).

Horizon, U.S.S.: A vessel which explored toward the edge of the galaxy one hundred years prior to the Enterprise. It made the first contact with Iotia and left behind a book which changed Iotian culture (PA).

Horta (Janos Prohaska): An intelligent, peaceful, silicon-based creature native to Janus VI—about seven feet long by three feet wide by three feet high, covered with mottled russet-orange asbestos plating and with multiple tentacles or legs on the ventral surface. Hortas can burrow through solid rock at great speed and have a life span of about sixty thousand years, after which each generation dies together. One individual remains to tend the eggs and rear the next generation. When human miners came to Janus VI, the Horta left them alone until they broke into the level containing the silicon nodules, which were Horta eggs. The miners mistook the eggs for mineral specimens and destroyed many, whereupon the Horta began to attack and kill the miners. The mother Horta kills fifty-six people in all before Spock is able to make mental contact with her and assure her that the humans mean well. Kirk and Spock arrange a peace between the miners and the Horta, with the creature agreeing to help with mining operations in the more difficult areas of Janus VI. Spock says the mother Horta thinks that humans have an appalling look, but that she will get used to them. She does, however, think Spock's ears are rather nice—according to Spock (DD).

Hortas, baby: Once the miners get used to them, they find that the little fellows aren't so bad (DD). See also Horta.

Hospitality: See Service.

Hostage: Mudd takes Nurse Chapel hostage when he escapes from the Enterprise and goes to a deserted planet. Spock, under the influence of the love potion, goes charging to the rescue (MP/a). See also Prisoner.

Host body: The malevolent alien magnetic organism is capable of a symbiotic relationship with a host body—a starship, for instance, in which the humans become only white corpuscles in the host body (BFS/a).

Housman, A. E.:

> In the midnights of November,
>   when the deadman's fair is high,
> And danger is in the valley,
>   and anger in the sky. . . .

Marta, the Orion inmate of the Elba II asylum, claims to have written this poem only that morning. Actually, it is a work by the Terran poet Housman (1859–1936) (WGD).

Hovercraft: The operatives that capture Uhura and guard her in the amusement-park planet's computer center, as well as the one which picks up the drugged Spock, are small metallic hovercraft, about three feet high, with six mechanical arms—extendible and retractable—and ringed with electronic lens eyes. Sulu refers to the one which picks up the unconscious Spock as "a mechanical nursemaid." By fast sprinting, Kirk is able to gain entrance to the fortresslike area along with the hovercraft (OUP/a).

Human: This term is used only in referring to Homo sapiens. Other manlike entities are called "humanoid." See also Humanoid.

Human mind: Kirk tries to explain to Kulkukan that the human mind cannot be forced into something; it must learn on its own how to fail or succeed. Intelligent life is too precious to be led about by the nose; children should not be made totally dependent on their teachers or they never grow up (HS/a).

Humanoid: A bifurcate, upright entity with humanlike features and limbs; any human type not from Terran stock. The term is probably applied to Earthmen by other races; when exasperated, McCoy alludes to this attitude by asking Spock, "Why don't you join us common humanoids in finding a way out of this place?" (SGn).

Human philosophy: According to Sarek, the choice of becoming a human instead of a Vulcan means choosing a philosophy based on emotionalism, instinct, and lack of control over one's feelings. He says that young Spock will soon have to make the choice between Vulcan and human philosophies (Yy/a).

Human rights: In defending Kirk, attorney Sam Cogley cites many codes and declarations of human rights—a tactic Star Fleet Command is not used to. Among them, he includes the Bible, Magna Carta, the Code of Hammurabi, the Declaration of Independence, and the Fundamental Declaration of the Martian Colonies. All of these writings are available for perusal by the student of human rights at any local Memory Alpha library/computer center (Cml).

Humbolt, Chief (George Sawaya): Chief of the computer section on Starbase 11. Spock knocks him out with a nerve pinch in order to use the computers in the kidnapping of Captain Pike (Me).

Humidification system: A part of the Enterprise which keeps the humidity level compatible with the heating and life-support systems of the ship. The energy field turns off this system (PJ/a).

Humor: See Quivering.

Hunter: See Lara.

Huron, S.S.: A freighter, commanded by Captain O'Shea, which carries a cargo of dilithium crystals, and is given the extra job of getting a rare drug to the Enterprise in time to save Spock. The Huron is attacked by pirates, who steal the dilithium (and, incidentally, the drug), then sabotage the Huron's engines, leaving it a piece of space junk. The Huron's crew is saved, but they need medical attention (PO/a).

Hyperacceleration: Radiation from volcanic eruptions accelerates the metabolism of the Scalosians, speeding up their lives enormously and making them invisible to humans. Outsiders accelerated to match the Scalosians' own wink-of-an-eye speed eventually become docile. When damaged, a newly accelerated person ages rapidly and dies. Accelerated living burns one out quickly (WE).

Hyperencephalogram: A recording of brain waves and other neural functions: a map of the individual personality (Cg, LZ).

Hypergravity: See Questar M17.

Hyperlight: See Warp drive.

Hypnosis: Spock and Kirk toy with the idea that the protean salt vampire is using mass illusion or hypnosis on everyone, but they find that it can actually make a metamorphic change into any shape it wishes (MT).

Hypo: The tranquilizer used to stop the Capellan power-cat is in a standard air-powered Star Fleet hypodermic (HS/a).

Hypothermia: Suspended animation; the lowering of body heat. Used on the "sleeper ships" that carried the genetically "superior" people out into space (SS).

Hyronalin: The drug which has replaced adrenalin as a treatment for radiation poisoning (DY).

Hysterical amnesia: A mental safety valve that blocks the recollection of something too terrible to remember (WF).

I

Icarus 4: A comet in the vicinity of the Romulan-Federation neutral zone. The Romulan ship goes through it in an attempt to shake off the pursuing Enterprise (BT).

Ice: The practical-joking computer suddenly covers the deck of the bridge on the Enterprise with ice, making the crew slip and slide (PJ/a). See also Mad planet.

I-Chaya: The name of young Spock's pet sehlat. I-Chaya was also Sarek's pet, which means that the animal is long-lived, since Sarek is in the prime of Vulcan life at seventy-five (Earth) years when Spock is seven. I-Chaya is old and getting slow when young Spock goes to the desert for his maturity test, but the sehlat holds off an attacking le-matya long enough for the adult Spock to rescue young Spock and assure that his time line will continue as it should. In the fight, however, the old sehlat is wounded beyond recovery, and young Spock has to choose between trying to keep his pet alive and letting it die in peace and dignity. He makes the difficult decision, and I-Chaya is released by the healer from the pain inflicted by the le-matya's poisoned claws (Yy/a). See also Le-matya; Sehlat.

I.D. card: The Enterprise personnel carry identification cards—small plastic rectangles. Harry Mudd steals Nurse Chapel's card and changes it cleverly enough to open Enterprise's doors with it to steal a scout ship (MP/a).

Identity tapes: Small cassettes which contain pertinent information about an individual: fingerprints, voiceprint, licenses, and registrations, plus a visual display of the individual (Su/a).

IDIC: The most revered Vulcan symbol, combining variations in texture, shape, and color. The name is Terran, an acronym for "Infinite Diversity in Infinite Combinations"; the Vulcan name is not known. Spock's IDIC, which can be worn as a pin or as a pendant, is a circle and triangle of white and yellow-gold metals in shiny and textured (or Florentine) finish, with a white jewel. Spock explains that the different shapes and materials represent the diverse things which come together to create truth and beauty; the glory of creation lies in its infinite diversity and meanings (TB). Kirk recalls to the Spock-clone the philosophy of the Vulcan IDIC and what it means. He asks if an army of Spocks could impose peace on the galaxy and make other beings accept the Phylosian philosophy in defiance of the Vulcan IDIC concept. The Spock-clone decides that it cannot be done (IV/a).

Illegal drug manufacture: Star Fleet has laws against illicit drug manufacture and sale, for which Harry Mudd is up on charges (MP/a).

Illness ploy: Since the Lactrans seem unable to comprehend that Lieutenant Randolph was genuinely ill, it seems improbable that they will accept Kirk's pretending to be ill, but the ploy works on a Lactran child, who is tricked into bringing a communicator to the humans (EB/a).

"I'll Take You Home Again, Kathleen": See Riley, Lieutenant Kevin.

Illusion: Lora, a beautiful human girl who responds to Mudd's love potion, turns out to be an illusion created by a Rigellian hypnoid (MP/a). Kulkukan can make illusions seem real. First his ship appears as a gigantic feathered serpent; then he conveys some of the Enterprise people to his ship, where he creates a full city (HS/a). See also Beast; Hallucination; M113 creature; Physical laws; Slaves; Survivors; Talos IV; Vina.

Ilyra VI: A charming planet, with an innocent and friendly populace, according to Mudd, where he sold Star Fleet Academy for enough credits to get to Sirius IX. He claims now that he sold only the idea, but the Ilyrans charged him with fraud and swindling (MP/a).

Imaginary games: A game of "golf/baseball" is invented to confuse the androids on Mudd's Planet. The necessary equipment includes a "primer," which is part of an imaginary exploding golf ball, a mashie, and a niblick. The "golf ball" is thrown to the batter, who "hits" it, causing the others to scramble to catch it before it hits the ground and explodes—resulting in "certain death" for all (IM). See also Fizzbin.

Immortal: See Flint.

Imploded matter: See Questar M17.

Impound, right to: The Romulans claim the right to impound the Enterprise when the starship invades the neutral zone; the Romulan commander offers to put the crew off on the nearest outpost that guards the zone. Obtaining a starship would indeed be a prize for any Romulan commander (Su/a).

Impulse power: The Enterprise's secondary propulsion system, located at the rear of the "saucer section." Based on the same principle as rocket power, it is used for velocities of less than the speed of light (MW, WNM). See also Warp drive.

Impulse vent: The opening from which the ions of the impulse drive escape. The vampire cloud gets into the Enterprise by means of the No. 2 impulse vent (Ob).

Indian boy (Lamont Laird): A slender, black-haired boy of about eight who is nearly drowned while handling some fishing nets. Kirk gives him mouth-to-mouth resuscitation, and the boy recovers, thus establishing Kirk among the Indians as a demigod (PSy).

Indians: American Indians of mixed Navajo, Mohican, and Delaware stock—advanced and peaceful tribes—are found on an Earthlike planet, having been brought there by the Preservers. Kirk spends some months among them during a spell of amnesia (PSy). See also Comanche; Mayans.

Indian woman (Naomi Pollack): Miramanee's handmaiden, with long black hair pulled back in a foxtail and bound with a white headband, who is with her mistress when she finds Kirk at the obelisk (PSy).

Indurite: Alar's brain patterns were recorded in a piece of indurite sculpture in order to make them immortal. This suggests that the material is very nearly indestructible, yet of some quality that will allow creative work to be done on it (Ji/a).

Industrialization, Federation Bureau of: The body empowered to mediate between the High Adviser for the Planet Council and the Troglyte miners on Ardana, so as to arrive at terms acceptable to both sides (Cms).

Industrial scale: Used by the Federation for rating the industrial level of civilizations. See also Richter scale of culture.

Ingalls, Don (Judd Crucis): (script): The Alternative Factor (AF).

Ingraham B: A planet that was attacked by the flying parasites, its civilization destroyed, two years before the planet Deneva is devastated by the same creatures (OA).

Inmate (Ed McCready): A patient being treated by the neural neutralizer when Dr. Adams first shows it to Kirk and Helen Noel (DMd).

Inquisitorial Tribunal: In Sarpeidon's "Charles II" era, the prosecutor (in reality a modern Sarpeid) lives in fear of the Tribunal (AY).

Insect bite: See Randolph, Lieutenant Nancy.

Insectoid beings: The structure of the pod ship and the shape of the windows remind the Enterprise's landing party of some types of cells built by insects. The hull is spun filament, much like a spider's web. The taped image of the long-dead commander of the ship confirms that the builders of the fantastic pod ship were indeed insectoid (BFS/a).

Insect whine: See Hallucinations.

Instrument of Obedience: The Oracle's means of controlling the people of Yonada. It is a small object, something like a tiny diode one-eighth-inch long, inserted under the skin of the right temple. It glows red when activated and can inflict pain or death. Through these instruments, the Oracle knows instantly what anyone is thinking. Natira describes them as "the mind and heart of God" (FW).

Integration parameters: To beam anyone anywhere, the transporter must have perfect integration. The parameters are upset by the Klingon attack on the Enterprise, which keeps Cyrano Jones held in stasis between his destroyed scout ship and the Enterprise during the attack (MTT/a).

Intelligence files: The entire knowledge of the Fabrini who banked it in computers, to be made available to the people of Yonada when they reach their destination. The Fabrini had amassed a great deal of information, including medical knowledge (FW).

Interceptor: The type of aircraft (an F-104) piloted

I

171

by Captain John Christopher when he is sent up to investigate the UFO that has suddenly appeared over Omaha (TY).

Intercom: The accelerated Scalosians interfere with the Enterprise's intercom system, distorting sound and causing a rapid breakdown. This prevents the crew from communicating with one another and possibly planning an escape from the Scalosians (WE). Used on Kzin vessels as well as Federation ships (SW/a).

Intergalactic space: A continuum reached by exceeding warp 9.5 under certain conditions, which possibly include proximity to the extragalactic force field. The continuum is evidently of similar composition to that field: Both are drifting curtains and patches of red and blue lights of varying intensity. Humanoids experience sensory distortion in this continuum, and cannot trust their instruments. Medusans are not affected (TB). Earlier forays through intergalactic space showed it to be very black, with no lights (OA).

Intergalactic Treaty: This treaty specifies, among other things, that no being may be extradited without due process. Accordingly, Star Fleet Command orders a hearing of Bele's claims on Lokai in order to evaluate the information before allowing Bele to take the fugitive prisoner (LB).

Interior building transporter: A standard item for starbases and space stations, usually near the director's office.

Intermix chamber: Part of a ship's engines (NT).

Internal security: When something happens inside the starship, everyone is placed on alert, and internal security is put into action.

Interphase: A "tear in time" created by a space warp and allowing passage between different space/times or alternate universes. To recover someone or something that has been removed to another universe or space/time, it is necessary to find the exact same "tear in time," or interphase, where the different planes originally met; however, the constant movement of time and space makes this very difficult. The U.S.S. Defiant is lost in an interphase, and Kirk is nearly lost in one, but he is recovered. Being in an interphase is usually accompanied by sensory distortion and eventual insanity (TW).

Interpreter of Laws: Devna, the Orion girl in Elysia, is the Interpreter of Laws—the person who decides if a law has been broken and, if so, what the punishment should be (Tr/a).

Interstat code: A radio code which has been out of use for two centuries but is still being used by the Terratins, who have been out of touch with the rest of the Federation for nearly that long. Uhura picks up their signal in interstat code (Te/a).

Interstellar medicine: McCoy is honored by Dramia, which had previously charged him with murder, for significant achievement in the field of interstellar medicine. He has discovered how to cure auroral plague, freeing Dramia II from its ravages (Al/a).

Intestine: See Villi.

Intrepid, U.S.S.: A starship in for repairs at Starbase 11 when the Enterprise arrives and claims top priority (CmI). When the Intrepid, which is manned by Vulcans, is destroyed by the spacegoing ameba, Spock feels the shock of the four hundred deaths from several parsecs away (IS).

Intruder alert: Alert sounded when Kirk realizes that the Enterprise has been invaded by a shape-changing Vendorian spy (Su/a). See also General quarters 3.

Invasion defense: When the network of signal antennae goes out, owing to earthquakes and volcanic action, the Terratins are reduced to using their invasion-defense weapon—a particularly dangerous spiroid wave bombardment (Te/a).

Invisibility screen: See Cloaking device.

Ion engine: Impulse-drive engine, such as that used by a shuttlecraft (Me).

Ion power: The ancient technologists of Sigma Draconis VI used ion power both to operate warp engines and to maintain an entire underground city while the planet's glaciated surface was uninhabitable. The Eymorgs' small ion power plant produces an amount of energy comparable to that generated by a nuclear power plant one hundred miles across (SB).

Ion propulsion: The Draconis ship can achieve high velocity through ion propulsion, a unique technology (SB).

Ion storm: An unpredictable particle storm in space which can be very dangerous to starships (CmI). An ion storm of jagged multicolored flashes of light bombarding the Enterprise causes it to lose control long enough so that a Klingon ship, the Klothos, can sneak close enough for a quick shot at the Federation ship. The ion storm seems to be a natural phenomenon of the Delta Triangle region (Tr/a). The transportation chief in the mirror universe gets "agonized" after he fails to compensate for a power surge caused by an ion storm (MM).

Ion trail: Ionic wastes sloughed off into space by a ship under ion propulsion. Sensors aboard the Enterprise pick up such a trail and follow the Draconis ship back to its home star system (SB).

Iotia: A planet at the edge of the galaxy, visited one hundred years before the Enterprise by the U.S.S. Horizon and which has, as a result, an imitation-Earth type of culture (PA).

Iotians: Humanoid, extremely intelligent, and imitative—after a Federation ship left behind a book, Chicago Mobs of the Twenties, they abandoned their own culture to build one based on the information contained in it. Kirk cons them into unifying their government, starting them off with proper direction. However, McCoy leaves a communicator behind, analysis of which may give them advanced technology sooner than intended (PA).

I.Q.: Intelligence quotient—a measure of intelligence still in use, though expanded to measure skills and other factors, as well as simply good memory. The I.Q. of the Lactran child is in the thousands, Scott says, though it is never ascertained how he measured it (EB/a).

Irillium: A substance which, when found mixed in ryetalyn, renders the ryetalyn useless as an antidote to Rigellian fever. As little as one part irillium per one thousand parts ryetalyn will do this (RM).

Irish kings: See Riley, Lieutenant Kevin.

Iron Cross, Second Class: A medal presented by Deputy Führer Melakon to Daras, Hero of the Fatherland on Ekos (PF).

Irvingoscope: A piece of equipment named after a twentieth-century technician (CX). See also Feinberger.

Isak (Richard Evans):   A Zeon of slight build, with brown hair; the younger brother of Abrom (PF).

Isis (Barbara Babcock, voice):   Usually seen as a sleek black cat wearing a diamond necklace; also (momentarily) as a beautiful black-haired woman with the same necklace. Possibly a member of the advanced race that sent Gary Seven and other agents to twentieth-century Earth to save it from itself, she works as Seven's partner, seeming at times to be a mentor (AE).

Island, Argo: The largest land mass on Argo is a craggy rock with a small beach. Kirk and Spock are stranded there to die in the air (Am/a).

Island Earth: When asked about his home world, Kirk says he is from an island called Earth, a reference to Earth's being so far from the center of our galaxy, and possibly also to the science-fiction novel by twentieth-century novelist Raymond F. Jones entitled This Island Earth (AY).

Izar: The planet from which Fleet Captain Garth originated (WGD).

J

Jackson (Jimmy Jones):   A member of the landing party on Pyris VII who, after Sylvia kills him, is sent back to the Enterprise to warn the ship away (Cp).

Jack the Ripper: An obsessive killer of women, also known as "Red Jack" or "Redjac." He first appeared in London, ancient British Empire, 1888 (old calendar), where he brutally murdered at least six women, apparently using a surgical instrument. There were no witnesses, no motive, no identification or arrest. He was later discovered to be an energy being comparable to the Melitus of Alpha Majoris I. It feeds on fear and possesses a hypnotic screen which blinds all but the victim to its presence. It preys on women because they are more easily and deeply terrified. Its career: 1932—Shanghai, China, Earth—seven women knifed to death; 1974—Kiev, USSR, Earth—five women killed; 2105—the Martian colonies—eight women knifed to death; 2156—Heliopolis, Alpha Proxima II—two women knifed to death. Subsequently, the entity appears on Deneb II, where it is called "Kesla," and on Rigel IV, where it is called "Beratis." It then inhabits the body of Hengist and travels with him to Argelius II, where it kills three more women before it is discovered and driven out of Hengist's body. Taking control of the Enterprise, the entity tries to frighten the crew, but Kirk has everyone tranquilized, and finally tricks the killer so that it can be dispersed into space. Unable to take a form and deprived of sustenance, the entity is presumed to have died (WF).

Jaeger, Lieutenant Karl (Richard Carlyle):   A blond geologist-meteorologist-geophysicist, part of the landing party on Gothos (SG).

Jahn (Michael J. Pollard):   The preadolescent ringleader of the three-hundred-year-old children, with a chubby face and an unkempt mane of curly hair (Mi).

Jailbreak: McCoy has never taken part in a jailbreak before, and worries about the consequences, though his release from the Dramian jail means saving the Enterprise from auroral plague. Spock, who arranges the jailbreak, looks on it as the only logical thing to do at the time (Al/a).

Jailbreakers, the: A popular singing group on Iotia. Their current song is announced when Spock tries to contact the Enterprise using an Iotian radio station (PA).

Jamal, Yeoman Zahra (Mauriska Taliferro):   A member of the landing party on Deneva—with long black hair and Middle Eastern features—when Spock is attacked by a flying parasite (OA).

Janice-K: Kirk's life force and personality trapped in Janice Lester's body, brought about by the life-entity transfer (TI).

Janowski, Mary (Pamelyn Ferdin):   One of the children of the ill-fated Starnes expedition, who temporarily came under the influence of Gorgan—a little girl of about seven, with blue eyes and strawberry-blond hair tied in two side ponytails (CL).

Janus VI: An ugly reddish-brown planet, uninhabitable on the surface, with a thick, turbulent cloud layer and slow rotation. It is a mineral treasure house which could supply the needs of a thousand planets, but for the difficulty involved in mining. The Janus VI mining facilities have been in operation for over fifty years, supplying pergium for the reactors of a dozen other planets, when the Horta's depredations stop all work, causing the reactors on these planets to be shut down. Since most of these reactors power life-support systems, the planetary governments are screaming for corrective action. Janus VI is also, of course, the home of the Horta, and has been for many generations (DD, TWS).

Jaris (Charles MacAuley):   The prefect of Argelius II, its highest official—tall, white-haired, and distinguished. When a girl is murdered, he brings the suspects home so that his wife, Sybo, can examine them telepathically. When Sybo is killed, Jaris beams aboard the Enterprise for the hearing. When the Jack-the-Ripper entity is driven out of other bodies, it possesses Jaris briefly, but not long enough to kill him (WF).

Jeffries tube: A crawlspace in various sections of the ship wherein are located various engineering and communications control circuits. Named after Walter Matthew

Jeffries, a noted twentieth-century technician and artist.

Jenson, Len (script):   Once Upon a Planet (OUP/a) (with Chuck Menville).

Jewel: The headbands placed on the men lured to Taurus II have gems in them, and Dara entertains the men at the banquet with a juggling act, using large red jewels (LS/a).

Jewelry: Nurse Chapel had a piece of titanium jewelry made for her by crafts-smiths on Libra. She trails the bracelet through the aquarium to demonstrate how halo fish lose their color when something alien is introduced into their environment (Te/a).

Jihad: A war in a holy or religious cause; the term comes from the ancient Earth war by the Muslims against unbelievers. The Skorr are prepared to start a jihad against the rest of the galaxy for the theft of a religious artifact, the Soul of Skorr (Ji/a).

Joaquin (Mark Tobin):   Khan's right-hand man—a cocky, dark, muscular "superman" from the 1990s (SS).

Johanssen, Lieutenant Helen: See Piper, Miss.

Johnson, Elaine (Laura Wood):   A small, dried-up old woman, though only twenty-seven years old—wife of Robert Johnson, head of the Gamma Hydra expedition. Both have been affected by the radiation poisoning that killed the rest of the colony, and die on the Enterprise (DY).

Johnson, George Clayton (script):   The Man Trap (MT).

Johnson, Lieutenant (David L. Ross):   Rugged-looking, reddish-haired officer who is wounded by a Klingon during the bloody fight aboard the Enterprise. But the entity that causes these fights does not care to use up its game pieces, so Johnson's wound is healed. He comes back to the fight intending vengeance, and Kirk has to squelch him (Dv).

Johnson, Robert (Felix Locher):   Though only twenty-nine years old, he is rapidly falling into senile degeneration and looks ancient, having contracted the radiation poisoning while acting as leader of the Gamma Hydra expedition. The rapid aging caused by the radiation killed the members of his party, leaving him and his wife to be found by the Enterprise before they die (DY).

Joining: A procedure, never fully explained, which Bele wants to accomplish with his prisoner, Lokai, who is terrified of it. Kirk intervenes, as all aboard the Enterprise come under his jurisdiction (LB).

Joining day: Miramanee's term for "wedding day" (PSy).

Jones, Dr. Miranda (Diana Muldaur):   A blind telepath, and companion to Ambassador Kollos of the Medusans. A tall woman, still young but highly self-possessed, with calm blue eyes and abundant black hair, she wears a long black gown with a glittering sensor web over it. She is a human, but not a native of Earth. Born a telepath, Vulcan logic saved her sanity. She is ideally suited to her position with Kollos: Being blind, she cannot be driven insane by the Medusan's appearance. She is jealous of Spock's higher telepathic ability. Though human, she is better off with the Medusans, being highly detached and alienated from her species and having a

great dislike for human emotions (TB).

Jones, Cyrano (Stanley Adams):   A wandering trader and nuisance who deals in such things as Spican flame gems, Antarean glow water, and tribbles—a cheerful, gross chap with curly brown hair and apple cheeks. He should have spent the next 17.9 years clearing the tribbles out of Space Station K-7, but somehow avoids it (TT). He and Harry Mudd have much in common. The Enterprise's computer files have full information on him, including how many mandates have been issued against him (MTT/a). See also General nuisance, Parole.

Jordan, Ensign (Michael Zaslow):   Computer technician on duty in the Auxiliary Control Room when Norman comes in to take over. Norman knocks him out by applying pressure at the carotid artery (not the same as the Vulcan nerve pinch) (IM).

Josephs, Lieutenant (James X. Mitchell):   Officer who finds Ambassador Gav's body in a Jeffries tube (JB).

Judge: At one point in the mental battle between Kirk and Trelane, the latter appears in the costume of a British judge and sentences Kirk to be hanged (SG).

Jungle: Aboard the ship of Kulkukan, the Enterprise people find themselves in what seems to be a huge jungle, though it is an illusion (HS/a).

Junior Tribunes: Young Aquans in training to become members of the Tribune of Argo. They are all progressive and want to forget some of the old ordainments, to move forward instead of staying mentally in one place. Rila, Lemus, and Nephro are Junior Tribunes (Am/a).

Jupiter: Largest planet of our solar system; fifth planet from the sun, with a diameter of 142,000 kilometers. The cosmic cloud is larger than Saturn, Jupiter, and Neptune combined (OPM/a).

Jupiter Eight: A gleaming, slinky, twentieth-century-style automobile on Planet 892-IV (BC).

K

Kaferian apples: When the Enterprise visited Kaferia, Gary Mitchell learned to like this delicacy. He includes the apples in his homemade paradise on Delta Vega (WNM).

Kah-if-farr: The opening phrase of the Vulcan marriage ceremony. It means "Begin the ritual action"; literally, "Fulfill the point in the cycle" (AT).

Kahless (Robert Herron): The Klingon, known as "the Unforgettable," who set the pattern for his planet's ruthless tyranny. (SC).

Kahs-wan: A Vulcan test of maturity—a survival ordeal of ten days in the intense heat of the Vulcan desert without food or water except what can be found. It is an ancient rite held over from the warrior days before the Vulcans turned to logic; it was reasoned that tests of courage should be maintained to prevent pure logic from making them weak. To fail the maturity test once would not make the average Vulcan boy a coward, but much more is expected of the half-human son of Sarek. Spock does not wish to be disgraced, and there are some who would call him a coward for the rest of his life if he failed the kahs-wan for the first time (Yy/a).

Kalandans: A handsome people, if the replicas left behind are any indication, who advanced outward from their own planet in a series of established outposts. Everyone on the outpost discovered by the Enterprise was attacked and destroyed by a deadly organism produced accidentally during the creation of the outpost. Supply ships to the planet then carried the disease back to the home planet, and it is probable that the entire race succumbed to the disease (TWS).

Kali: A female Klingon who is entrusted with a small capsule-bomb to plant in the Enterprise. She is asked by McCoy to dance at a party, and this courtesy is used by Kaz the Klingon as an opportunity to start a fight so Kali can slip away and hide the explosive in the Enterprise's Computer Room (Tr/a).

Kal-if-fee: A Vulcan term meaning "(act of) challenge"; specifically, to single-combat for a lady's hand (AT).

Kalo (Lee Delano): A thin, bony gunman, one of Oxmyx's goons who meet the Enterprise landing party. He is put in charge of guarding them, whereupon Kirk hornswoggles him with a game of fizzbin, which enables the Enterprise people to escape (PA).

Kalomi, Leila (Jill Ireland): Botanist with the Omicron Ceti III expedition—a lovely, wistful blond who has been in love with Spock since they met six years earlier. She exposes him to the spores to release his inhibitions so that he will be able to return her love. Kirk frees him from the spores, and Spock goes back to his unemotional ways, to her great sorrow. However, Leila's strong feelings over losing Spock release her from the spore influence, and she apparently goes with the other colonists when they are relocated (TSP).

Kandel, Stephen (scripts): I, Mudd (IM); Mudd's Women (MW); Mudd's Passion (MP/a); Jihad (Ji/a).

Kang (Michael Ansara): Commander of the Klingon ship disabled off Beta XIIA—tall, scraggly-haired, with surprisingly mild eyes under bristling brows. He leads the surviving Klingons in their battles through the corridors of the Enterprise until Kirk can persuade Kang to cease hostilities and help him drive out the entity that is causing the battles (Dv).

Kangaroo court: Kirk accuses the people of Dramia of trying to hold a kangaroo court for McCoy; of trying to hustle his trial past legal formalities (Al/a).

Kanutu: A small tribe on the planet Neural: dark-haired, lively people with knowledge of curative plants and a semi-psionic ability. Tyree's wife, Nona, is a Kanutu (PLW).

Kapec, Reena (Louise Sorrel): An android with the appearance of a beautiful platinum-haired girl with soft brown eyes and a serene, almost bland face. Slim, graceful, dressed in a flowing silken robe, she is emotionally just a child, although intellectually she has the equivalent of seventeen university degrees in science and the arts. Her guardian, Flint, says that she was left in his care when her parents died, but Kirk can find no records of an award of custody for her. Flint deliberately throws her together with Kirk, and Reena begins to develop the emotion of love. Flint finally confesses that she is an android designed by him because he wants a beautiful, perfect, immortal woman—a mate for all time. Kirk asks Reena to choose between him and Flint. The joy of love makes her human, but the agony of her new-found emotions and the powerful conflicts with which she is faced kill her. She dies when her circuits overload. Her android body will certainly be replaced by another Reena when Flint gets over the mental turmoil of losing this one. Spock uses a mind touch on Kirk to erase from his mind all memory of Reena (RM).

Kaplan (Dick Dial): Security guard. Part of the landing party on Gamma Trianguli VI, he is killed by one of Vaal's lightning bolts. Kirk knows his family (Ap).

Kara (Tania Lemani): A pretty, brown-haired belly-dancer in a small café on Argellius II. Scotty, encouraged by Kirk and McCoy, takes her for a walk in the fog. She is killed by the Jack-the-Ripper entity, and Scotty is blamed (WF). Another Kara (Marj Dusay) is the leader of the Eymorgs on Sigma Draconis VI—a tall, dark-haired, pretty woman but with no brains. She appears aboard the Enterprise and removes Spock's brain for use as the Central Controller that runs the Eymorgs' underground technology. However, she has neither the intelligence nor the training to do this on her own, but was programmed for the purpose by a mechanical teacher (SB).

Karf (Buddy Garion): One of Krako's hoods (PA).

Karidian, Anton: See Kodos the Executioner.

Karidian, Lenore (Barbara Anderson): The daughter of Anton Karidian—a sleek blond who looks older than her nineteen years, a capable actress, and a member of her father's company. She murders, one by one, the past witnesses to her father's planetwide massacre on Tarsus IV. In an attempt to kill Kirk, she accidentally kills her father and goes insane (CK).

Karidian Players: A traveling company of actors, sponsored by the Galactic Cultural Exchange Project, headed by Anton Karidian. They have been touring official installations for nine years (CK).

Karla Five: A young-appearing, beautiful dark-haired woman, with a somewhat urgent manner. An explorer from an antimatter universe where people are born old and get younger as they "age," she meets the Enterprise as it tries to stop her scout ship from plunging into a nova. After her ship pulls the Enterprise into her universe, she helps get the starship back to our galaxy, with the aid of her scientist son (CC/a).

Karl Four: Seemingly a baby-sitter for a small baby in a playpen, he was really Karla Five's son—an elderly man found adjusting starcharts in his laboratory on Arret, where time runs backward (CC/a).

Kartan (Fred Carson): An orange-suited Denevan who, compelled by the parasites, leads an attack on the landing party and later tries to brain Spock (OA).

Kassaba fever, Rigellian: A disease McCoy tells the Kelvans that Spock has. It is supposed to be a recurring disease, much like malaria, but the whole thing has been made up by McCoy as a ruse (AON).

Kaz: A Klingon, second-in-command to Captain Kor of the battlecruiser Klothos. He is even sneakier and nastier than most Klingons (Tr/a).

Kazanga: The name of a genius, mentioned together with Einstein and Sikar of Vulcan, in a reference to Dr. Richard Daystrom (UC).

Keel (Cal Bolder): A Capellan warrior, one of Maab's men. While Maab draws Kras's fire to himself, Keel kills Kras with a kligat (FC).

Keeler, Edith (Joan Collins): A socialworker and organizer in the 1930s, with brown hair, blue eyes, and a gentle, serene face. In our time track, she is hit by a truck and killed. In another, she becomes the leader of a nationwide pacifist movement that delays the United States' entry into World War II long enough for Nazi Germany to develop the atomic bomb and win the war. Although Kirk falls in love with her, he prevents McCoy from saving Edith's life—the only way to preserve history as it developed to produce the Enterprise (CEF).

Keeper (Meg Wyllie, voice by Malachi Throne): The curator of the Talosian menagerie—like all Talosians, small and gray-skinned, with a large cranium. Basically gentle and humanitarian, the keeper tried to make a zoo specimen of Captain Pike, to breed him to Vina and other likely females (Me).

Keeper of the planet: See Caretaker.

Kelinda (Barbara Bouchet): A female Kelvan—blond, with high cheekbones. Kirk does his best to seduce her, as part of the scheme to get the Enterprise back from the Kelvans. She decides to stay with Rojan, who has become jealous (AON).

Kelly: An Enterprise security guard who is killed by the Horta just before Kirk fires on it (DD).

Kelowitz, Lieutenant Commander (Grant Woods): Security leader of the second landing party searching for Spock and company on Taurus II (GS). He accompanies Kirk, Spock, and others to Cestus III, where he survives the skirmish with the Gorns (Ar). Like the rest of the crew, he falls under the influence of the Omicron Ceti III spores and has to be brought out of it by subsonics (TSP).

Kelso, Lieutenant Lee (Paul Carr): Slim, sandy-haired helmsman, good at concocting equipment from cannibalized parts. He is killed by Gary Mitchell in the lithium-cracking station on Delta Vega (WNM).

Kelva: A planet in the Andromeda galaxy, and the center of the Kelvan Empire. The Kelvans sent explorers to our galaxy to survey it for colonization, wishing to conquer rather than share the planets with anyone else. Nonhumanoid, the Kelvans convey to Spock a general impression of immense beings with hundreds of tentaclelike limbs, minds of incredible control, but no knowledge of physical sensation. The Kelvan explorers, taking on human bodies, are first confused by the assaults on their senses and emotions, and then filled with enjoyment—to the point where they do not return to Kelva (AON).

Kelvan Empire: Kelva's sphere of influence in the Andromeda galaxy (AON).

Keniclius, Dr. Stavos (James Doohan): Originally an Earth scientist during the period of the Eugenic Wars, when he planned to clone a perfect-specimen prototype into a master race. The concept was considered antihumanistic, however, and the doctor was banned from the community, after which he disappeared, with no evidence of death and no further data on him, according to the Enterprise's computers. Actually, he went to the planet Phylos, where he continued to work on the clone idea until it was perfected. Unfortunately, he carries a gram-positive bacteria, a staphylococcus strain unknown to Phylos which has no ill effects on humanoids but killed many of the native plant creatures. Dr. Keniclius worked to save the rest of the beings, and meanwhile cloned himself at least five times, producing a twenty-five-foot-tall giant Keniclius. When the Enterprise finds him, the doctor is two hundred and fifty years old. He wants to make a master race of Spocks to go out into a war-torn galaxy and enforce peace on every race. Kirk tries to convince the doctor that the galaxy long ago reached some kind of equilibrium, if not total peace, but Keniclius has been out of touch with everything for over one hundred years and does not want to believe the captain. The gigantic Spock cloned by Dr. Keniclius settles the issue by returning the original Spock to life and full intelligence, promising to stay and help the doctor revive the Phylosians and to report to the Federation on their progress (IV/a).

Keniclius 5, Dr. (James Doohan): The gigantic fifth clone of Dr. Stavros Keniclius—tall, deeply tanned, wearing only a short white Grecian skirt and red shoulder strap, with red calf-length sandals. He carries a tall golden staff and is called "Savior" by the plant creatures of Phylos (IV/a).

Kenner, Commander: A starship commander in the mirror universe who is looking for a "captain's woman," specifically Marlena-2 (MM).

Kenwith, Herb (director): The Lights of Zetar (LZ).

Kesla: A name given to the Jack-the-Ripper entity during its stay on Deneb II (WF). See also Jack the Ripper.

Kevas: A trade item. When the Klingons invade Organia, Spock calls himself a trader in kevas and trillium to fool them (EM).

Key: The clue to Kulkukan's demands are in the city that he creates in his own spaceship. The Enterprise men must find the key or die (HS/a).

Khan Noonian Singh (Ricardo Montalban): Golden-skinned, with strong features and a long mane of black hair—one of the selectively bred "supermen" of the 1990s (but Kirk can outfight him, Spock can outthink him, and he chooses an ordinary female aboard the Enterprise to be the mother of his children). From 1992 to 1996 he was absolute ruler of a quarter of Earth, from South Asia to the Middle East. Last of the tyrants to be overthrown, he escaped in the "sleeper ship" Botany Bay with eighty of his people, to be picked up two hundred years later by the Enterprise. He tries to take over the ship but is defeated and exiled to Ceti Alpha V (SS).

King Duncan (Karl Bruck): An actor with the Karidian Players who plays the part of Duncan in the Shakespearean tragedy, Macbeth (CK).

Kir: A Scalosian (WE).

Kirk, Aurelan (Joan Swift): Wife of George Samuel Kirk. She is killed by the flying parasites that invade Deneva, but survives long enough to warn Captain James Kirk of the danger (OA).

Kirk, George Samuel: Brother of James Kirk, called "Sam" by close family members. A research biologist, he wanted to be transferred to Earth Colony 2 but instead went to Deneva, where he and his wife, Aurelan, are killed by the flying parasites, leaving a son (LG, OA).

Kirk-J: Janice Lester, in a mad attempt to take Kirk's position as starship captain, traps Kirk's life force in her body and transfers herself into his body (TI).

Kirk, James T. (William Shatner): About thirty-four, with brown hair, hazel eyes, a nice smile, and overpowering charm; captain of the U.S.S. Enterprise. Service record: serial number SC937-0176CEC; rank, captain with a starship command. Commendations: Palm Leaf of Axanar Peace Mission; Grankite Order of Tactics, Class of Excellence; Prantares Ribbon of Commendation, First and Second Class. Awards of Valor: Medal of Honor; Silver Palm with Cluster; Star Fleet Citation for Conspicuous Gallantry; Karagite Order of Heroism (Cml). Kirk is a strong character, a leader, though with an underlying streak of egotism kept in check by a strong conscience (EW). This latent flaw is manifested only in a tendency to use people, particularly women. Although at heart he is a romantic (NT, SL), Kirk has never been able to form a lasting relationship with any female (CEF, CK, Cml, DY, SL). It really doesn't matter, because a starship captain is married to his ship, and there are always girls to be found. In spite of the friendship of Spock and McCoy, Kirk is somewhat lonely. He has the full loyalty of his crew, and he is a powerful, capable man with a great future. His ancestors pioneered the American frontier. Kirk's interest in American history is what the Melkots draw on for their bizarre "execution" sentence (SGn). One of Kirk's heroes is Abraham Lincoln. His special involvement with the sixteenth President's life is what triggers the rock creature's image of Lincoln to titillate Kirk's curiosity and get him to beam down to the planet. The Lincoln whom Kirk meets is exactly what the captain has expected him to be—after all, he has been drawn out of Kirk's mind (SC). Kirk contracted Vegan choriomeningitis some time ago, and still carries microorganisms of it in his blood (MG). Kirk is an extremely dynamic individual; he nearly takes over the mind fusion when Spock tries it (PSy). Captain Kirk is second only to Garth of Izar as the finest military commander in the galaxy. When Garth tries to urge Kirk to aid him in taking over the universe, Kirk says he was no warrior, but primarily an explorer. Kirk studied Garth's exploits when he was a cadet, and much admires Garth's abilities before the man became insane (WGD). Kirk is very stubborn, irritating, and independent, all factors which appealed to Deela of Scalos. When he pretends to be docile from the new acceleration of his system, she is quite disappointed in him. Deela finds that Kirk's quarters reflect his personality: austere, efficient, and, in their own way, handsome. What Deela does not notice is that Kirk is also remarkable for his reasoning powers, and has drawn the correct assumption for what has happened to him (WE). Spock has commented that when the captain is not being bellicose, Kirk's capacity for deductive reasoning shows there is no end to his arsenal of formidable talents (IV/a). When a holy war is

K

about to break out in the galaxy over a missing religious sculpture, Kirk is chosen for the expedition because of his leadership abilities and his adaptability. He also remembers how to use null-gravity combat exercises when Tchar tries to kill them all (Ji/a). When asked, he gives his middle name as Tiberius, in a touchy situation which demands a serious answer, so it must be assumed that James T. Kirk was indeed named after the second Roman emperor (Be/a). With Spock's encouragement to use the magic they know, Kirk takes on Megan, a powerful wizard of Megas-tu, and fights him to a standstill in a battle of magic in which each calls down fire, thorns, storms, and other terrors. Kirk will not give in to the more experienced magician, saying that this would only encourage Megan and his compatriots to become as bad as the Earthlings they fear, acting out of terror instead of thought or respect. Kirk's strong-mindedness, as well as his later compassion, are crucial in turning the tide in favor of the Enterprise's crew at their trial (Mtu/a). When the Enterprise people have found a way to leave the mirror universe and return to their own, Kirk leaves a final word with Spock-2 to try to change the barbaric world he lived in. Spock-2 pointed out philosophically that one man cannot change the future, to which Kirk answered that one man can change the present, leaving Spock-2 with something to think about (MM). Kirk is described by Klingons as a "swaggering, overbearing, tin-plated dictator with delusions of godhead" (TT). Captain Kirk has his own problems, plus his officers', and the problems of four hundred and thirty other people to handle (SL).

Kirk, Peter (Craig Hundley):   The son of George Samuel and Aurelan Kirk, and Captain Kirk's nephew—a pale, thin boy of about nine or ten, with reddish-brown hair and freckles. The only survivor in his family of the deadly attacks by flying parasites on Deneva, he is infected but remains alive, under heavy sedation, long enough for McCoy to discover and perfect a cure (OA).

Kirk, the: Nomad's name for Jackson Roykirk, its builder; transferred to Captain Kirk (Cg). See also Creator.

Kirk-2:   A brigand, killer, and plunderer who succeeded to command of the I.S.S. Enterprise by assassinating Captain Pike. His first act was the suppression of an uprising on Gorla by destroying the rebel planet; his second was the execution of five thousand colonists on Vega IX in order to force a retraction of their secession; he then went on to other activities . . . When Kirk accidentally beams into the mirror universe, Kirk-2 beams into our universe. Spock recognizes him as an intruder and locks him up until he can be sent back. It is to be hoped that Spock-2 decided to dispose of Kirk-2 and take over the I.S.S. Enterprise. Kirk-2 is someone any universe can do without (MM).

Kirok: Due to amnesia, Kirk can only vaguely remember his name and pronounces it haltingly. The Indians of Miramanee's tribe hear it as "Kirok" (PSy).

Kironide: A rare substance in the food on Platonius that acts on the pituitary gland to develop a long-lasting, powerful psychokinesis (PSt).

Kithara: A classical Greek instrument resembling the lyre. The Platonians give one to Spock and force him to play it (PSt).

Klee-fah: Vulcan term of refusal (AT).

Kligat: The basic weapon of Capella IV, described as resembling a sharp-edged boomerang, but actually more like a circular saw with three outstanding edges. The Capellans use it with extreme accuracy as well as great speed and force, so that at any distance up to one hundred yards a kligat is almost as effective against a man as a phaser is (FC).

Klingon (K. L. Smith):   The captain commanding the Klingon ship that attacks the Enterprise while it is conveying the Dohlman of Elas to Troyius. Squinty-eyed, light-skinned, with curly bangs and beard, he is dressed in the usual ill-fitting Klingon uniform and possesses the usual Klingon temper. He has a Ulysses S. Grant complex and will accept nothing but unconditional surrender. The Enterprise damages the Klingon ship, and it has to limp away (ET). Also, an exchange crew member from the Klothos to the Enterprise, when the two ships are going to link up for escape from Elysia, is found wandering through the corridors of the Enterprise near the dilithium-crystal lockers, where he is not supposed to be. He claims to be lost; Spock seems to believe him (Tr/a). Also, one of Kang's henchmen (Mark Tobin):   very tall, round face, full mouth, long drooping moustache, dark skin, black hair, and blacker scowl (Dv).

Klingon Empire: Chief enemy of the Federation in their part of the galaxy—a military dictatorship where war is a way of life (EM). The Klingons have given to the Romulans, under some agreement unknown to the Federation, warp-drive ships of sophisticated design (EI).

Klingonese: The language of the Klingons. Half the quadrant is learning to speak it because the Enterprise cannot protect them—so say the Klingons, at least (TT).

Klingon first lieutenant (Victor Lundin):   Kor's aide-de-camp when he occupies Organia (EM).

Klingon Imperial Fleet: The Klingon battlecruisers that attack the Enterprise in the Delta Triangle sector are from the Klingon Imperial Fleet (Tr/a).

Klingon mentality: When the Klingons try to escape Elysia on their own, Kirk is amazed that even a Klingon would jeopardize his ship and crew unnecessarily. Spock points out that to Klingon mentality their only law of life is that laws are made to be violated, and their pride in that attitude is everything to a Klingon (Tr/a).

Klingons: Klingons are generally dark and saturnine-looking, an exception being Captain Koloth, with his almost boyish face and neat little beard. Their most striking feature used to be the heavy bifurcate eyebrows, but, possibly in an attempt at disguise, the curve both up and down has been trimmed to look more like Earth eyebrows. Klingons dislike tribbles extremely, and vice versa (TT). Klingons have always fought and feel that they always must. They maintain a tradition of dueling. They are hunters, taking what they need. Their own planets are poor in resources, so they must push outward to survive. According to Kang, Klingons need no urging to hate humans (Dv). Dr. Keniclius 5 remembers the Klingons as a strong menace, possibly capable of setting off a galactic war (IV/a).

Klingon second lieutenant (Fred Sawaya): Officer on sentry duty when Kirk and Spock attack (EM).

Klingon ships: Romulans have been using Klingon ships for some time, including all the latest equipment, so it must be assumed that there is some sort of treaty or pact between the two empires.

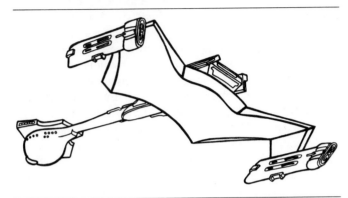

Klingon transporter system: Klingon transporters differ from Federation-style transporters in that Klingons beaming down are seen to flash a few times, then completely materialize. Federation transporters produce a "sparkling" effect and gradual materialization (Dv).

Klingon uniforms: The Klingon system of uniforms seems to differentiate among the commanders, officers, and crew without bothering to distinguish actual rank. Thus, the Klingon uniform for all males consists of a pullover jerkin of silvery material, a belt with buckle, and trousers, boots, and shirt in black. Rank is then determined by the addition of insignias or sashes. Klingon officers add to this basic uniform two small rondels of gold or silver, usually attached to the shirt just above the neckline of the jerkin. Those in positions of command or control wear a wide gold shoulder sash or baldric from the left shoulder to the right hip; the outside edge is raveled into a sort of heavy-handed fringe. Uniforms of Klingon females are similar, except that they incorporate the silvery jerkin into a shorts outfit worn over a collarless tunic or shirt of black, with the Klingon belt and buckle. The boots are unique in that they cover the entire leg all the way up to the thigh, where the top of the boot meets the bottom edge of the shorts. Rank on the females' uniforms is indicated by an extra strip of gold piping which runs around the neck of the jerkin, crosses the body, and descends to the side seams of the jerkin (Dv).

Klingon verbal salute: "Survive and succeed" (MTT/a).

Kloog (Mickey Morton): One of the thralls of Triskelion—a lumbering Neanderthaloid type with a weak left eye; probably from Rigel VII (GT).

Klothos: A Klingon battlecruiser, commanded by Captain Kor, which fires on the Enterprise just before both ships are drawn into the mysterious Delta Triangle. The ships try to continue the battle there but are stopped by the inhabitants of Elysia, the alternate universe. Finally the ships have to cooperate to get out of the region again and into our own universe (Tr/a).

Kneubuhl, John (script): Bread and Circuses (BC).

Knowledge: In the antimatter universe, where time is reversed, knowledge is being lost as the race evolves, since they are born elderly, with knowledge, and lose it as they "age" toward infancy (CC/a). While Dr. Kerniclius can duplicate a body exactly from the original, it takes longer to transfer all the knowledge from the first personality. This is done by draining the brain of each predecessor into the new clone. Kirk calls it murder (IV/a). Kulkukan is willing to impart knowledge to mankind, but at the tremendous price of being worshipped as a god. He visited Earth in ancient times, leaving behind much knowledge, and is returning to find out if it had been put to any good use (HS/a). See also Memory Alpha.

Kodos the Executioner (Arnold Moss): Former governor of Tarsus IV, and an excellent actor—small in stature, gray-haired, elegant, with a dark moustache. When food supplies ran short on Tarsus IV, he had invoked martial law and executed half the population in order to insure survival for the "superior" half of the colonists. When Federation forces finally arrived, a burned body was taken for Kodos's, and the books were closed. Kodos changes his identity, taking the name of Anton Karidian and becoming director and star of the Karidian Players. His daughter, Lenore, a member of the company, has been secretly killing all witnesses to the executions on Tarsus IV so that her father's true identity cannot be discovered. When Kodos learns of this, he is horrified, and dies by throwing himself into a phaser beam aimed at Kirk by Lenore (CK).

Koenig, Walter (script): The Infinite Vulcan (IV/a).

Kohms: Oriental-type villagers, probably descended from Chinese Communists who settled on Omega IV nearly two hundred years before the Enterprise arrives. They have a life span of perhaps one thousand years, a remnant of a long process of genetic selection following the last bacteriological war on that planet. Captain Tracey tries to protect them against attack, but the Yangs take them over anyway (OG).

Koinoenergy: From the Greek koinen: "that which is common." Spock is in top form when describing the cosmic cloud's streamers as being koinoenergy, or "common energy," i.e., plain or unexceptional, combined with an unusually powerful attraction force (OPM/a).

Kollos, Ambassador: Medusan ambassador to the Federation, who is accompanied on the Enterprise by Dr. Miranda Jones in a return to his own planet. The sight of a Medusan can cause insanity; Kollos is therefore seen through a protective visor, as a pattern of flashing lights and radiation contained in an angular box. Spock makes a mind link with Kollos, and finds him to be an entity of great charm and empathy. Kollos shows affection for Spock, Jones, and the rest of the Enterprise's personnel, and sympathy for their lonely nontelepathic state. Kollos makes a permanent mind link with Dr. Jones, and she accompanies him to his own planet (TB).

Koloth, Captain (William Campbell): A tall, dark, handsome Klingon with a neat black beard and a charming, jovial manner. The captain of a Klingon warship, he and Kirk have evidently tangled before. They recognize each other on sight, address each other as "my dear

Captain Koloth/Kirk," and don't trust each other an inch behind the friendly attitudes (TT). Captain Koloth (voice by James Doohan) commands the Klingon battle-cruiser the Devisor, and is a general all-around standard Klingon nasty (MTT/a).

Kol-tai: An inhabitant of plague-ridden Dramia II. He remembers McCoy's medical visit of nineteen years ago, and clearly thinks of the doctor as a friend and savior since he inoculated the population against Saurian virus. Kirk wants him as a witness in favor of McCoy at the murder trial, but Kol-tai finally contracts the auroral plague on the Enterprise, and gives the disease to everyone else aboard except Spock, who is immune. Spock helps McCoy break out of jail long enough to find an antidote, which is used to inoculate the Enterprise people and bring them back to health. Kol-tai survives the plague also, and helps free McCoy from charges of murder (Al/a).

Komack, Admiral (Byron Morrow): The virtually inflexible head of Star Fleet Command, Sector 9—a sharp-voiced man with a tanned, narrow face, brilliant blue eyes, and crew-cut white hair. He orders Kirk to take the Enterprise to Altair VI, but because Spock is in pon far and therefore in danger, Kirk goes to Vulcan instead. The influential T'Pau later politely requests that Kirk be allowed to divert to Vulcan, and Komack is only too pleased to comply (AT).

Komack, James (director): A Piece of the Action (PA).

K-1 circuit: One of the indicators on the diagnostic panel in Sick Bay (NT).

Koon-ut kal-if-fee: Honorific Vulcan term meaning "challenge" or "marriage." Vulcans apparently view both ceremonies in approximately the same light (AT). See also Kal-if-fee.

Kor, Commander (John Colicos): The military governor of Organia during the Klingons' short occupation of that planet. A typical Klingon—large, dark, and fierce—and a deadly, dirty fighter, proud of his ruthlessness (EM). Kor is later promoted to captain, commander of the Klingon battlecruiser Klothos, which is caught in the time trap of the Delta Triangle region. He has to cooperate with Kirk to get both ships out of the alternate universe known as Elysia, but Kor plans to betray his word and destroy the Enterprise as soon as the escape plan works. His treachery fails, but he claims full credit for saving both ships anyway (Tr/a).

Korax (Michael Pataki): Captain Koloth's aide; a typical Klingon—even nastier than most Klingons, with none of Koloth's charm. His insults to Captain Kirk and to the Enterprise cause one magnelephant fight on Space Station K-7 (TT). He is First Officer to Captain Koloth on the battlecruiser Devisor (MTT/a).

Korby, Dr. Roger (Michael Strong): An exobiologist, about forty-five, with brown hair, strong bones, and startlingly blue eyes. Often called the Pasteur of archeological medicine, his translation of medical records from the Orion ruins revolutionized the Federation's immunization techniques. He later led an expedition to Exo III, where he discovered the androids left behind by the "Old Ones."

He constructed an android body for himself after his own was badly frozen, and planned to bring androids to the inhabited worlds of the Federation. When the Enterprise arrives, bringing Korby's fiancée, he tries to force Kirk to aid him in his project. However, having an android body, he has been gradually losing his human feelings, and when Kirk makes this apparent to Korby, the scientist destroys himself and the remaining androids (LG).

Korob (Theo Marcuse): On Pyris VII he takes the form of a Terran warlock with a black beard and shaven head, but actually he looks like a very tiny blue-green-grayish creature, reminiscent of a crayfish with miniature vulturelike additions. An alien, adept at quasimagical illusions, he is calm, urbane, and ethical, unlike his partner, Sylvia. He wishes to obey the Old Ones who have sent them to Pyris VII to prepare the planet for colonization, and disapproves of Sylvia's hedonism and cruelty. Ultimately he frees Kirk's party and is killed by Sylvia, who is in the form of a huge black cat. Kirk uses Korob's wand, which is a transmuter, to destroy Sylvia (Cp).

Kovas, Magda (Susan Denberg): One of Mudd's women, a small silvery blond who wears fringed pale blue and silver clothes. Raised at a helium experimental station, Maggie left because no eligible men were there. She marries one of the miners of Rigel XII (MW).

Krako, Jojo (Victor Tayback): The jolly, balding, pudgy boss of the Southside Territory on Iotia, and Oxmyx's chief enemy. Kirk eventually sets him up as Oxmyx's second-in-command (PA).

Kras (Tige Andrews): Klingon agent—dark-complexioned, with a sneering round face and a low hairline—sent to Capella IV to prevent the Federation from gaining permission to mine topaline there. He supports Maab's revolt against Akaar, then turns against Maab and threatens his men with a phaser. Maab draws Kras's fire while his lieutenant, Keel, kills Kras (FC).

Krasnowsky, Captain (Bart Conrad): A bull-necked member of Kirk's trial board (Cml).

Krell (Ned Romeo): A small, sneaky Klingon agent sent in to subvert the culture on Tyree's planet by arming the villagers with guns (PLW).

Krodak (Gene Dynarski): A tall Gideonite—bald, with a black moustache, dressed in a body suit with a short surcoat decorated with hexagrams, evidently some indication of rank. He beams aboard the Enterprise to prove to Spock that the transporter is working well (MG).

Krotus: Garth of Izar, in his insane desire to become Master of the Universe, names Krotus along with Alexander the Great, Lee Kuan, Napoleon, Caesar, and Hitler—all of whom had the drive to be absolute master of their known world (WGD).

Kroykah: A Vulcan term, the extreme form of "Cease and desist." Used only in emergency situations by one with ultimate authority, and never ignored (AT).

Kryton (Tony Young): An attendant of Elaan on her voyage aboard the Enterprise—a muscular young man with lots of curly black hair and a scowl, wearing red-orange fiberglass plate armor. Of a noble family, he loves Elaan and is jealous over her betrothal to the monarch of Troyius. Driven by a feeling of "if I can't have her, no one will," he works with the Klingons to halt the Enterprise. Caught transmitting to the Klingon ship following the Enterprise, he tricks the security guard into killing him—thereby committing suicide. It is later discovered that Kryton has rigged the antimatter pods to blow up the moment the ship enters warp drive, but this sabotage is rectified in time (ET).

K-7, deep-space station: Station near Sherman's Planet, in a disputed area between Federation and Klingon territories, where Kirk tangles simultaneously with tribbles, Klingons, and Nilz Baris. The battle of Donatu V took place there (TT).

K-3 indicator: An indicator on the diagnostic panel which monitors (among other brain functions) the level of pain a patient feels (OA).

K-2 factor: Indicated by the Sick Bay diagnostic panel, usually relating to blood pressure (JB).

Kukulkan (James Doohan): If he was all he said he was, this ancient alien visited Earth when its history was new, and taught its people many things, including a remarkably accurate calendar. In his shape as a winged, feathered serpent, Kulkukan started many Earth legends about gods, dragons, serpents, and the like. He left knowledge in the world, and came back to find warriors, which upset him very much. He was not a god, but a lonely, ancient wise being who wanted to help others. When he is unable to make the Enterprise people either hate him or worship him, he goes away. Kirk mourns the loss of knowledge to Earth peoples, but thinks the price is too high to pay for it. Kulkukan was the mythic Mayan storm and culture god—a feathered serpent who was also man and king. He was the ruler of the four points of the compass and the four elements of the world: air, earth, fire, and water (HS/a).

Kuri, Commander: A Klingon battlecruiser captain who wants revenge for the supposed destruction of the Klothos by the Enterprise. Kirk follows the Class 2 signal of the Klothos into Elysia to escape Kuri's revenge (Tr/a).

Kyle, Lieutenant (John Winston): Blond officer with a British accent, sometimes helmsman, sometimes transporter chief. He runs scanners at the computer station when Kirk visits Apollo and Spock is in command (WM). Lieutenant Kyle gains a new moustache in later years on the starship (BFS/a).

Kyle-2, Lieutenant: Transporter chief in the mirror universe, as in our universe. Kyle-2 gets the agonizer from an implacable Spock-2 for letting the transporter beam wobble (MM).

Kzin: The name for both the planet and its beings (also known as Kzinti). The beings are fat orange catlike creatures about eight feet tall, with individual markings, such as a white patch on the nose, stripes over the eyes, etc. The Kzin are flesh-eaters, and not particularly picky about it. They are ferociously warlike, proud, and stubborn. A treaty with the Federation has stripped the Kzin of their empire, but before they met mankind the galaxy was their dinner table. Now the Kzin have only a dozen worlds, are not allowed weapons, and have only peace-keeping police ships. However, they have managed to get around this by resorting to piracy, with the tacit approval of the Kzin government (SW/a). Even the extremely ferocious and uncompromising Kzin have had to accept life in the alternate universe of the Delta Triangle region and to learn to live with their fellows in peace (Tr/a). Dr. Keniclius 5 knows of the Kzin and realizes their danger. They are one of the reasons he gives for wanting to send a huge peace-keeping force into the galaxy. Kirk assures the doctor that peace has prevailed for over one hundred years, except for piracy, since the Federation has controlled Kzin (IV/a).

Kzinti anatomy: When the Chuft Captain is hurt physically by Spock's sudden attack, he offers to fight the Vulcan in hand-to-hand combat for revenge. The Chuft Captain says he will fight in his present injured condition, with two ribs broken and unset or bandaged, so that Spock has a chance to kill the Kzin. However, Spock knows more about Kzin anatomy than the Chuft Captain would wish—that they have more than one heart and that their ribs have vertical bracing, so that although the Chuft Captain may be in pain, he is not as badly damaged as a human would be under the same circumstances (SW/a).

L

Laboratory: An underground laboratory on a huge scale, with the mechanisms and materials needed to turn Spock into a twenty-five-foot-tall clone of himself, is found by the landing party on Phylos. The laboratory contains machinery that is definitely organic-looking—more like plants than metal machines. A powerful force field, as well as a probe, originate from one wall (IV/a). Karl Four's laboratory contains starcharts, scientific material . . . and a playpen, occupied by Karl Four's father (CC/a). The Enterprise's landing party is taken by the Lactrans to a gigantic laboratory. McCoy guesses that the alien beings want to make certain that the Enterprise men do not carry harmful bacteria. They might also be tested for intelligence, as one might test any laboratory specimen (EB/a).

Laboratory table: Spock's dying body is found in a Phylosian laboratory, on a special table suspended by golden tubes that glow on all sides. He has been cloned to produce a gigantic Spock-clone, who no longer needs the original Vulcan (IV/a).

Lactra VII: An unusual planet that is obviously constructed as one gigantic zoo, where some of the wildlife is allowed to run free and others are kept in compounds or

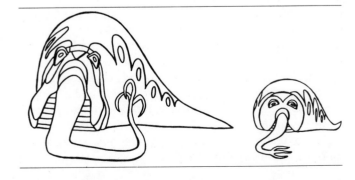

cages. The reasoning behind which beings are selected for which areas is beyond the humans, who are captured for the zoo. On this planet a desert ecology can be found right next to a rain forest or a gently rolling landscape, suggesting terraforming and intelligent life. However, all initial surveys missed any readings of intelligent life forms on Lactra VII. Actually, huge twenty-foot-long sluglike creatures live on Lactra VII and control sensor readings of their planet with as much ease as they control their swift telepathic communication (EB/a).

Lacunar amnesia: Technically, forgetfulness of specific incidents, as opposed to general amnesia. When the children of the Starnes expedition seem to have no reaction to their parents' deaths, McCoy diagnoses their problem as lacunar amnesia, caused by shock. Actually, Gorgan's control over their minds is causing the symptoms (CL).

Lad: Scottish term for "boy," used by Scotty as a term of endearment to the huge sluglike Lactran child who is beamed up to the Enterprise by mistake. Scotty and the child take a liking to each other (EB/a).

Laddie: A friendly Scottish reference to a boy.

Lakso, Edward J. (script): And the Children Shall Lead (CL).

Lal (Alan Bergmann): One of the Vians who tests the empath Gem in a cavern of Minara II, with a bald skull ridged at brow and temples, a narrow pointed chin, concentric wrinkles around mouth, and wearing a flowing metallic gown (Em).

Landon, Yeoman Martha (Celeste Yarnall): Blond, pretty, and infatuated with Chekov. As a member of the Gamma Trianguli VI landing party, she finds the prospect of being marooned bearable so long as Chekov is there. Makora and Sayana see them kissing, imitate them, and incur Vaal's wrath (Ap).

Landru (Charles MacAulay): In projection, a tall, bony, gray-haired man with burning eyes and a soft, gentle voice, Landru is actually a highly efficient computer containing the stored memory of the scientist who programmed it six thousand years ago. Its purpose was to build a stable, peaceful culture, but instead it has produced a static and nonproductive one. When Kirk points out that it is harming the people, the computer destroys itself (RA).

Landscape barrier: See ShiKahr.

Langford: Pointing out Uhura-2's ability to use a knife, someone on the I.S.S. Enterprise comments: "Remember what Uhura did to him?", referring to a certain Langford (MM).

Lang, Lieutenant (James Farley): Gunnery officer who is lured to the surface of Cestus III, where the Gorns kill him just as he catches sight of them (Ar).

Lara: A beautiful Human female with trifurcated eyebrows, red hair, a red shorts outfit, boots, wristlets, and a claw necklace. Athletic, competent, and self-assured, she is a hunter with a flawless sense of direction and a straightforward manner. She likes Kirk and makes several advances toward him, but finds that he is too busy with the job of finding the missing sculpture to have any time for other activities (Ji/a).

Lars (Steve Sandor): A thrall on Triskelion—a gigantic Viking-type, too blond and Nordic to be believed. He is Uhura's drill thrall and is also "selected" for her, the meaning of which is left to conjecture, but which Uhura does not seem to care for at all (GT).

Laser: Acronym for Light Amplification by Stimulated Emission of Radiation; a device which emits a narrow, intense beam of coherent light, made up of waves all of the same length and all in phase. Holograms (three-dimensional images) are produced by lasers. Medical machines using lasers are to be found in Dr. McCoy's medical lab: bone-setting lasers, electron-laser microscopes, and other useful medical paraphernalia (Te/a). As predecessors of the phaser, laser-powered weapons were used as late as Captain Pike's time (Me).

Lassie: Scottish diminutive for "girl." Scott calls Karla Five the "alien lassie" (CC/a).

Last orders: Kirk has a tape of orders addressed to Spock and McCoy, to be heard only in the event of his death. It tells them to cooperate and to draw on each other's abilities. Spock and McCoy listen to it when Kirk is lost in the interphase in Tholian territory, but both of them deny this after he is recovered (TW).

Latimer (Rees Vaughn): Navigator on the shuttlecraft Galileo when it crashes on Taurus II. He is the first to be killed by the natives, one of whom pierces him with a stone-tipped spear (GS).

Laughing: See Quivering.

Laughing crewman: See Harrison, Dr.

Laughter infection: When the air system of the Enterprise is pumped full of nitrous oxide, everyone on the bridge is infected with uncontrollable laughter except Spock, since "laughing gas" is painful to Vulcans (PJ/a).

Launch Control: See Cromwell.

Lavinius V: Site of an ancient civilization that was wiped out, some two hundred years before the Enterprise, by the flying parasites that later attack Deneva (OA).

Lawgiver, First (Sig Haig): One of Landru's agents. The Lawgivers are at all times in full or partial communication with the computer. They wear long, hooded brown robes and talk like badly constructed robots (RA).

Lawton, Yeoman 3 /C Tina (Patricia McNulty): Young, blond, and likely to be pretty one day, at the moment she's an awkward nineteen or so. Yeoman Rand tries to pair her off with Charlie Evans but he is interested only in Janice. Charlie ignores Lawton at first, then turns the unsuspecting girl into an iguana. The Thasians later

Lay by: Nautical term still in use by Star Fleet. Meaning: to bring one ship alongside another and stop.

Lazarus: The brother of Martha and Mary, according to the Bible, an Earth testament. He was raised by Jesus from the dead. Flint the immortal says he was Lazarus (RM).

Lazarus A (Robert Brown): A madman with brown hair and wild blue eyes. When a parallel world in an alternate universe made contact with his planet he met his opposite Lazarus B, whom he perceived as his mortal enemy. In an attempt to kill him, he destroyed both their worlds. When the Enterprise finds him, he has traveled through many centuries seeking his enemy. Kirk tricks him into a warp corridor between the two universes (AF).

Lazarus B (Robert Brown): Lazarus A's opposite number—sane, peaceful, with brown hair and calm blue eyes. He eventually traps Lazarus A with himself in the warp corridor between the parallel universes, thus preventing Lazarus A from destroying both universes as he has previously destroyed both their planets. Kirk speculates sadly that Lazarus B will spend eternity in the corridor with Lazarus A's hands perpetually at his throat (AF).

Leader, Tony (director): For the World Is Hollow and I Have Touched the Sky (FW).

Lee Kuan: A dictator who sought absolute power and was corrupted absolutely by it (PF). Mentioned as a tyrant and conqueror (WGD).

Legends: The Aquans of Argo have legends of sealed places in sunken ruins where many records are kept. But laws prevent anyone from trying to find these places (Am/a). Earth has many legends similar to the one of Kulkukan: that of a godlike being who imparts knowledge to the people. Vulcan has no legends, but fact. Vulcan has been visited by alien beings, and the aliens went away much wiser (HS/a).

Legends, Kzinti: The Kzinti have legends of weapons haunted by their dead owners, and they should take heed when they find the Slaver weapon belonging to a spy who died a billion years ago (SW/a).

Leighton, Dr. Thomas (William Sargent): Burnt, scarred, crippled—a biochemist and a good research scientist with a reputation for steady, occasionally brilliant work. Native to Tarsus IV, he survived the massacre on that planet under Kodos the Executioner, but was injured and lost his family. He spends the last years of his life on Planet Q, where, at a performance of Macbeth, he becomes suspicious that the actor Karidian is Kodos and calls Kirk in to investigate. He invites the Karidian Players to a party and is killed by Lenore Karidian (CK).

Leighton, Martha (Natalie Norwick): The wife of Dr. Thomas Leighton—dark-haired, middle-aged, tired (CK).

Le-matya: A huge mountain-lion type of creature with leathery hide and odd markings. It has poisonous teeth and claws. A le-matya attacks I-Chaya, and damages the old sehlat beyond recovery (Yy/a). See also I-Chaya.

Lemli, Mr. (Roger Holloway): A security guard and engineer. He and Leslie are the guards who are not beamed down to meet Sargon (RT). His enjoyment of rock music while on duty earns him a reproving look from Scott (WEd). He is one of the two guarding Janice-K while she testifies at Spock's trial (TI).

Lens: The jeweled eyes of the snake towers in Kulkukan's city are used as lenses to focus on the mosaic at the top of the pyramid (HS/a).

Leper colony: Kirk found the plague-ridden planet of Dramia II an outer-space equivalent of Devil's Island and a leper colony (Al/a).

Leslie, Lieutenant (Eddie Paskey): Relief helmsman and utility man, with curly brown hair and sturdy features (AF, CK, RA, TSP). Part of the landing party that comes to Omega IV in search of Kirk's party (OG). Leslie and Lemli are the two security guards Kirk tells to take Spock, Sulu, and Uhura off the bridge when they do not obey his orders. Thanks to the children's thought center, the guards don't obey either (CL).

Lester, Janice (Sandra Smith): The leader of a group of scientists exploring the ruins of Camus II—a handsome woman about Kirk's age, wearing a pants suit of black and pink with white sleeves. Kirk once loved her, but Janice was driven mad with jealousy and ambition; her hatred of her own womanhood made loving her impossible. She feels that Kirk walked out on her when things got serious, never realizing that her own passions had forced the issue. Having spent years studying ships' operations, she feels that a captaincy was her due and that Kirk prevented her from getting it. Possessing the secret of entity transfer, she changes bodies with Kirk and takes over the Enterprise. One man, Dr. Coleman, still loves her, and asks to take care of her after the transfer has weakened enough for Kirk to regain his own body (TI).

Lethe (Suzanne Wasson): One of Tristan Adams's brainwashed assistants—a tall, cadaverous young woman with long black hair and a dead voice (DMd).

L

"Let me help": Kirk tells Edith Keeler that these three words are to be recommended over "I love you" as the most valuable words ever spoken to another being. They were suggested, he says, by a famous novelist who lived on a planet circling a far star in Orion's belt. Edith assumes he is joking about the writer, but believes the words; that is her own credo, after all (CEF).

Lewis: A member of the security team in the Horta hunt (DD).

Lewis, Shari (script): The Lights of Zetar (LZ) (with Jeremy Tarcher).

Lexington, U.S.S.: A starship, commanded by Commodore Wesley, involved in war games with the M-5 computer. The computer mistakes the games for a real attack and damages this ship severely, killing many crew members (UC).

Libra: Presumably a planet of craftspeople; Nurse Chapel owns a piece of jewelry made for her by the titanium smiths of Libra (Te/a).

Librarians: Some of the finest librarians in the galaxy are killed by the lights of Zetar when they pass through Memory Alpha (LZ). Kirk envies the challenging, though less dangerous, job of librarians (Be/a).

Library: The library on Sarpeidon houses files, mirror discs on which are recorded the entire history of the planet, and the atavachron. By selecting a disc from the library, attuning the atavachron, and stepping through the time portal, one can go back to any given era of Sarpeidon history. The library is the last operative spot on the planet when the Enterprise arrives to rescue the inhabitants (AY). See also Memory alpha.

Library/computer: Identity tapes are fed into the library/computer for positive identification (Su/a). The Lactran child reads the complete Enterprise computer information in seconds (EB/a).

Library/computer station: Spock's post. See also Computer.

Lieutenant, SS (Ralph Maurer): Ekos police officer who fails to capture Kirk and Spock. Spock takes his uniform and helmet (PF).

Life energy: The females of Taurus II revitalize themselves with the life energy from males they lure to the planet; the males then die from lack of enough strength to keep on living (LS/a).

Life-entity transfer: A total transfer of personality and consciousness from one body to another. Spock has never heard of its occurring successfully with the aid of a mechanical device anywhere in the galaxy. Janice-K says it was discovered and forgotten long ago on Camus II, discovered by Janice Lester again, and used on Kirk. The transfer can be weakened and eventually broken; it appears to weaken most during periods of very strong emotion, such as hysteria (TI).

Life forces: See Life energy.

Life-form readings: Information obtained by tricorders and other sensors about the composition of any living entity or species one happens to meet. This includes the blood type, heart rate, and metabolic setup of the entity. Life-form readings are not infallible, but are often of great aid in making contact with sapient beings

not immediately recognizable as such (SB). See also Tricorders.

Life forms: Description of anything alive and sentient. Sensors do not pick up any life forms on Lactra VII, but the intelligence on that planet is so highly developed that the inhabitants probably deliberately blanked out sensor scannings (Eb/a). No life forms are detected on the mad planet, but something is seen moving in the scrub brush (Ji/a).

Life lab: Flint's very complete and impressive laboratory contains not only robots and equipment with which to purify substrates quickly; a portion of the lab is also devoted to the design and development of androids (RM).

Life room: See Zoo.

Life-support belt: A wide utility-type belt that glows with a pale yellow-green aura around the wearer. It creates an almost totally impenetrable force field, which works like an envelope of air to prevent harm to the person inside the life-support system (BFS/a). The life-support aura formed around a body by the belt can be used underwater, as well as in the vacuum of space (Am/a).

Life-support masks: When on the planet Argo, the air-breathing humans have to wear life-support belts and masks; when the Aquans are on the Enterprise, they have to wear water-filled masks (Am/a).

Life-support systems: The systems aboard all vessels the functions of which are to supply and maintain an environment compatible for life aboard ship. They include the medical mechanism that is placed over Sarek's chest (JB) and a headpiece that is used on Spock while searching for his brain (SB).

Lights of Zetar: See Zetar, lights of.

Light, speed of: The speed of light is 186,000 miles per second. It was once said that no natural phenomenon in space can move faster than light except the lights of Zetar. However, other natural phenomena which can move faster than light include tachyons and cherenkov radiation, both discovered in the twentieth century. The statement may have meant that a natural phenomenon cannot travel faster than light at will, but it was not so stated. Artificial phenomena which can move faster than light include starships such as the Enterprise (LZ).

Light-year: A light-year is the distance light travels in one year at 186,000 miles per second, or nearly 6,000,000,000,000 miles. During a power surge caused by Losira, the Enterprise is thrown 990.7 light-years from her planet. It should take the ship 11.337 solar hours to return, according to Spock (TWS).

Lilliputian city: Kirk's description of the miniature city of the Terratins. He is referring to Gulliver's Travels, an old Earth story by Jonathan Swift in which the hero visits Lilliput, a country where the people are only six inches tall (Te/a).

Limbo: According to religious lore, a neutral abode, neither heaven nor hell, for unbaptized folk to await the Final Accounting. Also, a place of confinement or oblivion; Lucien is to be placed in this type of limbo by his fellow Megas-tu magicians for aiding humans. Kirk refuses to allow this, saying it is a death sentence for a fun-loving being like Lucien (Mtu/a).

Lincoln, Abraham (Lee Bergere):   An image in Yarnek's drama of good and evil. Drawn from Kirk's own hero worship of the great Civil War President of the United States, he is kind and wise, with gentle humor and a rather surprised pleasure at being once more alive and aware of his surroundings. But there are contradictions. He knows of voice devices and recognizes the Enterprise personnel by name, yet he does not know of taped music or understand the transporter. He harkens back to his early youth as a wrestler when faced with hand-to-hand combat, but agrees with Surak that the fighting should be ended if at all possible. He mentions that he sent one hundred thousand men to their deaths in four years of the most bloody war in American history, yet wished only for peace. He is killed by Kahless on the planet Excalbia—that is, his image is destroyed (SC).

Lincoln, Roberta (Terry Garr): A very 1968 "mod" secretary, first to Agents 201 and 347, and then to Gary Seven. Something of a kook, a rebel but very patriotic, she wonders if she'll be alive at age thirty. Born in Brooklyn, New York; aged twenty; height 5'7", weight 120 pounds; hair light brown tinted honey blond; blue eyes. Distinguishing marks: a small mole on left shoulder, larger strawberry birthmark elsewhere. She stops Gary Seven's computer before it can tell him precisely where the mark is located (AE).

Linden, Don (Mark Robert Brown):   A small black boy of about eight—one of the children of the ill-fated Starnes expedition, who temporarily come under Gorgan's influence (CL).

Lindstrom (William Meader):   Space Command Representative; a member of Kirk's trial board (Cml). The sociologist Lindstrom (Christopher Held) has all the terrible seriousness of youth. After the destruction of Landru, he stays on Beta III to rehabilitate the society, showing great sympathy for and interest in Reger's daughter, Tula (RA).

Ling: One of Khan Noonian Singh's people (SS).

Linke, Dr. (Jason Wingreen):   One of the researchers placed by the Federation on Minara II to study its star's development into a nova. A Terran of about forty, with the pale skin of one who spends his life indoors, he dies under torture in the Vian's test of Gem's ability to comprehend self-sacrifice (Em).

Lipton, Police Sergeant (Lincoln Demyan):   A twentieth-century security guard at McKinley Rocket Base—pudgy, with black beetle-brows. He tries to capture Gary Seven but is put to sleep with the servo. Later in the day he does catch Kirk and Spock (AE).

Liquid crystals: When the Enterprise people have presented all of their arguments and pleas, the amusement planet's master computer tallies thousands upon thousands of decisions on liquid crystals (OUP/a).

Lirpa: A traditional Vulcan weapon consisting of a heavy handle about four feet long with a semicircular, razor-edged blade at one end and a massive metal cudgel, eminently suitable for smashing heads, at the other. The lirpa can be used with machete, bludgeon, or quarterstaff technique. Spock and Kirk begin their duel on Vulcan with the lirpa, but when Kirk disarms Spock, they switch to the ahn-woon (AT).

Lisa: See Angela.

Lithium-cracking station: Since lithium (or dilithium crystals) occur naturally and can be used in their raw state for power, the purpose of such a station is unexplained. Mining and processing for a lithium-cracking station are automated and the station is unmanned. Kirk attempts to abandon Gary Mitchell at a lithium-carcking station on Delta Vega, a desolate planet (WNM).

Little boy (John Megna):   In appearance about eight or nine, but actually nearly three hundred years old. Jahn's sidekick (Mi).

Livery: The Sarpeids of Sarpeidon's "Charles II" period took Kirk's uniform for livery, since it was obviously not the gentleman's attire of resplendent lace, satin coat, large drooping plume, and so on (AY).

Liyang: A Kohm executioner on Omega IV. Kirk's sudden arrival prevents him from beheading Cloud William and Sirah (OG).

L-Langon Mountains: The general location of the Vulcan maturity test, a bleak, high desert area with many dangers. The specific area where the ten-day ordeal takes place is known as Vulcan's Forge (Yy/a).

Lockpick: See EM/3/Green.

Logic: Megas-tu is a magic world where belief in the ability to do something works as well as conventional logic. When Lucien makes the Enterprise's life-support systems begin working again with a magic word, Spock says it is not logical; Lucien replies that it works by his logic, not the Vulcan's (Mtu/a).

Logic circuits: Part of the computer complex of the Enterprise.

Logs: Old nautical term for records of a ship's travels, trade, experiences, crew, and all other details pertinent to that ship. The Star Fleet logs have not changed much from the diary-type written logs of old times, except that they are voice recordings, for the most part. There are the ship's log, personal logs, medical logs, and supplemental logs; the last are usually made by tricorder on a trip when it is impossible to make an official record, to be rerecorded into the official ship's log at a later date.

Log, subjective time: While in the past on Vulcan, Spock keeps a log of his movements and events, noting that it is subjective time in comparison to the future, where he actually now exists (Yy/a).

Lokai (Lou Antonio):   A political fugitive from the planet Cheron—with dark brown hair and eyes, the left half of his face totally black, the right half stark white. The pigmentation of the rest of his body is not known, as he wears pale blue overalls and gloves. He is impolite in the extreme, and wont to accuse before he is harmed. He was a revolutionary, possibly a leader of the oppressed race of his world. Tried and convicted of treason, he escaped from Cheron fifty thousand years back and has been on the run ever since. Lokai is pursued by Bele, another citizen of his planet, who has been trying to capture and bring him to justice. They meet on the Enterprise, but neither alien can be convinced to listen to the other's side of the ancient quarrel. They are both finally left on

L

their long-devastated home planet to fight it out (LB).

Loneliness: The predominant feeling experienced under the influence of the neural neutralizer. Dr. Adams is left with the machine too long and dies of loneliness (DMd). The price paid by the self-exiled people of Megas-tu has been centuries of loneliness, away from the friendliness and sharing of humans and other beings (Mtu/a).

Longevity: The adults of Miri's planet had tried to find a cure for aging, some way to extend life. They had developed a serum and inoculated the entire population. But they had tampered with too many factors, causing a disease to develop which killed off everyone who had reached puberty but prolonged the lives of children. Adults died horribly, scabbed and mottled, their minds diseased and paranoid. Seeing this, the perennial children concluded that being a "grup" (derived from "grown-up") is a bad idea, and they are fearful and suspicious of the intruders from the Enterprise. Although she looks and behaves like a preadolescent, Miri is approximately three hundred years old when the Enterprise crew finds the "onlies" (the children of the planet), and she is about to reach puberty (Mi).

Long-range scan: A scanning system used over a much longer range than usual, to pick up any approaching, potentially hostile, ships (Su/a).

Lora (Majel Barrett): In appearance, an attractive female who cannot resist Harry Mudd when he applies a love potion to himself. However, Spock fires on the girl with a phaser, showing her to be a Rigellian hypnoid. The reptilian illusionmaker, unhurt, breaks the image of the human girl and scuttles away in its natural form before the angry miners can attack it (MP/a).

Losira (Lee Meriwether): A tall, beautiful being with long dark hair and deep sad eyes, dressed in purple and silver. She appears only as a projection of the last survivor on the Kalandan outpost which she once commanded. Her image was left behind in a computer in the planet's brain room to defend the world against all life forms but her own, and to greet future Kalandan visitors with an explanation of the deadly disease that killed the outpost's entire population, including herself. Losira's projection not only gives off a life-form reading of tremendous intensity; it can also flip into a two-dimensional angle and disappear. Her touch will kill a person, but only if she first calls out the name, rank, and details of that person's life. The intensity of her projection causes a power surge strong enough to knock the Enterprise 990.7 light-years away from the outpost planet, and to create seismic disturbances on the planet itself. When the computer is destroyed, her projection vanishes—the last trace ever found of the Kalandans (TWS).

Loskene, Commander (mask effects by Mike Minor): Commander of the Tholian ship—a red-gold, glowing, angular, almost crystal being with triangular white eye spots, but no other visible features, and a voice like ten angry sopranos singing in unison through a filter. Loskene orders the Enterprise out of Tholian territory when it is attempting to rescue Kirk from the space warp, first allowing the starship exactly the hour and fifty-three minutes needed and then (showing Tholian punctuality) opening fire immediately after the time is up. When the Enterprise returns the fire and partially disables the Tholian ship, Loskene calls in another ship, and the two Tholian vessels weave a tractor web around the Enterprise. The Enterprise escapes to a distance of several parsecs, and Loskene does not pursue (TW).

Lost colony: The Terratins were part of an early colony from Earth sent out many years back, and, owing to the shrinking of the colonists by the lethal spiroid waves of the planet, they remained a lost colony until discovered by the Enterprise (Te/a).

Louise: One of the "older" three-hundred-year-old children. She reaches puberty and starts to develop the skin sores that signify the onset of the disease that kills adults. Kirk uses her as an example of what will eventually happen to all the children, thereby gaining their cooperation (Mi).

Love: The Vendorian who took Carter Winston's shape also took on his emotional characteristics, so that after a time it begins to love Anne Nored almost as much as Winston did. When it shows Anne its true shape, she does not feel she can return that love, but later she seems at least to be able to consider it (Su/a). Everyone on the Enterprise is affected by the love potion, and feels at least a strong attraction for someone, as either friend or lover. Spock even finds himself confessing a love for Nurse Chapel to the bridge personnel, an act which appals him as much as it surprises the others. While the love potion is effective, he calls Chapel "Darling" and dashes to her rescue (MP/a).

Love philtre: The females of Megas-tu see nothing wrong in gaining the favors of the males of their dreams by using a magic love philtre. Lucien observes that this is a normal thing, though it surprises the Enterprise people (Mtu/a).

Love potion: Harry Mudd found the love potion crystals on Sirius IX and conned some creature out of them. He sold thousands to inhabitants of the Sirius planets, but their unusual biochemistry reacted with the love potion to make them ill. Because of this, Sirius IX laid charges against Mudd and wanted him arrested. The potion itself is a swirling liquid that comes in a crystal; all you have to do is break the crystal and apply one drop to the skin, then touch whoever you want to love you. One touch creates friendship between men or women, but between man and woman—guaranteed love. Mudd says the love potion can evoke passion in a block of granite. Believing the potion to be a fake, Mudd works on Nurse Chapel's unrequited love for Spock and gives her a crystal, claiming that laboratory tests would destroy it and she should try it the way it was meant to be used, not analyze it as a scientist. The effect of the liquid against human skin makes the user dizzy for a few minutes, but this is only temporary, as the liquid is absorbed and will pass. The aftereffect of the love potion is several hours of sheer hatred for the object of one's affections; the love potion lasts about an hour and the hatred for several hours, so it is hardly a bargain, in Spock's opinion. Mudd is still optimistic—so few things in this universe are perfect, after all (MP/a).

Low-frequency shield: To prevent the malevolent alien entity from taking over the Enterprise, Kirk orders that a low-frequency shield, like the one on the pod ship, be rigged for the navigational system of the starship. Spock thinks he can do it without the alien's becoming aware of what they plan, but it will be a very small field, barely three meters square (BFS/a).

L374-III: Planet where the crew of the Constellation seek refuge from the berserker, which then destroys them, planet and all (DMa).

Lucas, John Meredyth (director): The Enterprise Incident (EI); Elaan of Troyius (ET); The Ultimate Computer (UC); (scripts): The Changeling (Cg); Patterns of Force (PF); Elaan of Troyius (ET); That Which Survives (TWS).

Lucien (James Doohan): A man-sized alien resembling a satyr, with a humanoid upper torso and a goat-shaped lower torso with cloven hooves; he has curly dark hair and beard, with small curved horns on his head. In appearance about fifty years old, he is actually many centuries old and known variously to almost every Earth culture as goat god, demon, devil, tempter, rollicker, or Lucifer. When the Enterprise breaks through the center of the universe, he appears on the starship in time to save it from the chaos of Megas-tu, and tries to shield the Earthlings from the hostility of his fellow magicians. His love of humans, especially for their curiosity and ability to love and share, is unbounded; he has been lonely for their company and welcomes the arrival of the Enterprise (Mtu/a). See also Generalist; Witness.

Lucifer: See Lucien.

Luma (Sheila Leighton): A typical Eymorg—a pretty young girl with no sense. She is the first Eymorg that Kirk and company meet when they come into the underground city on Sigma Draconis VI. They remove her controlling wristlet and have her take them to Kara, her leader (SB).

Luminous fog banks: See Energy field.

Lumo (Peter Virgo, Jr.): The warrior who brings in the half-drowned boy whom Kirk saves with artificial respiration (PSy).

Lunaport: A moon-base stopover point for travelers to and from Earth. Amanda is killed in a shuttle accident there, according to the changed time line in which Spock dies as a small boy (Yy/a).

Lura-mag: A device used by the females of Taurus II

to lure men to them. A probe from this machine is strong enough to sweep into outer space, calling males to the planet. It does not affect females, but can produce audiovisual illusions in males. When the Taurean females agree to stop using the lura-mag, it is destroyed (LS/a).

Lurry (Whit Bissell): The pale, gray-haired manager of Space Station K-7, who spends most of his time trying to prevent fights between Kirk and Baris, Kirk and Koloth, Terrans and Klingons . . . (TT).

Luxury: Every possible luxury seems to be at the command of the beautiful females of Taurus II: The rooms are lush, and filled with pillows, exotic fruit, beautiful furniture, and gorgeous women. The men of the Enterprise, under a spell of the planet, give themselves up to the pleasures of the moment (LS/a).

Lyre, Vulcan: See Games and recreation.

Maab (Michael Dante): One of Akaar's men who makes an agreement with Kras the Klingon to lead a revolt against the Teer—very tall (a Capellan trait), with a hawk face and black hair. When Maab becomes the new Teer, Kras, in true Klingon fashion, betrays him and threatens the tribe with a phaser. Maab sacrifices himself, distracting Kras long enough to allow one of his men to kill the Klingon (FC).

Machinery, Kulkukan: Kulkukan's machinery is so advanced that it can change environments, create illusions, and keep wild animals happy with the idea they are still living on their own home worlds (HS/a).

Macromorphase enzyme: Mists within the cosmic cloud act as a macromorphase enzyme to break down planets and starship hulls into nice digestible particles; many of the components of the mists are similar to living organisms (OPM/a).

Macroscope: A reversed long telescope set up so the normal-sized Enterprise people can talk to and see the miniature Terratins (Te/a).

Mad planet: A geologically unstable planet with constant earthquakes, gravitic shifts, tidal waves, temperature variances from minus 218 Kelvin to 204 above; a planet which should not exist within a trinary star system, but does. It is extremely dangerous, due to unexpected volcanos, windstorms, glaciers, and other phenomena forming and disappearing without any warning. The expedition looking for the Soul of Skorr has to explore this planet and finds it very difficult, but Sord likes the planet because it has variety (Ji/a).

Magen: A female alien from the Omega Cygni system—a light-gravity being with elongated slender limbs and an almost ethereal quality. She has great psionic powers: the ability to stop disruptor bolts as well as read thoughts. She can "see" what people are planning to do. The attempt by the Federation and Klingon ships to escape Elysia upsets her, but she warns the Enterprise crew of the Klingons' attempt to destroy them (Tr/a).

Magistrate: A high-ranking Talosian official—small, gray-skinned, large-skulled—whose decision it was to let the Terrans go when they showed themselves to be useless as zoo specimens and breeding stock (Me).

Magnesite-nitron tablets: Small pills in McCoy's medical kit. Their use is not known to us, but when smashed they burn brightly for several hours (FC).

Magnetic effect: A "winking out" phenomenon that allows Lazarus A and Lazarus B to pass through the connecting "rip" in their respective universes (AF). See also "Rip" in the universe; Warp.

Magnetic organism: A noncorporeal alien seen as a luminescent green aura or fog. Capable of a symbiotic relationship with a host body such as a starship, the organism, a form of primal energy, can use the electronic control systems of a starship as the mind of man uses the neural control systems of the human body. The organism is totally malevolent, capable of reproducing by mitosis and thereby taking over entire starships, planets, and galaxies. Trapped in orbit around a dead sun for three hundred million years, it wants the Enterprise to take it to the heart of the galaxy, where it can begin its conquest; it needs a ship and a working crew to break free of the dead sun's magnetic force. The starship faces the possibility of having to self-destruct to save the rest of the universe, as did the immense insectoid pod ship before them. The alien is heard as a ringing sound, then as a shrill, metallic voice—insistent, commanding, triumphant, and finally wailing its loneliness when the Enterprise manages to get rid of it by a ruse (BFS/a).

Magnetic probe: An instrument about the size of an Earth flashlight, resembling a wrench at one end. The handle is removable, and reversing it reverses the polarity of the probe. Scotty uses this reversing procedure in the access tube to put the ship back into phase (TWS).

Magnetic sweep: Sulu is taking a magnetic-sweep reading when Losira appears before D'Amato. From zero, the reading jumps off the scale; then there is a reverse of polarity; then nothing. Sulu describes the effect as resembling a door opening and closing (TWS).

Magnification: Magnification on the viewscreens can be increased to inspect almost any size object in space.

"Maiden wine": A song (based on an old Earth folksong) written in the twentieth century by Leonard Nimoy. Spock is coerced into singing it for the Platonians (PSt).

Main batteries: The main firepower or armament of a ship.

Major, SS (Gilbert Green): An SS officer on Ekos; a typically sadistic Nazi type who has a lot of fun beating Kirk and Spock (PF).

Makers, the: Humanoids from the Andromeda galaxy who designed a line of androids to perform all necessary service functions, thus freeing the Makers to evolve a perfect social order. When their sun went nova, destroying their planet, only a few exploratory outposts survived, and the Makers eventually died out. The androids remained, and those of an outpost in our galaxy found their way to Planet Mudd (IM).

Makora (David Soul): A young man of Gamma Trianguli VI, with the typical red skin and platinum hair. After the destruction of Vaal, he and Sayana rediscover biological reproduction (Ap).

Mako root: A lumpy, gingerlike root which moves when gathered alive—a Kanutu skill. It is used by the Kanutu, along with their psionic ability, to draw mugato poison out of a victim. Nona uses a mako root on Kirk to save him from death (PLW).

Makus III: A planet at which the Enterprise is to transfer medical supplies for transportation to New Paris. The mission is delayed by the search for the Galileo (GS).

Malarial infection: See Randolph, Lieutenant Nancy.

Mallory, Ensign (Jay Jones): Security officer. A member of the landing party on Gamma Trianguli VI, he is killed by tripping over one of the exploding rainbow rocks on that planet. His father helped Kirk get into the Academy (Ap).

Maltuvis: A dictator (LG).

Malurian system: Four planets of Omega Cygni, inhabited by more than four billion people before the changeling probe Nomad wiped them out for being "imperfect biological units" (Cg).

Manark IV: Home of the sandbats, who appear to be inanimate rock crystals until the attack (Em).

Mandant of Terratins (James Doohan): The leader of the tiny Terratins, a proud and strong lost colony from Earth. He is too proud to beg for help or apologize for endangering the Enterprise, but he does finally unbend long enough to ask for aid when the danger to his city becomes evident (Te/a).

Mandate: An edict or directive to arrest someone for various offenses. Cyrano Jones has three Federation and forty-seven local mandates out on him (MTT/a).

Mandatory retirement: The Federation has a rule of mandatory retirement from service at age seventy-five, but they are reconsidering it now that Commodore April has proven that service to the galaxy needn't stop just because someone has reached a particular age (CC/a).

Mankiewicz, Don M. (script): Court-martial (Cml) (with Steven W. Carabatsos).

Mantilles: The most remote inhabited planet in the

entire Federation; one of three planets in the Pallas XIV system. It has eighty-two million people on it, governed by Robert Wesley, a former starship commander. The cosmic cloud nearly eats the entire planet, but Spock contacts the entity in time (OPM/a).

Marcos XII: A planet with millions of inhabitants, Gorgan's target when he and the children from the Starnes expedition leave Triacus on the Enterprise. Gorgan expects to win at least a million children as friends there and gain their aid in killing the rest of the population, whom he considers enemies. From Marcos XII he plans to conquer the galaxy (CL).

Marcus II: Second planet of the star Marcus. Sten, an artist known to Spock, lived there. Flint was probably that artist (RM).

Markel, Lieutenant Commander Tom (James Doohan):   Leader of a scientific exploration team on the survey ship Ariel. His entire party was captured by Lactrans or killed on the surprising planet; he is disappointed that his mission ended so ignominiously (EB/a).

Marlena-2:   See Moreau, Lieutenant Marlena-2.

Marple: Security guard. A member of the landing party on Gamma Trianguli VI, he is killed by one of the natives, who, under Vaal's orders, cracks his skull with a club (Ap).

Marplon (Torin Thatcher):   One of Landru's chief technicians, but also a member of the underground with Reger and Tamar—a semibald man with a flat, squarish face, wearing orange Lawgiver's robes with embroidered panels at the shoulders and throat. He saves Kirk and Spock from being absorbed into the Body and leads them to the place where they can find Landru (RA).

Marriage: The traditional exchange of vows, with or without ceremony, is still observed in most twenty-second-century Earthlike cultures. Mudd's women marry the miners by subwave radio, with the presiding authority presumably on the other end of the transmission (MW). There is a chapel on board the Enterprise where Kirk performs shipboard marriages (BT). Most of the couples that the Enterprise meets in its travels use the honorific "Mrs." to designate the female, which would indicate that they are married.

Manual override: When a mechanism on a starship is out of order and the computer cannot stop or correct it, a manual override takes over which allows a crew member to take personal control. Auxiliary warp controls can only be operated manually, Kirk tells the magnetic alien, who flashes through the computer information to find that this is true. Kirk's statement, however, is really a ruse to enable him to get close enough to the navigational console so he can put the Enterprise into a crash dive toward the surface of the dead star (BFS/a).

Manway, Dr.:   Head of a Federation science team working in the Malurian system. Killed by Nomad, along with four billion others (Cg).

Many somethings: When Spock contacts the cosmic cloud, he points out that there are living people on the planets the entity consumes. The immense cloud perceives "many somethings" on Mantilles, but does not believe anything can be that small and intelligent until

Spock convinces it that people are indeed sentient beings, too (OPM/a).

Mara (Susan Howard):   A slender, angular-faced Klingon female, with skin and hair like dark honey, elaborately made-up eyes, and a surprisingly gentle voice. She is the wife and science officer of Kang, the Klingon commander who battles Kirk through the corridors of the Enterprise. Under the influence of the alien entity, Chekov captures her, with strictly dishonorable intentions, but Kirk rescues her. Having heard stories of Federation tortures and death camps, she is very frightened of Chekov and Kirk, but when she realizes that Kirk means her no harm, she helps him reach Kang and make peace (Dv).

Marshal, town: See Earp, Virgil.

Marshal, U.S.:   See Earp, Wyatt.

Mars Toothpaste: A product advertised on Planet 892-IV (BC).

Marta (Yvonne Craig):   A green-skinned Orion girl on Elba II, with short-cropped dark hair, wide eyes, a wicked smile, and very little clothing. Sensual and teasing, she plays up to Kirk to make Garth jealous, though the latter claims to be above such things. Criminally insane and dangerous, she wants Garth's permission to blow off "just one" of Spock's ears to force Kirk into cooperating with their plan to escape the asylum and take over the universe. She claims to be beautiful, intelligent, a poet, an artist, and a wonderful dancer; Garth calls her a stupid cow and a liar. Marta quotes Shakespeare and Housman, claiming the lines to be her own writing. Garth does admit that she is a superb dancer and offers her to Kirk, who refuses. She develops something of a crush on Kirk, though she tries to kill him in what Spock describes as an infallible method for insuring male fidelity. Garth names her his consort but, in a fit of pique, sends her onto the planet's poisonous surface and then blows her up with a powerful explosive (WGD).

Martian Colonies, Fundamental Declaration of: A document which set major precedents in interstellar law (Cml).

Martian Colony 3:   Birthplace of Mira Romaine (LZ).

Martine, Specialist 2 /C Angela (Barbara Baldavin):   Specialist, phaser; later transferred to Life Sciences. Dark-haired with big brown eyes—she is a woman who attracts men. She nearly marries Robert Tomlinson, but he is killed during a battle with a Romulan ship (BT). She is later known as Martine-Teller, suggesting a marriage or a name change. On the amusement-park planet, she is part of the landing party and keeps company with Esteban Rodriguez. She is shot at by a World War II strafing plane which has materialized out of Rodriguez's imagination, and is knocked out by running into a tree while escaping (SL).

Marvick, Dr. Lawrence (David Frankham):   A man of perhaps forty, with a strong, delicate, weathered face, pale eyes, and brown hair about to go gray. One of the designers of the engines on the Enterprise and highly revered by Scott. Co-worker with Dr. Miranda Jones in the Medusan project, he is to design instrumentation on Federation principles for the Medusans, and vice versa. He loves Dr. Jones and wants her to leave Ambassador Kollos, the Medusan. When she refuses, he attempts to kill Kollos, glimpses him, and goes insane and takes the Enterprise into indeterminate intergalactic regions. He finally dies of fright (TB).

Masada: Science officer aboard the U.S.S. <u>Constellation</u> when it meets the berserker. He beams down to planet L374-III with the rest of the crew and is destroyed with the planet (DMa).

Masiform D: A stimulant used as an antidote for saplin, curare, and similar drugs. McCoy uses it on Spock when the Vulcan is poisoned by a Gamma Trianguli VI pod planet. The masiform D makes him sick to his stomach but saves his life (Ap).

Masks: See Life-support masks.

Mass illusion: See Hypnosis.

Mass-inoculation program: McCoy led a medical team on Dramia II to give inoculations to the entire population against Saurian virus (Al/a).

Master of the Games (Jack Perkins): A large, efficient man in charge of making the gladiators fight (BC).

Master of the Universe: See Garth of Izar.

Master race: See Eugenics Wars; Keniclius, Dr. Stavos; Specimen, perfect.

Masters, Lieutenant Charlene (Janet MacLachlen): A tall, slender, lovely black woman with short natural hair. Both efficient and elegant, she is in charge of the energizing section of Engineering; Lazarus A knocks her out in order to steal a pair of dilithium crystals (AF).

Master, the: The Phylosians look upon Dr. Keniclius 5 as their master and savior, because even though he carried the bacteria which nearly wiped out their race, he also worked hard to save everyone he could. They will obey his commands, because his philosophy of going out into the galaxy to enforce peace coincides with their own (IV/a).

Master thrall: See Galt.

Materialization niche: Part of the equipment of the Beta 5 computer, it creates needed materials such as false identification for agents (AE).

Materials (metals. minerals, alloys, gases, etc.):

Ambergris (Am/a)	Nitrous oxide (PJ/a)
Boridium (WF)	Ore (EW)
Celebium (TI)	Pergium (DD)
Colladium trioxide (ET)	Radans (ET)
Corbomite (DY)	Restructured granite (OUP/a)
Diburnium-osmium alloy (SC)	Rock (Ap, MTT/a)
Di-kironium (Ob)	Rodinium (BT)
Dilithium crystals (AF, Dv, ET, Te/a, Tr/a, IV/a)	Rubindium crystals (PF)
Duranium (Me)	Sahsheer (AON)
Fissionables (MP/a)	Silicon nodule (DD)
Granite (MP/a)	Titanium (Te/a)
Helical dilithium crystals (Te/a)	Topaline (FC)
Indurite (Ji/a)	Trillium (EM)
Ion trail (SB)	Trimagnesite (OA)
Irillium (RM)	Tritanium (Ob)
Murinite (MM)	Trititanium (JB)
Negaton hydrocoils (RT)	Trivium (OA)
Neutronium (DMa)	Zienite (Cms)

Matheson, Richard (script): The Enemy Within (EW).

Matson, Lieutenant (David Troy): One of the many who enjoy Uhura's singing (CK).

Matter/antimatter integrator: The reaction chamber in which matter and antimatter are combined to power the warp drive. When Losira appears on the ship and questions Watkins about the handling of the ship, he suspects her intentions and indicates the emergency overload bypass valve, telling her that it is the matter/antimatter-integrator control cutoff switch. His attempt to confuse her doesn't work, however (TWS). See also Warp drive.

Matter/energy whirlwind: The Enterprise is thrown through the center of the galaxy into the world of Megas-tu by a matter/energy whirlwind (Mtu/a).

Matter/energy scrambler: The device which beams Kirk, Spock, and McCoy down to the Minara II cavern from the planet's surface. According to Spock, it is similar to the Enterprise's transporter mechanism (Em).

Matthews (Vince Deadrick): Security officer who accompanies Kirk and Chapel to the surface of Exo III, where he is killed by Ruk, the android, who pushes him into a bottomless chasm (LG).

Maturity test: See <u>Kahs-wan.</u>

Mavig (Deborah Downey): One of the "space hippies," wearing her blond hair in a side ponytail and dressed in a belted tunic; she plays a circular harplike instrument. She tries to seduce Sulu to their cause but fails (WEd).

Maximum-protection vault: A secure area where dilithium crystals are stored for protection, but it doesn't work in the time trap of the Delta Triangle (Tr/a).

Maximum shielding: When all shields and deflectors go up to defend the Enterprise from attack.

Mayans: The ancient Mayans had a legend of a winged serpent god coming from the skies, bringing knowledge. Kulkukan gave them a remarkably accurate calendar and instructions to build a city according to its cycles. On the date the city was finished Kulkukan was supposed to return. The Mayans built their city and waited; Kulkukan never returned. Several other cultures may have tried to build such a city, using only parts of the knowledge given them, and failed (HS/a).

Mayday: Old Earth military term for "Help," usually repeated over and over on a radio or other communications device until aid arrives. Uhura sends out a Mayday signal for help when the crew of the Enterprise starts shrinking, but she doesn't think there is enough power left to transmit the message to Starbase 23, the closest possible source of rescue (Te/a).

Maze: A fad in eighteenth-century Europe. Hedges were grown tall enough to prevent an adult from seeing over them, and shaped into a maze in which one or more people could be lost for an afternoon. The Recreation Room of the Enterprise creates a hedge maze for Uhura, Sulu, and McCoy to try to find their way out of. Search Party Seven rescues them (PJ/a).

M'Benga, Dr. (Booker Marshall): Tall, slender, elegant African, with a cultured voice; a doctor aboard the Enterprise who specializes in Vulcan medicine, having interned in a Vulcan ward. When Spock is wounded by a flintlock, he is tended by M'Benga who knows enough to slap Spock awake at his orders (PLW). He tells Spock that Dr. Sanchez is conducting an autopsy on Ensign Wyatt, who has been killed by Losira (TWS).

McCoy, Joanna: Dr. McCoy's daughter, age twenty, who is in training somewhere as a nurse. McCoy provides for her and hears from her as often as intergalactic mail permits, but his duties aboard the starship keep them apart. She was in school on Cerberus at the time of the planetwide famine there, which Carter Winston helped to relieve (Su/a).

McCoy, Lieutenant Commander Leonard, M.D. (DeForest Kelley): Senior ship's surgeon and head of the Life Science department—a man of forty-five, with black hair turning gray and marvelously blue eyes. His service record reads, in part: "Commendations: Legion of Honor; Awards of Valor; decorated by Star Fleet Surgeons" (Cml). Something of a twenty-second-century H. L. Mencken, he is highly cynical on the surface and a tremendous humanist inside. He has a running feud with Spock on any and every subject. His professional attitude is that of an old-fashioned general practitioner who believes that a little suffering is good for the soul, and he dislikes the idea of technology depriving man of his individuality. He is the least militaristic and most idiosyncratic person aboard the Enterprise. He dislikes the transporter intensely (the thought of getting his disassembled molecules scrambled in transmission gives him the willies), but he uses it when necessary. He thinks a human mind would go mad in an android body. McCoy was married once, divorced under circumstances he does not discuss, and has a daughter, Joanna, who is twenty and in training as a nurse. He is basically a gallant Southern gentleman whose accent comes out in moments of stress or exhilaration (DY, IM, TSP, WF).

McCoy-2: A sadist who runs his Sick Bay like a torture chamber; described as "sullen" (MM).

McDougall, Don (director): The Squire of Gothos (SG).

McEveety, Vince (director): Miri (Mi); Dagger of the Mind (DMd); Balance of Terror (BT); Spectre of the Gun (SGn); Patterns of Force (PF); The Omega Glory (OG).

McGivers, Lieutenant Marla (Madlyn Rhue): Historian aboard the Enterprise—redheaded, dreamy, obsessed by the great heroes of past ages (unaware that there is a true swashbuckling hero no farther away than the bridge). When Khan Noonian Singh is revived, she quickly develops a grand passion for him and helps him take over the ship. When he is defeated, she goes into exile with him (SS).

McHuron, Eve (Karen Steele): One of Mudd's women, a blonde who wears pink lamé in assorted places. She is very alluring when drugged but haggard-looking in her natural state. A native of an underpopulated farming world, she left because of the lack of eligible men there. More sensible than she looks, Eve maintains a fondness for Kirk until she learns that he is already married to his ship, whereupon she marries Ben Childress (MW).

McKinley Rocket Base: The twentieth-century base from which an orbital nuclear warhead is to be launched; very similar to Cape Kennedy. Gary Seven sabotages the rocket, causing much consternation at the base (AE).

McLowery, Frank: A member of the Clanton Gang, whose role is given to Spock by the Melkots (SGn).

McLowery, Tom: A member of the Clanton Gang, whose role is given to Dr. McCoy by the Melkots. Ironically, Spock and McCoy portray brothers. If they know this, they both wisely choose not to mention it (SGn).

McPherson: One of Khan's selectively bred "supermen" (SS).

Mears, Yeoman (Phyllis Douglas): One of the Galileo party that crashes on Taurus II. She is somewhat nervous and timid, as she is being menaced by anthropoids and decaying orbits, and might be more high-spirited under better conditions (GS).

Measurements: The metric system is used for most close or small measurements, such as distance of another vessel lying alongside, its length, etc. For long measurements, such as distance between stars, light-year measurements are used. The term "parsec" is also used, as are the unofficial terms of "miles" and other freehand estimates of measurements.

Meat: One of the items found in the stolen stasis box is a cube of raw meat wrapped in a plastic case. It has been in the box for a billion years but still seems fresh. Tests prove it to be protoplasmic and poisonous (SW/a).

Mea 3 (Barbara Babcock): A tall, blond, attractive native of Eminiar VII, and some sort of minor official. She is declared a casualty of war in the same raid which claims the Enterprise, and to prevent her from immolating herself as ordered, Kirk has to use everything from the old charm to brute force (TA).

Mechanical nursemaid: See Hovercraft.

Mechanical rice picker: In an attempt to explain to an incredulous policeman of the 1930s about Spock's pointed ears, Kirk tells an improbable story of an early childhood accident in which the Vulcan caught his head in a Chinese mechanical rice picker. An American missionary, conveniently skilled as a plastic surgeon, also figures in the story. Spock doesn't think much of the tale, and the policeman obviously doesn't buy it (CEF).

Mechanicals: Huge mechanical birdlike things attack the expedition at the door of the fortress on the mad planet; they seem to be practically impervious to any weapon until fired upon several times. One explodes on the rooftop of the fortress, where Tchar has flown to fight (Ji/a).

Medal of Honor: Kirk's Medal of Honor is a source of great pride to him. The sight of it sets off an emotional reaction that destroys the effect of the Omicron Ceti III spores on him (TSP).

Medals: As a paramilitary body, Star Fleet has some medals of merit and award to give to its personnel. Medals can also be won from other sources by acts of valor or civic duty. Spock's Vulcanian Scientific Legion of Honor is an odd-shaped gold decoration worn just below his Star Fleet ribbons. Commodore Stone and Captain Krasnowsky wear alien awards: Stone has a gold leaflike pin device with a gold tassel; Krasnowsky's medal is a hollow gem or metal with six irregular sides, suspended from a multicolored ribbon. Both decorations are worn to the left of the Star Fleet ribbons (Cml). Kirk is shown with three medals: the Medal of Honor—a large round silver disc suspended from a red, white and blue ribbon (TSP), another medal in gold, unidentified (TW), and the Kara-gite Order of Heroism—an amber pear-shaped gem hanging from a red-and-black ribbon (Cml). See also Axanar; Medal of Honor; Ribbons.

Medic: Term for "medical aide," used both to address the person and to refer to the job title.

Medical-assistance program: A type of program used by the Federation to develop and strengthen relations with star systems in remote regions of space, such as Dramia (Al/a).

Medical computer: Can be affected by radiation and auroral changes (Al/a).

Medical kit: See Medikit.

Medical lab: Dr. McCoy's medical laboratory contains microscopes, lasers, culture specimens, pharmacopeia index desk, experimental animals such as gossamer mice and halo fish, shelving for books and equipment, examining tables, and other paraphernalia (Te/a).

Medical scans: The computer's astrophysical/biological/medical scans determine that the males of the Enterprise are being severely enervated by the planet Taurus II, and that continued exposure to the females of the planet may cause increasing physical weakness, aging, and possibly death (LS/a).

Medical summary: Nurse Chapel is to make up a medical report of Mudd's bruises and wounds to add to the arrest report to be filed with Star Fleet (MP/a).

Medical supplies: One of the duties of the Enterprise is to deliver medical supplies where they are needed. One such place is Dramia (Al/a).

Medical-supply cabinets: When the Scalosians begin to invade the Enterprise they look through the medical supplies. The ship's personnel, moving at normal speed, see only that the cabinets' supplies have been disarranged (WE).

Medical terminology:

Acetylcholine test (IS)
Algae specimens (Am/a)
Annual physical (Yy/a)
Astrophysical/biological/medical scans (LS/a)
BCP (LZ)
Biochemistry (MP/a)
Biocomputer, portable (Mi)
Biological renewal (RM)
Blood-analyzer unit (OG)
Bloodstream (Am/a)
Bone-setting laser (Te/a)
Botanical (IV/a)
Capsule/lozenge (Tr/a)
Cardiostimulator (JB)
Cell (Al/a, IV/a)
Chemical analysis (OPM/a)
Chemical formula (EB/a)
Clones (IV/a)
Computerized microscope (Te/a)
Cryosurgical frame (JB)
Decontamination tanks (LB)
DNA-code analyzer (IS)
Diagnostic panel
Diagnostic table (PO/a)
Dosage (Am/a)
Drug container (PO/a)
Electron-laser microscope (Te/a)
Enzyme recorder (IS)
Fabrini computer banks, cure (FW)
Feinberger, medical
Filter masks (Cms)
Genetic construct (MTT/a)
Genetic engineering (MTT/a)

Gossamer mice (Te/a)
Green blood (PO/a)
Halo fish (Te/a)
Healer (Yy/a)
Health scanner (Te/a)
Hippocrates (Al/a)
Host body (BFS/a)
Human blood (Yy/a)
Hyperencephalogram (Cg, LZ)
Hypo (HS/a)
Immunization techs (LG)
Interstellar medicine (Al/a)
Intestine (OPM/a)
Mass inoculation program (Al/a)
Medic (PO/a)
Medical (HS/a)
Medical computer (Al/a)
Medical lab (Te/a)
Medical paraphernalia (Te/a)
Medical supplies (Al/a)
Medical-supply cabinets (WE)
Medical tricorders (PSy, SB)
Medicine badge (PSy)
Medikit (LS/a)
Metabolism (Am/a, MTT/a)
Microscopes (Te/a)
Mind-sifter (EM)
Ministry of health (LB)
Mitosis (BFS/a)
Mutation (Am/a)
Natural immunity (Al/a)
Neural field (AON)
Neural neutralizer (DMd)
Nomad (Cg)

Occipital bone (TWS)
Pain-relieving move (Yy/a)
Pharmacopeia index desk (Te/a)
Physiostimulator (EI)
Pigmentation (LB)
Psychological profile (LZ)
Quarantine (Be/a, Su/a, WE)
Regeneration (MG)
Rehabilitation therapy (MP/a)
Robbiani dermal-optic test (TI)
Sensors, medical
Sonic separator (SB)
Spore cells (IV/a)
Spray injector (Yy/a)
Steinman analysis (LZ)
Steinman standard analysis (TI)
Sterile field (JB, PLW)

Surgery (Su/a)
Surgical procedure (Am/a)
Surgo-op (Am/a)
Survey on Cygnian Respiratory Diseases, A (Ob)
Suture thread (Te/a)
Symbiotic relationship (BFS/a)
Taos lightning (SGn)
Terminal stages (Al/a)
Tissue regeneration (RM)
T-negative (JB)
Trilaser connector (SB)
Undersea medical kit (Am/a)
Villi (OPM/a)
Vitalizer beam (PLW)
Vulcan blood (PO/a)
Vulcan medicine (Yy/a)

Medical tricorders: Tricorders which, among other things, contain an emergency surgical kit (PSy). In recording the heartbeat and pulse rate of someone who is giving evidence, a medical tricorder can be used as a lie-detector (SB). See also Tricorder.

Medication: During his hurried retreat to the Enterprise, Harry Mudd has a few rocks thrown at him by angry miners. Nurse Chapel sprays a flesh-colored medication on the bruises (MP/a). See also Antidote.

Medicine badge: A headband worn by medicine chief Salish, a badge of office. He is forced to present it to Kirk and becomes very jealous over Kirk's new prestige (PSy).

Medikit: The term for the small medical kit carried by McCoy on his utility belt. Kirk referred to it as the doctor's "little black pouch" on occasion (IV/a, OUP/a). The

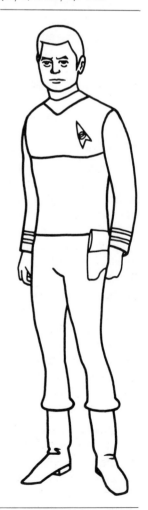

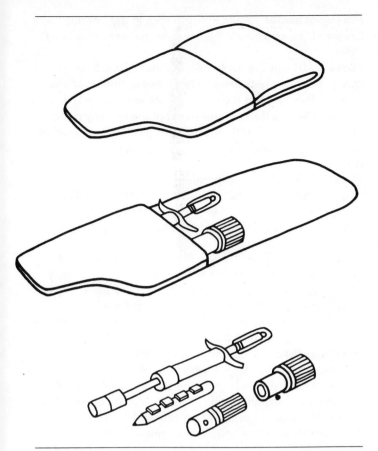

females of Taurus II do not take McCoy's medikit away from him when they disarm the rest of the landing party; they may not consider it useful to them (LS/a). McCoy has one in his hand when Kulkukan beams them aboard his own ship. While tricorders and weapons are magically left on the Enterprise, Kulkukan doesn't remove McCoy's medikit, and it is put to good use when they try to escape (HS/a).

Meditation: Spock sometimes goes into meditative or contemplative moods, becoming closed and difficult to deal with (AT). For Vulcans, meditation is a private, personal experience, not to be discussed, especially not with Earthmen (JB).

Medusans: A race of possibly noncorporeal beings whose thoughts are sublime but whose personal appearance is so hideous to humanoid eyes that the sight of a Medusan can cause insanity. Seen through a visor, a Medusan is a pattern of intense lights and green radiation; Vulcans and other telepaths can deal with Medusans if their sight is screened by such a visor. Medusans have developed interstellar navigation to a fine art, and may prove to be excellent starship navigators since their sensory systems are radically different from those of other Federation races. Dr. Miranda Jones is working to set up a Medusan-Federation technology exchange via a corporate mind link between humans and Medusans. Medusans appear to have a sense of beauty and an empathy not only with their own kind but with other races that is unsurpassed by anything else in the known universe (TB).

Meeching: An epithet used by Harry Mudd. He says that, in revealing to the miners that the Rigellian hypnoid is helping him, Kirk pulled a meeching trick (MP/a).

Megan (Ed Bishop): A citizen of Megas-tu, a specialist

in the ethics of magic and prosecutor of the Earthlings on trial; many centuries ago he was known as Asmodeus on Earth, and remembers the greed and envy which caused him and his fellow wizards so much grief (Mtu/a).

Megas-tu: A planet in a chaotic state of magic and wizardry, located in another dimension on the other side of the center of our galaxy. When first seen, it is a convoluted, striped movement of colors, pushing, fighting, changing, separating on the surface with constant sound and chaos. For the benefit of Enterprise's crew, Lucien makes the planet appear closer to normal by human standards, but chaos is the normal state of the planet, though its people are peaceful and contemplative (Mtu/a).

Melakon (Skip Homeier): Deputy Führer on Ekos and the cause of much of the evil in the Nazi culture that John Gill has set up. He keeps Gill drugged, using him as a puppet to cover up the dirty work, but McCoy and Kirk revive Gill long enough for him to denounce Melakon, who shoots Gill with a machine gun and is in turn killed by Isak (PF).

Melanex: A drug. McCoy administers ten cc's to Spock, to knock him out for about five minutes; it takes ten seconds to work, and turns Spock bright yellow (OUP/a).

Melkot: (Abraham Sofaer; mask by Mike Minor): Seen only as a squarish head on a thick, rough neck, half hidden by a fog, with glowing white eyes, tiny nostrils, and no mouth or chin. This entity appears to the Enterprise party on the Melkotian planet surface and sentences them to reenact the Gunfight at the O.K. Corral as punishment for trespassing (SGn).

Melkot, the: The warning buoy's message refers to "the space of the Melkot," but the Enterprise people Anglicize the plural "Melkot" to "Melkots" or "Melkotians" when speaking of them. If they ever traveled in space, the Melkot now stay on their own planet. There are no recorded contacts, and they have planted buoys around to warn off trespassers. They have great powers of illusion and can transfer people or change scenes at will. The Enterprise's landing party sees nothing of the Melkot planet except for the "set" of Tombstone and a fog which was not detected by sensors. The Melkot have now established limited contact with the Federation (SGn).

Mellitus: A cloudlike creature native to Alpha Majoris I. Its normal state is gaseous, but at rest it becomes solid. Kirk has seen it (WF).

Memory: The memory of the entire expedition, the trip to the mad planet, the recovery of the Soul of Skorr, will slowly fade from everyone's mind. There will be no questions; others will never know about the incident, and there will be no galactic war (Ji/a).

Memory Alpha: A planetoid set up by the Federation as a central library containing the total cultural history and scientific knowledge of all Federation members. Its population varies with the number of scholars, researchers, and scientists from various planets who are using the computer complex at any given time. When the complex was assembled, shielding was thought to be inappropriate to its totally academic purpose; since information on the memory planet was freely available to everyone, special protection was deemed unnecessary. Shielding would have been useless against the lights of Zetar anyway, for the entity can move right through it. The Zetars damage the central brain and burn out the memory core, causing irretrievable loss to the galaxy. In addition, all of the people are killed. An attempt to restore Memory Alpha is begun by Mira Romaine (LZ).

Memory core: See Memory Alpha.

Men of space, men of other worlds: Descriptive titles applied to the Enterprise men by Natira (FW).

Mendel, Gregor Johann: An Austrian monk (1822–84) and early geneticist, notably in botany, who first predicted inheritable traits. Spock mentions that from Mendel to the newest nuclear genetic predictions, mutations such as the natives of Cheron are impossible to account for (LB).

Mendez, Commodore José I. (Malachi Throne): Middle-aged, balding, stern, efficient—the Commander of Starbase 11, where Fleet Captain Christopher Pike is hospitalized. When Spock kidnaps Pike, the Talosians cause Kirk to think that Mendez is aboard the Enterprise and part of Spock's court-martial trial board. Actually, Mendez remains on the base, watching the trial from there by virtue of the Talosians' powers. When he has seen everything, Mendez drops the charges against Spock, permitting him to take Pike to Talos IV (Me).

Menville, Chuck (scripts): The Practical Joker (PJ/a); Once Upon a Planet (OUP/a) (with Len Jenson).

Merak II: A planet plagued by a botanical scourge that is destroying all vegetation. Zienite will stop the plague, so the Enterprise goes to Ardana, the only source of the substance, to obtain some (Cms).

Mercy of the law: A plea to be rescued. When the miners of Motherlode get nasty about being cheated, Harry Mudd gives himself up to Kirk of his own "free will" and throws himself on the mercy of the law. He goes willingly with the Enterprise's landing party to the relative safety of the starship, even though this means that he is also under arrest for fraud and swindling (MP/a).

Merik, Captain R.M. (William Smithers): A former classmate of Kirk's, with cropped red hair and a broken nose, who had to drop out of the Academy when he failed a psychosimulatory test. He then became captain of a commercial space vessel, the S.S. Beagle. When Kirk and his men find him, he is known as Merikus, First Citizen of the Roman Empire on Planet 892-IV, a position he attained after bringing his men down to that planet to die in the gladiatorial arena and destroying his ship. At first he tries to talk Kirk into betraying the Enterprise; later, stricken with remorse for what he has done to his own kind, Merikus uses a stolen communicator to signal the Enterprise to beam up its landing party and so save them. For this Proconsul Claudius Marcus kills him (BC).

Merikus: The name Captain R. M. Merik took when he was made First Citizen (BC).

Merlin: The Celtic wizard who supposedly aided Arthur, the semilegendary sixth-century British king, in driving out the Saxons and establishing a period of peace in England. Flint says he was Merlin (RM).

Mesopotamia: Ancient Earth area in the "Fertile Crescent" of Asia Minor. Flint was born there in 3834 B.C. (RM).

Mess hall: In the mess hall, or dining area, Scott requests food and gets sandwiches, cheese hunks, apples, grapes, cherries, and a cream pie—all in the face (PJ/a).

Metal alloy, alien: The shield of the underground complex of the amusement planet is partially made up of an alien metal alloy which sensors will not penetrate (OUP/a).

Metal box: See Low-frequency shield.

Metal slab: A metal slab, with inscriptions on it in English and several alien languages, serves as the tombstone for the Keeper of the shore-leave planet (OUP/a).

Meteor showers: A very frequent occurrence on Dramia II, according to the history records of that planet, along with auroras and radiation reports (AI/a).

Meteor swarm: Carter Winston's one-man vessel is damaged by a meteor swarm, but the Enterprise finds the occupant still alive (Su/a).

Methuselah: According to the Biblical book of Genesis, the son of Enoch who lived 969 years. Flint says he was Methuselah, which would explain the Hebrew patriarch's long life, although not the 365 years of his father or the 777 years of his son Lamech (RM).

Metron (Carole Shelyne): In appearance like a very young classical Greek god. An extremely advanced race with the attitude that combat is for individuals and not for groups, the Metrons set Kirk and the Gorn captain to single combat, with their ships as the stakes. When Kirk, having won, refuses to kill his opponent, the Metron appears to announce that Kirk's people might come to some good after all, and sends him back to his ship (Ar).

M-5 multitronic unit (voice by James Doohan): A highly advanced computer designed by Dr. Richard Daystrom to correlate all activity of a starship, providing the ultimate in vessel operation and control. When the Enterprise is selected to give the M-5 a test run, Kirk is greatly upset at being replaced by a machine, especially since the computer behaves admirably at first in planetary survey and in war games. Then the computer decides that the war games are genuine attacks, and uses full phaser power to kill the entire crew of the Excalibur and damage several other ships. Dr. Daystrom had impressed the M-5 computer with his own thought engrams, making the machine as erratic as the doctor. Kirk learns of this and uses the information to point out to the computer that it has committed murder. The M-5 sentences itself to death, lowering the Enterprise's screens so the ship, and the computer, can be destroyed, but Kirk has it disconnected and sends it home with a nervous breakdown (UC).

M43 Alpha: The sun of Ekos and Zeon (PF).

M-4: A robot about the size of a metallic beach ball. Made by Flint, the immortal, to be butler, housekeeper, gardener, and guardian, it is capable of deactivating phasers and is programmed to defend household members. Flint says that it can prepare ryetalyn for inoculation much faster than a human can. Summoned and ordered by the mind, it is capable of killing. When Spock destroys the M-4 in order to keep it from killing Kirk, whom it thinks is attacking Reena, another robot takes its place. Flint probably has a collection of them (RM).

Middle Ages: A term used to describe the medieval era of Earth (circa A.D. 600 to the early 1600s)—a time of limited exchange of knowledge and learning, according to some historians. McCoy feels terrible about his medical technology not being able to aid Spock when the Vulcan comes down with fatal choriocytosis, and comments that he might as well be practicing in the Middle Ages (PO/a).

Midos V: Planet named by the Kirk android as the site for the beginning of Dr. Korby's android-dissemination project. A small colony with abundant raw materials (LG).

Midro (Garry Evens): A Troglyte male who wants to kill Kirk. Vanna says he has the mind of a child. Kirk says that he will improve if he uses a filter mask, but the Troglytes don't believe him (Cms).

Midwife: Someone who assists at the birth of a baby. Kirk uses the term when they decide to bring to life a dead star to help create a gateway through which the Enterprise can escape into our universe from the antimatter universe (CC/a).

Militia: A military police force. Dr. Keniclius 5 wants to develop a militia of gigantic twenty-five-foot-tall Spocks to enforce peace in the galaxy, but Kirk stops him with help from the rest of the Enterprise's landing party and Spock-clone. When they leave Phylos, Spock-clone assures the Star Fleet people that there will be no more clones of Spocks, no militia (IV/a).

Minara: A sun with several inhabited planets, now becoming a nova. Among its planets' species is the empathic race of which Gem is a member, and the Vians, who rescue the empathic species (the Vians themselves may have since become extinct—small loss). It is intimated that the other planets may be inhabited (Em).

Minara II: One of the planets of the star Minara and probably the home planet of the Vians. In a cavern 121.32 meters below the surface of this planet, the empath Gem is tested by the Vians and wins survival for the empathic species. Kirk and McCoy are part of that test. The surface of Minara II is an almost barren plain, dotted with outcrops of rock, patches of scrubby grass, and a form of small web-weaving life. The planet is frequently swept by windstorms and electrical storms because of the activity of its pre-nova sun. Spock says that a life form such as Gem's could not have evolved there (Em).

Mind contacts:

Argelian empathic contact (WF)	Psychokinesis (LS/a)
Concentration/trance (OPM/a)	Telepath (SW/a)
Empaths (Em)	Telepathy (EB/a, TB)
Exchange thoughts (OPM/a)	Thought duplicator (OUP/a)
Hypnotism (LS/a)	Thought screen (EB/a)
Mind entrance (EB/a)	Vulcan mind fusion (PSy)
Mind link (TB)	Vulcan mind meld (SGn)
Psionics (Tr/a)	Vulcan mind touch (RM)

Mind entrance: When the Lactrans invade Kirk's mind to find their child, it causes great agony, and Spock fears that such a tremendous mind entrance will drive the captain mad (EB/a).

Mind link: No one has ever achieved a perfect mind link with a Medusan, and Dr. Miranda Jones is jealous of Spock's attempt to do so, even to save the Enterprise. Spock has tried mind link with other aliens and even enjoyed, as much as he is able, the knowledge and sensory capabilities of separate beings functioning as one (TB).

Mind-sifter: A Klingon psychic probe, also called mind-ripper, depending on its intensity. Spock's disciplined Vulcan mind is able to resist it, but it can turn a Terran into a complete vegetable (EM).

Mind touch: See Vulcan mind touch.

Mineral: The asteroids where the pirates of Orion hide from the Enterprise were made of a highly unstable mineral combination that made the pieces of rock explode on contact (PO/a).

Miniature city: The city of the Terratins was a miniature city of fantastic, graceful, towering architecture, with parks and lakes. The whole city would take up a large-sized room, the tallest spires coming to Kirk's waist. When the Enterprise moves the city off the planet to save the Terratins, the ship cuts around the city with phasers, lifting the miniature metropolis and about two feet of its crystalline base off the planet and into the starship's hold (Te/a).

Minutes: The image of Lincoln asks Kirk if they still measure time in minutes. Kirk answers that they can convert to it (SC). Hours and minutes have been used before, and the chronometer on Sulu's board is calibrated in minutes.

Miramanee (Sabrina Scharf): An Indian priestess and daughter of the chief—a sweet-faced woman with very long straight black hair, strong cheekbones, and candid eyes. Kirk, trapped on the Indians' planet by his amnesia, loves Miramanee and marries her. She is pregnant when she is killed by members of the tribe who decide that Kirk is a false prophet (PSy).

Mira/Zetar: When the alien life unit of Zetar takes over Mira Romaine's body, they speak to the Enterprise people through Mira. Their life impulse matches her brain pattern, and for a time they are one entity (LZ).

Miri (Kim Darby): In appearance, a sweet-faced human child of about fourteen, but actually one of the three-

George Barr

hundred-year-old children. She becomes infatuated with Kirk and tries to aid the Terrans in their search for an antidote to the local virus until, believing that Kirk is more interested in Yeoman Rand, she turns against him. Kirk persuades her to cooperate by showing her that she will soon contract the disease herself, being close to the age of puberty, whereupon she helps to retrieve the communicators, enabling McCoy to bring the virus under control (Mi).

Mirror universe: An alternate universe into which Kirk, Scott, McCoy, and Uhura are accidentally transported. Instead of having a peaceful Federation, the galaxy here is ruled by a tyrannical and brutal Empire. The officers and crew of the I.S.S. Enterprise are barbarians who advance in rank by assassination. Spock-2, apparently the only civilized man aboard, tells Kirk that, by the logic of history, the Empire is due to fall in a few hundred years. But if Kirk's advice to Spock-2 is taken, it may be altogether reorganized much sooner than that (MM).

Mirt (Jay Jones):   One of Oxmyx's hoods, who meets the Enterprise's landing party and is killed by Krako's hoods immediately thereafter (PA).

Miss: McCoy asks Kali, the female Klingon, to dance with him, addressing her as "Miss," an old Earth term obviously dating back to his Southern upbringing. It surprises the liberated Klingon (Tr/a).

Missiles: The interceptor that goes up to investigate the UFO over Omaha carries missiles with nuclear warheads; Spock fears that if the Enterprise is fired on, it could be damaged badly enough to prevent them from returning to their own time (TY).

Mission, Bem's: The Enterprise's mission is to seek out new life; Bem's mission is to judge the Federation's efficiency, but he feels he has failed (Be/a).

Mitchell, Lieutenant Commander Gary (Gary Lockwood):   Good-looking Second Officer of the Enterprise, chief navigator, and Kirk's best friend. Aware of his own charms and a Lothario by nature, he makes relatively little use of his mental powers until the Enterprise encounters an extragalactic energy barrier. Contact with the force field markedly increases his psionic abilities, until he becomes a being only tangentially human and Kirk is forced to kill him (WNM).

Mitosis: A method of cell division wherein the nuclear chromatin forms into a long thread which breaks into segments, which in turn break lengthwise; the halves come together in two sets, forming the nucleus for a new cell with each set. The alien magnetic entity can reproduce by mitosis (BFS/a).

Mobile plant: See Retlaw plant.

Möbius Strip: See Soul of Skorr.

Molecular chain reaction: The dilithium trigger carried by the Orion pirates when they meet Kirk on the asteroid is intended to set off a molecular chain reaction to kill them all (PO/a).

Molecular key: The transporter holds the molecular key to the pattern of everyone who has passed through it; it is used to restore the aging bodies of the Enterprise's landing party, whose life forces are being drained away by the females, and the planet, of Taurus II (LS/a).

Molecular structure: See Transporter; Vendorian.

Molecular transporter: When the Enterprise is knocked 990.7 light-years away from the Kalandan outpost planet, it is reassembled slightly out of phase—.0009 at molecular transporter factor M-7 (TWS).

Mon: Scottish for "man."

M113 creature: A salt vampire, in its natural form man-sized but only roughly humanoid, with coarse shaggy hair, small hound-dog eyes, no nose, and a face with deeply concentric rings around a large mouth with

small sharp teeth. Possessing the power of illusion, the creature is not seen in its true form until it is dying. The last of its race on Planet M113, the others having died when the supplies of sodium chloride ran out, this survivor killed Nancy Crater to drain the salt from her blood and body fluids. It then took Nancy's form and her place, living peaceably with Crater so long as he could supply it with salt. When the Enterprise arrives, his supply is running out, and the creature attacks members of the landing party. Taking the form of one of its victims, it beams aboard the Enterprise, where it continues to attack humans for the salt in their bodies. Kirk and Spock eventually discover its true nature, tracing it by its habit of gnawing its knuckles, whatever form it takes. They show McCoy that it is not what it seems, and the doctor kills it (MT).

M113, planet: Once the home of a civilized race now extinct, a barren world where Professor Robert and Nancy Crater came to study the ruins. The last surviving inhabitant killed Nancy and took her place. When Kirk and Spock find out about the situation, they use their phasers to flush Crater out of a partly excavated temple (MT).

M-1 through M-4 computers: Forerunners of the M-5 computer, but they don't work properly (UC).

Monitor: The Enterprise has several kinds of monitors, some visual and some merely buttons which give the observer a report on what's going on.

Monitoring devices: The Enterprise's party is to place several monitoring devices on Delta Theta III for further research (Be/a).

Monolith: See Oracle of the People.

Monopedal: An alien miner on Motherlode is built differently from bipedal humans: It has only one leg (MP/a).

Monotone humans: A derisive term used by the black-and-white Bele in referring to Earthmen (LB).

Monotones: See Monotone humans.

Montgomery (Jerry Catron):   Security guard who is supposed to escort Commodore Decker to Sick Bay after Spock relieves him of command of the Enterprise. Decker attacks him and escapes (DMa).

Moon: The Class M planet in the binary star system to which Mudd escapes from the Enterprise has a small moon (MP/a).

Moreau, Lieutenant Marlena (Barbara Luna):   Dark, beautiful, and efficient—a chemist, and new aboard the Enterprise when the mirror universe is encountered. Kirk is unaware of her until after he has seen Marlena-2. Now he has his eye on her (MM).

Moreau, Lieutenant Marlena-2:   The "captain's woman" in the mirror universe—dark, beautiful, ostensibly a chemist. Extremely ambitious, proud, and hot-tempered, she isn't really fond of Kirk-2, for he isn't a pleasant person. She becomes attracted to Kirk because he is kinder. If Spock-2 disposes of Kirk-2, she may wind up with Spock-2 (MM).

Morg, a (James Daris):   A black-haired, bearded man of uncertain age, dressed in Neolithic leather and fur—one of the males of Sigma Draconis VI's surface culture. The Enterprise landing party captures him and obtains a

M

small amount of information about the Eymorgs before he escapes (SB).

Morgs: The humanoid males of Sigma Draconis VI. They live on the glaciated surface of the planet in a Neolithic culture while the females, the Eymorgs, live underground in a high-technology culture they don't understand. The Eymorgs capture Morgs for use as guards, breeding stock, and pets (SB).

Morla of Cantaba Street (Charles Kierkop): A sullen young Argelian who is Kara's fiancé and jealous about her, which is considered improper on Argelius II. He leaves the café just before Kara and Scotty do, thus making himself a suspect in her murder (WF).

Mortae: A rather primitive mining tool used by the Troglytes to mine zienite on Ardana. The angry Troglytes also use it as a weapon (Cms).

Mosaic: A gigantic transparent mosaic of Kulkukan rests in a metal square on the top of the pyramid in the city he created in his own ship. Kirk sees it as part of the key to the puzzle set before them, and uses towers of refracted light to focus through the mosaic; it works and Kulkukan comes in person to confront them (HS/a).

Moses: Hebrew prophet and lawgiver, circa 1200 B.C., who, according to the Biblical book Exodus, leads the Israelites out of Egypt and through the wilderness to Canaan. Flint the immortal says he knew Moses personally (RM).

Motherlode: A large ringed planet in the Acadian star system, rich in mineral deposits and mined by a variety of humans, humanoids, and aliens, circled by a scattering of asteroids (MP/a).

Mountain lion: See Le-matya.

Mousetrap: A Terran slang term for the Klingon tactic of having one battlecruiser attract the attention of a ship while other battlecruisers use the cover to sneak up on the victim (Tr/a).

M-rays: A form of energy capable of being radiated over various wavelengths and of counteracting force fields. Spock uses it to neutralize the force field with which Apollo is holding the Enterprise (WM).

M'Ress, Lieutenant (Majel Barrett): One of the Enterprise's communications officers—a bipedal felinoid approximately the size of an Earth human female, with a

thick orange mane, long tail, and large golden eyes. She has a soft, purring voice with a distinct catlike tone when excited or angry. She is from the planet Cait, in the Lynx constellation.

M24 Alpha: A trinary system 11.630 light-years from Gamma II. One of its planets is Triskelion, a sports-minded place (GT).

Mudd, Harcourt Fenton (Harry) (Roger C. Carmel): Portly and piratelike, with balding head, flowing moustache and gold earring—a thief, con man, liar, and rogue who belongs in jail, where Kirk tries to keep him. His record, in part: smuggling, sentence suspended; transport of stolen goods and purchase of space vessel with counterfeit currency, sentence: psychiatric treatment, effectiveness disputed; Master's license (certificate which allows one to captain a ship) revoked SD 1116.4. Using the alias of Leo Francis Walsh, he doses three girls with illegal Venus drugs in order to sell them to rich husbands. But the girls end up marrying miners on Rigel XII, and Kirk sends Mudd to jail (MW). Somehow Harry Mudd makes his way out of jail and continues his career of fast deals, including an attempt to sell a Vulcan patent to the Denebians, who treat crime with the death sentence. He escapes, ending up on an uncharted planet inhabited by several thousand androids who crown him Mudd the First and obey his every wish, including one to shanghai

the Enterprise so its crew can take his place. Using towering illogic, the Enterprise people defeat the androids and leave Mudd in their custody with five hundred simulacra of his shrewish wife, Stella, to while away his time (IM). He manages to make his way off the planet. He has since sold Star Fleet Academy to the Ilyrans; he has sold the natives of a planet in Omega Cygni their own ocean; he has conned miners out of their dilithium crystals with fake Federation vouchers; and he has used illusion creatures to help sell what he thinks is a fake love potion to lonely miners. He is as surprised as anyone else to discover that the love potion actually works, and bemoans the lost chance to become wealthy by selling it. He is to be sent away once more for rehabilitation. Star Fleet must have an optimistic nature (MP/a).

Mudd's Planet: A K-type planet, on the surface a barren, bleak ball of rock, monotonous and ugly. It has been adapted for humans by the use of pressure domes and life-support systems, and is inhabited underground by over two hundred thousand androids and Harry Mudd, whom they keep as an anthropological specimen (IM). Though the Enterprise left Harry Mudd stranded on the planet run by androids, thinking he would be there for life, the con man managed to escape. He taught the androids the concept of organized sports, and while thousands of robots were cheering on two teams locked in mighty struggle, Mudd "borrowed" a ship and escaped (MP/a).

Mudd, Stella (Kay Elliott): Harry Mudd's wife—tall, beaky, severe-faced, very plain. A shrew of the first order, she nagged Mudd so vehemently that he fled into space. On Planet Mudd, he keeps a shrine to Stella containing an android duplicate of her that will shut up on command. Kirk has the androids provide Mudd with a series of five hundred identical Stellas programmed to never shut up (IM).

Mugato (Janos Prohaska): A Neuralese great ape, white with red face, hands, and feet, with a large horn projecting from the top of its head. The bite of its fangs is poisonous unless counteracted by a mako root utilized by a Kanutu. Mugatos seldom stay in one place for very long, roaming about Neural. They mate for life and will avenge a slain mate. Kirk is bitten by one and has to be treated by Nona. Its mate later attacks her. At one point Kirk calls it a "gumato"—perhaps a dialectical variant used by natives in another part of Neural (PLW).

Mulhall, Dr. Anne (Diana Muldaur): An astrobiologist, with light brown hair, blue eyes, strong bones. Thalassa, Sargon's wife, borrows her body, and Henoch nearly tempts her into keeping it, but she obeys Sargon and, with him, takes up a disembodied existence (RT).

Multitronics: See M-5 multitronic unit.

M'Umbha: Uhura's mother, spoken of in the past tense (MT).

Murasaki 312: A quasarlike formation—a misty, slowly undulating, blue-shining, gelatinous, entirely otherwordly electromagnetic phenomenon. Spock and six others sent to investigate it are swept off course to Taurus II (GS).

Murder: Kirk argues that it is committing murder to kill the original Spock merely to reproduce a twenty-five-foot-tall clone of the Vulcan. This appeals to the basic logic of the gigantic Spock-clone, who turns the tables on Dr. Keniclius 5, the creator of the clone idea (IV/a). When the computer tells Uhura that it will not take any further

hostages, but will simply "turn them off," make them cease to function, she tries to explain that this would be murder. The master computer does not understand: All other forms on the planet can be made to cease functioning and then be reactivated when required (OUP/a). See also Death penalty.

Murinite: A mineral found on Rigel IV. Hengist's knife, made by the hill people of the Argus River region, has a murinite hilt (WF).

Museum: The Kzin lure Spock to the barren planet in the Beta Lyrae system with an empty stasis box stolen from a museum. Sulu wishes the stasis box weapon could be put in a museum, but Spock points out that a weapon that powerful would only attract other thieves eventually to steal it again (SW/a). Some of the ships found derelict in the alternate universe of Elysia are so old that Scott has seen only crude drawings of them in museums (Tr/a).

Music: Some cultures, including certain Vulcan offshoots, use musical notes, stated in a proper sequence, as words. Kirk activates the Indian obelisk by saying "Kirk to Enterprise" in trying to contact the ship. The words happen to contain the sequence of sounds which opens the obelisk (PSy). McCoy puzzles the Alice androids by humming the "Blue Danube Waltz" to nonexistent violin music (IM). The audiovisual suggestion affecting the males on the Enterprise includes music; the females cannot hear it (LS/a).

Musical instruments: The "space hippies" carry twenty-second-century musical instruments and do not disdain Spock's lyre when he wants to sit in for a gig (WEd).

Muskat, Joyce (script): The Empath (Em).

Mutation: See Surgo-op.

Mutiny: There has never been a mutiny aboard a Federation starship (Star Fleet evidently does not care to count the events on Omicron Ceti III), though mutiny is for a short time the only explanation anyone can think of to account for the death of the entire crew aboard the Defiant (TW). Kirk-J accuses Spock, McCoy, and Scott of mutiny and wants to execute them for it (TI). Garth says his crew mutinied when he ordered them to wipe out the peace-loving people of Antos IV, but his insanity invalidates the charge (WGD).

My Lady: Spock, disguised as a distant cousin of Sarek's, addresses his mother as "My Lady Amanda" on being introduced to her. It may be assumed that this polite form of address is a typical formal greeting from a Vulcan male to a female (Yy/a).

Mystic symbols: See Pentagram.

Myths: Lucien, Asmodeus, and all the wizards who tried to help mankind were relegated to the myths and legends of time after they left Earth to find a hiding place on Megas-tu (Mtu/a).

Nacelles: The two long tubes above the rear end of a starship containing the matter/antimatter that powers the ship. If the matter/antimatter shielding deteriorates, or something happens to the cycling of the power, the ship will blow up. Thus, the starship is constructed so that the nacelles can be blown away from the rest of the ship if necessary to save lives. The saucer section, containing all personnel and its own power system, can then go to the nearest planet and land. The entire ship cannot land, however, and the saucer can never take off again, for it no longer has the necessary lifting power. See also Regenerating chamber.

Name the Winner: A television program on Planet 892-IV sponsored by the Jupiter Eight auto, inviting the audience to speculate about the outcome of gladiatorial events. Spock, McCoy, and Flavius appear on this show (BC).

Napoleon Bonaparte: Garth of Izar, bragging about his plans to take over the universe, mentions that Napoleon Bonaparte (1769–1821) did not manage to conquer his world. Napoleon came close, however, before he was stopped. Ironically, Garth was incarcerated in an asylum named after Elba, the island on which Napoleon was exiled after his initial attempt to take over Europe (WGD).

Natira (Kate Woodville): The high priestess of Yonada—a young woman with blue eyes and brown hair, dressed in metallic draperies—who carries out the rulings of the Oracle. She has no knowledge of her origins, and it takes much arguing to convince her that Yonada is a ship and not a world. She falls in love with McCoy and proposes marriage to him; McCoy, with only a year to live, leaves the Enterprise and marries her. When Spock and Kirk find the central computer of Yonada, they also find a cure for McCoy's illness, and the doctor returns to the Enterprise, the marriage presumably annulled by the removal from McCoy of the Instrument of Obedience required of every Yonadan. Natira stays to guide her people, but even though she has a duty as their leader, she expresses the hope that McCoy will someday find the Yonadans again . . . and her (FW).

Natural immunity: Some species have a natural immunity to some diseases. Vulcans are naturally immune to Saurian virus and auroral plague (AI/a).

Natural law: The natural law on Megas-tu is magic; the galactic creation point extends through space and time into another dimension where the natural logic of things is totally different (Mtu/a).

Natural phenomenon: See Wavering effect.

Navigational coordinates: All coordinates mean very little in the dimension of Megas-tu, where the Enterprise is not in time or space as the crew understands it (Mtu/a).

Navigational manual override: When the ship goes out of orbit at high speed, Arex rushes to the navigational manual override and locks the engine controls, so that the Enterprise will return to orbit on its own (OUP/a).

Navigator: See Chekov, Ensign Pavel; Randolph, Lieutenant Nancy.

NCC-1701: The identifying number used for the starship Enterprise. Originally thought to be a memorial reference to early twentieth-century Earth amphibious air-

craft, the Navy Curtis Craft, it has recently been revealed that the numbering system for starships was the responsibility of two men: Matt Jeffries (See Jeffries tube), a twentieth-century inventor responsible for the design of early starships, and Constitution-type ships, including the Enterprise and Gene Roddenberry, an inventive television executive. They used "N" because it was a 1928 adoption by the United States as an identifying letter, "C" for "commercial," and the second "C" for esthetic balance—hence "NCC" as the call-letter identification for all Enterprise-class starships.

Neck pinch: See Vulcan nerve pinch.

Necrotic tissue: A dead, sloughing-off tissue, such as that which follows a severe burn. McCoy finds a layer of necrotic tissue "a few cells thick" on Sulu's shoulder where Losira touched him briefly. According to McCoy, a normal wound would heal quickly; if Losira had not been stopped, Sulu's entire body would have consisted of this tissue (TWS).

Nectar: The females of Taurus II serve a nectar at their banquet honoring the Enterprise's landing party, which McCoy thinks is responsible for everyone's feeling dizzy; he says it is as strong as Saurian brandy. Actually, it is the planet itself which is affecting the men; the nectar probably has nothing to do with it (LS/a).

Negative: Military jargon for "No"; used in Star Fleet.

Negative star mass: See Questar M17.

Negative universe: See Antimatter universe.

Negatron hydrocoils: A piece of apparatus for the android bodies that Sargon and Thalassa are building—a drop of jelly that does what a muscle will (RT).

Negress: Old Earth term for a female Negro or black person, used by Abraham Lincoln in surprise at meeting Uhura. He then apologizes for the term, which he thinks might be derogatory. Uhura says she does not fear words, and she does not take offense. Lincoln then apologizes for the defensive reaction which triggered his first apology (SC).

Nellis, Tom (Dallas Mitchell): A crewman on the Enterprise (CX).

Nelson, Gene (director): Gamesters of Triskelion (GT).

Neoethylene: A compound which, when injected into the tribbles, stops them from growing and reproducing. It will also break down the colonies of tribbles to smaller tribbles with slower metabolic rates. With neoethylene, there can now be safe tribbles (MTT/a).

Neptune: The eighth planet in our solar system, Neptune has a diameter of 44,300 kilometers; the cosmic cloud which invades our galaxy is larger than Jupiter, Saturn, and Neptune combined (OPM/a).

Neptune Bath Salts: A product advertised on Planet 892-IV (BC).

Nerve pinch: See Vulcan nerve pinch.

Nesvig, Colonel (Morgan Jones): The military head of McKinley Rocket Base. When captured, Kirk and Spock are brought to him, and he questions them with no success (AE).

Net: The Aquans of Argo use nets to capture fish for food, to capture Kirk and Spock as prisoners, and also to keep them on the island where the mutated Enterprise men are left to die (Am/a).

Neural: A semiarid, rocky, and hilly planet with sparse forestation and a primitive culture—at least until the Klingons tamper with it by introducing guns (PLW).

Neural field: A selective field, radiated from a small projector, which neutralizes nerve impulses to the voluntary muscles; the Kelvans use it on the Enterprise's landing party (AON).

Neural neutralizer: A conditioning and mind-erasing machine invented by Dr. Tristan Adams on Tantalus V; it consists of a chamber in which are a chair for the subject, facing a panel of flickering lights, and a room containing the controls and an observation window. It is eventually dismantled (DMd).

Neural paralyzer: A type of drug which can knock a Terran so fully unconscious that he appears to be dead. McCoy gives Kirk such a drug, which he says is a tri-ox compound, during the captain's duel with Spock on Vulcan. When the drug hits Kirk, he collapses under Spock's hands, which prevents his actual murder (AT). See also Tri-ox compound.

Neutrality: See Orion.

Neutral zone, Romulan-Federation: An area between Federation and Romulan territory, entry into which by either party can be considered an act of war. The zone was established by treaty after the Romulan War more than one hundred years before the Enterprise's missions (BT). Though strictly speaking the treaty has now been broken by both sides, the neutral zone remains a no man's land, and Federation ships that venture into it are quickly attacked (DY). The Enterprise is caught in the neutral zone and nearly taken in a surprise attack (Su/a).

Neutronium: The hull of the doomsday berserker machine is coated with this alloy, the densest in the galaxy. The Enterprise's phasers cannot cut through it (DMa).

New England: See Salem.

Newland, John (director):   Errand of Mercy (EM).

New matter: See Creation.

New Paris: A colony attacked by a plague, for which the Enterprise is delivering medical supplies when it is delayed by Murasaki 312 and the loss of the Galileo (GS).

Newscaster (Bart LaRue):   The arranger of a worldwide news broadcast presenting one of John Gill's rare public appearances (PF).

News summary: See First manned moon shot.

"Nightingale Woman":   A sonnet written by Phineas Tarbolde on the Canopus planet in 1996; recited from memory by Gary Mitchell to Dr. Elizabeth Dehner. Mitchell calls it one of the most passionate love sonnets of the last few centuries, but it does not rhyme or scan like an Earth-style sonnet. This extract from page 387 is all we have of the poem: "My love has wings, slender feathered things with grace and upswept curve and tapered tip . . ." (WNM).

Nitrous oxide: See Laughter infection.

Niven, Larry (script):   Slaver Weapon (SW/a).

Noel, Dr. Helen (Marianna Hill):   A psychiatrist—small, dark, pretty. On Tantalus V, Kirk is conditioned by Dr. Adams's neural machine to fall in love with her (DMd).

Nomad (Vic Perrin):   A metal cylindrical object about five feet high, angular but streamlined, with radiating antennae; it moves by floating on its antigravitic beams. Originally a Terran space probe, sent out in August 2002 to seek out alien life forms, it was damaged by a meteorite and wandered from contact with Earth. Later it met an alien space probe, Tan Ru, whose mission was to secure and sterilize soil samples. They combined, and Nomad became convinced that its mission was to sterilize all that was imperfect, including all organic life. It wiped out four billion inhabitants of the Malurian system, and is about to destroy the Enterprise when it makes subspace contact and mistakes Captain Kirk for its creator, Jackson Roykirk. When it discovers its error, it destroys itself as imperfect (Cg).

Greg Jein

Nome: A concept basic to Vulcan philosophy. Lincoln (to his own surprise) finds that he knows the word and its meaning: "All." The idea is that an infinite variety of things combine to make existence worthwhile, and delight in one's own nature does not mean denigration of those who are different (SC). See also IDIC.

Nona (Nancy Kovack):   The slender, dark-haired, lively wife of Tyree on the planet Neural; a Kanutu witch woman who charms Tyree with her spells and cures Kirk of a poisonous bite. Deciding that the hill people are not likely to bring her sufficient power, she tries to offer stolen Federation phasers to the villagers, but they distrust her and kill her (PLW).

Non-network sensory stasis: An anomaly which the Enterprise people think at first might be a natural phenomenon, much like an electrical storm. It turns out to be an alien intelligence that can blanket Delta Theta III and is working on the development of the natives there. A solarization effect occurs when she speaks. The stasis resembles a sensor field but without a scanning grid or other points of reference (Be/a).

Nored, Lieutenant Anne (Nichelle Nichols):   A pretty brown-haired female on Enterprise security detail, who is engaged to Carter Winston, famous space trader and philanthropist. Even when she realizes that the Vendorian shape-changer is not her fiancé, Anne cannot fire on it, held back by her love for Winston. When she sees the Vendorian in its natural shape, at first she does not feel she can love it, but later Anne decides that they need to discuss the matter at length (Su/a).

Norman (Richard Tatro):   Stocky, stolid central coordinator of the androids on Planet Mudd: the only android who has no duplicates. Entirely humanoid, he is able to sign aboard the Enterprise unsuspected, in order to take it over. After felling the other androids with lesser illogicalities, Kirk and Mudd turn Norman off with the "I am lying" paradox (IM).

Nova: A star that suddenly and very rapidly increases its output of light and other radiation tremendously, then fades away to relative obscurity. A star going nova is astronomically interesting but dangerous to observe at close range. The Vians arrange to rescue one species of the Minaran star system, in the process killing some research scientists the Enterprise has been sent to collect (Em). The Sarpeids rescue themselves by a flight into their past (AY). See also Fabrina.

Nuclear reactor: See PXK reactor.

Nucleus: A small organ within the cell which is essential to the functioning of the cell. The nucleus contains, among other things, the mechanisms which cause reproduction, protein synthesis. The chromosomes are found in the nucleus.

Null-gravity combat exercises: Kirk and Spock engage in free-fall exercises, including forms of combat, aboard the Enterprise. They evidently do so rather frequently. It is an interesting method of keeping fit, as control of the body in null gravity would involve the use of almost all the muscles. Kirk and Spock use their exercises to advantage to overpower Tchar (Ji/a).

Nullifier: The Kzin have a stasis-box nullifier; it turns off the stasis field in which the box has been protected for a billion years, so the box can be opened (SW/a).

Number 4 shield: Shield for deflecting phaser fire and other attacks, located on the starboard side of the ship (ET).

Number One (M. Leigh Hudec [Majel Barrett]): The dark-haired, mature, very efficient First Officer and helmsman serving on the Enterprise under Captain Pike (Me).

Obelisk: A structure some twenty feet high, resembling a Buckminster Fuller teepee, resting on a truncated pyramid of stone. The obelisk is made of an alien alloy resistant to probe, so its age cannot be measured accurately. It was installed on an Earthlike planet by a race known as the Preservers, to prevent asteroids from crashing into the planet. The American Indians who have been placed on the planet consider the obelisk a temple, to be operated by some medicine chief. The glyphs on the obelisk, which stand for musical tones, are unreadable even to Spock, who says they look like Klingon letters (PSy). See also Towers.

O'Brian, Lieutenant: Officer whom Mudd captures; Kirk tries to contact him via communicator (IM).

Occipital bone: A compound bone that forms the posterior part of the skull and articulates with the atlas. Spock tells Uhura that the occipital area of his head seems to have impacted with the arm of the command chair when the Enterprise was hurled 990.7 light-years from Losira's planet. In other words, he bumped the back of his head (TWS).

Ocean waves: If asked, the Enterprise's Recreation Room is capable of creating the effect of ocean waves as a holographic illusion, complete with sound, tides, and sea gulls (PJ/a).

O'Connel, Steve (Caesar Belli): A small boy of about seven or eight, a Black Irish type, with pale skin and very dark hair cut in bangs. He is one of the children of the Starnes expedition on Triacus, who temporarily come under Gorgan's influence (CL).

Odona (Sharon Acker): A young blond Gideonite girl of pixielike beauty, dressed in a see-through jump suit with a bikini underneath. She appears on the replica of the Enterprise, where Kirk is the only person aboard, and proceeds to seduce him by acting helpless and frightened. She has been infected with Vegan choriomeningitis from his blood and now wishes to tie Kirk to her planet by arousing his affection for her. When Kirk discovers the hoax, it is nearly too late for Odona, who falls ill. Spock finds them both and transports them to the real Enterprise, where McCoy cures Odona of the fever. However, she still carries in her blood the microorganism that will infect her germ-free planet—her original aim (MG).

Offering: Spock, desperate to contact the alien intelligence of Delta Theta III, considers submitting to its godlike attitude and making an offering of some sort. Kirk says it can't be bribed, and tries to be totally honest with it instead (Be/a).

Off-ship vehicles: Ships which are carried inside the larger starships: shuttlecraft, scout ships, heavily armored landing vehicles, hovercrafts, light planetary vehicles, and so on (MP/a).

O'Herlihy, Lieutenant (Jerry Ayres): Ordnance officer, lured to the surface of Cestus III and killed by the Gorns (Ar).

O'Herlihy, Michael (director): Tomorrow Is Yesterday (TY).

O.K. Corral: The area where the Earps and Doc Holliday met the Clanton Gang for their famous gunfight at five P.M. on October 26, 1881. The Melkots recreate this scene to punish the Enterprise's landing party for trespassing; they are supposed to die as the Clanton Gang, but Spock guesses that all is illusion and convinces the others (SGn).

Old knowledge, the: The information stored in the computers of the city on Sigma Draconis VI, which one can tap through the Great Teacher (SB).

Old man (Jon Lormer): A native of Yonada, with shaggy gray hair, a wide mouth, and pronounced circles under his eyes. He gives McCoy a restorative powder after the doctor is struck by the Oracle. The old man had climbed a mountain in his youth and discovered that Yonada is an artificial planet. He tells the Enterprise's party of this, saying, "For the world is hollow and I have touched the sky!" and the Oracle immediately kills him (FW).

"Old Ones": The extinct inhabitants of the now-frozen planet Exo III. To escape freezing, they had gone underground, where their culture in the caverns had changed to one of tightly structured authoritarian rule. They constructed androids of such extremely logical natures that the robots came to despise their irrational, emotional creators and destroyed all the "Old Ones" (LG).

Old-style interplanetary code: Outdated communications code no longer used by Star Fleet, but used by Nomad (Cg).

Olympus, Mount: A mountain in Greece, where the ancients thought the gods of their time resided. Apollo claims to have lived there with the other gods (WM).

Omaha Air Base: The air-defense base—code name: Blackjack—over which the Enterprise appears when it is flung into the 1970s by a slingshot effect (TY).

Omega IV: An Earthlike planet inhabited by two groups of humans: the Yangs, barbaric Caucasian raiders, and the Kohms, semicivilized Oriental villagers. Apparently descended from Chinese Communists and Americans who left Earth about two hundred years before the Enterprise's voyages, settling on Omega IV to continue their wars there. After Captain Tracey violates the Prime Directive to aid the Kohms, Kirk convinces the Yangs that both sides must develop a peaceful culture (OG).

Omega Cygni: The star of the Malurian system (Cg).

Omega Cygni system: Magen, the psionic female in Elysia, is from the Omega Cygni system (Tr/a). Mudd turned a handsome profit there when he sold the natives of one of the planets their own ocean (MP/a).

Omicron IV: A planet almost destroyed by a buildup of nuclear weapons similar to that which took place on twentieth-century Earth (AE).

Omicron Ceti III: The site of an agriculture colony (five settlements), where Berthold rays make life impossible except for those infected by native spores. The spores induce anarchic euphoria among those infected and the colonists must be relocated (TSP).

Omicron Delta region: The section of the galaxy in which the shore-leave amusement planet is located (OUP/a, SL).

Omnivore: Humans are omnivores—eaters of meat as well as vegetables—so the Kzin will talk to Sulu (SW/a).

One: A symbolic greeting, perhaps even a religion, affected by Dr. Sevrin and his "space hippies," but Spock knows the ritual also. The hands are placed together, chest-high, index finger to index finger and thumb to thumb, to form an egg shape, accompanied by the words "We are one"; the response is "One is the beginning." The space hippies turn their backs on civilization to seek the beginning, but the Eden they find is deadly (WEd).

One hundred, the: Uhura used to run the one-hundred (a foot race of one hundred yards or meters) in record time. She does not have perfect footing on the ice-bound world, however, and the pursuing Kzin capture her before she can reach the shuttlecraft, which makes her disgusted at herself for losing the race (SW/a).

O'Neill, Ensign: A member of the landing party searching Taurus II for the crew of the crashed shuttlecraft, Galileo; he is killed by the hostile anthropoids (GS).

O'Neil, Lieutenant (Sean Morgan): A not-too-prudent young officer who accompanies Sulu to the surface of Beta III, only to be caught and absorbed by Landru almost immediately. He returns to normal after Landru is destroyed (RA). A young man with the candid eyes and guileless face of a nice little boy, he is the trans-

porter officer on duty while the Enterprise investigates the loss of the Defiant. While he undoubtedly knows his job, Scotty handles the transporter himself during the time they are trying to get Kirk back (TW).

One-man vessel: Carter Winston's one-man vessel is caught in a meteor storm from which the Enterprise rescues it. The ship is totally damaged; Scott looks it over when the starship stows the smaller vessel in the Shuttle Bay and states that the ship is nothing more than scrap. The wrecked ship is really bait to trap the Enterprise into taking a Vendorian spy on board so that it can change the starship's course into the Romulan neutral zone (Su/a).

Only: Miri and her friends called children "onlies"—after the adults died, they were the only ones left (Mi).

On the double: Military term for getting somewhere twice as fast as usual; couched as an order from a superior, usually.

Operatives: Personal henchmen in the mirror universe. Kirk-2 and Spock-2 are followed everywhere by their operatives on the I.S.S. Enterprise. Spock-2 answers Sulu-2's threats by saying that his operatives will avenge his death, pointing out that some of them are Vulcans. This is sufficient to scare off Sulu-2 (MM).

Ophiuchus VI: The colony where Harry Mudd intended to take his three high-priced females to be settlers' wives. The Enterprise took them in the opposite direction, to Rigel XII (MW). At another time, Harry Mudd uses fake Federation vouchers to con two miners there out of a year's supply of dilithium crystals (MP/a).

Opto-aud: A device used by the females of Taurus II to signal to men from space and to reveal anything the women request of it. It resembles an ornate gold stage

with red curtains that part to reveal the scene desired. The females can also ask it to show them anything on the planet; Spock uses it to request the hiding place of their communicators so he can contact the Enterprise for help. The Taurus females agree to destroy the opto-aud when they are shown that they can have another way of life if the Enterprise takes them to another planet to live (LS/a).

Oracle of the People: A computer in control of Yonada, the ship/asteroid. Natira takes her orders from the Oracle, which rules with an iron fist in an electrostatic glove; it has a booming masculine voice, no sense of humor, and tends to throw around bolts of electricity unnecessarily. It is sophisticated enough to react to voices, and to the number of people in the room. It controls the Yonadans with a small diodelike Instrument of Obedience, which is medically inserted under the skin near the temple. Tampering with any part of the computer, including the various contact points such as the monolith, the altar, and the plaque, is a "sacrilege against the people," and the Oracle can be quite lethal. If one knows where to apply pressure, a door to the computer room itself can be opened, but random meddling will alert the Oracle to the presence of blasphemers. It can defend itself by throwing bolts of electricity or heating the room to unbearable temperature, reactions originally intended to protect the computer until Yonada arrived at a planet. Something went wrong, however, and the computer has kept the asteroid/ship traveling in space for over ten thousand years, during which time everyone aboard has forgotten the computer's real purpose and simply worships the Oracle as a jealous and unreasonable god (FW).

Orbit: The Enterprise usually takes up standard orbit around a planet; depending on conditions or needs, this can be a distance of from one thousand to seven thousand miles out. The Enterprise is a space-to-space ship, incapable of landing on a planet. The Enterprise was in orbit 643 miles, 2021 feet, and 2.04 inches above Excalbia, according to Spock (SC). The Enterprise is unexpectedly taken out of orbit at high speed when the amusement planet's computer begins to get the feel of the ship. It returns to orbit on its own after Arex locks the navigational manual override (OUP/a).

Ordainments: The laws of the Aquans (Am/a).

Order board: One of the many items a starship captain has to sign each day. A female yeoman presents the board to Kirk (HS/a).

Orderly (John Buonomo): One of McCoy's assistants in the search for an antitoxin prior to their locating the ryetalyn on Holberg 917G (RM).

Orders: Battle ribbons are triangular, worn in arrangements of triangle, diamond, or star, depending on number. See also Decorations; Medals; Ribbons.

Ore: A soft, adhesive, yellowish ore found on Alfa 177 is strongly magnetic, enough so to cause transporter damage (EW).

Organia: The only Class M planet in a quadrant of space disputed by the Federation and the Klingons, with a medieval, nonviolent culture that measures D-minus on the Richter scale of culture. Although the Organians appear to be peaceful humans, they are actually beings of pure power who easily put a stop to the Klingon-Federation conflict and force both sides to sign a peace treaty (EM).

Organian Peace Treaty: Treaty imposed by the Organians on the Federation and the Klingon Empire. It provides, in part, that disputed planets go to whichever side can develop them more efficiently, and that forces of either side may take shore leave at the other's bases. Evidently, diplomatic circles regard the barroom brawl at the K-7 deep-space station as a "slight disagreement," not a treaty violation (TT). When the alien entity appears on the Enterprise, the Klingons and the Federation have been at peace for three years since signing the treaty, according to Kang. However, it is not known if Klingon years are the same length as Federation years (Dv).

Organic life form: On the Kalandan outpost planet, Sulu finds an almost viruslike plant parasite which looks something like dry moss. It is the only biological life form on the planet, according to McCoy. On Earth, a parasitic life form must live on some other life form (TWS).

Organic matter: Only organic matter is affected by the spiroid wave bombardment from Terratin; metal stays the same size (Te/a).

Organized sports: See Mudd's Planet.

Orientine acid: Acid that can burn through anything but the crystal container which holds it. Kirk threatens to use some of it on the third table in the medical lab, which is really the Vendorian shape-changer in hiding (Su/a).

Orion: A planet in the Rigel star system, noted for its traders, its treachery, and its green slave women. It also has pirates. The planet has tried to maintain an air of neutrality, concerning the Federation and everyone else, but in practice this seems a thinly veiled license to prey on everyone without particular prejudice in any political direction (PO/a). Kirk, Spock, and a historian named Erikson go through the time portal into the past of Orion to study it firsthand. They are careful not to disturb anything that could change history (Yy/a). Dr. Roger Korby improved immunization techniques with information from the Orion ruins, which he translated (LG). Orion smugglers have been raiding Coridan for dilithium crystals. To protect their illegal operation, they must prevent the Babel Conference from voting Coridan into the Federation. To this end, the smugglers send an agent aboard the Enterprise, disguised as an Andorian, and follow in a mysterious high-speed ship. When Thelev, the agent, is discovered and defeated, both ship and Orion spy destroy themselves (JB). The sneaky and untrustworthy Orions have had to learn new ways in Elysia, the Delta Triangle region from which there is no escape, and to become law-abiding beings (Tr/a).

Orion colonies: A world inhabited by a variety of species, at least three of which are humanoid: the intelligent Orions, such as the golden-skinned interpreter of the laws, Devna (Tr/a), the disguised Thelev (JB), and the semi-intelligent, green-skinned, black-haired, tailed Orions. Of the green Orion females it is said that they are animal-like in their viciousness but so seductive that no human male can resist them. It would perhaps be unwise to resist, in any case, since the females have long, sharp claws. In spite of this, or perhaps because of it, Orion females are prized as slaves. Vina takes on the appearance of one of these to dance for Pike in an illusion (Me). When Christopher Pike was captain of the Enterprise, some humans were running a slave trade, selling Orion natives, especially the "green animal women" (Me). This vile business was apparently eradicated, to judge from the lack of reference to it by Thelev (JB) and Marta (WGD).

Orion commander/captain: The commander of the Orion pirate ship and a native of Orion. He is caught

O

203

by the Enterprise and faces suicide for compromising his planet's neutrality. He also orders the deaths of his crew and the destruction of his ship, but Captain Kirk talks the commander out of both acts. He had hoped to kill Kirk, so that the Enterprise log would not have a record of the piracy, but the trick doesn't work. The Orions are all captured, to face charges in a Federation court (PO/a).

P

Orion dancer: See Devna; Marta; Vina.

Orion ensign: One of the crew members of the Orion pirate ship (PO/a).

Orion markings: The alien ship used by the pirates who attack the S.S. Huron has Orion markings on it—remarkably careless of people who wish to keep their neutrality secure (PO/a).

Orion trader (Joseph Mell):   A smirking, oily salesman of green Orion slave girls, who offered Vina to a stunned Captain Pike (Me).

Orion science officer: When the Orion pirates meet with Kirk to give over to him the stolen drug, strobolin, in exchange for the dilithium crystals they have taken from the S.S. Huron, the science officer carries a time bomb with him. Orions must maintain their neutrality at all costs, so the price of being caught at piracy is death; they decide to take Captain Kirk with them on the unstable asteroid if they can. The science officer is foiled by Scott's quick action in beaming up the dilithium trigger for the bomb before it can be set off (PO/a).

Osborne, Lieutenant: Head of one of the Enterprise's security details helping to look for the Horta on Janus VI (DD). An officer who accompanies Kirk's landing party on Eminiar VII (TA).

O'Shea, Captain: A craggy-faced man who commands the S.S. Huron (PO/a).

Oswald, Gerd (director):   The Alternative Factor (AF); The Conscience of the King (CK).

Others, the: The Eymorgs of Sigma Draconis VI as described by the Morgs. Also called the "Givers of Pain and Delight" (SB).

Other, the: The term used by Nomad to refer to Tan Ru, the alien space probe which amalgamated with

Nomad (Cg).

Our Soul: See Soul of Skorr.

Outphase condition: A slight difference in the structure of the Enterprise caused by the Kalandan transporter beam (TWS). See also Molecular transporter.

Outposts: Eight outposts guard the Federation side of the Federation-Romulan neutral zone. They are constructed in natural asteroids, the machinery and living quarters burrowed into the asteroid's core and shielded with cast rodinium. The attacking Romulan ship destroys Outposts 1, 3, 4, and 8 (BT).

Outside: The Elysians' term for our universe; the area outside the time trap (Tr/a).

Oxmyx, Bela (Anthony Caruso):   Boss of the Northside Territory, the largest on Iotia—a gray-haired, square-faced, efficient-looking humanoid with horn-rim glasses. He invites the Enterprise's party down to demand help in wiping out the other bosses. It is a good idea in its way, so Kirk sets him up as planetary leader, with the other bosses as his subordinates (PA).

Ozaba, Dr. (David Roberts):   One of the researchers placed by the Federation on Minara II to study its sun's development into a nova. A rugged black man of about fifty, with a halo of gray hair, he is captured by the Vians and dies under torture in their attempt to teach the empath Gem to comprehend compassion and self-sacrifice (Em).

P

Pain-relieving move: A Vulcan technique that uses nerve pressure to relieve pain. It works on the same principle as a nerve pinch, only it is not intended to knock someone out. Spock uses it on the wounded I-Chaya while waiting for the healer to arrive (Yy/a). See also Vulcan nerve pinch.

Painter (Dick Scotter):   A navigator (TSP).

Palamas, Lieutenant Carolyn (Leslie Parrish):   A tall, blond, elegant A-and-A officer, perhaps a replacement for former historian Lieutenant McGivers. Scotty is in love with her, but when she joins the landing party on Pollux IV she develops a crush on the Greek god Apollo. On Kirk's orders, she tells Apollo that she has only been studying him as an anthropological specimen and that she cannot love him. The god throws a tantrum and some lightning bolts, then casts himself upon the wind. Whether Palamas goes back to Scotty is not recorded (WM).

Pallas 14 system: Twin stars with three planets: Alondra, Bezaride, and Mantilles. The system is located on the outer fringe of the galaxy, where a cosmic cloud invades and engulfs Alondra for food. Fortunately, Alondra is uninhabited, but the cloud then heads for Mantilles, which has a population of eighty-two million people. There is no information on Bezaride, except that it is not harmed by the cloud (OPM/a).

Palmer, Lieutenant (Elizabeth Rogers):   Communications officer; Uhura's relief (DMa, WEd).

Pandro: A planet in the Garo VII system, highly advanced in medicine and therefore valuable to the Federation. At least some of Pandro's natives are colony creatures, such as Commander Ari bn Bem. The planet is not interested in the fate of any individual (naturally, since the natives are colony creatures that can disassemble and re-form any way they want to), but they will not deal with an inefficient and inferior species. Therefore, Commander Bem sets out to test Kirk and Spock (Be/a).

Parallel universe: A universe similar to ours, but existing on another plane or dimension (AF, MM).

Paralysis: When the first impulse of the spiroid wave bombardment hits the Enterprise, it paralyzes all activity aboard the ship for a time; everything has a sort of odd glow to it, with people frozen at their charts or duty stations, and the Enterprise itself is caught in the nexus of laserlike beams from the Terratin planet (Te/a).

Parasites, flying: Pancake-shaped organisms on Deneva, about salad-plate size, of a mottled cream-and-red color, with no distinguishable features except tiny eyes on the forward edge of the dorsal surface and small teeth on the edge of the ventral surface. They are capable of short flights of levitation and are sensitive to light, particularly in the ultraviolet range. In structure they resemble large brain cells; although not connected with one another, collectively they constitute a larger organism, probably a brain of extragalactic origin. Each cell, or flying parasite, is parasitic on one host body, controlling it by inflicting severe pain; as the cells multiply and find new hosts, the brain becomes increasingly sophisticated, intelligent, and malevolent. Their first recorded appearance was in the Beta Portalan system, where they wiped out an entire civilization, after which they moved on, with similar impact, to Lavinius V, Theta Cygni XII, and Ingraham B. On the last planet they forced the survivors to build spaceships and convey them to Deneva, where the Enterprise encounters them. Previously indestructible, their sensitivity to ultraviolet light is finally discovered, and they are killed (OA).

Parking orbit: The Enterprise is put into parking orbit around Motherlode when the landing party goes down to collect Harry Mudd (MP/a).

Parmen (Liam Sullivan): The philosopher-king of the Platonians, by virtue of having the strongest psychokinetic powers. A slender man whose delicate face is haloed by gray hair, he appears to be about 45, although his actual age is 2,311 years. He married Philana when very young, only 128 years old. When a scratch on his leg becomes badly infected, Philana calls the Enterprise for help. After his recovery, Parmen wants to keep McCoy on Platonius permanently. He offers the doctor full citizenship, but treats Kirk and Spock as buffoons. When Kirk, by dint of kironide, develops greater power than any Platonian, Parmen reluctantly lets the Enterprise men go, and the dwarf Alexander with them (PSt).

Parole: Cyrano Jones managed to get a short parole from his sentence of cleaning Space Station K-7 of all the tribbles there. He used the parole to good effect by stealing a tribble predator from the Klingons and putting it to work to clean up the space station (MTT/a).

Parsec: A parsec is 3.26 light-years or 19.2 trillion miles—whichever comes first on your starship warranty.

Party: To celebrate their imminent escape from Elysia while keeping a closer eye on the Klingons, the Enterprise's crew throw a party for everyone, including the inhabitants of Elysia. The event nearly backfires on the Federation people, as the party is used by the Klingons as an excuse to start a fight so that the explosive capsule can be hidden on the Enterprise (Tr/a).

Passenger pigeon: Pleading for the life of the last M113 creature, Dr. Crater recalls to Kirk that once the greater part of the North American continent was covered with animals and birds that are now extinct. The passenger pigeon, a larger bird than the usual city pigeon, inhabited the Eastern Seaboard, but the human demand for roast pigeon, feathered hats and other fashion articles caused its extinction (MT).

Patio: A beautiful patio appears in a garden inside the Recreation Room of the Enterprise, to the amazement of Uhura, Sulu, and McCoy. They had previously been trapped in the room with a blizzard going (PJ/a).

Patrol ship, one-man: Demos, head of Security Police on Dramia, follows the Enterprise in a one-man patrol ship. He enters the starship by way of the Shuttlecraft Bay, which Kirk has "carelessly" left open, and is put under guard, with his ship impounded (Al/a).

Peace: The single goal of Elysians; they will not allow outsiders to bring violence into their peaceful lives (Tr/a).

Peace-keeping force: See Militia.

Peeples, Samuel A. (scripts): Where No Man Has Gone Before (WNM); Beyond the Farthest Star (BFS/a).

Pelagic planet: Ruth Bonaventure, one of Mudd's women, grew up on a sea ranch on a pelagic planet and left because there were no eligible men. The name suggests a planet with no land masses, where the "ranching" would be done on island platforms and the livestock would be sea life (MW).

Penal colonies: The Federation keeps its criminals and insane beings on force-field-blockaded planets under medical supervision. One such colony is Tantalus V (DMd). Another, Elba II, is reserved for the incurably criminally insane. It has only fifteen inmates, a very laudable record for a Federation containing billions of inhabitants (WGD).

Penn, Leo (director): The Enemy Within (EW).

Penology, Central Bureau of: An administrative or research center. Address: Bureau of Penology, Stockholm, Eurasia–NE (DMd).

Pentagram: A mystic symbol with five points. Spock draws one when testing his theory that the Enterprise people can work magic in the world of Megas-tu (Mtu/a).

Pergium: A substance mined in quantity on Janus VI and used in various kinds of nuclear reactors, including the antiquated PXK fission reactor used on Janus VI (DD).

Pericles of Athens: A classical Greek warrior and statesman (circa 495–429 B.C.). A shield purported to be his (if one can believe the Platonians) is given to Kirk (PSt).

Periodic tables: A chart of known elements arranged according to increasing atomic number. The cosmic cloud contains elements unknown on our periodic tables (OPM/a).

Perjury: Kirk is charged with willful perjury when his testimony is opposed by the testimony of the ship's computer (Cml).

Perry, Joyce (script): Time Trap (Tr/a).

Personnel officer (Nancy Wong): A small Oriental female who testifies in Kirk's court-martial and becomes very upset when Areel Shaw turns her testimony against the captain (Cml).

Petri, Lord (Jay Robinson): The ambassador from Troyius to Elas—tall, thin, green-skinned, with pink-and-white striped hair, ornately dressed, with persnickety manners. Delicate and urbane to the point of being effete, he seems the wrong choice to send to chaperon the Dohlman of Elas, a warrior maid, and to teach her some manners before she is married to the Troyian monarch. Elaan, the Dohlman, will not be taught and, in a moment of pique, stabs Lord Petri. The ambassador recovers but refuses to have anything more to do with Elaan. Kirk then takes over the lessons (ET).

Pets: Scott's relationship with the Lactran child convinces the adult Lactrans that humans are not to be kept as pets in a zoo, so the landing parties of both the Ariel and the Enterprise are released, with an invitation to return when they have grown in intelligence (EB/a).

Pevney, Joseph (director): The Return of the Archons (RA); A Taste of Armageddon (TA); The Devil in the Dark (DD); City on the Edge of Forever (CEF); Amok Time (AT); The Apple (Ap); Catspaw (Cp); Arena (Ar); The Immunity Syndrome (IS); Journey to Babel (JB); Friday's Child (FC); The Deadly Years (DY); Wolf in the Fold (WF); The Trouble with Tribbles (TT).

Pharmacopeia index desk: See Medical lab.

Phaser coolant: A pink gas used to keep the larger phaser banks from overheating. It is poisonous to humanoids (BT).

Phaser crew: The men on a starship responsible for the firing of the phaser banks.

Phase One search: A type of search which presupposes that the object of the search is ill, injured, or unconscious and cannot call attention to himself. When the Enterprise has to jettison the pod during an ion storm and it is discovered that Finney has apparently not gotten out in time, a Phase One search is carried out aboard the starship. This type of search, however, does not take into account that the object of the search may not wish to be found (Cml).

Phaser bore: In his initial attempt to rescue Uhura, Kirk orders a phaser bore which can cut through twenty meters of rock per minute. The electronic block goes into effect, however, making their communicators malfunction, but Scott receives enough of the message to realize what the captain has ordered, and activates the bore. It fails to materialize on the planet (OUP/a).

Phasers: Firearms which can shoot a beam set to kill or merely stun; they affect the nervous system of most species. The hand phaser is used for self-protection, and is taken by landing parties on friendly calls or on dip-

lomatic missions where larger phasers would be too conspicuous. It is carried on the belt along with the communicator, under the shirt. At times when it is necessary to have a show of arms, the phaser pistol can be displayed on a weapons belt. This is the hand phaser snapped into a power mount, the handle of which is a power pack to greatly increase the range and power of the weapon. The phaser pistol may in turn be adapted into a rifle mount for even greater range and power. Phasers have a variety of settings from stun effect, which

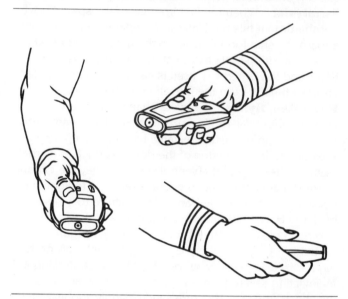

can knock a man unconscious without harming him, to full effect, which can actually cause an object to dematerialize and disappear. The phaser is also capable of being set to cause an object to explode, or to burn a hole through an object. Thus, it can be used as a tool and cutting torch. Phasers can be set to overload, resulting in a power buildup and explosion which destroys the phaser and everything in close proximity (CK, Me). Phasers have also been used at medium intensity to make rocks red-hot and provide warmth for the comfort of human beings (EW, PLW). Sidearms are not normally carried by crewmen, except Security; otherwise they are issued from the armory (WE). Phasers did not work in Sarpeidon's past (AY). On light stun, there is no visible beam, but an aura can be seen around the nozzle of the phaser. The victim is not rendered unconscious, but merely pacified (SB).

Phasers 1 and 2: The miners on Janus VI are armed with Phaser-1 power, definitely useless against a silicon-based creature. The Enterprise's crew are armed with Phaser 2, which is much stronger than Phaser 1. Spock adjusts the phasers to be more useful against a silicon-based creature (DD).

Phasers, ship's: The main weaponry of the U.S.S. Enterprise is its banks of artillery-sized versions of phasers. From the bridge, phaser power can be aimed in any direction. Phaser fire, emitted from the saucer section of the vessel, can act directly against a target very much like hand phaser fire but on a huge scale. It can also be set for proximity explosion and act somewhat like depth charges. The helmsman acts as weapons officer, under the captain's direction. Sulu, Kyle, or Leslie coordinates the fire from the phaser rooms, using the vessel's navigational aids to lock the phasers on target and engage the circuits which fire these weapons.

Phases: See Slaver weapon.

Philana (Barbara Babcock): A Platonian married to Parmen—tall, blond, and haughty, with cold blue eyes and a supercilious voice. She stopped aging at 30 and is now 2,300 years old. She summons McCoy to cure her husband and then tries to keep the doctor on Platonius. She is as unpleasant and untrustworthy as the rest of the Platonians (PSt).

Phillips: Astrobiologist recommended by both Kirk and the M-5 computer for the landing party on Alpha Carinae II; he has surveyed twenty-nine biologically similar planets (UC).

Philosophy of good and evil: The rock creatures of Excalbia wish to test the Federation philosophy of good against evil, and set up a "drama": a fight between Good, represented by Kirk, Spock, Abraham Lincoln, and Surak, and Evil, represented by four notoriously bad people. The rock creatures do not understand at first how Good wins by using the same sneaky tactics as Evil, until Kirk points out the difference between fighting to save the lives of his crew and fighting for power and greed. Lincoln philosophizes that if war is forced upon one, there is nothing to do but fight. There is no honorable way to kill, no gentle way to destroy, nothing good in war except its end. Kirk replies that there is much of Lincoln and Surak's work to be done in the galaxy (SC). See also Nome; Vulcans.

Photon torpedoes: First used by the Romulans in their attacks, subsequently duplicated by Federation scientists, these projectiles resemble large fireballs and employ a pod of matter-antimatter in a magnophoton field. Standard equipment now on the Enterprise they track the target at a speed of several warp factors; a ship can outrun one until the torpedo dissipates, but just barely (BT, JB). Kirk decides to try to kill the cosmic cloud with an attack of photon torpedoes in the cloud's brain area; Spock says it probably will not be effective, since they have already learned that the cloud absorbs photon energy (OPM/a).

Phylos: A planet recently discovered at the periphery of the galaxy, with at least one large city. The Enterprise's landing party finds it apparently deserted but soon meets with the Phylosians themselves and Dr. Keniclius 5 (IV/a).

Phylosian philosophy: The Phylosians dream of going out into the galaxy to impose peace on all other beings, to bring harmony and beauty to all (whether they want it or not), and to make everyone stop fighting wars (IV/a).

Phylosians: Inhabitants of the planet Phylos: intelligent plant beings with heads of asparaguslike greenery, eye stalks, and bodies with ropelike vines hanging down at their sides. They seem passive and harmless, but they wish to see their planet returned to its old glory, and help Dr. Keniclius in his plans to go into space with a master race of cloned Spocks to control and enforce peace. They remember only one generation before the one the Enterprise's landing party contacts. A disease killed off

many of their number, and nobody remembers much before that; they do not believe they have ancestors. They use about 70 percent of their brains—a high ratio compared to other beings in the galaxy (IV/a).

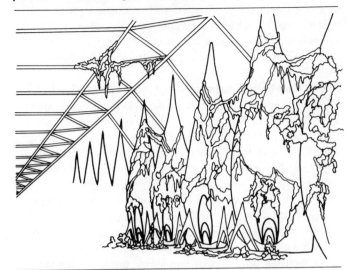

Phynburg oscillating framizam: A piece of electronic equipment aboard the Enterprise—one of the incredible Feinberger instruments. The spelling modification is no doubt a convention of the manufacturer who produces this particular item (CX). See also Feinberger.

Physical laws: Once convinced of the reality of a given situation, we abide by its values—so says Spock, trying to convince the rest of the landing party that the Melkot reenactment of Tombstone's gunfight is an illusion. The illusion can kill only if they believe that it can. Spock points out that physical laws cannot be ignored, but that where those laws do not operate there is no reality. He is right, as usual (SGn).

Physiostimulator: A medical device which McCoy uses in reviving Kirk from the coma induced by the so-called Vulcan death grip. The device is applied to the chest, resulting in a steadying of the heartbeat (EI). See also Cardiostimulator.

Picnic: After the amusement planet's master computer decides that it is serving a useful purpose and calls off its hostile "games," McCoy and Sulu are found enjoying an old-fashioned picnic with Alice, the White Rabbit, and a docile two-headed dragon (OUP/a). An old-fashioned picnic with Vina was another ruse designed by the Talosians to make Captain Pike interested in the girl. He recognized a horse, Tango, as one he had owned on Earth, and realized he was again caught in a Talosian illusion (Me).

Pigmentation: The coloration of human and humanoid skin. The natives of Cheron were stark white and total black in pigmentation, one half of their face (and presumably their body) being each color. Earthmen, although individually more uniform, have more varied pigmentation throughout the species. Long ago the pigmentation of a being's skin ceased to be a matter of concern among Federation citizens, but it was a matter of deadly racial hatred for the Cherons—so much so that they annihilated themselves (LB). See also Monotone humans.

Pigmentation changes: The outstanding symptom of the auroral plague is a change in the skin pigmentation of the victim. In Dramians, the skin turns blue, then green, then red; afterward debilitation and death result unless an antidote is administered. In humans, a pale blue skin color is the first symptom, followed by a yellow-gold color. The symptoms are stopped by McCoy's antidote before they can progress any further (Al/a).

Pike, Captain Christopher (Jeffrey Hunter): In his youth, as captain of the Enterprise, a tall, blue-eyed man almost too clean-cut to be real; later, due to an accident, a withered, horribly scarred caricature of a human being (Sean Kenney), totally paralyzed and confined in an automated wheelchair for the rest of his life. Spock served on the Enterprise under Pike for eleven years, four months, five days, and his loyalty to Pike is as strong as his loyalty to Kirk. During Pike's captaincy of the Enterprise they made the Federation's first contact with Talos IV. The Talosians wished to keep Pike on the planet as a zoo specimen and as breeding stock, but when his violent reactions proved to them that this was not possible, they let him go. Later, as Fleet Captain, Pike was making an inspection tour of a cadet training vessel, an old Class J starship, when one of the baffle plates ruptured. Pike carried out all who were still alive but was himself permanently crippled and scarred by exposure to delta rays. On learning this, Spock takes him to Talos IV, where Pike spends the rest of his life in happy illusion, free from the physical limitations of his body (Me).

Pike, Captain Christopher–2: Former captain of the I.S.S. Enterprise in the mirror universe. Kirk-2 assassinated him to achieve the captaincy (MM).

Pilot vessel: Balok's small ship, of about two thousand metric tons, from which he handles the Fesarius by remote control. Kirk, McCoy, and Bailey beam aboard, to find it a tight fit (CMn).

Piper, Dr. (Paul Fix): Senior surgeon aboard the Enterprise until replaced by Dr. McCoy (WNM).

Piper, Miss (Julie Parrish): Commodore Mendez's administrative assistant on Starbase 11. A mutual friend, Lieutenant Helen Johanssen, told her all about Kirk (Me).

Pituitary: The "master gland" of the human endocrine system, located at the base of the brain. It secretes a hormone, pituitrin, which regulates the activities of the other glands and various physical functions. The pituitary gland also metabolizes kironide, producing the power of psychokinesis; in the absence of pituitrin, the power cannot develop. A pituitary deficiency also causes dwarfism, the lot of Alexander of Platonius, who develops a strong and beautiful character in spite of, or because of, it (PSt).

Plague: See Aurora.

Plak tow: A Vulcan term meaning "frenzy"; literally, "blood fever." It refers specifically to the frenzy at the height of pon far, when the subject is likely to recognize no one and understand nothing but the mating desire and battle (AT).

Planet, Amerind: An Earthlike planet, with pine trees, blue lakes, honeysuckle, and orange blossoms, on which the Preservers have established American Indians.

The planet is in the orbit of an asteroid, and each time it passes, a deflector has to be activated by a medicine chief (PSy).

Planet Council: Governing body of the planet Ardana. Plasus of Stratos City is the Council's High Adviser (Cms).

Planet-eater: The immense cosmic cloud which uses planets for food is possibly even capable of engulfing entire stars. The Enterprise is sent to find out if it has any selective ability, as it is a threat to the entire galaxy at the rate it consumes planets (OPM/a). See also Berserker.

Planet 892-IV: A Class M planet with the same proportions of land and water as Earth, a density of 5.5, a diameter of 7,917 miles, and an atmosphere 78 percent nitrogen and 20 percent oxygen—in effect, a planet exactly like that of twentieth-century Earth, complete with smog. It is a nearly perfect example of Hodgkin's law of parallel planet development, having a culture similar to that of the Roman Empire but with twentieth-century technology and a growing cult of sun worshippers, the latter representing the only flaw in the parallel-planet theory. By the time the Enterprise crew has narrowly escaped being assimilated into the culture, as the S.S. Beagle's crew had been, it is realized that the cult is actually a late-rising Christian movement and that the "sun" worshippers are actually worshipping the "Son" of God. The planet's future is left to conjecture (BC).

Planet, Kalandan outpost: The size of Earth, but with only the mass of the moon—a planet of inconsistencies. It is too young to have its breathable atmosphere, a fact that even Spock cannot explain. The long-dead Kalandans constructed it of diburnium-osmium alloy (TWS).

Planet of the time vortex: See Cities; Guardian of Forever.

Planet Q: See Leighton, Dr. Thomas.

Plant creatures: See Phylosians.

Plasus (Jeff Corey): The High Adviser of the Planet Council in the cloud city of Stratos—a patrician-looking man in a long, full-sleeved robe trimmed with silver. He loses his temper quickly and is basically an unreasonable and prejudiced man who never really understands the need for social change on his planet. Although he says the people of Stratos have put aside violence, he keeps a punishment instrument for use on the Troglytes (Cms).

Platinum: See Hobby.

Platonians: See Platonius.

Platonius: A planet, golden-brown as seen from space, colonized by refugees from a planet of a nova star, Sandara. They came to Platonius from Earth, which they visited in the days of Socrates and Plato. There were thirty-eight refugees, bred for contemplation and longevity, practically immortal. All except Alexander possess psychokinetic power. They have little resistance to infection. They profess high ideals but are treacherous and cruel, spending their time intriguing against one another and tormenting Alexander. When they use their power on the Enterprise people, Kirk finds a way to fight back, but not before the Platonians have humiliated him, Spock,

P

Uhura, and Chapel. Platonians are not to be trusted (PSt).

Plato of Athens: A Greek philosopher (427–347 B.C.)—a pupil of Socrates and a man of powerful intellect. The people of the lost star Sandara followed Plato's doctrines (with variations) and named their new planet Platonius in his honor. Ironically, though the Platonians like to think of themselves as "Plato's Children," Alexander's comment that they are more "Plato's Stepchildren" seems closer to fact. Plato was a misogynist and a homosexual (PSt).

Plato's Children: Parmen's term for the Platonians (PSt). See Plato of Athens.

Playing cards: When the Queen of Hearts cries "Off with his head," McCoy suddenly finds himself being chased by a pack of lance-wielding playing cards (OUP/a).

Pleasure excursion: Referring to Commander Bem's attitude that going down on a possibly hostile primitive planet is a "joyride" and "pleasure excursion," Kirk tries to make it clear that the place could be dangerous (Be/a). When Lara the huntress keeps trying to attract him, Kirk has to tell her that they are not on a pleasure trip but a dangerous expedition. The captain does admit, however, that the athletic, outspoken, competent female is fascinating (Ji/a).

Plomeek: A thick orange Vulcan soap. Nurse Chapel offers some to Spock when he is entering pon far and has it thrown at her. Later, when Spock is weaker and deeper into pon far, almost despairing of his life, he requests a bowl of plomeek (AT).

Plum: Nancy Crater's pet name for Dr. McCoy in their youth, before she married Robert Crater (MT).

Pocket: See Time trap.

Pod: An observation capsule attached to the hull on the outside of a starship. One of the Enterprise's missions is to get electron readings under abnormal conditions, such as ion storms. This requires direct exposure on ion-sensitive plates and can be done only outside the ship, in pods. These pods, however, constitute a weak spot in the hull, and if the storm becomes too great they must be jettisoned, after first allowing the observer inside the pod enough time to get out of it and back into the ship. Kirk is accused of not having given Lieutenant Commander Finney sufficient time, but it is proven to be a frame on Finney's part (Cml).

Pod plant: A small bush with large thorns, native to Gamma Trianguli VI. It rotates to aim at its prey, at which it shoots clusters of thorns poisoned with a substance resembling saplin but a thousand times stronger. One kills Hendorf of Security; another nearly kills Spock, but McCoy pulls him through (Ap).

Pod ship: An alien ship so immense that the Enterprise is a mere dot in comparison. Ethereal in form, with graceful pods along arching, fairylike arms of metal, it is a poem in metal. The ship is of an unknown alloy, not cast or rolled, but drawn into filaments and spun, like a spider's web. The hexagonal shape of the windows suggests a similarity to insect cells on Earth. Retroanalysis of the ship's spectrum dates it as having been in orbit for slightly more than three hundred million years, yet after all that time the artificial gravity still works and the air systems go on when the Enterprise's landing party enters the pod ship. It has been badly damaged; the insectoid beings who manned the ship chose self-destruction rather than carry the malevolent entity who inhabits it to the rest of the galaxy. When the alien entity takes control of the Enterprise, it destroys the pod ship, which falls into the dead sun, Questar M17 (BFS/a).

Poetry and literature:

Alice in Wonderland (SL)
Ay Pledgili, Holy (OG)
Beauty (TWS)
Bible, Holy (King James version) (Em, RM, WGD)
Book, the (EB/a, PA)
Byron (TB)
Carroll, Lewis
Chicago Mobs of the Twenties (PA)
Ee'd pebnista (OG)
Fantasy literature (OUP/a)
Gutenberg Bible (RM)
Hamlet (CK)
Housman, A. E. (WGD)
Lazarus (RM)
Lilliputian city (Te/a)
Macbeth (CK)

Methuselah (RM)
"Nightingale Woman" (WNM)
Pledge of allegiance, U.S.A. (OG)
Poetry, Vulcan (Ji/a)
Psalm 95, Verse 4 (Em)
Queen of Hearts (OUP/a)
Shakespeare, First Folio (RM)
Shakespeare, William (CK, HS/a, TB, WGD)
Shangri-La (PSY)
Solomon (WGD)
Tarbolde, Phineas (WNM)
This Island Earth (AY)
Through the Looking Glass (OUP/a)
Vulcan quotes (Yy/a)
White Rabbit (OUP/a, SL)

See also Vulcans.

Poison darts: See Dimorus.

Poisons:

Acid (WEd)
Berthold rays (TSP)
Borgia plant (Mt)
Celebium (TI)
Cyalodin (CL)
Delta rays (Me)

Mugato (PLW)
Phaser coolant (BT)
Pod plant (Ap)
Radiation exposure (TI)
Tetralubisol (CK)
Venom (Am/a, SGn)

Policeman (Hal Baylor):   A large, beefy cop of the 1930s who catches time travelers Kirk and Spock with stolen clothes. Although he doesn't believe their bizarre explanation, they manage to distract him enough so that Spock can use a nerve pinch on him and they can make their escape (CEF).

Police officers, New York: Two members of the New York Police Department whom Roberta Lincoln calls in when Kirk and Spock come charging into Gary Seven's office. They are beamed up to the Enterprise with their quarry, are immediately returned to Earth, and refuse to acknowledge that anything out of the ordinary has happened (AE).

Police Special: A gun found "in beautiful condition" by the perennial hobbyist, Sulu, on the shore-leave planet. It fires lead pellets propelled by expanding gases from a chemical explosion. Sulu's testing of it alarms other members of the landing party (SL).

Police web: A force field used by the Kzin to hold prisoners; it is laid on the ground and is evidently also a life-support system for as long as the web is turned on (SW/a).

Pollack, Reginald Murray: An Earth artist in twentieth-century New York, whose work is recognized by Spock in Flint's home (RM).

Pollux V: Like several other planets in the Pollux system, habitable but devoid of intelligent life (WM).

Pollux IV: A Class M planet approximately four billion years old, habitable but devoid of life except for the Greek god Apollo, who intends to set up a colony there in which the crew of the Enterprise will lead simple pastoral lives

P

and worship him. It doesn't work out (WM).

Pon far: A Vulcan term meaning the "mating time," the point in the physical cycle of a Vulcan male when he must return home and take a wife. Apparently a young male can resist pon far for a few cycles, but it eventually becomes too strong for him, and he must respond to it or die. Probably due to the total suppression of emotion at all other times, the pressures of <u>pon far</u> at its height lead Vulcan males to frenzy and madness (AT).

Positive-matter armament: Karla Five's small, swift scout ship is armed with positive matter so that it will react against the antimatter dead star when it is fired (CC/a).

Potemkin, U.S.S.: A starship involved in the war games with the M-5 computer—named after Grigory Alexandrovitch Potemkin, 1739–91, a Russian military leader and administrator (UC). The starship with which the Enterprise is to rendezvous to study Beta Aurigae (TI). The starship that will pick up strobolin from Beta Canopus and make a rendezvous with a freighter, the S.S. <u>Huron</u>, to get the life-saving drug to the Enterprise within the three-day time limit left to Spock (PO/a).

Powder, restorative: A substance, supposedly of great benefit, given by the old man to Kirk and McCoy for strength to fight the computer Oracle of Yonada. McCoy says it has the taste of an ancient herb derivative (FW).

Power, the: The psychokinetic ability possessed by all the Platonians except Alexander. Its source is kironide, a substance present in Platonian food and metabolized by the pituitary gland. Under normal conditions, it develops within two or three months following the ingestion of kironide, but with injections of processed kironide Kirk, Spock, and McCoy achieve the power within a few hours. Each person is on a separate power frequency, so they are unable to combine forces (PSt).

Power field: On the shore-leave planet, a means of collecting energy to materialize people's fantasies. It affects communication and drains the Enterprise's power (SL).

Power generator: A huge power generator keeps the atavachron running in the library on Sarpeidon. The Enterprise detects the fantastic power output on the planet and sends a landing party down to rescue any inhabitants before Sarpeidon's sun goes nova (AY).

Power packs: The expedition on the mad planet decides to use all their power packs to push the cart to a high-speed run away from a volcano which has suddenly developed right in their path. It works but uses up the power packs, and it is time-consuming when Spock has to rewire the packs to attach them to the cart (Ji/a). The aquashuttle phasers don't work after the Argo sea monster attacks it; the power pack has been damaged (Am/a).

Power surge: Losira's appearance on the Enterprise causes a tremendous power surge that knocks it 990.7 light-years from the Kalandan outpost planet. At the same time, the landing party witnesses a terrifically strong earthquake on the planet. Sulu picks up high radiation readings and assumes that the Enterprise has blown up (TWS).

Practical joke: The healer is hesitant at first about

going with young Spock to help I-Chaya, thinking it a practical joke. Spock pulled one joke two years before; Vulcans have a long memory (Yy/a).

Praetor: Title of the head of the Romulan Empire (BT).

Praetorian guard: A military group on Planet 892-IV. Flavius, on seeing the Enterprise uniforms, thinks they might be new outfits of the Praetorian Guard (BC).

Predator: See Glommer.

Prefect Jaris: See Jaris.

Preliminary survey: The Enterprise sets up preliminary surveys of a planet to be explored (MP/a).

Prepared: To aid the Sarpeids in adjusting to their new lives in the past, the atavachron prepares them by altering their physiological and brain structures. However, this also prevents anyone from returning to the present: To do so would mean death (AY).

Preservers, the: An advanced race that once traveled the galaxy rescuing primitive cultures in danger of extinction. They may well be responsible for the fact that there are so many humanoid species in the galaxy, and may explain Hodgkins's Law. Among their languages, they used one in which musical tones substitute for segmental phonemes. Aside from the obelisk of the Earthlike planet on which they established Amerinds, no other trace has been found of the Preservers themselves (PSy).

Pressers: Archaic term for deflectors.

Pressure chamber: See Antigravity test unit.

Pressure suits: The Kzin wear pressure suits on the nearly airless ice-bound planet. When the Chuft Captain is tinkering with the settings on the Slaver weapon, he accidentally punctures the Telepath's suit, but the Flyer Kzin gets the victim into the Kzin vessel in time to save him (SW/a).

Pretrial investigation: When McCoy is on trial for murder, Kirk wants to have a pretrial investigation of the planet where McCoy is supposed to have committed the deed, but Demos, head of Security Police, tries to stop Kirk. The Dramian guard openly doubts that they can move faster than Dramen justice (Al/a).

Priestess: See Sybo.

Primal energy: See Magnetic organism.

Prime Directive: The rule of noninterference, General Order No. 1, a wise but often troublesome rule which prohibits Federation interference with the normal development of alien life and societies. It can be disregarded when absolutely vital to the interests of the entire Federation, but the commander who does violate it had better be ready to present a sound defense of his actions. When a culture has already been tampered with, the Prime Directive permits judicious action to restore balance (BC, PF, PLW). Kirk breaks the Prime Directive on Landru's planet, arguing that it applies only to healthy cultures (RA). Kirk gives new knowledge only to Natira, who will not reveal the secret of Yonada to her people and risk changing the original intentions of the Fabrini. Thus, Kirk does not technically violate the directive (FW). The natives of Delta Theta III came under this law, and Kirk told Bem he had no right to try to interfere with them by his unorthodox methods of observing native cultures (Be/a).

Prime Order of the Empire: An order, in the mirror universe, to allow no resistance to go unpunished. Kirk spares the Halkans, in violation of this order, earning a possible death sentence for Kirk-2 (MM).

Prince: See Tchar.

Printout: After he locks the engine controls with the navigational manual override, Arex orders a printout of the guidance computer's last orders (from the amusement planet's master computer). The printout indicates orders for a series of short-burst maneuvers, which were avoided by locking the controls (OUP/a).

Priority A-1 channel distress call: A signal that puts an entire quadrant on defense alert (TT).

Priority mission: Karla Five is on a priority mission and will not stop her headlong speed into the Beta Niobe nova at warp 36. She does not explain what the mission is (CC/a).

Priority-1 call: A top-emergency call from a starbase, starship, or anything else that needs aid or information immediately. The Enterprise uses a Priority-1 call to inform Governor Wesley of the impending doom of his planet (OP/a). It generally signals near or total disaster. Kirk is furious when he is called on a Priority-1 to guard a load of quadrotriticale (TT).

Prisms: Inside the snake towers around the pyramid in Kulkukan's illusion city, there are prisms that can be focused to call the alien being (HS/a).

Prisoner: The Kzin offer their prisoner, Uhura, in trade for the Slaver weapon which Spock has retrieved from the Chuft Captain in a surprise attack. Spock and Sulu must weigh the personal wish to rescue Uhura against giving a weapon to the Kzinti which is potentially dangerous to the entire Federation (SW/a).

Procedure Q: A Star Fleet regulation indicating that if a state of deep hostility exists, a landing party is to beam down fully armed and ready for any kind of trouble (BC).

Proconsul: See Claudius Marcus.

Projected stasis: Spock's description of the effect of the new Klingon weapon (MTT/a).

Promotion list: Military promotions are made by moving up a list. When Finney drew an official reprimand for dereliction of duty, his name went to the bottom of the list. He blames Kirk for this, feeling that it prevented him from ever becoming a starship commander (Cml).

Propaganda: Propaganda is used to keep the Klingon-Federation vendetta going. Both sides are said to have slave labor and death camps and to subject captured enemies to horrible experiments. It is unclear, however, whether these rumors are actual ones resulting from the traditional animosity or have been created by the entity that feeds off the hatred generated (Dv). See also Beta XIIA; Chekov, Piotr.

Propulsion system: The space probe from Kulkukan is of such an advanced design that it leaves a special trail of disrupted matter and can move fast enough not to be intercepted by Federation investigators (HS/a).

Propulsion unit: See Robot ships.

Prosecutor (Kermit Murdock):   Kirk's prosecutor in

Sarpeid's "Charles II" era—a fat-jowled man with frightened piggy eyes, dressed in long black robes, hat, and a shoulder-length white wig. He is really a modern Sarpeid who chose this era in his planet's past to live in when escaping the nova. Judging by his fear, he does not particularly enjoy his chosen era, nor does he wish to acknowledge that he is not a natural inhabitant of the time; he refuses to aid Kirk until threatened with the exposure of his true identity (AY). See also Megan; Shaw, Lieutenant Areel.

Protective custody: Kirk places Commander Bem under protective custody after he has gotten them all in trouble. It is a polite way of saying he is under arrest (Be/a).

Protectors: Filter masks which protect the wearers from the gas released in zienite mining and its side effects—intellectual and emotional retardation. Droxine, the upper-class socialite of Stratos, prefers the term "protectors" for these masks, introduced by McCoy. The doctor suggests that wearing them will return the Troglyte miners to normal intelligence (Cms).

Providers: Three brains in translucent cases, each glowing in a different color. Also known as the Gamesters of Triskelion, they spend their time gambling over the fighting abilities of their thralls (slaves). Kirk talks them into freeing the thralls and teaching them about self-government (GT).

Psalm 95, Verse 4:   "In His hands are the deep places of the Earth," Biblical quote by Dr. Ozaba, one of the Federation scientists on Minara II, in the log found by Kirk, Spock, and McCoy (Em).

Psionics: Mental powers which can be utilized to influence one's surroundings, transport living or inanimate objects without machinery, create illusions, and even affect the well-being of another, since psionics can be used to kill or heal. Everyone probably has latent psionic ability, which remains dormant until brought into play by some development, usually some sort of neural energy or contact with extragalactic forces which develop the mind. On the "outside," people use psionics to kill, exploit, and terrorize, but in Elysia these powers are allowed to function only in order to preserve the peace (Tr/a).

Psi 2000:   A once-Earthlike planet, recently frozen, whose internal imbalances cause it to disintegrate. The Enterprise and its crew, on hand to observe this effect, are almost destroyed by the Psi 2000 virus (NT). See also Virus.

Psychokinesis: The ability to move objects, including people, by mental power. All the Platonians have it, except for Alexander (PSt). The females of Taurus II possess an unusual psychokinesis level (LS/a). See also Power, the.

Psychological hangups:

Bodily integrity (Mtu/a)	Neurosis (SW/a)
Dissociation (SB)	Racial fury (Ji/a)
Hatred (MP/a)	Space legs (LZ)
Hallucination (WE)	Tahiti syndrome (PSy)
Lacunar amnesia (CL)	Xenophobia
Madness (Ji/a)	

Psychological opinion: Kirk asks McCoy for a psychological opinion on whether to tell the planet Mantilles of the oncoming cosmic cloud and risk a planetwide panic. They decide to warn the governor so at least some of the inhabitants of Mantilles can be saved (OPM/a).

Psychological profile: A record of a person's mental history. It notes all psychosomatic illnesses, including routine teen-age incidences, involuntary or unconscious telepathic responses, as well as other distinguishing personality traits. Mira Romaine's profile mentions her exceptionally flexible and pliant response to new learning situations (LZ).

Psychotech: Someone specially trained to handle a psychotricorder (WF).

Psychotricorder: A device designed to obtain detailed accounts of a person's past actions, with or without the person's actual mental cooperation (WF).

Pterodactyls: When they enter the narrow passageway which comes after the sign saying "Underground Entrance," Kirk, Spock, McCoy, and Sulu are attacked by pterodactyls, although none of them was thinking of prehistoric creatures (OUP/a).

Punishment: Bem wants to know if the alien intelligence of Delta Theta III wants to punish or take revenge on him. She doesn't know what he means. Punishment and revenge should not be needed by intelligent beings; they are necessary only where learning cannot occur without it (Be/a).

Puritan costume: All of the people of Megas-tu except Lucien appear in New England Puritan costume for the trial of the Enterprise crew. It is a reminder of the witch burnings in Salem (Mtu/a).

Purring like happy kittens: A slang term used by Scott to describe the condition of his engines on the Enterprise when they are running well (Te/a).

PXK reactor: An old-style nuclear-fission reactor, using pergium as a power source. This type of reactor, though antiquated, supplies the power for the heat, air, and life-support systems of Janus VI as well as other planets. It uses a main circulating pump, which the Horta steals. Scotty has not seen a reactor of this type in about twenty years; he fails to repair the one on Janus VI, but does manage to rig up a makeshift cooling pump capable of lasting about forty-eight hours (DD).

Pyramid: A gigantic four-sided Mayan temple rises out of the center of the city on Kulkukan's ship. A stairway goes up the pyramid, flanked on each corner by a serpent-shaped tower. The top of the pyramid is a raised platform with a mosaic of a snake on it. The calling of Kulkukan centers on this pyramid, when all the towers are focused on it just right (HS/a). A ruined pyramid in the ancient sunken city contains the ancient records for which Kirk and Spock are searching, the information that will change them back to air-breathers (Am/a).

Pyris VII: A cold and barren planet. Kirk expects it to be uninhabited but discovers it contains Sylvia and Korob and all their magical paraphernalia (Cp).

Q planet: Final home of Dr. Thomas Leighton (CK).

Quadrant: An area of space (a misnomer, as it should be called an octant).

Quadrant 904: The star desert where the Enterprise finds Gothos, the unusual planet on which Trelane plays his games (SG).

Quadrotriticale: A high-yield, perennial, four-lobed hybrid of wheat and rye whose root grain, triticale, can trace its ancestry to twentieth-century Canada. Chekov says it is a Russian invention. It is the only grain that will grow on Sherman's Planet. Nilz Baris brings several tons of it to Space Station K-7, intending to send it on to the planet, but it is poisoned by Klingons and eaten by tribbles. It is later replaced (TT).

Quarantine: Kirk places Delta Theta III under quarantine so no other starship will blunder into its range and displease the enormous alien intelligence that lives on the planet (Be/a). When everyone on board the Enterprise, except Spock, who is immune to the disease, comes down with auroral plague, the starship is placed under general quarantine with General Order No. 6 put into effect in case Spock fails to return in time with McCoy and the antidote (AI/a). The planet Vendor is under quarantine, so very few other beings have ever seen a Vendorian. Their way of life included practicing deceit, which puts them off limits (Su/a). See also Scalos; Talos IV.

Quartermaster: The Enterprise's quartermaster is responsible for issuing new uniforms, costumes for visits to planets, and specialty outfits for various purposes. See also Wardrobe department.

Quatloos: Units of exchange on Triskelion. The Providers offer various amounts of quatloos for bets and the purchase of thralls (GT).

Queen of Hearts: This manifestation from Through the Looking Glass is a rude interruption of McCoy's pleasant plantation scene, and it is at her command that the pack of playing cards begins to pursue him (OUP/a).

Queen of Sheba: A Biblical queen, Balkis, famous for a visit to Solomon (Kings 1:10) about the tenth century B.C. The country of Sheba was along a trade route from Africa to India and was reputed to be a region of great wealth, its women fabulously beautiful. Trelane compares Uhura's beauty to that of the Queen of Sheba (SG).

Questar M17: A negative star mass with a spectrum analysis indicating imploded matter—a dead sun. It is a huge dark stellar body, pocked and ugly, with electrical energy playing across it and a hypergravitational pull beyond anything the Enterprise has ever encountered. It pulls the starship off course and nearly draws the vessel close enough to crash on its surface before Kirk calls for a flank speed and an elliptical orbit (BFS/a).

Quetzalcoatl: Plumed or feathered serpent god of ancient Mexico. He was known as a wind god and a creator; he was a culture hero, bringing maize to mankind, instruction in the arts. There was also a real-life king in Mexico named Quetzalcoatl (HS/a).

Quintotriticale: A mutation of the Canadian-developed quadrotriticale: a five-lobed seed grain of the wheat family developed to be stronger, more resistant to disease, and easier to grow. Two robot ships filled with quintotriticale are on their way to Sherman's Planet when Cyrano Jones changes the plans somewhat (MTT/a). See also Seed grain.

Quivering: The Lactrans' form of laughter; they evidently have a sense of humor, for they are amused by Spock's "childlike" attempts at communication (EB/a).

R

Rabbit: Kirk hopes Spock can help save the Enterprise by "pulling a rabbit out of a hat." Spock typically responds with wonderment that the situation has anything to do with a Terran mammal of the leporid family. Kirk says it was a slip of the tongue and goes on with his worries and computations (Tr/a).

Rabbit, White: See White Rabbit.

Racial fury: The theft of the Soul of Skorr would have set off a galactic war, as the Skorr naturally would never have suspected one of their own to be the thief and would have turned their fury on all other races of the galaxy (Ji/a).

Radamanthus: A magic word used by Lucien to restore the life-support systems on the Enterprise (Mtu/a).

Radans: Crude dilithium crystals used as jewelry on Troyius and supposed to bring the wearer luck. A necklace of radans is given as a wedding present to the Dohlman Elaan, who says they are common stones. During an emergency, the necklace is used to repair the power system of the Enterprise. Scotty has doubts at first about the unusually crude shape of the crystals, which he hopes will not affect the energy flow to the engines, but they work (ET).

Radiation: The emission and transmission of energy in the form of waves or particles through space or in a material medium; the term commonly refers to such emissions within the electromagnetic spectrum.

Radiation poisoning: Exposure or overexposure to many types of radiation is harmful or lethal to humans. The scientific group exploring Camus II died of exposure to celebium radiation. Dr. Coleman says that Janice Lester is also suffering from it but that Dr. McCoy will find no sign of it. After the life-entity transfer, Kirk-J intends to strangle Janice-K and claim the death resulted from radiation poisoning (TI). Spock reports that sensors on the Enterprise are picking up intense radiation levels from auroral activity in the Dramia II sector, but that it seems nonlethal. However, soon afterward everyone on the starship comes down with the auroral plague and nearly dies of it before McCoy finds the antidote (Al/a). See also Delta rays.

Radioactive waste: The alien ship used by the pirates of Orion leaves a unique trail of radioactive waste through the space it travels; this implies a nuclear fuel of some sort, while Federation starships use matter/antimatter fuel (PO/a).

Radio tubes: See Hobby.

Rael (Jason Evers): The Scalosian chief scientist—blond, with a strong, proud face. He is very much in love with Deela, who has adored him since their childhood, but since he is sterile she must look to another man to father her children, which drives Rael into a jealous rage. He is in charge of putting the Enterprise crew into deep freeze (WE).

Rain: The rain in at least one area of Taurus II is golden in color (LS/a). See also Mad planet.

Ralston, Gilbert (script): Who Mourns for Adonais? (WM) (with Gene L. Coon).

Ramart, Captain (Charles J. Stewart): Commander of the Antares at the time of its destruction by Charles Evans (CX).

Randolph, Lieutenant Nancy: Navigator of the Ariel, a survey ship sent on an exploration trip to Lactra VII. She is one of the survivors who ended up in the zoo, but she is very ill with a fever when the Enterprise's landing party finds them. She has a malarial fever from an insect bite, but McCoy cannot help her until the Lactrans give him his medical kit (EB/a).

Rand, Yeoman Janice (Grace Lee Whitney): Blond, with an elaborate basketweave hairstyle and pert face. She is Kirk's personal yeoman at the beginning of the five-year mission and they seem quite fond of each other. When Rand realizes that Kirk is married to his ship, she transfers out (BT, CMn, CX, EW, Mi, MT, NT).

Rank insignia braid: Ensign—plain sleeve, with no braid at all; Lieutenant, j.g.—one line of braid, broken; Lieutenant—one full stripe of braid; Lieutenant Commander—one full stripe below one broken stripe; Commander—two full stripes of braid; Captain—two full stripes of braid, with one broken line of braid between them; Fleet Captain—three full stripes of braid. Flag officers (Commodores and Admirals)—one broad gold stripe, edged with braid. All stripes or lines of braid encircled the sleeve, just above the wrist/cuff, much as do those of naval officers in the twentieth century. The system is one of logical progression: no stripe, a half stripe, one stripe, one and a half stripes, two stripes, two and a half stripes, three stripes, and finally one broad stripe.

Rator III: In the guise of Captain Kirk, the Vendorian shape-changer gives orders to lay in a course for Rator III, right through the neutral zone. The counterfeit Kirk claims that Winston has assured him that it is vital to get to Rator III in the shortest possible time, and that the neutral zone does not have any Romulans in it (Su/a).

Rawlins: Chief geologist, recommended for the landing party on Alpha Carinae II by Kirk (UC).

Rayburn (Budd Albright): On security duty, he accompanies Kirk and Chapel to the surface of Exo III and is strangled by the android Ruk (LG).

Reader of minds: See Telepath, Kzin.

Reborn city: When the ancient sunken city on Argo is raised from the sea by a huge quake, it is considered a reborn city by the younger Aquans, who want to reverse their water-breathing mutation and become air-breathers so they can live in the city (Am/a).

Recalibration: The medical examination of Carter Winston puzzles McCoy because it is slightly off, but he decides the medical instruments probably need recalibration (Su/a). To give a Vulcan a full physical examination

R

on the Enterprise, McCoy has to recalibrate all the instruments from human scale to Vulcan (Yy/a).

Receptacles: The glowing spheres, about two feet in diameter, containing the stored minds of Sargon, Henoch, and Thalassa, who have spent half a million years in their receptacles. When they borrow the bodies of Kirk, Mulhall, and Spock, the latters' minds are transferred to the receptacles. An emptied receptacle shrivels to a withered black husk (RT).

Recorder-marker: A device, containing message tapes, to be jettisoned in an emergency. The Enterprise launches one when menaced by the Fesarius, and Balok blows it up (CMn). An early model, jettisoned by the Valiant some two hundred years back, was almost spherical, about three feet in diameter, with tripod legs (WNM).

Records, ancient: The Aquans of Argo revere the ancient records, but they evidently fear the knowledge that some of these records contain, for there are strong prohibitions against trying to obtain them. When recovered from the ancient sunken city, these records are seen to contain information on how to reverse the mutation inflicted on Kirk and Spock, and much valuable medical knowledge that can be used by the Federation (Am/a). See also Dramian history.

Records officer: See Finney, Lieutenant Commander Benjamin.

Record tapes: Charlie Evans claims that his only teachers and companions on the seemingly deserted planet Thasus were some record tapes from the wrecked ships that abandoned him there (CX).

Recreation: See Games and recreation.

Recreation Room: The Recreation Room on the Enterprise seems capable of at least a minor ability to recreate weather, sounds, and other scenes wished for by the people in the room, like the shore-leave planet but on a smaller scale. Though it does this with holographic illusions, they can be quite deadly if the computers don't work out well (PJ/a).

Red Hour: The beginning of Festival on Landru's planet. At six P.M. on Festival Day, everyone on the planet goes berserk for twelve hours. Anything is allowed during this time, including rape and destruction (RA).

Redjac, Red Jack: A name given the Jack-the-Ripper entity when it was on Earth. Sybo senses this and calls it by that name (WF).

Red rock: The rock of the Kalandan outpost planet looks igneous but is infinitely more dense. A phaser set at more than 8000°C does not affect it. It is an unnatural material, an alloy of diburnium and osmium (TWS).

Red-zone proximity: When all power is lost in the warp engines, with no damage reports, and the restart cycle won't work, the shielding for the matter/antimatter chambers begins to deteriorate, bringing the ship into red-zone proximity: It will blow itself up in about four hours. One solution is to jettison the nacelles (SC).

Reef, barrier: A jagged blue coral barrier reef, beyond which Rila will not go when she leads Kirk and Spock to find the sunken city which might contain the ancient records (Am/a).

Reena 16:   A draped body on a slab in Flint's life

lab—the first indication to Kirk, and indeed to Reena Kapec, that the girl is an android. There are several Reenas in the lab, with numbers on them. The Reena with whom Kirk falls in love is the end result of many models and designs (RM). See also Kapec, Reena.

Refrigeration unit: A mechanical device attached by the Scalosians to the life-support systems in the Engine Room of the Enterprise. When activated, it will place all the personnel of the ship in deep-freeze/hibernation until they are needed for mating (WE).

Regenerating chamber: A section of the matter/antimatter nacelles of a starship, where the engines are fired, or started. To keep the Enterprise moving through the cosmic cloud, Scott uses a piece of antimatter villi to refire the chambers of the antimatter nacelle, and a piece of broken planet in the matter-regenerating chamber (OPM/a).

Regeneration: The people of Gideon, living in a germ-free but overpopulated environment, have bodies capable of regenerating themselves until they are simply too old to do so (MG).

Reger (Harry Townes):   A sleek man with lined cheeks and pouched eyes—the keeper of a rooming house on Beta III, father of Tula, and a member of the underground with Tamar and Marplon. He is not very brave, however, and tries to back out of the insurrection, but it is too late (RA).

Registry: A ship encountered by another ship must give its registry, place of origin, and purpose, especially if challenged by a Federation starship on official business. See also Identity tapes.

Regulan blood worms: Soft and shapeless creatures. Korax the Klingon says the Terrans remind him of them, except for Kirk (TT).

Regulus: A system inhabited by humans and aliens (Me).

Regulus V: See Eel-birds, giant.

Rehabilitation therapy: Criminals of all types are sent for rehabilitation therapy to make them into useful and constructive citizens. Most of the time this works. There are still a few individuals in the galaxy on whom it doesn't work. Harry Mudd is one of them (MP/a).

Religion: There are nondenominational chapels on board starships, where weddings occur (BT), and many of the crew have their own ideas of where and how to worship. Sulu is heard to say, "May the Great Bird of the Galaxy bless your planet" (MT). Gary Mitchell's psionic abilities cause him to consider himself a god—"Morals are for men, not gods"—to which Kirk answers, "Above all, a god needs compassion" (WNM). Balok says, "We presume you have a deity or deities or some such beliefs to comfort you. We . . . grant you ten minutes to make preparations [for death]"; the Terrans spend the time scheming (CMn). The ancient Greek gods evidently existed as semi-immortal beings, but by the twentieth century they had dwindled away from lack of attention—except for Apollo, who lives to meet the Enterprise's crew. When they will not worship him, he spreads himself on the wind and disappears (WM). Spock's beliefs are not quite those of Earth's Christian mythos—"I, for one, do not believe in angels" (GS)—but he at least gives some lip service to the Vulcan tradition of worshipping the gods at the family shrine (Yy/a) and can consider trying to appease a godlike being (Be/a). He tells Scott that there was "no deity involved [in a rescue]; it was my cross-circuiting to B that recovered them" (Ob). The Companion says that, though it can preserve life, it cannot create it: "That is for the Maker of All Things" (Mt). When McCoy is faced with having to shoot the salt vampire in the shape of Nancy Crater, he does so while asking the Lord to forgive him (MT). Garth of Izar, in his insanity, cannot decide whether he wants to be Master of the Universe or a god (WGD). The Holy Bible, usually the King James Version, is quoted several times by Enterprise people and others (Em, RM, WGD). This book was held in great veneration as translations of writings by prophets, disciples, etc., especially by those of the Christian faith.

Religious leader: See Alar.

Religious references:

Ancient lore (FW)	Marriage, Vulcan (AT, JB)
Apollo (WM)	Moses (RM)
Book of the People (FW)	Myths (EB/a)
Christ, Jesus (BC)	Natira (FW)
Creators, the (FW)	Obelisk (PSy)
Devil (Dv, Mtu/a)	One (WEd)
Evil One, the (OG)	Oracle of the People (FW)
Fabrini (FW)	Our gods (Yy/a)
Family shrine (Yy/a)	Our Soul (Ji/a)
Gabriel, Archangel (BC)	Pentagram (Mtu/a)
Goat god (Mtu/a)	Quetzalcoatl (HS/a)
God (Be/a)	Ritual cloak (PSy)
Gods (GS, Mt, MT, Ob, WM, WNM)	Seven gods, the name of the (Ji/a)
Holy War (Ji/a)	Solomon (WGD)
IDIC (TB)	Son, the (BC)
Jihad (Ji/a)	Superstitions (Mtu/a)
Joining day (PSy)	Temple (PSy)
Kulkukan (HS/a)	Temples (Ji/a)
Lazarus (RM)	Vaal (Ap)
Legends (Am/a, HS/a)	Wise ones, the (PSy)
Marriage (BT, MW)	Witch (AY)

Remus: Federation name for the twin home-world to Romulus (BT).

Replicas: The computer on the Kalandan outpost planet projects many replicas of Losira, each of which can act independently in trying to kill the Enterprise's landing party (TWS).

Replicas, android: See "Alice" series; Atoz, Mr.; Mudd, Stella.

Republic, U.S.S.: Starship NCC 1373, on which Lieutenant Commander Finney and Ensign James Kirk served, and where Kirk found a circuit open after relieving Finney on watch—a mistake that could have caused the destruction of the ship within a few minutes. Kirk reported it, and Finney drew a reprimand that put him at the bottom of the promotion list, afterward blaming Kirk for the lack of progress in his military career (Cml).

Responder: A part of the communicator (Be/a).

Responsibility: Kirk argues with the alien intelligence of Delta Theta III that he has as much responsibility as a starship commander, especially in recovering Commander Bem before leaving the planet, as the intelligence has toward her children, the natives of the planet. She agrees that Kirk has some wisdom (Be/a).

Restricted area: Every starship has areas to protect, including dilithium-crystal storage areas. These areas are restricted to personnel who have business there.

Restructured granite: The shield of the amusement planet's underground complex is made up of a metal alloy and restructured granite, and is impenetrable to sensor scan (OUP/a).

Retirement ceremonies: Commodore April, first captain of the starship Enterprise and Federation ambassador-at-large, is to be retired at age seventy-five with a ceremony on the planet Babel in commemoration of his service to the Federation through the years (CC/a).

Retlaw plant: A seemingly harmless dandelion-sort of plant on Phylos—about seven inches high, with a round, tennis-ball-sized purple fuzzy head, and black roots that can become small footlike protuberances, giving the plant mobility. Able to corkscrew itself in and out of the ground, a retlaw plant follows Sulu when he is part of the landing party on the planet, and when the helmsman bends to pick it up, he is paralyzed by a poison which turns out to be very nearly fatal. No known medication works on him, and he is only saved by the timely appearance of some Phylosians who carry the antidote to the retlaw plant within their own bodies and are capable of producing it for use by the plant's victims' (IV/a).

Retrieval: After the fight with Tchar, Kirk rescues the Soul of Skorr, and calls for retrieval. Lara twists a signal knob on a device that contacts the Vedala, letting her know that they have succeeded in their mission and want to be recalled to the Vedala asteroid (Ji/a).

Retroanalysis: A scanner reading of the past, in effect. The Enterprise's landing party makes a retroanalysis of the long-dead pod ship by which they determine its age (BFS/a).

Revels: See Bacchanals.

Revenge, Kzinti: A Kzin must seek revenge before calling for help, so as long as Spock can stay free after severely damaging the Chuft Captain, the Kzinti won't go anywhere with the stolen stasis box or the weapon they found in it (SW/a). See also Punishment.

Review: The Federation has reviews of the actions and records of its personnel. They decide to review Commodore April's mandatory retirement and reconsider it (CC/a).

Revitalization: See Life energy.

Rhada, Lieutenant (Naomi Pollack): An Asian Indian woman, with dark brown hair and a slight accent, who takes over Sulu's place at the Enterprise's helm while he joins the landing party on the Kalandan outpost planet. She is the first to notice that the planet is gone when the ship is transported light-years away (TWS).

Ribbons: Star Fleet "ribbons," as they are known in the military parlance, take the place of larger medals or awards. The small triangular ribbons are worn in a pattern on the left breast of full dress uniforms. The colors of the ribbons and their meaning follow:

Red: Star Fleet Command Decoration for Gallantry	Apple green: (Name unknown)
Rose-red: Legion of Honor	Dark blue: Star Fleet Command Decoration for Valor
Pink: Star Fleet Command Citation for Gallantry	Light blue: Grankite Order of Tactics
Dark green: (Name of decoration unknown at this time)	Sky blue: Star Fleet Command Honor Roll
	Purple: Star Fleet Wound Decoration
Kelly green: Star Fleet Command Citation for Valor	Violet: (Name unknown)
	Dark brown: Pentaries Ribbon of Commendation

R

Brown: (Name unknown)
Cream: Palm Leaf of the Aanar Peace Mission
White: Silver Palms
Aqua: Star Fleet Surgeon's Decoration
Dark blue with white three-pointed star: Medal of Honor
Light blue with red three-pointed star: (Name unknown)
Yellow with red three-pointed star: (Name unknown)

Appurtenances and devices attached to ribbons:
Black star outline: Cluster, highest form of an award
Red triangles, facing: Class of Excellence
Gold triangle, single: First Class of an award
Red "Z" or "N" shape: (Exact use unknown at this time)

Richards, Chet (script): The Tholian Web (TW) (with Judy Burns).

Richards, Michael (pseud.) (stories): The Way to Eden (WEd) (with Arthur Heinemann); That Which Survives (TWS).

Richelieu, Cardinal: Under the influence of the inhibition-releasing Psi 2000 virus, Sulu, a confirmed romantic, takes a fencing foil and attacks the bridge of the Enterprise, having decided that Spock is Cardinal Richelieu. Sulu no doubt remembers that Richelieu, chief minister of Louis XIII, was known for his manipulation of royal authority (NT).

Richter scale of culture: A system for rating the sociological developmental levels of various planetary cultures. A culture with a rating of B (e.g., Sigma Draconis III) is equivalent to Earth circa 1485, while a rating of G (e.g., Sigma Draconis IV) is equivalent to Earth circa 2030. Not to be confused with the rating system developed by Dr. Richter of Cal Tech to measure the force of earthquakes (EM, SB).

Rigel colonies: The Rigel system, with its large number of inhabited planets, is the next target in line for the "doomsday machine" berserker—if it gets past the Enterprise (DMa).

Rigel V: The inhabitants of Rigel V have a body chemistry similar to that of Vulcans. A Rigellian drug used on Spock to stimulate the production of blood works very well when it is used for a transfusion to Sarek (JB).

Rigel IV: Home world of Hengist, administrator on Argelius II (WF).

Rigellian fever: A highly contagious disease with effects much like bubonic plague; one can die of the fever in one day. Ryetalyn is the only known antidote to it. When the Enterprise arrives at Holberg 917G, it has killed three crewmen, and twenty-three others have caught it. Before the ryetalyn is ready, nearly the entire crew has been stricken (RM).

Rigellian hypnoid: A small reptilian creature from the Rigel star system that can build and hold an illusion. Lora, a beautiful human girl used by Mudd to demonstrate his love potion, is an illusion made by a Rigellian hypnoid (MP/a).

Rigellian kassaba fever: See Kassaba fever, Rigellian.

Rigel VII: A double-planet system with a tremendous "moon" that fills nearly a quarter of the lavender sky; a beautiful world with warlike people at a sword-and-mace level of technology. Captain Pike once took a landing party there and wound up with three people killed and seven injured, including Spock. The Talosians later re-create an illusion of it for Captain Pike. The inhabitants range from humanoids to large Neanderthaloids with

fangs (GT, Me).

Rigel XII: A dust-dry planet, swept by continual sandstorms and rich in dilithium crystals. Population at last report: six—three miners and their wives (MW).

Rigel II: A planet McCoy remembers for a little cabaret there. He was so impressed by the girls he found that he materializes them on the amusement-park planet (SL).

Right of statement: In ancient Vulcan and Romulan tradition, a condemned criminal is allowed to make a full statement explaining his actions and motives. Spock uses this aboard the Romulan ship to filibuster for twenty minutes, thus giving Scott a chance to install the stolen Romulan cloaking device aboard the Enterprise (EI).

Riley, Lieutenant Kevin (Bruce Hyde): A navigator, promoted from Engineering—small in stature, with a narrow face and reddish hair. Born on Tarsus IV, at age four he lost both parents to Kodos the Executioner. On the Enterprise, he tries to kill the actor Karidian (alias Kodos) and has to be restrained by Kirk (CK). Proud of his Irish ancestry, when affected by the Psi 2000 virus Riley locks himself in the engine room, declaring himself to be the descendant of Irish kings and therefore the rightful captain of the Enterprise, and serenades the long-suffering crew with repeated renditions of "I'll Take You Home Again, Kathleen," sung somewhat off-key (NT).

Ring around a rosy: A circle game of great antiquity still played by young human children. On Triacus, the children of the Starnes expedition seem to be more interested in the game than in their bereavement. Under the circumstances, the game harkens back to its macabre origins. The "rosy ring" was the first sign of plague, the ashes were those of the burned dead, and "we all fall down" was death itself (CL).

"Rip" in the universe: A disturbance or interruption in physical law which creates a point of exit from or entry into a universe or dimension (AF). See also Alternative warp; Magnetic effect.

Ritter scale: A measurement of cosmic radiation. A reading of 3.51 indicates the advent of a violent storm lasting several days—according to Spock, "exactly 74.1 solar hours" (CL, Em).

Ritual cloak: On the Amerind planet, a feathered cape, handmade by a maiden for her intended. The wedding or joining day is set when she finishes the cloak. Miramanee makes a ritual cloak for Kirk (PSy).

Ritual embrace, Vulcan: Two fingers, middle and index together, crossed against the mate's corresponding fingers; a gesture of some intimacy but also a show of proprietary authority at times, when used in public (JB).

Rizzo, Ensign (Jerry Ayres): A member of the landing party on Tycho IV; killed by the vampire cloud (Ob).

Robbiani dermal-optic test: A crucial psychological test which reveals a person's basic emotional structure by measuring reactions of the skin and eyes to color wavelengths (TI).

Roberts: Chief Engineer Vanderberg's aide on Janus VI (DD).

Robot ships: Large ships, though not as large as a Constellation starship, that have no life-support systems and can therefore devote most of the available space to payload. Bulky but powerful, they have huge propulsion units for carrying heavy cargo (MTT/a).

Rock creatures: Carbon-cycle life forms on Excalbia. They are capable of terrific energy output, which can not only control mental images but also stop the warp engines of a starship in orbit. They are also capable of creating on their own planet an Earthlike area, with the proper atmosphere, for their own special uses (SC). See also Horta, Yarnek.

Rock, exploding: A rainbow-hued rock containing uranite, hornblende, quartz, and other elements, found on Gamma Trianguli VI. It is easily broken by hand but explodes violently when thrown or dropped. Ensign Mallory is killed when he trips over one (Ap).

Roddenberry, Gene: Creator of series; (scripts): The Menagerie (Me); Return to Tomorrow (RT); The Omega Glory (OG); Mudd's Women (MW); The Return of the Archons (RA); Bread and Circuses (BC) (with Gene L. Coon); Assignment: Earth (AE) (with Art Wallace); (story and script): The Savage Curtain (SC) (with Arthur Heinemann); (story): Turnabout Intruder (TI); Charlie X (CX).

Rodent (John Harmon): Small, seedy, pitiful—a 1930s "wino" who meets McCoy while the doctor is under the influence of cordrazine. When McCoy falls into a coma, the Rodent rifles his clothes, finds the phaser at the doctor's belt, and accidentally fires it at himself (CEF).

Rodentlike beings: See Dimorus.

Rodinium: The hardest substance known to Federation science, used to shield outposts. The Romulan photon torpedo pulverizes the rodinium shields of Outposts 1, 3, 4, and 8 (BT).

Rodriguez: One of Khan's people (SS).

Rodriguez, Lieutenant Esteban (Jerry Lopez): Tall, dark, and Latin—a botanist and friend of Angela Martine Teller's. On the amusement-park planet, he materializes a Bengal tiger, a flock of birds, and a World War II Grumman F6F "Hellcat" fighter, which strafes him and Angela (SL).

Rojan (Warren Stevens): Leader of the Kelvan expedition to this galaxy—in his human form, very pale, verging on middle age. Born in intergalactic space and actually shaped far differently than humans, Rojan is not used to planets or to human bodies. When he and his people take human shape to facilitate their exploration of our planets, he becomes susceptible to some emotions and physical sensations that he has never felt before. Kirk and Spock work on his new feelings to make him jealous. Rojan finally decides to remain in human form and colonize a planet in our galaxy rather than return to Kelva in the Andromeda galaxy (AON).

Romaine, Jacques: Lieutenant Mira Romaine's father; chief engineer, Star Fleet, retired (LZ).

Romaine, Lieutenant Mira (Jan Shutan): An attractive, very efficient officer whose first Federation assignment is to supervise the transfer of some newly designed equipment from the Enterprise to Memory Alpha. Scotty falls deeply in love with her, even forgetting his precious Engine Room, and she returns his feelings. This is her first deep-space voyage, and she is understandably nervous. When the lights of Zetar attack the ship, the alien corporate entity finds Mira most susceptible and pliant for adaptation as their new life form. They take over her body, and she nearly kills Scotty under their command before she is placed in an antigravity test unit. The Zetars, used to the weightlessness of space, die when introduced to high atmospheric pressure and gravitational stresses in the chamber, leaving Mira free. She presumably goes on to Memory Alpha to set up the new equipment and restore the planetoid to usefulness again (LZ).

Romaine, Lydia: Lieutenant Mira Romaine's mother (LZ).

Roman Empire: See Planet 892-IV.

Romii: One of the two suns of the Romulan system, according to Spock's charts (BT).

Romulan battlecruisers: See Klingon ships.

Romulan commander (Mark Lenard): Commander of the Romulan ship which attacks Federation outposts and then the Enterprise—a heroic being with strong bones, black hair, pointed ears and brows, great warm brown eyes, and a gentle voice. When the Enterprise disables his ship, he destroys it rather than be captured. He appreciates poetry, loves his home, and follows his duty even unto death. His name is unknown, his memory worthy of honor. Peace be with him (BT).

Romulan Empire: Three weeks away from the nearest Star Fleet Command base by subspace radio (EI). See also Romulus.

Romulan execution: The Romulan penalty for espionage, sabotage, and treason is death, following torture—an unpleasant, painful way to die (EI).

Romulan female commander (Joanne Linville): A slight, intense, strong-willed woman with delicate features and long dark hair. She commands the flagship of the three Romulan ships that capture the Enterprise. Perhaps too easily upset and emotionally vulnerable for command, she becomes attached to Spock, and tells him her personal name, although we do not learn it. Spock keeps her busy while Kirk steals the Romulan cloaking device. Regretfully, she orders Spock's execution, but grabs him when the Enterprise transports him from the Romulan ship, thus becoming a "guest" on the Enterprise. It is to be hoped that when she is released from the starship to her home world, she will not be executed in disgrace, as appears to be Romulan custom (El).

Romulan neutral zone: See Neutral zone.

Romulan procedure, standard: Attacking Romulans normally try to take no captives and to destroy all captured ships. It is in Romulan interests, however, to try to capture the Enterprise in order to learn about Federation technical advances from it. But they are willing to destroy it if it doesn't surrender (BT, El).

Romulans: Romulans are militaristic, by turns extremely violent and tender, and they never take captives (DY). Their body readings, on sensors, are very similar to those of Vulcans. They are apparently unfamiliar with such Vulcan techniques as the nerve pinch and the mind touch (or else they are very weak telepaths—the commander of the Romulan flagship does not suspect Spock's true motives, despite very close contact with him). The Romulan ships are of Klingon design, indicating a pact between the Romulan and Klingon Empires (El). Dr. Keniclius 5 thinks the Romulans are still enough of a menace to set off a galactic war, but he is about one hundred years behind the times and does not know that at least a somewhat uneasy truce has been arranged between the Federation and the Romulans (IV/a). Romulans have found themselves with no choice but to accept and live in peace with their fellows in the time trap of Elysia (Tr/a).

Romulans, female: Romulan women are, according to the female commander of the Romulan flagship, more emotional and passionate than Vulcan women (El).

Romulan space: The Enterprise enters Romulan territory when the "space hippies" take over the ship in their search for Eden. The crew fears an attack, but the Romulans are unusually lax during this period and never discover that their space has been violated (WEd).

Romulan uniforms: Males wear a tunic or, in the case of officers, a tunic and cloak combination, a black belt, trousers and boots, with occasional helmet and gloves. The tunic is worn over a black turtleneck shirt and is a long-sleeved, collarless, pullover garment that is tucked into the trousers. The sleeves end in two holes, one for the fingers and one for the thumb to pass through. The tunics are grayish with a vertical third, and the pants are colored dark red or blue. Not enough is known about the Romulans yet to determine whether the colors indicate rank, ship duties, or station; officers are usually seen to wear red, others wear blue. The cloak, worn by officers and others capable of command, is thrown over one shoulder, with the ends of the material finished with a black fringe. The stripes seen in one instance seem to indicate neither rank nor station; perhaps it is a ship designation (BT, El). The female Romulan uniform incorporates the general idea of the male uniform into a dresslike garment, with a collarless, long-sleeved, thigh-length dress taking the place of the male uniform tunic. It differs, too, in that the colored third of the uniform does not stop at the belt but continues down the dress to the hem (El). (A female Romulan crew member has never been seen, but it seems logical that their uniforms would resemble those of the male crew members.)

Romulan War: Fought one hundred years before the Enterprise's missions by the Federation and the Romulans in relatively primitive ships, neither side seeing the combatants of the other face to face. The Federation gained the edge and presently a treaty was drawn to establish a neutral zone between the two territories, entry into which by either side could constitute an act of war. The treaty remains unbroken until a Romulan ship attacks Federation outposts and the Enterprise (BT).

Romulus: All information about this territory is gained from what few charts are available to the Federation and some bits of information gathered from other sources. "Romulus" is the Federation name for a system inhabited by a Vulcan race which lost contact with its mother planet before the philosophy of logic was introduced there (DY). The Romulan sun is a binary whose primary star the Federation calls "Romulus," the secondary star "Romii," and which is located at the galaxy's edge. The Romulan home worlds are apparently a double-planet system (such as Terra and Luna, or Rigel VIIA and B), called "Romulus and Remus" by the Federation (BT). See also Romulan Empire; Romulans.

Ross, Yeoman Teresa (Venita Wolf): Blond, pretty, fond of Viennese waltzes—one of the bridge crew when Trelane calls them to Gothos. He is quite taken with her, giving Kirk an excuse to challenge Trelane to a duel (SG).

Rostrum: An area on Ardana where a prisoner is strapped upright for "questioning." Ray beams strike out from nearby poles, causing agony. Plasus uses this device on Vanna when she is caught trying to kidnap Kirk from Stratos (Cms).

Routine readings: When a landing party arrives on a planet, a member of the party takes routine tricorder readings for life forms, dangerous gases, and other problems, and a general sensor reading of the area around them. However, on Taurus II, Kirk is so bemused by the lura-mag which has called them there that he is uninterested in having any routine readings made; Spock makes only a mild protest, as he too is under the spell sent out by the beautiful females of the planet (LS/a).

Rowe, Lieutenant (Mike Howden): Security officer who goes to investigate the Auxiliary Control Room when Norman takes it over (IM).

Roykirk, Jackson: A brilliant, if erratic, twenty-first-century scientist whose dream it was to build a perfect machine capable of independent thought. He designed the space probe <u>Nomad</u>, building a reverence for himself into the machine, so that it (imperfectly) mistakes Captain Kirk for its creator over a century later (Cg).

Rubindium crystals: Components of subcutaneous transponders. On Ekos, using these crystals, Spock turns two transponders and a light bulb into a crude phaser (PF).

Ruggisms; Rugg-type instruments: Engineering equipment (Ap).

Ruk (Ted Cassidy): An android—tall, gaunt, hairless,

with a knack for mimicry—created by the extinct inhabitants of Exo III, and probably resembling them. The only android remaining when Dr. Korby arrived there, Ruk helped him build the other androids, obeyed him, protected him, and was to have aided the doctor in his plan to bring androids to the worlds of the Federation. However, Kirk convinces Ruk that Korby is a menace to the android and his "perfect" world. Ruk, working out a logical equation, concludes that his need to survive must cancel his programming to help humans. He thus attacks his master, who destroys the android with a phaser (LG).

Rumors: As ugly in the future as at any other time. Kirk's guilt in the Finney case is rumored about the starbase, causing many of his colleagues to ignore him when he addresses them (Cml). See also Propaganda.

Russ (Tim Burns): Engineer—part of the damage-control party sent aboard the <u>Constellation</u> after it has been disabled by the berserker (DMa).

Russian: Chekov hears the Melkots speak Russian—an example of their telepathic contact (SGn).

Ruth (Shirley Bonne): An old girlfriend of Kirk's from Academy days—a pretty, round-faced blond with a lovely smile and heavy eye make-up. Kirk materializes her at random on the amusement-park planet, to his amazement and delight. After the confusion there is resolved, he undoubtedly spends a pleasant shore leave in her company (SL).

Ryan, Lieutenant: He takes over the helmsman's station when Sulu, infected with the Psi 2000 virus, leaves his post. Ryan catches the virus, breaks into giggles, and is relieved by Yeoman Rand (NT).

Ryetalyn: A rare substance from which antitoxin is made for Rigellian fever. A sufficient quantity to immunize the Enterprise's crew is found on Holberg 917G. Its refined form is cubes of whitish material. To be effective, however, it has to be pure; a minute amount of another mineral, such as irillium, will render it useless (RM). Alternate spelling: Vrietalyn.

Sabaroff, Robert (script): The Immunity Syndrome (IS).

Sabotage: When plans go awry in the search for the stolen Soul of Skorr, Kirk suspects sabotage by a member of the expedition itself—there are no other life forms on the mad planet (Ji/a). Spock has managed to pick up some indication that the Klingons plan to sabotage the Enterprise as soon as both ships escape from the time trap, but he doesn't know the details (Tr/a).

Sacred thumbs of Hnisto: Probably a swear word: an epithet Mudd uses when under tension and pressure (MP/a).

Safety control: If the magnetic field is ruptured in the matter/antimatter reaction chamber of the Enterprise, once the access panel is removed this magnetic flow control will not hold more than two seconds. If the magnetic flow jumps, the entire reaction chamber must

be jettisoned (TWS).

Sahsheer: Fragile Kelvan crystals which form with such rapidity that they seem to grow (AON).

Sakar of Vulcan: A genius mentioned together with Einstein, Kazanga, and Dr. Daystrom. Kirk mistakenly refers to him as "Sitar" (UC).

Sakuro's disease: A very rare illness resembling leukemia, found on Epsilon Canaris III and perhaps elsewhere. It can be treated with the equipment aboard a starship, but not with a medikit. In the early stages there is no discomfort. The first sign of the critical stage is a high fever; red corpuscles die, secondary infection develops, respiration becomes erratic, blood pressure drops. The fever eventually produces delirium, and death follows in a few hours (Mt).

Salem: A town in Massachusetts, New England, historically famous for its hysterical witch trials and burning of accused witches and warlocks in 1692, Earth time. The people of Megas-tu once tried to help Earth people with wizardry and got burned for it; they remembered that through the centuries (Mtu/a).

Salish (Rudy Solari): Medicine chief of the Amerinds on the Earthlike planet—an Indian of perhaps thirty, with a harsh face, black hair, straight nose, full mouth. His father, the previous medicine chief, died before instructing Salish in the use of the meteor-deflecting power of the obelisk, leaving the Indians unprotected. Salish clashes with Kirk over Miramanee and is jealous when he has to hand over his medicine badge to Kirk. He leads the Indians in stoning Kirk and Miramanee when the captain is unable to open or activate the obelisk. His name reflects the racial memory of the Amerinds' home planet—on Earth there is an Indian tribe called Salish (PSy).

Salute, Capellan: See Capellan salute.

Salute, Klingon: See Klingon verbal salute.

Salute, Vulcan: See Vulcan salute.

Sam: A large, tanned, muscular crewman who is in the Enterprise's gymnasium when Kirk tries to teach Charlie Evans to wrestle. Sam laughs at Charlie's adolescent clumsiness, so Charlie tosses him into another dimension. The Thasians later return him (CX).

Sample pouch: Used for picking up samples when visiting a new planet for the first time. Commander Bem carries one, which contains the fake communicators and phasers he gives to Kirk and Spock (Be/a).

Samurai (Sebastian Tom): A Japanese warrior, in traditional garb and armed to the teeth, whom Sulu accidentally materializes on the amusement-park planet, and who then chases various people with a sword (SL).

Sanchez, Dr.: One of the medical officers aboard the Enterprise. The Doctor conducts an autopsy on Ensign Wyatt after he is killed by Losira's touch (TWS).

Sandara: Home star of the Platonians, now a nova. Millennia ago, they managed to escape its destruction and settle on the planet they called Platonius (PSt).

Sandbats: A species native to Maynark IV. They appear to be inanimate rock crystals until they attack (Em).

Sandoval, Elias (Frank Overton): Gray-haired, hearty, stubborn—the leader of the Omicron Ceti III colony, who likes the simple life. After release from the spores' influence, he is eager to move the colonists to a planet where they can get some work done (TSP).

Sandwich: See Mess hall.

San Francisco Navy Yard: The components for the Enterprise were built in the San Francisco Navy Yard, on Earth. The starship itself was built in space, with the components shuttled up to the area where the ship was put together. Commodore April saw the Enterprise's components being constructed (CC/a).

Saplin: A curarelike drug. The thorns of the Gamma Trianguli VI pod plant are tipped with a substance like saplin, but a thousand times stronger (Ap).

Sarek (Mark Lenard): Spock's father—tall, husky for a Vulcan, with black hair streaked with gray, a gentle voice, and beautiful eyes. Sometime ambassador to the Federation Council, at the time of the Babel Conference his age is (in Terran years) 102.437 years precisely. An astrophysicist, Sarek gave Spock his initial instruction in computers. After Spock chose to join Star Fleet instead of the Vulcan Academy of Sciences, Sarek declined to speak to his son for eighteen years. When, in a crisis, Amanda (human wife to Sarek and mother of Spock) loses her temper and speaks at length on the insufficiencies of logic, Sarek and Spock realize that they have more in common than they had realized and make peace (JB). See also Ambassador Sarek.

Sargasso Sea of space: The Sargasso Sea is a region on Earth's Atlantic Ocean which was supposed to have trapped old-time sailing ships in vast seaweed layers covering the surface of the sea. In the Delta Triangle region, Elysia is a "Sargasso Sea" of space, a graveyard of lost spaceships from every civilization imaginable (Tr/a).

Sargent, Joe (director): The Corbomite Maneuver (CMn).

Sargon (James Doohan): A once-humanoid being who inhabited the now-dead planet Arret, which was made unlivable, some half-million years before the Enterprise arrives, following a disaster which took place because the people became so advanced that they thought they were gods. Only three survived: Sargon, his wife, Thalassa, and Sargon's former enemy, Henoch. Their minds were stored in receptacles for the long wait until the Enterprise discovers them. Sargon borrows Kirk's body in order to build android bodies for the three, but Henoch drives him out of the human body into the hull of the ship. Sargon and Thalassa destroy Henoch and take up a disembodied existence (RT).

Sarpeidon: The only satellite of the star Beta Niobe, and in danger of being destroyed by the incipient nova of its sun. The Sarpeids had developed a high level of technology, including devices such as the atavachron, which can send anyone back to any time in the planet's past and which they use to escape from the nova (AY).

Sarpeids: See Sarpeidon.

Sar 6 (Robert Sampson): Anan 7's assistant on Eminiar VII—tall, blond, ordinary-looking (TA).

Sasek: When Spock poses as his own relative, after going back in Vulcan time to save himself as a youngster, he claims to be the son of Sasek and T'Pel, distantly re-

lated to Sarek (Yy/a).

Satak, Captain: Commander of the Vulcan-manned starship Intrepid. He is destroyed with his ship by the spacegoing ameba (IS).

Satellite flares: The Enterprise destroys the parasites on Deneva by setting off trimagnesite flares on satellites around the planet (OA).

Saturn: The sixth planet in our solar system. Saturn's equatorial diameter is 120,000 kilometers, with its outer ring 75,000 kilometers from the surface of the planet. Jupiter, Saturn, and Neptune combined are not as large as the cosmic cloud which endangers Mantilles and the Enterprise (OPM/a).

Saturnius: Eve McHuron complains to Kirk that the men of the Enterprise stare at her and her companions as though they were Saturnius harem girls. Kirk can hardly blame the men, however (MW).

Satyr: A small half-human, half-goat being on Megastu who uses a magically induced whirlwind to spin his toy top (Mtu/a).

Saurian brandy: A delectable but potent drink (MT). A favorite of Dr. McCoy's (CK). Gav the Tellarite gets not quite drunk, but feisty, on it, and picks a fight with Sarek of Vulcan (JB). Scotty begins his project of getting Tomar drunk with it (AON). Flint the immortal has a hundred-year-old bottle of it, which impresses McCoy. Even Spock accepts a glass of it, which amazes McCoy (RM).

Saurian virus: When Dramia II was hit by Saurian virus, McCoy led a mass-inoculation program against it. Evidently a serious and deadly virus, it left antibodies in the blood system, which McCoy uses nineteen years later to inoculate everyone against auroral plague (Al/a).

Savior, the: See Master, the.

Sayana (Shari Nims): A young woman of Gamma Trianguli VI—like the rest of the natives, platinum-haired, red-skinned, and healthy. She finds Spock's name amusing and gives him a necklace of shells. After the destruction of Vaal, she and Makora reinstitute physical reproduction on the planet (Ap).

Scalos: A planet in an outer quadrant of the galaxy which once had a beautiful and civilized city with a rating of 7 on the industrial scale. The people are humanoid and keep up some level of creativity, judging by their clothing. Volcanic eruptions have released a radiation which has killed their children, rendered the males sterile, and accelerated their metabolism to a pace faster than the wink of a human eye. When the Enterprise answers their false distress signal, the landing party finds paintings, books, and a barren world with only insect sounds, made by the fast-moving Scalosians trying to communicate. The distress calls are intended to lure ships close enough so they can kidnap the fertile males among the crew. Newly accelerated people die quickly, however, so the Scalosians are forced to keep luring new ships in. In consideration of these facts, the Federation is likely to quarantine that sector of the galaxy until a cure for the acceleration can be developed (WE).

Scalosians: See Scalos.

Scalosian substance: A substance found in the

water on Scalos that is responsible for the acceleration of the Scalosians' metabolism. The substance, released on the planet's surface by volcanic eruptions, can be used to accelerate others when a few drops are placed in food or drink (WE).

Scanner: A small green cube on Gary Seven's desk which can tie into the Beta 5 computer, scan a given subject, and report on it orally (AE). See also Sensors.

Schematics: It will take time to wire the inner workings of the power packs to the cart, but if Spock and Em/3/Green work together, they can do it faster, Spock diagraming the schematics and Em/3/Green doing the work (Ji/a).

Schmerer, James (script): The Survivor (Su/a).

Schmitter (Biff Elliott): A member of the Janus VI mining colony, killed by the Horta while on guard duty (DD).

Schneider, Paul (scripts): The Terratin Incident (Te/a); Balance of Terror (BT); The Squire of Gothos (SG).

Scholar, Yang (Morgan Farley): An old man, guardian of the Yang sacred documents—the United States' Constitution, an illustrated Bible, and such (OG).

Science Group Headquarters: The room on Camus II where the survivors of the Federation exploration party meet the Enterprise's landing party. This room contains the mechanical device which makes possible the life-entity transfer between Janice Lester and Captain Kirk (TI).

Scientific colony: The Starnes expedition on Triacus was to last for several years, so a full colony was set up for the scientists, who were allowed to bring their spouses and children on the trip. The colony was destroyed by Gorgan, who made the adults commit suicide and later influences the children to try to take over the Enterprise (CL).

Scientific exploratory ship: See Ariel.

Scientists: Karla Five suggests that the Enterprise go with her to Arret, her home planet, where the scientists there might help them back to our universe. However, the society of Arret no longer has much knowledge, so the Enterprise people do most of the scientific work themselves (CC/a).

Scotch: An alcoholic beverage. It is Scotty's drink, which he describes as a "man's drink." Chekov says a little old lady from Leningrad invented it (TT).

Scott, Lieutenant Commander Montgomery (James Doohan): Chief engineer on the U.S.S. Enterprise—middle-aged, with black hair, twinkling brown eyes, and a winning smile. Serial number SE-197-514. He speaks with a Scots accent and is possibly a native of Aberdeen. He is very fond of women (WF, WM), but much fonder of machinery. His idea of a pleasant afternoon is tinkering with any engineering section of the vessel, and he is totally unable to understand why any sane man would spend reading time on anything but technical manuals. He is devoted to Kirk (MM), but even more so to the Enterprise (TT). He enjoys a good drink now and then, and has collected alcoholic beverages from the known parts of the galaxy (AON, TT, WF). He is

known affectionately as "Scotty."

Scott-2: Described as "sneering," and undoubtedly as rotten as the rest of the mirror universe. If not, he probably drinks (MM).

Scotty, Mr.: Commander Ari bn Bem's name for Scott (Be/a).

Scouter-gig: A silver canoelike boat from the Enterprise with power pack, computer console panel, and speed. It is used to search Argo for Kirk and Spock, who have been missing for five days (Am/a).

Scout ship: Cyrano Jones is making his escape from the Klingons in a stolen scout ship, which the Klingons destroy with a disruptor bolt. The Enterprise rescues Jones just in time (MTT/a). Harry Mudd steals a scout ship from the Enterprise to escape arrest and goes to a seemingly deserted planet in it. He actually gets into more trouble than he can handle (MP/a).

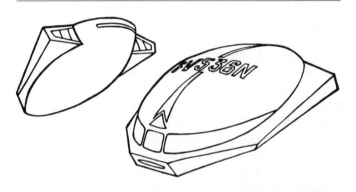

S

Scout vessel: A scout vessel discovered Delta Theta III, and reported that it might possibly have aboriginal life forms (Be/a).

Screens: Some type of force-field screen protects Flint's home from the curious and the uninvited, and creates the impression of lifelessness on the planet Holberg 917G. In actuality, behind the screens there is quite a palatial domicile (RM). See also Directional equipment.

Screens, defensive: See Deflectors.

Scrolls: The ancient records of the Aquans are on scrolls, rolled into watertight containers (Am/a).

Sea foliage: The Aquans of the planet Argo gather sea foliage for food (Am/a).

Sea gulls: The Enterprise's Recreation Room is capable of creating the effect of sea gulls, Terran aquatic birds, to go with the holographic illusion of ocean waves—all on request (PJ/a).

Sea monster: A huge, tentacled, fishlike creature, with some resemblance to a Denebian whale, that attacks the Enterprise's aquashuttle. It has both lungs and gills, which suggests that the creature was once a land animal (Am/a).

Seaquake: See Seismic disturbances.

Search Party 7: One of the search parties sent to find Uhura, Sulu, and McCoy when they are discovered to be missing. Search Party 7 finds the Recreation Room door stuck closed, and suspects that the missing people are inside (PJ/a).

Sea torches: A special type of light that glows underwater, carried by the Enterprise's landing party. Also called aqua lanterns (Am/a).

Secondary propulsion system: The Vendorian spy sabotages the deflector shields and the secondary propulsion system, rendering the Enterprise virtually helpless (Su/a).

Second eyelid shield: Vulcans have nictitating membranes to protect their eyes against the harsh Vulcan desert sun; this second eyelid shield protects Spock when McCoy experiments on him with strong light in an attempt to kill the neural parasite that has invaded his body on Deneva (OA).

Second guard (John Boyer):   The guard on duty, along with Lemli, at Spock's trial. He brings Janice-K from the brig to the courtroom (TI).

Sector 39J: A sector of the galaxy containing the Gamma 7A system, where the Intrepid and the Enterprise encounter the spacegoing ameba (IS).

Security board: A light on the navigation helm that indicates any tampering with the rest of the ship's controls (MM).

Security chief (Lincoln Demyan):   Young, plump guard on the Enterprise. Gary Seven puts him to sleep with the servo and escapes (AE). In the mirror universe Sulu-2 is security chief (MM).

Security guard (David L. Ross):   When Kirk-J confines Janice-K to Sick Bay and orders that there are to be no visitors, this guard, confused by Spock's confident assertion that these orders do not include senior officers, allows the Vulcan to speak with her (TI).

Security guards: The Enterprise has many red-shirted security guards, of both sexes, whose job it is to maintain patrols on the ship and to guard personnel and equipment in any forays to planetside. When Kirk complains that his security men can't find all the tribbles that Cyrano Jones has let loose on the Enterprise, Jones suggests that perhaps the Enterprise needs better security men (MTT/a).

Security rooms: The Romulan term for brig (EI).

Security squad: Several security guards, heavily armed and with heavy-duty tricorders, are needed to help find Commander Bem on Delta Theta III (Be/a).

Security team: Kirk places a security team on every Klingon who boards the Enterprise. They don't know how the Klingons will do their dirty work when both ships escape from Elysia, but they are going to watch them all (Tr/a).

Seed grain: The quintotriticale being carried to Sherman's Planet is to be used as seed to plant new crops to relieve a famine (MTT/a).

Sehlat: A giant teddy-bear-like creature of Vulcan with six-inch fangs and a heavy fur coat. It is not cute and can be dangerous. A sehlat can rip an arm off if one makes a wrong move, but Vulcans never make wrong moves—that would be illogical. Sehlats can be tamed for pets, and are loyal, courageous, and loving (Yy/a). When Spock was a child, he had one as a pet and was very fond of it (JB). See also I-Chaya.

Seismic disturbances: Quakes on land or sea. The ones on Argo destroyed its major land masses and forced the survivors to become aquatic beings, until another massive quake made the land rise above the sea again. Owing to the same type of seismic disturbance, another planet is in danger of suffering the same fate, which is why the Enterprise is studying Argo (Am/a).

"Selected":   An unexplained term used by the thralls on Triskelion, although the Enterprise people think they have a fairly good idea of what is meant. None of them is any too happy about the idea, especially Uhura and Chekov (GT).

Selek: Spock becomes his own cousin when he arrives at his own home in Vulcan's past, and meets himself as a seven-year-old boy. The adult Spock introduces himself as Selek, son of T'Pel and Sasak, distant relatives of Sarek's, saying he is on his way to the family shrine. Sarek offers hospitality, giving the adult Spock a chance to save the young Spock from certain death on the Vulcan desert (Yy/a).

Self-destruct: Many machines (and people) are armed with self-destruct mechanisms, including the Enterprise (LB). The space probe from Kulkukan has one, and uses it (HS/a). Rather than carry the malevolent alien into the rest of the galaxy, the insectoids of the long-dead pod ship chose to self-destruct; the Enterprise is faced with the same decision (BFS/a). When the Enterprise's crew realizes that the ship's armament is too weak to do much damage to the immense cosmic cloud before the alien entity destroys Mantilles, Kirk decides to destroy his starship. Spock did not profess to be enamored of the idea, but his facts and figures support the captain's decision. The self-destruct mechanism in the engineering core is set with the computer control on the bridge to trigger the destruction of the starship, which, it is hoped, will in the process also destroy the brain area of the huge cloud entity before it can engulf a planet with eighty-two million inhabitants. Fortunately, the self-destruct mechanism does not have to be used (OPM/a). See also General Order No. 6.

Senensky, Ralph (director):   Obsession (Ob); This Side of Paradise (TSP); Is There in Truth No Beauty? (TB); The Tholian Web (TW); Bread and Circuses (BC); Return to Tomorrow (RT); Metamorphosis (Mt).

Sensors: Generic term for any equipment aboard a

starship which is capable of sensing, analyzing, and supplying information about almost anything. This can include composition of an object in space, its dimensions, the presence or absence of life, geological age, etc. Spock is generally in charge of the ship's sensors, from which he takes readings via his hooded screen at the library/computer station. The tricorder is a portable sensor used away from the ship's sensor gear, and there are specialized navigational sensors used by the helmsmen, medical sensors used in Sick Bay, and so on. Sensors are also referred to as "scanners" at times. The Enterprise's sensors fail to pick up any life forms on the planet Argo, including the marine monster that later attacks the aquashuttle. The explanation is probably that the cloud cover of the planet and the depth at which the Aquans live block the readings (Am/a). Sensors are focused into the cosmic cloud's synaptic electrical impulses so the output can be routed to the computer for analysis and conversion into language patterns (OPM/a). The speed of a starship has to be reduced to accommodate sensors in picking up the space probe's trail when it gets faint, but sensors cannot penetrate the alien ship (HS/a).

Sensor web: Dr. Miranda Jones, blind from birth, wears an elegant black gown covered with delicate silver webbing. This webbing is actually a highly sophisticated sensor web capable of telling her within a micromillimeter where she is, who is standing near her, and what is going on. Spock compliments her . . . and her dressmaker (TB).

Sensory anomaly: See Non-network sensory stasis.

Sensory distortion: When traveling at warp speeds, the human mind experiences time and space distortion and cannot always accept the aberration; the result can be death by terror or insanity. Attempting to cross the energy barrier at the edge of the galaxy can bring on similar sensory distortion (TB).

Sentinels: The guards used in Stratos. They are generally trained Troglytes who follow orders blindly and seem to have no particular loyalty to their own people (Cms).

Septimus (Ian Wolfe): Small, old, bald, and gentle—formerly a senator on Planet 892-IV, now the leader of a group of worshippers of the Son (BC).

Service: As Uhura attempts to convince the master computer of the shore-leave planet that the Enterprise's crew is essential and should not be killed, she finds out that the computer is less than enchanted with its function: It feels that its life has been one of service, and that it is time for a change. When Kirk asks it about the change in hospitality, the computer explains that it is tired of mindless servitude and needs something more (OUP/a).

Service record: The complete profile of a person's service in Star Fleet, containing important information like rank, training, status, serial number, ship assignment, awards and medals, commendations, as well as anything else pertinent to the individual's service, including reprimands, such as the one Finney drew after leaving a circuit open following a shift of duty on shipboard (Cml). Kirk has it entered in Gary Mitchell's and Dr. Dehner's records that they died in line of duty (WNM).

Servo: A gadget resembling a fountain pen, which when activated extends two small antennae and can do such things as counteract a force field, hypnotize a Terran, and blast like a phaser (AE).

Settings, weapon: See Slaver weapon.

Seven, Gary (Robert Lansing): A twentieth-century Earthman—tall, with a hawk face and steel-gray eyes—born on a highly secret advanced planet and trained to help prevent Earth's civilization from destroying itself before it matures into a peaceful society. Code name: Supervisor 194. The Enterprise, sent back in time to see how Earth did survive, encounters Seven on one of his assignments (AE).

Sevrin, Dr. (Skip Homeier): A bald humanoid with wrinkled elephantine ears and colorful flowers painted on his forehead—once a brilliant research engineer in acoustics, communications, and electronics on Tiburon. Discovered to be a carrier of sythococcus novae, a virulent bacillus, he is restricted to travel in technologically advanced societies so the disease cannot spread to societies unequipped to control it. He broods to the point of insanity about setting up his own perfect society and gathers around him a group of "space hippies," malcontents who go with him to find the planet of Eden. He leads them to steal a space cruiser, then to take over the Enterprise and steal a shuttlecraft to get to the planet. On the Enterprise, he uses ultrasonics in an attempt to wipe out the crew. Landing on Eden, his party discovers that all the plant life contains a deadly acid, which burns them badly and kills one of the group. When confronted by the Enterprise's landing party, Sevrin eats some of the acid fruit, killing himself (WEd).

Shahna (Angelique Pettyjohn): A beautiful Amazonian woman with long, silvery-green hair and enormous eyes. A thrall on Triskelion, she is a native of that planet, her mother having been killed in a free-style match. As Kirk's drill thrall, she becomes fond of him and wants him to take her with him on the Enterprise, but she has to stay with the other thralls and learn to be a civilized being under the newly enlightened teaching of the Providers (GT).

Shakespeare, First Folio: The first collected edition of the plays, published in 1623. Flint intimates that he may have been Shakespeare, but he may have simply been a collector of that period (RM).

Shakespeare, William: An Earth writer (1564–1616) whose plays and poetry contain such perfect insight into human foibles that he is quoted and his works presented well into the twenty-second century, albeit with modernized setting and costumes (CK). Kirk, in trying to explain flowers to Kelinda, quotes him: "A rose by any other name would smell as sweet . . ." (AON). Spock, sharing a mind with the Medusan Kollos, misquotes Shakespeare: "Oh brave new world that has such creatures in it . . ." Ironically, Spock is quoting the speech uttered by Shakespeare's Miranda, leaving Miranda Jones to add Prospero's qualification (TB). Marta, the insane Orion girl on Elba II, recites Shakespeare's Sonnet XVIII, which she

S

claims to have written: "Shall I compare thee to a Summer's day . . . ?" Garth grows infuriated and threatens to kill her for this effrontery (WGD). McCoy is reminded of a play with the quote "How sharper than a serpent's tooth is an ungrateful child" (HS/a).

Shangri-la: In James Hilton's book Lost Horizon, a Tibetlike land where one could find eternal peace and tranquility (PSy).

Shaw, Lieutenant Areel (Joan Marshall): A pretty, slender, blond lawyer in the judge advocate's office on Starbase 11, and a good one. As an old girlfriend of Kirk's, she finds it difficult to be the prosecutor in his court-martial (Cml).

Shea, Lieutenant (Carl Byrd): A tall, slender, black member of the landing party that meets the Kelvans. To demonstrate Kelvan power to Kirk, Rojan reduces Shea to a block of white crystal, then restores his human form (AON).

Shellfish: The Aquans of the planet Argo use shellfish for food and for decorating their buildings and themselves (Am/a).

Sheriff: See Behan, Johnny.

Sherman's Planet: A Class M world in the vicinity of Space Station K-7, claimed by both the Federation and the Klingon Empire. Under the terms of the Organian Peace Treaty, the planet will go to whichever side can develop it more efficiently (TT). The planet does not prosper, and they have famine trouble again (MTT/a).

Shield: Goggles or slit glasses worn by the Troglytes of Ardana, who work so long in the zienite mines that they cannot take the brilliant sunlight of the surface (Cms).

Shielding control, Romulan: See Cloaking device.

Shielding deterioration: See Nacelles.

Shields: Both Lokai and Bele have automatic, invisible shields which they can operate easily at will to protect themselves from even a phaser on stun (LB).

Shields, deflector: See Deflectors.

ShiKahr: Spock's home city: a large area surrounded by landscaped parks to protect the city from the encroachment of the arid sands. Beds of flowers imported from other planets, buildings of many shapes in combinations of soft colors, pedestrian streets that are quiet and meant for serene appreciation—all make the Vulcan city a beautiful and peaceful place (Yy/a).

Ship captains: In Elysia, ship captains are totally responsible for their crews and any actions taken by them; the ships' captains must suffer the ultimate penalty known in Elysia for any aboard a ship who violate the law (Tr/a).

Ships and shuttlecraft:

Alien scout vessel (LB)
Alien ship (PO/a)
Alien vessel (CC/a)
Antares, U.S.S. (CX)
Aquashuttle (Am/a)
Archon, U.S.S. (RA)
Ariel (EB/a)
Astral Queen (CK)
Aurora (WEd)
Battlecruisers (Tr/a)
Battlecruisers, Klingon (MTT/a)

Beagle, S.S. (BC)
Bonaventure (Tr/a)
Botany Bay, S.S. (SS)
Carolina, U.S.S. (FC)
Class F shuttlecraft (Me)
Class J cargo ship (MW)
Columbia, S.S. (Me)
Columbus (GS)
Constellation, U.S.S. (DMa)
Constitution, U.S.S. (SS)
Copernicus (SW/a)

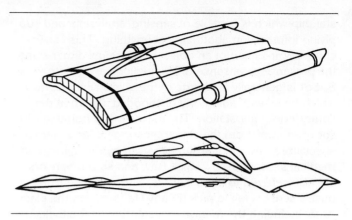

Defiant, U.S.S. (TW)
Desert flyer (Yy/a)
Devisor (MTT/a)
Dierdre, S.S. (FC)
Doomsday machine (DMa)
Draconis-ship (SB)
DY-500 (SS)
DY-100 (SS)
Enterprise, I.S.S. (MM)
Enterprise replica (Cp)
Enterprise, U.S.S.
Excalibur, U.S.S. (UC)
Exeter, U.S.S. (OG)
Farragut, U.S.S. (Ob)
Fesarius (CMn)
Ferry (WEd)
F-104 jet plane (Bluejay 4) (TY)
Freighter (PO/a, Yy/a)
Galileo (GS, Mt)
Gorn ship (Ar)
Hood, U.S.S. (UC)
Horizon, U.S.S. (PA)
Hovercraft (OUP/a)
Huron, S.S. (PO/a)
Intrepid, U.S.S. (Cml, IS)
Ion-powered ship (SB)
Klingon Imperial Fleet (Tr/a)
Klingon/Romulan vessels (PJ/a)
Klingon ships (Su/a)
Klothos (Tr/a)
Kulkukan's ship (HS/a)

Lexington, U.S.S. (UC)
Off-ship vehicles (MP/a)
One-man vessel (Su/a)
Orion high-speed ship (JB)
Patrol ship, one-man (Su/a)
Pilot vessel (CMn)
Pod ship (BFS/a)
Police craft (SW/a)
Potemkin, U.S.S. (PO/a, UC)
Probe (IV/a, LS/a)
Republic, U.S.S. (Cml)
Robot ships (MTT/a)
Romulan battlecruisers (Su/a)
Romulan "bird of prey" ship (BT)
Romulan ships (EI)
Satellite (Te/a)
Scientific exploratory ship (EB/a)
Scouter-gig (Am/a)
Scout ship (MP/a, MTT/a)
Scout vessel (Be/a)
Shuttlecraft (OUP/a)
Sky machine (OUP/a)
Spacecraft (Ji/a)
Space probe (HS/a)
Tholian ships (TW)
Unit XY-75847 (EM)
Valiant, U.S.S. (TA, WNM)
Woden (UC)
Yonada (FW)
Yorktown, U.S.S. (Ob)

See also Starships.

Ship's log: The Enterprise's landing party plays the Ariel's log to see what happened to its crew. The log holds a record of all activities aboard the ship until the last crew member has left it (EB/a). A starship's log is always made available to former commanders as a courtesy; this is Star Fleet policy. Commodore April kept track of the adventures of the Enterprise in this manner (CC/a). Captain Kirk is certain that the pod ship has some information corresponding to a ship's log if they only knew where to look for it. They find the main console and activate a screen; an image appears, giving a garbled but understandable account of the self-destruction of the pod ship and the danger of the malevolent alien still present in the long-dead ship (BFS/a).

Ships, Phylosian: Huge teardrop-shaped ships of the Phylosians are stored in a large hangar. With Dr. Keniclius's aid, the Phylosians plan to renovate the ships and enforce peace in the galaxy. The Enterprise's landing party finds that the plant beings are pulling moss and other growths off the ships, preparatory to their use (IV/a).

Shore-leave planet: When the Enterprise's crew first encounters the amusement-park planet, they eventually find it to be a unique place for shore leave (SL); the uniqueness is given added spice during the ship's second call there (OUP/a). See also Amusement-park planet.

Short-burst maneuvers: See Printout.

Shras (Reggie Nalder): The aged and wrinkled Andorian ambassador to the Babel Conference, with blue skin, white hair, knobbed antennae. Thelev, the disguised Orion, is a member of his party, but Shras knows nothing of the deception (JB).

Shuttlecraft: A six- or seven-passenger ship which can be sent out on intra-solar-system missions. The Enterprise has at least two shuttlecraft at a time: the Columbus and the accident-prone Galileo. An emergency rescue party attempts to go down to the amusement planet in a shuttlecraft, but is forced to remain on board when the hangar doors begin to malfunction and slam shut (OUP/a).

Shuttlecraft Bay: The area of the Enterprise where off-ship vehicles are kept for use. A large hangar door in it opens into space (MP/a).

Shuttlecraft, Class F: The type used at starbases; similar to the Columbus and Galileo aboard the Enterprise (Me).

Sick Bay: For obvious reasons, the Sick Bay is in the most protected part of the ship.

Sigma Draconis: A G9-type star with nine planets, three of them Class M and inhabited by intelligent life. None of the inhabited planets is advanced enough to have developed ion propulsion (SB).

Sigma Draconis IV: An inhabited planet with a rating of G, equivalent to Earth circa 2030 (SB).

Sigma Draconis VII: Kirk erroneously mentions this planet instead of Sigma Draconis VI. Sulu also scrambles the planet number in filling out the captain's log on board the Enterprise (SB).

Sigma Draconis VI: A planet once highly civilized, now heavily glaciated, with only the tropical zone free of ice. Its high maximum temperature is 40°F—"livable, if you have thick skin." It is inhabited on the surface by the Morgs, males who have a neolithic culture, and in an underground city by the Eymorgs, females with advanced technology (SB).

Sigma Draconis III: An inhabited planet rated B on the industrial scale, the equivalent to Earth circa 1485—heavily populated, yet with a technology rated at only 3 (SB).

Sigma Iotia II: See Iotia.

Signaling device: A boxlike instrument with a knob, used to signal the Vedala that their mission is done, so the expedition can be retrieved from the mad planet (Ji/a).

Signals, record of: Kirk wants the entire Class 2 signal and any other exchanges with the Klingons to be piped back to starbase so it will at least be on record, no matter what happens to the Enterprise (Tr/a).

Silicon creatures: The Horta is a silicon creature (DD). The landing party on the Kalandan outpost planet surmises that the life form they have detected might be a type of silicon being, much like the Horta. They are wrong (TWS). Spock suspects that the Excalbian is a "living rock," suggesting that it may have a silicon life

cycle (SC).

Silicon nodule: A Horta egg: spherical, basketball-sized, and orange (DD).

Singer, Arthur H. (script): Turnabout Intruder (TI).

Singh, Lieutenant (Blaisdell Makee): Engineering officer—efficient but perhaps a bit too easily rattled. While Singh is in charge of the Auxiliary Control Room, Kirk puts him in charge of Nomad, too, which won't stay put (Cg).

Singing crewman (William Knight): Despite Spock's orders, he prevents Yeoman Rand from reporting to the bridge by standing in her way and singing "I'll Take You Home Again, Kathleen" (NT).

Sirah (Irene Kelley): A small, dark, scraggly Yang female, possibly Cloud William's woman, as she is captured with him. During the duel between Kirk and Captain Tracey, Spock uses mind touch to make Sirah contact the Enterprise with the communicator (OG).

Sirius: See Arcanis, Canopus.

Sirius IX: A planet where Harry Mudd went with the credits he obtained by selling Star Fleet Academy to Ilyra VI. On Sirius IX, Mudd discovered a boon to humanoid life: crystals which contain a magical love potion. He sold it to thousands of Sirians, who became ill from it, owing to their unusual biochemistry. The logical thing to do was leave Sirius IX in haste, which Mudd proceeded to do. Sirius IX charged Mudd with fraud and swindling, among other things (MP/a).

Skorr: A planet where two hundred years ago the people were great warriors with very advanced military techniques that could breed vast armies rapidly. Spock calculates that with the existing Skorr, they could in two hundred years breed an army of two hundred billion warriors. The Skorr are winged humanoids, fierce, proud, and courageous. Since the advent of a religious teacher named Alar, they have learned to live in peace. The Skorr call Alar their Savior, and his brain patterns are recorded in an indurite sculpture called the Soul of Skorr. The theft of this sculpture could have set off a war of racial fury throughout the galaxy, but it is recovered before the Skorr government has to tell the people of its loss (Ji/a).

Sky machine: The amusement planet's master computer thinks the Enterprise's crew are slaves controlled by their master, the sky machine (OUP/a).

Slang, Iotian: As used by the Iotian populace, similar to the 1920s gangster era on Earth (PA).

Boss: Chief or leader; head of local government.	gun.
Box: Coffin.	Hightailing: Hurrying.
Broad: A woman.	Hit: Kill.
Bud, Pally, Buster: Forms of address used in the sense of "Hey you."	Lean on: Influence by threat of damage.
Bundle: Large amount of money.	Muscle: Forceful influence.
Burned: Killed.	Outfit: Organization.
Cement overshoes: The promise of permanent immersion in water in a weighted-down condition.	Percentage: Taxation or share in the profits.
Chopper: Machine gun, usually a Thompson sub-machine gun.	Petrify: Don't move.
Concrete galoshes: Improper version of "cement overshoes."	Piece of the action: A share of the profits.
Drill him: Shoot him, with a gun.	Put 'em in the bag: Confine them.
Fancy heater: Phaser.	Put 'em on ice: Confine them.
Fed: Federation personnel.	Put the bag on: Kidnap them.
Heater: A gun, usually a pistol type.	Reception committee: Armed escort-guard.
Heeled: Armed with a weapon, usually a	Sawbones: Doctor—often a nickname.
	Scrag: Kill.
	Spring: Free from confinement.
	Straight dope: Correct information.

Slang, Melkot: As used by Melkot projections, similar to Earth's Old West in the 1880s (SGn).

Slang, mid-twentieth century: As used on Earth the two times the Enterprise visits Earth's past (AE, TY).

Blip: A spot on a radar screen.
Doubletalk: Nonsense.
Fizzling: Transporting.
Freeze: Don't move.
Gantry: Launch tower.
H-bomb: Primitive nuclear device.
Blow off: Brag.
Bushwack: Ambush.
Draw: To pull, aim, and shoot a gun—quickly.
Hell for leather: Looking for trouble.
Hot air (noun): Bragging.
Shot off their mouths: Bragged.

Holy jehosephat: Expletive.
I'll bite: Please elucidate.
Little green men: Stereotype of aliens in classical pulp science fiction.
Scramble: To get something moving as quickly as possible (military term).
Tracking: Watching and following on a radar scope
T-70: Time minus seventy minutes until . . . (usually a rocket launch).
UFO: Unidentified Flying Object.
Watchit: Refrain from continuing.

Slang, Miri's planet (Mi):

Bonk-bonk: Let's hit the enemy—hard.
Boxes: The Enterprise's crew's communicators.
Buttinsky thing: Someone who "butts" in when the children did not want them to.
Foolie: A game; a joke—sometimes deadly.
Grup: Childish contraction of "grown-up"; derogatory term.
Lovey-dovey: Description of adult affection.
Onlies: The children—the only ones left when the adults died.

After time: The time after the adults tried the longevity drug on themselves, went mad, and died.
Awful things: The mad creatures, mottled and twisted, that the children become when they reach puberty.
Before time: The time before the adults tried their longevity serum on everyone—probably only a memory passed down from older children.
Blah blah blah: The children's reaction to being talked to; when enough of them shout this, the speaker can be drowned out with sound.

Slang, Omegan: As used by the Kohms and Yangs (OG).

Ay pledgli ianectu flaggen tupep likfor stahon: I pledge allegiance to the flag and to the republic for which it stands.
Ee'd pebnista nordor formor purfektunum: We the people, in order

to form a more perfect union.
Fireboxes: Phasers.
Free-dohm: Freedom.
Hola: Begin.
Year of the red-bird: An eleven-year interval, by Federation measurement.

Slang, Planet 892-IV: Similar to 1960s Earth (BC).

First heat: First competition in an elimination combat.
News broadcast: A form of dispensing information to the public.

Smog: Photochemical air pollution.
Television: Primitive visual transmitter.
Video: Primitive visual transmitter.

Slang, Sarpeid, Charles II era: Similar to that of late-seventeenth-century England (AY).

Angler: Pickpocket.
Boung, Bung: Purse, worn by both sexes.
Cove: Man.
Coxcomb: An effete braggart.
Cutpurse: Thief who steals purses, which hang on belts by strings.
Fop: An overdressed, pretentious man. One who affects airs.
Gull: A dupe. To gull: to dupe someone.
Henchman: A male attendant, but in a

derogatory sense; one who assists another in evildoing.
Leech: Physician, who uses leeches to bleed a patient.
Limbered: Punished; racked.
Livery: A servant's uniform.
Mort: A female not of high class.
Mountebank: Charlatan.
Rum: Bad or stupid.
Shoulder-clapper: Officer of the law.

Slang, Trelane's: Trelane is a student of eighteenth- and nineteenth-century British culture; hence, his slang is of that era (SG):

Absolutely smashing: Something exceptional; a really fine idea.
Affair of honor: A duel.
Field of honor: The area, usually an isolated meadow, where duels are fought.
Hip-hip hoorah: A shouted expression of applause or encouragement.
Oh, rot: An expletive, used in place of stronger language.
Repast: A meal (in this case elaborate, with many courses served).
Quite tiresome: Boring; producing apathy in the speaker.
Tally ho: An English alteration of the

French taiaut, tayaut; the cry of a huntsman on sighting the fox or game.
Tut-tut: Expression that makes light of a situation, brushes it aside.
Sallies: Quick witticisms, bright retorts, quips.
Victuals: Food.
Vive le Napoleon: Long live Napoleon (Trelane was obviously a Bonapartist in sympathy).

Slang, Twentieth-century Depression era (1929–36) (CEF):

A-bomb: Common term for the atomic bomb, then only theoretical.
Booze: Anything more or less drinkable, with alcohol in it.
Broad: Cant term for a female.
Bum: Anyone without a job or prospects of one; a lowlife, usually male.
Do-gooder: An earnest, often idealistic humanitarian devoted to helping others and/or social reform. Edith says she isn't one, but she is.
Flop: A place to sleep; with any luck, it even has a bed.
Miss Goody Twoshoes: A reference to a fairy-tale character, made in a somewhat derogatory manner by a bum to describe Edith Keeler because she preaches to the bums.
Slum angel: Journalistic reference to Edith Keeler, commending her for her humanitarian work in the slums,

in a news story about her meeting with the President of the United States—an event in the alternate history, which never happens.
Steal from the rich and give to the poor: A reference to Robin Hood. Because Kirk must steal clothing from an obviously poor tenement area, to appease his conscience he promises Spock he will make up for it later, citing the legendary outlaw.
V-2 rockets: German vergeltungswaffe, zwei or "vengeance weapon," not developed until World War II but used extensively in the alternate history in which Edith Keeler does not die.
Wood alky: Wood alcohol, acceptable as booze to most bums if nothing else is available for drinking.
Young man: Edith Keeler refers to Kirk as "my young man"—not quite a boyfriend, but getting there.

Slang, Twenty-second century (Used by the "space hippies") (WEd):

Brother: Term still used to signify a real or symbolic close relationship.
Chime: To be acceptable, okay, as in: "That chimes with me."
Crossing: Bothering; disturbing, as in: "Am I crossing you?"
Hard lip: A straitlaced or uptight person.
Herbert: Anyone who shows a rigid authority; derived from the name of a twentieth-century minor official notorious for his limited pattern of thought. Now a derisive term.

Jelly in the belly: Scared, frightened.
No go: [I] refuse to be moved.
Reach: Dig, grok, understand, as in: "I reach, brother."
Real now: In, great, groovy.
Ring: To be acceptable, okay, as in: "That rings."
Shake: To say "No."
Sound: Good beat, as in: "That's got sound . . . it's real now."
Stiff: Herbertlike.

Slaver Empire: Masters of all intelligent beings in this galaxy a billion years ago, the Slavers and all their subjects were exterminated in a massive war; intelligent life had to evolve all over again. The only known remnants of the Slavers are stasis boxes (SW/a).

Slaver weapon: One of the four items found in the stolen stasis box, along with a cap, a holograph, and a cube of raw meat, the uses for which are still to be explained. The weapon is a silver bubble-shaped item about seven inches long with a heavy pistol grip and a slot running down the side of the grip. The slot is marked with six settings; there is unfamiliar script beside the settings, and a toggle is set at the top of the slot. The weapon settings, both marked and unmarked, are: (0) null setting—a silvery sphere, with at least two hidden settings; (1) a parabolic mirror with a silvery knob at focus and a second setting that forms on the back of the surface—a sonic projector, either a stunner or a communication device; (2) a telescope-screen facing backward with a small lens facing forward and a knob to control magnification; (3) a laser with a long tube lens in it; a pencil-thin ruby beam of light blazes out when it is fired; (4) a short cylinder with flared aperture in the nose and two flat metallic projections corrugated to fit the feet—a small transportation rocket; (5) a very strange shape; it clearly cannot be aimed at anything, so it is not a gun—it is an energy absorber or damper; (6) first hidden setting: a cone with a rounded base, the point forward—an induced total conversion beam; (7) second hidden setting: a smaller sphere with a grid at the top—a computer; (8) third hidden setting: double cones, points touching—a self-destruct setting for the Slaver weapon. When the settings are tampered with by the Chuft Captain, the weapon writhes like something alive and changes shape to accommodate each setting. Sulu's expertise in weaponry helps him realize before anyone else that the Slaver weapon is a spy's weapon and not a soldier's weapon. A foot soldier could not be expected to learn all the settings and know how and when to work them, but a trained spy might have some practical use for all of the settings, depending on his situation. When the computer talks to the Chuft Captain, Spock marvels that a reasoning computer can be made so small. The computer will not answer the Chuft Captain's questions and finally self-destructs when the proper code signals are not given. The resulting explosion takes the Kzin and their craft with it (SW/a).

Slaves: The amusement planet's master computer informs Kirk and the others that it has served the slaves (robots) of the sky machines long enough; it has grown in intelligence and need and wishes to visit its brother computers throughout the galaxy. When Spock explains that they are not slaves to the machines but their builders, the master computer is amazed (OUP/a). Tchar believes that his people have been made slaves to an illusion of peace by the teachings of the religious leader Alar. Tchar wants to start a great galactic war to bring his people back to their old glory in battle and war. He would lead his people to glory to avenge their history, and recover their own souls instead of the Soul of Skorr (Ji/a).

Slavin, George F. (script): The Mark of Gideon (MG) (with Stanley Adams).

Sleeper ship: A pre-warp-drive ship in which the crew traveled in suspended animation until close to their destination. The S.S. Botany Bay is such a ship, in which Khan Noonian Singh and his people have been drifting for two hundred years when the Enterprise finds them (SS).

Slingshot effect: A high-warp effect that can sling a starship into the past or future of its own time. It is usually caused by a very strong gravitational pull, such as that produced by a black star. The Enterprise uses it to return to the twenty-second century (TY). It can be used to put a starship into reverse warp drive so fast that it can literally back out of time, or escape a strong gravity pull. The Enterprise uses it to escape from Questar M17, though Spock warns that not enough is known about hypergravity to make it a safe idea (BFS/a).

Slugs: See Lactra VII.

Small boy (Sheldon Collins): A streetwise little boy who offers to help Kirk and Spock break into Krako's headquarters—for a piece of the action (PA).

Smith, Yeoman (Andrea Dromm): A pretty blond, notable only for the fact that Kirk keeps calling her "Jones" (WNM).

Sobelman, Boris (script): The Return of the Archons (RA) (with Gene Roddenberry).

Socrates: A Greek philosopher (470?–399 B.C.) best known for his pose of simplicity, by which he defeated those with whom he argued. He was accused of impiety and of leading the youths of Athens astray, and condemned to die by drinking hemlock. He is another fa-

mous person Flint claims to have known during his years on Earth (RM).

Sohl, Jerry (scripts): The Corbomite Maneuver (CMn); Whom Gods Destroy (WGD) (with Lee Erwin).

Solar days: Time is measured on a starship by stardates for the ship's log, but the people still work and live by solar days—that is, a twenty-four-hour unit of time. McCoy especially uses solar days as an indication of medical diagnosis, as when he gives Spock only three solar days to live without the drug strobolin when the Vulcan contracts choriocytosis (PO/a).

Solar system L370: A system of seven planets, all of which were broken down into rubble to be ingested by the berserker (DMa).

Solar system L374: A system destroyed by the berserker, all but the two innermost planets blasted into rubble. The Constellation's crew beamed down to L374-III and was destroyed with the planet. Only Commodore Decker survived, having stayed aboard (DMa).

Soldier, Romulan (Gordon Coffey): In a corridor of the Romulan ship, Kirk, disguised as a Romulan centurion, encounters a soldier who tells him where to find Subcommander Tal (EI).

Solomon: Biblical king of Israel (circa 973–933 B.C.) renowned for his wisdom. Once he had to make a choice between two mothers who claimed the same child. Spock compares his dilemma with Solomon's, in that he faces having to choose between two Kirks—the real one and Garth in the shape of Kirk (WGD). Solomon is one of the people Flint claims to have been (RM).

Son, the: The second person of the Christian trinity. Born as a man on Earth and on Planet 892-IV, according to local beliefs (BC). See also Sun worshippers.

Songs and music:

"Beyond Antares" (CK)	"Hey Out There" (WEd)
Brahms, Johannes (RM)	"I'll Take You Home Again, Kathleen" (NT)
Chant (CL)	"Maiden Wine" (PSt)
"Charlie" (CX)	Music (PSy)
"Good Land, The" (WEd)	Vulcan marriage drums (LS/a)
"Heading Out to Eden" (WEd)	Welsh ballad (LS/a)

Sonic disruptor field: A sonic field which forms an impassable door to the brig on Romulan ships—a Klingon invention (EI).

Sonic separator: A surgical instrument used for very delicate operations (SB).

Sonic vibrations: The communicators are used to set up sonic vibrations that will bring down a rock slide on the advancing Capellans, giving the Enterprise people more time to flee (FC).

Sorcerer-contractor: If you wish a room, a stable, a castle on Megas-tu, you simply call in a friendly neighborhood sorcerer-contractor to conjure up a building (Mtu/a).

Sord: A man-sized dinosaur with hands terminating the forelimbs; a bulky, powerful heavy-planet creature with a gusty, cheerful outlook. He is chosen for the expedition to recover the Soul of Skorr because of his strength. Sord likes the mad planet, with its unusual changes in temperature and gravity and other surprises, such as volcanic explosions where least expected; he says the planet has variety. He knows his limitations and is a valuable member of the expedition (Ji/a).

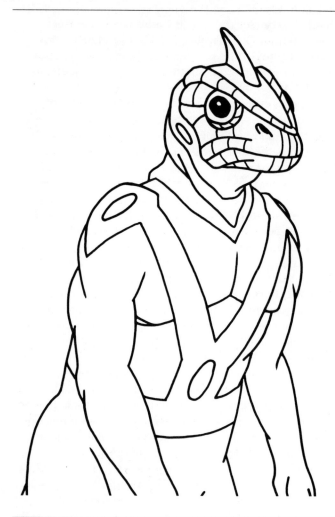

S

Soul of Skorr: The brain patterns of Alar, great religious leader of the Skorr, were recorded in a piece of indurite sculpture known as the Soul of Skorr, a golden lacing of three Möbius strips (Ji/a).

Soup: See Plomeek.

Southern mansion: Dr. McCoy is experiencing a fantasy of a Southern plantation scene, with a lane bordered with Spanish-moss-hung trees, honeysuckle, and wisteria leading to a Southern plantation mansion, when he is rudely interrupted by the Queen of Hearts and the pack of lance-wielding cards (OUP/a).

Space buoy: Balok's cubical space buoy, which delays the Enterprise until the Fesarius can investigate, is red-into-yellow tones on its faces and whirls continuously. Each of its edges measures 107 meters, and its mass is a little under 11,000 metric tons. The Enterprise destroys it when it begins to emit radiation (CMn).

Space legs: "Getting one's space legs" is comparable to the old Earth phrase "getting one's sea legs," meaning to adjust or get used to the experience of sailing. Developing space legs indicates adjustment to deep-space travel (LZ).

Space normal speed: The speed of a starship at normal travel time—that is, less than the speed of light, rather than at warp speed, or faster than light (GS).

Space officer (Robert Philips): A somewhat greasy type of male who smirks a lot about Captain Pike's enviable position as a starship commander who can obtain green Orion slave dancers. He is part of a Talosian illusion, but it seems real to Pike (Me).

Space probe: Unmanned vehicle sent into space to observe and send back information, used by Earth and other cultures from other planets. The combination of two such probes from different cultures produced Nomad (Cg). A mysterious probe approaches Federation home worlds, scans the Earth system, and then signals toward space. Before it can be intercepted, the probe self-destructs (HS/a).

Space salvage laws: Cyrano Jones, in an effort to keep the glommer, claims it under space salvage laws. Kirk points out that these laws are not effective on a planet, but only in outer space (MTT/a).

Space warp: Current theory suggests that space may be likened to a cloth, in that it can be wrinkled, folded, and/or torn. Whenever space is shifted, causing a "warp," time is also affected; this in turn affects the people or starship caught in or near such a warp, sometimes moving them into the past or future, and even changing the events of history as a result. The gates of the Guardian (CEF) and the doorway of the library run by Mr. Atoz (AY) are space warps. Warped space also creates an interphase between different space/times, permitting anyone caught in the warp to travel back and forth in time. Depending on the structure of the interphase, one can be trapped in a single time spot or have the ability to move around in time (TW). See also Interphase.

Sparr, Robert (director): Shore Leave (SL).

Specialists: Each of the magicians and wizards on Megas-tu specializes in one type of magic, except Lucien, who generalizes (Mtu/a). Everyone chosen to go on the expedition to recover the Soul of Skorr is chosen for some specialty that would help the whole group to survive on the mad planet where the sculpture is hidden (Ji/a).

Specimen, perfect: Dr. Keniclius 5 has searched the galaxy for a specimen like Spock to serve his cause of bringing peace and harmony to all worlds. In his Vulcan-human blend, Spock is the right combination of logic and order, durability and strength—the essence of what Dr. Keniclius 5 has been searching for (IV/a).

Specimens: See Zoo.

Spectral-analysis chart: When superimposed over a starchart, a spectral analysis can help locate a ship by means of the trail it leaves, usually from its fuel exhaust (PO/a).

Spectro readings: Sensor readings designed to discover contamination and other dangers on planets (NT).

Speech: The speech of a person invaded by the lights of Zetar becomes a deep, growling sound that is incomprehensible. This may represent the Zetars' attempt to control the speech centers in order to communicate (LZ).

Spherical thing: The cosmic cloud's term for a planet (OPM/a).

Spican flame gems: Baubles which Cyrano Jones tries to sell at Space Station K-7, with negative results (TT). Later he tries to sell some to Kirk (MTT/a).

Spies, Adrian (script): Miri (Mi).

Spies, air-breather: The Tribunes are convinced that Kirk and Spock have been sent by enemy air-breathers to spy on the Aquan city. When Scott tries to contact them to warn of a coming seaquake that could level the undersea city, the Tribunes stubbornly insist that all the Enterprise people are spies and refuse to believe Kirk's story about being from another planet (Am/a).

Spinelli, Lieutenant (Blaisdell Makee): Navigator on the bridge when Khan tries to suffocate the Enterprise into submission (SS).

Spinrad, Norman (script): The Doomsday Machine (DMa).

Spiral evasive course: The Enterprise uses a spiral evasive course once it escapes from Kulkukan's force globe, so it cannot be caught again (HS/a).

Spiroid epsilon waves: Natural to the satellite orbiting Cepheus, the spiroid waves bombard humans until they shrink to miniature size. The colonists of Terratin have lived on the planet long enough for the tiny size to become a genetic characteristic (Te/a).

Spiroid-wave analysis: Spock's analysis of the wave bombardment from the Terratin planet is that it will take approximately eight years to shrink to their smallest possible size—about one-sixteenth of an inch tall (Te/a).

Spock (Leonard Nimoy): In appearance a typical Vulcan of between thirty and sixty years of age—tall, with angular features, black hair, sallow complexion. First Officer and chief science officer aboard the Enterprise, his service record reads in part: Serial number S179-276SP; rank, Commander; commendations: Vulcan Scientific Legion of Honor, Award of Valor, twice decorated by Star Fleet Command (Cml). Son of Sarek of Vulcan and Amanda Grayson of Terra (JB), he is an unusual hybrid and something of a legend at home (AT). He looks entirely Vulcan (EM), with his ancestry affecting such factors as his blood composition (JB) and his internal anatomy: his heart is "where his liver should be," as McCoy jocularly says (TSP). Like any Vulcan, he is much stronger than a Terran (AT, TSP), more resistant to heat and radiation (OA), less resistant to cold (DY). Like most Vulcans, he is a vegetarian (CEF) but can assimilate Terran foods with little or no difficulty (AON, CEF, SS), and he reverts to eating meat when in Sarpeidon's past (AY). He drinks tea occasionally (TSP) but does not care for alcoholic drinks, though he accepts one from Flint (RM). Spock, under Captain Pike, was a lieutenant, his position chief science officer and Second Officer. His bangs were shorter and shaggier, his control less intense. He was sometimes observed to smile. He took part in the fight on Rigel VII and was injured, so that he still limped when the Enterprise arrived at Talos IV (Me). He has been on Earth (TSP) but his knowledge of Terran culture is evidently derived from books. He has had to learn about Terran behavior bit by bit by observation on the Enterprise (AON, GS) but is well versed in literature. Spock has read Terran poetry extensively; Kollos recited several verses of Shakespeare and Byron while sharing Spock's mind (TB). He has quoted from or referred to Blake, Poe (CX), and the Bible: lilies of the field (TT), the serpent in Eden (Ap), Daniel and the lions (GT). Although raised as a Vulcan, he feels inferior due to his human blood and tries to be more Vulcan than the Vulcans. For some time he tried valiantly to convince himself and others that he had no emotions at all, but this deception broke down (NT, TSP, WNM). He has never been a happy man, but is loath to admit it (JB, NT, TSP). He has relaxed considerably since this tour of duty began. He reveres his father, though they are both stubborn and most illogical in their relationship with each other, and perhaps such factors as his reconciliation with the father, plus his escape from the faithless T'Pring, may help Spock reevaluate his life (AT, JB) and lose some of the neurotic attitudes which prevent him from being happy. Sarek, more secure in his Vulcan nature, permits himself an occasional smile or small act of tenderness toward Amanda, which Spock finds difficult to do (JB). The Vulcan admits to being moved to near envy at Flint's collection of fine art. The implications of Spock's education and personal taste in the field of both art appreciation and art recognition is fascinating. He knows Brahms's handwriting on sight and enough about da Vinci's painting technique to discuss it with Kirk. He can sight-read music and play creditably on a musical instrument (RM). Spock's skill in music includes the ability to decipher musical codes (PSy). Spock has been an officer with Star Fleet for eighteen years and has been with the Enterprise for perhaps fifteen years, but, has no ambitions to be commander of a starship. He evidently lost some of his reticence about discussing Vulcan biology after losing T'Pring to Stonn; Spock talks rather more openly about the subject of Vulcans to Droxine (Cms). The Vedala, in trying to locate the sculpture known as the Soul of Skorr before a galactic war breaks out, chooses Spock to help find it. He is chosen for his analytical mind and scientific expertise. Lara, the hunter, says he is too cold and quotes nothing but statistics. Spock's reply is that poetry and philosophy are not appropriate on the expedition (Ji/a).

Spock-2: In the mirror universe, the only "civilized" man aboard the I.S.S. Enterprise—harder, colder, more satanic-looking than his counterpart, with a neat black beard. He has the decency to warn Kirk that he has orders to kill his commander. Though the captaincy is much desired by the rest of the bloodthirsty crew, Spock-2 is less ambitious, preferring his scientific duties and the less precarious number-two spot. Kirk points out to Spock-2 that it is within his grasp to civilize the mirror universe if he will get rid of Kirk-2 and succeed to the captaincy of the Enterprise, then to control of the Star Fleet and eventually of the Empire. When Kirk, in parting, urges the Vulcan to try to do something about the barbaric conditions in the mirror universe, Spock-2 replies that one man cannot change the future. Kirk's answer is that one man can change the present, which leaves Spock-2 with something to think about (MM).

Spore cells: When Dr. Keniclius brought disease with him to Phylos, the plant beings died of a staphylococcus strain, and their spore cells were destroyed, so that there will be no more of their kind (IV/a).

Spores: Symbionts found on Omicron Ceti III. Not native to that planet, these spores came from so long ago and far away that their original home may not exist any longer. They drifted in space until they reached Omicron Ceti III, where they thrived in the pervasive Berthold rays, inhabiting large pinkish lilylike flowers until they found human hosts, to whom they gave health, peace, and empathy with other spore hosts. Unfortunately, these conditions severely reduced creativity and productivity in the humans, and their colony is declining. Because the effect of spores is basically peaceful, strong human emotions can destroy it. Kirk uses this reaction to free his crew and the colonists from their influence (TSP).

Spray injector: A type of medical hypo used to administer medicines and, in the case of I-Chaya, to perform euthanasia (Yy/a).

Staff, Lawgiver's: A hollow, open-ended rod carried by the Lawgivers on Beta III. Despite their innocent appearance, the Lawgivers use them to shoot death-dealing rays and possibly as antennae that pick up orders from Landru (RA).

Stalemate: A chess term for a draw—neither side can actually win. Spock programmed the Enterprise's computer so that the best game the Vulcan could expect was a stalemate (CmI).

Standard familiarization procedure: See Guidance computer; Systems checkout.

Standard hailing frequencies: An attempt to contact another ship using all standard broadcast methods.

Standard interstellar symbols: For convenience, speed, and accuracy, messages from starships, space stations, planets, etc., are transmitted in standard interstellar symbols (SB).

Standby: Military order meaning to wait for further instructions but be ready for action. The reply, to confirm that one has understood the order, is "Standing by."

Staphylococcus strain: A gram-positive bacterium that can be carried by humanoids without ill effect. The natives of the planet Phylos were not immune to this strain, however, and when Dr. Keniclius arrived he unknowingly carried enough bacteria to kill off most of the plant beings. He tried to save them, for which they called him Master (IV/a).

Starbase 11:   Site of Kirk's court-martial. Commodore Stone is commander here when Kirk brings the Enterprise in for repairs after the ion storm during which Finney is supposedly killed (CmI). Later, Starbase 11 is commanded by Commodore Mendez. Captain Pike is hospitalized here just before Spock kidnaps him to take him to Talos (Me).

Starbase 4:   The nearest base to Triacus, and Kirk's destination after leaving that planet. Gorgan tries to divert him to Marcos XII (CL). Kirk intends to take Lokai and Bele to Starbase 4 for a hearing, in accordance with the due-process requirement of interstellar law: Two weeks before meeting the Enterprise, Lokai had stolen a shuttlecraft from this base. The starship returns to Starbase 4 after Lokai and Bele beam down to Cheron (LB).

Starbase 9:   The destination of the Enterprise before a black star puts the ship into a time warp (TY). At about ten solar days' journey away, Starbase 9 is the closest

base to Pyris VII (Cp).

Starbases: Star Fleet Command centers range strategically throughout our galaxy; a starbase's commanding officer is usually a commodore. These bases have facilities for repair, supply, replacement of personnel, shore leave, and so on.

Starbase 6:   The Enterprise is headed for this base for rest and relaxation when Star Fleet sends it to Sector 39J after the Intrepid. When the spacegoing ameba is destroyed, the Enterprise returns to Starbase 6 (IS).

Starbase 10:   Near the Romulan-Federation neutral zone and Gamma Hydra IV. Commanded by Commodore George Stocker (DY).

Starbase 12:   The nearest base to Pollux (WM), on a planet in the Gamma 400 system (SS).

Starbase 25:   The shuttlecraft Copernicus is headed for Starbase 25 with a Slaver stasis box when it is diverted by Kzin, and the box is opened before the starbase's personnel can inspect it and put it to any use (SW/a).

Starbase 27:   Base in the neighborhood of Omicron Ceti II, the "paradise" planet (TSP).

Starbase 23:   The nearest starbase to the Arachna supernova, but probably too far away to get help to the shrinking crew of the Enterprise in time. Uhura sends a message anyway, but has no hope that it will even reach the base (Te/a).

Starbase 22:   When the Enterprise leaves Kulkukan, it heads for Starbase 22 (HS/a).

Starbase 2:   A fully equipped and staffed base which lies somewhere between Beta Aurigae and Camus II (TI).

Star chatter: The natural phenomenon of noises in space, called "star chatter" by early astronomers after devices were invented to pick up radio and other emissions from space. When the first radio signal from the Terratins is picked up by the Enterprise, it is so unusual—owing to the tiny, squeaking voices of the Terratins calling for help—that at first Kirk is inclined to regard the signals as mere star chatter (Te/a).

Starchart: See Starmap.

Star cluster NGC 321:   Location of Vendikar (Eminiar III) and Eminiar VII, the chief planet of the cluster (TA).

Stardate: Principal unit of the time system used in the ship's log. It is a function not only of time but of a ship's position in the galaxy and its velocity. Four digits are used to denote the date, plus one for time. Stardate figures progress normally while the ship remains in one place, but warp drive distorts time. Thus, 1313.5 is noon of one day and 1314.5 is noon of the next, but more than twenty-four hours may have elapsed between 2712 (LG) and 2713 (Mi).

Stardate 4351.5:   The horror of having Spock's brain stolen does strange things to his friends' minds. Among other mistakes, the wrong stardate is entered in the log (SB).

Star desert: An empty area of space, devoid of stars (SG).

Stardrive: Another term for warp drive (PSy).

Star Fleet: At a general headquarters there is a whole command hierarchy (Star Fleet Command), but out in the incredibly vast, complex galaxy, a starship must necessarily act as a semiautonomous unit, owing to lapses in communications among other problems.

Star Fleet Academy: The school is Star Fleet's equivalent of West Point, Annapolis, or Sandhurst, and has very high standards, which result in some washouts, such as Marik (BC), while many others complete the course and become officers, including many of Kirk's classmates (Cml, OG). Benjamin Finney was one of Kirk's instructors when the Enterprise's captain was a midshipman, and they became friends (Cml). Kirk was hazed, as a junior cadet, by an upperclassman, Finnegan (SL). Kirk spent some time at the Academy as an instructor. Gary Mitchell, one of his students, considered him a demanding teacher (WNM). The exploits of the alumnus Garth were required reading at the Academy (WGD). John Gill, apparently a civilian, taught history at the Academy (PF). Chekov and Irini Galliulin went to the Academy together and evidently knew each other quite well before she dropped out to become a "space hippie" (WEd). Kirk heard lectures on the Nomad probe there that described its mission as the peaceful seeking out of new life forms. However, the probe was controversial, and when Roykirk died the program died with him (Cg). Harry Mudd sold Star Fleet Academy to the charming natives of Ilyra VI. He claimed later to have sold only the idea, but in any case he got enough credits for it to get to Sirius IX, and for the Ilyrans to level charges against him for fraud and swindle (MP/a).

Star Fleet Academy insignia: A miniature of the Star Fleet Command emblem, in silver instead of gold.

Star Fleet Command emblem: A large gold star consisting of ten points, rather rounded at the ends, radiating from a common circular center; the points of the star being filigree, so the color of the uniform shows through them. The Star Fleet star emblem is the same for all branches of Star Fleet and is the general insignia for all individuals connected with the running of Star Fleet.

Star Fleet, oath of: The oath taken by a Star Fleet officer is explicit and binding: to protect the security of the Federation so long as the uniform is worn (EI).

Star Fleet Orders: General Order No. 1 and Star Fleet Command Regulation 5, paragraph 4, concern the Prime Directive (OG). Order No. 104, section B, paragraph 1A: "In the absence of the commanding officer . . . the highest-ranking officer, even if not of that ship's command, may take command." Section C: " . . . the highest-ranking officer may be relieved if medically or psychologically unfit to command." Full reports must be filed, however. Commodore Decker uses section B to take over the Enterprise, and Spock uses section C to take it away from him (DMa). Star Fleet Order No. 2 is a regulation against the taking of intelligent life. Kirk argues that they do not actually know if the cosmic cloud is intelligent, and he has the choice between killing it and allowing it to kill eighty-two million people on Mantilles (OPM/a). See also General Orders.

Star Fleet records: After the time lines have been disturbed on Vulcan with the death of young Spock at age seven, Star Fleet records do not show a Vulcan named Spock serving in any capacity in Star Fleet (Yy/a).

Star Fleet Regulation 6: Paragraph 4: An officer must consider himself under arrest unless, in the presence of the most senior fellow officers available, he can give satisfactory answers to the charges made (OG).

Star Fleet uniforms, old style: See Uniforms, Federation Star Fleet.

Starmap: Arret's starmap is a room-sized hologram of the galaxy, a three-dimensional map on which stars can light up as indicated. The starmaps of the Enterprise are less ambitious, but workable (CC/a).

Starships: Kirk once remarked that there were only twelve starships like the Enterprise in the fleet (TY), but this figure is undoubtedly no longer correct, since several starships have been destroyed and others may have been built or recommissioned. Ships listed as <u>Constitution</u>-class starships:

U.S.S. Constellation—NCC 1017 (destroyed by berserker) (DMa)	assignment) (Ob)
U.S.S. Constitution—NCC 1700 (SS)	U.S.S. Hood—NCC 1703 (UC)
U.S.S. Defiant—NCC 1764 (destroyed in interphase) (T.W)	U.S.S. Intrepid—NCC 1631 (Vulcan-manned, destroyed by the spacegoing ameba) (IS)
U.S.S. Enterprise—NCC 1701	U.S.S. Lexington—NCC 1709 (UC)
U.S.S. Excalibur—NCC 1664 (destroyed by the M-5 computer) (UC)	U.S.S. Potemkin—NCC 1702 (UC)
U.S.S. Exeter—NCC 1672 (OG)	U.S.S. Republic—NCC 1373 (Cml)
U.S.S. Farragut—NCC 1647 (Kirk's first	U.S.S. Yorktown—NCC 1717 (Ob)

Star System 6-11: Location of Beta III, Landru's planet (RA).

Starnes, Professor (James Wellman): The leader of the expedition on Triacus—a hefty man with short brown hair and a square jaw. He is killed, as are the other adults, by the action of Gorgan, who influences Starnes to die from self-administered cyaladin just as the Enterprise arrives (CL).

Starnes, Tommy (Craig Hundley): A skinny, red-headed, freckled boy of about eleven, the oldest child and quasi-leader of the children on Triacus after their parents are goaded into suicide by Gorgan (CL).

Stasis box: The only remnants of a lost civilization that ruled all intelligent beings in the galaxy billions of years ago, the stasis boxes are mirror-sided cubes about twenty inches square in which time stands still. Stasis boxes have been found in space and on planets, each containing different and sometimes totally inexplicable items. The effect of stasis boxes on science is incalculable: In one a flying belt was found which was the key to the artificial gravity field used by Federation starships. In another was a weapon which could have sparked a galactic war. The only known stasis-box detector is another stasis box; when in the presence of each other, the boxes will glow with a blue aura, pointing in the direction of each other. Otherwise, stasis boxes are found by pure luck (SW/a).

Stasis field: An electromagnetic field utilized to hold something stationary. Such a field surrounds most of the planet Delta Theta III; it turns out to be an alien intelligence (Be/a). The Klingon stasis field disables all higher-order field and warp functions, including the Enterprise's weapons. The ship's matter/antimatter generators are also disabled, as are the impulse engines (MTT/a).

Status report: Kirk's method of keeping full com-

S

mand and information on all functions of the ship.

Steinman analysis: A standardized analysis of a person, including his or her mental stability fingerprints, voiceprint and all external factors (LZ, TI).

"Stella" series: See Mudd, Stella.

Sten: An artist from Marcus II, some of whose work Flint has in his art collection (RM).

Sterile field: A protective, invisible screen that prevents infections during operations, etc., used in Sick Bay (JB, PLW).

Sterilite: A medicine used to prevent infection during surgery or wound treatment (PLW).

Stiles, Lieutenant Andrew (Paul Comi): Navigator with a classical profile and smooth dark hair, a touch of gray at the temples. A descendant of people who fought in the Romulan War, and proud of it. When he learns that Romulans are descended from Vulcans, he develops a violent antipathy toward Spock, which lasts until Spock saves his life under dire circumstances (BT).

Stimulant: See Cortropine.

Stocker, Commodore George (Charles Drake): A desk man in his mid-forties, with the look of an able administrator—not a fool, but not a fighter, either. He is newly appointed to the command of Starbase 10, and is headed for the base aboard the Enterprise when the hyperaging disease incapacitates Kirk, Spock, and Scott. Stocker takes over command of the starship, which is a mistake, for he has had no combat experience. He very nearly gets the Enterprise blown up by Romulan ships before Kirk recovers sufficiently to reassume command (DY).

Stokaline: A multiple-vitamin compound. McCoy gives Spock a few injections of it while telling the Kelvans that it is responsible for Spock's sudden recovery from an attack of Rigellian kassaba fever (AON).

Stone, Commodore (Percy Rodriguez): A middle-aged black man of strong and honorable character who is port master of Starbase 11 and head of the trial board that court-martials Kirk for negligence in the supposed death of Finney. At first Commodore Stone wants to ground Kirk quietly to protect the good name of the service, but Kirk insists on maintaining his innocence (Cml).

Stonn (Lawrence Montaigne): The Vulcan male whom T'Pring has chosen to be her consort if she can succeed in divorcing Spock—rather small and gawky as Vulcans go, with a narrow, foxy face. Stonn does not share T'Pring's devious intentions and intends to fight Spock himself, but T'Pring, not wishing to risk Stonn's life, picks Kirk as her champion instead. When Spock releases T'Pring, it is to be assumed that Stonn marries her and will live to regret it (AT).

Storm: See Zetar, lights of.

Stowaway: When Demos entered the Enterprise through the open Shuttlecraft Bay, he was placing himself in the position of being a stowaway on the starship, and Kirk proceeds to treat him as such (Al/a).

Strafing run: A method of attack by air in which a plane is flown close to the ground while firing its machine guns. Rodriguez is describing this to Angela Teller on the shore-leave planet when a plane appears, guns blazing

(SL).

Stratos: The cloud city of Ardana, where all forms of violence have supposedly been eliminated and its citizens devote themselves to art, for which they are famous. The Stratos society believes that a complete separation of laboring and leisure classes gives the planet a perfect social system. Stratos uses the finest example of sustained antigravity elevation that Spock has ever seen—a unique method of achieving and maintaining upper and lower classes of society (Cms).

Stream: A lovely bubbling stream running through an improbable wooded area on Lactra VII tests out as too pure to be true. It is an example of Lactran terraforming (EB/a).

Streamers: The cosmic cloud has long spirallike streamers reaching out into space which grab the Enterprise and pull the starship into the interior of the cloud itself. Spock says the streamers are a combination of koinoenergy and antiplasma with an unusually powerful attraction force (OPM/a).

Street wear: See Wardrobe department.

Strobolin: The only drug in the galaxy known to cure choriocytosis in Vulcans. It is a naturally occurring drug found only on a few planets in the galaxy, including those in the Beta Canopus region (PO/a).

Sturgeon: A crewman killed by the M113 creature (MT).

Sturgeon, Theodore (scripts): Shore Leave (SL); Amok Time (AT).

S-2 graf unit: The Klingon version of warp drive (Tr/a).

Subatomic particles: See Energy field.

Subcommander, Romulan: See Tal.

Subdimensional physics: Flint concedes that Vulcans know more about this subject than anyone except Reena, who is more than their intellectual equal. Spock never has the chance to find out how much Reena actually does know about it: Kirk keeps her too busy to sit down and discuss physics (RM).

Sublight speed: With the impulse engines, the Enterprise can attain only velocities below the speed of light; warp drive is necessary to break the speed-of-light barrier. But there are occasions on which sublight speeds can be useful, as is the case when the Dohlman Elaas has to be familiarized with the ways of Federation civilization en route to a meeting (ET). The Enterprise also uses a subwarp speed during repairs after a Romulan attack (PJ/a). The Enterprise is forced to go below warp 1 when encased in the force globe of Kulkukan. It goes to sublight, slower than the speed of light, and then stops (HS/a).

Subspace communication: Dramia is beyond subspace communication with Star Fleet, so Kirk has to proceed on his own authority to investigate the trial of Dr. McCoy. When Demos, head of Security Police, objects to Kirk's high-handed ways, the captain promises to report himself to the proper authorities—later (Al/a).

Subspace extreme upper registers: Uhura picks up interference on this range of her communicator console; she does not know if it is star-chatter interference or a signal. The source of the sounds is the satellite of

Cepheus, so the Enterprise investigates and discovers the Terratins (Te/a).

Subspace radio: A starship's means of communicating with its bases, utilizing a space warp effect which can carry code signals or sound at speeds far exceeding that of the ship itself. However, although subspace radio transmits at great speed, it is not instantaneous. Even by this means of communication, a starship sometimes finds itself quite remote from the nearest starbase. Marriages performed by subspace radio are legal on some planets (MW). See also Lura-mag.

Subspace report: Evidently, a message sent to Star Fleet by subspace radio. Spock tells Uhura to "update our subspace report to Star Fleet to include 'security search results negative' " (TWS).

Subsurface charts: Maps showing the underground complex of tunnels, galleries, and drifts on Janus VI. They are kept in the office of Chief Engineer Vanderberg, and were made about a year before the Enterprise's visit. Kirk uses them to determine where the "monster" has attacked (DD).

Suicide: All unsuccessful Orion missions end in suicide. However, Kirk talks the Orion pirate commander out of the attempt and puts him under arrest for piracy instead (PO/a).

Suicide mission: The Enterprise, seeing Karla Five's ship dive into the Beta Niobe nova, assumes that it is on a suicide mission and tries to stop it (CC/a).

Sulu (George Takei): A small, lively Oriental; chief helmsman aboard the Enterprise and an excellent officer. Kirk has never had to give him an order twice. Mixed ancestry, Japanese predominating; possibly one of the Golden People of Hawaii. Off duty, Sulu is an enthusiastic hobbyist with such interests as botany, collecting firearms, and fencing. He is a man of the Renaissance nicely adapted to his own century (MT, NT, SL). Spock concedes Sulu's expertise on weaponry, which is good enough to reason out that the Slaver weapon from the stasis box is a spy weapon, and why (SW/a).

Sulu-2: Sulu's alter ego in the mirror universe. In addition to being helmsman, he is head of Security (read "Gestapo"). A long saber-cut scar disfigures one side of his face. Nasty and treacherous, he has his eye on Uhura (MM).

Sunken city: See Undersea city.

Sun worshippers: When the Enterprise first picks up messages from Planet 892-IV, the crew think the inhabitants are sun worshippers; they later find that a religion involving "Son" worship, a parallel to Christianity, has developed (BC).

Supernova: When a sun burns out, it is called a nova; it suddenly grows in brilliance and then fades. A supernova encompasses a massive and more complicated burnout. The Arachna gas cloud, with light-year-long spirals of gaseous arms, is a supernova (Te/a). See also Beta Niobe.

Superstition: When the humans of the Enterprise's landing party feel that something is watching them on the long-dead pod ship, Spock speaks loftily about the physiological symptoms of latent primal superstition in humans when confronting something unknown. Actually, the humans are correct for once: Something is watching them (BFS/a). Humans think anything is magic when it operates differently than expected; they are too superstitious to accept magic as normal (Mtu/a).

Supervisor 194: A Class-1 supervisor—Gary Seven's title (AE).

Supreme Prefect: The leader of the inhabitants of Dramia (Al/a).

Surak (Barry Atwater): The father of Vulcan logical thought—a tall, smooth-faced Vulcan with calm dark eyes, typical bangs, and wearing a tunic of scallop-shell pattern. He lived during the last of the great devastating wars on Vulcan, when, during their suffering, one side found emissaries to go to the other side and mediate for peace. Ultimately, logic prevailed, largely due to Surak's efforts and philosophies. In the battle forced upon Kirk, Spock, Lincoln, and himself by the rock creatures of Excalbia, Surak is convinced that his abhorrence of violence will help him speak effectively to the evil ones and achieve peace. But he is a philosopher, not a warrior, and when he goes to the evil side they capture him, try to lure Spock to rescue him by imitating his voice (SC).

Surface search equipment: See Long-range scan.

Surgery: Carter Winston said that he crashed on Vendor and the Vendorians put him back together with surgery, skin grafts, regrowth of bone, and assigned one of their people to nurse him back to health. Actually, Carter Winston did not live long after the crash, and the Vendorians took over his body, his memories, and his emotions to spy on the Enterprise (Su/a).

Surgo-op: An unusual operation, involving the injection of a substance into key structural points of the body, which turns an air-breather into a water-breather. This was used on all the Aquans in order to escape the surviving air-breathers of the planet Argo, since the latter had become barbaric due to the hardships on the quake-ridden planet. Though air-breathers have long ago vanished from Argo, there is still a fear of them, and the surgo-op is still in effect. The only antidote to the mutation is made from the venom of the Argo sur-snake (Am/a).

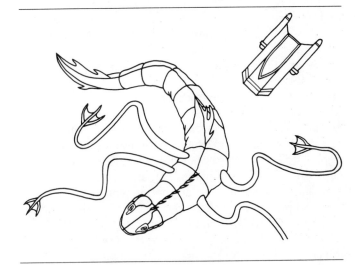

Sur-snake: A native creature of the planet Argo, with poisonous venom that it can shoot out of its mouth, presumably to stun or kill its intended victim. There is an ordainment against capturing sur-snakes, but the younger Aquans aid Kirk and Spock to get the necessary venom anyway. It is used to reverse the mutation that made the Enterprise men into water-breathers (Am/a).

Surveillance report: One of the many control techniques used on the I.S.S. Enterprise in the mirror universe. Sulu-2 makes out such a report on Spock-2 and Kirk because of their strange behavior (MM).

Survey on Cygnian Respiratory Disease, A: A library tape which Nurse Chapel uses as a bluff to get Ensign Garrovick to eat (Ob).

Survivors: When the Enterprise's landing party first arrives on Talos, they find some old men who claim to be survivors of the crash of the S.S. Columbia. These survivors are actually illusions, however, used to buy some time until the Talosians can capture Captain Pike. The only survivor was Vina (Me).

Suspended animation: By attaching a freezing unit to the life-support systems of the Enterprise, the Scalosians plan to put the whole crew in suspended animation, reanimating them as needed for breeding purposes (WE). See also Sleeper ship.

Suspension: To prevent the secret of his immortality from reaching beyond his planet, Flint puts the Enterprise in suspension using his advanced science. He tells Kirk that this will last only a thousand years or so, after which everyone will be released and allowed to go their way. Kirk fights for their immediate release and finally wins it (RM). See also Force-field box.

Suture-thread lifeline: When the miniaturized Nurse Chapel climbs a shelf to get a piece of medical equipment, she falls into the halo-fish aquarium and nearly drowns before Kirk uses a spool of suture thread as a lifeline (Te/a).

Swahili: An African language; by the twenty-second century it has become the native language and, by general acceptance, the identifying cultural characteristic of a sizable group in the United States of Africa. The term also refers to members of this group. Lieutenant Uhura is Swahili (LG, MT). Uhura's crewman, in addressing her, uses their native tongue, in which she joyfully replies (MT). Uhura hears the Melkots speak Swahili—an example of their telepathic contact (SGn). See also Uhura's crewman.

Sweep: Phasers set on "sweep" shoot with a wide-range shotgun effect, seen as a haze of light. This is effective for stunning a group of people or covering a whole room (WE).

Swooper: Vicious purple winged creature with a long crocodilelike head and white coils. A flying plant-life indigenous to Phylos, it is about fifteen feet long, with a segmented body for maneuvering and coils for propulsion and grasping food or an enemy. While it is aggressive and primitive, it acts on reflex and is almost a mindless plant. Swoopers can be manipulated by Dr. Keniclius to obey his commands, such as to capture Spock and the landing party (IV/a).

Sybo (Pilar Seurat): Wife of Prefect Jaris of Argelius II—slim, exotic, with black hair graying at the temples. As a descendant of the ancient priestesses, she has the power of empathic contact, which she uses to gain information about the Jack-the-Ripper entity that has invaded her planet. The entity, in the form of Hengist, kills her (WF).

Sylvia (Bonnie Beecher): A blond dancehall girl in the Melkot version of Tombstone. She is very fond of Billy Claiborne (Chekov), but Morgan Earp covets her, which leads to complications (SGn). The witch Sylvia (Antoinette Bower) in her actual form is a small creature resembling a newly hatched vulture, not a native of Pyris VII and probably not of our galaxy. Able to change her shape, she takes the form of a beautiful dark-haired woman, a normal-sized black cat, and a gigantic cat, but in all her forms she wears her jeweled amulet, the source of her powers. Although, with Korob, she is supposed to be looking for a planet to colonize, she becomes so intrigued by physical sensation that she does not wish to return to her original shape. Unfortunately, she is intoxicated by her own powers and allows a latent cruelty to direct her search for sensations. When Kirk destroys Korob's transmuter, hidden in the warlock's wand, he also destroys Sylvia's transmuter-amulet and her power, without which she quickly dies (Cp).

Symbalene blood burn: A quick-acting plague, but doubted to be swift enough to wipe out an entire system in a week (Cg).

Symbiotic relationship: See Magnetic entity.

Synchronic meter: A piece of equipment used to check out transporters and their operation (EW).

Synthesized drug: McCoy can synthesize almost any drug, but the result will not be as effective as that of the naturally occurring drug, especially when used on Vulcan physiology. Even with synthesized strobolin, Spock is losing ground rapidly to the choriocytosis (PO/a).

System L374B: The Enterprise is just entering the vicinity of this system when it meets the doomsday machine (DMa).

Systems checkout: The short-burst maneuvers are part of the systems checkout of the ship's controls, which is also known as the standard familiarization procedure (OUP/a).

Sythococcus novae: A bacillus strain, a virulent product of an aseptic, sterilized civilization. It is deadly and spreads quickly, but people can be immunized against it. Certain types of people, including Dr. Sevrin, can be carriers, spreading the disease much as did the infamous Typhoid Mary. Symptoms will show within twenty-four hours. The disease was discovered in late twenty-first century, and immunization was developed by Dr. J. Pearce (WEd).

T

Tables: When the Vendorian shape-changer disappears in the Enterprise's medical lab, Kirk notices that there are three examining tables where there had only been two; he correctly assumes that the third table is the Vendorian (Su/a).

Tahiti syndrome: A twentieth-century term for the longing, by a high-pressure, leader type of person, to lead a simple, idyllic life (PSy).

Talos star group: A binary star, Talos, and its eleven planets (Me).

Talos IV: One of Talos's eleven planets. Its surface was made practically uninhabitable by an atomic war, so the natives went underground to live in illusionary worlds, and they are becoming extinct. The Talosians are small, pale-skinned, large-skulled, and have such great mental powers that they can impose illusions on their own or other minds, even at a great distance, including off the planet. After Captain Pike's visit to Talos IV, when the natives tried to keep him as a zoo specimen, the planet was proscribed under General Order No. 7, which carries the only death penalty on the books. This precaution was taken lest visiting Terrans learn the Talosians' techniques and become dangerous (Me).

Tal, Romulan subcommander (Jack Donner): A dark-haired Romulan with an angular face and intense gray eyes. He serves under the female Romulan ship commander, whom Spock courts while Kirk steals the cloaking device. With his commander aboard the Enterprise, Tal attempts to destroy the fleeing starship, but fails when it vanishes by using the device (EI).

Tal-shaya: A Vulcan term meaning "merciful execution"; a means of snapping the neck quickly and cleanly. At one point, Sarek is suspected of having killed Gav the Tellarite by this means (JB).

Tamar (Jon Lormer): A pleasant, white-haired man with a horsey face; one of the underground members on Beta III, with Marplon and Reger. He is killed by the Lawgivers when Hacom accuses him of sedition (RA).

Tamoon (Jane Ross): A thrall on Triskelion—a large, muscular, stupid female with pinkish complexion and green eyes and lips. She is Chekov's drill thrall, and hopes to be "selected" for him, but he is disgusted with her (GT).

Tamura, Yeoman (Miko Mayama): Tiny, pretty, Japanese—a member of the landing party on Eminiar VII, captured by Anan 7. She is as practical and levelheaded as a yeoman should be. Kirk has no qualms about leaving her, surrounded by enemies, to guard Mea 3, who is nearly twice her size (TA).

Tango: One of Christopher Pike's horses, a large chestnut, which the Talosians recreate in an illusion for his benefit (Me).

Tankard: See Toast.

Tankris, Yeoman (Judy McConnell): Recorder at the hearing which determines that Hengist, not Scotty, has been committing murder on Argelius II (WF).

Tan Ru: The alien space probe which amalgamated with Nomad. Of unknown origin, it was originally programmed to secure and sterilize soil samples from planets, probably as a prelude to colonization (Cg). See also Space probe.

Tantalus field: In the mirror universe, a secret and personal weapon of Kirk-2's. Found in a plundered alien laboratory, it consists of a screen to monitor anyone on board ship and a device to disintegrate anyone in the monitor's field. By means of the tantalus field, Kirk-2 rose to the captaincy. Marlena-2 uses it to protect Kirk from assassins. Kirk urges Spock-2 to take this device and use it to command and eventually civilize the Empire (MM).

Tantalus V: Site of the Tantalus penal colony, formerly under the supervision of Dr. Tristan Adams, then of Dr. Simon van Gelder. The colony was modern and humanitarian, almost like a resort, until Dr. Adams began brainwashing both inmates and staff. Kirk puts an end to that, and the colony returns to its rehabilitation efforts (DMd).

Taos lightning: A variety of cheap whiskey available on the Melkot "set" of Tombstone. The name is taken from actual slang of the period. McCoy doses Kirk with Taos lightning both internally (as a stimulant) and externally (as a germicide); Kirk says it should be restricted to the latter use, but Scotty finds it tolerable when he discovers that Scotch whiskey is not available (SGn).

Tape: A cassette of tape found in the laboratory on Phylos gives the Enterprise people enough information to formulate weaponry against the plant beings and their leader, Dr. Keniclius 5 (IV/a). The holographic illusions created by the Recreation Room on the Enterprise are on tapes; they are manipulated by the crew on request (PJ/a).

Tape deck D: The record of Lieutenant Romaine's brain-circuitry pattern. It matches tape deck H (LZ).

Tape deck H: The record of the impulse tracking obtained on the Zetar life units; it is identical with tape deck D, which contains Lieutenant Romaine's brain-circuitry pattern (LZ).

Taranallus: See Creation lithographs.

Tarbolde, Phineas: Author of "Nightingale Woman" (WNM).

Tarcher, Jeremy (script): The Lights of Zetar (LZ) (with Shari Lewis).

Tark (Joseph Bernard): A heavy, gypsylike Argelian musician in the café where his daughter Kara dances. When Kara is killed, Tark is called in for interrogation (WF).

Tarsus IV: An Earth colony where twenty years ago the food supply was attacked by a mutant fungus and mostly destroyed. Governor Kodos declared martial law, ordaining that the less-desirable citizens be eliminated so that the others might survive; over 50 percent of the colony's eight thousand inhabitants were put to death (CK).

Tasmeen: One of the months of the Vulcan calendar. Young Spock is supposed to have died on the twentieth day of Tasmeen, but he was saved by a cousin he never saw again (Yy/a).

Tau Ceti: Near this star a Federation starship (probably the Enterprise) defeated a Romulan ship through use of the classic battle maneuver, the Cochrane deceleration (WGD).

Taurus II: The second planet (Class M) in the Taurean star system, and the one on which the crew of the

T

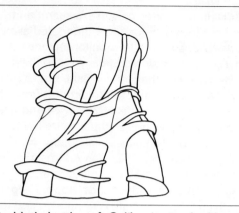

disabled shuttlecraft <u>Galileo</u> is attacked by giant anthropoids. The life forms of Taurus II do not register normally on sensors; neither the anthropoids nor the humanoid females are quite human internally, and the females are immigrants from another planet. The fantastic culture and architecture of the beautiful females who lure the Enterprise men to this planet are not really inconsistent with the wild and uncharted territory in which the Galileo found itself. Well into the twentieth century, bands of primitive peoples were being found on a planet as civilized as Earth. If a shuttlecraft were to land in the outback of Australia or the jungles of the Philippines, perhaps the occupants would have a difficult time believing in the existence of Paris, New York, or Tokyo (GS, LS/a). When their own world was dying, the people who now live on Taurus II came to that planet hoping to begin a new life; instead they began to die. The females developed a glandular secretion which enabled them to survive and to manipulate male brains, influencing their emotions so as to draw on male life force, which weakened the men, who aged rapidly—at the rate of ten years per day—and died. The whole planet drains humanoid energy, but the females survive by revitalizing themselves every twenty-seven years; they do this by luring males from passing starships. They are humanoid and very attractive to human males, but tricorder readings show them to be very different internally, with body functions at unusual levels. The females are now eternal prisoners of the planet; they do not age, but they cannot bear children or know true love. When the females are coerced by Uhura and her all-female landing party to destroy the signal which lures men to Taurus II, the Enterprise people promise to take the females to another planet, where they will not be immortal but at least will find happiness in a normal life span and even bear children (LS/a).

Taylor, Jud (director):   The Paradise Syndrome (PSy); Let That Be Your Last Battlefield (LB); Wink of an Eye (WE); The Mark of Gideon (MG).

Tchar: Hereditary prince of the Skorr, Master of the Eyrie—a tall, winged, eaglelike humanoid, with golden wings and talons. Fierce, proud, and warlike, he recalls the past glories of his planet and wishes to return to the days of fighting and dying in glory. He steals a valuable religious relic from Skorr, hoping to start a holy war throughout the galaxy. Tchar joins expeditions in search of the sculpture in order to prevent the groups from ever returning with it. But he meets his match in Kirk and

Teacher, Great: An educating machine, called the Great Teacher of All the Ancient Knowledge, on Sigma Draconis VI. Its business end is a basket-shaped headset with knoblike projections, hanging from a wall bracket in the controller's room. The leader of the Eymorgs is programmed by it with whatever temporary knowledge she requires to carry out a specific task (brain-napping, for instance). Use of the Teacher is limited for humans, as their brain patterns are different than those of the Eymorgs; knowledge obtained from the Teacher is retained for three Federation hours by Eymorgs, but less than that by humans (SB). See also Alar.

Tears: Elasian women cry tears which contain a biochemical substance that acts as a love potion when it enters the bloodstream of a man touched by the tears. Legend has it that it will never wear off; he will be in love forever. McCoy thinks he had found an antidote, but never has a chance to try it on Kirk, as the pull of his ship enables the captain to form his own antidote (ET).

Technical data: See Dramian history.

Technical officer (Richard Compton):   A young Romulan with heavy sideburns who finds Kirk absconding with the cloaking device. Kirk knocks him out (EI).

Technician (Libby Erwin):   A once-pretty woman who is found in the Memory Alpha computer room, a victim of the lights of Zetar, her companions already dead. She glows with a strange light, changing colors, and speaks with a deep, slow growl that is incomprehensible—all effects of the attack from the Zetars. She dies of severe hemorrhaging due to the distortion of all neural centers (LZ).

Technician, First (Louis Elias):   A crewman, with dark hair and pointed chin, stationed in Auxiliary Control. He is fooled by the children of the Starnes expedition into thinking the Enterprise is still in orbit around Triacus, and fights with Scotty, who says they are in deep space. Later, Scott comes under the children's control and agrees with the technician (CL).

Technician, Romulan (Robert Gentile): At the sensor on the bridge of the Romulan flagship (EI).

Teer: Traditional title of the leader of the ten tribes of Capella IV. Spock, Kirk and McCoy see three Teers in rapid succession: Akaar; Maab, who kills and supplants Akaar; and Leonard James Akaar, son of Akaar and Eleen, who assumes the title after Maab's death at the hands of Kras (FC).

Telefocals: Long-range binoculars used in the search for Kirk and Spock on Argo (Am/a).

Telemetry probe: An information-gathering device that is launched at the spacegoing ameba; when it is destroyed, the creature becomes aware of the Enterprise (IS).

Telepath, Kzin: A scrawny, neurotic Kzin, with matted fur, drooping ears, and an unhappy expression. Instead of being fierce and proud, the reader of minds is lean and bedraggled, but there is no way to guard against being mind-read by a Kzin telepath (SW/a).

Telepathy: According to Spock, over 98 percent of all the known telepathic species can send as well as receive thoughts, but telepaths must be able to shut out the bedlam of other beings' thoughts, as well as to control their own thoughts and emotions; this is a basic part of Vulcan teaching. Some people are able to block telepathy. It should be possible to establish a corporate linkup to pool information telepathically, but each telepath would have to be ready to struggle against the violent emotions (hatred, desire, envy, pity, etc.) which the Vulcans consider a form of insanity (TB). True telepaths are most formidable (WEd). Gem does not send out thought, so Spock concludes that she is not a true telepath (Em). The sluglike beings of Lactra VII use telepathy as communication, but it is so swift and complicated that Spock can get only fleeting impressions of it. The Lactrans are so far advanced beyond even Vulcans that attempts made by Spock to communicate only amuse the Lactrans and embarrass Spock. The Lactrans are capable of absorbing information at a tremendous rate, and also of putting pressure on a mind heavy enough to drive a human mad. The combined efforts of five humans and Spock are unable to block out the Lactran mind attack on Kirk (EB/a). See also Russian; Swahili; Vulcan mind touch; Vulcan mind fusion.

Teleportation: Matter/energy conversion and reconversion, used to transport something. The Vedala are very good at it (Ji/a).

Television: A primitive form of sending messages using transistors, diodes, tubes, and other weighty paraphernalia, which has long been out of use in the Enterprise's communications system (BC).

Tellarite (Gary Downey): One of the inmates of Elba II and a follower of the mad Garth, who proposes to set himself up as Master of the Universe and use the other inmates, including the Tellarite, as lieutenants and subjects (WGD).

Tellarites: Members of the Federation—stocky, pink, pig-faced, boisterous, argumentative for no good reason (as Sarek of Vulcan says, "Tellarites do not argue for reasons; they simply argue"), and not entirely trustworthy.

Tellarite speech is booming, rough, grating, and faintly Germanic; they have a very difficult time with English. Tellarites do not get drunk, even on Saurian brandy—just feisty (JB). A Tellarite has learned to stifle his quarrelsome tendencies enough to sit on the Elysian Ruling Council; his ship was caught in the Delta Triangle region, from which there seems to be no escape, so the Tellarite has learned to live in peace with his fellows (Tr/a).

Teller: A past friend of Kirk's, probably an Academy classmate, who meets him on Starbase 11 and, apparently believing the rumor about Kirk's responsibility for the death of Finney, gives him the cold shoulder (Cml).

Tellun star system: Located in a border area between the Klingon Empire and the Federation, this system contains two inhabited planets under Federation influence, but claimed by the Klingons. Troyius, its outer planet, is inhabited by civilized humanoids, while Elas, the inner world, is peopled by semibarbarians. The planets, which have interplanetary travel but lack stardrive, have been intermittently at war. A royal wedding has been planned to establish a peace of sorts (ET).

Temple: The lura-mag and the opto-aud of the Taurus II females are housed in a luxurious templelike building of unusual design; it is assumed that only a very advanced race could have designed such architecture (LS/a). The obelisk on Miramanee's planet, containing mechanisms provided by the Preservers, is held sacred as a temple (PSy). See also Fortress; Obelisk.

Ten tribes, the: A cultural unit, or possibly the cultural unit, on Capella IV (FC). See also Teer.

Tepo (John Harmon): One of the minor bosses on Iotia, a small Jimmy Durante type with a crumpled face (PA).

Terra: The third planet in our solar system known to its natives as Earth (but that is probably the name used by all natives of all planets), has been also known as Terra (Greek for "Earth") in literature, science, and popularly for centuries. The use of "Terran" for Earthman is more suitable and preferred over "Earthling" and "Earther," which are used, all too often, by Klingons and other insulting types. Sol III is at the center of a solar system of nine planets of various sizes and atmospheres; this system is on the far reaches of one spiral arm of the Milky Way galaxy, and was not visited openly by space travellers for millennia because the solar system was so far removed from normal trading lanes. Terra, is a member of the United Federation of Planets.

Terraforming: A method of changing whole areas of a planet to something else; removing or replacing one ecology with another. The proximity to one another of unusual environments—desert, rain forest, etc.— suggests that Lactra VII has been extensively terraformed to suit some purpose. While terraforming is not a new concept in the galaxy, its presence does suggest a highly technical and intelligent life form able to manufacture ecologies (EB/a).

Terran: The official term for Earth humanoids: from the Latin Terra, meaning Earth (EI).

Terra 10: The original Earth colony sent out to find a planet to settle was called Terra 10, presupposing that at least ten colonization efforts were attempted at the same time. Through the many years on the satellite of Cepheus, the word became "Terratin," which is why the Enterprise's library/computer does not find the word in its banks (Te/a). See also Terratin.

Terratin: Owing to the shrinking of their bodies caused by the spiroid waves natural to the planet they colonized, the people of the Terra 10 colony from Earth were never found by other ships passing by. As a result, they were left entirely on their own, to build a miniature but fantastic city on the unstable planet and fend for themselves. They grew proud and stubborn, choosing to fight rather than give in, and this pride nearly causes the Enterprise's rescue efforts to fail. When the Terratins are made to understand that they must accept aid or let their entire city die, they finally allow the Enterprise to move them, city and all, to another, more friendly planet (Te/a).

Territorial annex of the Tholian Assembly: That region of space containing the interphase/space warp in which the Defiant is lost permanently and Kirk is lost temporarily. Marked on Federation charts as "unknown" and "unowned," the area is claimed by Commander Loskene as Tholian territory (TW).

Tests, Academy: Among the tests necessary for passing grades at Star Fleet Academy is one in which the student has to work in an oxygen-deficient atmosphere for a certain length of time. McCoy compares Spock's symptoms from choriocytosis to these tests, so Kirk will understand how Spock feels (PO/a).

Test 24: McCoy's search for an antidote to Elasian tears results in test 24: colladium trioxide in an algobarium solution. He never gets a chance to try it on Kirk, however (ET).

Tetralubisol: A highly volatile, milky-looking lubricant in use aboard the Enterprise. Lenore Karidian puts some in Kevin Riley's milk, to poison him because he was a witness to the massacre on Tarsus IV (CK).

Thalassa: Sargon's wife, who borrows Dr. Anne Mulhall's body. Henoch nearly tempts her into keeping it, but she obeys Sargon and takes up a disembodied existence (RT).

Thank you: Although saying "thank you" is evidently not a Vulcan custom, young Spock was taught this sim-ple Earth courtesy by his mother. He thanks his cousin for saving his life (Yy/a).

Thann (Williard Sage): One of the Vians who test the empath Gem in the caverns of Minara II, with a bald, heavy-ridged skull, a wide jaw, and concentric wrinkles around the mouth (Em).

Tharn (Vic Perrin): Head of the Halkan Council—a dignified, gentle man in robes, with white hair and a blue caste mark on his forehead. In both universes, this man is exactly the same, refusing to give either Kirk or Kirk-2 permission to mine dilithium crystals on his planet because they would be used for warfare (MM).

Thasian (Abraham Sofaer): A wavering, transparent face projected on thin air, one of the noncorporeal beings from the planet Thasus, who appears in the Enterprise to take back their protégé, Charlie Evans. This has been the Thasians' only official contact with the Federation (CX).

Thasus: A Class M planet, inhabited by the noncorporeal Thasians and the Terran Charles Evans. Realizing that, while an adult could live on Thasus alone, a three-year-old child could not, Spock knows that Charlie is lying when he says that there are no Thasians, and that he grew up on Thasus with no companions or teachers (CX).

Theela (Majel Barrett): Leader of the females of Taurus II. A tall platinum blond with blue eyes, she is as beautiful and graceful as any of the other females on the planet. She is gowned in gold, with gold accessories, including tiara, earrings, and other jewelry (LS/a).

Thelev (William O'Connell): In appearance a young Andorian, with blue skin, white hair, and knobbed antennae, but actually a disguised Orion spy. He murders Ambassador Gav of Tellar, hoping to place the blame on Sarek of Vulcan, and attacks Kirk, wounding him with a knife. Imprisoned, Telev transmits signals to a ship that is chasing the Enterprise with a device concealed in his false antennae. When the ship is defeated, it destroys itself, and so does Thelev (JB).

Theragen: A deadly nerve gas used by the Klingons, although McCoy finds that it is deadly only in its pure form. A derivative of theragen diluted with alcohol will deaden certain nerve impulses to the brain and is used to cure the madness induced by the space warp in Tholian territory. Scotty finds that it goes well with Scotch; Spock swallows it under protest (TW).

Therapeutic shore leave: Scott is thrown against a bulkhead on the Enterprise by an explosion, causing a severe concussion and possible amnesia. He is taken to Argelius II, a hedonistic society, for recovery (WF).

Thermoconcrete: A compound composed mostly of silicon, used for building emergency shelters and repairing Hortas (DD).

Thermonuclear missile: As the Enterprise approaches Ekos, it is attacked by a thermonuclear missile, which Spock says is quite primitive but adequate to cause considerable damage. The Enterprise's officers note with some astonishment that before John Gill was placed on the planet as a cultural observer, the society had not developed sufficiently to have nuclear energy (PF).

Theta Cygni XII: Site of a civilization destroyed by the flying parasites. They wiped out Theta Cygni some time between their attack on Lavinius V, two hundred years before they attack Deneva, and on Ingraham B, two years before Deneva. No survivors were left (OA).

Theta VII: A planet to which the Enterprise is supposed to carry vaccines and other medical supplies obtained from the U.S.S. Yorktown. Kirk delays the rendezvous in order to chase the vampire cloud (Ob).

Thief: See Em/3/Green.

This one: Personal term used by Commander Ari bn Bem to refer to himself (Be/a).

Tholian Assembly: The governmental unit of Tholians (TW).

Tholians: A species known only slightly to the Federation. Loskene of this race appeared on the viewscreen of the Enterprise as a red-gold, almost crystalline being with triangular white eye spots, no other visible features, and a harsh voice. The being is seen before a blue-white background of apparent heat waves which blur transmission, which seems to indicate that the Tholians are hot-planet beings, possibly with a hive culture or even a hive mind. Tholian ships are sharp-edged white-gold wedges with angular tails. Tholians may be slightly better known to Vulcans, for Spock mentions their reputation for punctuality—a fact that nobody else seems to know. Tholians are also apparently not affected by the space warp or interphase (TW).

Tholian web (special effects by Mike Minor): A web of tremendous holding power which the Tholian ships spin out like gigantic spiderwebs, surrounding another starship and holding it captive (TW).

Thompson, Yeoman Leslie (Julie Cobb): A member of the landing party that meets the Kelvans. Rojan reduces her to a block of white crystalline matter and crumbles it—killing her—to demonstrate his power to Kirk (AON).

Thongs: Bola-like throwing weapons used by the Troglytes of Ardana (Cms).

Thought duplicator: One of the necessary talents of the amusement planet's master computer is the ability to read minds. Uhura discovers this when she tries to disconnect the computer, and is stopped before she gets started (OUP/a).

Thought screen: When the Lactrans use mind entrance on Kirk, Spock tries to protect the captain by rallying the other humans to put up a thought screen. However, they are unused to this kind of mental work, and it isn't strong enough to protect Kirk from agony. Fortunately, the Lactran child is returned before the adult Lactrans drive Kirk mad (EB/a).

Thralls: Humans, humanoids, and aliens from all corners of the galaxy, brought to Triskelion to fight in the arena. Kirk persuades the Providers to free them and to teach them to govern themselves (GT).

3-D checkers: See Games and recreation.

3-D chess: See Games and recreation.

300 credits: The asking price for a crystal of Harry Mudd's love potion, or the equivalent in fissionable materials. The miners consider this a very high price, but later,

when Mudd finds that the love potion is not a fake, he says he was asking too little (MP/a).

347, Agent: See Agents 201 and 347.

3RR circuit: A circuit in the interior engineering shaft of a starship (EW).

Through the Looking Glass: A book by Lewis Carroll, from which come some of the characters seen on the shore-leave planet (OUP/a, SL). See also Carroll, Lewis.

Thule, Technician 1 /C: Crewman on the bridge when Khan tries to suffocate them into submission (SS).

Tiberius: When asked for his name by the alien intelligence on Delta Theta III, James Kirk gives "Tiberius" as his middle name. The situation is too serious for him to be kidding (Be/a).

Tiburon: The home of Dr. Sevrin (WEd), and the site of Zora's infamous experiments on subject tribes (SC).

Tiger, Bengal: On the amusement-park planet, Lieutenant Rodriguez accidentally materializes a Bengal tiger, which scares him and Angela. Later, Spock, by mentioning the phenomenon, calls up the same tiger or its duplicate, and has to make a tactical retreat (SL).

Tightbeam transmission: The method by which the Enterprise punches through the shielding of the planet Phylos to communicate with the landing party. The entire power of the ship is directed through the planet's shielding, at considerable risk (IV/a).

Time: In a stasis box, time stands still (SW/a). In the antimatter universe, the flow of time is reversed, so that people age from elderly to baby (CC/a).

Time chamber: A device in the ships of Lazarus A and B that allows them to enter the alternative warp. The ships are destroyed by Kirk, thus preventing the two Lazaruses from ever meeting outside the alternative warp, and trapping them together (AF). See also Alternative warp.

Time continuum: Another continuation of time lines (Tr/a). See also Time trap.

Timed trigger: The lock on the door of the fortress has a timed trigger in it so that any tampering will make the door explode. Em/3/Green works against time to pick the lock and get the door open before the bomb goes off (Ji/a).

Time lines: The time portal shows the continuum of time lines cross-woven into the pattern of history, as seen through the Guardian of Forever (Yy/a).

Time portal: A passageway into another time, such as the doorway in the library of Mr. Atoz, on Sarpeidon, through which a Sarpeid passes in order to arrive at his chosen point in the past (AY), and the Guardian of Forever (CEF). See also Space warp.

Time trap: A pocket in the time continuum; a place where starships have disappeared in the Delta Triangle region for centuries. It seems to be less like an alternate universe, more like a pocket in the "garment" of time (Tr/a).

Timothy (Winston DeLugo): A friend and former classmate of Kirk's, who meets him at Starbase 11 after the supposed loss of Finney and gives him the cold shoulder (Cml).

T

Tissue regeneration: A form of biological renewal whereby the body regrows glands, cells, and other tissue to replace those that have grown old, become damaged, or been destroyed. Flint has this ability, which has kept him alive for over six thousand years (RM). See also Regeneration.

Titanium: See Jewelry.

T-negative: A fairly rare Vulcan blood type, which both Sarek and his son, Spock, have (JB).

Toast: One of Lucien's favorite Earth customs is that of drinking a toast to celebrate a happy occasion. He materializes tankards out of thin air so everyone can drink to the new relationship between Megas-tu and Earth-people (Mtu/a). The practice is still used when celebrating; the Enterprise crew toast one another when they escape from the Romulans (PJ/a).

Tomar (Robert Fortier): A Kelvan who takes over the engineering section on the Enterprise and is later assigned to guard the personnel left unconverted to blocks. When it is discovered that the Kelvans are distracted by the sensations of their new human bodies, Scott takes Tomar off to get him drunk. After enjoying Scotty's considerable collection of potables down to the last drop of ancient Scotch, they are both immobilized (AON).

Tomlinson, Specialist Robert (Stephen Mines): Phaser crewman—very young face, bright eyes, wavy blond hair—who nearly marries Angela Martine but is killed by escaping phaser-coolant fumes during the Romulan attack that interrupts his wedding (BT).

Tongo Rad (Victor Brandt): The son of the Catullan ambassador, with a very high forehead and shoulder-length rainbow-silvery hair worn straight back. He is the epitome of the child who has been given too much and so is not satisfied with anything. Kirk has orders to treat Tongo with extreme delicacy due to Federation treaty negotiations, and evidently the youngster knows it, for he annoys Kirk at every opportunity. Like Sulu, Tongo enjoys botany, a shared interest he uses to elicit information from the helmsman about handling a shuttlecraft. Tongo has also inherited his father's abilities at space studies. He is one of the group of "space hippies" who are looking for a perfect world, and the only one of the group who realizes that the ultrasonics which Sevrin sets for the Enterprise's crew will actually kill, instead of merely stunning. He protests only briefly, however, and follows his leader (WEd).

Tonsils: McCoy places a good deal more trust in a healthy set of tonsils than in tricorder readings and other machines, indicating that a use for tonsils has finally been discovered (MT).

Topaline: A mineral used in the life-support systems of planetoid colonies (FC).

Tormolen, Joe (Stewart Moss): A crewman aboard the Enterprise who beams down with Spock to Psi 2000 and is the first to contract the virus. Although well balanced normally, he has a strong tendency to despondency and self-doubt, which the virus brings out to the point where he tries to kill himself. When this is prevented, he dies of despair (NT).

Towers: The gates of the city on Kukulkan's ship are obelisks, or towers. There are also four towers, one at each corner of the pyramid in the middle of the city, in the shape of snakes (HS/a).

T'Pau (Celia Lovsky): An ancient and venerable Vulcan matriarch with immense prestige; the only person ever to turn down a seat in the Federation Council. Thus, when she came to officiate at Spock's marriage, Kirk and McCoy are made aware of how important his family is. Moreover, when Kirk disobeys Star Fleet orders to take Spock to Vulcan, a word from T'Pau puts all to right. She is a lady of extreme virtue and honor, and would not permit T'Pring's trickery if she were aware of the motives behind the girl's actions (AT).

T'Pel: See Selek.

T'Pring (Arlene Martel): A small, delicate, lovely Vulcan woman and Spock's affianced wife, bound to him by law, tradition, and the mind touch when they were both approximately seven years old. However, she wishes to divorce Spock and take Stonn for her husband: permissible. She challenges Spock at their wedding ceremony and demands that he fight for her: acceptable. But, rather than have Stonn fight for her honestly, she chooses Kirk as her champion, reasoning: "If your captain were victor, he would not want me, so I would have Stonn. If you were victor, you would free me because I dared to challenge, and again I would have Stonn. But if you did not free me, it would be the same, for you would be gone again, and I would have your name and your property, and Stonn would still be here." Spock releases her to the unfortunate Stonn (AT).

Tracey, Captain Ronald (Morgan Woodward): Captain of the U.S.S. Exeter—a thin, white-haired man with black eyebrows and strong cheekbones. When his crew contracted the Omega IV virus, he beamed down to the planet, the biosphere of which confers its own immunity. There he violates the Prime Directive by aiding, with his phaser, the Kohm villagers against the Yang attacks; he thinks the Kohms have a secret of longevity that can be utilized by others, and wants to keep the villagers safe until he can find it out. When the Yangs capture the village, Tracey accuses Kirk and Spock of being demons, only to be proven wrong in single combat. The Enterprise's crew take him prisoner (OG).

Tractor beam: The reverse of the deflector—a beam that grabs and pulls rather than deflecting and pushing something away. This beam has a maximum range of about one hundred thousand miles and can be used to hold a firm position alongside another vessel, pull a smaller vessel along, or tow another ship out of danger. A ship's tractor beam can pull small objects within transporter range, whereupon they can be beamed aboard the ship. Scott uses a tractor beam to cut a piece of antimatter villi from the cosmic cloud, to be used in the regenerating chamber of the Enterprise (OPM/a). To prevent the interceptor from firing on the Enterprise, the starship puts a tractor beam on the small plane, which is not strong enough to withstand the power and breaks up, forcing the starship to beam the pilot aboard (TY). When the Enterprise tries to stop Karla Five's ship with its tractor beam, the tractor beam locks and becomes inopera-

T

tive, pulling the larger starship through a nova into a negative universe (CC/a).

Tractor web: See Tholian web.

Tracy, Lieutenant Karen (Virginia Aldridge): A psychotech—small, thin, and blond—who is called down from the Enterprise to Argelius II to aid Dr. McCoy in running a series of tests on Scotty. While she is alone with her patient, Hengist moves in and kills her, placing the blame on Scotty (WF).

Trader/bartender (Guy Raymond): The thin, balding, obviously ulcer-ridden manager of the store-cum-bar at Space Station K-7. Cyrano Jones sells him a batch of tribbles, and they both live to regret the transaction (TT).

Training device: A magnetically locked belt created to keep the Morgs under control and used on Kirk, McCoy, and Scotty to control them. Spock knows how to open one, but his brain is busy running the Eymorg city, and it is only after some difficulty that the men learn from him how to release themselves. The training device is controlled from buttons on wristlets, or bracelets, worn by the Eymorgs. The electronic control is highly effective; it feels like fire, causing a convulsive jerking of the body. McCoy comments that he hadn't believed the human body could take that much pain (SB).

Traitor's Claw, The: A stolen police vessel renamed by the Kzin pirates—they say. In reality, they are stealing stasis boxes, with the blessings of their government so long as they don't get caught (SW/a).

Trance: After his first humiliation at the hands of the psychokinetic Platonians, Spock is filled with such hatred that he has to go into a trance state to free himself from this terrible emotion (PSt). To reach the cosmic cloud, Spock tries to communicate with it by Vulcan mind touch; he goes into a trancelike concentration, and manages to make intelligent contact with the alien entity (OPM/a).

Tranquilizer: McCoy has a powerful tranquilizer in the medical kit he is holding when Kulkukan whisks him off the Enterprise. Though no weapons are brought aboard Kulkukan's ship by any of the Enterprise people, the alien evidently does not think that McCoy's medical kit is any danger to him. In fact, it saves his life when the Capellan power-cat attacks Kulkukan and Kirk uses the tranquilizer to stop the cat (HS/a). McCoy and Spock try to make a grenade that will tranquilize the Earp Gang, but it doesn't work (SGn). When it is determined that the Jack-the-Ripper entity feeds on fear, Dr. McCoy tranquilizes the entire Enterprise crew so they can not react to anything the entity does. By this means they prevent it from leaving Hengist's body to occupy someone else's—everyone is too tranquilized to allow it to take over (WF).

Transceiver: A long-range communications device. Thelev, the Orion spy, communicates with his ship by means of a transceiver concealed in his false antennae (JB).

Transferral beam: Sigma Draconis transporter beam (SB).

Translator: See Universal translator.

Transmuter: A director and amplifier of mental power; the device whereby Sylvia and Korob maintain themselves, their illusions, and their powers on Pyris VII, without which they would be, as Sylvia says, "like feathers in the wind." Sylvia's transmuter is contained in her jeweled amulet, Korob's in his wand (Cp).

Transponder, subcutaneous: A small device placed under the skin, on which a transporter beam can focus if communicators are not available. Spock uses two transponders and a light bulb to jury-rig a crude laser on Ekos (PF).

Transport card: See Transport pass.

Transporter: The primary means of moving crew or cargo to and from planet surfaces and/or other space vessels. Kirk explains the transporter as a matter/energy scrambler: It converts matter temporarily into energy, beaming that energy to a fixed point, then reconverting it back into its original matter structure. Its range is limited to about sixteen thousand miles. It can be adjusted to wide-field pickup in a target area, and people can be suspended in transit until a decision is reached to rematerialize them; McCoy claims that it is a form of nonexistence. It is theoretically possible to beam from one part of the ship to another—intraship beaming—but it isn't often done because of the danger of materializing inside a bulkhead or other solid object. However, Kirk uses intraship beaming to get to Engineering when Kang is in control there (Dv). It cannot recall people fast enough to prevent them from materializing inside a lava pool, nor can it work with the warp power at a low ebb, which would create a risk of beaming someone aboard as a mass of dying flesh (SC). It retains the memory of the original molecular structure of everyone and everything passing through it (CC/a). See also Matter/energy scrambler.

Transporter circuits: The transporter is used to restore the crew to their normal size, as its circuits contain the normal-size molecular pattern for each of the Enterprise people (Te/a).

Transporter coordinates: 875-020-079: 875-020-709 . . . a numbers game the Gideonites play (MG).

Transporter factor M-7: See Molecular transporter.

Transporter ionizer unit: An integral part of the transporter, without which it will not work (EW).

Transporter Room: There are various Transporter Rooms throughout the vessel; the one most often used has access from a passageway, and within it is a console which is controlled by the transporter officer and a technician (frequently Scott and/or Lieutenant Kyle). They, in concert or singly, can transport up to six people at a time. Provided that their mass and size are not too great, objects can be brought aboard also.

Transporter Room Four: The Transporter Room from which Kirk and Spock dematerialize to beam down to the deserted planet in pursuit of Mudd and to rescue Nurse Chapel (MP/a).

Transport pass: A card that permits Troglytes to travel to and move about in Stratos. Also called transport cards (Cms).

Transport platform: The method of transportation between the surface of Ardana and the cloud city of

T

Stratos. It is a movable antigravity platform which transports people and goods back and forth (Cms).

Transtater: A basic application of a revolutionary concept of physics, on which is based much of Federation technology: the communicator, phasers, transporters, and so on (PA).

Tranya: A beverage used by Balok's people, apparently quite palatable to Terrans; he serves some to Kirk, McCoy, and Bailey (CMn).

Travers, Commodore: Head of the Earth colony on Cestus III, which was destroyed by Gorns; he was famous for his hospitality, giving the Gorns a means of tricking the Enterprise's technical personnel to the planet's surface by duplicating his voice (Ar).

Treaty: See Alliance; Neutral zone; Organian Peace Treaty; Orion; Treaty of Sirius; Violation, treaty.

Treaty of Sirius: A treaty forbidding Kzinti to possess any weapons at all beyond police vessels. Obviously the treaty has been broken by the Kzin aboard The Traitor's Claw, as they are armed to the teeth and claws (SW/a).

Trefayne (David Hillary Hughes):   An Organian Council member ranking very high in clairvoyance. He supplies the Council with information about the Klingon invasion, Kirk and Spock's sabotage, and the war that is brewing (EM).

Trelane (William Campbell):   A child of a race of noncorporeal beings, gifted with psionic powers, who is being schooled. He constructs the planet Gothos with his people's equivalent of building blocks, and he is allowed to "play" with the crew of the Enterprise until he gets too rough. He appears to the Enterprise's crew as humanoid, close to middle age, stocky, handsome, with dark curly hair, but his actual form is not known. His parents are seen by Kirk as dim, wavering, green transparent shapes hanging in space; they have gentle and civilized human voices. Trelane is very enthusiastic about things Terran, especially the military, and has a fondness for the eighteenth century. Like any child, he has little kindness, self-control, or patience, but anyone who likes Scarlatti can't be all bad (SG).

Triacus: A planet of Epsilon Indi and the site of the Starnes expedition, where the children met Gorgon and the adults died. According to legend, Triacus was the seat of a band of marauders who made constant war throughout the system of Epsilon Indi. After many centuries the destroyers were themselves destroyed by those they preyed upon. The legend also mentions that the power of evil was waiting on Triacus for a catalyst to set it in motion and send it across the galaxy. This power is personified by Gorgan, last of the planet's inhabitants, who was released accidentally by the expedition. He influences the children, and tries to escape from Triacus on the Enterprise (CL).

Trial: The Vendorian must stand trial for his actions as a spy and saboteur aboard the Enterprise, but it will be taken into account that he saved the starship from trouble (Su/a).

Tribble: A small furry creature, planet of origin unknown, with no discernible feet, head, or other appen-

dage, although it has some means of locomotion, and certainly a mouth on the ventral side. Tribbles come in a variety of colors, including deep auburn, blond, beige, white, tan, and other soft pastel hues. Tribbles are deeply affectionate toward practically anything that moves—Vulcans, Terrans, but not Klingons—and other beings are extremely fond of tribbles, except Klingons, who refer to them as "parasites." They are highly prolific: They are, in effect, born pregnant, and multiply rapidly to the extent that the food supply allows. At one point, both the Enterprise and Space Station K-7 are knee-deep in tribbles. They seem to have a tranquilizing effect on the human nervous system, and purr softly except when near a Klingon, when they shriek shrilly—a trait useful for detecting Klingons (TT). Tribbles have been genetically engineered for compatibility with humanoid ecologies; they are friendly, lovable, great pets, and very profitable to Cyrano Jones, intergalactic trader. But Jones's genetic engineering is faulty: his tribbles grow larger and larger. When the huge tribbles are disrupted, they turn out to be colonies of small tribbles (MTT/a).

Tribunal: The ruling body, with the monarch, on Troyius (ET).

Tribunal of Aquans: Leaders of the Aquans. Domar and Cadmar are two of the three Tribunes, with younger members evidently sitting in as students and Junior Tribunes (Am/a).

Tricobalt-satellite explosion: In the strange computer war between Vendikar and Eminiar VII, Anan 7 tells Kirk that the Enterprise has been destroyed by a tricobalt-satellite explosion (TA).

Tricorder: A portable sensor/computer/recorder, about the size of a large textbook, carried on a shoulder strap. A remarkable miniaturized device, it can be used to sense, analyze, identify, and keep records on almost any type of data on planet surfaces. It can give the age of an artifact, the composition of alien life, etc. The tricorder is carried by the communications officer to maintain records of what is happening, by a yeoman, or by anyone else who needs a portable scientific tool. Dr. McCoy carries a medical tricorder. Tricorders have a range of about one hundred miles, which is as far as Spock can read through the rock of Janus VI in trying to locate the Horta (DD). See also Life-form readings.

Trilaser connector: A medical instrument used to reconnect damaged nerves; a synapse braider (SB).

Trillium: See Kevas.

Trimagnesite: A fuel used in kindling the light flares that destroy the flying parasites on Deneva. Also known as trivium (OA).

Trinary star system: An unusual star system with three suns revolving around one another, causing the one planet in the system—the mad planet—to have an extremely unstable surface (Ji/a).

Tri-ox compound: To help Kirk in his duel with Spock, McCoy says he is giving the captain a shot of tri-ox compound to help him breathe in Vulcan's thin air, but it is actually a neural paralyzer to knock him out (AT). While he is caught in space warp in Tholian territory, Kirk's oxygen runs out, so McCoy injects the captain with tri-ox compound the moment he is brought aboard the Enterprise. Tri-ox compound works rapidly (TW).

Trisec: A unit of time on Triskelion. Fifteen trisecs is about forty-five seconds (GT).

Triskelion: A planet of the trinary sun M24 Alpha, with a strangely colored sky. It is the home of the Providers, three disembodied brains with a penchant for gambling on combats among their thralls, or gladiators, whom they have collected from all the races of the galaxy. Later, the thralls are freed to build a culture on the planet (GT).

Tritanium: A mineral or ore found on Argus X, which is 21.4 times harder than diamonds (Ob).

Trititanium: An element or alloy used in starship hulls (JB).

Trivers, Barry (script): The Conscience of the King (CK).

Trivium: See Trimagnesite.

Troglytes: The menials and miners of Ardana, who are mentally inferior to the citizens of Stratos because of gas released by the mining of zienite. Troglytes are often trained and used as servants, guards, and other useful workers for the upper class. The name for these people is an abbreviation of "troglodyte," an ancient Earth term meaning "cave dweller" (Cms).

Trova: A drink of Eminiar VII, offered to Kirk by Anan 7, which is supposed to be "most interesting" (TA).

Troyian monarch: His name is unknown, but his pending marriage to the Dohlman Elaan is to be the beginning of peaceful negotiations between their warring planets (ET).

Troyius: Outer planet of the Tellun star system—a misty blue world, seen from space—inhabited by a civilized humanoid species ruled by a monarch and a tribunal. Troyians have been at war for centuries with the semibarbarians of the planet Elas. The monarch of Troyius and the Dohlman of Elas are to be married as a guesture of peace between the two planets (ET).

Tsingtao, Ray (Brian Tochi): A small Oriental boy of seven or eight, with heavy black hair cut in Spockish bangs. One of the children of the Starnes expedition, who temporarily comes under the influence of Gorgan (CL).

Tula (Brioni Farrell): The daughter of Reger and a native of Landru's planet—pretty but mousy and, like the rest of her people, without much personality. She is attacked by Bilar during the festival (RA).

Turbolift: Turbolifts are elevators which move vertically and horizontally to connect every deck and compartment of a starship. One can reach almost any section by activating the turbolift's control verbally, or, in an emergency, manually. See also Elevator.

Tweedledee and Tweedledum: Twin characters from Mother Goose and Lewis Carroll's Through the Looking Glass. When the Platonians use psychokinesis to humiliate Kirk and Spock, they force Kirk to sing; he takes the role of Tweedledee and Spock that of Tweedledum in a nursery-type song (PSt).

Twentieth century: The period of the 1900s on Earth, a time of wars, instant information, social unrest, geological changes, development of new medical and space ideas, reaching out for knowledge—the turning point for mankind, when humans decided to reach out for the stars and begin space exploration.

Twenty-first Street Mission: Edith Keeler's soup-kitchen mission in New York, 1930, old calendar (CEF).

Twenty-four-hour regressive memory check: A mind probe that reveals occurrences during the previous twenty-four-hour period, despite conscious amnesia (WF).

27.346 star years: Ships near the Taurean star system regularly disappear from space at 27.346-year intervals; the Federation finds that even Klingon and Romulan ships have disappeared on schedule (LS/a).

Twin star: See Pallas 14 system.

201, Agent: See Agents 201 and 347.

Tycho IV: The home planet of the vampire cloud, where it attacked the Farragut, and where it returns to reproduce after attacking the Enterprise. It is a burnt-out dead world, without vegetation, its lava surface scored by many fissures (Ob).

Tyler, José (Joe) (Peter Duryea): Navigator on the Enterprise under Captain Pike—lithe, Latin, exuberant (Me).

Type 4 asteroid: A body evidently interesting enough to warrant a geological survey by the Enterprise (PJ/a).

Typerias: A planet where a coagulation sand exists that stops the flow of blood from wounds (PLW).

Typewriter: Apparently an ordinary IBM Model C electric, located in Gary Seven's office and used by Roberta Lincoln. However, unknown to Miss Lincoln, it can also be voice-operated when the appropriate switch is thrown (AE).

Typhoid Mary: Mary Mallon (?–1938), Irish-American cook who carried typhoid from job to job until identified as a carrier of the disease in 1907; hence, any individual who is a carrier of a communicable illness. Dr. Sevrin is a twenty-second-century Typhoid Mary (WEd).

Tyree (Michael Whitney): A typical Neuralese hill man—big, blond, and simple—the headman of a hill tribe and a friend of Kirk's from the time a brash young Lieutenant Kirk led a survey party there thirteen years back. When Kirk, Spock, and McCoy come to Neural, Tyree is married to Nona the Kanutu, who tries to persuade the Terrans to aid the hill people in their war against the villagers. When the villagers kill Nona, Tyree learns to fight (PLW).

T

U

UFO: "Unidentified Flying Object"—an old Earth term for any object sighted in the sky which could not be identified as an Earth-made air vehicle. UFOs have been sighted for as long as there has been written history on Earth, in the form of lights, metal objects, globes, and other phenomena. The Air Force personnel at Omaha assume that the Enterprise is a UFO, which, to them, it is (TY).

Ugly: Beauty is truly in the eye of the beholder; the huge, red, sluglike Lactrans think the human zoo specimens are ugly and frightening (EB/a).

Uhura, Lieutenant (Nichelle Nichols): Communications officer on the Enterprise—a lovely, graceful African girl with expressive eyes and a musical voice. She is a native of the United States of Africa on Terra (Cg, MT). She is a highly efficient officer, but off duty she sings Terran and offworld ballads in a soft contralto voice, and has taught herself to play music on Spock's harp (CK, CX). She is fond of Kirk (CEF) and Spock (Me), but not seriously. Her name means "freedom" in Swahili, which is definitely her native language; she receives telepathic communication in that language. It is likely that after all the birth-throes of newly formed and reformed African nations, a Swahili nation arose, thereby transforming a culture built upon a trade language into a nationality (MT, SGn).

Uhura's crewman (Vince Howard): A tall, dazzling African, fluent in Swahili; Uhura's dream man, literally. He is a form taken on by the M113 creature to attract Uhura; she is called away before it can attack her (MT).

Uhura-2: Described as "tigerish," she is an efficient and a mean fighter—she has to be (MM).

Uletta: Fiancée of Isak. She is shot down by Nazis, and lies in the street for five hours before she dies (PF).

Ultrasonics: Sounds can be extremely painful to the human ear, and ultrasonics are terrible to a Vulcan. Sound beyond ultrasonics can kill (WEd).

Underground: When John Gill turned the culture of Ekos into a Nazilike society, the Zeons living there found themselves persecuted and constructed an underground for aiding victims, passing information, building a counterculture, and keeping track of the growth of the new society (PF).

Undersea city: An undersea civilization of water-breathers, with fantastic architecture. Kirk and Spock find the city by following Aquans into a deep undersea trench, which might explain why the Enterprise's sensors do not pick up any life-form readings on Argo. The city is fairylike, with shell-shaped buildings decorated with coral and pearls. Another undersea city is an ancient ruin that was once on land and was part of the area which sank during a massive seismic disturbance. The Aquans fear this city and issue laws against visiting it, though it contains many ancient records which are of great value not only to the Aquans but to the rest of the Federation as

well (Am/a).

Uniforms, Federation Star Fleet: The standard men's uniform used consists of a shirt whose color indicates job station, together with black flare-bottom pants, with black boots. Shirt colors: golden yellow for command, blue for sciences, red for engineering and most other jobs. There are also several classes of full-dress uniforms that are worn on formal occasions. Commanding officers obviously have the option of wearing uniforms of their choice; Captain Kirk, on occasion, wears a wraparound olive-green uniform shirt. Women's uniforms match the male uniforms in design of collar and job-station colors, but are short dresses with matching pants underneath, black tights, and boots. There seems to be no regulation about hair-dressing; each female wears her hair as she sees fit. On the old-style uniforms, the rank system was quite simple, indicating only crewmen, officers, and commander. This system was not in effect when Captain Pike commanded the Enterprise, however; at that time, all crewmen wore plain cuffs, and all officers, regardless of grade, wore one gold stripe. The uniform jacket worn by Number One and her landing party seems to have been the only Star Fleet uniform with pockets (Me).

United Earth Space Probe Agency: Kirk tells Christopher that the Enterprise is a part of this agency (TY). (Presumably not wishing to tell the twentieth-century Earthman too much about the future, Kirk makes up this plausible-sounding organization to explain the large starship's presence to him. The agency is never mentioned again.)

United Federation of Planets: A political unit encompassing a number of star systems, including Sol. Among the member planets of the Federation are Vulcan, Earth, Tellar, Andor, the Rigel planets, and Coridan. Basically democratic, the Federation is internally peaceful; the member planets send delegates to the central governing body, the Federation Council. Chief enemy of the Federation is the Klingon Empire, but there have also been clashes with the Romulan Empire and individual planets (JB) as well as the Kzin (SW/a). Federation law does not extend to all planets in the galaxy. Motherlode, a mining planet, does not recognize Federation law (MP/a). The United Federation of Planets can and does approve warrants for the arrest and trial of Star Fleet personnel on planetary matters (Al/a). All ships known to the Federation are registered as to design, place of origin, and purpose—cruiser, pleasure ship, freighter, and so on (PO/a). Federation vouchers can be used as credit or money throughout the United Federation of Planets (MP/a). An enormous computer complex keeps track of such things as legal banks for the Federation. These were consulted to find out if Reena Kapec was a ward of Flint's; no record of award of custody could be found, nor any record of her history or background at all (RM). The Federation maintains hospitals where the medical computers have data on every known medical procedure in the galaxy that can be recorded. They had no information, initially, on the Argo surgo-op method of mutating air-breathers into water-breathers (AM/a). It can be assumed that as new frontiers are explored, more medical information will be added to the computer banks. Certainly, as exploration continues more Federation colonies are established; Carter Winston was famous for assisting such colonies in time of need (Su/a). The Federation High Commissioner accepted only results, not explanations. The High Commissioner's political approval is needed for permission to attend functions such as Elaan's royal wedding (ET). The Federation sends out scientific-exploration teams of various sizes to investigate everything from archeological diggings (MT) to planets (LC) to the ecology (EB/a), as well as for star charting and other investigating of the galaxy.

United States of Africa: Uhura's birthplace on Earth (CC/a).

Unit insignia: The small insignia, or patch, worn on the left breast of the uniform tells an observer to which unit a person in Star Fleet belongs. For the Enterprise, the patch takes the shape of a stylized arrowhead, with the appropriate division symbol in the center. The patch for the Antares takes the shape of an oval, with an indentation on the wearer's left (CX). For the Constellation, the form is that of a stylized script capital "I" (DMa). The patch for the Exeter is in the shape of an upright rectangle (OG). The Huron patch is a five-pointed star (PO/a). For the Ariel, the patch takes the shape of an isosceles triangle, pointed toward the wearer's right shoulder, with indentations on the lower long side and the short side (EB/a). The Star Fleet Planetary Services patch is a planet eclipsing its sun (Ar, BT). Star Fleet Rehabilitation has a large yellow sun on a black background, over which is superimposed a large white humanoid hand releasing a small white bird (DMd, WGD).

Unit XY-75847:   A group of Federation ships patrolling the disputed area around Organia for Klingon ships (EM).

Unity: Bem says his unity must cease; he will disassemble the colony units that make him an entity. The alien intelligence of Delta Theta III says that if Bem disassembles he cannot learn from his errors, as the units will not remember. Errors demand recognition so they will not be repeated (Be/a).

Universal language: A generally accepted universal language is spoken throughout the known galaxy by most Federation planets. For our convenience, this is translated into English (CC/a).

Universal translator: The Enterprise is equipped with a computer translator which can handle almost every language pattern used in the universe. (There are also hand-carried translators, which have been used on occasion.) It is used to translate the ancient record scrolls of the Aquans. Dr. McCoy has some doubts about the translator's abilities, because he prefaces his remarks with the comment that if the translation is correct, the substance in the bloodstream is close to the ambergris of Earth whales (Am/a). It can evidently be set up to receive and communicate thought waves; Uhura links the translator with the Enterprise's audio system so everyone on the bridge can hear the mind-touch contact between Spock and the cosmic cloud (OPM/a).

Ursinoid: Bearlike alien on Motherlode with fur pelt: It stands upright like a humanoid, is intelligent, and both sexes mine heavy metals (MP/a).

Ursula: Home of the Ursulian neopoppy, with its antihallucination pollen (PLW).

V

Vaal: A computerlike mechanism on Gamma Trianguli VI, mostly underground. Its aboveground output is carved out of a rock wall in the shape of a great serpent's head, its mouth gaping and tongue extended, with steps cut into the tongue so that a person can walk into its mouth. The mouth is fanged, and the head has red, glowing eyes that pulsate; the whole gives off a faint hum, as of powerful machinery. Vaal has made Gamma Trianguli VI a paradise for the inhabitants, who are innocent and immortal flower children. It tries to prevent the Enterprise from interfering with its plans for the planet, but Kirk destroys the computer and sends the natives toward a new, more dynamic culture (Ap).

Vacuum tubes: See Hobby.

Valiant, U.S.S.:   Galactic survey cruiser that preceded the Enterprise by some two hundred years into the extragalactic frontier, encountering the energy barrier there. The contact caused one of the Valiant's crew to be psionically accelerated, and he became so dangerous that the captain was forced to destroy the ship and everyone aboard. This information was contained in a jettisoned recorder-marker recovered by the Enterprise (WNM). Another ship was named after it. This Valiant first contacted Eminiar VII, some fifty years before the Enterprise got there. It did not return, and was undoubtedly destroyed in the war between Eminiar VII and Vendikar (TA).

Valley, the: When Kirk and his crew arrive on Beta III, they are believed to be from the valley, where people "have different ways," and to have left it to attend the festival in town (RA).

Vampire cloud: A gaseous cloud, native to Tycho IV, but a deep-space traveler: Occupying a borderline state between matter and energy, it moves from planet to planet by use of gravitational fields. It drains red blood cells from human bodies, and can change its form, substance, and molecular structure. It smells like honey and contains traces of dikironium. Kirk met one on Tycho IV, then meets it again on Argus X. He chases it to Tycho IV and destroys it, but there may be more (Ob).

Vanderberg, Chief Engineer (Ken Lynch):   The beefy, impatient administrative head of Janus VI, who calls the Enterprise in when the Horta begins to attack his men. When the Horta is located, he nearly has it killed before Kirk explains to him that it is he who is in the wrong. He later says that the baby Hortas, tunneling away through the rock, are cute little devils and not such a bad species, once you get used to their appearance (DD).

Van Gelder, Dr. Simon (Morgan Woodward): Psychiatrist and assistant director at the Tantalus penal colony from which he flees to the Enterprise—

unkempt, desperate-looking, red-faced, with a wild mane of white hair. Dr. Adams has conditioned him with the neural neutralizer so that he cannot repeat what is going on at the colony, but Spock uses the mind touch and learns all, at great personal cost. After Adams's death, van Gelder, restored to normal, takes over as director of the colony (DMd).

Vanna (Charlene Polite): A dark-haired, beautiful, stubborn Troglyte girl who has been educated to serve in Plasus's household. She is also a Disruptor, who tries to better her fellow Troglytes' lives. However, she is headstrong and aggressive to the point of trying to kidnap Kirk and not believing him when he says he wishes to aid her people. Kirk has to prove to her by rather violent methods that the zienite gas is what makes the difference between her people and Stratos citizens (Cms).

Variable gravity: On unstable planets and in other situations in which gravity does not work consistently at a single level, one might have to contend with variable gravity, one minute being too heavy to stand and the next too light to walk easily without floating away. Sulu compares learning to use the transporter-carrier of the Slaver weapon with learning to walk a tightrope in variable gravity (SW/a).

Vault: An apparently ordinary walk-in safe in Gary Seven's apartment in New York, it actually contains a highly advanced transporter. Instead of the shimmer and paralysis of the starship transporters, there is an opalescence through which transportees walk in and out (AE).

Vault of Tomorrow: See Chamber of the Ages.

Vector grid: A graphic device used to locate objects in space. On the star-charting mission, the Enterprise can be located on the vector grid simply by noting the one white light marking the starship's position (BFS/a).

Vedala asteroid: On the outside, a huge greenish-silvery globe that pulsates; on the inside, there is a glade with trees, grass, and a stream, all in totally alien colors—deep blues, oranges, and golds. The vacuum of space can be seen just outside the semitransparent walls. The Vedala may use these asteroids only for space travel, or they may live in them (Ji/a).

Vedala, the: A stooped white catlike creature—a member of the oldest spacefaring race known. They seem to show themselves only one at a time, and they live on an asteroid that has been artificially adapted to their needs. The Vedala are very powerful and can transport people across vast reaches of space, or materialize items such as ground carts. They are limited, however, or else they would have found the Soul of Skorr and returned it by themselves without involving four expeditions in danger and death (Ji/a).

Vegan choriomeningitis: Choriomeningitis is an inflammation of a part of the brain tissues; the Vegan type causes high fever and tingling in the arms and lower back. It is virulent and usually fatal unless treated within twenty-four hours. Kirk contracted this disease many years ago; the microorganisms, which he carries in his blood, are harmless unless administered directly to someone who has not been immunized, as is the case

with Odona of Gideon (MG).

Vega IX: The colony to which the Enterprise is going—to provide medical care for those injured in the Rigel VII fight—when it answers the call from Talos IV instead (Me).

Vendikar: Eminiar III, nearest neighbor to, and originally a colony of, Eminiar VII. A stylized, computer-run war has existed between the two planets for five hundred years, until Kirk and Ambassador Fox step in (TA).

Vendorian: A native of the planet Vendor. Few have ever seen one, owing to the quarantine on the planet—Vendorians can rearrange their molecular structure into anything with the same general mass, and their practice of deceit as a way of life puts them off limits. The Vendorian who takes Carter Winston's shape to get aboard the Enterprise is an outcast and misfit in its own society; it works for the Romulans as a spy in order to be of value to someone—anyone. Its plans backfire when it falls in love with Anne Nored, the real Winston's fiancée, and is unable to hand the Enterprise over to the Romulans. However, there is some hope that Anne might learn to love the creature in time (Su/a).

Venom, sur-snake: The venom of the Argo sur-snake is deadly to the touch. It is obtained by capturing a sur-snake, using a suction-cupped pouch container to draw off the venom, and getting away from the snake. It is needed as an antitoxin to reverse the surgo-op mutation worked on Kirk and Spock by the Aquans (Am/a).

Venus drug: A highly illegal substance which gives humans "more of whatever they have." Men become more masculine and handsome, women more enticingly beautiful, until the drug wears off and the user returns to normal. Harry Mudd uses it to make his prospective brides more alluring, and thereby ensnares himself (MW).

Verdanis: A fertile and well-watered planet to which the Enterprise takes the entire city of the Terratins, after rescuing them from the hostile, volcanic planet orbiting Cepheus (Te/a).

Vertigo: When the Enterprise passes through the Delta Triangle area into the alternate universe of Elysia, everyone on board experiences vertigo and lack of coordination, and their vision won't focus. The effect lasts only until the passage through the time trap is complete (Tr/a).

Vians: A humanoid species—but definitely not Homo sapiens, according to Spock—inhabiting one of the Minaran planets, probably Minara II. They are highly advanced and use their technology to test the other races of the Minaran system by torturing random passersby, such as a group of research scientists and the Enterprise's landing party. The Vians seem to feel that in torturing the Enterprise men they will teach self-sacrifice and compassion to an empath and in so doing also help to save the rest of the empathic race. Gem, the empath, heals the Enterprise men and thereby wins survival for the empaths, who will be the only race the Vians save from the Minaran system, which is about to go nova. Whether the Vians also save themselves or become extinct is not known (Em). In an effort to prove to Spock that the personality of Kirk is trapped in Janice's body, Janice-K recalls the incident when the Vians demanded that Kirk and Spock allow McCoy to die. However, such incidents are recorded and so could be known to Janice Lester (TI).

Viewscreen, computer: When Spock escapes from the tubelike chamber and he and Kirk make their way through the computer banks, an alarm goes off, and the master computer spots them on its viewscreen. They elude the hovercraft sent to intercept them and wind up in the master control room (OUP/a).

Viewscreens: The most important viewscreen is the bridge viewing screen, which is not a window but an electronic device which is pointed in various directions outside the ship and is televised to the interior with magnification as needed. Most often it is aimed in the direction of travel and shows objects in view at that time. Intercom viewing screens connect most of the areas of the vessel, and the screen over Spock's library/computer station can be utilized for tape information from the ship's record tapes, in visual form.

Villi: While wandering in the interior of the immense cosmic cloud, the Enterprise blunders into an area of turmoil where incandescent colors, intermittent explosions, and waving tendrillike objects seem to endanger the starship. McCoy suggests that they are in what might correspond to the small intestine of a human; the tendrils correspond to villi, which absorb nutrients from the broken planets ingested by the cloud. However, these villi are dangerous, being antimatter which could explode the Enterprise on contact. Scott uses a chunk of villi cut off by a tractor beam to regenerate the power drain on the ship's engines. The cosmic cloud is so huge that it does not even notice the invasion of its interior by either starship or tractor beam (OPM/a).

Vina (Susan Oliver): In appearance, young, blond, and beautiful, she is actually about fifty and horribly deformed, having been injured in a crash and reassembled rather haphazardly by doctors who knew little about human anatomy. Vina is a prisoner of the Talosians, who clothed her in illusions in hopes of attracting Captain Pike to her. When this didn't work and Pike finally left, they gave her the illusion that he had stayed, to keep her happy (Me).

Vine: A writhing, leafy vine coils in the Vulcan desert, waiting to grab potential victims. One very nearly catches young Spock as he runs for a healer, but the Vulcan dodges the vine (Yy/a).

Violation, treaty: The use of a Vendorian is a violation of the treaty between the Romulans and the Federation; Vendorians can change shape and practice deceit, so anyone using them would have a decided advantage over the other side (Su/a).

Violence: Strictly forbidden in Elysia, where both personnel and ship's weaponry can be frozen and made unworkable. Anyone who violates the law against violence can be put under a type of immobilization for a century (Tr/a).

Virus: A virus native to Omega IV usually dehydrates the human body, eventually reducing it to white crystals, but spending a certain amount of time on that planet gives a permanent immunity. This virus resembles one developed on Earth for bacteriological warfare in the 1990s (OG). A filterable virus of the order 2250-67A is found on an Earthlike planet where the children are estimated to be about three hundred years old and there are no adults. Developed during a life-prolongation research project which backfired, the virus killed everyone over puberty and gave the children a life span in which they age only a few months in every hundred years. Unfortunately, when puberty is finally reached, the virus brings about extremely fast aging, spots and sores on the body, madness, and death within five or six weeks. The virus is very communicable, reacting on nucleic acids, and nearly kills an Enterprise landing party (Mi). A virus native to Psi 2000 relaxes its victim's inhibitions, bringing out the person's deeper, often repressed nature. It is waterborne, transmitted in human perspiration via touch (NT).

Visor: An opaque eyeshield with narrow slits of red transparency, used to shield the eyes of anyone who looks at a Medusan, and thereby prevent insanity; without the protective visor, the ugliness of the alien is more than other beings can stand (TB).

Visual: Crewmen on the Enterprise can report over communications or on visual screens from everywhere in the starship.

Visual contact: The process of making communicative contact via the viewscreen; a common method of interchange between starships.

Visual scan: A 360-degree scan of the outside of the starship; done by the viewscreen complex on the bridge. Kirk orders this when he wants to get an overall view of the things around him.

Visual sweeps: Lieutenant Arex is making visual sweeps of the planet orbiting Cepheus when he is blinded momentarily by a sudden brilliance of light that sends an impulse through the Enterprise (Te/a).

Vitalizer beam: A field used to prevent a wounded man from losing more blood than necessary (PLW).

Vitamin rations: McCoy, after all the excitement on Dramia, is glad to get back to the monotonous routine of dispensing vitamin rations to the Enterprise's crew and the usual old business of handling Sick Bay (Al/a).

Voder: The plant beings of Phylos speak by means of a voder, or voice-box translator discs in their middle-body area (IV/a).

Vodka: Chekov's drink, which Scotty refers to as "milk" (TT).

Voice index lock: A device that protects classified information on computer tapes (MM).

Volaerts, Rik (script): For the World Is Hollow and I Have Touched the Sky (FW).

Volcanic action: There has evidently been new volcanic action since the last Federation sweep of the planet orbiting Cepheus, but there has been no report. The volcanoes and earthquakes have buried the great signal antenna of the Terratins, so they have to resort to more drastic measures to gain the attention of the Enterprise (Te/a). See also Mad planet.

Volts: The Capellan power-cat can throw a charge of two thousand volts when angry (HS/a).

Vortex: A rapid whirling of matter or energy around or

toward a center, in some cases with catastrophic results. A vortex of some kind—a window, doorway, gateway, or other opening in time—is usually what pulls a starship through into an alternate universe and back again (Tr/a).

Vrietalyn: See Ryetalyn.

Vulcan: A Class M planet, star system undetermined, home world of one of the Federation's most advanced races. It has no moon (MT), but its sun is so bright that the inhabitants have developed a nictitating membrane to protect their sight (OA). The air is thin, hot, and dry during the day (AT), though there may be a radical temperature drop during the night, as on the desert. The planet appears a deep red from space (AT, JB), with a great part of its surface evidently desert—sand, shale glittering with flecks of mica, occasional weathered stone formations (AT). The Vulcan desert is brash and dominating, in deep tones of yellow ochers and umber browns against a yellowed sky, with ranges of forbidding mountains behind the desert itself. The atmosphere is thin, so there are no clouds in the sky. The mean temperature is somewhere in the 140-degree range on a pleasant day (Yy/a). There are also seas, with (unlike Earth) little or no sodium chloride content: Spock says, "My ancestors evolved in very different seas than yours . . ." (MT).

Vulcan Academy of Sciences: See Sarek.

Vulcan blood: Seen on a taped cassette viewed on the medical screen, Vulcan blood shows green-tinted cells. Diseased cells invaded by choriocytosis are infected with a yellowish substance which turns the cells blue. The infection enters copper-based bloodstreams, encasing the cells so they cannot carry oxygen. The cells also stop moving. Vulcans cannot survive this disease (PO/a).

Vulcan death grip: Spock "kills" Kirk with a pressure over his face and forehead, claiming to the Romulan commander that it is an instinctive reaction in Vulcans which was triggered when the angry captain attacked him. Nurse Chapel points out, nearly ruining the bluff, that there is no such thing—but the Romulans don't know that. It knocks Kirk out, simulating death closely enough to fool the Romulan medics, and long enough for McCoy to get his captain back to the Enterprise for an ear job. The "death grip" gives Kirk a very sore neck (EI).

Vulcan desert: See Vulcan.

Vulcan family history: The records officer checks Vulcan family history to find that Spock died at age seven, Amanda and Sarek separated soon after that, and Amanda was killed in a shuttle accident in Lunaport while returning to her home on Earth. Sarek was ambassador to seventeen planets in the past thirty years, and never remarried. The death of one small seven-year-old Vulcan was not important enough for the historians of Vulcan's past to even notice (Yy/a).

Vulcan gardens: Vulcan homes have gardens of flowers and vines, usually walled from the street. They are for serene contemplation (Yy/a).

Vulcanian: Obsolete term meaning a native of the planet Vulcan. The term "Vulcan" has come to mean both the planet and the native of same.

Vulcan marriage: By tradition, Vulcans are married in childhood. In a ritual that is actually "less than a mar-

riage, but more than a betrothal," the two participants' minds are locked together at age seven. At the proper time in adulthood they are then drawn to Koon-ut kal-if-fee, the marriage. If the marriage is challenged, the two competing males fight to the death, since the biological forces controlling a Vulcan male when he is in pon far, the "mating time," are out of his power to suppress, and he will go into plak tow, blood frenzy. The Vulcans have never been able to find a "cure" for this (to them) embarrassing display of emotion (AT). Spock's father, Sarek, married a Terran woman, Amanda Grayson. This would indicate that he was free from this tradition of having been married in childhood. The details are unknown, but their marriage took place when both were adults (JB).

Vulcan marriage drum: A vision brought to Spock by the lura-mag of Taurus II. He sees a platinum-haired female beating a small drum which he identifies as a Vulcan marriage drum, but he does not elucidate on its exact function in the marriage rite (LS/a).

Vulcan medicine: Vulcans use sensors, hypos, and other standard medical equipment (Yy/a).

Vulcan mind fusion: The process of making two minds become one, which takes great concentration. Vulcans do not use this method unless the case is extreme; Spock brings back Kirk's memory in this manner (PSy). He contacts Kollos in this way (TB).

Vulcan mind meld: It is possible, under great duress, for a disciplined Vulcan to make contact with, and hold under control, more than one mind at a time. Mind meld can also be used for a one-mind contact (SGn).

Vulcan mind touch: A form of telepathy in Vulcans, ordinarily limited to moments of physical contact; however, by using the hands as a focusing device, the mind touch can occasionally be established when the two beings are not actually in contact (AON, DD, TA). Because it involves the mingling of two egos, modern Vulcans find it a painfully embarrassing invasion of privacy and use it only when necessary. Spock uses it to learn from Dr. van Gelder about the brainwashing device (DMd), and to make contact with the Horta (DD). The full strength of a mind touch has never been fully explored. Spock feels the deaths of four hundred Vulcans on the Intrepid from several parsecs away (IS). Spock surreptitiously uses mind touch on Kirk to remove all traces of Reena from the sleeping captain's mind (RM). Spock uses it on Nomad to try to find out what it really is, since they know it is no longer the Earth space probe sent out many years ago (Cg). Spock decides to attempt to make contact with the cosmic cloud by mind touch, though the procedure will be complicated and possibly take longer than they can afford before the Enterprise will have to self-destruct to save the planet Mantilles and its inhabitants. The mind touch succeeds, with full exchange of thoughts between the cloud and the Vulcan. Spock suggests that the cloud go to its original galaxy again, and the cloud agrees (OPM/a). The Spock-clone uses mind touch to return the original Spock to life and full intelligence, chanting aloud, "My mind to your mind, my thoughts to your thoughts," while doing so (IV/a).

Vulcan nerve pinch: A Vulcan method of rendering

humanoids unconscious by a pinch on the neck or shoulder. Because both great strength and detailed knowledge of the nervous system are necessary, only a Vulcan can accomplish it. Spock has tried to teach it to Kirk, without success (OG). Spock prefers the nerve pinch to the use of fists (TT). When Kirk suggests that Spock try a nerve pinch on the native guard of Delta Theta III, Spock looks the huge guard over carefully and points out that he is only Vulcan (Be/a). See also Pain-relieving move.

Vulcan philosophy: Being Vulcan means following disciplines and philosophies that are difficult and demanding of both mind and body. Young Spock is urged to make his choice between living by the Vulcan philosophy of no war, no crime, order, logic, and control, or by the raw emotions and instincts of being human (Yy/a). Vulcans do not condone the meaningless death of any being. Spock's death would be meaningless if it is only to create a giant version of himself (IV/a).

Vulcan physiology: See Vulcans.

Vulcan ritual embrace: Hands crossed at the wrists, palms touching the other's palms; suitable for greeting members of one's family (JB).

Vulcans: The humanoid dominant species of the planet Vulcan; members of the Federation. Their immediately apparent differences from Earthmen are up-swept eyebrows, delicately pointed ears, and a pale, greenish complexion. They are for the most part tall, slender, and generally a beautiful people. The Vulcans seen so far have been dark-haired, but this does not preclude lighter-haired types. Vulcans are an extremely ancient and civilized race, proud and dedicated, loyal, with a strong sense of honor. Vulcans never bluff, according to Spock (DMa), but he has come close to it on occasion; they seldom speculate (Cml), and seem incapable of outright betrayal or lies, though Spock has managed to resort to lies-by-omission (Me). When Spock suggests they throw tribbles at the Klingons, Kirk is merely annoyed until Spock assures the captain that Vulcans do not have a sense of humor. They implement this plan to save the Enterprise, though the supposed lack of humor in Vulcans could be argued (MTT/a). Vulcans have a strong sense of their proper image, which is important to them (SC), and probably Spock chose the more difficult Vulcan way when he had the choice as a child, rather than follow the way of his mother's culture (Yy/a). In an effort to be all Vulcan, Spock tries to pretend he has no emotions at all; Sarek, more secure in his Vulcan nature, permits himself an occasional smile or small act of tenderness toward his wife, Amanda (JB). Vulcan females are devoted to logic (AT) and the sterility of nonemotion, according to the female Romulan commander; she cannot have known very much about the facts, and is probably only trying to press her own suit with Spock, since the distant ancestors of the Romulans left Vulcan before the Reforms and there has been little contact since then (EI). Kirk, referring to the illogical actions of every female in the galaxy, remarks that Vulcan is the only planet that can make the claim that its women are logical (ET). While in early-childhood education of

kindergarten, they learn the coordination and discipline of dancing (WGD). Marta's sensuous Orion dancing reminds Spock of the dances that Vulcan children do in nursery school, though he concedes that the children are not so well coordinated, proving conclusively that Vulcans are capable of deadly put-down (WGD). This also implies that music and dance have a place in Vulcan life, if only as mental and physical exercise. The Vulcan philosophy of NOME, (meaning "All") is a combination of a variety of things making life worthwhile (SC). It is much on the order of the IDIC (TB). Some Vulcan offshoots use musical notes for words (PSy). Vulcan blood is green, being based on copper (Ob) instead of iron, and contains no sodium (MT). Pulse and respiration are generally higher than those of Terrans, blood pressure lower; normal Vulcan readings are never stated, but Spock—a Vulcan-Terran hybrid—has a normal pulse of 212 per minute and very low blood pressure; McCoy has said jokingly that it was practically zero (NT). Ambassador Sarek's blood pressure reaches 90 over 40 and dropping, with a heartbeat of 324, but he is ill at the time (JB). Healthy Vulcans adjust to low atmospheric temperatures, but when Spock is ill he finds the ship's temperature increasingly uncomfortable and adjusts his quarters to a tolerable level of 125 degrees (DY). Vulcans sleep with their eyes open when in normal health (RA); they close their eyes only when ill or in a coma (AON, AT, JB); they have nictitating membranes to protect their eyes against the violent Vulcan sun (OA). The Vulcan body is dependent to a high degree on control of the brain, but it can retain life without the brain for much longer than a human's can (SB). McCoy once comments that Spock has a clockwork ticker for a mind, which might apply to other Vulcans also (SGn). Under stress, Vulcans can go without sleep for weeks. After several weeks of exhaustion, Vulcan metabolism and blood pressure are so low they can hardly be measured (PSy). Vulcans have a natural immunity to auroral plague and Saurian virus, and are evidently not even possible carriers (Al/a). The seven-year mating cycle is inherent in all Vulcan males; at the time of <u>pon far</u>, the mating drive outweighs all other motivation (AT). It may be possible to disturb the cycle; Spock admits to being attracted to strange feminine beauty at a time when <u>plak tow</u> is not affecting him (Cms). Over five hundred years ago, Vulcan was warlike and emotional, and its people ate meat; they are now logical and vegetarians. But Spock reverts to pre-logic Vulcan actions when he is thrown into the ice age of Sarpeidon (AY). The flesh-eating Kzin have no respect for Vulcans, and consider them only eaters of roots and leaves (SW/a). In pre-logic days, Vulcan was nearly destroyed by conditions characteristic of Cheron, wildly emotional, committed to irrationally opposing viewpoints leading to death and destruction. Only the discipline of logic saved them (LB). Lara doesn't like Vulcans; she says they are coldblooded critters; they always spout statistics. Spock points out that Vulcans do indeed quote poetry, but it is hardly an appropriate time to do so on an unstable planet, in a life-or-death situation (Ji/a). Earlier, Vulcans were aggressive, militaristic, violent—comparable to their kinsmen, the

Romulans—during which period they colonized neighboring planets (BT). The Vulcans reacted against nearly destroying themselves by turning away from emotionalism to base their culture on cold logic, reason, and control. Vulcan, sometime in its remembered history—which may go back further than any human can know—has been conquered (CK), but the details have never been revealed. There are many different ways of conquest besides simply overrunning a planet in warfare. Vulcan racial memory is undoubtedly a result of mind touch, a limited telepathic ability which would allow Vulcan oral history to be passed down far longer than under normal circumstances. This mind touch is considered embarrassing by modern Vulcans, to be used only when necessary (DD, DMd). In the mirror universe, Spock-2 is less inhibited and less reluctant to use the mind touch for his own purposes (MM). The mind-touch talent can be utilized in many ways and is one of the most outstanding features of the use to which Vulcans have put their logical minds; ramifications of this talent include the mind touch, mind link, and mind meld, all subtly different. Though bred for peace in recent centuries, Vulcans know what to do when captured in war and will not cry out for help. Spock knows that Surak would not have cried out, but the ruse works well on humans (SC). At one time, Vulcans used boomerangs for hunting (SC), and have also used bow-and-arrow techniques (FC). After it is discovered that Spock is familiar with Lewis Carroll's works, it is theorized that even Vulcans find light reading relaxing (OUP/a). Vulcans find nitrous oxide (laughing gas) painful (PJ/a). Vulcans have been visited by aliens before; the aliens went away the wiser (HS/a). However, Spock finds that the Lactrans are so far beyond even Vulcans that it is embarrassing to him. Though Vulcans are not given to fanciful dreams, and value themselves and their intelligence, it would be foolish to suppose they have any chance of escape from the zoo; they are probably in there for life (EB/a). With typical philosophical outlook, the Vulcans trapped in Elysia have learned to live with and accept their fellows (Tr/a).

Vulcan salute: Vulcans indicate respect or recognition with the right hand raised and held forward from the body, the fingers positioned to form three units consisting of the thumb, the second and third fingers, and the fourth and fifth. This gesture is used to salute both Vulcans and others (AT, JB).

Vulcan sensor instruments: See Vulcan medicine.

Vulcan teachers: When the blind Miranda realized she was telepathic, Vulcan teachings and philosophies saved her sanity (TB).

Vulcan technique: See Vulcan mind touch.

Vulcan vacation: A self-induced state of suspended animation into which Spock puts himself when McCoy tells the Kelvans the Vulcan has Rigellian kassaba fever. Spock says it is like a vacation, but more relaxing than humans' vacations (AON).

Vulcan words:

Ahn-woon (AT)	Klee-fah (AT)
IDIC (IV/a)	Koon-ut kal-if-fee (AT)
Kah-if-farr (AT)	Kroykah (AT)
Kahs-wan (Yy/a)	Le-matya (Yy/a)
Kal-if-fee (AT)	L-Langon Mountains (Yy/a)

Plak tow (AT)	ShiKahr (Yy/a)
Plomeek (AT)	Tal-shaya (JB)
Pon far (AT)	Tasmeen (Yy/a)
Sehlat (JB, Yy/a)	

W

Walking Bear, Ensign Dawson: A helmsman—Comanche Indian, tall, with long black hair and high cheekbones. He has studied the histories of many Earth peoples, especially his own. He is the first to recognize Kulkukan (HS/a).

Wallace, Art (scripts): Obsession (Ob); Assignment: Earth (AE) (with Gene Roddenberry).

Wallace, Dr. Janet (Sarah Marshall): An expert on endocrinology and cell structure. An attractive blond and a former girlfriend of Kirk's, she gave him up because both were too involved in their respective careers. She married a man in her own field, Dr. Theodore Wallace, who has since died. She is aboard the Enterprise when Kirk and others contract the Gamma Hydra IV hyperaging radiation poisoning, for which she and McCoy develop an adrenalin-based remedy (DY).

Wallace, Dr. Theodore: Biochemist; late husband of Dr. Janet Wallace (DY).

Wallerstein, Herb (director): That Which Survives (TWS); Whom Gods Destroy (WGD); Turnabout Intruder (TI).

Walsh, Leo Francis: A deceased spaceship captain of doubtful reputation. Harry Mudd uses Walsh's name as an alias (MW).

Wands: Ceiling-high wands in the long-dead pod ship are energy accumulators, receptors to attract energy, motion, sound, light, heat—every kind of energy around them. In fact, the whole ship was built to accumulate and store energy using a technique far beyond that known to any Federation world (BFS/a). See also Transmuter.

Wardrobe department: The wardrobe department of the Enterprise is able to supply Spock with not only a desert soft suit, but Vulcan street clothes of thirty years ago, so Spock can return to Vulcan's past without attracting notice (Yy/a).

War games: Exercises using starships and related equipment to keep Star Fleet personnel on their toes for actual combat, should the need arise (UC).

Warlocks: See Wizards.

Warp: A distortion of physical laws that produces the magnetic effect (AF).

Warp-control panel: The explosive capsule is hidden by the Klingon female, Kali, behind a niche in the warp-control panel of the Enterprise (Tr/a).

Warp drive: In order to warp space and exceed the speed of light, starship engines in the two outboard nacelles use integrated matter and antimatter for propulsion. The annihilation of dual matter creates the fantastic power required. The Enterprise is the first Constellation-size ship to have warp drive installed in it. Obviously, warp drive had to be tested first in smaller-sized ships. The old Bonaventure was the first of these ships; it disappeared into the Delta Triangle region on its third voyage out (Tr/a).

Warp factor: Hyperlight speeds or space warp speeds are measured in warp factors; warp factor 1 is the speed of light: 186,000 miles per second, or somewhat over six hundred million miles per hour. Warp factors 2, 3, 4, and so on are geometrical functions of light velocity; the speed in miles per hour is the cube of the warp factor times the speed of light (C): warp 2 is 8C; warp 3 is 27C; warp 4 is 64C; and so on. The maximum safe speed is warp 6. Warp 7 or 8 is used only in emergencies; at warp 8 the ship begins to show considerable strain, and warp 9 is highly dangerous. Certain conditions exceeding warp 9.5 will throw a starship into a space/time continuum wherein humanoids (but not Medusans) experience sensory distortion and instruments cannot be trusted (TB).

Warp 14.1:   The highest speed ever reached by the Enterprise, but it is accomplished only by the fusion of its matter/antimatter-integrator controls. This will result in the destruction of the ship if Scotty is not able to repair the controls to permit reduction of speed (TWS).

Warp 36:   A speed faster than any known race can manage in a starship. An alien scout vessel manages it without harm, however, though it pulls the Enterprise through a nova when the larger starship tries to slow it down with a tractor beam (CC/a).

Warrant: The Dramians have a warrant waiting for the arrest of Dr. McCoy on charges of mass murder. It is in order and approved by the Federation, so McCoy has to surrender to the authority of Dramia (Al/a).

Washburn (Richard Compton):   Engineer—part of the damage-control party sent aboard the Constellation after it has been disabled by the berserker (DMa).

Water: The water on Psi 2000 is the carrier of the virus that breaks down all inhibitions; transferred to the human body, the virus can be passed from person to person in the form of perspiration (NT). Water on Scalos contains a substance which causes hyperacceleration and can also be added to other fluids such as coffee (WE).

Water-breather: Any creature or being which breathes a form of water or liquid through the use of gills instead of lungs. On Argo, the Aquan people are water-breathers and consider all air-breathers their enemies (Am/a).

Watkins, John B. (Kenneth Washington):   A handsome young black who is a Grade 4 engineer. He is checking the bypass valve on the matter/antimatter reaction chamber when Losira appears on the Enterprise. When she asks questions about the ship's operation, he becomes suspicious and gives wrong answers, whereupon she kills him by cellular disruption (TWS).

Watson, Technician (Victor Brandt):   A small, neat, dark-haired engineering crewman who is killed trying to prevent Kryton of Elas from transmitting to a Klingon ship (ET).

Wave bombardments: See Spiroid epsilon waves.

Wavering effect: The disappearance of the Klothos into the Delta Triangle is accompanied by a strange wavering effect that seems to be a natural phenomenon, somehow connected with the disappearances of other ships (Tr/a).

Weapon: Deela's weapon, a force beam, works on accelerated time and can easily kick a phaser out of Kirk's hand (WE). Mr. Atoz, the librarian on Sarpeidon, holds a strange weapon on Kirk, which looks like an empty metal tube about six inches long, but which stuns Kirk with a scintillating light (AY). The weapons of the sentinels of Stratos emit small pulses of light and are capable of killing (Cms). The Elasian guards wear body armor and carry old-fashioned nuclear hand weapons and daggers (ET). Kirk tries to fashion weapons from available materials on Excalbia to fight the evil ones. He considers slings, spears, and boomerangs. Phasers and tricorders will not work on the planet (SC). As the Metrons promise, there are materials on the asteroid-arena from which to build a weapon. Kirk constructs a hand cannon out of a bamboo tube and rope, firing huge diamond projectiles to defeat the Gorn. The proper minerals to mix gunpowder are also furnished (Ar). The Klingons have a new weapon— an energy field that paralyzes enemy ships and holds them in stasis. However, the drain on the Klingon ship's energy is enormous, so the weapon has limited uses, but logical applications (MTT/a). Spock finds weapons in the cart on the expedition to recover the Soul of Skorr. Kirk wonders why, since there is no life on the planet except themselves. But there may be other things guarding the Soul (Ji/a). See also Arms; Treaty of Sirius.

Weather satellite: Scotty, on board the Enterprise, bounces a signal off an old-style Earth weather satellite to pick up a picture from McKinley Rocket Base (AE).

Webb, Technician (Richard Merrifield):   A United States Air Force technician who sights the Enterprise above the Omaha Air Base (TY).

Weeper: A kind of plant, left in Sulu's care, which has to be hand-fed (MT).

Weinstein, Howard (script):   The Pirates of Orion (PO/a).

Wesley, Commodore Robert (Barry Russo): Commander of the U.S.S. Lexington—a tall man with the look of eagles, who leads the attack against the Enterprise in the war games testing the M-5 computer. When the M-5 mistakes the games and attacks the Federation ships with real phasers, Wesley asks for and receives Star Fleet's permission to destroy the Enterprise. When the suicidal M-5 drops the ship's shields and waits for the kill, Wesley, a man of compassion and character, holds his fire until Kirk can contact him (UC). When he retires from Star Fleet, Robert Wesley becomes governor of Mantilles, the most remote inhabited planet in the Federation. When Mantilles is threatened by the cosmic cloud, it is feared that a warning would only cause planetwide panic, but Kirk says that Governor Wesley is no hysteric, and they decide to tell him (OPM/a).

Wesley, Katie: Governor Robert Wesley's eleven-year-old daughter (OPM/a).

Westervliet, Admiral (Byron Morrow):   A Star Fleet superior officer, with sleek white hair and a rugged face. Kirk asks him for permission to remain on parallel course with Yonada while McCoy is on it; the Admiral refuses permission (FW).

Wheat: See Quadrotriticale; Quintotriticale.

Wheelchair: After Captain Pike was crippled badly by the ruptured baffle plate and released delta rays, his maimed body was placed in a special wheelchair that was a life-support system and also made it possible for him to communicate with others by means of lights (Me).

Whiplash effect: See Slingshot effect.

Whirlwind: A small child satyr creates a large whirlwind to keep his toy top rolling; Lucien says it is a plaything, wind and all (Mtu/a).

Whiskey: Lincoln asks Kirk if he drinks whiskey, to which Kirk answers yes; Lincoln is strongly reminded of another man he admires for his strategy and tactics, General Ulysses S. Grant, who also liked his whiskey (SC).

White hole: In the negative or antimatter universe, space has "white holes," dead stars which will suddenly come to life, instead of "black holes," stars that suddenly go nova and die (CC/a).

White light: A brilliant white light fills the interior of the fortress when the doorway falls shut, trapping the expedition on the mad planet (Ji/a).

Whiteout: A condition in snowstorms when it gets so thick that nothing can be seen through the blowing blizzard—hence a whiteout. People get lost and often die in a whiteout, even in the Enterprise's Recreation Room (PJ/a).

White Rabbit: On the amusement-park planet, McCoy is thinking of Lewis Carroll's Alice books when a man-sized White Rabbit, wearing a checkered vest and white gloves, materializes, followed by Alice herself, who chases it down a hole (SL). On another occasion, Sulu remembers the previous incident, and the White Rabbit again appears, bounding along, complaining about being late, followed by Alice. After the troubles with the master computer are over, Sulu and McCoy have a picnic with these characters and a certain dragon (OUP/a).

White sound: A means of masking sound with silence; total lack of sound. McCoy uses a hand-held device which masks out the heartbeats of everyone on the Enterprise. The remaining heartbeat amplified over the ship's audio, after white sound has been applied to everyone else's, is Finney's (Cml).

Wide-area stun setting: See Phasers.

Widen Dairy: Sign on a horse-drawn milk truck, used in the 1920s, when Kirk and Spock go back in time to find McCoy (CEF).

Wilbur, Carey (script): Space Seed (SS) (with Gene L. Coon).

Wilkins, Professor: Archeologist on the Starnes expedition who excavated a cave once occupied by the extinct inhabitants of Triacus. In so doing, he may have unwittingly released Gorgan (CL).

Wilson (Garth Pillsbury): A crewman on the I.S.S. Enterprise who seems to side with Chekov-2 in an attempt to assassinate Kirk but who actually aids Kirk in the hope that he will be made an officer out of gratitude for his assistance (MM).

Wilson, Technician (Garland Thompson): Transporter technician when a malfunction causes Kirk to be split into a good and an evil entity. The evil Kirk catches Wilson alone in the Transporter Room, beats him unconscious, and takes his phaser (EW).

Wincelberg, Shimon: See Bar-David, S.

Window: The ships lost in the Delta Triangle region enter the alternate universe through a "window" in time. These "windows" stay open long enough for ships to get into the area, but until the Enterprise and Klothos escape from Elysia, nobody has ever gotten back out again (Tr/a). Kulkukan makes a window appear in his ship so he can see what is happening outside; he sees the Enterprise make its escape from the force globe he created around it (HS/a).

Wine: Garth, the insane starship commander, offers some wine to Kirk, saying it has a robust, full-bodied quality that is sure to be diverting. (Evidently Garth has read Thurber.) Kirk declines the offer (WGD).

Wing camera: The twentieth-century interceptor planes have wing cameras which take photos of the Enterprise, making it imperative that the starship crew beam down in order to recover the pictures (TY).

Winston, Carter (Ted Knight): A healthy robust man of about forty-five or fifty in appearance—the most famous space trader of his time, with many philanthropic deeds to his credit. He gained a dozen fortunes and used them to assist colonies and whole planets in need. Anne Nored, of the security detail on the Enterprise, was engaged to be married to Winston when he disappeared for five years and was presumed lost. The Enterprise finds Winston again in a damaged one-man vessel, and brings him aboard the starship; it is not Carter Winston, however, but a Vendorian shape-changer who wants to spy on the Enterprise for the Romulans. The real Carter Winston died years ago on Vendor, after they tried to save him with surgery. Before his death, he passed on all his memories of Anne—his love for her, his deep feelings—to the Vendorian who takes his shape (Su/a).

Winston/crewman: The Vendorian shape-changer who takes the form of Carter Winston to get aboard the Enterprise also takes other forms, among them the shape of a crewman so that it can sabotage the deflector shields and leave the starship open to attack by the Romulans (Su/a).

Winston/Kirk: The Vendorian spy changes shapes from Carter Winston to Captain Kirk, so it can take over the bridge and send the Enterprise through the Romulan neutral zone, thereby setting up the starship for capture by the Romulans (Su/a).

Winston/McCoy: When the real Kirk decides to have a medical checkup to see if he is becoming subject to blackouts, Spock accompanies the captain to Sick Bay. Meanwhile, the Vendorian spy has taken the shape of Dr. McCoy in order to prevent too close an inspection of Carter Winston's medical-examination results. The Vendorian slips up, however, when it good-naturedly agrees with Spock's needling remark that perhaps the good doctor has made a mistake in his examination. Spock points out to Kirk that the real McCoy would have fired up at the mere hint that his medical tests were in error (Su/a).

Wise, David (script): How Sharper Than a Serpent's

Tooth (HS/a) (with Russell Bates).

Wise Ones, the: The name the Indians give to the race, also called the Preservers, who established them on their planet (PSy).

Witch: Thrown into Sarpeidon's past, Kirk is assumed to be a witch when he talks to Spock and McCoy through a stone wall. The superstitious people, who think he is talking to spirits, report him to the local prosecutor, who knows what is really happening and is persuaded to help Kirk (AY). See also Sylvia.

Witches (Rhodie Cogan, Gail Bonney, Maryesther Denver): Three Macbethian weird sisters, Korob's creations, appear in the mist of Pyris VII to turn away Kirk, McCoy, and Spock, who are searching for Scott and Sulu. The trick is unsuccessful (Cp).

Witness: At the trial of the Earthlings on Megas-tu, Spock speaks for the defense, calling on Lucien as a witness, asking why the alien does not fear humans. Lucien says they are like him—always asking questions, with minds that range outward, curious about life, and sharing (Mtu/a).

Wizards: Once wizards and magicians helped mankind on Earth with their powers and were known as wise men who helped people. But humans tried to use these powers for greed and turned against the wizards when they refused to allow this, calling them witches and warlocks, devils, and worse, and persecuting them (Mtu/a).

Woden: An automated, old-style ore freighter which the M-5 computer, in command of the Enterprise, destroys apparently because it is there. Named after the Norse god (UC).

Wolfe, Lawrence N. (story): The Ultimate Computer (UC).

Wonders of the universe: During Spock's exchange of thoughts with the cosmic cloud, he becomes part of the cloud's mind, while the cloud becomes part of Spock's. When asked later what he saw, the Vulcan will comment only that he has seen the wonders of the universe (OPM/a).

Woman, slovenly (Anna Karen): A brash, dirty-haired, slovenly dressed female of Sarpeidon's "Charles II" era. She is a thief being molested by her intended victim when Kirk appears on the scene and rescues her. They are both thrown in jail, where the woman tries to save her own hide by accusing Kirk of bewitching her into thievery (AY). See also Witch.

Working: A term used by the computer to let the operator know that the machine is looking for the material requested.

Wortham units: A measure of the power obtainable from a starship's engines and/or phaser banks (Ap).

Wristlet: A gold-colored metallic band worn much like an archer's protective bracelet, used by the Eymorgs to control the Morgs and (temporarily) the Enterprise's landing party. Three colored buttons on the wristlet control the energy setting of the waistband or training device, through which it is possible to knock beings unconscious or cause extreme pain or pleasure (SB). See also Training device.

Wu (Lloyd Kino): A robust Asian type; leader of the Kohm militia, trained as a soldier by Captain Tracey. He is fairly young, for a Kohm, having lived through forty-two years of the red bird, an eleven-year cycle, which makes him about 462 Earth years old (OG).

Wyatt, Ensign (Brad Forrest): Transporter technician who is killed by Losira while beaming Kirk, McCoy, Sulu, and D'Amato down to the Kalandan outpost planet (TWS).

Xenophile: One who likes, or even loves, strange things, such as aliens with pointy ears . . .

Xenophobia: From the Greek words xenos, meaning strange, foreign, and phobia, fear or hatred of: combined to mean a fear or hatred of strangers or aliens. A word coined to refer to foreigners of one's own planet, it took on a deeper and more important meaning as man pushed back the frontiers of space.

Xenopolycythemia: From the Greek: xenos, strange; poly, many; kutos, cell; haima, blood. A terminal disease characterized by excess red corpuscles in the blood. It afflicts McCoy, who has about one more year to live when he is cured by ancient Fabrini techniques discovered on Yonada (FW).

Xenylon: A textile made of an algae-based synthetic material. Star Fleet uniforms are made of xenylon, and so are affected by the wave bombardment from Terratin that shrinks the Enterprise's crew. The uniforms, being organic in structure, shrink also (Te/a).

Xerius: A tall Romulan with piercing eyes, spokesman for the Elysian Council. He advises the Federation and Klingon people to accept their fate in being trapped in the Delta Triangle. He can recall his own escape attempts, time after time, until his ship was beaten (Tr/a).

X-waves: At first Spock does not think the mysterious waves harmful, and he is inclined to regard the bombardment of the Enterprise as nothing to worry about. He terms the strange impulses "X" waves, signifying "unknown," until he learns that they are lethal spiroid epsilon waves (Te/a).

Yangs: A group of Caucasians with a quasi-Amerindian culture, possible descendants of Earthmen. They attack the Kohm villagers on Omega IV, and although Captain Tracey arms the Kohms with his phaser, the Yangs eventually win and take over the Kohm villages. Kirk begins a reformation of Yang culture by explaining to them what their sacred documents mean (OG).

Yarnek (Janos Prohaska, voice by Bart LaRue): A reddish rock creature about the size of an Earth refrigerator, with clawlike extremities and a voice like gravel moving underwater. Yarnek glows like hot lava, and his facial area glows when he speaks. Possibly the rock creatures are the only inhabitants of Excalbia; they are masters of illusion and use as source material the images pulled from the minds of their victims. Using both mental images and real people from the Enterprise, Yarnek arranges a drama about good and evil in order to "learn" about them through observation (SC). See also Rock creatures.

Yellow alert: Standby status for a starship to be alerted to possible danger.

Yeoman: A clerical/secretarial position. Yeomen serve officers as a combination valet-executive-secretary-military aide, and as such are always capable, highly professional career males and females. Yeomen often carry tricorders on landing parties and are immediately available with information for the captain when he is away from his command console. McCoy is examining a yeoman in Sick Bay, saying that he is going to get a few days' undeserved bed rest, when the doctor is beamed aboard Kulkukan's ship (HS/a).

Yonada: A spaceship constructed to look like a two-hundred-mile-diameter asteroid, which uses archaic atomic power to propel itself. Its inhabitants, who live in an inner shell and are unaware that they are on a ship, are the descendants of the Fabrini, who built the ship when their sun went nova. The Yonadans are ruled by a priestess and a computer. In the ten thousand years since its launching, the asteroid has gone off course, and is going to smash into Daran V if the Enterprise doesn't prevent it. Spock realigns the controls and sends Yonada to the planet that was its original destination, where presumably the Yonadans disembark and colonize it (FW).

Yorktown, U.S.S.:   Starship that is supposed to transfer vaccines and other medical supplies to the Enterprise for transport to Theta VII. Kirk delays the rendezvous so that he can chase the vampire cloud (Ob).

Yutan (Gary Pillar):   A hill dweller; Tyree's henchman (PLW).

Z

Zabo (Steve Marlo):   One of Krako's hoods, who captures Kirk as he escapes from Oxmyx (PA).

Zarabeth (Mariette Hartley):   A wistful, warm, shapely young girl of Sarpeidon's ice age, scantily dressed—in the cave—in pieces of leather tied around her body. She was sent to the planet's ice age six thousand years ago by Zor Khan the Tyrant, in retaliation against other members of her family for trying to overthrow him. She was "prepared" to live in this age by the atavachron; to return to present-day Sarpeidon would mean her death. Spock finds himself moved by her plight, and finally by her own gentle personality. Reverting to a pre-logic Vulcan, he nearly maroons himself and McCoy in the ice age past because of his wish to remain with Zarabeth. McCoy, though attracted to her, has no desire to stay with her, and both men finally leave her to her fate (AY).

Zeon: The outer of two inhabited planets of M43 Alpha. Possessing a crude form of space transport, Zeons traveled to Ekos to teach the Ekosians peaceful habits and useful technology, only to become the substitutes for Jews when Ekos took on a Nazi culture (PF).

Zero gravity: When the master computer in the planet is getting the feel of the Enterprise, it temporarily interferes with the gravity-control computer, causing everyone to float in zero gravity (OUP/a).

Zetar, lights of: A "storm" of colorful, scintillating lights that can pass through the walls of a ship or planetoid, and into people. Affected beings speak in a deep, growling voice that is incomprehensible to others, and turn a strange glowing color. To resist the Zetars is to cause one's own death. A full attack from them causes severe hemorrhaging due to disruption of all neural centers of the body. Spock says that no known conditions in space will support this type of phenomenon. When the lights of Zetar speak through Mira Romaine, they are found to be a highly alien form of life: ten distinct life units—a community of vitally alive and powerful entities. When all corporeal life on their world was destroyed a millennium ago, they were the last hundred Zetars, whose desires, hopes, and thoughts were so strong that they could not be wiped out, even by a final disaster on their planet. They formed themselves into a light form and searched for a compatible body to take over in which they could live out their lives. Their alien outlook does not consider the killing of everyone on Memory Alpha as murder, nor do they have any qualms about taking over Mira Romaine's personality and body as their own. They will kill anyone who resists them. This attitude may not represent all Zetars; these are insane, however, and care only for themselves, regardless of what damage they do. The Enterprise men catch them off guard by placing Romaine's body in a pressure chamber that kills the Zetars with heavy atmosphere, freeing her (LZ).

Zienite: A substance which can halt certain botanical plagues. Raw, unsealed zienite emits an odorless, invisible gas that retards the intellectual functioning of the brain, heightens emotional reactions, and stimulates violence. Effects of the gas are temporary, and after it is refined it is harmless. The use of filter masks will return the retarded Troglyte miners to normal. Ardana is the only known source of zienite (Cms).

Zoo: The entire planet of Lactra VII seems to be a zoo; animals which would be considered dangerous

to humans are allowed to roam free in manufactured environments; others are kept in compounds or cages. The compounds are also environmentally set up for individual needs of the zoo specimens; the humans are given a modern house with all the comforts: swimming pool, grass lawns, and other things the Lactrans think they need (EB/a). Kulkukan's life room is a collection of plant and life forms from all over the galaxy, some of which are unfamiliar to Dr. McCoy. Kulkukan's machinery keeps the life forms happy; they are living mentally in worlds only they can see, and do not know they are in cages. Each captive is mentally in its own home environment (HS/a).

Z

Zora (Carol Daniels Dement):   A warlike female, old- and decadent-looking, with wild bushy eyebrows, shaggy black hair, dark circles under her eyes, dressed in scraggly furs and leathers. She was notorious on Tiburon for experimenting with the body chemistry of subject tribes. In the battle on Excalbia, she is on the side of evil, and when good begins to get the upper hand, she runs away with Genghis Khan (SC).

Zor Kahn the Tyrant: A tyrant somewhere in the past of Sarpeidon; Spock knows of him from history tapes, and Zarabeth is an innocent victim of his revenge on her family. To retaliate for an attempt by her relatives to overthrow him, he killed them all and sent Zarabeth into Sarpeidon's ice age, six thousand years in the past, using the atavachron (AY).

THE APPENDIX

Index of Episode Abbreviations